THE COMPOSITION OF EVERYDAY LIFE

A Guide to Writing | Fifth Edition

John Mauk
Miami University

John Metz
Kent State University at Geauga

2016 MLA Update Edition

CENGAGE Learning

Australia • Brazil • Mexico • Singapore • United Kingdom • United States

CENGAGE
Learning®

The Composition of Everyday Life: A Guide to Writing, Fifth Edition
2016 MLA Update Edition
John Mauk, John Metz

Product Director: Monica Eckman

Product Team Manager: Christopher Bennem

Product Manager: Laura Ross

Senior Content Developer: Leslie Taggart

Content Developer: Stephanie P. Carpenter

Associate Content Developer: Rachel Smith

Product Assistant: Kerry DeVito

Senior Managing Media Developer: Cara Douglass-Graff

Marketing Manager: Erin Parkins

Senior Content Project Manager: Andrea Wagner

Senior Art Director: Marissa Falco

Manufacturing Planner: Betsy Donaghey

IP Analyst: Ann Hoffman

IP Project Manager: Farah Fard

Production Service/Compositor: MPS Limited

Text and Cover Designer: Bill Reuter

Cover Image: ©iStock.com/johnwoodcock

Library of Congress Control Number: 2014946322

Paper Edition:
ISBN: 978-1-337-28088-4

Loose-leaf Edition:
ISBN: 978-1-337-28089-1

Cengage Learning
20 Channel Center Street
Boston, MA 02210
USA

Cengage Learning is a leading provider of customized learning solutions with office locations around the globe, including Singapore, the United Kingdom, Australia, Mexico, Brazil, and Japan. Locate your local office at **www.cengage.com/global**.

Cengage Learning products are represented in Canada by Nelson Education, Ltd.

To learn more about Cengage Learning Solutions, visit **www.cengage.com**.

Purchase any of our products at your local college store or at our preferred online store **www.cengagebrain.com.**

Printed in United States of America
Print Number: 01 Print Year: 2016

Brief Contents

Contents

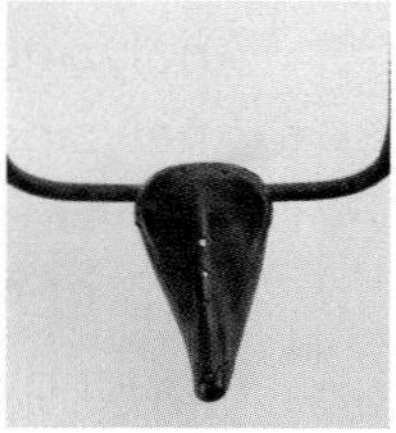

Chapter 4 Observing 94

Chapter 5 Analyzing Concepts 128

HORSES>
< HIKERS

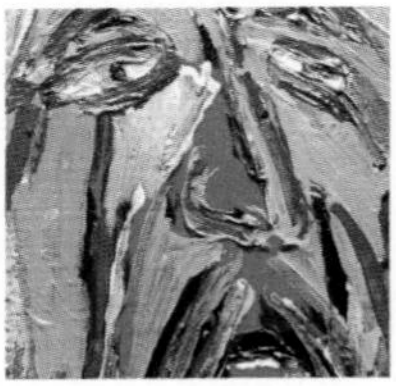

Chapter 20 Anthology: Everyday Rhetoric 598

SPEED
LIMIT
35

Using *The Composition of Everyday Life* as a Thematic Reader

Here we suggest how readings from different chapters might be grouped together thematically. As you explore a particular subject (education and learning, for example), you might focus on a particular rhetorical aim (such as evaluating or proposing a solution). Or you might explore a subject area without a particular aim in mind, eventually discovering a specific topic and rhetorical aim.

Education and Learning

Are students customers? What is the practical value of studying great works of literature? Is school too easy? The following essays explore the complexity of education and learning. Through reading, writing, and discussion, you might explore and come to think differently about education and its role in people's lives. You might discover an important point about education by exploring a memory, a relationship, an observation, a concept, and so on.

Justice and Equality

A quick survey of the readings about justice and equality suggests a range of areas: Native American rights, body type, legal drugs, the mentally and physically challenged, wildlife, and so on. These readings can help you identify and explain a relationship, analyze a concept (such as "justice" or "equality"), respond to an argument, identify a cause, propose a solution, and so on. What is justice, and how might exploring the concept of justice in today's world be of value? What revelatory idea about justice and equality might you discover and share with others?

Environment and Animals

These readings, which offer different ways of looking at the environment and animals, encourage you to explore ideas beyond your initial thoughts and beyond conventional beliefs. What is your relationship to the land? To the air? To the animals? How might you think differently about that relationship? And what might be the consequence of your new way of thinking?

Consumerism and Economy

Several readings in this book encourage you to think about yourself as a consumer. What and how do you consume? And what, if anything, do you produce by consuming? As with other subjects in *The Composition of Everyday Life,* you might spend an entire semester exploring this area, or you might explore it for just one assignment. It could be of great value to spend an entire semester exploring just one question: What does it mean to be a consumer?

America

These readings deal with America and being American. They allow you to explore the relationship between yourself and your country. (International students may find this subject to be especially interesting as they bring a unique perspective to the topic.) To what degree do the two—individual and country—influence each other? You can make observations, evaluate, identify causes, propose solutions, and so on. And, you can explore how America communicates with and influences you.

"Whales R Us," *Jayme Stayer* (8)

"What Orwell Didn't Know," *George Lakoff* (9)

"Reality Check," *Alison Hester* (9)

"Talibanned," *Benjamin Busch* (10)

"American Consumerism," *Jamie Bentley* (11)

"Reverence for Food," *Rachel Schofield* (12)

"The Grapes of Mrs. Rath," *Steve Mockensturm* (20)

"Cookies or Heroin?" *Marie Winn* (20)

"What Is Education?" *Petra Pepellashi* (20)

"Cartoons 'n Comics: Communication to the Quick," *Joy Clough* (20)

"Crimes Against Humanity," *Ward Churchill* (20)

"The Worst Crime of the 20th Century," *Carolyn Dean and Elissa Meininger* (20)

"A More Perfect Union," *Barack Obama* (20)

"Revealing the Ugly Cartoonish Truth: *The Simpsons*," *Simon Benlow* (20)

"Not Homeschooling? What's Your Excuse?" *Tricia Smith Vaughan* (20)

"Hip-Hop: A Roadblock or Pathway to Black Empowerment?" *Geoffrey Bennett* (20)

Self

Readings in this book encourage you to explore your own life in a way you have perhaps not done before. These readings about self go beyond mere expressive writing. They encourage you to connect with others, even though—or perhaps *especially when*—you are looking inward at yourself. You can explore how these readings, your own writing, and focused discussion with others helps you to see differently—to learn something about yourself and connect it to the world around you.

"Selling Manure," *Bonnie Jo Campbell* (2)

"How I Lost the Junior Miss Pageant," *Cindy Bosley* (2)

"Thrill of Victory . . . The Agony of Parents," *Jennifer Schwind-Pawlak* (2)

"Mugged," *Jim Crockett* (3)

"Delicate Friend," *Lauren Jackson* (3)

"Corpse Colloquy," *Justin Scott* (4)

"Cruelty, Civility, and Other Weighty Matters," *Ann Marie Paulin* (8)

"What Orwell Didn't Know," *George Lakoff* (9)

"*The Andy Griffith Show:* Return to Normal," *Ed Bell* (10)

"Throwing Up Childhood," *Leonard Kress* (11)

"American Consumerism," *Jamie Bentley* (11)

"Celibate Passion," *Kathleen Norris* (13)

"Pass It On," *Molli Wallen* (20)

"A *Beat* Education," *Leonard Kress* (20)

"What the Honey Meant," *Cindy Bosley* (20)

"Cookies or Heroin?" *Marie Winn* (20)

“Trees Please,” *Michael Rust* (20)

“A New Map of How We Think: Top Brain/Bottom Brain,” *Stephen M. Kosslyn and G. Wayne Miller* (20)

“Are Female Long-Dist Prone to Suicidal *de la Bruyere* (20)

Others (Community)

Can we look at ourselves without looking at our community? Both subjects (self and others) explore relationships between an individual and his or her surroundings. What is community? How is community created? These readings will help you to explore what we commonly call *community,* to consider how it works, and to examine your place in it. An entire writing course might be an exploration of one very important question: What is the relationship between community and communication?

“Delicate Friend,” *Lauren Jackson* (3)

“Corpse Colloquy,” *Justin Scott* (4)

“Black Like I Thought I Was,” *Erin Aubry Kaplan* (5)

“Cruelty, Civility, and Other Weighty Matters,” *Ann Marie Paulin* (8)

“What Orwell Didn’t Know,” *George Lakoff* (9)

“Where Anonymity Breeds Contempt,” *Julie Zhuo* (12)

“An Apology to Future Generations,” *Simon Benlow* (13)

“Unemployed, and Working Hard,” *Simon Wykoff* (13)

“Pass It On,” *Molli Wallen* (20)

“A More Perfect Union,” *Barack Obama* (20)

“Dog-Tied,” *David Hawes* (20)

“Technology, Movement, and Sound,” *Ed Bell* (20)

“Television: Destroying Childhood,” *Rose Bachtel* (20)

“The Parting Breath of the Now-Perfect Woman,” *Chester McCovey* (20)

“Hip-Hop: A Roadblock or Pathway to Black Empowerment?” *Geoffrey Bennett* (20)

“Why Tough Teachers Get Good Results,” *Joanne Lipman* (20)

Language and Culture

What is the relationship between language and culture? For example, how does the way that a group of people communicates affect their shared values, beliefs, customs, attitudes, and practices—and vice versa? (How, for example, does what a group values about education influence the way that group uses, and thinks about, language?) These readings and others will help you step back and explore the relationship between words, ideas, and actions. Through exploration

. this subject, you might discover that your college writing class is something more than you had originally imagined it to be.

"The Real, the Bad, and the Ugly," *Cassie Heidecker* (5)

"Rise of the Image Culture: Re-Imagining the American Dream," *Elizabeth Thoman* (7)

"The Mighty Image," *Cameron Johnson* (7)

"An Imperfect Reality," *Rebecca Hollingsworth* (7)

"Whales R Us," *Jayme Stayer* (8)

"What Orwell Didn't Know," *George Lakoff* (9)

"Reality Check," *Alison Hester* (9)

"Is Google Making Us Stupid?" *Nicholas Carr* (11)

"Attending to the Word," *Deirdre Mahoney* (12)

"Pass It On," *Molli Wallen* (20)

"Why We No Longer Use the 'H' Word," *Dan Wilkins* (20)

"What Is Education?" *Petra Pepellashi* (20)

"Cartoons 'n Comics: Communication to the Quick," *Joy Clough* (20)

"Crimes against Humanity," *Ward Churchill* (16)

"Hip-Hop: A Roadblock or Pathway to Black Empowerment?" *Geoffrey Bennett* (20)

"Sex, Lies, and Conversation: Why Is It So Hard for Men and Women to Talk to Each Other?" *Deborah Tannen* (20)

Gender and Identity

What does it mean to be male or female? How does gender affect our identities? What influence can we have on issues of gender and identity? This group of readings can be used in combination with other reading groups—from America or pop culture, for example. Instead of exploring just gender and identity, you might narrow your focus to readings that relate to gender and identity *and* pop culture.

"Selling Manure," *Bonnie Jo Campbell* (2)

"How I Lost the Junior Miss Pageant," *Cindy Bosley* (2)

"The Thrill of Victory . . . The Agony of Parents," *Jennifer Schwind-Pawlak* (2)

"Delicate Friend," *Lauren Jackson* (3)

"Cruelty, Civility, and Other Weighty Matters," *Ann Marie Paulin* (8)

"Throwing Up Childhood," *Leonard Kress* (11)

"Celibate Passion," *Kathleen Norris* (13)

"Sex, Lies, and Conversation: Why Is It So Hard for Men and Women to Talk to Each Other?" *Deborah Tannen* (20)

"Are Female Long-Distance Runners More Prone to Suicidal Depression?" *Emily de la Bruyere* (20)

Parents and Family

What role do our parents play in our lives? Such a question might be explored endlessly with interesting results for both writer and readers. You might spend an entire semester exploring issues about parents and family. Such a simple subject area can prove to be far more complicated—and interesting—than you first imagined. What might be the value of thinking analytically and finding public resonance regarding the subject of parents and family?

Popular Culture

What is the relationship between an individual and his or her popular culture? In what ways are we products of our own pop culture? From beauty pageants to theme parks, these readings allow you to consider the world that surrounds you from a fresh perspective. You can explore the *why* of your own behavior, considering how you and others are influenced by pressures of which you are both very aware and barely aware.

"Talibanned," *Benjamin Busch* (10)

"*Star Trek:* Where No Man Has Gone Before," *Jaren Provo* (10)

"*The Andy Griffith Show:* Return to Normal," *Ed Bell* (10)

"Is Google Making Us Stupid?" *Nicholas Carr* (11)

"American Consumerism," *Jamie Bentley* (11)

"Where Anonymity Breeds Contempt," *Julie Zhuo* (12)

"Attending to the Word," *Deirdre Mahoney* (12)

"Reverence for Food," *Rachel Schofield* (12)

"A *Beat* Education," *Leonard Kress* (20)

"Onward, Gamers, Onward!" *Royce Flores* (20)

"Cookies or Heroin?" *Marie Winn* (20)

"What Is Education?" *Petra Pepellashi* (20)

"Cartoons 'n Comics: Communication to the Quick," *Joy Clough* (20)

"Condaleezza Rice's Cleveland Browns," *Holly A. Putnat* (20)

"Crimes against Humanity," *Ward Churchill* (20)

"Internet Addiction," *Greg Beato* (20)

"Revealing the Ugly Cartoonish Truth: *The Simpsons,*" *Simon Benlow* (20)

"Hip-Hop: A Roadblock or Pathway to Black Empowerment?" *Geoffrey Bennett* (20)

"The Parting Breath of the Now-Perfect Woman," *Chester McCovey* (20)

"Television: Destroying Childhood," *Rose Bachtel* (20)

Technology

We cannot overlook technology. How does it influence the way we live? Through reading, writing, and discussion, you can explore beyond your initial thoughts and perceptions to consider the complex relationship in today's world between an individual and technology—or between one individual and another *because of technology*. What idea about technology might you discover and share with others, helping them to think or act differently?

"Americans and the Land," *John Steinbeck* (3)

"The Front Porch," *Chester McCovey* (4)

"Rise of the Image Culture: Re-Imagining the American Dream," *Elizabeth Thoman* (7)

"Cruelty, Civility, and Other Weighty Matters," *Ann Marie Paulin* (8)

"Whales R Us," *Jayme Stayer* (8)

"What Orwell Didn't Know," *George Lakoff* (9)

"*The Andy Griffith Show:* Return to Normal," *Ed Bell* (10)

"*Star Trek:* Where No Man Has Gone Before," *Jaren Provo* (10)

"Is Google Making Us Stupid?" *Nicholas Carr* (11)

"Where Anonymity Breeds Contempt," *Julie Zhuo* (12)

Note to Instructors

Like most college writing instructors, we see English composition as a vital component of an academic career. Without a transformative composition experience, many college students will struggle, fumble, or worse. And beyond the college classroom, we see writing instruction as intimately connected to students' everyday lives. We believe that composition courses are not only preparation for more academic work but also a genuine study of one's own rhetorical situations. More specifically, we assume that student writing should do two things:

1. It should emerge from the discursive entanglements of students' everyday lives. Student writing is often stiffened by the popular-but-distant topics of the day: gun control, abortion, cloning, cell phone use, and so on. Of course, for some students, these topics intersect with everyday life, but for the vast majority, they are glorified encyclopedic preformulations. They offer no possibility for new connections, no possibility for radical rethinking, no hope for discovery, and no exigence whatsoever. They are dead. Therefore, we hope to offer a pedagogy that genuinely guides students into the tensions, cracks, and unseen notches of their own lives. Perhaps, then, they will see that this whole enterprise is worthy of the immense intellectual energy it requires.
2. It should prompt students to think more adeptly, to invent a better way of knowing. We believe the only reason to write an essay is to generate a better way of thinking about a topic. In professional academic work, essays are not written to prove grammatical prowess or syntactic proficiency, but to share an important new insight, to contribute to an ongoing conversation, to reveal an otherwise hidden position or viewpoint. In the composition course, it should be no different. And it's been our experience that classroom engagement increases dramatically when students understand this rhetorical mission.

Over the editions of this book, we've been asked: Why such focus on invention? What led us to place invention at the center of the pedagogy? Initially, this focus came from understanding our own students—from witnessing how they struggle, succeed, and fail. We asked ourselves some basic questions: What do we value but fail to teach explicitly? What do other writing instructors value and assess? What are the gaps between proficient high school writing and proficient college writing? What we discovered was a type of hidden curriculum. Instructors want revelation, discovery, depth, rigor, and intellectual richness. But such qualities are not taught explicitly and consistently at the high school level. Students entering college often lack the discursive tools for generating the richness and complexity that college composition instructors hope to see. Our conclusion: Students need specific guidance in developing that complexity.

As we looked closely at our students, we noticed that successful writers tend to:

- Start thinking about their topics and their own responses early on
- Turn ideas and positions around—investigating intellectual possibilities
- Rethink based on the values, assumptions, and claims of others
- Address and even envelop opposing ideas

In short, successful writers invent. They do what the classical rhetoricians taught: use language to explore what's possible.

Contrarily, unsuccessful writers skip invention. Their relationship with language is at best tentative . . . at worst, antagonistic. And they often carry some counterproductive notions about thinking and writing: ideas emerge fully formed from an individual's head; good writers do not struggle or rethink; the only way to develop an idea is by adding facts; an essay is good if it's properly arranged and grammatically correct. Such assumptions work against writers—even more than their unfamiliarity with grammatical conventions or other "basics." Before they even begin a course or an assignment, these quiet notions stymie many students' foray into an intensive writerly experience.

With *The Composition of Everyday Life*, we hope to vitalize students' assumptions about writing, and to dramatize a simple but crucial point: Language is not merely a conduit for expression but a tool for developing ideas. We hope that students imagine writing as an act of public exploration, a process of inventing and sharing what can be thought, what can be said, what can be known. This book, then, is grounded in and driven by a set of principles that we've deemed *invention pedagogy*. It emerges not only from our understanding of students but also from the pre-Socratic Greek sophists—those folks who invented rhetoric (and the practice of democracy). The broader goal is to get students using language in public writing to develop increasingly sophisticated ideas. More specific goals are tied up in the sections of each chapter:

Point of Contact sections encourage students to slow down and notice the nuances of life around them while considering possibilities for writing topics. The questions pull students away from stiff and distant topics and toward the real entanglements of their own lives.

Analysis sections help students develop meaning and significance while prompting them to explore their topics with questions and dialogic activities.

Public Resonance sections draw attention to the rhetorical situation—to the assumptions, values, and beliefs of others. Writers are prompted to explore what others believe and how the particular writing project can influence common belief.

Thesis sections in each invention chapter help students to hone their ideas to a fine edge. Each section contains prompts, sample thesis statements, common thesis problems, and an "Evolution of a Thesis" chart, which illustrates the gradual development of an idea.

Rhetorical Tools sections explain the support strategies that are most applicable and appropriate to the writing situation. The sections teach students that all rhetorical tools (such as narration, argumentative appeals, allusions, and so on) can be applied according to the writer's particular needs.

Revision sections suggest ways to work back through essay drafts, applying even more invention strategies. Each section also features chapter-specific questions for peer reviewers.

Reflection sections ask students to articulate ideas about how their essays work. These prompts get students writing about writing, dealing metacognitively with the particular intellectual maneuvers required/prompted in that chapter. Many of the "Reflection" sections also invite students to go "Beyond the Essay"—to take their ideas from the chapter and recast them in some other format: a poster, a cartoon, and so on.

As they work through the sections, students may feel their ideas getting more complex, even unwieldy. That's okay. In fact, if we are doing our jobs well, our students' thinking will likely get messier. But if we walk through the entire intellectual journey (that is, an assignment) with them, students may see their ideas regain focus. They may see assignments as intellectual pathways.

As all writers know, good ideas require intellectual grappling, occasional cognitive slippage, and plenty of revision. We think students at this particular point in history, in these particular economic and cultural times, must learn how to grapple and rethink. We cannot assume that such critical and nuanced skills will seep into student consciousness—that some lucky students will "pick up on" the most crucial discursive moves. If writing instructors value rigorous (*inventive, rich, deep, intensive, analytical, critical*) thinking, and if we reward it with a grade, then we owe students the tools for making it happen. We cannot simply provide interesting samples and expect them to extract the epistemology. If we value invention, we must teach students how to explore, how to unpack their initial thoughts, and how to persist beyond the commonplace.

A quick glance at the economy, labor relationships, world politics, and demographic shifts portends a new kind of literacy: People will need intellectual agility; they will have to think around topics, beyond themselves, beyond their initial assumptions, to simply get along in a fast-changing cultural landscape. Having an opinion and writing it neatly in five coherent paragraphs will be its own kind of illiteracy. Those who can only say what they think will get left behind. Those who can invent new intellectual postures for themselves and others will thrive.

New to This Edition

New "Analyzing Written Texts" chapter: Chapter 6 focuses on rhetorical analysis of a written text, providing instructors with examples and assignments to help students formally think through rhetorical concerns such as context, audience, use of appeals, and so on.

New Part III, "Organization and Delivery": Part III now includes new chapters on organizational strategies (Chapter 17), developing voice (Chapter 18) and creating sentence vitality (Chapter 19). The chapters provide a single place for students to find these strategies that are useful for all projects in the book.

More support for writing "Beyond the Essay": Each writing project chapter concludes with a section to help students consider how the work they have done to invent essays can transfer to other types of writing, including sound recordings, visual presentations, and other multimodal genres.

More reading tools: To supplement the existing guidance on how to read an essay and annotated examples, *The Composition of Everyday Life* now includes a passage at the beginning of each chapter that prepares students to read for the particular qualities, dimensions, and rhetorical tools of that chapter.

More attention to the role of invention in revision: The opening pages of Chapter 1 help students better understand how commonly taught steps in the writing process, such as revision, figure into invention-centered writing.

More on source evaluation: New coverage integrates evaluation of online sources so that students can see how the principles of relevance, reliability, credibility, and timeliness apply to all source types. In addition, the chapter includes more brief exercises to help instructors gauge students' understanding quickly. Finally, the sample source evaluation (with annotations and discussion) is on a more accessible topic, binge drinking.

New assignments for literacy narratives and ethnographic essays: Chapter 2 ("Remembering Who You Were") and Chapter 4 ("Observing") feature new assignment prompts aimed at helping students write literacy narratives and ethnographic essays, respectively. Chapter 4 also includes a new sample ethnographic essay.

The latest MLA guidelines and new sample research papers: Chapter 16, "Integrating and Documenting Sources," includes the updated documentation guidelines put forth in the eighth edition of the *MLA Handbook* (2016). It also features new student essays in MLA and APA style.

New reading selections: Fifteen new readings from celebrated writers in a range of fields as well as from students responding to assignment prompts from *The Composition of Everyday Life*, illustrate the rhetorical tools essential to inventive writing.

Key Features

Emphasis on invention: Unlike any other writing guide, *The Composition of Everyday Life* offers thirteen invention chapters, guiding students to be inventive thinkers and writers. In addition, "Point of Contact" sections encourage students to slow down and notice the nuances of life around them while considering possibilities for writing topics.

Step-by-step invention instruction: Included in each invention chapter, "Point of Contact" sections will help students discover a topic from everyday life. "Analysis" will launch them beyond initial thoughts and help explore the topic. "Public Resonance" will help students extend the topic outward, to make the topic relevant to a community of readers. "Thesis" will help you focus students' thinking and develop a revelatory point. "Rhetorical Tools" will help students support their point with a variety of common strategies.

Thorough revision and editing coverage: "Peer Review" activities specific to each chapter as well as "Public Resonance" sections illustrate that writing is public in nature, and help students shape their writing for their audience. Adding an intensive editing step to the invention process, the new Chapter 19, "Vitalizing Sentences," explains and illustrates particular strategies for pruning, weeding, trimming, and giving life to students' writing.

Beyond the "final" draft: Prompting students into some theorizing about their own language and intellectual moves, the "Reflection" sections can help students transfer to other writing situations what they have learned while writing a single essay. These activities can also help students identify areas for revision toward a course portfolio.

Attractive design in a concise package: *The Composition of Everyday Life* still offers the clean and elegant design students and instructors value, but the look and feel is lighter and more approachable.

Instructor Resources

The Composition of Everyday Life: A Guide to Writing, Custom Options

Additional chapters on writing in a digital age and creating and delivering effective oral presentations are available. These chapters complement *The Composition of Everyday Life* and are designed for courses in which coverage of multimedia writing or speech communication is desired.

The Composition of Everyday Life: A Guide to Writing, Brief Fifth Edition

The brief version of *The Composition of Everyday Life* includes twenty chapters, omitting the handbook.

The Composition of Everyday Life: A Guide to Writing, Concise Fifth Edition

The concise version of *The Composition of Everyday Life* includes nineteen chapters, omitting the handbook and anthology.

Instructor's Manual and Survival Guide for Teachers

John Mauk and John Metz have revised the instructor's manual alongside the fifth edition of *The Composition of Everyday Life*, updating its numerous resources to help you prepare for class. Teaching tips, syllabus planning, and lesson organization are all included. Additionally, the instructor's manual clearly specifies the ways *The Composition of Everyday Life* supports the five primary outcomes of the Council of Writing Program Administrators' (WPA) Outcomes Statement for First-Year Composition.

MindTap for The Composition of Everyday Life, Fifth Edition

MindTap for *Composition* is a personalized teaching experience with relevant assignments that guide students to analyze, apply, and improve thinking and writing, allowing you to measure skills and outcomes with ease. Easily integrate your own content into the learning path and e-book and select readings to include from a vast database, providing a single place for students to access all their course materials. Encourage students to get individualized feedback on their writing from a professional tutor, manage electronic paper submission, grading and peer review, assign multimodal activities that help students apply writing skills to real life, and track student progress and engagement with powerful, visual analytics. MindTap for *Composition* helps you teach your course, your way.

Acknowledgments

A textbook is a big invention workshop, and we are fortunate to have extremely savvy collaborators. We offer our humble gratitude: to our development editor, Stephanie Carpenter, for her powerhouse clarity, nuanced decision making, and persistent wisdom; to Leslie Taggart for supporting all the layers of the development process; to Monica Eckman, Christopher Bennem, and Laura Ross for reinforcing the company's commitment to our work; to Samantha Ross Miller for overseeing production; to Heather McElwain for checking the soundness of every assertion; to Michael Lepera and Edward Dionne (MPS Limited) for deftly steering us through production; to the marketing crew at Cengage, particularly Erin Parkins who keeps her radar on these editions; to Ann Hoffman for managing rights and permissions; and as always, to the intensive sales folks throughout the country who give arms and legs to our books.

Thanks also to our students and colleagues who graciously stumble along with us in our efforts to transcend what is and to invent what could be. Thanks to our families and friends for enduring yet another project.

Any textbook project requires hearty professionals who give up their time and energy to help steer the pedagogy in valuable directions. We relied heavily on the insights of our reviewers and were often humbled at their prowess. We are indebted to the following teachers, theorists, rhetoricians, and scholars:

Susan Achziger, *Community College of Aurora*

Belinda Adams, *Navarro College*

Steve Amidon, *Indiana Purdue University–Fort Wayne*

Andrew Andermatt, *Clinton Community College*

Gillian Andersen, *Eastern New Mexico University*

Sonja Andrus, *Collin College*

Lauryn Angel, *Collin College*

Scott Banville, *Nicholls State University*

Thomas Barthel, *Herkimer County Community College*

Larry Beason, *University of South Alabama*

Goretti Benca, *State University of New York–New Paltz*

Jeff Birkenstein, *Saint Martin*

Russell Bodi, *Owens State Community College*

Robert Bonds, *New England Institute of Art*

Jim Bosinger, *University of Toledo*

Jon Brooks, *Okaloosa-Walton College*

Ron Brooks, *Oklahoma State University*

Bessie Brown, *Hinds Community College*

Harryette Brown, *Eastfield College*

Patricia Buck, *East Tennessee State University*

Jolene Buehrer, *Bowling Green State University–Firelands*

Gary Cale, *Jackson Community College*

Walter Cannon, *Central College*

William Carpenter, *High Point University*

Peter Caster, *University of South Carolina Upstate*

Carole Chapman, *Ivy Tech Community College of Indiana*

Colin Charlton, *University of Texas-Pan American*

Marjorie Church, *High Point University*

Kirk Colvin, *American River College*

Robert Comeaux, *Northwestern State University*

Lucinda Coombs, *Central Maine Community College*

Sheilah Craft, *University of Indianapolis*

Bryan Davis, *Georgia Southwestern State University*

Martha Dede, *California State University–Long Beach*
Dominique Dieffenbach, *Florida Community College at Jacksonville*
Mariellen Dietz, *Wartburg College*
Suzanne Disheroon, *Cedar Valley College*
Lori Doddy, *Texas Woman's University*
Steve Edgehouse, *Bowling Green State University*
Dianne Fallon, *York County Community College*
Daniel Fitzstephens, *University of Colorado*
Saundra Foderick, *Argosy University–Twin Cities and Online*
Erwin Ford, *Albany State University*
Luisa Forrest, *El Centro College*
Anne Marie Fowler, *Keiser University*
Todd Fox, *California State University–Long Beach*
Christina Francis, *Bloomsburg University*
Linda Fricker, *North Dakota State University*
Jackie Garfat, *Dakota High School*
Sharon George, *College of Charleston*
Patricia Golder, *Victor Valley College*
Nate Gordon, *Kishwaukee College*
Rebecca Gorman, *Metropolitan State University of Denver*
Jack Grier, *Wilkes University*
Susan Grimland, *Collin County Community College*
Eduard C. Hanganu, *University of Southern Indiana*
Robin Hanson, *Minnesota State Community and Technical College*
Betty Hart, *The University of Southern Indiana*
Jennifer Hazel, *Owens Community College*
Anne Helms, *Alamance Community College*
Michael Hill, *Henry Ford Community College*
Valerie Hockert, *Thomas Edison State College and Axia*
Savona Holmes, *Lewis-Clark State College*
Dedria Humphries, *Lansing Community College*
William Hutchings, *University of Alabama–Birmingham*
Tammy Jabin, *Chemeketa Community College*
Lowell Jaeger, *Flathead Valley Community College*
Hershman John, *Phoenix College*
Darlene Johnston, *Ohio Northern University*
Peggy Jolly, *University of Alabama–Birmingham*
Jason Kahler, *Saginaw Valley State University*
Peggy Karsten, *Ridgewater College*
Timothy Kenyon, *Saginaw Valley State University*
Mark Kessler, *Washington State Community College*
Elizabeth Kleinfeld, *Red Rocks Community College*
David Konitzer, *Art Institute of Tampa*
Elizabeth Kuipers, *Georgia Southwestern State University*
Kim Lacey, *Saginaw Valley State University*
Jane Lasarenko, *Slippery Rock University of Pennsylvania*
Sarah Layden, *Indiana University–Purdue University Indianapolis*
Jeanette Lugo, *Valdosta State University*
Criostoir Mac Suibhne, *State University of New York–Canton*
Mercedes Martinez, *Global Language Institute*
Sean Mathews, *Adirondack Community College*
Diane Matza, *Utica College*
Sheila McAvey, *Becker College*
Jim McKeown, *McLennan Community College*
Pat McQueeney, *Johnson County Community College*
Robert Mellin, *Purdue University North Central*
Neil Michaels, *Saginaw Valley State University*
Mutiara Mohamad, *Fairleigh Dickinson University*
Christina Montgomery, *Saginaw Valley State University*
Missy-Marie Montgomery, *Springfield College*

Cleatta Morris, *Louisiana State University–Shreveport*
Mary Ellen Muesing, *University of North Carolina–Charlotte*
Joanna Murray, *Heald College*
Beverly Neiderman, *Kent State University*
Julie Nichols, *Okaloosa-Walton College*
Pam Nichols, *Alma High School*
Deborah Noonan, *University of South Florida*
Shelley Palmer, *Rowan-Cabarrus Community College*
James Pangborn, *State University of New York–Oswego*
Michael Pennell, *University of Rhode Island*
Carolyn Perry, *Westminster College*
Mary Peterson, *Avon Unit Community Schools*
Robert Petersen, *Middle Tennessee State University*
Andrew Preslar, *Lamar State College–Orange*
Arthur Rankin, *Louisiana State University–Alexandria*
Robin Reid, *Texas A&M University–Commerce*
Diane Reuszer, *Northeastern Junior College*
Andrey Reznikov, *Black Hills State University*
Katherine Riegel, *State University of New York–Potsdam*
Rebekah Rios-Harris, *Cedar Valley College*
Natasha Robinson, *Collin College*
Amy Rule, *Collin College*
Danielle Saad, *Alvernia College*
Linda Sacks, *Monmouth University*
Michael Schanhals, *North Muskegon High School*
Lisette Schillig, *Lock Haven University of Pennsylvania*
Summer Serpas, *Orange Coast College*
Elizabeth Shannon, *West Allegheny High School*
Beverly Slavens, *Arkadelphia High School*
Jeff Smithpeters, *Delta State University*
Holly Spaulding, *Northwestern Michigan College*
Debra Suffety, *Saginaw Valley State University*
Helen Szymanski, *College of DuPage*
Jeff Tate, *Northern Oklahoma College*
Luke Tesdal, *University of Texas–Arlington*
Donna Townsend, *Baker College of Clinton Township*
Rita Treutel, *University of Alabama–Birmingham*
Amanda Walton, *Longwood University*
John Wegner, *Angelo State University*
Natasha Whitton, *Southeastern Louisiana University*
Vernetta Williams, *Southwest Florida College*
Robert Wilson, *Cedar Crest College*
Carmen Wong, *John Tyler Community College*
Kristy Wooten, *Catawba Valley Community College*
Elizabeth Wurz, *Columbus State University*
Sandra Young, *Sacred Heart University*

THE COMPOSITION OF EVERYDAY LIFE

1 Inventing Ideas

Réunion des Musées Nationaux/Art Resource, NY/Estate of Picasso/ARS - Artist's Rights Society

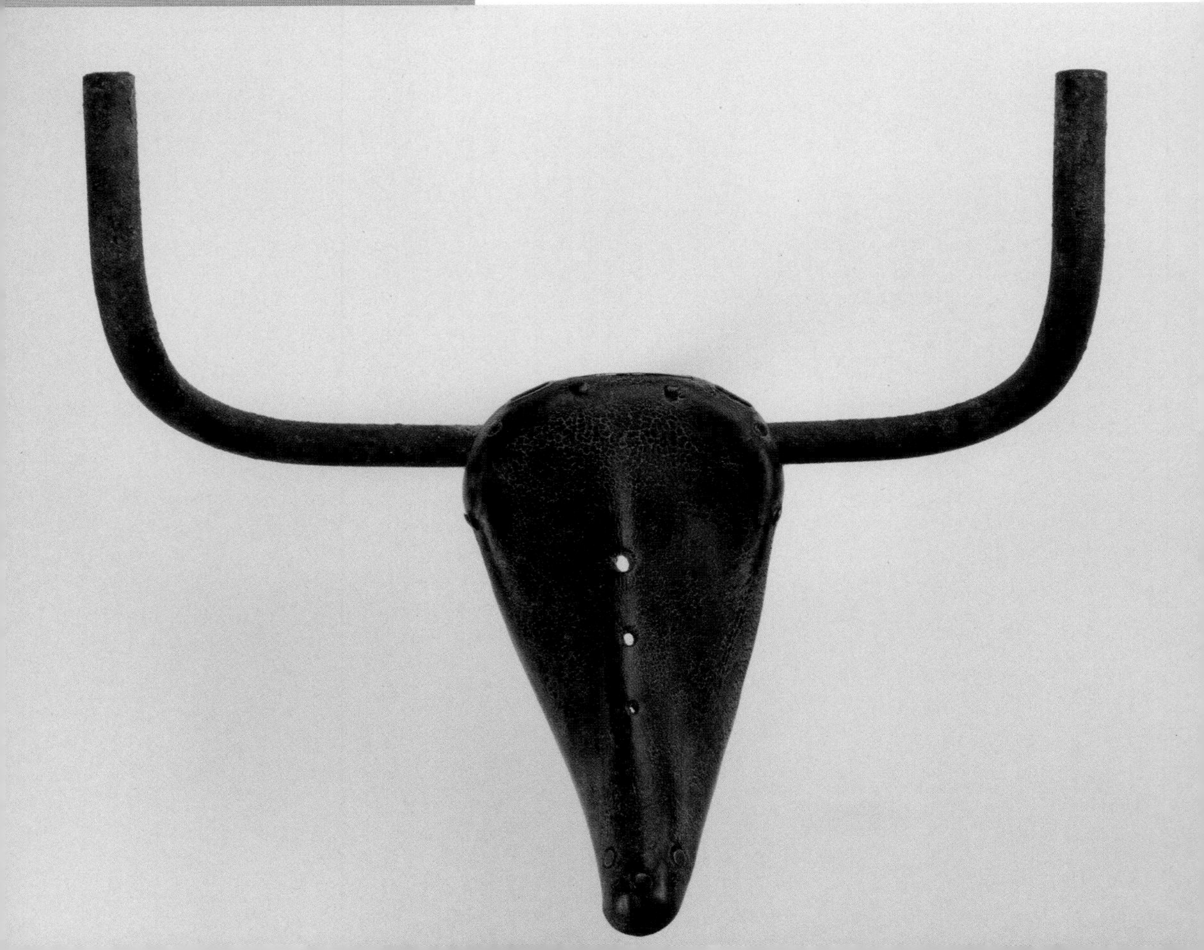

“Writing is not simply a one-way flow of information from the brain to the hand. Quite the opposite . . .”

Thousands of students across the country are required to take introductory college writing courses. These courses are nearly universal requirements, and it seems reasonable to ask: Why? What’s the purpose of these courses, and more specifically, what’s the purpose of writing? How does writing well relate to engineering, nursing, photography, business management, or aviation? Why do business and governmental leaders throughout the country want all students to take more, not less, writing? If students will not be writing essays in their jobs, why should they write essays in college?

When asked such questions, people tend to respond that writing is important for two reasons: because it helps to *express* thoughts and *communicate* ideas. However, they often forget a third point. Beyond expression and communication, there is another, perhaps far more powerful, reason: Writing is an invention tool. It helps us to generate new ideas and add dimension to the ideas we already have. Writing is not merely the performance or expression of something we know or believe. It’s also an *act of inventing, developing, and reinventing what can be known.*

Writing is not simply a one-way flow of information from the brain to the hand. Quite the opposite: It actually produces new ideas, changes everyday life, and vitalizes the thinking of writers, the readers, and the people who interact with them both. These are the reasons that writing is nearly a universal requirement in college. And it is not simply because our culture needs better communicators, but because we will always need better ideas and better ways of thinking about the situations we face every day.

Have you ever asked yourself where ideas come from? Do they pop out of thin air? Do they come from divine beings whispering in our ears? Do they come from lab experiments? From someone’s heart? Another organ? Most scholars who wrestle with such questions believe that ideas come from language, that people build, refine, pull apart, and rebuild ideas with words. And although we can use words silently in our heads, the act of writing dramatizes and amps up the whole idea-making process. In other words, writing is like an idea calculator. It allows us to put ideas “out there” on a page or a screen and then process them—adding, subtracting, multiplying, and dividing. Writing allows us to put an idea into a formula, add exponents, and radicalize. It allows us to keep several abstractions floating around at once, to link thoughts, to collapse them, to evaluate them, and even to cancel them out.

Writing is also an invitation, a convergence of many minds. In fact, in academia, writing is seen as a tool for creating social and institutional momentum: for directing people's energies, for guiding policies, for urging on new and better enterprises. Writing changes the way people act, spend, vote, teach, think, and even hope—which means this is all pretty serious and heavy business.

The Invention Manifesto: Invention in the Writing Process

What we call *invention* was not created for schoolwork, for essay assignments, or even for business. It was conceived 2,400 years ago by the ancient Greeks as a tool for analyzing and debating everyday issues. Invention was the first part of a bigger practice called *rhetoric*—the study or art of persuasion.

The Greeks had the radical notion that common people, not holy or military leaders, could think for themselves and even make policies best suited for their own affairs. In other words, the Greeks invented the thing we now call democracy. And when they started to solve problems and debate issues publicly, some people realized that successful thinkers and speakers employed certain moves; they weren't just the loudest talkers or the most charming personalities. It didn't take them long to realize that good thinking was about inventing new insights, not simply rephrasing a common opinion in fancy words. Good thinkers could ask hard questions. They could use language to show complexity and possibility. It was soon obvious to the Greeks that everyday life in a democracy requires good thinking—inventive thinking.

This book is about inventive thinking. It puts invention at the heart of college writing and each writing project. In fact, the Invention chapters (Chapters 2 through 13) walk through specific steps designed to make projects more insightful, more sophisticated, and ultimately more engaging to an academic audience. As you will see, these chapters invite writers to insert intellectual space into their process. Many people, especially those who find that they don't like to write, approach writing in two simple steps: (1) get the writing task and (2) write the essay. Think of students who turn on their computer the night before an essay is due (or a couple days earlier) and produce the required writing. Their process looks like what is shown in Figure 1.1.

This approach to academic writing leads to a problem with length, which is really a problem with ideas (a problem coming up with interesting claims and persuasive support).

writing task—final draft

Figure 1.1 One approach to writing.

Invention changes all of that. It puts intellectual space between the writing task (assignment) and the final draft, which means that the students' process now looks more like what is shown in Figure 1.2.

writing task-------*intellectual space*-------**final draft**

Figure 1.2 Invention-based approach to writing.

With this invention-based process, the students take more time (insert more space) to first explore the complexities of the topic. First they do invention writing to explore possibilities. They invent to create a focused thesis and then they draft and revise, steps that also involve acts of invention. Figure 1.3 illustrates this process.

------------------------*intellectual space*------------------------

invention:	**thesis:**	**drafting/revision:**
Using language—alone and with others, through writing and speaking—to explore, discover, & develop ideas.	Ideas created through invention are ultimately narrowed to a focused & insightful main claim (or thesis statement).	Writers draft and revise over time. When they are revising—and even when editing—they continue to invent ideas. And when they invent—before drafting—they are often revisiting and re-thinking their initial ideas.

Figure 1.3 Invention is an ongoing process (not a single step) that extends throughout the writing process including prewriting, drafting, and revision.

In this process, writers use language to create ideas, not just to deliver them. In this sense, the Analysis and Public Resonance sections you will find in Chapters 2 through 13 are Invention sections. They help writers explore, discover, and develop ideas *before* they attempt to convey anything to an audience. (You can think of this as pre-audience writing. Or you can think of it as: the audience for this writing is *you*, the writer.) Doing things the other way around—attempting to convey ideas first—leads to writer's block, lack of ideas, and generally poor writing that gets stretched out to make little-to-say long enough. And this can lead to an often fruitless revision experience because the ideas being revised lack depth and sophistication. The new intellectual space consists of time (days instead of hours, or weeks instead of days), and that time involves invention work that is absent in the old process.

In this invention-based process, writers spend time digging up raw material. Imagine a builder who starts building a house with whatever is lying around. Now imagine someone who gathers rocks (the right kinds of rocks), fells timber, hauls it to the building site, mills it, makes nails, and so on, creating high-quality raw materials. The second builder's job isn't any simpler or easier, but it results in a house that doesn't fall down. For writers, invention doesn't make writing simpler or easier. It complicates the writing (and thinking) process, which leads to better results. It leads to interesting college-level writing, and it leads to important development as a writer and thinker.

Ideas *come to* writers who insert intellectual space into the process. Why? Their minds will be at work on the topic, even while they are doing other things: walking the dog, shopping, watching TV, running, reading, hanging out with friends, eating, driving, listening to music, surfing, and so on. When writers invent first, they begin to notice how ideas from everyday life relate to their writing topic, and this helps them think new and more interesting ideas.

Learning to think of writing this way requires some adjustment, especially if you have only been imagining language as a way to convey what you already think or what you have researched. You might think of this concept—the concept of language as creator of ideas—as a threshold concept. A threshold concept is one that brings you to a new way of seeing, thinking, and being. Threshold concepts are transformational. You actually see and understand something you didn't see and couldn't understand before crossing the threshold. And, threshold concepts are troublesome. Because they involve a new way of seeing, it's normal to struggle a bit at first—and even for a while—before finally seeing the light.

The FedEx logo is not itself a threshold concept, but it can be used to illustrate what it's like to cross the threshold. (See Figure 1.4.) If you have never noticed the arrow in the logo, look until you see it, or just have someone point it out to you. Once you see it, you will easily see it every time you see the logo again. The same is true once you really use language to invent and not just convey ideas, as the questions in the Analysis and Public Resonance sections will help you do. You will cross an important intellectual threshold that transforms your writing and thinking.

© Tupungato/Shutterstock.com

Figure 1.4 Can you make out the arrow in the FedEx logo?

Asking Questions

One of the most powerful ways to insert intellectual space into the writing process is to ask questions. For instance, let's explore a basic or common concept such as *freedom.* We might ask, *What is it?* First, we might write out some initial thoughts:

What is freedom?

Freedom is the ability to do whatever one wants. It's the feeling we get when we know that we can do whatever we want.

But can we go further? What else can be known or thought about freedom? Let's apply more questions, the kinds of questions you'll encounter in Chapters 2 through 13:

What particular behaviors are associated with freedom?

Politically speaking, voting, protesting, speaking one's mind, worshipping whatever or whomever one desires—or not worshipping at all. Personally, free people do what they want whenever they want. They make their own choices: what they want to buy or drive or eat, how they want to spend their time, where they want to go, what they want to read, whom they want to love or marry.

What responsibilities come with freedom?

Maybe none. If people are free, they do what they want and let others clean up the mess or worry about the consequences. That sounds somehow wrong or bad, but that's what true freedom is. There's no impending rule that says one must do something or think something. Put this way, freedom—true freedom—might be pretty messy. People would get away with murder. Literally.

What hidden role does freedom play in people's lives?

Most people are always trying to get free—from work, duty, homework, etc. They want to be "done" with the things other people assign to them. They want Saturday afternoon—when no one is saying, "Be here and do this." And politically (again), people throughout the world are dying for it. They stand in front of tanks, blow up government buildings, or pack their families onto wagons and trudge for hundreds of miles so they can experience freedom. So those are the obvious ways freedom works. But "a hidden role"? Is freedom hidden? Do we hide it from ourselves? Why would we do that? Don't we want it? I think most Americans spend their time in some kind of duty—work, school, both. When they're not working under someone else's guidelines, they look to fill up the freedom time. They schedule it. I wonder if people know what to do with freedom . . . with time not gobbled up by duty. Skateboard? Listen to music? Read? Watch TV? Is that what freedom is? What about retirement? Isn't that supposed to be total freedom? If so, why do people get lonely? Why do senior citizens want something to do? Why do they volunteer? (They're always the ones at voting booths, libraries, bake sales, etc.) Maybe people want to be given things to do. Maybe they want to be a part of something. Beyond having the right to speak, marry, vote, work, and travel at will, people want to feel commissioned—to be of some good use. And in some way, that's the opposite of freedom. People yearn for freedom but suffer when they experience it in the extreme.

When the writer applies more Invention Questions, the concept grows. The writer's thinking gets richer, more complex. After the third question here, the writer gets past the obvious, taken-for-granted layer and digs up some truly interesting ideas, for instance, that unmitigated freedom could be ugly.

Obvious Layer: Freedom is about escaping duty.

Deeper Layer: Escaping all duty comes with a price.

This intellectual process is invention. Asking questions and writing responses makes writers go from an obvious idea (*Freedom is doing whatever one wants*) to something less obvious (*Freedom is the sometimes spiritually hollow lack of duty*). And in academic writing, readers are hoping for something less obvious. The goal isn't to state what most people, or even some people, already think. Rather, it is to bring hidden layers to the surface.

This is no easy task. The process requires a certain degree of endurance—a willingness and ability to continue thinking through intellectual walls and past "answers." The excerpts about freedom shown here, for example, are just one small part of the larger invention writing process that involved a great deal more writing and thinking. Much of this invention writing (not shown here) stalled out, went in new directions, hit dead ends, started up again, and eventually *through persistence* led to discoveries and potential discoveries. This example is like the highlights of a baseball game that show a home run or a diving catch but not all the foul balls and pop-ups. Invention writers should not expect a few sentences or paragraphs to automatically lead to a new idea. It might take a few paragraphs or pages to work through their initial thinking on the way to less obvious, more insightful ideas. Because ideas come from language, the more language one uses *in the spirit of invention,* the more ideas will be created.

Activity

With a small group, take a concept (such as education, individuality, authority, crime, or art) and try to dig up something new—some hidden layer or less obvious quality, something that others in your class may not imagine. Use the following questions:

- What is it?
- What particular behaviors are associated with it?
- What responsibilities come with it?
- What hidden role does it play in people's lives?

Reading for Rhetoric

If your situation is like that of nearly every other college student, instructors will ask you to read essays that have little or no obvious connection to your life. You may be interested in football, and your college English instructor may assign an essay about the punk movement in Europe or vineyards in Washington. Why? Why should urban students read about agricultural practices, rivers, or forests? Why should rural students read about the streets of Chicago, the Manhattan subway, or the opera? Why should twenty-year-olds read about the role of the World War II generation in shaping the suburbs? Is it because instructors want students to get specific information on those topics? Probably not. In fact, reading assignments in college English courses are often connected to a larger academic goal: to broaden students' perspectives.

Most readers ask themselves questions. Two questions seem to arise consistently:

Do I like this essay?

Can I relate to this information?

But those questions can limit readers. In fact, if they're the *only* questions available, they put readers at a big disadvantage by limiting what they can learn. Most instructors want students to think about topics from different angles, and to examine life outside of their own spheres. In other words, instructors hope that students gain some *intellectual agility*—the ability to move from position to position without tremendous difficulty, to imagine a realm of experience and perspective beyond their own biases and reflexes.

If readers have some other questions in mind, some other reasons to continue (besides liking something or relating to it), they might discover something and gain intellectual agility. Imagine, for instance, how the following questions might take a reader somewhere more valuable than the two preceding questions:

How does this essay prompt me to think?

What new idea does it offer?

What new connections does it make?

Why am I resisting the point? Why do I agree with the point?

Where is this essay taking me? How far will it go?

With such questions swirling in their heads, good readers are more apt to push onward through foreign ideas, to examine new assumptions, to carry away something significant.

Good readers do more than read. They read and monitor their own thinking as they move through the text, and they allow themselves to go further than their personal likes or ability to relate. They tolerate (maybe even bask in) intellectual discomfort. They consider ideas and assumptions that might seem foreign, weird, abstract, or unnecessarily provocative.

So the purpose of reading in college goes far beyond the two most common questions readers may ask themselves. In an academic setting, we do not read merely to relate or associate with the information. We read to rethink issues, to discover positions we had not previously imagined, to revise common perceptions. And to fulfill such goals, we must expect to work through ideas, even struggle at times. Most importantly, we must expect to be surprised, to have our tidy mental rooms messed up occasionally. Reading in academia means being intellectually adventurous and expecting something new or radically different.

Another goal of reading assignments involves the *rhetorical* layer: Behind the obvious content of an essay, there lurks a complex set of *rhetorical tools*—strategies that persuade readers to accept the writer's ideas. Even though an essay may be about pollution, cats, childhood obesity, or any other topic, it has another dimension, a rhetorical dimension. You might think of this as the machinery of the essay, the stuff that makes it go. And most often, that rhetorical dimension is the reason instructors assign particular essays. It's not the "information" that instructors want students to focus on, but the way information is dealt with (analyzed, revised, dramatized, even radicalized). For example, in Chapter 4, Anne-Marie Oomen's essay focuses on a sand dune. If you are asked to read Oomen's essay, it's probably not because your instructor loves sand, nature, or hiking. So the essay must have some other value. It must be up to something other than celebrating sand dunes. And that something must be important to college writing—and to higher education. What is that something?

The answer lies in Oomen's rhetorical prowess: her ability to help readers think differently, to yank readers' attention away from the mundane aspects of everyday life and conventional ways of thinking:

> I have come to love the wind here, the power it has to erase through its insistent presence. Just as it has blown out the hilltop, the very place that represented the great mother, Michimokwa, the wind has fragmented the story itself, altered what the place means. The meaning shifts, catches in the wind, lifts and transforms until there will be nothing left of even her heart. This is not sad, but rather the wind waking the imagination and simultaneously, paradoxically, waking us to emptiness, to the limits of story. To mystery. This is the wind making the place where story meets void, the opposite of meaning. The hollow bowl that also shapes our being.

It wouldn't matter if the essay were about canyons, skyscrapers, or subways; what's important are her strategies for nudging readers to think—to resee themselves, their lives, their mysteries, their stories. So when you do get to the Oomen essay, don't be fooled. *It ain't about sand.*

Activity

When we see only the obvious content (or information) of an essay and miss the rhetorical dimension, we miss the most transferable and usable part. It is like going for a drive and seeing only the windshield of your car; like seeing a movie and remembering only the names of the actors; like walking through a town and seeing only the street signs. To illustrate your understanding of this point, generate another analogy and share it with the class. *When we see only the obvious content of the essay and miss the rhetorical dimension, it's like* __________.

The rhetorical dimension of an essay is the layer of strategies that prompt readers to accept its ideas. When we read an essay, we get not only the information but also the set of intellectual moves and rhetorical strategies the writer employs. We can learn from and use these strategies in our own writing. In the following passage from "How I Lost the Junior Miss Pageant" (page 33), Cindy Bosley makes a sophisticated rhetorical move. She focuses on her own misunderstanding or naiveté, but then quickly pulls reader outward and focuses on the town of her childhood—a hard-knuckled town that seemed out of sync with the idea of beauty contests:

> Clearly, I lacked the save-the-whales-and-rainforest civic-mindedness required not only of Miss America, but of Junior Miss America, too. Even, although one wouldn't think it, in Ottumwa, Iowa, where my mother would go on to work in a bathtub factory, and then a glue factory, and then an electrical connectors factory (the factory worker's version of upward mobility), and finally, a watch factory where they shipped and received

> not just watches but cocaine in our town that at that time had more FBI agents in it than railroad engineers. And even in this town where my sister would go to work the kill floor of the pork plant where, for fun, the workers shot inspection dye at each other and threatened each other's throats with hack-knives. And even in this town where my cousin, age 13, would bring a bomb to seventh grade for show-and-tell, and get caught and evacuated, and be given community service to do because the public-school-as-terrorist-ground phenomena hadn't yet been born.

Bosley's passage holds some valuable lessons for writers. At the grammatical level, she takes significant risks (such as some intentional sentence fragments) that parallel some of the essay's insights. At the rhetorical level, she lines up particular details about her hometown. These details are intensely specific and even gruesome, and more importantly, they add up to a feeling about the place, about Bosley's childhood, which was completely at odds with the notion of a beauty contest.

If we remove specific content (information about beauty contests, pork plants, and bombs for show-and-tell), what do we have left? We have some rhetorical moves that we can transport to other topics:

- Personal testimony works if the details are riveting.
- Grotesque details can be highly engaging, even necessary.
- If the details are specific enough and lined up together, they can add up to an undeniable conclusion about a place or an event.
- As writers, we're allowed to wonder ourselves.

In an essay from Chapter 4: Observing, Chester McCovey contrasts the past and the present. Like Bosley, he does not simply say that something happened. He imagines how it happened and what it means:

> My grandparents' garages were small, just enough for one car and a few tools—not much of a garage for today's homeowner. In those days the garage kept a car and a small lawnmower, some rakes, and so on. The garage today must keep much more. One can see, then, how the exchange occurred. Like an old-fashioned trade in baseball, gone is the home team's beloved front porch, replaced by a big, new garage. Of course the trade is much more interesting than that. And a look at how it occurred enlightens us a little about the world in which we live. More importantly, it tells us not so much about how life is now but about how it came to be. And, I would argue, it shows us the way in which things will continue to change.

After making the simple contrast between the past and present, McCovey offers an analogy (a comparison to trading in baseball). And then he suggests some hidden complexity—some "interesting" dynamics going on behind the shift from porch to garage. (He later deals with these dynamics in the essay.) For both Bosley and McCovey, meaning lies beyond the facts of the case. The writer must probe behind the physical things and events.

In his essay, "Americans and the Land," John Steinbeck describes how early Americans ravaged the continent, and he laments that modern Americans carry on those early traditions. In the following passage, he notes how carefully scientists work to avoid polluting outer space:

> Since the river-polluters and the air-poisoners are not criminal or even bad people, we must presume that they are heirs to the early conviction that sky and water are unowned and that they are limitless. In the light of our practices here at home it is very interesting to me to read of the care taken with the carriers of our probes into space, to make utterly sure that they are free of pollution of any kind. We would not think of doing to the moon what we do every day to our own dear country.

Steinbeck reveals the absurdity of common practice—a standard yet critical move for writers. His point is not simply "don't pollute," a common sentiment. Instead, he shows the blindness and hypocrisy of polluting one's own country. He references one behavior (being careful not to pollute the moon, where no one lives) and juxtaposes it to a common behavior (openly poisoning our land, where all humans live). From this passage, we might carry away a single powerful question: What act do we allow or even defend in one situation that we forbid in another?

Good reading leads to good writing. If we keep our radar on and look at the content and the rhetorical dimension of essays, we are more apt to see the moves, questions, and strategies that can be used for any topic.

Activity

Read the following passage from Jayme Stayer's essay, "Whales R Us" (page 256), an argument about SeaWorld. Behind the specific information about SeaWorld, what is Stayer *doing?* What kinds of rhetorical moves does he make? How might a writer use those moves for another topic?

> I'm an educator, and I pay close attention when someone is trying to teach me something. So on my way out of SeaWorld, I asked myself what I had learned. Like a student who has crammed for an exam, I was able to recall lots of idiocies, but could only say I had truly learned two things. (1) Thanks to the film, I learned that sharks attack humans only when provoked, and, (2) thanks to their anthropomorphizing skits, I learned that sea otters are *cute* little buggers. Even if these elements were judicious pedagogical objectives (which they are not), they still don't add up to anything resembling education. In fact, the entire experience of SeaWorld is suspiciously similar to the exact opposite of education: mind-control.

How to Use *The Composition of Everyday Life*

As is probably clear, this book is about discovering and developing ideas through reading, inventing, and writing. Each of the Invention chapters (2 through 13) begins with three sample essays that illustrate key rhetorical moves. The Invention sections follow the sample essays and constitute the majority of each chapter.

Sample Essays

The essays in this book were written for fellow scientists, philosophers, economists, business leaders, politicians, family members, students, and public citizens. They show the real writing that is done in the public sphere—how professionals in all walks of life talk to their colleagues and to the public. Despite their individual discipline or career field, the writers all seek to develop ideas that involve and impact the world around them.

Each chapter features a professional writer (someone whose writing was published prior to this textbook), a commissioned writer (a writer or teacher who used the chapter to develop an essay), and a student writer (a college student who used an earlier version of the textbook to create a successful project). Each type of writer (professional, commissioned, student) brings something unique to the chapter and shows a set of qualities that you might adopt for your own projects. And although some of the writing techniques and personal styles differ, some qualities are constant: valuable insights, well-supported ideas, and engaging voices.

To help you read these essays closely, each is followed by Writing Strategies and Exploring Ideas questions. Also, each chapter features an *annotated* essay (an essay with comments and analysis in the margins). These annotations show a reader stopping at certain places, noticing particular claims and strategies, and speaking back to ideas.

Writing Topics

The Composition of Everyday Life offers several possibilities for inventing and developing writing topics. You can (1) read the essays in a designated chapter and then use the Ideas for Writing after one or more of the essays; (2) use the Point of Contact section, which will help generate topics from everyday life; or (3) read several content-related essays, according to the thematic table of contents at the front of the book, and then develop topics that emerge from the readings. For all three options, the Invention section of each chapter can be used to develop writing projects.

As you consider your own writing projects, imagine that topics are not prepackaged issues—as though writers simply choose something they like and start drafting. Instead, imagine topics as ideas that emerge slowly through an invention process. If you imagine topics as something to *develop,* rather than something to *choose,* your intellectual experience and your writing will likely be more intense.

Invention

"Invention is the mother of necessities."

—Marshall McLuhan

As we explain at the beginning of this chapter, invention is the process of discovering some new idea and developing that idea through focused exploration. It is often associated with one particular activity: coming up with an idea to write about. However, invention is a complex activity that extends far beyond the initial topic idea. It involves committing to an idea, exploring it in depth, and discovering its worth.

When writers take the time to explore topics, they discover something worth sharing, something that is not already floating around in everyone's minds. In short, invention makes all the difference between powerful, engaging writing that introduces new ideas, and dull, lifeless writing that offers nothing but a writer's attempt to fulfill an assignment.

Because invention is the most difficult but most crucial part of academic writing, this book devotes several sections per chapter to it. The following sections appear in each chapter and are designed to help you through the invention process:

- **Point of Contact** will help you discover a topic from everyday life.
- **Analysis** will launch you beyond initial thoughts and help you explore the topic.
- **Public Resonance** will help you extend the topic outward, to make the topic relevant to a community of readers.
- **Thesis** will help you focus your thinking and develop a revelatory point.
- **Rhetorical Tools** will help you support your point with a variety of common strategies.

The questions in each section, those marked by orange arrows, are not meant to be answered directly in a final essay. Instead, they are meant to generate ideas, focus, and support strategies for your writing.

Invention Workshops

In Chapters 2 through 13, you will see Invention Workshops—prompts to enlist the help of others in the development of your projects. Rather than answer the Invention Questions alone, you can gather in a small group and take turns explaining your topic to others. The whole group then can explore your topic by focusing on a single question or set of questions.

Invention Workshops can be the most powerful element in a composition course. If all parties are invested in the struggle to focus and vitalize ideas, the process can dramatically improve the thinking and writing for each project. But be mindful of the process. If approached uncritically or lackadaisically, workshops can decrease energy and deflate ideas. For example, in the first four workshop transcriptions that follow, the ideas get derailed. One of the participants shuts down the thinking or diffuses it somehow. But in the fifth workshop, the participants take Linda's topic to a compelling place. By following the ideas put forward, they build to a new insight:

Workshop 1

LINDA: What is the significance of a tattoo?
MARCUS: The significance is just whatever people think it is.

Workshop 2

LINDA: What is the significance of a tattoo?
DIANA: Well, it depends on the actual tattoo, doesn't it? A flower has a different significance than a skull.
LINDA: Maybe. But why do people get any tattoos?
DIANA: They just want to. Everybody has their own reasons.

Workshop 3

LINDA: What is the significance of a tattoo?
JACK: What do you mean?
LINDA: What do tattoos mean? What's the meaning behind inscribing ink permanently onto the skin?
JACK: My cousin has this huge tattoo on his back.

Workshop 4

LINDA: What is the significance of a tattoo?
MARCUS: What do you mean, "significance"?
LINDA: You know, what's the fundamental meaning of a tattoo? What's the *meaning* behind inscribing ink permanently onto the skin?
DIANA: I think it's gross, myself. I mean, don't get me wrong, people can do whatever they want with their own bodies, but it's really disgusting to me.

Workshop 5

LINDA: What is the significance of a tattoo?
MARCUS: What do you mean, "significance"?
LINDA: You know, what's the fundamental meaning of a tattoo? What's the *meaning* behind inscribing ink permanently onto the skin?
DIANA: Well, when people get a tattoo, they're doing something permanent to themselves—or at least they assume they are.
MARCUS: They're making a statement of some kind.
DIANA: A statement that has permanence.

JACK: Yeah, that's gotta mean something. People must want to have something about themselves, on themselves, that is not going to go away. It must feel . . . sorta . . . important, ritualistic, big, you know . . .

LINDA: So, people long for permanence. That's interesting. And a tattoo is a little (maybe tiny) way of establishing that . . . on their own bodies.

MARCUS: It's also something that is totally personal. I mean, you can have a tattoo of anything, and it's all your own.

DIANA: Yeah, that's why people get tattoos of their loved ones' names.

JACK: My brother has a tattoo of his old girlfriend's name.

DIANA: Yeah, my dad has a tattoo of some kind that doesn't really mean anything, and he won't even tell us what it's from. He got it when he was a teenager.

LINDA: OK. But what do those examples show? Tattoos are still there, but the people's lives go on.

MARCUS: Well, life is change. You can't escape change.

LINDA: And tattoos are a way of resisting change? A way of marking the present on one's body—storing it, keeping it with you.

MARCUS: Right! That's the significance.

Point of Contact

The Point of Contact section in each chapter invites the writers to slow down, to stop, to notice common and not-so-common aspects of life. The point of contact refers to a writer's moment of awareness. It is where the writer's vision collides with issues, events, situations, behaviors, and other people. The idea in this section is that writing begins with a discovery—a realization about something that might otherwise go unnoticed. Therefore, writers have to be ready; their radar has to be on.

As you go through the Point of Contact sections, you will notice lists of questions that are designed to generate possibilities for writing topics. Think of the questions as exploration tools; they raise possible points of interest for writing. However, the lists are by no means exhaustive; they are simply examples of what can be asked. Follow up (in peer groups or alone) to generate more questions. (And if you are outside of an academic setting, it is certainly fair play to borrow a family member or friend to help with the invention process.)

Analysis

We are all familiar with analysis. We participate in it constantly. We see auto mechanics analyze our cars to discover the cause of the knocking sound. We see our doctors analyze conditions to understand why we feel sick. Basically put, such analysis is a process of discovering why and/or how something occurs. But analysis also involves discovering meaning. Writers are not content to simply see a person, situation, or object. They explore the significance; that is, they imagine what ideas a thing might suggest. For instance, a writer sees an empty storefront in a strip mall and imagines that it suggests corporate irresponsibility or a declining economic system or even the end of an era when businesses lasted for several years before leaving a community. In other words, the storefront has potential meaning when analyzed (and often that analysis, as we will make clear in the next section, can make a topic relevant to a broader community).

The Invention Questions in each Analysis section are designed to help you reveal the complexities of your topic. (For example, see the questions and responses about *freedom* on pages 7–8.) As in all the Invention sections, the goal in the Analysis section is to generate some idea that is distinct, surprising . . . even weird.

Public Resonance

Perhaps the most important feature of writing is that it matters to a reader. This may sound obvious, but topics are not intrinsically relevant to people's lives. They need to be made relevant. They need to be expressed in a way that involves readers. Consider capital punishment: It is not, in itself, a relevant topic to the average college student, or even the average American citizen. Most people have not had a personal experience with the death penalty, but many people still have much to say about it. Why? The answer is rather simple: Capital punishment has been made relevant. Human rights activists, civil liberties groups, and religious groups have spoken or written the relevance of capital punishment into being. They have made the life of a death row inmate in Texas relevant to a suburban schoolteacher in Minnesota or a biology major at UCLA.

Good writers can make an issue resonate with their readers' feelings, thoughts, and situations. They can transform a bad day at the office into an important efficiency issue for all workers. Or they can make a seemingly distant event, like the destruction of rain forests or the death of a prison inmate, real and immediate. They make a connection between two things: (1) what they see, know, do, believe, and feel; and (2) how that matters to other people. It may not matter to every other person, but generally, it *resonates* with the public. It speaks to and engages the members of a community who, like the writer, are able to look beyond themselves (the "me") and into the public arena (the "we").

The assumption behind public resonance is that we are deeply connected to others in our communities, and even beyond those communities. Our very identities are bound to a complex system of relationships that extend into all different realms of social life. We are tied by economic, social, institutional, political, familial, religious, and even physiological connections. We share laws, fears, dreams, and hopes. And when writers tap into those connections, when they make topics part of that large social network, they achieve public resonance.

Finally, consider the Public Resonance sections as Analysis. In these sections, we're not simply analyzing the topic; we're analyzing how people tend to think about the topic.

Analysis: Focuses on the topic itself.

Public Resonance: Focuses on how people think.

In other words, writers should consider the values, assumptions, beliefs, and opinions that people have about the topic in question. Only then can they understand what to emphasize, what to minimize, what to insist upon, what to dramatize. Generally, writers can do this even without extensive research. The following questions (taken from Chapter 5: Analyzing Concepts) might help us to discover some important layers to freedom:

Is the concept generally agreed upon?

Not really. People in the United States talk about freedom, but there are many disputes about it. Should people have the freedom to burn the flag, marry the person they love, get an abortion, own a machine gun or two, stockpile hand grenades, stage a protest at a funeral, or hold the majority of a company's stock and be the CEO at the same time? The answers to such questions are wrapped up with one's political beliefs.

What is the possible connection between the topic and some public concern?

People are deeply concerned about not simply their own freedom but also other people's freedom. In the 2004 election, millions of people voted to make sure that other people didn't have the freedom to marry whom they want. In this sense, personal freedom is a kind of misnomer. It's not personal at all. An individual's freedom in the United States depends entirely on what everyone else thinks! I'm only free as far as others allow me to be.

Here, we're beginning to explore how complex freedom gets when it's analyzed against a backdrop of human affairs. This is the spirit of the Public Resonance sections throughout this book. The goal is to seek out the most resonant layers of the topic—the most powerful way the topic embeds itself into the deep structure of public life. This is no easy task. Often, the most resonant layer is the most hidden. For example, we can easily discover how freedom comes up in everyday life in songs, anthems, and public documents, but it's more difficult to discover how freedom works in public thinking, beneath those songs and anthems.

Thesis

A thesis statement is more than a one-sentence summary of an essay. It represents an essay's most pointed and dense idea, the one that gives everything else in the essay purpose. Whether the essay project is observing, arguing, or problem solving, thesis statements focus writer and reader on some new insight.

Throughout the chapters, we make a distinction between flat and revelatory thesis statements—between statements that announce an obvious opinion and those that provoke a new way of thinking. Revelatory statements contribute something; they prompt readers to imagine topics differently; they pose alternative notions, reveal hidden sides:

Flat statements: obvious, plain

Revelatory statements: provocative, insightful, contributive

For example, in the following sentences, the first statement is flat, a simple announcement of common thinking. But the follow-up sentences dig up something new. The last three statements are ripe for a powerful essay on an otherwise typical topic:

Cell phones can make people behave rudely.

Cell phones enable people to perform their social lives for an audience.

Cell phones reinforce the quiet notion that everyone is starring in his or her own reality show.

Cell phone calls crowd out time for the most important dialogue in life—the one in our own heads.

Creating revelatory statements is not magic. In fact, language drives the process. When writers replace words with other words in a sentence, they replace patterns for thinking. The revelatory statements about cell phones were created by trading out the main verb in the original sentence. The writer removed *can make* and started dropping in other verbs: *enable, reinforce, crowd out.* These verbs actually made the writer think differently: What acts or attitudes do cell phones enable? What ideas, behaviors, or assumptions do cell phones reinforce? What voices do cell phones crowd out?

Thesis statements do not emerge out of thin air. They come from an intensive evolution in which writers develop ideas with hard questions, focused dialogue, and reflective writing. Therefore, each chapter of *The Composition of Everyday Life* includes a Thesis section with prompts, sample thesis statements, and common thesis problems. Each section also shows the Evolution of a Thesis, the gradual development of one writer's idea. (The section comes after the Analysis and Public Resonance sections to allow writers the opportunity to think through and around their topics, to imagine a range of possible positions and perspectives, before committing to a particular statement.)

Rhetorical Tools

As we mentioned, a rhetorical tool is a persuasion technique, a strategy for making people believe or accept an idea. Throughout the book, we will often refer to writers' rhetorical strategies—the techniques they use to develop their ideas and attempt to convince others to accept their positions. Good writers use good rhetorical tools. They come in many forms:

Narration is the act of storytelling. Stories are often used to persuade people, to help them appreciate the value of an idea.

Description involves giving specific details to readers. Sensory details (sounds, smells, sights, tastes, touches) prompt readers to experience a topic and so accept the ideas that the writer offers.

Illustration is the graphic depiction of an idea. Although illustration certainly suggests pictures and charts, it can also be accomplished with words.

Allusions are references to some bit of public knowledge such as a historical event, a news event, a popular culture icon, or a literary text.

Scenarios are hypothetical situations.

Testimony is an eyewitness account of a particular scene or situation.

The operating assumption is that these tools can be used for any topic, that writers can apply them according to their specific needs. For example, allusions function for a huge number of writing situations. Imagine that we're developing an analytical essay about freedom. We might refer to various moments in history: the Revolutionary War, the Emancipation Proclamation, women's suffrage, Woodstock, the Patriot Act, civil unions, medical marijuana legislation, and so on. These are well-known situations that writers can reference as a way to make meaning about the idea of freedom.

The Rhetorical Tools section in each chapter explains the strategies that are most applicable and appropriate to that writing situation. However, no strategy is exclusive to any particular kind of writing. (The tools depend on the task at hand—the purpose, the audience, the topic.) The strategies introduced throughout the book can be used for unlimited writing situations. In Chapter 8: Making Arguments, the rhetorical tools become a bit more complicated. They involve *appeals, counterarguments,* and *concessions.* As you will see, the latter chapters of the book (starting with Chapter 8) all involve argumentative rhetorical tools; however, those introduced earlier in the book (such as narration and allusion) can also apply to argumentative writing. As you move through the book, think of your collection of rhetorical tools growing.

Revision and Peer Review

Revision is about reapproaching ideas. As academic writers work, they constantly rethink their original ideas. To some degree, revision is fused into every act of the writing process. Writers are constantly asking questions: "Is this the best way to do this? Is there a better way to engage my readers?" Writers also benefit from a holistic rereading of their work: a process that involves first stepping away from the text for a period of time, and then reexamining everything (the main ideas, the supporting points, the organization, and even the voice). This probably sounds intimidating—rethinking everything after a significant amount of work has already gone into a draft. But revision is often where writers finally have a grasp on the whole, where they can make the ideas cohere, tighten, and come to life.

Each chapter provides a variety of revision prompts. They appear throughout the Invention sections and invite you to stop, refocus on the ideas you've created, and to investigate the value and complexity of those ideas, with the hope that everything can be more intense, more focused, more engaging. Each chapter also includes a final Revision section with Peer Review questions so that writers can share their projects with others and receive focused and helpful feedback.

Reflection

We often need time and distance from daily events before we understand them. As our brains and bodies rush onward, we rarely have time to think about our own thinking—to get *metacognitive*. But when we're lying down at night, we can review the day and realize causes, effects, and nuances that we ignored in the moment. And it's often weeks, months, or years after an event that we begin to understand it.

The same goes with academic work. Often, the real intellectual benefit occurs after we are done writing. Only when we are in the fumes of the chaos, in the cerebral aftermath, do we understand what happened, what we had thought, and what we think now. For this reason, writers often reflect on and even write about their own work *after* it is completed and submitted. They look back on what they wrote, and they keep thinking. In fact, much of the work that we now call scientific discovery was written as a reflection on a previous study.

When writers look back on their writing, they can see what worked and what didn't. When they review their writing as a finished product, they can see it differently than a work in progress. They can step back and see how their rhetorical moves played out—how they worked and how they might have worked better. This kind of reflection is critical to one's development as a writer and thinker. Without a formal pause to examine their own rhetoric, writers risk jumping into the next project without developing from the previous one. Thus, each chapter of this book offers an opportunity to reflect—to look back and see your own rhetoric from the vantage point that a finished project allows.

Part II: Research

While the chapters in Part I focus on invention, the chapters in Part II focus on research—on all the critical steps for engaging and integrating what other scholars have written:

Chapter 14: Finding Sources

Chapter 15: Analyzing, Synthesizing, and Evaluating Sources

Chapter 16: Integrating and Documenting Sources

These chapters can be applied to any of the writing projects in Part I: Whether you are analyzing a concept (in Chapter 5), searching for a cause (in Chapter 11), or proposing a solution (in Chapter 12), you can integrate primary and secondary sources. And while these chapters explain practical steps for sound academic research, they also explore some important intellectual and rhetorical problems related to researching across digital landscapes. Taken together, the three chapters will help you to understand the nature of potential sources and the many ways that they can intensify, shift, and shape your writing projects.

Part III: Organization and Delivery

So far we've been exploring, discovering, and developing ideas about a writing topic. In Part III, we consider issues of delivery: organization, writer's voice, and sentence vitality. *The Composition of Everyday Life* offers a chapter on each:

Chapter 17: Organizing Ideas

Chapter 18: Developing Voice

Chapter 19: Vitalizing Sentences

Whether narrating an event, describing a scene, offering evidence, or making an allusion, writers can arrange rhetorical tools in many different ways. Chapter 17 (Organizing Ideas) provides strategies for presenting ideas that read like a journey: beginning with a sense of direction (an introduction), passing through various locations over different terrain (separate paragraphs), connected with road signs (transitions), and leading somewhere (a unique and valuable conclusion). The Organizing Ideas chapter suggests ways ideas might be arranged—shaped, ordered, connected.

Every writer creates a voice—the character that is projected by the language and style of the essay. Whether or not you know it, simply writing a sentence creates *voice*. Chapter 18 (Developing Voice) helps writers become aware of strategies for stylizing voice based on the audience and writing situation. Chapter 19 (Vitalizing Sentences) makes writers aware of writing habits that zap the life from an essay. This chapter shows you specific—nuts-and-bolts—strategies for writing lively and readable sentences.

A Final Note

As you work through the chapters, remember that writing is not merely a tool for expressing opinions; rather, it is a tool for making new ideas, and for adding new dimensions to old ideas. Our purpose in writing is not merely to express what we think, but to shape what can be known. We are hoping to explore intellectual possibilities. In this light, a college essay can be seen as a record of intellectual exploration—a writer's attempt and invitation to figure out something new.

Invention Writing Project

The purpose of this assignment is for you to experience how language/writing is the way we explore, discover, and create ideas (not just convey them). It may be helpful to picture yourself as a creator of ideas rather than a writer of essays. In other words, instead of writing a traditional essay for this project, imagine that your entire goal is to generate an increasingly focused and revelatory idea about the topic.

This project involves two parts:

Part 1: Invention Writing

Part 2: Writing about Your Invention Writing

PART 1: Invention Writing (Using Language to Create Ideas)

A. Choose one of the following topics:

high school sports or a particular high school sport: basketball, girls soccer, etc.

college or a particular aspect of college: tuition, cheating, texting, students, etc.

art or a particular type or work of art or a particular artist: graffiti, Mona Lisa, Basho, etc.

music or a particular type of music or a particular band/artist: hip-hop, country, Elvis, etc.

pay or the pay/salary or work conditions for a particular job/profession: teachers, fast food workers, etc.

nature or a particular aspect of nature: trees in your neighborhood, rivers, Hudson River, mice, etc.

technology or a particular technology: smartphones, course websites, television, etc.

entertainment or a particular type of entertainment: gambling, amusement parks, Daytona Beach, etc.

drugs or a particular type of drug: marijuana, Ritalin, alcohol, etc.

some other topic: Instead of one of the previously mentioned topics, choose a different topic, one that you're interested in, that matters to you, and that you want to explore further and understand in a different, more complicated way.

A. **Note on Choosing a Topic to Explore:** At this point you are faced with an early decision: what topic to explore. As you decide, keep in mind that all the topics involve the same type of thinking, writing, and work. None of the topics are easy, and none of them are hard. You can explore the topic you are the least interested in or know the least about just as easily (and with all the same difficulty) as you can explore a topic you really like and know a lot about.

B. **Respond to the following Invention Questions:** The six questions that follow will act as springboards for thinking about your topic. To get the most out of this activity, write out your responses in complete sentences and paragraph form; do not just jot down phrases, make an outline, or cluster. Why? Jotting down phrases, outlining, and clustering involve identifying *topic areas* you might include in your essay. Writing complete sentences, however, allows you to explore nuance, subtlety, contradiction, and tensions related to the topic. To explore, discover, and develop ideas (to explore into the complexity of the idea and complicate your thinking about it), you will likely need to write several paragraphs in response to each of the questions. Now is the time to go beyond what *is* and explore what *might* and what *could* be:

1. Specifically, how does the concept influence or change people's lives?
2. What particular emotions, behaviors, or ideas are associated with it?
3. What hidden role does it play in everyday life?
4. Are there complexities to the concept that people overlook?
5. Is it generally agreed upon?
6. Why is it important that people have an appropriate understanding of this concept?

PART 2: Writing About Your Invention Writing (Using Language to Convey)

Review your invention writing and write an essay:

Where in invention writing did you reveal something? In other words, which statements or passages pose alternative notions or reveal hidden sides? Why do you conclude this?

The audience for your invention writing was you: you were writing to explore, discover, and develop ideas. Now, the audience for this essay is someone else: you are writing to explain to readers how through invention writing you complicated your thinking. This audience will understand your points best if you quote or paraphrase specific passages from your writing and explain why you think they are revelatory—what new idea or way of thinking they reveal and what is interesting or important about that.

2

Remembering Who You Were

Carlos Javier Ortiz/Aurora Photos/Corbis

"Those who fail to learn the lessons of history are doomed to repeat them."

—George Santayana

You have probably heard this famous statement—perhaps when someone in a history class asked plaintively, "Why do we have to learn this stuff?" Santayana's point, of course, is that the past is filled with situations that teach us about ourselves, and that ignoring the past results in blindness to the present and future. While Santayana's statement is most often applied to a collective history (e.g., American or world history), it also suggests something for the individual. In the same way that countries learn from their pasts, individuals come to new insights because of their own experiences. Obviously, we learn basic *dos* and *don'ts* from experience (not to ride a bike over the icy patch in the driveway, not to talk during math class, not to indulge too much the night before an exam). But our pasts are filled with more opportunity for insight beyond simple I'll-never-do-that-again situations. A vast array of moments lurks in the past, moments that may mean far more than what we have always assumed.

Writers looking into their pasts attempt to learn something new, to understand the importance of some moment, or to understand the significance of a situation. They are retrieving an event or situation, uncovering a moment, and examining it from their present perspective. The hope is that writers will see more about the situation than they possibly could have seen in the past. Imagine an adult writer looking back at a childhood baseball game: As a child, he fretted over striking out in the last inning. But as an adult, he can see how important that moment of failure was to his life, to his intellectual and spiritual growth. The present (adult) writer is able to see this because the elapsed time has allowed him emotional and intellectual distance.

In academia, writers often look to their own pasts for insight:

- In a sociology course, students recall their childhood communities; they pay close attention to the institutions (churches and schools) they attended and include their memories in a theory about institutional affiliation.
- A psychology professor prompts students to recall their early experiences with non-parental authority (such as teachers, extended family, and babysitters) and form a theory of authority based on those experiences.
- In a Western civilization course, students recall their early experiences with organized religion. They include their experiences in their collective examination of religious principles.

Memories do not, in themselves, teach us anything. We must create the lesson. We must look back at the past with a certain perspective: one of curiosity and possibility. Although we have lived through the past, we must entirely rediscover it if we are to learn.

This chapter will help you rediscover a specific situation or event from your past, explore it in depth, develop a particular point about it, and communicate your ideas in writing. The essays will provide insight into various writing strategies. For example, they all develop a particular insight from some personal memory. Although the main insight of an essay is often placed in the opening paragraph, the essays in this chapter might communicate this insight elsewhere. Look for this insight as you read. Then identify, as much as possible, a particular moment the insight hinges on. Also look for the public resonance of the essay—the connection between the particular memory and a shared, or public, concern. After you read the essays, you can find a topic in one of two ways:

1. Go to the Point of Contact section to find a topic from your everyday life, or
2. Choose one of the Ideas for Writing that follow the essays.

After you find a topic, go to the Analysis section to begin developing your ideas.

Readings

Selling Manure

Bonnie Jo Campbell

Writers try to see beyond the obvious—beyond simple reflexes and common associations. As they reach beyond the usual responses to everyday life, they may discover vulgarity in nice places and beauty where others least expect it. In this essay, Bonnie Jo Campbell, a celebrated short story writer and novelist, helps readers to see value in a dirty and potentially menial job—selling manure. Obviously, such work would stink. But Campbell helps us to consider the quiet honor and honesty of the job.

Mid-May, after school was out, I found myself staring six weeks of unemployment in the face. This bothered me only until I began to envision myself reading novels in the shade of my favorite hickory tree, or making and eating entire batches of chocolate fudge, staying up late to watch black and white movies. How long had it been, I tried to recall, since I spent an entire day on my horse or in the treehouse? My mother, however, had no patience for such idleness, and she lined up myriad farm chores to occupy me—including mucking out her big horse barn. The manure was so deep in places that the horses were scraping their heads on the ceilings.

"How are we going to get rid of this stuff?" I asked.

"You're going to load it in the back of the truck," said Mom, who was conveniently under doctor's orders to refrain from activities such as scooping, lifting, and flinging. "And then we're going to sell it."

She placed ads in the *Kalamazoo Gazette* and *The Kalamazoo Shopper,* offering manure for 35 dollars a truckload. My portion for doing the physical work was a generous 20 bucks; Mom got 15 for providing the truck and the product. Right away we got calls. A surprising number of people wanted the stuff we were so anxious to get rid of.

I spent much of that unseasonably hot May and June sweating inside the barn, moving layer after layer of manure and urine-soaked straw. Periodically, Mom brought me quart jars of iced tea to keep up my spirits and electrolytes—I could tell she was even feeling a little guilty about my working so hard. I didn't tell her that, far from feeling wretched as I loaded the truck, I was feeling revived. For one thing, I was in good company. The horses and donkeys wandered through and sniffed at me; the dogs lay in holes they'd dug outside the barn door and chewed on chunks of manure; a little garter snake who lived in a hole in the dirt floor slithered in and out of the barn under the wall. And I was enjoying letting my thoughts wander. After months of sitting in class, focusing on the drone of professors and poring over books and notes, I finally had rejoined the world of the living.

Delivering the manure was a little embarrassing at first. The body of my mother's pick-up truck was rusting away and the two sides of the bed were held together with shock cords. Most of our deliveries were to west side neighborhoods, and it was problematic that construction crews had narrowed West Main to one lane in each direction. Stuck in a traffic jam, in ninety-five degree heat with a half a ton of manure in the back, we made quite a sensation. In the beginning, I put my hand over my face and hoped that I wouldn't see anyone I knew.

Within about a week, however, I began to see the absurdity of our situation as liberating. As we rattled through well-kept neighborhoods in a pickup full of stinking manure, I loosened the safety belt and hung my leg out the passenger side window, and I felt like master of all I surveyed. Perhaps this was how a prostitute felt toward a wealthy, respectable client; I might be dirty, but I have something you need.

Mom and I provided an excellent quality product at a fair price to decent folks. The people who bought our product were nice—after all, only very earthy people would order manure from the farm rather than buying it deodorized and sterilized in bags from the store. Customers often tried to help me shovel, but after I rebuffed their advances they stood back and smiled at the cascading dung. Hands on hips, eyes sparkling, they might have been fantasizing about late-summer gardens brimming with tomatoes and squash.

One man who lived just off Stadium Drive was planting a full acre of garden on land he'd rented from the utility company. After I unloaded the truck under the power lines, he took Mom and me to admire a mound across the way. "Do you know what that is?" he asked. "That's llama manure. And this pile over here, that's pig manure. And that's chicken." The pig pile was so fragrant that I figured he'd soon have trouble with his neighbors in the nearby apartment complex, but his enthusiasm was touching. I felt proud that our manure was out in the world, mingling with other manures, making things grow.

There is no vocation more honest than selling manure. Consider what most people do for a living. They go to work where they build crap, or sell crap, or move crap, or spin a line of bull over the telephone, all the while trying to convince the customer that their product is something other than crap. When I deliver a load of manure to someone's garden, the customer and I are both upfront about what we were dealing with. All I have to ask is, "Where do you want this shit?"

This experience has made me reflect on the idea of work in general. Any job is an important job, whether it is selling manure or selling insurance. People should take pride in what they do, and not assume that a low-paying job or a dirty job makes them second class citizens. And even the smelliest job has its rewards.

My darling Christopher works second shift at a paper converting plant in Parchment. "What are you doing today?" he asked me, as I walked him out to his truck. I told him I was going to spend the afternoon shoveling manure.

"Aren't we all," he said, nodding. "Aren't we all."

Writing Strategies

1. What is the main idea of Campbell's essay? And how is it something beyond the obvious?
2. Explain how detailed description works in the essay. For instance, how do the details about the barn, the dogs, and the heat figure into her main idea?

3. How does Campbell support the notion that her work was *liberating?*
4. How does Campbell create public resonance? Point to a particular passage in which Campbell makes her own experience relevant to others.
5. Explain how the customers' responses work in the essay (in ¶8 and ¶9). Focus on specific sentences or descriptions, and explain how they relate to Campbell's main idea.

Exploring Ideas

1. Campbell boldly states, "There is no vocation more honest than selling manure." How is that true?
2. Campbell says that the absurdity of her situation made it liberating. How does that work? Explain how absurd predicaments free us from something—from our usual routines, from the oppression of our daily concerns.
3. In ¶7, Campbell compares herself to a prostitute. What makes that an appropriate or inappropriate comparison?
4. This essay suggests something about socioeconomic status—working-class, middle-class, and upper-class jobs. How is this essay a defense or celebration of working-class life?

Ideas for Writing

1. What experience was a little (or a lot) embarrassing at first but later became liberating? Help the reader understand how you came to feel differently about the experience. (Avoid making obvious points, such as it was no longer embarrassing because you were better at doing it.)
2. What job of yours was either very honest or very dishonest? Help the reader see the less obvious value the work had for you and for others.

If responding to one of these ideas, go to the Analysis section of this chapter to begin developing ideas for your essay.

How I Lost the Junior Miss Pageant

Cindy Bosley

Most people have never participated in a beauty pageant. But nearly everyone has experienced the angst associated with the quiet pageantry of everyday life—the constant pressure to perform well in public, to look the part of a happy, stable, well-to-do member of society. Cindy Bosley, a teacher and published poet, is brave enough to share her early attempts at dealing with this pressure. On one hand, this essay is an examination of beauty pageants and the awkward system of values and beliefs that surround them; on the other, it is an intimate look at a mother/daughter relationship defined by the social goings-on of a small city in the middle of America.

Every evening of the annual broadcast of the Miss America Pageant, I, from the age of seven or so, carefully laid out an elaborate chart so that I might also participate as an independent judge of the most important beauty contest in the world. From my viewing seat on a green striped couch in my parents' smoky living room where the carpet, a collage of white, brown, and black mixed-shag, contrasted so loudly with the cheap 70s furnishings that it threatened my attention to the television set, I sat with popcorn and soda, pen in hand, thrilled at the oncoming parade of the most beautiful women in the world.

In the hours before the show began, I'd carefully written out in ink, sometimes over and over, names of all 50 states, Washington, D.C., and Puerto Rico along the *y* axis of my paper. And my categories of evaluation of the contestants ribbed themselves along the *x* axis—beauty, poise, swimsuit, evening gown—plus categories of my own—hair, likability, teeth. Over the years, an increasingly complex system of points and penalties evolved: an extra point for being tan, a loss of points for sucking up, more points for breasts, more points for unpainted nails, fewer points for big noses, fewer points for skinny lips, an extra point for smartness, subtraction of a point for playing the piano. Who wants to hear a sonata? Dance for me, bounce your bootie.

My mother had secret hopes. Finally divorced for the second time from the same man, my father, she sat with me and gave her own running commentary about who was cute, who smiled too much, who would find a handsome husband. My mother, having always been a little to a lot overweight, excelled at swimming, and she told me much later that she chose swimming because she didn't feel fat in the water. Her sister was the cheerleader, but she was a swimmer, too heavy for a short skirt of her own, she said. My mother's secret was that she wanted the winner to be her daughter. Sitting with me on the couch at 137 North Willard Street, she already knew I wasn't tall enough or pretty enough in the way of models and movie stars to ever stand a chance, but her real fear, which I only became aware of as an older teen, was that I would always be too chubby and too backward and too different and too poor, for which she blamed herself, to win a beauty pageant. Still, there were always those surprises of the contests—Miss Utah? She was no good! Why did she win? What were those judges

Cindy Bosley, "How I Lost the Junior Miss Pageant." Reprinted with permission of the author.

thinking! It should have been Miss Alabama, anyone can see that. Who would have guessed Miss Utah, with that mole on her shoulder?

After my mother's never-subtle hints that if I'd just lose 20 pounds boys would like me and I might even win a beauty contest, it was my friend Bridget who wanted us to enter the Ottumwa (pronounced Uh-TUM-wuh) Junior Miss Pageant together. I secretly believed that I stood a better chance than Bridget did, though she had the right name and the right body, though she wore the right clothes and was more magazine-beautiful than I. I had *some* hope for the contest: I had *some* talents and a kind of baby-cute innocence complete with blond hair and blue eyes that I was sure the judges would find "charming and fresh." Yeah, okay, so I was already engaged to be married—so what—I was still on my way to college, and Bridget was not. And Judy was funny but had a flat face. Marcy was smart but had no breasts or hips. Carol was pretty but totally uncoordinated and her knees came together when she jumped. Desirea had enviable boobs, almost as nice as mine and probably firmer, but her chin did weird things when she smiled and her eyes were brown.

We practiced, all of us together, several times a week with a lithe woman—somebody's mom with good hair and body—getting us into form for the stage. This was the era of *Flashdance,* so we all wore our own leg warmers and torn sweatclothes and fancy headband scarves. If you were one of the north-side girls (that meant your daddy was a businessman or doctor), you had gotten your leg warmers from Marshall Field's in Chicago. If you were Bridget, your dad worked at John Deere like mine but was in management and not out in the factory threading bolts on a greasy, noisy machine, so you got your leg warmers from the mall in Des Moines. If you were me, with a factory dad who didn't even live in the same house, you got your leg warmers from Kmart down the road because Target was all the way across town and too expensive, and Wal-Mart hadn't yet been born as far as we knew. The fancy mom-lady made sure everyone had a brochure about her charm school (this is small-town Iowa, mind you, so anyone operating a charm school and modeling agency in this town was kidding themselves. But making lots of money.).

So 14 of us, nervous, jealous, ears ringing with Mirror-Mirror-on-the-Wall, met daily for two weeks prior to the pageant to go over our choreographed group fitness routine to be performed, not in swimsuits, but in short-shorts and white T-shirts, Hooters-style (also not invented yet as far as we knew), and to discuss such techniques as Vaseline along the teeth and gum lines to promote smooth smiles, lest our lips dry out and get stuck in a grin during discussions with the judges of the agonies of world hunger. We were each responsible for our own talent routines and props, and each one of us had to provide a 5×7 black-and-white photo for the spread in the town paper.

The photographs were a problem. My father did not believe in such things for girls as shoes, clothes, haircuts, college, or photographs for Junior Miss, and so there was no way he was going to give a penny for a pageant-worthy dress or a professional photographer's 10-minutes-plus-proofs. I believe my mother even humiliated herself enough to ask. This was hard for her, since he'd admitted before leaving to a five-year affair with a woman who looked surprisingly like my mother but heavier. So Mom and I tried some Polaroid headshots against the side of the house, but me dressed up in my prettiest sailor blouse couldn't counteract the hospital green of the aluminum siding. We moved up to our only other option, which was my mother's flash camera with Instamatic film, and still nothing suitable (I could have agreed on one of the Polaroid shots, but my mother knew it would knock me out of the contest for sure even before the night itself).

I don't know who she borrowed the money from or what she did to get the favor, but my mother had me down at Lee's Photography the very next afternoon, and he took one shot and offered us the one proof. Abracadabra, there was my face among all the other faces as a contestant in the Uh-TUM-wuh Junior Miss Pageant. From the layout in the paper, it looked to me, and to my flushed mother, as though I had as good a shot as any.

The contest night went quickly: my foot, couched, pinched, and Band-Aided uncomfortably in a neighbor's hand-me-down high heels, slipped (hear the auditorium's quick and loud intake of breath in horror!) as I walked forward to say my name with a strong, vibrant hello just like I'd been coached by the fancy-mom; my dress was last year's prom dress, which earned me no cool points with my peers but didn't lose me any either since I had none to subtract; I managed not to land on my bottom (as I had in every practice before the contest) in my gymnastics routine, self-choreographed with my own robot-style moves to the synthesizer-heavy tune "Electricity," by a band that was popular in Sacramento, California, in that year, 1985, but not yet in my hometown. (The cassette tape had been given to me by my Hispanic, juvenile delinquent, just-released-from-young-boy-prison-in-California ex-boyfriend Jim.)

My exercise routine went off very well in front of the crowd, and I don't think anyone could even tell that my shorts were soaking wet from having been dropped by me into the toilet just an hour before as I arranged my items for quick-change. My mother and fiancé were actually sitting together, their mutual hatred of each other squeezed like a child between them. I'd even kept myself from leaving my mother behind when, backstage after the contest as I hugged and cried in joy for the co-winners and out of desperate relief that it was over now, my mother, beside herself with embarrassment for me and disappointment for herself, and misunderstanding my tears, hissed loudly enough for the benefit of everyone, "STOP your crying, they'll think you're not a nice LOSER!"

So I had done it: I had been a contestant in the Junior Miss Pageant and my mother had the snapshots to prove it.

I'd lost the contest because I didn't yet know how to tell people what they wanted to hear. The small girl that boys secretly liked but wouldn't date doesn't win Miss America. The girl hiding in her room reading and writing poetry doesn't win Miss America. The girl playing violin despite her mother's anxiousness that other people will think she's weird doesn't win Miss America. The girl on Willard Street doesn't ever win Miss America.

But the truth is that I'd lost the contest when I told the judges, when they asked, that my most personal concern was my mother's loneliness, and if I could change anything at all, I would give her something—a man, God, anything to free her from that loneliness.

Clearly, I lacked the save-the-whales-and-rainforest civic-mindedness required not only of Miss America, but of Junior Miss America, too. Even, although one wouldn't think it, in Ottumwa, Iowa, where my mother would go on to work in a bathtub factory, and then a glue factory, and then an electrical connectors factory (the factory worker's version of upward mobility), and finally, a watch factory where they shipped and received not just watches but cocaine in our town that at that time had more FBI agents in it than railroad engineers. And even in this town where my sister would go to work the kill floor of the pork plant where, for fun, the workers shot inspection dye at each other and threatened each other's throats with hack-knives. And even in this town where my cousin, age 13, would bring a bomb to seventh grade for show-and-tell, and get caught and evacuated, and be given community service to do because the public-school-as-terrorist-ground phenomena hadn't yet been born. And even in this town where if you want to go to college, you better know someone who knows how to get you there because otherwise it's too far away and too much money and too much trouble and way, way, way beyond your own intellect and sense of self to do it alone. How scary (get married). How wasteful (get married). How expensive (get married). How strange (get married). How pretentious (get married). How escapist (get married).

If your parents are crazy and poor, and if you can't win the Junior Miss Pageant, and if it's the kind of town where you stay or they don't ever want you coming back, you get married, you move to Texas where your husband sells drugs, you hide away from the world until your self grows enough to break you out, and then you leave and you pray for your mother's loneliness and you spend your life learning to come to terms with your own, and you are smart and willful and strong, and you don't ever have to draw another chart before the pageant begins.

My mother told me later that she was just sure I would have won the Junior Miss contest if I hadn't made that awful mistake in my gymnastics routine (I don't know what mistake she was talking about—it was the least flawed part of the evening), but I knew the truth about why I'd lost, and I knew I'd lost even before the contest or the practices began. I'd lost this contest at birth, probably, to be born to my father who had a date that night, and to my mother who believed some girls—girls like me, and girls like her—had to try very hard to catch and keep a boy's attention. I'd lost the contest in borrowed shoes and an out-of-date dress. I'd lost the contest with the engagement ring on my seventeen-year-old finger. I'd lost the contest with wet shorts and too funky music. I'd lost the contest with a bargain photograph and Kmart leg warmers. I'd lost the contest with an orange Honda Express moped parked between the other girls' cars. I'd lost the contest in a falling-down green house. I'd lost the contest in the grease on my father's hands and hair and the taste of grease in his lunchbox leftovers. I'd lost the contest in my growingly cynical evaluation of Miss America as I'd gotten older—"chubby thighs touching, minus five points," "big hair, minus three points," "too small nipples, minus two," "flabby arms, minus five," and subtract and subtract and subtract. It's a contest no one should want to win. Our mothers should not have such dreams for us. Our mothers should not have such loneliness.

Writing Strategies

1. Complete the following sentence: The main idea of Bosley's essay is that ____________________________.
2. Bosley uses details to hold the reader's interest. Select three details that got your attention and explain how they help the reader understand and accept Bosley's main idea.
3. How does Bosley make her essay matter to someone who doesn't care about pageants?
4. Describe Bosley's writer's voice. For example, would you say it is angry, comedic, intense, dark, professional, light? Come up with your own descriptive term (or terms) and explain how three sentences from the essay support your description.
5. Divide Bosley's essay into at least four parts and briefly summarize the purpose of each part.

Exploring Ideas

1. What basic value or belief drives the way Bosley now thinks about pageants?
2. Explain how Bosley's point about pageants speaks to one of the following issues: competition, class, tradition, media. To what other issue does the essay speak? What point does it make about the issue?
3. Interview several people to find out how they view pageants. Record their responses, then explain what viewpoints are the most common, most unusual, and most thought provoking.

Ideas for Writing

1. Discover the significance of an experience or activity in which you participated with disappointing results.
2. Discover the significance of an experience or activity at which you exceeded your own expectations.

If responding to one of these ideas, go to the Analysis section of this chapter to begin developing ideas for your essay.

Student Essay

The Thrill of Victory . . . The Agony of Parents

Jennifer Schwind-Pawlak

We often get caught up in the moment. As children—and as adults—we first react to situations one way, and then later make better sense of what happened. Jennifer Schwind-Pawlak, who wrote the following essay for a college writing course, explores one of these moments from her past. As you read the essay, notice how Schwind-Pawlak uses her own particular experience to tap into a more universal one. From a new perspective, allowed for by the distance of time, she finds the positive value of what appeared back then to be a negative experience. In this essay, she stands back and talks about the experience, engaging readers with key details, a mature writer's voice, and an important lesson.

The relationship between parents and children. Parents commit "fouls" or "crimes."

Introduces general subject matter leading up to the main idea: parent/child dynamics.

Parents—one word that can strike many emotions in children when said aloud. Some children will smile and think about how silly their dad looked when he put carrot sticks up his nose that very morning, while others will cringe when they think about how their mother picked them up from school last week wearing orange polyester pants and a green shirt, oblivious to the hard work that some fellow went through to create the color wheel. My own emotional state of mind seemed to run the gamut throughout childhood. I chose to blame my parents for all of the traumatic events that unfolded but took pride in my obvious independence during the successes. One of the most heinous crimes that my parents committed was "the soccer foul." If I could have ejected them from the game of life at that point, I would have.

Ironically, I was not particularly fond of soccer. Being the youngest of four children, I often chose to run around the field with friends while my brothers and sisters performed feats of soccer, the likes of which had only been seen during the World Cup. I would happily contort my fingers into chubby pretzels while singing "The Itsy Bitsy Spider" as the game's events were recounted on the drives home. Still, whether by guilt or by the need to belong, I joined the team when I became of age.

The team that I played on was designed to turn the young and awkward into the swans of the soccer field. My father (a one-time soccer coach) explained several times that this was the time that I would learn the rules and workings of the game and that I shouldn't expect much more than that. Since it was a child's league, learning and the team experience were the focuses. Winning was a pleasant bonus but should not be achieved at the cost of the main objectives. This litany was taken and stored somewhere in the recesses of my brain. For me, however, the main objective was looking cool while running down the field chasing a spotted ball. Everything else seemed secondary.

Develops essay through narration and description.

We have all participated in these childhood activities that were supposed to teach us lessons, about sportsmanship, teamwork, etc.

Details are carefully selected: father's explanation becomes key later in the essay.

Due to the family history, I attended every Tuesday and Thursday practice and managed to make each a social occasion while going through the motions of the game. I succeeded in understanding the game and, though not the most skilled of players, began to enjoy the half game of playing time that was required by the league for each player. Though I was far from a star player, I felt that my contribution mattered to the overall outcomes of the games, all of which had been lost to this point.

Her relationship with soccer seems to be developing, changing.

Sums up practice and games thus far.

Sunday, the morning of the fifth game of the season, came with no warning. I got up, went to church with the family, then came home to suit up for the game. Upon arrival at the field, I was greeted by the coach and went to take my place along the sidelines with the rest of my team. There was a buzz of excitement that left me with the feeling that I would get when my brother would poke me with his fingertip after dragging his stocking feet across the carpet. The team that we were playing had a record identical to ours. We could win this game. I didn't care what the parents said. Winning would be a blast.

Sets up the fifth game. Excitement, suspense are building.

The coach kept me on the sidelines the entire first half of the game, which my pre-adolescent mind attributed to my obviously increasing skill at the game. He was saving his trump card, me, for the last half of the game. I knew this was rare, but I was sure that his reason was to bedazzle the crowd and the other team with my pure firepower on the field. The other players, except one other girl, continued to cycle in and out of the game. While I was excited because we were winning the game, I was concerned that the coach had forgotten about me. I inched, ever so slowly, toward him and started

Description of the fifth game.

We all—most of us—have not gotten to play at some point: common experience?

■ Writing Strategies ■ Exploring Ideas

mindless conversation to let him know that I was there. He spoke to me, so I knew that he could not have forgotten about me. As the game was winding down, I was sure that he must have decided to put me in for the last play of the game.

Three-word paragraph has dramatic effect.

The game ended.

She is "horrified" not to play.

I was horrified to realize that I had not played one moment of the first win of the season. After all of that practice and the ugly uniform, I was deemed such a poor player that I was not even good enough to play one moment of that game. How would I ever live this down at school? How would I face all of my classmates on Monday? My stomach began to churn, the way that it does when you are going down the first hill of any great roller coaster. I looked to my parents for support, which only added to the horror of that day.

Description of "the foul."

She is "horrified" and looks to her mother for help. Turns out, her mother is "horrified" too, and reacts in a way that makes things worse. What does she learn about her mother, parents, and relationships from her mother's reaction—and from her reaction to it?

Joann (the name I call my mother when she does something embarrassing) was screaming at the coach. In a voice so screeching that it rivaled fingernails on a blackboard, she told him that he was a disgraceful coach and that he should be ashamed of himself. She continued to point out the error of his ways by reminding him that I had not played at all in the game. How could she do this to me? My mother had managed to enlighten the few people that hadn't noticed on their own that I had not played at all. What was she thinking? She might as well have rented billboard space saying, "So what if Jeni sucks at soccer? The coach wouldn't let her play." My only thought was, "I don't want to go to school tomorrow!"

Reflects on her experience—what "looking back" means.

She sees the experience differently now. Sometimes—many times—we see differently when something's happening than we do later on.

Looking back, I realize that it wasn't so bad the next day at school. I walked out to recess and talked about how nuts my mother was and everyone seemed to agree, sympathize, and get on with the important task of freeze tag. At that moment I wasn't sure that I would ever be able to forgive my mother for what happened that day, but, as far as I can recall, I began loving her again within the week. I am sure that she either cooked my favorite dinner, told a corny joke, or told me how much she loved me to make that lump of anger fade away.

She gives possible reasons for never playing another organized sport again.

One consequence is that she quit soccer, sports. She's not sure why? Complexity.

I never went to soccer again. As a matter of fact, I never played another organized sport again. Maybe it was the fear of rejection. Maybe it was the uncertainty of my talent. Maybe I was just too busy with other things. I never really felt the urge to compete on that level after that day.

The relationship that I have with my parents has changed very much throughout the years. The polyester pants don't bother me anymore, but the carrot sticks still make me laugh. While their "soccer foul" embarrassed and angered me at the time, I understand and appreciate it now. My mother was angry *FOR* me. She was hurt *FOR* me. Through the pages of time, I can look back and see that, more often than not, I embarrassed her. She never stopped feeling for me, loving me, or protecting me. I have grown enough to realize that, though I often pointed out my parents' fouls, they scored countless goals that I didn't even notice.

She sees the experience differently now. Parents and children embarrass each other sometimes. This is part of the relationship. In this situation, though, her mother was angry/hurt FOR her.

Finds meaning through reflection.

Writing Strategies

1. Explain why Schwind-Pawlak's opening paragraph makes the reader want to continue reading.

2. Why does Schwind-Pawlak tell us that her father "explained several times that this was the time that [she] would learn the rules and workings of the game and that [she] shouldn't expect much more than that" (¶3)?

Julie Elliot/StockXchng

3. Is Schwind-Pawlak's writer's voice funny, serious, pensive, silly? Describe it in your own words and then refer to three sentences that support your decision.
4. What subject would you say Schwind-Pawlak's essay is about: parents, soccer, life, growing up, or something else? What is Schwind-Pawlak's main point about the topic?
5. What details does Schwind-Pawlak use to help the reader understand and accept her main idea?

Exploring Ideas

1. In groups or on your own through writing, discuss experiences like Schwind-Pawlak's. Can you recall a similar embarrassing experience of your own? Are such experiences inevitable? What makes them valuable? What can make them harmful?
2. What activity did you have the ability, opportunity, and interest to do again, but only did once? What is it, or was it, about yourself that kept you from doing it again?

Ideas for Writing

1. What is the significance of a big game or event from your past?
2. What emotional or intellectual experience has prevented you from ever doing something again? How has the experience influenced your later decisions?

If responding to one of these ideas, go to the Analysis section of this chapter to begin developing ideas for your essay.

Invention
"I'm digging in the dirt / To find the places I got hurt / To open up the places I got hurt."

—"Digging in the Dirt," Peter Gabriel

Invention is not simply about finding a topic. It also involves exploring and analyzing that topic, examining your thoughts, and developing points. For a remembering essay, the process will be self-reflective. It will begin with a personal exploration, but the broader goal is to discover something that others can share. The following three sections are designed to help you through invention—specifically, to discover a particular topic, situation, or event from your past (in Point of Contact), to develop points about the topic (in Analysis), and to make it relevant to a community of readers (in Public Resonance). The Invention Questions in each section are not meant to be answered directly in your final written assignment, but using them to explore ideas will help you begin writing and keep intensive ideas flowing.

Point of Contact

You might think that nothing interesting has ever happened to you, but even if you have never won the lottery, wrestled an alligator, or been on a first date, your life is filled with thousands of situations that can reveal something to you and to your audience. Use the following questions and images (Figure 2.1) to help find a specific situation, event, or set of events from your life.

Call or Write Someone from Your Past Ask him or her about your shared history.

- What do you remember most about our lives back then?
- What was the best part of our lives? The worst?
- How have we both changed since then? Why did we change?
- What forces, feelings, or situations kept us together?

Do Something that You Have Not Done for Many Years Go fishing, play baseball, listen to a particular song, reread a particular book. Then consider the following: How was doing the activity now different from doing it in the past?

Analysis and Public Resonance: Choose one experience from your long list of possibilities, one that allows you to focus on a particular moment that changed your relationship with literacy (with reading, writing, and ultimately with ideas). Then use the Analysis and Public Resonance sections to explore deeper into the experience. As you respond to the Analysis and Public Resonance questions, pay attention to particular attitudes, people, places, sounds, colors, feelings, smells, and so on. You won't include all these particulars in your essay. You are noting them now because you are using writing to explore, discover, and develop ideas. Making note of particulars is another invention strategy. The particulars you record will help you think of more ideas. Then, when you write your literacy narrative, you will select *some* of these particulars to bring your narrative to life.

Thesis: Because your thesis will be derived from all the thinking and writing you do in response to the Analysis and Public Resonance sections, it's important to wait until after you generate ideas to make rhetorical decisions about how to convey your literacy narrative to readers. At that point, turn to the Thesis section for help focusing your ideas on one particular insight. Your thesis should make clear the significance of your literacy narrative by stating the significance in a one-sentence statement.

Delivery: The Analysis, Public Resonance, Thesis, and Rhetorical Tools sections are key to creating the raw material (the ideas) you will need *before* trying to convey ideas to readers. In addition to the information in those sections, for a literacy narrative consider the following:

- Organization—How will you arrange the story? Will you go chronologically from beginning to end? Will you start in the middle then fill in the details leading up to the significance? Will you start at the end and then go back to the beginning?
- Writer's Voice—Consider how your voice as a writer helps readers understand and accept your thesis.
- Vitality—Make sure you delete and combine ideas to emphasize main points and keep the story moving along. Use descriptive details to bring the narrative to life for readers, but be selective. Don't bog readers down in unnecessary details.
- Images and Design—What images (photos, drawings, diagrams, video) and document design features (spacing, font, headings) can help readers understand and accept your thesis?
- Revision—

  —Where can you combine/delete ideas for clarity, conciseness, and vitality?

  —Where can you add ideas to fill in gaps for readers?

  —If you told a story and then stated the significance at the end, how can you weave the significance throughout the story? (Avoid a closing *the-moral-of-the-story-is* paragraph.)

—If the point (the significance) of the narrative is dull, obvious, or uninteresting, how can you narrow your focus and dig deeper to make the narrative more meaningful and interesting to readers?

Analysis

Analysis is an art and a science. It involves intellectual freedom and careful, deliberate probing. Good analysis calls for writers to venture into possibilities while monitoring their thinking. This difficult intellectual work yields insight and meaning. As you examine a particular event or situation from your past, try to find the *significance* (why something is important for both the writer and the readers).

- How did I change? (Who was I before and after the situation?)
- Why did the event or situation occur? What forces were at work?
- Did I realize the significance of the event at the time? Why or why not?
- What do I see now that I didn't see then? What did that younger person not understand?
- Why was the event or situation important to me?

  —Did it help me to understand myself as a man or woman?

  —Did it help me to grow intellectually? Spiritually? Socially?

  —Did it help me to see myself in a different way?

As you analyze, remember that the goal is not simply to tell a story about your past, but to discover something meaningful—something that can be shared with and valued by others. Avoid moving too quickly through your thoughts. Imagine a writer, Jack, who visited his old elementary school:

What do I see now that I didn't see then?

I see that school is important, and back then I didn't.

Jack answers the question and *begins* walking the path of analysis, but his brief answer does not go far enough. It does not reveal the real complexity of his experience. He says that "school is important," but such a phrase is broad and hollow. What particular aspect of school, we might ask, is important? What specific moments or situations are valuable to a growing individual? Struggling through impossibly difficult classes? The reward of a good grade? Being prompted to read material one would otherwise ignore? Or maybe what's important is the slow and charted evolution of one's identity through various classes, teachers, friends, and hallways. Jack's answer blankets such rich possibilities, covering them up with a broad, sweeping phrase.

Another writer, Diana, goes further in her thinking:

What do I see now that I didn't see then?

When I was younger, I didn't see the big picture, how my life in school connected to anything outside of school. I went, did the work, and came home, but mostly daydreamed about the time I'd spend away from schoolwork. For me, and probably most of my friends, life was separate from schoolwork. Every day, the goal was to get it done so we could be away from it. I remember the feeling of freedom in running out the door after school or during recess, but what I was running toward was a bunch of silly games, posing, and meaningless searches for excitement. I never thought, maybe I was never taught, that learning is really what makes life worth anything, that an intellectual challenge is real excitement. When I was a teenager, I was focused on the surface—the shallow giddiness of thrills and "parties." I thought school was a drag—and I looked for every possible excuse to be bored. I actually *convinced* myself to be bored. But now that I am older, I realize that school is the only place where people actually care about your mind—where they want you to grow, imagine, and experience new ideas. These are the things that make life outside of school worth living. I see that now.

All the jobs I had after high school just wanted me to perform a certain duty. No one wanted me to explore my intellectual potential. And unfortunately, I see a lot of younger college students still thinking the way I did in high school. They moan at challenging assignments; they just want to duck out of everything. Today, a boy said to me, "Can you believe how long that reading took?" as though the goal were to get through it. What's that about? Well, I know what it's about—blindness to the big picture.

Diana's thoughts are developing. She is making specific distinctions between her present and her past understanding. In the past, she did not question her own boredom. But in the present she has distance from her old self and can see false assumptions and misplaced values.

Thinking Further

Although Diana has already analyzed further than Jack did, she should not stop yet. Through analysis she has unearthed some interesting new ideas. Now she can review her invention writing and identify her best ideas, using them not as final conclusions but as springboards into further exploration. Now she can seek out some insight that lurks even further below the surface of her previous discoveries.

For example, if Diana's goal is to share the significance of a memory, she could say that she realized *school is where people care about your mind—where they want you to grow, imagine, and experience new ideas—and that these are the things that make life outside of school worth living.* And she could illustrate her thesis by discussing how certain teachers encouraged her to grow and imagine while she scorned their encouragement. But what if Diana sought out the underlying reasons for her childhood behavior? She could quickly claim that she was a wild and typical adolescent. Or, she could think past that assumption, returning to the Invention Questions on page 47. Now that she has generated some new thinking, the same questions (and new ones that Diana comes up with on her own) can lead to even further insights. For example,

Why did the event or situation occur? What forces were at work?

Why didn't I see the big picture? Who or what is to blame? It isn't as if everybody in high school failed to take advantage of it. Many students were highly motivated. (Although even students who seemed motivated might have had misplaced priorities.) Still, had I known then what I know now, I might have worked harder and learned more, perhaps gone to a better college, and excelled in all kinds of ways. Perhaps my parents should have forced me to study harder, or helped me to better understand the importance of high school. Perhaps—probably—they didn't understand it themselves. But couldn't my teachers have gotten through to me? So many of them seemed disinterested. Others tried, but what could they do? And what about the media, pop culture, sports, the mall? All these factors competed and, in my case, won out over education.

By analyzing further, Diana is getting closer to the root of a complex issue: She is discovering that her attitude toward high school was impacted by competing factors, such as the media, pop culture, sports, and the mall. However, the writing above does not provide final answers. Diana has even more exploring to do, which might include additional invention writing, discussion with others, and secondary research.

To go further with your own thinking, focus on a key issue in your invention writing. Then return to the Invention Questions on page 47 and create probing questions on your own. Use them to reveal something deeper, more hidden, more complex, about the situation. For example:

- What other forces were at play?
- Why were they hidden from my view back then?
- What makes people blind to such forces in their lives?

In her response to the Invention Questions on page 50, Cindy Bosley hones in and finds meaning in a "small moment." Bosley's notes are exploratory. They are not simple answers to questions. Much of the language in her response does not appear in her final essay, but she is willing to explore and stretch her reasoning:

Why did the event or situation occur?

If I isolate the event or situation as the gulf between my own grasp of fun and happiness and my mother's severe disappointment and embarrassment, her concern that others would think I was not a "nice loser" in that small moment, I think it clearly speaks so much more about my mother—as though I saw her, her disappointments and worries about image and desirability in herself through me. She was no stage mother, not at all, but she must have had these fears about how people in the town looked at her, and at us, her three children, because of my father to a certain extent, but also just because she herself was a woman who'd grown up to some degree "unacceptable" in her and her family's eyes because she was heavy, or because she liked lots of boys, or because she got pregnant and married, or because she moved so far away. My mother was and is a creative, talented, vibrant woman and she worked very hard, and very successfully, sacrificing so much for herself so my sister, brother, and I could have the things that we wanted like the other kids, things that might help us break out of our own family's economic situation. Things like acrobat lessons, and cheerleading camp, and swimming lessons, and overnight birthday parties. I have absolutely no idea how she pulled all those things off.

Bosley does not focus only on the beauty pageant but on the layers of emotions beneath it—those tied to her mother. She discovers a fresh perspective about the pageant by looking closely at the life that led up to and surrounded it. And from these notes, the ideas evolve in her essay:

> But the truth is that I'd lost the contest when I told the judges, when they asked, that my most personal concern was my mother's loneliness, and if I could change anything at all, I would give her something—a man, God, anything to free her from that loneliness.

Discovering the significance of the past can be tricky because it is not obvious. In fact, the most significant events might be those that seem totally normal or insignificant. For example, a single soccer game spent standing on the sidelines would seem to have no meaning, other than frustration, for the younger Schwind-Pawlak; but to the older writer looking back, the game reveals something about her relationship with her parents.

Invention Workshop

After exploring the past on your own, you might hit a wall. Here's where an invention partner can help you break through and discover a focused insight worth sharing with readers. Review your invention writing thus far, and with your invention partner, or several partners, discuss: *What could I now tell that younger version of me?* In your discussion, explore, discover, and develop possibilities, then ask: *What hidden forces were at work? Why didn't I understand things differently back then?* Remember that the goal of this invention workshop is to reveal something new.

Activity

Using a smartphone or webcam, record a video of an invention workshop. One group member can shoot the video while the others prompt the writer with questions, beginning with those in this (Analysis) section and then any others that emerge through the invention process. After the workshop, the writer should review the video, identifying interesting points worthy of further exploration.

Public Resonance

What you discover about your past should suggest something for the lives of your readers. Dealing with public resonance means addressing the connection between your particular memory and a public or shared issue. You may have already found public resonance by answering the Invention Questions. If not, closely consider your response to the following:

- What public issue is related to my memory and how?
- What does my memory reveal or show about the nature of ________? (Childhood? Teenagers? Towns? Families? Schools? Teachers? Religious institutions? Education? Parenthood? Growing up? Failing? Succeeding? Suffering? Dying? Healing?)
- Who might relate to my memory?

In this excerpt from Cindy Bosley's invention notes, she does not merely reinforce her early feelings of confusion; she discovers "the truth of" her confusion:

> **What public issue is related to my memory?**
>
> This isn't about my mother so much as it is about women more generally, and the images we're given through history at birth and before and never ever really break. I always felt shame after what I told the judges about wanting my mother to not have to be so lonely—how narrow of me, how far I missed the point—and yet, now I feel the truth of it, and I hope if I could go back, I'd still tell them that's the one thing I'd want to be able to change—for my mother to be able to feel beautiful and free and lovely and bright, overweight or not, advanced education or not, and with or without a man.
>
> I remember my joy in graduate school when my friend Karen hosted a Miss America party the night of the pageant, and maybe my essay began to grow here. It was that night that I discovered I wasn't the ONLY little girl making up my own score sheets for the contest, hoping to predict who would win, and always imagining, because we thought it was the thing to wish for, that we could someday be Miss America. And all the usual stuff about women's narrow, "perfected" images in the media, Barbie dolls, fairy tales, all of it comes to bear here. There's such a feeling of shame and degradation (I don't think it is too big a word to describe it) in allowing oneself to be judged in this way, whether literally in a contest, or even just by agreeing to play, which we all do, by all the ancient rules of "fitting in," whether you're male or female. And there seems to be this desperate hole of loneliness and fear that seems anchored to it all. We often recognize it first in other people.

Your answers to the Invention Questions may not appear word-for-word in your final writing. However, they should generate focused thinking that finds its way into the final draft. For example, in her notes, Bosley discovers that her situation (and her mother's loneliness) is not unique. And in the conclusion of her essay, she makes this evident by changing the personal pronoun from *I* to *our,* thereby including others in her thinking. This links her realization about pageants and mother/daughter relationships to others so that her essay is not simply about herself, but about people who grew up in similar conditions. Bosley shows us how an unusual memory can resonate with readers: the importance and meaning of the memory translates into something beyond her personal feelings.

Activity

Before you write a thesis and begin drafting an essay, imagine how the significance of your memory might have meaning for readers. Doing this will help you develop a thesis that can guide your essay. With others or on your own through writing, explore: What might readers learn about themselves from my memory? How can I connect the significance of my memory to the readers' interests?

Thesis

Like any essay, one that is based on a personal experience should have a main point or *thesis.* And that point should reveal something to the writer and readers. It may be tempting to offer an overly broad statement about life, but more valuable statements will narrow in on a particular quality, situation, relationship, or layer of everyday life. The first broad statement in each set can be developed into more revelatory possibilities:

1. People are deeply influenced by their friends.

- Friends develop our sense of ambition—what we want for ourselves.
- Friends create the intellectual terrain of our past and present.
- Friends mirror our own worldviews back to us.

2. Family is all that matters.

- Our early struggles with brothers and sisters create the limitations we place on ourselves later in life.
- As we grow into adulthood, our siblings keep alive the memory of our childhood selves.
- Fathers create a sense of place, a sense of location that looms throughout our lives, even when we are spinning far out of control.

3. Teenage years are wild.

- During adolescence, the world makes sense, even though that sense is a complete illusion.
- A fourteen-year-old boy can barely contain all the energy coursing through his veins. He spends most of his time struggling to tame instincts that he cannot even name.
- Before leaving our formative years, we might glimpse the best and worst habits we have acquired from our families . . . if we are lucky.

So how does someone go from a broad, flat statement to a revelatory idea? Intensive analysis! More intensive analysis always (not sometimes, but *always!*) leads to more intensive and focused statements. But when writers have difficulty expressing an intensive single statement, they can retool the specific words—the key verbs and nouns. Notice how the more intensive and revelatory statements often avoid linking verbs (*is, am, are, was, were,* and so on). Instead, they rely on active verbs *(develop, create, mirror, keep, glimpse)* to pull the readers' mind through ideas. So changing the verb in a sentence can actually prompt the writer to think differently, in more intensive ways.

Activity

Create a broad, flat sentence, something that offers very little new insight. Then, from that sentence, develop three or more intense, focused, and insightful statements. In these more insightful statements, try to reveal something that normally goes ignored or that rarely gets considered. To create more insightful statements:

1. replace broad nouns with more specific nouns;
2. replace linking verbs with active verbs. Use adventurous or unusual verbs . . . and see where your mind goes.

Evolution of a Thesis

The thesis of a remembering essay suggests the *significance of the memory.* Notice how the following statement evolves from a description of what happened to an explanation of its significance:

- I remember as a kid sitting in my grandparents' backyard listening to them and my parents tell boring family stories.
- I realize now that I learned a lot about my family history from sitting around as a kid listening to my grandparents and parents tell family stories.
- We learn important things about who we are and where we came from by listening to family stories.
- Though we might prefer not to hear them, we can better understand who we are and why by taking in family stories as children.

An *explicit* thesis is stated directly in the essay; an *implied* thesis is suggested by the details in the essay but is not directly stated. Having an implied thesis does not mean a writer can simply wander through many different ideas. The details throughout the essay must be focused and coherent enough to suggest a main point, both for the writer and the readers.

Because you have already explored the significance and public resonance of your memory, you may already have a thesis. Ask yourself: *What is the most important point about this memory that should be communicated?* Try to express that point in one statement. (Even if you have an implied thesis, stating the main idea will help you develop the essay.)

Common Thesis Problems

When it comes time to craft a focused statement, writers also should avoid the temptation to flatten out their experiences into an overused phrase, or *cliché.* Clichés have a comfortable ring to them, but they rarely prompt new insight or reveal complexities. In fact, clichés often *cover up* complexities because they are applied as blanket statements to many different situations:

- You don't know what you've got until it's gone.
- Blood is thicker than water.
- What doesn't kill you only makes you stronger.
- Home is where the heart is.

Such statements may be true and worth considering, but academic writing seeks to reveal something new. Clichés are worn-out expressions. They might sound like profound statements, but when a thesis is a cliché, the main idea of the essay doesn't reveal something new. Instead, it restates an old, worn-out idea.

Revising Your Thesis

Share your thesis statement with a group of peers:

- What general words can be replaced with specific ones?
- What clichés can be replaced with intense, revelatory language?
- How can the thesis better express the significance of the memory?
- What is the most important point about this memory?

Rhetorical Tools

Even though the writing for this chapter is personal in nature, it needs to involve the audience, developing a point that connects to the public. As author Joan Didion said, "Quite often you want to tell somebody your dream, your nightmare. Well, nobody wants to hear about someone else's dream, good or bad; nobody wants to walk around with it. The writer is always tricking the reader into listening to the dream." To do this, writers can explore various tools.

Narration

Narration is a retelling of events, a story. As Joan Didion argues, we must do more than tell a story. We must trick readers into listening to the story and accepting its significance. The art of storytelling involves pace, or the movement of events. At important points in a narrative, the amount of detail tends to increase, and so readers slow down and experience each moment. But good storytellers move quickly through unimportant events. It might be helpful to think of this strategy as it works in movies: At the climax of an adventure movie, the events slow down (we see the lead character's hand grasping for the light saber; we hear each breath of the character as she runs down the hallway and toward the open window), but during less important moments, an entire day or week can flash by in a second.

In her narrative, Jennifer Schwind-Pawlak moves quickly through unimportant events. She quickly relates the pregame events (going to church, suiting up) because they do not have a significant impact on the main idea of the essay:

> Sunday, the morning of the fifth game of the season, came with no warning. I got up, went to church with the family, then came home to suit up for the game. Upon arrival at the field, I was greeted by the coach and went to take my place along the sidelines with the rest of my team.

However, the narrative slows down (and offers more details) at important moments:

> Joann (the name I call my mother when she does something embarrassing) was screaming at the coach. In a voice so screeching that it rivaled fingernails on a blackboard, she told him that he was a disgraceful coach and that he should be ashamed of himself. She continued to point out the error of his ways by reminding him that I had not played at all in the game. How could she do this to me? My mother had managed to enlighten the few people that hadn't noticed on their own that I had not played at all. What was she thinking? She might as well have rented billboard space saying, "So what if Jeni sucks at soccer? The coach wouldn't let her play." My only thought was, "I don't want to go to school tomorrow!"

As you consider your own narrative, slow the pace when relaying events that are directly related to your main idea.

Allusions

Allusions are references to some public bit of knowledge (such as a historical event, a political situation, or a popular culture figure). An allusion can give a personal essay a more public and broader feeling; that is, it can make the ideas and events of a personal situation relate to the readers through a shared culture. Because the allusion is shared knowledge, it communicates this broader, public feeling more quickly than a longer explanation would. This helps to keep the essay moving along. For example, Bosley's allusion to the Hooters restaurant chain ("to be performed, not in swimsuits, but in short-shorts and white T-shirts, Hooters-style . . .") quickly creates an image in the readers' mind because of the shared knowledge about the Hooters uniform. Later, when Bosley refers to "the save-the-whales-and-rainforest civic-mindedness required not only of Miss America, but of Junior Miss America, too," she quickly communicates an idea that without the allusion would take much longer to explain. Because the allusion is public knowledge, the writer connects with the readers because they feel that they, too, are *in on it.*

Dialogue

Dialogue, discussion between two or more people, can make an event or memory more real and engaging to the readers. It is most valuable when used to emphasize a main point and show something significant rather than simply to convey events. Conveying general events is better left to narration. Formatting for dialogue involves several steps:

- Use quotation marks before and after the actual spoken words.
- Put end punctuation (such as a period) inside the end quotation marks.
- Indent when a new speaker begins.

Integrating a speaker's words can be accomplished in several ways:

- Use a comma between the quotation and the speaking verb (*explained, asked, said, yelled, proclaimed,* etc.).

  Louisa asked, "What are we going to do now?"
- Use a colon before the speaker's words. In this case, the narrator usually forecasts the ideas or mood of the speaker in the sentence preceding the colon.

  I was clearly agitated by her accusation: "What the heck are you talking about?"
- Work the speaker's words directly into the grammar of your sentence.

  But Louisa was convinced that our decision would "hurt us either way."

  See all of these rules operating in the following exchange:

  "Come on in," Mr. Smith said.

  "Hey, something smells great," I said as I walked into his lamp-lit living room. The small terrier looked up out of its lazy place on the sofa as Mr. Smith reached to get his wallet.

  "Yep, I've been cookin' my chili again. It's Max's favorite." He gestured at the complacent blurry-eyed dog. "So, is the price of papers still the same?"

  "Well, as far as I know, it's still $4.25 for the month." And then without considering the consequences, I asked the wrong question: "How have you been, Mr. Smith?" It took him 45 minutes to explain his "return to normal" after a long spell of stomach flu.

In this example, notice how attributive phrases (such as *he said*), which give ownership to the spoken words, are absent after the second indentation. Generally, after the dialogue pattern is established and the readers can easily tell who is speaking at each indentation, attributive phrases are unnecessary.

Activity

Before drafting your essay, use writing to plan:

- Write down your thesis.
- What narrative events will you move through quickly, and what narrative events will you slow down for?
- What historical, popular, or fictional situations, events, or characters relate to your situation?
- If you are considering dialogue, how will that dialogue help show the significance of the main idea?

Revision

Revision is a necessary part of good writing and of one's development as a writer and thinker. Revision is when you step back and analyze your own rhetorical decisions, and perhaps even your own mind. Writers can revise alone or with others.

Peer Review

Peer review, revising with the help of others, can be done in various ways. Your instructor may provide specific guidelines and, of course, you are free to try different approaches outside the classroom. If your instructor asks you to exchange essays with a peer or form small groups and read your essays aloud, the following advice can help you work efficiently and get results:

- Provide peer reviewers with a readable copy of your draft.
- Help focus the reviewers by writing down your carefully worded questions about your draft.
- If you read your essay aloud, don't read too fast.
- Be specific when responding. In addition to saying what you think, say why you think it.
- Be honest and encouraging. Providing only praise will not help the writer, yet phrasing your comments too negatively might be discouraging.
- Do not defend your essay, but instead view it as a work in progress. Be open to all ideas.
- Consider all comments, then make the changes you think are appropriate.

After you exchange drafts with another writer, use the following questions to guide your review:

1. How does the essay prompt you to think differently? (For instance, do you see something with more complexity, more beauty, more ugliness, or more intensity than you did before?) Explain what the essay helps you see differently. If you have a difficult time answering this question, perhaps the essay has not yet gone far enough.
2. What clichés should the writer replace with a new, revelatory idea? (Look closely. Clichés sometimes masquerade as profound thoughts.)
3. Which details best illustrate the main idea? (Which details reinforce the main idea and make you picture something specific?)
4. Which details could be added to illustrate the main idea? What particular behaviors or events could be further dramatized with details? For instance, the essay probably has a focused moment—a specific event that holds intense meaning. Could that moment use more detail?
5. Which details do not seem related to the thesis of the essay? Why not?
6. How could the writer create more public resonance?
7. Do any paragraphs lack coherence? Do they ramble or wander pointlessly through the past? Look for details that may hold meaning for the writer but don't develop the point of the essay.
8. How could the essay begin with more intensity? (For instance, if the essay begins with a broad statement such as *Children are curious creatures,* could it instead begin with a specific narrative or a more focused or surprising statement?)
9. Describe the writer's voice. Is it appropriate and consistent? Could the writer use figurative language or details that are more fitting? Where could sentence length be varied?
10. What sentences could be rewritten to create more vitality?
    - Where can the writer combine sentences with coordination?
    - Where can the writer combine with subordination?
    - What verbs can be more intense?
    - Where do basic grammatical issues (such as run-on sentences, sentence fragments, or pronoun/antecedent agreement) distract readers?

Peer Review Truisms

- **The process can make writers think differently about their own work.** Humans are great modelers. We model our behavior after others, and we make all kinds of subtle changes to our thinking when we read others' work. As modelers, peer reviewers can discover new approaches to an assignment, new writerly moves, new patterns of thinking, or new strategies for creating an engaging voice. (Reviewers can also discover qualities that they want to avoid in their own writing. They might discover some sentence or organization patterns and try to avoid them!)
- **Even the most inexperienced writer can offer valuable comments.** Some people believe that they have little to offer: "I'm not the teacher!" they'll announce. However, peer review is not about pointing out wrongs and rights. It's about reading closely and responding as a thoughtful human in a shared situation. If you can read and focus your attention, you can be a valuable reviewer. In fact, fellow students may even have more to offer one another because they're in a similar situation—faced with a similar task, experiencing the same pressures, at the same moment, in the same place.
- **Chat is the great enemy of good analysis.** Some instructors may set up sessions so that writers can converse about their drafts. Such sessions can be valuable and engaging—even intense and animated. But the danger is that they can devolve into chat sessions about the topics (or something else!). While chatting about one's topic is helpful (and can be worked into a class), a focused and intensive peer review session has its own kind of value.
- **Peer review can be the most valuable component of a writing class.** Writing in college is a social occasion. An academic essay (or any writing assignment) is an intersection of writers, instructors, and students. Peer review brings that to life. It makes the interaction of thinkers real and dramatic. When reviewers take the process seriously, it increases the value of the experience.
- **All writers need help.** Even the best of the best writers rely on the insights and assistance of others. Name a great writer from the past or the present (Steinbeck? Tolkien? Morrison? Dillard?). All of them used the ideas and thoughts of others to help shape their projects and even their sentences.
- **Done carelessly, peer review can be a terrible thing.** If peer reviewers read drafts quickly and only point to small, surface-level issues, they waste their partners' time. It is a similar waste if they read for "agreement" and "disagreement"—simply looking for passages they agree or disagree with—and then announce their approval or disapproval of certain points.

Reflection

Students develop as writers and thinkers not just by writing an essay but also by reflecting on an essay *after* it has been written. This involves thinking, and even writing, about how rhetoric was used not just to communicate an idea but also to come up with the idea. Now that you have written a remembering essay, step back and explain its rhetoric:

1. What focused insight does your essay arrive at? Is it clearly expressed in a sentence? If so, write it down. Or is it implied through the details of the essay? If so, write down the focused insight in one sentence and then explain what details convey this idea throughout the essay.
2. How did you discover and develop your essay's insightful point? Your response to this question should trace the specific development of your insight throughout the writing process, which involved using rhetoric. Rather than give a general statement, try to give a detailed description of your process.
3. When used effectively, narration—a rhetorical tool—helps readers understand a writer's insight about a topic. When used ineffectively, it can take over the essay, drowning out the insight. Explain how narration in your essay helps readers understand your insight without overshadowing it. Explain how the insight shines through.
4. Even though your essay focuses primarily on *your* past, how does it have meaning for others? What passages from the essay connect your particular memory to a public concern?
5. The best writers work hard at saying more in fewer words. They are concise, using only the words necessary to make a point. Find a sentence in your essay that is concise, and then find one that is wordy. Rewrite the wordy sentence.

Beyond the Essay: Invention Video

1. If you recorded a video of an invention workshop for the activity on page 50, try editing that video into a four-minute (or so) movie, using video editing software such as iMovie. (If you're not familiar with editing software, work with an editing partner or team.) Your movie might end up paralleling the remembering essay, taking the same basic structure of the essay and making the same points. Or, because you shot video of some early invention work, your movie might tell a different story: You might edit the video to show how ideas evolved through the discussion, eventually leading to the discovery that became the essay's thesis.

Whether your movie parallels the remembering essay or documents the invention process, it can be a simple series of edited shots or a more complex production including titles, transitions between shots, close-ups, background music, and other effects and editing techniques. Each editing decision—what (and what not) to include, the pace (*Will a shot be three seconds or five?*), the type of transition between shots, the selection of music if there is any, when to begin the music and when to fade it out, and so on—requires careful thought. This thought is a type of analysis that allows you to see how all the little pieces of a thing work together to create the overall message.

2. After creating your movie, describe the editing decisions you made. What was your overall purpose—to communicate the main points of the remembering essay, to document the process of discovery, or something else? What shots did you decide to use and why? Describe the pace of your video and the effect of the pace: Did you use a lot of brief shots edited together, fewer longer ones, or a combination of both? What other video editing decisions did you make, and how did they contribute to the overall message, pace, and tone or voice of the movie?

3 Explaining Relationships

John Metz

"It is little wonder that [the American settlers] went land-mad, because there was so much of it. They cut and burned the forests to make room for crops; they abandoned their knowledge of kindness to the land in order to maintain its usefulness. When they had cropped out a piece they moved on, raping the country like invaders. The topsoil, held by roots and freshened by leaf-fall, was left helpless to the spring freshets, stripped and eroded with the naked bones of clay and rock exposed. The destruction of the forests changed the rainfall, for the searching clouds could find no green and beckoning woods to draw them on and milk them."

—John Steinbeck

In the above passage, from "Americans and the Land," John Steinbeck characterizes the relationship between early European settlers and the North American continent. Contrary to the conventional view of settlers as brave frontiersmen, Steinbeck describes them as land-mad invaders. Later in his essay, he describes them as "overindulged children."

Explaining relationships is common daily work: people on city councils explore the relationship between neighborhoods to help their cities better understand ethnic diversity; corporate executives try to understand the relationship between their own companies and their competitors; and certainly everyone is aware of the ongoing attempts by political leaders to explain the relationships between countries or regions. In a shrinking world, in which people of vastly different value systems attempt to coexist, explaining relationships is more than an exercise. It is an act of survival. To understand our place in the world, in a culture, in a family, in any system, we have to understand relationships.

One might even argue that the greatest discoveries have involved the discovery of relationships—between, for example, atomic elements, religious practices, geological events, historical figures, or heavenly bodies. Albert Einstein spent his life exploring the relationship between the impossibly small and the seemingly infinite; Carl Jung explored the relationship between the conscious and unconscious; Hélène Cixous explored the relationship between sexuality and language. And we might see the history of science as a series of questions about relationships: How does the sun relate to Earth? How does matter relate to energy? How do particles relate to waves? How do fish relate to mammals? How does climate relate to the atmosphere? The same goes for philosophy. From ancient civilizations to modern institutions, people have asked, for instance, how language relates to thought, how ethics relate to religion, and how the individual relates to the community.

In all academic disciplines, people work to understand and communicate the nature of relationships:

- In a computer technology course, students study the relationship between an individual computer and a network of computers, or between a group of users and the Internet.
- In an anthropology course, students explore the relationship between a particular waterway and the ruins of a past civilization.
- In a biology course, students and faculty work to see the relationship between two forms of bacteria.
- In an interior design course, students examine the relationship between a large interior office space and a front entrance to a particular building.

This chapter explores relationships—among places, things, events, people, and even ideas. The goal here is to investigate, to seek out some of the hidden dynamics of relationships, to discover the nature of a relationship, or to discover a relationship where one is not necessarily seen.

This chapter will help you discover a topic (a particular relationship), explore that relationship in depth, and explain the nature of the relationship in writing. The essays will provide valuable insight and necessary strategies for going beyond obvious relationships and exploring hidden connections. For example, Jim Crockett's essay, "Mugged," makes two important discoveries: that any possible psychological "disorder" is less important than some basic human need, and that his simple coffee mug provides a form of security. Crockett's discoveries give his essay insight (a less-obvious and worthwhile point) and public resonance (a connection to the concerns of others). As you read, seek out the hidden connection (the less obvious relationship) that gives the essays insight and public resonance. After reading the essays, you can begin looking for a particular relationship in one of two ways:

1. Go to the Point of Contact section to find a relationship from everyday life.
2. Choose one of the Ideas for Writing questions that follow the essays.

After finding a topic, go to the Analysis section to begin developing the evaluation.

Readings

Americans and the Land

John Steinbeck

In John Steinbeck's novels, such as *The Grapes of Wrath* and *Of Mice and Men,* the setting is a vital element of the stories. Steinbeck often draws attention to the ways in which the land influences people's lives. In this essay, from *America and Americans,* Steinbeck focuses on the American settlers' impact on the land. Notice that the land, here, is not something to simply live *on* or even *from.* Instead, it is something to live *with*—or, in the case of many early Americans, to live *against.* As with so many of his novels and stories, Steinbeck's essay invites readers to see the relationship that people cultivate with the world around them.

I have often wondered at the savagery and thoughtlessness with which our early settlers approached this rich continent. They came at it as though it were an enemy, which of course it was. They burned the forests and changed the rainfall; they swept the buffalo from the plains, blasted the streams, set fire to the grass, and ran a reckless scythe through the virgin and noble timber. Perhaps they felt that it was limitless and could never be exhausted and that a man could move on to new wonders endlessly. Certainly there are many examples to the contrary, but to a large extent the early people pillaged the country as though they hated it, as though they held it temporarily and might be driven off at any time.

This tendency toward irresponsibility persists in very many of us today; our rivers are poisoned by reckless dumping of sewage and toxic industrial wastes, the air of our cities is filthy and dangerous to breathe from the belching of uncontrolled products from combustion of coal, coke, oil, and gasoline. Our towns are girdled with wreckage and the debris of our toys—our automobiles and our packaged pleasures. Through uninhibited spraying against one enemy we have destroyed the natural balances our survival requires. All these evils can and must be overcome if America and Americans are to survive; but many of us still conduct ourselves as our ancestors did, stealing from the future for our clear and present profit.

Since the river-polluters and the air-poisoners are not criminal or even bad people, we must presume that they are heirs to the early conviction that sky and water are unowned and that they are limitless. In the light of our practices here at home it is very interesting to me to read of the care taken with the carriers of our probes into space, to make utterly sure that they are free of pollution of any kind. We would not think of doing to the moon what we do every day to our own dear country.

When the first settlers came to America and dug in on the coast, they huddled in defending villages hemmed in by the sea on one side and by endless forests on the other, by Red Indians and, most frightening, the mystery of an unknown land extending nobody knew how far. And for a time very few cared or dared to find out. Our first Americans organized themselves and lived in a state of military alertness; every community built its blockhouse for defense. By law the men went armed and were required to keep their weapons ready and available. Many of them wore armor, made here or imported; on the East Coast, they wore the cuirass and helmet, and the Spaniards on the West Coast wore both steel armor and heavy leather to turn arrows.

On the East Coast, and particularly in New England, the colonists farmed meager lands close to their communities and to safety. Every man was permanently on duty for the defense of his family and his village; even the hunting parties went into the forest in force, rather like raiders than hunters, and their subsequent quarrels with the Indians, resulting in forays and even massacres, remind us that the danger was very real. A man took his gun along when he worked the land, and the women stayed close to their thick-walled houses and listened day and night for the signal of alarm. The towns they settled were permanent, and most of them exist today with their records of Indian raids, of slaughter, of scalpings, and of punitive counter-raids. The military leader of the community became the chief authority in time of trouble, and it was a long time before danger receded and the mystery could be explored.

After a time, however, brave and forest-wise men drifted westward to hunt, to trap, and eventually to bargain for the furs which were the first precious negotiable wealth America produced for trade and export. Then trading posts were set up as centers of collection and the exploring men moved up and down the rivers and crossed the mountains, made friends for mutual profit with the Indians, learned the wilderness techniques, so that these explorer-traders soon dressed, ate, and generally acted like the indigenous people around them. Suspicion lasted a long time, and was fed by clashes sometimes amounting to full-fledged warfare; but by now these Americans attacked and defended as the Indians did.

For a goodly time the Americans were travelers, moving about the country collecting its valuables, but with little idea of permanence; their roots and their hearts were in the towns and the growing cities along the eastern edge. The few who stayed, who lived among the Indians, adopted their customs and some took Indian wives and were regarded as strange and somehow treasonable creatures. As for their half-breed children, while the tribe sometimes adopted them they were unacceptable as equals in the eastern settlements.

Then the trickle of immigrants became a stream, and the population began to move westward—not to grab and leave but to settle and live, they thought. The newcomers were of peasant stock, and they had their roots in a Europe where they had been landless, for the possession of land was the requirement and the proof of a higher social class than they had known. In America they found beautiful and boundless land for the taking—and they took it.

It is little wonder that they went land-mad, because there was so much of it. They cut and burned the forests to make room for crops; they abandoned their knowledge of kindness to the land in order to maintain its usefulness. When they had cropped out a piece they moved on, raping the country like invaders. The topsoil, held by roots and freshened by leaf-fall,

"Logging in the Everglades" Photo courtesy of HistoryMiami Archives and Research Center

was left helpless to the spring freshets, stripped and eroded with the naked bones of clay and rock exposed. The destruction of the forests changed the rainfall, for the searching clouds could find no green and beckoning woods to draw them on and milk them. The merciless nineteenth century was like a hostile expedition for loot that seemed limitless. Uncountable buffalo were killed, stripped of their hides, and left to rot, a reservoir of permanent food supply eliminated. More than that, the land of the Great Plains was robbed of the manure of the herds. Then the plows went in and ripped off the protection of the buffalo grass and opened the helpless soil to quick water and slow drought and the mischievous winds that roamed through the Great Central Plains. There has always been more than enough desert in America; the new settlers, like overindulged children, created even more.

The railroads brought new hordes of land-crazy people, and the new Americans moved like locusts across the continent until the western sea put a boundary to their movements. Coal and copper and gold drew them on; they savaged the land, gold-dredged the rivers to skeletons of pebbles and debris. An aroused and fearful government made laws for the distribution of public lands—a quarter section, one hundred and sixty acres, per person—and a claim had to be proved and improved; but there were ways of getting around this, and legally. My own grandfather proved out a quarter section for himself, one for his wife, one for each of his children, and, I suspect, acreage for children he hoped and expected to have. Marginal lands, of course, suitable only for grazing, went in larger pieces. One of the largest landholding families in California took its richest holdings by a trick: By law a man could take up all the swamp or water-covered land he wanted. The founder of this great holding mounted a scow on wheels and drove his horses over thousands of acres of the best bottomland, then reported that he had explored it in a boat, which was true, and confirmed his title. I need not mention his name; his descendants will remember.

Another joker with a name still remembered in the West worked out a scheme copied many times in after years. Proving a quarter section required a year of residence and some kind of improvement—a fence, a shack—but once the land was proved the owner was free to sell it. This particular princely character went to the stews and skid rows of the towns and found a small army of hopeless alcoholics who lived for whisky and nothing else. He put these men on land he wanted to own, grubstaked them and kept them in cheap liquor until the acreage was proved, then went through the motions of buying it from his protégés and moved them and their one-room shacks on sled runners on to new quarter sections. Bums of strong constitution might prove out five or six homesteads for this acquisitive hero before they died of drunkenness.

It was full late when we began to realize that the continent did not stretch out to infinity; that there were limits to the indignities to which we could subject it. Engines and heavy mechanical equipment were allowing us to ravage it even more effectively than we had with fire, dynamite, and gang plows. Conservation came to us slowly, and much of it hasn't arrived yet. Having killed the whales and wiped out the sea otters and most of the beavers, the market hunters went to work on game birds; ducks and quail were decimated, and the passenger pigeon eliminated. In my youth I remember seeing a market hunter's gun, a three-gauge shotgun bolted to a frame and loaded to the muzzle with shingle nails. Aimed at a lake and the trigger pulled with a string, it slaughtered every living thing on the lake. The Pacific Coast pilchards were once the raw material for a great and continuing industry. We hunted them with aircraft far at sea until they were gone and the canneries had to be closed. In some of the valleys of the West, where the climate makes several crops a year available, which the water supply will not justify, wells were driven deeper and deeper for irrigation, so that in one great valley a million acre feet more of water was taken out than rain and melting snow could replace, and the water table went down and a few more years may give us a new desert.

The great redwood forests of the western mountains early attracted attention. These ancient trees, which once grew everywhere, now exist only where the last Ice Age did not wipe them out. And they were found to have value. The Sempervirens and the Gigantea, the two remaining species, make soft, straight-grained timber. They are easy to split into planks, shakes, fenceposts, and railroad ties, and they have a unique virtue: they resist decay, both wet and dry rot, and an inherent acid in them repels termites. The loggers went through the great groves like a barrage, toppling the trees—some of which were two thousand years old—and leaving no maidens, no seedlings or saplings on the denuded hills.

Quite a few years ago when I was living in my little town on the coast of California a stranger came in and bought a small valley where the Sempervirens redwoods grew, some of them three hundred feet high. We used to walk among these trees, and the light colored as though the great glass of the Cathedral at Chartres had strained and sanctified the sunlight. The emotion we felt in this grove was one of awe and humility and joy; and then one day it was gone, slaughtered, and the sad wreckage of boughs and broken saplings left like nonsensical spoilage of the battle-ruined countryside. And I remember that after our rage there was sadness, and when we passed the man who had done this we looked away, because we were ashamed for him.

From early times we were impressed and awed by the fantastic accidents of nature, like the Grand Canyon and Yosemite and Yellowstone Park. The Indians had revered them as holy places, visited by the gods, and all of us came to have somewhat the same feeling about them. Thus we set aside many areas of astonishment as publicly owned parks; and though this may to a certain extent have been because there was no other way to use them, as the feelings of preciousness of the things we had been destroying grew in Americans, more and more areas were set aside as national and state parks, to be looked at but not injured. Many people loved and were in awe of the redwoods; societies and individuals bought groves of these wonderful trees and presented them to the state for preservation.

No longer do we Americans want to destroy wantonly, but our new-found sources of power—to take the burden of work from our shoulders, to warm us, and cool us, and give us light, to transport us quickly, and to make the things we use and wear and eat—these power sources spew pollution on our country, so that the rivers and streams are becoming poisonous and lifeless. The birds die for the lack of food; a noxious cloud hangs over our cities that burns our lungs and reddens our eyes. Our ability to conserve has not grown with our power to create, but this slow and sullen poisoning is no longer ignored or justified. Almost daily, the pressure of outrage among Americans grows. We are no longer content to destroy our beloved country. We are slow to learn; but we learn. When a super-highway was proposed in California which would trample the redwood trees in its path, an outcry arose all over the land, so strident and fierce that the plan was put aside. And we no longer believe that a man, by owning a piece of America, is free to outrage it.

But we are an exuberant people, careless and destructive as active children. We make strong and potent tools and then have to use them to prove that they exist. Under the pressure of war we finally made the atom bomb, and for reasons which seemed justifiable at the time we dropped it on two Japanese cities—and I think we finally frightened ourselves. In such things, one must consult himself because there is no other point of reference. I did not know about the bomb, and certainly I had nothing to do with its use, but I am horrified and ashamed; and nearly everyone I know feels the same thing. And those who loudly and angrily justify Hiroshima and Nagasaki—why, they must be the most ashamed of all.

Writing Strategies

1. Focus on Steinbeck's opening paragraph. How does it function? Does it state or imply the main idea? How does it establish Steinbeck's voice? Does it invite the readers into the essay? If so, how?

2. Throughout the essay, Steinbeck describes detailed situations (anecdotes) that illustrate his point. Which of these anecdotes best supports his point about the relationship between settlers and the land?

3. In ¶10, Steinbeck describes the people that the railroad brought west as "land-crazy." He says they moved "like locusts." Identify other figurative expressions he uses to describe the people. Explain how these expressions function in the essay. How do they work with his overall point about the relationship between Americans and the land?

4. In ¶16, Steinbeck gives some examples that show contemporary Americans are, perhaps, more thoughtful about the land. How does this paragraph impact your understanding of the essay? How does it impact Steinbeck's voice?

5. In his conclusion, Steinbeck talks about shame. Explain how this passage supports his overall point about Americans' relationship with the land.

Exploring Ideas

1. What does Steinbeck say about Americans and the land? What is he trying to accomplish in this essay?

2. Imagine Steinbeck as a guest on a current political talk show. What kinds of people would call in? Who would support Steinbeck's point? Who would angrily deny it?

3. What is your relationship with the land? What everyday actions of your own have a positive impact on the land? What everyday actions of your own have a negative impact on the land?

4. How have you been taught to think about American settlers? How does Steinbeck's essay fit into or push against the history you've been taught?

Ideas for Writing

1. What is the relationship between Americans and the land today?

2. Describe your relationship with your immediate surroundings (your house, bedroom, apartment, dorm, etc.). How is it typical (or not typical) of your broader attitude concerning the relationship of humans to the land?

3. Observe the way land is used in your community. Take field notes. Discuss your observations with others, looking for ways that you might participate in Steinbeck's discussion of Americans and the land. How might you contribute to this discussion? What idea, for example, could use further explanation or clarification?

If responding to one of these ideas, go to the Analysis section of this chapter to begin developing ideas for your essay.

Mugged

Jim Crockett

Jim Crockett, a Spanish instructor, songwriter, farmer, and carpenter, has been drinking coffee for fifty years. As with millions of other Americans, coffee is fused to his everyday life. In this essay, Crockett focuses on a particular part of his relationship with coffee. But the essay goes far beyond his personal rituals and habits; it reveals something about the "small behaviors we cling to" and the size and scope of those seemingly simplistic habits that create meaning and familiarity. (Portions of Crockett's invention work appear later in the chapter.)

I have been mugged. Not accosted as I walk to my parked truck across a dark lot; not waylaid by thugs in the night. But mugged, nevertheless. I have been mugged by insinuation, by the insertion into my life of a cylindrical drinking vessel: one that holds coffee. I have been mugged by a to-go cup.

The relationship, or mugging, that has developed with my coffee mug is one-sided and is, because a mug's needs are simple, an easy relationship to maintain. Oh, I rinse and wipe it out every morning, and occasionally wash it with detergent, but these are minimal maintenance requirements, ones easily met. So why, if all this object does is simply hold coffee, would I consider our relationship worthy of the time and effort spent in its exploration and explication? Why would I seek depth of meaning in a seemingly superficial attachment to such a mundane object? Maybe the very mundanity of the object, the very quotidian nature of the relationship, deepens the attachment, suggests that the relationship goes symbolically deeper, symptomatically deeper, than I think.

In exchange for its minimal upkeep, my coffee mug gives back much more than it takes. Its secure lid keeps my mustache drip-free and, therefore, my books, shirts, and papers clean. My mug is insulated so it delivers hot, delicious, organically shade-grown, fair trade coffee for a couple of hours at a time, and in so doing, helps me directly support the small coffee growers and their cooperatives around the world. It is also an environmentally friendly mug. When I buy a cup of coffee, I only buy coffee: the paper cup and insulating sleeve, both little bits of tree, remain in the store. I remain weaned from dependence upon the earth- and human-pillaging multinational coffee cartel.

Wrought in stainless steel and plastic, this bit of industrial-designer paraphernalia (it holds my drug of choice) is every cup holder's dream. Its shape, curvaceous, tapered, slim-waisted and a bit heavier on top, is designed to fit cup holders in most vehicles, while being a natural-feeling extension of the human hand; or, in my case, a necessary adjunct to, a logical appurtenance thereof. My coffee cup is in my hand a lot.

In fact, when it is not in my hand, when I misplace it momentarily, or when, like the other day, I leave it on the bumper of my truck and see a flash in the rearview mirror as my

---

mug goes airborne into the filthy slush of the winter street, I feel a twinge of separation anxiety. When I stop traffic to rescue it from the gutter after a close call with a Chevy Suburban, impatient and angry faces glare through wiper-slapped windshields to remind me that the small choices we make, the small behaviors we cling to, affect the way in which we are perceived in the world.

I worry, at times, when students and colleagues ask how much coffee I drink, or say they've never seen me without my coffee mug, that my attachment to my little friend is symptomatic of some neurosis or other, or that it indicates an obsessive/compulsive disorder. I don't, however, worry for long. Because, even though my mug is always nearby, whether on the lectern or table in front of the classroom, in the cup holder on the dashboard of my truck, on the desk where I am writing this essay, or just dangling from my hand, all it really signifies is an addiction to caffeine and the need, because I am human, for some small and securing daily grounding ritual. In an *econoculture* so far removed from its agrarian and wilderness roots, from its time-worn rituals of life, my coffee mug provides a needed, however tiny, bit of continuity in my daily doings, a small tie to place and home.

Writing Strategies

1. How does the connotation of *mugged* impact the essay? How does the idea add to Crockett's point about his own relationship with coffee?
2. Although this essay focuses primarily on Crockett's personal relationship, how does it make broader, more public, points? What particular passages or sentences pull readers beyond Crockett's personal situation?
3. Describe Crockett's voice. How does word choice impact the "sound" of his voice?
4. In his conclusion, Crockett characterizes the society around him as an *econoculture.* What idea is he creating with that term? How does it resonate with other passages or points in this essay?
5. What is Crockett's most compelling rhetorical move?

Exploring Ideas

1. Crockett claims that humans need "some small and securing daily grounding ritual." What is a grounding ritual? Do you think it is, indeed, a fundamental human need?
2. Some sociologists, psychologists, and writers claim that the small moments in everyday life tell us the most about human behavior. Does this seem like a fair claim? In considering your own life, your own habits, is it true?
3. Why do people "cling" to their own habits?
4. Some historians have noted that the arrival of coffee and tea in medieval Europe could have been primary catalyst of the Renaissance. Caffeine, they say, woke up Europe! To what extent does caffeine impact our present culture—or your own ability to participate in the *econoculture?*

Ideas for Writing

1. What is the most consistent daily ritual in your life? What does it reveal about your identity?
2. What common ritual do you share with millions of others?
3. Crockett says, "Maybe the very mundanity of the object, the very quotidian nature of the relationship, deepens the attachment, suggests that the relationship goes symbolically deeper, symptomatically deeper, than I think." What mundane object is symbolically, symptomatically fused to your identity?

If responding to one of these ideas, go to the Analysis section of this chapter to begin developing ideas for your essay.

John Mauk

Student Essay

Delicate Friend

Lauren Jackson

Jackson wrote the following essay for her first-semester college English course. As she wrote drafts, responded to Invention Questions, and participated in invention workshops, she discovered increasing complexity. Jackson's relationship to cigarettes is not simply a matter of nicotine, personal choice, or even peer pressure. The relationship is instead driven by some basic human needs.

Perched on the white and brass speckled counter of my mother's kitchen is where I found my niche in the social circle. My mother smoked Marlboro Light 100s in a box and only in the kitchen when it was cold. She was courteous to the rest of the house: keeping the children out, always emptying the ashtray right away, and spraying air freshener. I used to sit in the dining room around the corner of the wall, to be out of view, and listen to her gossip and smoke while she danced around the linoleum with the telephone cord. When her girlfriends would come over, they would drink coffee, smoke, and talk about any and everything—usually discourse unsuitable for innocent ears. They would shoo the kids out of the kitchen and explain we couldn't be around the smoke. It seemed to me that smoking was an invitation to the secrets they shared. It was what they had in common, what they did. As I got older, I would sneak in for a glass of water and slink into a corner until they noticed and kicked me out. I wanted desperately to be included in the bond of the adult women and trusted with the whispered character assassinations. I wanted to be an integral part of a whole. I wanted to belong to something exclusive.

Focuses on the main idea immediately—without broad overarching statements.

She watched how a social group worked.

Describes the particular desire that drives the relationship.

This shows how people become attracted to exclusivity. It's the sociology of exclusion!

A public resonance strategy.

During middle school, a place when all children loathe themselves, anything and everyone, I decided it was time to define myself. I started stealing an occasional Marlboro Light from my mom. She kept them in a drawer in the kitchen that squeaked, so it took time and skill. There is a system to smoking below the legal age. And I had it perfected. I had a tin box containing various brands of stolen cigarettes, a few pairs of rubber gloves so my hands wouldn't hold the smell, a travel bottle of mouthwash, and dollar store body spray. I felt ingenious living

Lauren Jackson, "Delicate Friend." Reprinted with permission of the author.

■ Writing Strategies ■ Exploring Ideas

this reticent life. There were safe places throughout the neighborhood. A barbeque pit at a nearby abandoned house was ideal. A circle of trees hid it from public view. It became my private smoking place.

Moves from private/secret smoking to public/collective smoking.

At school, smoking garnered status. After some bragging and showing off the goods, I quickly joined up with "The Bad Girls." I was someone. We stole cigarettes from our relatives and smoked before and after school. Having the smell on us was impressive and intimidating. The small patch of trees just outside the gym door was our lair. We practiced French inhaling. Instead of chemistry, English, or math, we talked about the cutest boys and who had gone how far with whom. What I found in those tight little rolls of tobacco was acceptance and courage. And when I started college, my initial friends were the smokers. I was relieved to discover them, and our conversations started easily. Smoking did the talking for me. *Hey, got a smoke? A light? Cold out here, isn't it?* Those turned into *Where ya from?* and *Maybe we can get together later.* I was granted a reassuring feeling that whatever the other people in class might think of me, the three smokers approved. I was not alone.

Junior high: when kids discover the need to adopt a label, an identity.

Moves from public behavior to the cultural/political issue.

Identities have status, power, force.

Gradually the media became an enemy to my pal and social crutch. Anti-smoking hysteria dominated televisions. Screens were filled with commercials of men singing out of voice boxes, bodies strewn about the streets depicting actual numbers of deaths from lung cancer. Smoking was banned from within 15 feet of all public entrances, most restaurants, a few bars, and then the entire downtown area. Government programs were issuing free nicotine patches along with information packets about quitting. Many folks, it seemed, were acknowledging the obvious health risks. They either quit or made it their business to make others quit (or both). My associates and I were characterized as irresponsible, reckless addicts. But the fact is that I am more addicted to the social environment of smoking than I am the actual nicotine. That is what enticed me initially. I was not attracted to the strong odor that saturates my clothes and hair, the stain on my hands and teeth, the risk of ruined health or an imminent death. I was attracted to something else. I learned how to be social, intimate, helpful, constant, and rebellious by smoking. Those are possibly not the most ideal values to uphold, but they worked for me.

Responds to the cultural/political messages—and reveals the quiet layers of the relationship.

She admits to the craving for affirmation—for belonging.

The final insight addresses the tension developed in preceding paragraphs.

No one likes to be a social outcast, unless of course you can be involved in a separate society of them. We want validation. We crave belonging and confirmation. Perhaps the Good Samaritans

Group identity cancels out the fear of being outcast.

trying to save the world from a chemically enhanced haze are seeking that confirmation themselves. The validation I craved was freely given to me in a box pack of twenty.

Writing Strategies

1. How does the opening paragraph function in this essay? How does the memory of Jackson's mother help to establish the main idea?
2. Jackson describes the particular places that she smoked. What do these passages do for your understanding of the essay? How do they help you to see her point about smoking?
3. How does Jackson create public resonance? What particular passages seem most important for making her experience relevant to readers?
4. How is Jackson's essay revelatory? Explain how she gets to something more complex than the common sentiments about self, identity, or belonging.
5. This essay is largely narrative, but a college essay should do more than tell a story—more than relay events. It should also analyze how something (like a relationship) works. So how is Jackson's essay doing more than telling a story? Point to specific passages that reveal how the relationship works.

Exploring Ideas

1. Jackson describes herself as craving connection, belonging, even exclusivity. How is that craving similar to or different from an addiction to nicotine?
2. Jackson explains that she learned to be "social, intimate, helpful, constant, and rebellious" through smoking. But she admits that such qualities may not be valued by her readers. Why might someone object to these qualities? Do you object to any of them?
3. Jackson describes an important distinction: while people don't want to be isolated from the mainstream, they enjoy being part of a rebellious group. What other groups, besides smokers, might consider themselves rebels? How do they illustrate Jackson's point?
4. Jackson describes her desire for validation both as a child and as a college student. This suggests that adults crave validation as much as children do. Describe a situation that supports or refutes this suggestion.

Ideas for Writing

1. Have you ever been a social outcast? Do you know a social outcast? What is the relationship between the outcast and the culturally accepted?
2. What has the craving for acceptance or validation prompted you to do? Has the craving for validation prompted you into a relationship?

If responding to one of these ideas, go to the Analysis section of this chapter to begin developing ideas for your essay.

Invention

Invention is the activity of discovering ideas, developing points, and thinking through a topic. For academic writers, it is a necessary activity, one that leads to vital and valuable ideas. In this chapter, the invention process will involve focusing on a particular relationship and exploring its possible meaning. The following sections are designed to help you through the process: specifically, to discover a topic (in Point of Contact), to develop particular points about the topic (in Analysis), to make it relevant to a community of readers (in Public Resonance), to develop a focus (in Thesis), and to generate support (in Rhetorical Tools). The Invention Questions in each section are not meant to be answered directly in your final written assignment. Rather, they are meant to help you develop increasingly intense ideas for your project.

Point of Contact

When you hear the word *relationship,* you may imagine an intimate personal bond between significant others, family members, or friends. But consider the relationships that are less obvious, those that surround or define us but remain hidden by the patterns of everyday life. Imagine the intense, but also subtle, relationships that define life as we know it: between an old man and his backyard, among people in a corporate office, between a lake and a local economy, between pigeons and people in a park.

As you explore possible topics, ask yourself, "What is the nature of this relationship?" If you cannot answer the question easily, you may have a good topic—one worthy of continued thinking and writing. Use the following suggestions, questions, and images (Figure 3.1) to begin exploring:

Norbert Machinke/StockXchng

Jonas Jordan, USACE/U.S. Army

Figure 3.1

- **Visit a Public Place**
  - —How do the people interact or depend on each other?
  - —How do the people relate to their surroundings? To objects? To buildings? To nature?
  - —How do the objects (buildings, tools, products, shops) relate?
  - —How do people or objects influence each other?
- **Examine Your Own Relationships**
  - —Consider the groups or allegiances that you claim: Are you a smoker, a cyber punk, a metal head, a gamer, a comic book fanatic?
  - —What are the tensions, contradictions, or quiet associations that come along with that identity?
- **Examine a Job Site**
  - —How do workers relate to their tools or equipment?
  - —How must the people relate to each other? (How must they influence or depend on each other?)
  - —How do workers relate to their environment?
  - —How do workers relate to the public?
- **Examine Everyday Civic Bonds**
  - —Between a customer and a sales clerk, a customer and a mail carrier, the public and a city police force, a politician and her constituents, or an artist and the public.

Dawn M. Turner/MorgueFile

© Cengage Learning®

Valeria Obregon/StockXchng

Hal Wilson/StockXchng

- **Imagine Human/Object Relationships**

  —Between a person and a computer, a person and a musical instrument, a person and a car; or between two objects, such as a college course and a textbook, a book and a computer, an old car and a new one, or a road and a house.

- **Examine Relationships in Your Academic Major**

  —Between the professionals in your field of study and the public (such as nurses and their patients, or business marketing professionals and potential consumers).

  —Between two things in your field of study. Students of criminal justice, for instance, can explore how one case (or one kind of case) relates to another; environmental scientists can explore the relationship between waterways and surrounding land or between trees and animal life.

  —Between your field of study and another field. Most academic disciplines and professional fields define themselves in conjunction with other fields. For instance, biology explores its relationship with ethics, computer technologies involve visual or graphic design, and political science involves religious studies.

Analysis

Analysis is the process of inspecting how or why something works, but analysis also involves discovering connections and meaning. In this chapter, analysis involves investigating all the possible ways entities relate to each other. It means going beyond the obvious relationship and exploring the hidden connections. For example, we might begin with some basic understanding of a relationship:

- Students have a relationship with education.
- Smokers have a relationship with cigarettes.
- Pet owners have a relationship with their pets.
- Athletes have a relationship with their equipment.

Inside of the broad idea, we can look for relational clusters—for more specific relationships that maintain or give meaning to the broader idea. For instance, a student has a relationship with education, but more specifically, a computer sciences student may have a relationship to technology *and* change *and* Generation Y. Or a pet owner may have many specific relationships because of her dog—say, with a certain open field, a leash law, or a neighborhood park. When we begin to see clusters of relationships within the broader idea, we get closer to revealing important connections. Use the following Invention Questions to explore deep layers of the relationship that you will explain in your essay:

- What relationships exist within the broader relationship? How do those smaller relationships drive the broader relationship?
- Is the broader relationship difficult? Why?
- What keeps it going?
- How does the presence of one entity (person or thing) influence the other? In what hidden or indirect ways do they influence one another?
- What would occur to one if the other were gone?

If you examine an intimate personal relationship, try to go beyond the initial common thoughts ("it is supportive"; "it is difficult"; "it has ups and downs"; "it is loving") and find some hidden complexity. Use the following Invention Questions to explore the complexities of a human relationship:

- In what ways do I communicate with this person?
- To what degree do I share in his or her personal crises?
- Do I ever feel obligated to do, think, or say something for this person?
- Why am I in this relationship?
- What kinds of disagreements arise in the relationship? Do they become sources of debate and tension, or do they fade away?

As you work through these Invention Questions, use them to develop ideas. For example, in the following excerpt, Jim Crockett's invention writing helped him discover the insights he shares in his essay. In his responses to the Invention Questions, we can see how important concepts emerge and lay the groundwork for his essay:

> **In what hidden or indirect ways do [the persons or things] influence one another?**
>
> At the outset, I'm really wondering why I need to use the same mug every day and not one of the many on the shelf that perform the same function, i.e., keep my mustache dry and drip-free while keeping coffee hot. Maybe it's because I received this mug for my birthday a few years back—received it from good friends. Maybe it's the functional good looks of the stainless steel and plastic—industrialized design good looks. Maybe it's because I have a need to carry a security object (Linus's blanket). What if I have an obsessive/compulsive disorder? What if? Does it really matter? Do I really care? Is this really a big deal? Maybe not, but it's probably worth looking into—probably worth unraveling the thread of the warm blanket (warm sweater?) of my relationship with my coffee mug.

Here, Crockett explores various layers. He raises some questions that later evolve into the essay, and he makes two important discoveries: that any possible psychological "disorder" is less important than some basic human need and that he connects his mug with security.

Now let's look at a different topic and writer. In the following, Marcus uses the Invention Questions to explore the relationship between a police department and the surrounding community. Notice how Marcus's response to the last question (Why am I in this relationship?) takes him further into his own thinking. Although the question seems unrelated to his topic, it actually prompts him to see an essential point: *People can be in a relationship without consciously thinking about it.*

Is the relationship difficult?

Yes. My father is a police officer, and he is constantly stressed about the work. Patrolling in some neighborhoods is hard work—and dangerous. And even though many officers face dangerous situations, they are expected by people in the community to be totally passive. It's nearly impossible work.

What keeps it going?

People stay in the job for obvious reasons: They need money, They have the training, they get some satisfaction out of the job (most of them still assume that they are "protecting and serving"). But the real question is: What keeps the tension going? And that's a mixture of things: On one side, economic problems in the city create bad neighborhoods where people are desperate. On the other side, every time the news reports anything involving the police, it's going to be bad, so people learn to associate police cars and uniforms with negative feelings.

Why am I in this relationship?

Technically, I'm not in it. Or maybe I am. I am "the community." But I guess most people probably don't think they are in the relationship until they see the flashing lights behind them. That's also part of the reason that the tension keeps going. People in the community don't see themselves as part of the relationship—maybe they don't even see a relationship.

Thinking Further

How do writers identify potentially interesting ideas? Of all the ideas swimming around, how do they decide which to pursue and which to ignore? You might consider two key strategies:

1. **Capitalize on Uncertainty.** If you are uncertain how to answer a question, or you can answer it several ways, explore further. (The uncertainty is a sign of complexity!) For example, Marcus writes, "Technically, I'm not in it. Or maybe I am." As Marcus reviews his notes, he can focus on this indefinite answer and explore the ambiguity.
2. **Look for Fresh Perspectives.** Occasionally you might see a topic differently than most other people. Because writers are looking for a new perspective, such realizations are vital. For example, when Marcus writes, "the tension keeps going" because "people in the community don't see themselves as part of the relationship," he has discovered an important idea worth pursuing further.

If writers discover some uncertainty or fresh perspective, they can then ask even more questions to pursue their thinking. For example, Marcus might explore further by asking the following questions:

"Technically, I'm not in it. Or maybe I am."

- Am I in the relationship or not? What is the nature of the relationship?
- Can I ever get out of the relationship? What would happen if I did?
- How does the relationship influence me in hidden ways? How does it influence law enforcement?

"People in the community don't see themselves as part of the relationship—maybe they don't even see a relationship."

- Why don't people in the community see the relationship? How is their not seeing helpful or harmful?
- Who does see the relationship? How do people who see the relationship act differently?
- If more people saw the relationship, would it be less difficult? Would people be influenced differently?

Invention Workshop

Meet with at least one other writer and use one of the Invention Questions (on page 81) to initiate a focused discussion on your topic. Briefly explain your topic to the other writer(s), and then ask one of the Invention Questions. Try to stay focused on that question until you've reached some new insight about the relationship.

Look into the deep connections, both present and past; look at the consequences of actions; consider the effects of attitudes. And remember two key strategies: (1) Capitalize on uncertainty, and (2) look for fresh perspectives.

Sample Invention Workshop

WRITER: [Explains the Topic] I want to write about my relationship with snowboarding. I really like snowboarding. I do it all winter. It's what I do with my friends. I love the snow, the speed, and the excitement. It's expensive though, and risky.

PEER: [Applies an Invention Question] Let's use one of the Invention Questions to probe deeper: What relation-ships exist within the broader relationship? How do those smaller relationships drive the broader relationship?

WRITER: Well, if the broader relationship is me and snowboarding, then some smaller relationship that exists within it might be . . .

PEER: [Helps the Writer Identify Smaller Relationships] You mentioned speed and excitement and risk. Do you think speed is part of the risk? Is excitement part of the risk? Or vice versa?

WRITER: Well, I'd say both. Maybe they're all tangled together. The speed creates a kind of risk—of physical harm, I guess—and that creates excitement. The rush comes from zooming down the hill, not poking along.

PEER: [Prompts Writer to Explore Uncertainty] So the speed wouldn't be as intense if there weren't some peril involved? Are peril and intensity linked in some way?

WRITER: Probably. Well, it's not totally about the potential harm. I mean, you don't go out there looking to get hurt or fall down a mountain. It's also about the skill it takes to avoid crashing—and to go faster, to do more with your own body.

PEER: [Prompts Further Thinking] Your own body? Why's that important?

WRITER: Well, it's just you and the board—and the hill. Nothing else. You and natural forces. No computers, no monitors, no nothing. And if you move the wrong way, just a little, you feel the consequences.

PEER: And the opposite could also be said, right? That moving just the right way makes you feel something?

WRITER: Definitely. You really learn what your body's capable of—split-second decisions and reflexes.

PEER: So maybe that's how the speed figures in. It cranks up the need for your body to respond? To rely on reflexes?

WRITER: Exactly. And you don't get that anywhere else. I don't anyway. The rest of my life is about sitting, watching, pushing buttons, reading—all eyes, ears, and fingers. I need more than that.

PEER: So snowboarding makes your body wake up to itself—and in a really intense way. Okay. Here's another Invention Question. What would occur to one if the other were gone?

WRITER: Well, if I didn't have snowboarding, I don't think I'd be aware of my own reflexes. I don't know if I'd understand how my reflexes and body even work.

The writer is now digging into the relationship. From here, she could go into the Public Resonance questions (on the following page) and explore the issue further. For instance, the writer may examine how people need a certain degree of raw intensity—something beyond the digital, clinical, and predictable routine of everyday life. That further exploration might yield a revelatory thesis.

Public Resonance

Remember that you are not writing entirely for yourself. You are writing to explain something for others. The particular relationship you are explaining may be specific and narrow (perhaps between two people), but it may suggest something beyond the particular—something that is relevant or important to your readers. As you consider your own topic, ask the following questions:

- Does the relationship reveal something about people's strengths, weaknesses, or needs?
- Why is it important that people see the meaning of the relationship?
- Is there something unusual or usual about this relationship?
- Does this relationship show how difficult, easy, or valuable human relationships can be?
- Does this relationship show how rewarding or valuable a particular kind of relationship can be?

Exploring public resonance can be hard work. But the process takes writers somewhere important, even vital: to new insights. In his project, Jim Crockett discovers the bigger significance of a relationship—that his simple mug is not merely a personal habit but a representation of human habit and a basic need. He also considers how the specific relationship functions within the broader sphere of relations between humans and their economy, humans and their home, and humans and their past:

> Why is it important that people see the meaning of the relationship? We all need daily ritual in our lives in an increasingly alien world—a culture, econoculture removed from the time-worn agrarian rituals, from the ties to place and home. How much coffee do you drink anyway? The cup/mug is natural—a natural extension of the human hand, a necessary adjunct to, a logical appurtenance thereof. Small choices—these small behaviors we cling to—affect the way in which we are perceived in the world.

And in further writing, Crockett picks up on an idea that surfaces in the previous passage—the idea of ritual. He realizes that *ritual,* the term itself, has significance, meaning beyond the obvious, so he says more about it. Notice that he finds his way back to the concept, to the word, and thinks about its role in the world. In this sense, Crockett's own language is pulling him further into ideas. He is inventing by exploring the meaning and significance of his words:

> I'm tired of people asking how much coffee I drink. Do they really care? Caffeine or antioxidants? Whose side are you on? They should care where their coffee comes from. They should care about buying coffee in tree-killing paper cups. They should know that the small choices they make affect the world; that the smallest choices have power. !!! Ritual power—the power of small rituals. We are grounded by our rituals—in the wider world—

in the econoculture—the world of corporate greed—we (individuals) have no control. My mug ritual gives me some control in the huge arena of coffee trading. My money goes to the small farmer in Chiapas (at least more of my money) not to the national cartels. The ritual grounds me and ties me to the place and affects, as well, the wider world, the world far removed from its agricultural roots, a world where wilderness is a theme park and where the agrarian rituals have been replaced with what? Maybe they haven't been replaced. Maybe just forgotten. Maybe ritual behaviors are no longer deemed important in a society driven by technology—a society enamored of subject only. Who's doing the verbing here? It doesn't matter who's the recipient, the object. That's why this matters. Maybe we should ask—maybe we should be asking: Whom or what do the small behaviors, ones we cling to, affect? How do they affect the way we are perceived in the world?

Thesis

As you focus your topic, you will also be narrowing in on a thesis statement or main idea. Like many writers, you may write your way to a thesis, or you may try to focus the idea before drafting. Either way, you need to have a single statement that not only gives focus to your topic but also gives particular insight on that topic. Your project might do one of the following:

- **Explain the significant qualities of a particular kind of relationship.**

  —Human/dog relationships rely on so little understanding and effort from humans and so much work, agility, and determination from the dog.

  —Rock stars and their fans both rely on a sense of urgency and exclusivity.

- **Explain what is sometimes hidden in a particular kind of relationship.**

  —Beneath the obvious authority issues between teachers and students, there exists a mutual kind of awe in which each marvels at the will of the other.

  —Homeowners often forget the powerful underground struggle between plumbing and trees—until they see stems and leaves swimming in the toilet.

- **Explain the difficulties or problems of being a child, friend, parent, or significant other.**

  —Our children's birthdays are a tangle of joy and unutterable sadness that comes with knowing how time will eventually do its work and create absence.

  —College friends are surrogate families, which means they always fall short in some quiet way.

- **Explain how a particular relationship is much like something else.**

  —Presidential candidates and their potential supporters are both authors of fiction, each conjuring visions of what the other will certainly do.

—If the surrounding neighborhood is a family, the 7-11 is like a bad in-law that has slowly been accepted.

- **Explain how a particular relationship reveals something important about a subject.**

  —The river's color beyond the city shows how water willingly carries the by-products of human endeavor.

  —The association between gun and police officer speaks of our culture's assumption about power.

Regardless of your approach, avoid the fog. Steer clear of unfocused generalizations. A narrower and more particular thesis will create a more intensive experience for both writer and readers. Notice the difference among the following:

General	**Specific**	**More Specific**
Students	Third-grade girls	The attitudes of third-grade girls
Employees	Retail sales associates	Retail sales associates' energy
Campus	The new buildings	The look of the new buildings

The more specific subjects help readers (and writers!) focus on more specific insights. They help readers and writers tune in to intricacies and intimacies. (They actually help sharpen consciousness.) In considering the focus of your project, examine the nouns you use. Can they be more specific?

If nouns (or subjects in sentences) help create focus, then verbs can help create *revelation.* A revelatory thesis statement shows something new—a commonly overlooked layer, connection, or idea. Notice the following statements:

- The attitudes of third-grade girls *depend* upon the number of close friends.
- Retail sales associates' energy *relies* on the number and nature of customers.
- The flat, corporate look of the new buildings on campus *competes* with the traditional stone giants and illustrates the clash between the old academic tradition and the new corporate designs on education.

In these statements, the verbs *(depend, relies, competes)* are active and intensive. They help show how two things or groups of people relate.

Evolution of a Thesis

Writers should allow their initial ideas to become increasingly more focused and revelatory. Notice how a broad statement can become more intense and sophisticated as it becomes more focused:

- **Runners develop an intense relationship with the road.**

  Here, "intense relationship" can be defined or narrowed. It's potentially interesting, but we need to see the intensity.

- **Runners share space with humans and machines.**

  The writer can keep thinking about that space—what happens in that shared space?

- **Runners must confront the overwhelming presence of both cars and car culture when they take to the road.**

  The writer has helped us to see a kind of difficulty or tension in the relationship. We're examining not only the physical presence of cars, but some set of assumptions or attitudes related to cars.

Revising Your Thesis

A key part of writing is developing an intellectual rearview mirror—a habit of looking back and redirecting your course. Apply the following questions:

- In my thesis, which nouns could be narrower, more specific?
- In my thesis, which verbs could be intensified to reveal more about the relationship?
- How does the statement offer something beyond a commonsense or simplistic assumption? How is it revelatory?

Other writers can help you with this process. Try exchanging your initial ideas with others and using the preceding questions for peer evaluation.

Rhetorical Tools

The next step is to develop and support ideas. Remember that potential readers already know about relationships in general. (They are certainly mired in several.) But in your essay you have the opportunity to shed light, to go beyond ordinary thinking, and to reveal something that most people do not necessarily consider.

Using Narration

Narration, or storytelling, is appropriate for many kinds of writing. It is not simply relegated to remembering events. You might consider beginning your essay with a brief retelling of a situation regarding the relationship, or using a brief account to illustrate something about the relationship. It will be important to determine how much narration to use. For example, Lauren Jackson relies heavily on narration. Jim Crockett uses narration more sparingly. If you decide to use narration, make good choices:

1. Start the narrative at an appropriate place. That is, limit your story to include only relevant parts of the situation.
2. Focus on only the relevant details of the events.

3. Use consistent verb tense. (In most cases, past or present tense can work in retelling a story. However, you must be consistent throughout the narrative.)
4. At some point, make sure to explain the significance or relevance of the narrative to the readers.
5. Refer to Chapter 2 for other valuable narrative strategies.

Using Description

Readers like details. The more detailed the images, the more intensely readers will experience them. In this essay, you might decide to describe the people involved in the relationship—their particular postures, facial expressions, and gestures. Or you might need to detail more abstract qualities—their imaginations, their appetites, their pride, their esteem, their effect on strangers. In the following, a writer is describing the relationship between a coffee shop and the students who frequent the place. The first passage is broad and without detail:

> The coffee shop makes them feel more academic. It is more than a location to do homework and drink caffeine. It is a place where students totally surround themselves in college work.

These are valuable statements, but they remain abstract, general, and ultimately unhelpful to readers. But the ideas come to life more with details:

> The coffee shop is more than a location for doing homework. It is like a satellite campus where students and professors alike work, talk, reflect. On any given day, several tables will be pushed together while a group of students work together on a project, their papers and notebooks scattered between coffee cups and half-eaten bagels. Invariably, a professor, graduate student, or staff member from the college will sit at one of the corner tables reading a newspaper. Several students will be perched on the windowsill, their backs against the outside world as they read through textbook chapters.

You might need to describe a particular situation in detail. In that case, narration and description will work together. For instance, Steinbeck includes several situations or anecdotes in his essay that dramatize the relationship between American settlers and the land:

> Another joker with a name still remembered in the West worked out a scheme copied many times in after years. Proving a quarter section required a year of residence and some kind of improvement—a fence, a shack—but once the land was proved the owner was free to sell it. This particular princely character went to the stews and skid rows of the towns and found a small army of hopeless alcoholics who lived for whisky and nothing else. He put these men on land he wanted to own, grubstaked them and kept them in cheap liquor until the acreage was proved, then went through the motions of buying it from his protégés and moved them and their one-room shacks on sled

> runners on to new quarter sections. Bums of strong constitution might prove out five or six homesteads for this acquisitive hero before they died of drunkenness.

Using Figurative Language

Any explanatory essay can benefit from figurative language, which is language that goes beyond words' basic definitions and uses them to suggest imaginative connections between ideas. Figurative language does more than just make interesting comparisons. It also reveals a new dimension to the topic; it helps writers and their readers to see the topic in a new light.

Metaphor: A metaphor is a comparison in which one thing is made to share the characteristics of another. In his essay, Jim Crockett slides in a subtle metaphor that graphically describes most consumers' relationship with big coffee corporations:

> When I buy a cup of coffee, I only buy coffee: the paper cup and insulating sleeve, both little bits of tree, remain in the store. *I remain weaned from dependence* upon the earth- and human-pillaging multinational coffee cartel.

Simile: A simile is a comparison that uses *like* or *as.* John Steinbeck's similes help to characterize the nature of the relationship between American settlers and the land:

> I have often wondered at the savagery and thoughtlessness with which our early settlers approached this rich continent. They came at it *as though it were an enemy,* which of course it was.

> There has always been more than enough desert in America; the new settlers, *like over-indulged children,* created even more.

As you consider your own topic, apply the following questions:

- What brief story will help readers to see my point about the relationship?
- What vivid details will help demonstrate the precise nature of the relationship?
- Can I compare the relationship (or the entities in the relationship) to an animal? A thing? A place? A person? What new dimension would this comparison reveal?

Activity

Before developing a draft, plan out your writing. A brief plan, in fact, can make all the difference between writerly hiccups and writerly flow. If you have an overall plan, you'll be able to more smoothly move along. Chart out your ideas: What is your thesis? What are your main support strategies? What examples will you use? What stories will you tell? And where will you begin and end those? What comparisons will you make?

Revision

Revision is the most difficult intellectual step in writing. It requires a commitment to rethink some basics, to step back and ask if the writing does, at its most basic level, what it should. For instance, does the draft, as it stands, offer a revelatory insight about a relationship? Does it go beyond describing a relationship and, instead, offer a focused insight beyond what readers already know? Does it help readers to rethink the nature of the relationship?

Before you get a peer review, go back through the main sections of the chapter and ask some basic questions: How well does my draft explain the hidden complexities of a relationship? Does the draft connect to or involve issues or relationships beyond my personal relationship? Is the thesis sufficiently focused and revelatory? Does the draft provide details, narration, and explanation that support the thesis? Is it organized so that readers can follow the ideas? How does the voice engage readers? How does it do more than fulfill an assignment? Which sentences can be vitalized? How can the draft be woken up, turned up, or intensified?

Peer Review

Exchange drafts with at least one other writer. Before passing your draft to others, underline the thesis, or write it on the top of your essay. This way, reviewers will get traction as they read.

As a reviewer, use the following questions to guide your response.

1. Point out any phrases in the thesis that could be more specific. (See the Thesis section for more guidance.)
2. Where can the writer do more analysis and reveal more about the relationship? (Point to passages that seem most obvious to you.) As you read, look for claims that anyone could immediately offer without intensive analysis.
3. Help the writer illustrate his or her claims with details. As you read, look for broad characterizations. If you see phrases such as "influence one another" or "depend on one another," ask yourself: Could this be more specific? Can we *really* see the influence or dependence? Suggest further details to the writer. Explain what you would like to see.
4. Offer some figurative language to help characterize the relationship. After you have read the entire draft, offer your own metaphor or simile about the relationship. Make sure it is something that fits the writer's voice—something that he or she could use.
5. Are the paragraphs coherent? Do you ever get the sense that a paragraph is wandering? Mark any passages or details that seem unrelated to the point of the essay.
6. Help the writer kick-start the essay. The writer might begin with a broad statement about the relationship—or about something even broader. But the most focused statement possible often makes for a better introduction. Suggest a surprisingly focused opening statement.

7. Consider the writer's voice. Where could the writer employ a whisper or a yell (see pages 566–568) to better engage readers?
8. Point to particular sentences and phrases that could gain vitality and intensity. Use the following questions:
   - Where can the writer change *be* verbs to active verbs?
   - Look for clauses (especially those that begin with *which are, which is, that are, that is,* etc.). Suggest a strategy for boiling down the clause to a phrase.
   - Look for phrases (especially prepositional phrases that begin with *about* or *of*). Suggest a strategy for boiling down the phrase to a word.
   - Consider vitality strategies from the previous chapter:

     —Combine sentences.

     —Repeat structures.

     —Intensify verbs.

     —Help the writer avoid common grammatical errors: comma splices, sentence fragments, or lack of pronoun/antecedent agreement.

Reflection

For writers, the big insights often come after they have completed a project—after they have thought through an idea, developed an essay, revised, edited, and given it to the world beyond them. After all of these steps, writers should have a better sense of what they have discovered and accomplished. Understanding one's writing in this better sense involves analyzing its rhetoric—the way it communicates an idea and persuades others to think differently *and* the way you, the writer, came to think differently through the process of exploring and developing an idea. Look back on your essay—from the invention to the final draft—and analyze its rhetoric based on the following questions:

1. How is the main insight revelatory? (How does it go beyond what people normally imagine about this kind of relationship? How might it have even taken you, as a writer, to a new intellectual place?)
2. What support strategies were the most important? If you used narrative, what made you focus on particular scenes or situations?
3. What would you say is the public resonance of the essay? How does your main insight resonate with some broader issue, idea, tension, trend, or behavior?
4. Describe your voice. If every essay has a voice, what does yours sound like? Is it sober? Formal? Lazy? Intense? Meditative? Forceful? Earnest? What particular passages best show the character of your voice?

Beyond the Essay: Images as Support

Images can function like words (the way sentences and paragraphs do) to help readers understand a writer's main idea.

1. For your explaining relationships essay, use one to three images to help readers understand and accept your thesis. Place photographs, drawings, or other visuals within the essay to illustrate key points.

   Think of the images as rhetorical tools that help support your thesis, like the words in a sentence or a paragraph would.

   Make sure the images are rhetorically and aesthetically effective. Consider where in the essay the image should be placed; what size the image should be; how the image contributes to or detracts from the momentum of the essay; whether the image should be colorful, bold, restrained, black-and-white, and so on.

   Include a concise caption beneath each image.

2. After incorporating the images into your essay, write a separate document to explain how the images help readers understand and accept the essay's thesis. To help with your explanation, for each image think about content, framing, composition, focus, lighting, texture, and vantage point, which are discussed in Chapter 7: Analyzing Images.

4 Observing

John Metz

"The goal here is to see something in a new way, to see beyond the casual glance."

Observing is about observing is about discovery—about finding something unique and particular about a subject. It involves more than simple description. Careful observers go beyond the casual glance; they study their subjects and learn something by seeing them in a particular way. In some ways, then, learning how to observe involves learning how to see things, how to notice what is beneath the surface.

We casually observe our daily lives constantly. We watch our communities carrying on with life; we watch our coworkers, friends, children, and families. Occasionally, we take time to study, to focus on subjects and take in something beyond surface meanings: at those times we go beyond what something means to us and discover something outside of our expectations and biases. We see, for instance, how a man sitting on a street corner means something to the city that surrounds him; we suddenly see the systematic design in the movements of a seemingly chaotic crowd of people. Such seeing involves more than open eyes; it involves an open consciousness.

Observation is an essential strategy in academic life:

- Child psychology students observe the behaviors of young teens at a video arcade.
- Education students observe the interaction between high school teachers and their students.
- Biology students study the growth of bacteria over a 24-hour period.
- Chemistry students observe the effects of mixing different compounds.
- Sociology graduate students and faculty observe the language habits of a small island town.

Observers find the hidden meaning, the significant issues, and the important aspects of a particular subject. They point out how and why a particular subject is of interest to a broader public. We experience this kind of observing and reporting when we watch documentaries or nature specials. Writers and researchers for such programs first make general observations. Then they focus their perspective on a particular issue or subject. They analyze that issue or subject to find the most important or valuable thing to say. Throughout this process, the observing writer is always looking to discover, to find and communicate a fresh and interesting idea.

This chapter will help you choose a subject to observe, discover something particular about that subject, and develop a focused essay about your discovery. The essays will provide insight to various strategies for observing, which can range from the somewhat formal methods on display in Taylor Perry's ethnography essay to the evocative details of Anne-Marie Oomen's meditation on a sand dune. As you read, take note of the hidden meaning, significant issue, or important aspect of the subject being observed and how it resonates with the lives of others. After reading the essays, you can find a topic in one of two ways:

1. Go to the Point of Contact section to find a topic from everyday life, or
2. Choose one of the Ideas for Writing that follow each essay.

After you find a topic, go to the Analysis section to begin developing your observation.

Readings
Heart of Sand
Anne-Marie Oomen

In "Heart of Sand," Anne-Marie Oomen takes readers to a place, a massive sand dune. Through careful observation she explores the meaning of that place and the legend about it. Oomen is author of *An American Map,* a collection of essays; two memoirs, *Pulling Down the Barn* and *House of Fields;* and a collection of poetry, *Uncoded Woman.* She teaches creative writing at Interlochen Arts Academy and in the Solstice MFA program of Pine Manor College.

Before the legend of the Sleeping Bear became Michigan's state story, I was struck by its sad contradictions. It is the tale of the great she-bear, Michimokwa, who, to escape a Wisconsin forest fire, swam with her cubs across Lake Michigan to a new peninsula. Though she reached the open sand on the Michigan side, her young cubs drowned a short way from the Michigan shore.

In the story, the great spirit, Gitche Manitou, transformed the cubs into the two islands we call the Manitous, but it is that west-facing dune on the shore that is the pivot point for the legend, the one that represents the great she-bear watching those two islands. She is said to watch from the dunes for her cubs to make it to shore. She is said to call for them. She is said to sleep in peace under the sand. I know how stories twist, how they must mean many things in order to last, but how could she sleep in peace and be ever watchful at the same time?

Would I understand it better if I went there?

In the autumn, I decide to visit Sleeping Bear Dunes National Lakeshore and walk to the Sleeping Bear, the single dune identified by sailors among the seventy thousand acres of dune and forest and islands that are named for her. I decide to go on my birthday, to mark the moment with a look at the great mother.

5 I drive the park's forested scenic road to the point where it opens to the light and sand of the dunes. I park, hike the boardwalk to a lookout with benches offering a view of the Bear to the north. This civilized platform is where most people stop, read the story printed on the signs, and then return to their cars. From here I can see the rough rise and darkness of the dune in the distance.

A mile? Two?

Cold and bluster bully me as I squeeze under the railings and step off the lookout, cutting directly across the dunes, trudging through this northern desert. From the lookout, the dune seemed close enough, but when I leave the deck and start walking through sand so soft it leaves a clean print only after rain, I realize there is a good reason not many people visit the specific dune I have chosen. The hard walk up and down the crumbling slopes dampens my determination to find a place I have never been.

But it is my birthday.

I stumble along the shoreline bluff, walking slowly through varied soil, sometimes soft sand, sometimes coarse gravel or crusty silt—all of it light. The wind gusts fiercely along these bluffs, and even though the dunes are still snowless, winter is already pushing its way toward these arid places. As I move over the drifts of glacial debris, walking absorbs my attention. I watch my feet, notice snail shells in abundance, along with small stony fossils. Here and there are scattered rust-colored beer cans leftover from the days when the dunes were privately owned and dune buggies carrying thrill-seekers tore across the fragile dune ecosystem. There are tracks everywhere in this part of the dunes—though I see no animals and hear little except the alarm of the crows, the distant roar of waves below the bluffs. The wind picks up, slams sand against my jeans.

10 I think I may be lost.

Deep swales. I cannot see the lake or the distant reference point of the dune. I stop, disoriented, pull my hood back to let the wind cool my face, and then start again, but without a clear sense of direction. I am out here alone, and even my husband does not know I have decided on this birthday sojourn. I wonder if I have lost my bearings and study the slopes for landmarks, just as I think I should turn back before my tracks are obliterated by wind, a slow rise carries me up a low ridge and there, across the distance, high green foliage marking the Bear. I keep going, fighting wind and poor footing and now, colder air.

Half an hour later, having spanned the final mile and struggled up through rough scrub, I crest the rim—gasping for breath, and look down into what is the bowl of the bear. I had expected something else, a plateau marked with thick and tattered shrubbery. But this dune is deceptive, secretive. What from a distance looks like a hilltop and rises like a rough upturned dish, like some solid and long-standing pedernal, is instead something in motion. Open space. Instead of the flat-topped mound that would have been the geological metaphor for the bear, a hollow. The Bear is a huge basin, winnowed out and case empty by wind, an immense sink of sand.

It has become a blowout.

A blowout is a dune summit or ridge that may have once looked like a lush foliage-covered hilltop. But because of the lightness and fragility of the soil—almost dust—and the death, due to drought or other weather conditions, of that vegetation, plus exposure to the constant westerlies, the dune sand erodes away from the roots, especially at the crest of these hills. After years of enduring this relentless wind, the vegetation blows away, and the dune begins to hollow itself out, like a bowl, weathered down from the high point, leaving the lower, less exposed sides to rise like a rim. Dune walkers commonly stumble on blowouts all over the open duneland, but this one is startling for its immensity and grandeur, a huge basin carved by wind.

15 And then, there is the beauty of her bones.

From the crater of sand where her body would have rested, ghost trees rise, scattered and leaning and awful. The remnants of this spirit forest are scattered like ribs and femurs and spine. They shimmer silver gray, smoothed by the gales, their grain polished to gleam against the half-lit day.

John Mauk

I stand there for a long time, asking quietly if I may enter, and when the wind drops, I take it as acceptance and climb inside, where the wind drops but never ceases.

How long can one explore a void? The inside of the word *hollow?* I wander, spiraling lower, touching the driftwood trees that were once green and are now an uncanny architecture, shards of some immense being. I sniff cold air, dryness, dune dust. Wind mutes and huffs through this place, and over the years, it has not only hollowed the bowl but shaped a broad opening at the west side of the blowout—as though the sand that once made the mound was poured out of a wide spigot. But this is the opposite of the truth. The broad opening is where the constant westerlies enter the blowout and lift sand particles up and carry them east and farther into the dunes—shifting the landscape every season.

Finally, I do what I have been avoiding. There is here a place within a place. I look to the center of the blowout, which contains a smaller mound, still intact, around which the wind has worked all these years. It is perhaps two stories high, and despite the fact that all else around it is hollowed out and left to bones, it stands over this desert and the skeletal trees, a rough, grass-pocked cone with its top sheered off. I have been circling its irregular slopes cautiously because I feel the anomaly.

This entire rise has been blown away, but this core has remained, grasses still clinging to its surface. I choose the least steep slope on the backside, the slope protected from the lake winds, and scramble up, slipping with every step. Finally I am perched on this upturned funnel in the middle of windy emptiness. Breathless, I lie down and watch the rush of combed skies.

20 Is this place within a place what's left of her mammoth heart? Is this heart of sand the stalwart core of emptiness? It is a place that simply resists. Resists just enough to hold, even against the force of the west winds. Resists a bit longer than the rest of the earth against the inevitable wearing down. A symbol of the Bear, who waits—held in the paradox of eternal sleep and eternal watchfulness—for her cubs, those distant islands of Manitou.

Before I climbed the interior mound, I had been imagining that her bones would someday rise and gather themselves into body, whole and muscled and covered with the mat of her great hide. I saw her walk on water, raise up her startled cubs, cuff them into motion, and then lumber over the land to call us all out of sleep. This is how I hoped the legend would wake us, wake me. As something fierce and alive, resurrected in power. But now, sitting on the mound, staring out, I imagine her heart defined by a will to stay, to endure a little longer the inevitable winds.

What does a thousand years mean to a mother waiting?

Since then, I have tried to make the trek once a year, usually in the fall when the isolation is more remarkable. I know better ways to get there now. I have learned to go quietly, with reverence, and not to move anything, not to touch much. I always climb the mound, sit in what I perceive as the center of not just this dune, but of all the shifting acres for miles around.

I have come to love the wind here, the power it has to erase through its insistent presence. Just as it has blown out the hilltop, the very place that represented the great mother, Michimokwa, the wind has fragmented the story itself, altered what the place means. The meaning shifts, catches in the wind, lifts and transforms until there will be nothing left of even her heart. This is not sad, but rather the wind waking the imagination and simultaneously, paradoxically, waking us to emptiness, to the limits of story. To mystery. This is the wind making the place where story meets void, the opposite of meaning. The hollow bowl that also shapes our being.

Writing Strategies

1. Observing involves going beyond the casual glance to discover something new. What does Oomen discover, or learn, about her subject?

2. How does Oomen go beyond "simple description" and communicate a new way of seeing? Provide excerpts of description from the essay to develop your response.

3. Good description appeals to the senses. To which senses (hearing, sight, touch, smell, taste) does Oomen appeal? What appeal is especially evocative because of the detail Oomen provides?

4. Complete the following sentence: Oomen's main point is that ____________________.

5. Oomen uses several one-sentence paragraphs. How do these paragraphs function and why? (Are they main ideas, support strategies, miscellaneous information, headings, or what?)

Exploring Ideas

1. With a group of peers, discuss the feeling created by Oomen's essay. How was the essay more than informational or informative? What passages stirred your feelings and why?

2. How does Oomen resolve the "sad contradictions" she originally had about the legend of the Sleeping Bear?

3. When have you carefully observed or studied a subject as carefully as Oomen did the Sleeping Bear dune? Why did you observe it? What did you discover?

Ideas for Writing

1. In ¶20, Oomen describes "a place within a place." Observe a place so closely that you discover a new way of seeing it and can take the readers to "a place within a place."

2. As part of Oomen's observing state of mind, she even observes herself: "As I move over the drifts of glacial debris, walking absorbs my attention." As you observe a subject, also observe yourself observing it.

3. In ¶18 Oomen asks, "How long can one explore a void?" Find a void, or what you might at first imagine to be a void, and explore it. For example, you might explore an empty gym, a field, or an abandoned part of town.

If responding to one of these ideas, go to the Analysis section of this chapter to begin developing ideas for your essay.

The Front Porch

Chester McCovey

Chester McCovey's observing essay illustrates how one can use an observation as a point of contact and then, through analysis, explore why the observation matters. McCovey makes a simple observation: that people don't sit out on their front porches like they did when he was a kid. Then he explores and determines that the loss of the front porch equals a loss of community. Through analysis, he goes from a specific observation (about garages and porches) to a general insight (about a loss of community).

The essay begins with a personal observation and connects with the readers.

If you walk through my neighborhood, you won't see many porches, at least not the kind people sit on in the evenings. Those days are gone where I live, and likely where you live, too.

States the main observation: porch replaced by garage.

The front porch was a place where people used to talk (pass the time, shoot the breeze).

The writer uses personal details to develop the observation.

The front porch has been replaced—by the two-car garage. Both sets of my grandparents, who lived in the same small town, had big front porches, and summer visits often meant sitting on the porch, talking, and watching cars and people out walking. After a while someone might have suggested getting some ice cream. The adult conversation was often dull, sometimes painfully so for a child, but sometimes it was interesting. The everyday people a child sees in church or at the Little League field in a small town have a few years behind them, and what person who has lived a little doesn't have a story to tell—or a story to be told about them? Sometimes those stories would come out and bring to life a previously uninteresting Frank or Gretchen. Small towns are full of life's everyday dramas. A child hears and figures out many things on a place like a front porch on a thing like a warm summer night.

The essay moves toward analysis. Why did this happen, and what does it mean?

The shift from porch to garage tells us about the world in which we live, how it came to be and how it will continue to change.

My grandparents' garages were small, just enough for one car and a few tools—not much of a garage for today's homeowner. In those days the garage kept a car and a small lawnmower, some rakes, and so on. The garage today must keep much more. One can see, then, how the exchange occurred. Like an old-fashioned trade in baseball, gone is the home team's beloved front porch, replaced by a big, new garage. Of course the trade is much more interesting than that. And a look at how it occurred enlightens us a little about the world in which we live. More importantly, it tells us not so much

From Chester McCovey, "The Front Porch." Reprinted with permission of the author.

■ Writing Strategies ■ Exploring Ideas

about how life is now but about how it came to be. And, I would argue, it shows us the way in which things will continue to change.

Back then, our own garage held two cars, a riding lawnmower, a push mower, bicycles, and lots of tools. We had a front porch and sat on it, but mostly just when we had company. Our house, then, represents the transition between two generations: my grandparents' generation that traveled less, received only three television stations (*sans* remote control), and didn't have air conditioning and my own generation that is more likely to be on the go (driving from one place to another) or sitting inside, on the computer or watching TV.

The writer's own childhood house illustrates the transition from porch to garage.

The front porch fell victim to its two natural enemies: the internal-combustion engine (automobiles) and electricity (air conditioning, lights, and TV). Now, instead of gathering on our front porch as our grandparents did, we are either gone somewhere thanks to our transportation or we are at home but indoors.

Main Ideas: What happened to the front porch and why: automobile and electricity. What happened because of that: we are either gone or indoors.

how life must have splashed
out of the cup
on warm summer nights
before the cool air
of electricity
urged us all to relax
in the fluttering glow
of color tv

Because of automobiles and electricity, we spend more time driving alone or watching TV than we do talking with our friends and neighbors. Is this a problem? A loss of community?

We have traded sitting on the front porch for sitting in traffic, or to be more positive about it, for sitting in our automobile as we speed along to some very important place to be. The shift from porch to garage is beautifully simple. It goes like this: I need a place to park my transportation machine (car, truck, SUV) and I don't need a large, outdoor room for sitting. The reasoning (the reality of the situation) is just as simple: There's not as much action on the sidewalk as there once was (the neighbors are indoors or driving somewhere) and I don't need to sit outdoors to stay cool on muggy nights (the air conditioning indoors takes care of that). So, a need or desire—to stay cool, to be entertained, to keep up with what's going on—is replaced not by a different need or desire but instead by a new way of meeting it.

Explanation: how/why the shift occurred.

Need or Desire—To Stay Cool

Previously met by evening breeze; now

met by air conditioning
Need or Desire—To Be Entertained
Previously met by conversation with
neighbors; now met by TV, computer,
shopping at the mall, conversation with
friends who we drive to see
Need or Desire—To Keep Up with What's
Going On
Previously met by discussion with
neighbors and friends; now met through
national media (TV and Internet)

To avoid oversimplifying, the writer qualifies the point and concedes that there are still front porches, *but* that their days are numbered.

I am not saying there are no front porches. Obviously there are. And I am not saying everyone has a two-car garage instead. In my neighborhood, small garages not connected to the house still reign. But obviously, their days are numbered. The new houses sometimes look as much like a house attached to a garage as a garage attached to a house. Today's garage often dominates the house.

Anticipates a potential concern of readers: what about the back deck?

The back deck takes us out back, away from community.

Main point: We lose something very basic—very fundamental—when we lose the front porch culture. Leaves readers to consider the cost of this change.

Finally, the careful reader is insisting that I deal with the backyard patio deck. What about *it?* When we do sit outdoors, we choose to do it out back, away from the rest of the world. This is interesting. We need a break, I would suggest, from the hustle and bustle of daily life, so we retreat to our own backyard to be left alone with our families. But that hustle and bustle is mostly the hustle and bustle of traffic, radio, television, and a few quick transactions with total strangers. Of course another reason for opting to relax in the backyard is that, as previously mentioned, there just isn't that much going on out front these days. (If there were, I wonder if we would sit on the front porch and watch it . . . *and* contribute to it.) I am arguing that we lose something very basic—very fundamental—when we lose the front porch culture.

Sunday drives in the country bring to mind an earlier time, when people hung out on the front porch talking with neighbors.

On Sunday drives through the country, I see big new houses with big new porches. As Americans we can have it all—the house with the big front porch *and* the big garage. But I never (I am tempted to qualify this statement and say "almost never" or "rarely" but I have been thinking about it and I do mean "never")—I never see anyone out sitting on those porches. I am not prepared here to argue that we are a civilization in deep trouble because of this, though it does seem to me appropriate that we should lament, at least a little, the loss of the front porch.

Imagine: Being entertained by sitting on a porch and talking.

Ironically, McCovey is *driving around.*

Where do people talk like they used to on a front porch: At the kitchen table, the student lounge, Facebook, Twitter?

Writing Strategies

1. What is the essay's thesis?
2. What details help readers value the thesis and why?
3. In a paragraph, summarize McCovey's explanation of *how* the shift from porch to garage occurred and *why* it matters.
4. Why is it important that McCovey writes about the backyard patio deck? How does this paragraph help readers accept the main claim?
5. Where does McCovey use a metaphor or simile (comparing two unlike things: *The clerk was a bear* [metaphor]; *The clerk was like a bear* [simile])? Where else does he use figurative language?

Exploring Ideas

1. Based on this essay, what does McCovey value? To what degree do you value the same thing?
2. In your own words, summarize McCovey's main idea. Then share your summary with several classmates who have also read the essay. Discuss your understanding of McCovey's main idea, and then reread his essay and revise your summary as necessary.
3. To further explore this issue, share your summary with people of various age groups, asking them to respond to McCovey's ideas. Describe how their views are similar to or different from McCovey's.
4. Think of a metaphor or simile of your own that might work well in this essay.

Ideas for Writing

1. Besides the move from porch to garage, what other change has taken place? How has that change impacted everyday life?
2. Observe some difference in a way of living, whether it be the result of time (your grandparents and you, for example) or location (Southern Californians and Midwesterners). Do not be afraid to generalize, as long as you do it thoughtfully and are mindful of exceptions.

If responding to one of these ideas, go to the Analysis section of this chapter to begin developing ideas for your essay.

Student Essay

Corpse Colloquy

Justin Scott

Justin Scott, a biology major at Western Michigan University, uses the Invention Questions in this chapter to look beneath the surface and find new meaning in a familiar place, the graveyard. "Corpse Colloquy" is an example of how an observation essay goes beyond mere description. Through careful observation and analysis, Scott helps readers see cemeteries differently, as "the key to a more exposed and fulfilling life."

The cemetery nestles within the confines of the city. "Oakwood," the sign announces. One can hardly help but wonder if the name is meant to reference the now-sparse trees, or if perhaps it refers to the dense forest of tombstones laden with a 6-foot-shallow bone root system. One must battle traffic and stoplights to gain entrance rather than multi-headed dogs and demanding ferry captains. The other thing that separates this still world of the dead from the busy world of the living is the winter skeleton of a hedge.

One thing is immediately obvious in this cemetery: Those laden with the gifts of life often choose to utilize them in death, and those less fortunate make do with what they must. Class warfare spills into the afterworld: Business owner is segregated from bricklayer, clergy is separated from atheist. There are large domineering crypts bearing the surnames of the wealthy dead inside, branch-scraping obelisks with ornate script, tombs carefully sculpted to resemble tree stumps, small temples dedicated to their dead in ancient Greek style, and, inevitably, the sunken, flat, and nondescript markers of the poor or humble. Some of the dead have even had exclusive gated communities constructed; large, elegant gravestones are surrounded with walls of iron or marble to keep the pauper corpses at a proper distance. The military and various secret societies have also their own niches; war memories, ranks carved into stones, and Mason symbols can be found throughout the cemetery, often placed more prominently than the name of the dead or when they were alive. Did people value their association with a group more than their own identity?

Toward the center of the field is an open plot with a marker denoting a common grave. Here lie the forgotten. Time will not remember their names any more readily than they were remembered while alive, for here are the mentally ill, the locked away and the vagrants. One large marker bids us to forget identity entirely.

Religion separates the dead as surely as the living. While in the living world the borders are less physically concrete, here signs announce the religious preference of those buried underneath. A walking tour reveals that here lie the Catholics, there the Jews, and over yonder are sundry reformists. Crosses, six-pointed stars and IHS[1] are distributed freely.

Neatly shorn trees line the carefully built roads. Were they interred there to keep the bony remains underneath from warring over wealth and religion as they would in life? Were

---

1. An abbreviation for the name of Jesus in Greek letters.

it not for the snow, one would surely find grass cared for with the precision of a golf course and symmetrically trimmed bushes. The roads inside are paved but do not bear names; only the dead have that privilege here.

Modern society has a calculated and placated feel to it. Most things are carefully contrived in order to generate the most profit, and we are medicated to be placid and unfeeling; in the end, we are dedicated consumers in all things. Our deaths are as sterile and distant from us as the cemeteries in which our remains rest forever; manicured nails and lawns make way for manicured plots of land and stones and preservation via formaldehyde. We supposedly live in *post-ironic* times. "Irony is dead," some would say. But irony is alive and well and can unmistakably be found among the dead in cemeteries worldwide.

It is said that only two things are certain in life: death and taxes. The cemetery, despite pomp, segregation, and sundry other shows for the living, does not belie that old aphorism. Everyone resting in that place, under or above earth, Catholic, Protestant, or Jew, poor or rich, remembered or forgotten, has succumbed to the scythe. Everyone dies. Yet in the frenzied pace of modern life this truth is lost, and we as ever fall into the patterns of exclusivity, neglect, bigotry, and *schadenfreude.*

More time should be spent learning the dead. Their testament is spoken to us from within the maelstrom of coffins and gravestones. Their ghosts bade us not to be concerned with materialism, creed, or race; through them and the past they represent is the key to a more exposed and fulfilling life. *Graveyards are the doppelganger of the living world.* Seeing and recognizing the shadow-self of the graveyard allows us to enrich our lives and live beyond the lessons it presents. The cemetery, above all, tells us of acceptance and judgment: to embrace the former and neglect the latter. Life is finite, precious, and far too short to waste on arrogant trappings already so thoroughly explored by those entombed under earth.

Dona eis requiem sepiternam.

John Mauk

Writing Strategies

1. In Scott's essay, what does a cemetery reveal about life?
2. What details are most effective in helping readers understand and accept Scott's main point?
3. Describe Scott's writer's voice. Refer to three sentences to support your description.
4. What other paragraph in the essay could Scott have used as the opening paragraph? Why would or wouldn't that paragraph be an effective new beginning?
5. How is Scott's essay a call to action?

Exploring Ideas

1. What does Scott value? How might his essay connect with readers because they value the same thing?
2. How is the way you see a cemetery different from the way Scott sees one? Go beyond the casual glance. What else might a cemetery symbolize or reveal?
3. Talk to several people to find out their views on cemeteries. Do they visit cemeteries often? What word would they use to describe a cemetery: *peaceful, spiritual, creepy?* Why do people view cemeteries differently?
4. Research the modern cemetery. When did cemeteries become parklike, and why?

Ideas for Writing

1. Spend several hours observing a cemetery. How can your observations help readers see something about cemeteries and life differently?
2. Observe your college's campus or a particular building. Take notes and make connections among details. What new idea can you share about college, your college campus, education, life?

If responding to one of these ideas, go to the Analysis section of this chapter to begin developing ideas for your essay.

Red Raiders Fans

Taylor Perry

"Red Raiders Fans" is an ethnography essay—a type of observing essay that focuses on a particular culture. Taylor Perry observed high school football fans over the course of three weeks, writing down observations then analyzing those observations for insight—for what it is to be an Oakville Red Raiders high school football fan. Perry acknowledged that he had preconceived ideas about the topic before and during his observation. But by remaining open to the situation and successfully putting aside those ideas, he discovers something new.

A high school football game strikes me as a rite of passage, a sort of initiation experience that one might read about in *National Geographic* or see on the History Channel. While we imagine primitive cultures dancing around fires, the elders presiding as the young boys perform acts of courage, perhaps walking across fire or ritualistically yet still realistically fighting each other, we might think how primitive they are, and how primitive we aren't. We can easily see the primitivity in their rituals, and I anticipated discovering something I already knew: that high school football is just another one of these primitive rites of passage, initiation rituals. The adults gather to watch the boys ritualistically, yet realistically too, battle each other on behalf of their communities. By doing this, they become men. A band performs. The elders who oversee all this participated in it themselves years ago. When it's over, someone wins and someone loses. There's a hero . . . and a goat. They've all proven themselves by participating. Some have achieved great status. The communities live in peace. Oakville and Harborview (both names have been changed for this essay) don't go to war. One has bragging rights, and the other has next year.

However, what I ended up observing and concluding was the way two groups of fans (a few loud ones and everyone else) interacted. Some verbal exchanges at the beginning of the third game were typical of the way the fans communicated. It was cold and windy. Fans were arriving an hour early. Forty-five minutes before the game I chose a seat across the aisle from the middle section. Red Raiders fans wore hats, gloves, heavy coats, and brought blankets. Some had hand warmers stashed inside their gloves and probably had foot and body warmers too, but if so, these were hidden from view. Red Raiders fans could be divided into three clothing groups. The largest group wore their team's color, and the same was true for each of the opposing teams' fans: team colors. Another group wore heavy hunting or work clothes, either camouflage or Carhartt brown. A third group wore other cold weather gear, in brands like North Face, Patagonia, or Columbia.

Dressed this way, fans chose their seats, some with hot dogs, pizza, soft pretzels, coffee and hot chocolate. They greeted each other before the game: "Hey, baby, where's your husband? I'll help you keep warm," a guy behind me, the back row I think, yelled to a woman heading toward her seat. Based on her response ("Now you *know* I'd rather freeze, Jerry! Michelle gonna come by after work?"), she didn't seem to take offense. Another guy from the back row yelled at someone else, "You need another blanket," not quite a question and not quite an explanation. And that fellow responded, "No, I got enough." Caught up in these greetings, I heard a woman behind me, referring to what she's wearing, say, "How stupid do I look?" I couldn't help turning around and saying, "I have to look, since you asked. You look great!" Exchanges like these seem to take the place of "Hello. How are you? Nice to see you. I am fine."

In addition to these greetings, people talked about what they did earlier in the day, what their children are up to, and I hear two men behind me reminiscing about previous football seasons. One man said, "I took a team down there twenty years ago. We played X, Y, Z (he mentioned particular schools I wasn't able to write down)." And then the discussion branched off from there and they talked about the teams, their playing styles (one man mentioned a particularly good team's Achilles heel, its lack of discipline), and some star players. A man with a blanket spoke to two women (a mother and daughter it turns out) a few rows in front of me:

> "Hello, Stranger. Are you on break?"
>
> The girl replied, "No. I graduated. I live at home now."
>
> "I thought you were trying to get rid of her," he said to the mother.
>
> The girl replied, "I keep coming back." And the man moved on to find a seat for the game.

This verbal behavior turned out to be interesting, though not earth-shatteringly insightful. I've been to many high school games before and this is just typical of what gets said. It was interesting to me, it turns out, because I was observing it. The act of observation made the verbal exchanges interesting. I really noticed how Red Raiders fans consistently said something besides "Hello" to say hello. Their exchanges were usually humorous. They were quick and friendly. They conveyed an acknowledgment of some aspect of the other person's life (college, spouse) and of the present situation (cold).

During Game 3, which ended in a loss for the Red Raiders, I was able to observe some contrasting cheering styles. When the announcer made the traditional pre-game announcement about fans practicing good sportsmanship, for example not harassing the referees, one of these fans yelled, "We'll be good if the officials are good," which got some laughs from the rest of the section. This fan turned out to be one of four real yellers in the top row of the section to my right (closer to the fifty yard line). It turns out these four fans—and just these four fans—were very dissatisfied throughout the game with the officiating. One woman led the crowd in front of her in a "Get that ball back, get that ball back" cheer. No one in my section cheered along. After one tackle, she and the man next to her (both dressed in Red Raiders' gear) shouted, "Horse collar! Horse collar! Don't let them horse collar tackle!" No one else around us objected to the tackle or called it an illegal horse collar tackle, though.

At one point, one of the four hollered, "Hey, wake up over there!" I heard her yell it, but didn't know what she meant until the woman sitting next to me said she was talking to our section which was more quietly watching the game, cheering for big plays, but not yelling loudly throughout the game. The Red Raiders fans in my section were at that point listening to, glancing at, talking about, and mostly trying to ignore the four loud yellers behind us and to our right, and so were the fans in front of them in the middle section, I'm pretty sure. "Hey, ref! Watch the game. You're missing a good one!" the man yelled. "Just like at Waysville Lake," one of the women yelled. "Get in the game! They can't do it on their own!" the other women yelled.

Were these yellers ruining my observation, or were they my observation? At halftime, a high school girl stood next to me in the aisle, "Mom, mom, Amy!" When she said her mom's name, she got her attention. "Want some hot chocolate?" Her mother said she did. I imagined making a joke when the girl brought her mother some hot chocolate, joking that she'd brought it for me and then passing it down to her mother. The girl never came back though. In the second half, one of the yellers yelled, "Hey, Amy! We need you over there." Amy smiled and acknowledged the yeller's comment, but she like the rest of us was watching the game more quietly, cheering for big plays and talking (what I would consider to be) more reasonably about the game.

I observed that at a high school football game, and at a Red Raiders' game in particular, most fans were pretty quiet. They cheered for their team but not maniacally. They didn't yell at the players or at the referees. They talked amongst themselves and only got loud for a touchdown, an interception, or a big hit. What surprised me, or what I observed (not sure how surprising it really was), was that most people put up with a few yellers. At one point a man in the middle section had words with the yelling man (I couldn't hear the exact exchange). Then one of the yelling women yelled, "You shut up! And you shut up!" to each of the men. No one else spoke up to try to silence the yellers and the two men went back to watching the game, one quietly and one loudly.

This behavior is probably not unique to Red Raiders fans; however, I think in some other communities (some other cultures) fans might have objected verbally to the yellers. Of course in those communities, there might just have been even more yellers. My hypothesis going into these observations was something about high school football being a rite of passage activity. I observed the dress, the food, the verbal exchanges, the seating, and I ultimately had imposed upon me an observation about several hundred people's response to four people's over-the-top yelling.

Writing Strategies

1. What is Perry's thesis? Write down one sentence, either from the essay or of your own, that expresses the essay's main insight.
2. Perry's ethnography essay could be organized differently. What paragraphs could appear elsewhere in the essay? What headings might Perry use to organize the essay? How might these changes impact the reading experience?
3. What information would you delete to preserve Perry's main idea while making the essay more concise?

4. What word would you use to describe Perry's writer's voice? Provide two passages and explain why they support your description.

5. Perry's essay includes specific observations from the Red Raiders game and knowledge from previous experiences. Identify a passage where a specific observation depends on Perry's preexisting cultural knowledge.

Exploring Ideas

1. With a group of peers, discuss the following: Are fans of a particular high school sports team a culture? If so why, and why is that culture worth observing and writing about? What about fans of a college or professional team? Are they a unique culture? Why might they be worth observing?

2. Perry says the pregame verbal practices of the Red Raiders fans were interesting "it turns out, because [he] was observing them." With a group of peers, make sense of Perry's statement. Discuss it and try to discover examples in which group members found a familiar topic more interesting because they were more deliberately observing it.

Ideas for Writing

1. What non–sporting group of spectators constitutes a culture worth observing?

2. In addition to fans or spectators, what are some groups that constitute a culture?

Invention

Observation requires a good deal of analysis and planning. It goes far beyond simply choosing a subject and writing down details. Writers usually go through a cyclical invention process, in which they return repeatedly to their original notes to find patterns and significant points. The following sections are designed to help you through this process: specifically, to discover a topic (in Point of Contact), develop particular points about the topic (in Analysis), make it relevant to a community of readers (in Public Resonance), focus your ideas (in Thesis), and develop them into an essay (in Rhetorical Tools). The Invention Questions in each section are not meant to be answered directly in your final written assignment. They are designed to help generate ideas—to guide you through an intellectual process.

Point of Contact

The goal here is to see something in a new way, to see beyond the casual glance. You may choose to visit places and do things you have never done before, or you may visit the usual places but with focused attention. Use the following questions and images (Figure 4.1) as possible starting points for your observation.

Observing People

Supervisor, manager, line worker, server, religious leader, teacher or professor, principal, athlete, bingo player, student. Use notes, audio and video recorders, and/or photographs to gather details about the person. You might also interview the subject. (See the section on interviews in Chapter 14.)

- In what hidden ways is the subject working with or against the surroundings?
- Does the subject reinforce or work against rules?
- How do others treat the subject (with respect, disdain, indifference, or something else)?
- If the subject is a group, how do the individuals maintain harmony or unity? How do they conflict?
- What explicit or hidden rules do they follow?

Figure 4.1

Observing a Place

Job site, family restaurant, factory, office, break room, playground, park, movie theater, shopping mall, video arcade, college hall, college club, campground, woods. Gather details about the place. In addition to obvious details, consider the less obvious:

- What subtle behavior patterns do you detect?
- Is there a hidden competition or collaboration going on?
- What mood might the creatures (people, animals, plants) share? How do they unknowingly maintain that mood?
- Are people free to do as they please, or does something restrain them? (Do they know that something is restraining them?)
- What is the unstated, normal mode of behavior?
- Does anyone or anything break out of the norm? What are the hidden consequences?
- What is missing?

Observing an Animal

Family pet, friend's or neighborhood pet, stray cat or dog, birds, animals at a park or zoo, wild animals, farm animals. Gather basic information about the animal's behavior, but also look beyond the simple glance:

- What does it know?
- What secrets does it have?
- How does it signal its mood?
- Does it have dramatic mood changes?
- How does it get along with humans? With the world around it?
- What habits does it have?
- Is it a public or private creature?
- Does it compromise or alter its behavior to accommodate others?

Observing a Person or Event Involved in Your Major

Use the questions in this section to help gather information about a subject related to your major, but also develop more questions. By observing a particular person or event, what can you discover about the nature of your major?

Activity

Choose a category (a place, person, animal) and develop ten more questions that will reveal something interesting about a subject.

Observing a Culture: Writing an Ethnography Essay

One type of observing essay is an *ethnography* essay. *Ethnography*, from *ethno* (nation, culture, people) and *graphos* (something written down), observes the characteristics of a group of people. Although some ethnographies involve months or years of living within and observing a particular culture, we can also write an ethnography essay—a sort of mini-ethnography—based on a few weeks or days of careful observation. Because an ethnography is a type of observing essay, the Invention sections in this chapter (Analysis, Public Resonance, Thesis, and so on) will help you first invent ideas and then convey them as an essay. One essay in this chapter, "Red Raiders Fans," is an example of an ethnography essay. Also, see Sharon Angel's essay, "Graveyard Shifts" (page 534), which focuses on the characteristics and interactions of third-shift workers.

Point of Contact: After reading "Red Raiders Fans," make a list of cultures you can observe—groups of people who meet at a place and time where you can observe them at least three times for more than an hour each time. It's important to be sure the group of people share an identity, instead of just happening to show up at the same place at the same time. A shared identity is based on certain common characteristics such as language, food, religion, fashion, dress, habits, values, beliefs, music, and so on. The purpose of your observation is to observe the practices of a culture (what members routinely say and do) and discover how the particular culture *does* (the practice of) their culture. For example, "Red Raiders Fans" explains how Red Raiders fans *do* (the practice of) Red Raiders fans. An ethnography essay on cowboys in Wyoming would explain how cowboys in Wyoming *do* (the practice of) cowboys in Wyoming.

Analysis and Public Resonance: Once you decide on a culture to observe, you can use the Analysis and Public Resonance sections to record your observations and discover insights. Keep in mind that it's difficult to have insights if you allow memories and expectations to get in the way of recording what you are experiencing with your senses. Although you will have preconceived ideas as you begin your observation, the key is to acknowledge this and continue to record your observations, letting the practices of the culture you observed influence your thinking. An ethnographer observes and records the following—

- the location, including specific descriptions of the physical environment
- verbal exchanges, including what group members routinely say and more specific exchanges among members
- how the group uses writing if they do
- routines, including what group members do routinely; what they do every day as part of their normal experience
- rituals, including activities that are viewed as highly important or sacred
- rites of passage, including significant practices that change a member's sense of identity, social role, or status
- values and beliefs
- timelines, including what happens when

Don't let these categories or the questions in the Analysis and Public Resonance sections limit your observations. These are just examples of the kinds of observations you can make. Remember, *recording particulars* is an invention strategy. The particulars will help you think of more ideas. And these particulars are important later because you will select *some* of them to use in your ethnography essay.

Thesis: Because you want your insight to emerge from the observations themselves, not from what you think you might observe or conclude, it's important to wait until *after* you record your observations to make rhetorical decisions about how to convey your ethnography to your readers. The Thesis section will help you focus your essay on a particular insight. Your insight can be what it means to be a member of the group; what makes someone an insider or outsider; what unifying characteristic surprised you about the group; how your preconceived idea(s) about the group changed; and so on.

Delivery: After you record your observations and discover a focused and insightful thesis, turn to the Rhetorical Tools section for help delivering your ethnography to the readers. The following guidelines can help you make effective rhetorical decisions:

- An ethnography presents your observations while focusing on a particular discovery or insight about the culture.
- Your readers will expect you to explain why you chose the subject, what happened during your observations, and what you discovered.
- Your observation should identify the group and important background (orienting) information about your observations, where/when you observed them, and your relationship to the group; then your specific observations; and your conclusions.
- While you try to be an objective observer, you can acknowledge your role as an observer and the influence of your own biases on your observations. Your ethnography essay is about the culture you observed but need not ignore your role as observer.
- Document design features such as headings, font styles, and spacing can help readers understand and accept your thesis.
- If your professor allows it, photos or video clips can help convey your main idea.

Other parts of *The Composition of Everyday Life* will help you with your essay:

- Use the Revision questions later in the chapter to rethink a draft of your essay and make changes.
- Use Part II for help finding, analyzing, synthesizing, evaluating, integrating, and documenting information from sources.
- Use Part III for help organizing and delivering your idea.

Analysis

Details do not have their own meaning. It is up to people to *make* meaning from details. As we analyze, we move from observation notes to focused ideas, from a collection of potentially unrelated details to a set of particular points. Analysis prompts us to see patterns, connections, and paths within the particulars. The following questions can help you to make meaning out of your observation notes and look at the subject as something more than its physical characteristics.

- What is unique about the subject?
- What is ordinary about this subject? (How are its qualities common to other places, people, or animals?) What does that quality show?
- Is this subject symbolic of something? (Does it stand for some idea or ideal?)

- Does the subject seem different after the observation (more complicated, less intimidating, more human, less human, more predictable, and so on)?
- What does the subject "say" about life (about human interaction, social behavior, institutions, nature, and so on) in this place and time?

Although focusing on and gathering details may be a challenging aspect of observation, analyzing those details poses a difficulty of its own. Because a list of details offers so many options and no obvious path for making meaning, the process can be uncertain and confusing. However, it can be an intensive and valuable process. Imagine a student, Linda, who observed people at her place of work, a small factory. Her observation notes include long lists of details about the environment, the lighting, the physical actions of the workers, and their interaction with the machines and with each other. But as she begins to analyze, using one of the Invention Questions, she finds connections in those details. Notice how she goes beyond her first simplistic answer to a more complex idea:

What does the subject "say" about life (about human interaction, social behavior, institutions, nature, and so on) in this place and time?

At first, I thought that my coworkers were just miserable people at a job. They work at their individual stations, occasionally interact to communicate something about a machine part or materials, and then go to breaks—or home. But outside of that, I couldn't see anything important. But the more I looked over my notes, I realized something was going on in those small and infrequent interactions between people. While they might seem miserable and disconnected at times (maybe even most of the time), they all offer some support to one another: a small glance, a shared roll of the eyes when the supervisor inspects one person's work; the way Rob, the oldest in the shop, actually runs over to someone who needs help with something, the extra cup of coffee Bob got Maria because she didn't have time during break. All these things mean something—the underground, almost secretive, strategies to keep each other afloat in their shared situation. After I realized this, I went back over all my notes and remembered things I had not written down. The days are actually filled with these little gestures; they happen at all times: at breaks, on the way into the shop in the morning, while the machines are operating.

Linda could then develop this point in her writing. The idea may even develop into a thesis statement. This would mean that many other details (about physical structure, about the machines themselves) might be abandoned unless they have some significance for worker interaction. In this way, Linda's observation goes from a list of seemingly unrelated details to a focused idea.

Activity

Observe the activities in your classroom. Consider actions and behaviors among work groups, among demographic groups, before the instructor arrives, or as the class ends. As a class or in a group, discuss the possible meaning or significance of particular events, behaviors, or interactions.

Chester McCovey's invention notes explore the meaning of the garage—not simply what it does for people (store their cars) but how it works in their lives, how it says something about the way people live.

Is this subject symbolic of something? (Does it stand for some idea or ideal?)

It is, perhaps. These big garages are obviously a necessity for today's homeowner. I mean, most of these homes are not within walking distance of where the owner works. Many, I suspect, can only be afforded if both husband and wife work—two cars! Now, fill the garage up with all the other machinery you need to maintain the yard. The garage quite simply says "go," "drive," "automobile," "transportation." I am at home, but not for long. No doubt the cars have air conditioning, as does the house. One need never be hot (or cold). The garage has replaced the porch. You pull into the garage and go inside and stay inside the house. Then get in the air-conditioned space bubble car when you want to leave. Of course there is recreation, but recreation is getting away from life and not a part of it. Let's take a break in our day and burn some calories, not let's burn some calories in the natural course of our day. The garage symbolizes driving, moving, loss of neighborhood, community, wealth, poverty . . .

Thinking Further

In the previous paragraph, McCovey uses invention writing to seek out the significance of today's big garage. His exploration leads him to write, "The garage symbolizes driving, moving, loss of neighborhood, community, wealth, poverty. . . ." Now McCovey, alone or with others, could explore this idea further, digging deeper and uncovering new details and complexity. (Or he might choose a different idea from his invention writing to explore further.)

Activity A

Use the following questions to explore McCovey's invention writing:

- Using McCovey's paragraph and your own ideas, explain how the big garage might be symbolic of or stand for driving. For moving. For loss of neighborhood. For wealth and poverty. Develop your responses in the spirit of exploration.
- Of the six ideas McCovey mentions, which one is the least obvious and why? Which one is the most important and why? Which one is the most interesting and why? (Consider focusing on the least obvious, most important, or most interesting.)

Remember, your purpose in this writing is not just to say what you think or know. Your purpose is to explore and figure out what can be thought about the topic.

Activity B

Consider your own invention writing, as you just considered McCovey's. For help, explore ideas further through discussion.

- What new way of thinking (what insight, what revelation) did you discover?
- How might you explore the complexities of that idea further? For example:

  —How might that thinking be wrong?

  —How can you probe more deeply by asking why, how, or so what?

  —What contradictions or inconsistencies must be explained?

Public Resonance

Writers do more than focus on a subject, such as a sand dune, porch, or cemetery. They make the subject resonate with the lives of others. The following Invention Questions will help broaden your subject's perspective and make it resonate with a potential audience.

- Why is this subject important to people? (Why is its uniqueness important?)
- Why should your peers know about this subject?
- What do people normally experience, understand, or assume about the subject?
- Does the presence or action of this subject teach people something—about themselves, about life, about work, about happiness, about materialism, about sincerity, about identity, about relationships, about the past, about the future, about death?

Notice how McCovey explores the breadth of his subject—how the question helps him to see the broad implications of porches and garages:

> **Does the presence or action of this subject teach people something—about themselves, about life, about work, about happiness, about materialism, about sincerity, about identity, about relationships, about the past, about the future, about death?**
>
> What we see is a loss of community. The big garage shows us we're leaving our own neighborhood a lot. The fact that the garage is connected to the living space shows us that we go from our living area directly, by pushing a button that opens the door, into the street and to another community far enough away that we drive to it. We don't interact with our neighbors (we might not even know their names). We drive past them with our windows rolled up. We maybe don't even smell or feel our neighborhood (I guess that's an exaggeration, but there's something there). Remember, we're not talking about all houses. We're talking about the ones built today. Is loss of neighborhood a loss to the people who live in those neighborhoods? Does big garage/no front porch mean loss of neighborliness? Yes, these relationships—or ones like them—can exist outside one's own neighborhood. But what is the effect of this? What is a neighbor anymore?

Here McCovey explores connections to broader cultural trends. While some subjects have more automatic public resonance, others need to be *made* relevant to the audience, and it is up to a writer to make the connection.

Invention Workshop

An essay does not just relay information; it invites readers to see something new in a familiar world. If you think a topic is boring, you have an opportunity to unpack the boredom, finding something new and worth sharing with others. Instead of allowing a dull topic to stop one's thinking, a good observer uses analysis to make the topic interesting.

1. Share your observation with others and discuss what the subject shows about the way people live, about the way people see the world around them. The goal is to develop new insights for your project.
2. After exploring the public resonance of your topic with others and writing down any new insights, return to the Analysis questions on page 117. Respond in writing to these questions again, now that you have focused on the public resonance of the subject. See what else you can find. As you write, think about how you can re-approach the questions from a new, more informed perspective. For example, how might you see something else unique about the subject now? Does the subject now seem unique in some less obvious way?
   - What new insights emerged from your second round with the Analysis questions?
   - What new questions emerged?

Thesis

The thesis, whether stated directly or implied, reveals a specific insight on a subject. The more narrow the insight, the more focused and intensive the writing will be. Although it is easy to offer a first-glance statement, try to narrow in on a particular quality. Notice how the following bulleted statements offer broad and predictable ideas. But the purple statements reveal something unique and specific:

- The people at the local tavern keep to themselves.

  In the dark, smoky quiet of Timothy's Pub, the regulars face straight ahead but share intimate crises in their quick coded exchanges.
- The neighborhood is a quiet place.

  The disappearing porches in the neighborhood signal a shift to a more disconnected, isolating, but technologically advanced time.
- The Fun Factory has a spirit of competition.

  Once the games begin at The Fun Factory, the players shift radically: from unfocused adolescent "dorks" to focused competitive intellectuals.

The more specific theses focus on more particular subjects: people vs. regulars; neighborhood vs. disappearing porches; Fun Factory vs. players. These specific sentences bring the reader up close. (We can even imagine a television camera literally zooming in to the more particular subjects.) Also, the purple sentences have stronger verbs: *keep* vs. *face/share; is* vs. *signal; has* vs. *shift.* The stronger verbs do more than create action; they enrich the content, making the nouns work harder. As a result, the sentences push readers through the sentence with more energy.

Revising Your Thesis

Before drafting your essay, develop a thesis to guide you. Then, in groups, discuss your working thesis statements. For each noun, suggest a more specific word. Suggest stronger verbs.

Evolution of a Thesis

Imagine a writer is observing students at a community college. She notices many things about the students: their clothes, their ages, and so on. But she decides to focus on a particular point: *The students at Beach Community College spend their time coming and going primarily alone.* Such a statement offers a particular idea about the college students. The essay then would focus on the solitary nature of the students. The point might grow and develop layers throughout the invention process:

Point of Contact:

- The majority of the students coming in and out of the buildings are alone; they do not talk together or in groups. If people are talking, they are talking on cell phones.

Analysis:

- Although I have always associated college with social life, the students at Beach Community College show that college is often a solitary experience.

Public Resonance:

- When most people talk about college, they inevitably bring up campus life: the parties, the Greek system, the study groups, etc. They think of all the movies and stories about those crazy college years, but the reality may be fundamentally different for many students.

Working Thesis:

- Despite the popular notions of social life on college campuses, the students at Beach Community College show that higher education can be a solitary experience.

Rhetorical Tools

An observing essay shares an insight about a particular subject. While writers discover and develop this insight through careful observation, they communicate it to the readers through a variety of rhetorical tools.

Using Details

The details of an essay are what paint the writer's point, giving the essay focus and value. When Anne-Marie Oomen details her walk to the Sleeping Bear dune, she says, "The hard walk up and down the crumbling slopes dampens my determination to find a place I have never been."

Oomen has never been to the Sleeping Bear dune, nor has she sorted out the contradictions of the Sleeping Bear legend. The details that follow contribute to both explorations:

- I stumble along the shoreline bluff, walking slowly through varied soil, sometimes soft sand, sometimes coarse gravel or crusty silt—all of it light. (¶9?)
- I stop disoriented, pull my hood back to let the wind cool my face, and then start again, but without a clear sense of direction. (¶11?)
- I choose the least steep slope on the backside, the slope protected from the lake winds, and scramble up, slipping with every step. (¶19)

Throughout her narrative, Oomen provides details of sight, sound, and touch that not only describe the scene but express the significance. To choose details for your writing, consider:

- ▶ What details will not only describe your observation but also help to focus readers on its significance?

Using Narrative

Some writers narrate an observation, explaining the events leading up to a particular moment of discovery. When narrating, writers avoid unnecessary events and details, limiting the narration to key events and details that help convey the significance of the observation. Oomen's essay is a narrative beginning with her decision to visit the Sleeping Bear Dunes National Lakeshore. She tells how she "drive[s] the park's forested scenic road," "squeeze[s] under the railings and step[s] off the lookout," "stumble[s] along the shoreline bluff," and "crest[s] the rim—gasping for breath, and look[ing] down into what is the bowl of the bear." While narration is a savvy rhetorical move for Oomen's observation (she narrates her physical trek as well as her intellectual one), narrating an observation is not necessary: neither McCovey nor Scott relies on narration to communicate his insights. If you are considering using narration in your writing, ask yourself the following questions:

- ▶ Would narrating the events leading up to the observation help engage readers?
- ▶ Would narrating part of the observation help to engage readers?

Using Allusions

Allusions are references to bits of public knowledge, things, events, or people outside of the main subject being observed. Writers use allusions to help illustrate a point or create a feeling. For instance, McCovey alludes to baseball when discussing the front porch:

> One can see, then, how the exchange occurred. Like an old-fashioned trade in baseball, gone is the home team's beloved front porch, replaced by a big, new garage.

McCovey's allusion calls readers back to an earlier time when people sat outside on front porches and talked to neighbors passing by. The allusion to baseball helps to create the feeling of which McCovey speaks in his conclusion: "I am not prepared here to argue that we are a civilization in deep trouble because of this, though it does seem to me appropriate that we should lament, at least a little, the loss of the front porch." Some (not all) readers will immediately identify with the feeling the allusion conjures, of a time in baseball before free agency when many players began and ended their careers with the same team, when fans became more attached to their hometown players and were more likely to lament their departure, when life was simpler, the pace was slower, and baseball was the national pastime.

McCovey's allusion to the old-fashioned trade in baseball illustrates both the value of and the concern with using allusions. Some readers won't pick up on the baseball allusion. McCovey decides to use it anyway, understanding this. The allusion adds texture and depth of meaning for some readers, but McCovey does not allow the overall meaning of his essay to be lost on a reader who doesn't understand the allusion. (A reader would not say: I didn't understand his main idea because I don't know what an old-fashioned trade in baseball is.) The following questions will help you develop allusions for your own writing:

- Does my subject relate to any political event or situation?
- Does my subject relate to any social or cultural event or situation?
- Does my subject relate to any person or event in history? In literature? In popular culture (movies, television, music)?

Using Figurative Language

Figurative language makes an imaginative connection between ideas, creating pictures for readers and making points more intense. For example, Oomen uses figurative language to help the reader imagine the bowl of the Sleeping Bear dune: "Wind mutes and huffs through this place, and over the years, it has not only hollowed the bowl but shaped a broad opening at the west side of the blowout—as though the sand that once made the mound was poured out of a wide spigot." To help readers experience the dune, Oomen creates a visual image. By describing the shape of the dune as "sand pouring out of wide spigot," she even creates a sort of motion picture, an image of the sand moving.

Although figurative language can be bold and dramatic, it is frequently quiet, quick, and effective—creating a clarifying image in few words. In the following examples, Oomen uses a type of figurative language called *simile,* which compares two things using *like* or *as*:

- After years of enduring the relentless wind, the vegetation blows away, and the dune begins to hollow itself out, like a bowl, weathered down from the high point, leaving the lower, less exposed side to rise like a rim.
- The remnants of this spirit forest are scattered like ribs and femurs and spine.

For your own writing, remember that figurative language should be used to help readers understand main insights. Apply the following questions:

- A thing? A place? A person?
- What purpose would this comparison serve?

Activity

As writers develop, they learn to insert intellectual space between the writing instructions and their essay. Where the inexperienced writer might read the instructions and then write an essay, the more experienced writer inserts space by first using writing to plan, to ask questions, to invent, and to reflect. Before you draft your essay for this chapter, write down a working thesis and several supporting ideas. For example, how might you use narration, allusions, dialogue, or some other strategy to help readers understand and accept your thesis? Then share your sketch with others to get feedback before you draft an entire essay.

Revision

Writers create essays through invention, drafting, and revision. A draft is very much a work in progress, and it must be viewed that way. Writers don't just buff a draft—correcting spelling, punctuation, grammar—instead, they ask hard questions about their basic approach: Does my thesis and essay *really* express a focused insight about the subject? Drafts often express a variety of general ideas, so revision can involve making brutal, sometimes painful cuts to focus entirely on the single most important, most valuable insight. Another tough question is whether the thesis and essay are *really* revelatory. Many drafts have not yet revealed something unique and particular enough to make the essay stand out, so revision involves examining the supporting points, returning to the Analysis and Public Resonance questions, and exploring *one* less-obvious, potentially interesting point more deeply. Before exchanging drafts with a peer, ask yourself hard questions about your essay's focus and insight.

Peer Review

Exchange drafts with at least one other writer. Before passing your draft to others, underline the thesis, or write it above your essay. This way, reviewers will get traction as they read. As a reviewer, use the following questions to guide your response:

1. Point out any words or phrases in the thesis that could be more specific. (See the Thesis section, page 121 for more guidance.)
2. Where can the writer do more analysis and reveal more about the subject in the observation? (Point to passages that seem most obvious to you. As you read, look for claims that anyone could immediately offer without intensive analysis. Beside these passages, write "more analysis?" If you can suggest an interesting idea, explain it on the back of the writer's draft.)
3. Help the writer to illustrate his or her claims with details. As you read, look for broad characterizations—those that anyone could imagine without a close observation. Ask yourself: Could this be more specific? Can we *really* see the particular nuances of the subject? In the margin, write "more details" where the writer could more intensely show the points.

4. Offer some figurative language to help characterize the subject. After you have read the entire draft, offer your own metaphor or simile about the subject. Give your suggestion on the back of the draft. Make sure it is something that fits the writer's voice, something that he or she could use.
5. If the writer uses narrative, does it help support the main idea of the observation? How? (If you have difficulty explaining how it supports the main point, perhaps the writer should rethink its use in the essay!)
6. Are the paragraphs coherent? Do you ever get the sense that a paragraph is wandering—giving you details that seem unrelated to one another or unrelated to the point of the essay? If so, write in the margin "check paragraph coherence."
7. The most focused statement possible often makes for a better introduction. Suggest a surprisingly focused opening statement. (The writer might decide to use it.)
8. Consider the writer's voice.
   - If the writer is present (using "I"), is this necessary? Explain how the presence of the writer helps make the point of the observation.
   - If the writer is invisible (no "I"), how is that beneficial?
   - Where could the writer be more informal (breaking some conventions) or more formal?
9. Help the writer avoid common grammatical errors: comma splices, sentence fragments, or pronoun/antecedent agreement.
10. Write down the specific subject of the observation: a sand dune, porches, cemeteries, for example. Then complete the following statement: Ultimately, this essay is not about [the specific subject: a sand dune, for example]. It is about ______________________ ________________.

Reflection

As a developing writer and thinker, you should be able to not just write an essay but also articulate ideas about your essay's rhetoric—the way it uses language to communicate an idea and persuade others to think differently. Now that you have written an observing essay, step back and answer the following questions:

> What does your observation say about life in this place and time?
>
> What do people normally experience, understand, or assume about the subject, and how does your essay present a new way of thinking about it?

List three rhetorical tools you used in the essay, and explain specifically how each one helps readers understand and accept the thesis.

Identify several sentences that are especially lively and well written. What is it about the nouns, verbs, sentence length, word order, and other sentence particulars that make the sentences lively and well written?

As you respond, remember to practice the habits of good writing. Invent, draft, and revise your responses. Write carefully edited complete sentences, not fragments.

Beyond the Essay: Cover Image

1. Images are often used to represent a movie (think movie poster), novel, album/CD, video game, and so on. How might you use an image to express the main idea of an essay? This assignment asks you to create a *collage* as a cover or title image for your observing essay that expresses the essay's main idea.

   A collage is a single image made up of various images, sometimes from various media. For example, a collage expressing the main idea of an observing essay could include photos, newspaper headlines, objects from nature (a leaf, a seed), trash (a candy wrapper or other packaging), and so on. It could be entirely electronic—an *e-collage.*

   As with an essay, creating a collage involves selecting and combining smaller parts (or ideas) to create a larger, overall message (or idea). The particular pieces to include in the collage will be an early decision, and then you will decide how to arrange the parts into the larger image.
2. Once you have created a collage expressing the main idea of your observing essay, explain the visual rhetoric of your collage. How do the particular visual elements work together to convey one main idea? What is the relationship, physically (on the page or screen) and conceptually (in the reader's mind), among the elements? How do colors, shapes, textures, and the physical juxtaposition of images work together to create the overall message?

5 Analyzing Concepts

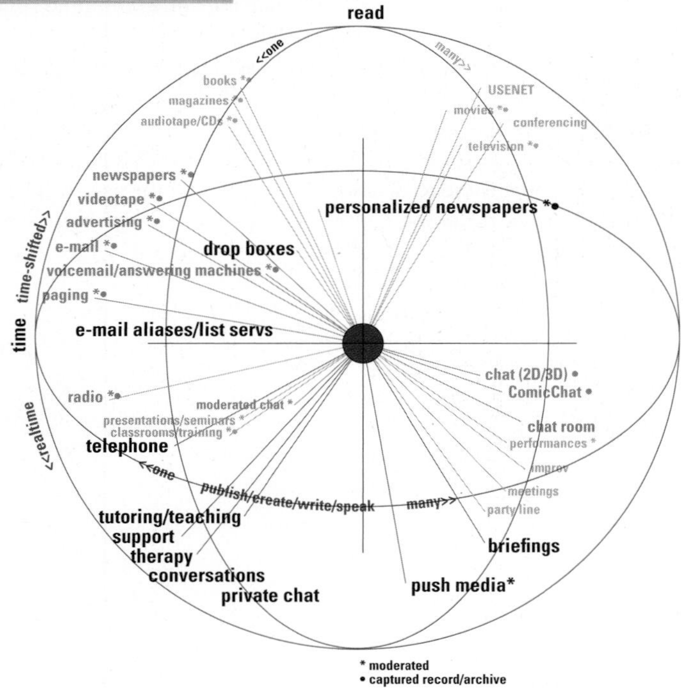

Figure 5.1 Conceptual map of relationships in cyberspace. From Nathan Shedroff, http://www.cybergeography.org/altas/conceptual. html

"Concepts have no 'real' definitions; instead, they have uses. They are our ways of coming to understand the world and deciding how to behave within it."

—Susan R. Horton

Concepts are ideas or abstract formulations. They are generalized notions beyond specifics. For example, we have concepts of *college, marriage, friendship,* or *technology* that go beyond any particular college, spouse, friend, or piece of equipment. And when our colleges, spouses, friends, and machines do not measure up to our concepts, we get frustrated, and we may even alter our concepts.

Within a particular culture, concepts change, sometimes drastically. Consider how the concept of *president* has changed for many people. Before the Watergate scandal (involving President Nixon), the Iran Contra scandal (involving President Reagan), the Monica Lewinsky scandal (involving President Clinton), or the invasion of Iraq (involving President Bush), most Americans' concept of *president* probably did not include scandal. But in the wake of such events, the concept has changed. Or consider how the idea of America changed after September 11, 2001. Before that date, most Americans probably did not consider how their country related to the concerns of people in the Middle East; however, after the terrorist attacks, *Americans'* concept shifted to accommodate our role in global politics.

Of course, people do not always agree on concepts. A dispute over a concept is often the catalyst for major conflict between people, cultures, and countries. Think about the intense and extended battles brought on by differing notions of *God* or the political struggles brought on by differing concepts of *woman, man, family, life, torture, or freedom.* Analyzing concepts turns out to be a rather important and sticky business.

In academia, students and professors are mired in the process of analyzing, discussing, and arguing about concepts. Consider, for example, *sex:*

- In a biology course, students discuss sex as reproduction. The concept in biology involves the study of hormones and reproductive systems (egg, sperm, gestation periods, embryo, and so on).
- In psychology, sex might be understood as a complex of drives. Students explore it using Freud's understanding of sexual development, repression, and parental affiliation.
- In sociology, students might approach sex as socially patterned behavior. A sociological understanding of sex may involve the study of social customs (such as dancing, choosing clothing, dating, and marriage).

These concepts are obviously different; in fact, many people claim that a discipline's take on a concept partly defines that discipline. (In other words, part of what defines a sociologist is how he or she understands *sex* or *community* or *family*.) Disciplines also focus on and develop their own concepts. *Ego,* for instance, is a concept developed by psychology. And much of your college career will involve exploring and analyzing the main concepts of different disciplines and your chosen field.

This chapter will help you analyze a particular concept, develop a focused explanation, and communicate your ideas in writing. The following essays will provide insight into various analytical strategies. For example, each essay looks closely at the parts or elements of a concept. This close examination of the particulars leads to a focused and insightful point about the concept. As you read, try to identify the parts or elements being broken down, and trace what the examination of them reveals. After reading the essays, you can find a concept in one of two ways:

1. Go to the Point of Contact section to find a topic from everyday life, or
2. Choose one of the Ideas for Writing that follow the essays.

After finding a subject, go to the Analysis section to begin developing the analysis.

Readings

World Gone Mad

Derrick Jensen

Derrick Jensen is a writer and an activist. He holds degrees in mineral engineering physics and creative writing. He has published fifteen books including *End Game, The Land of Make Believe,* and *Resistance Against Empire.* His work consistently questions the collective actions of mainstream American culture. In this essay, published in the September/October 2010 issue of *Orion* magazine, Jensen analyzes the concept of sociopathic behavior—and shows how the concept applies to our way of life.

I don't know about you, but whenever I attend some "green" conference, I know I'm supposed to leave feeling inspired and energized, but instead I feel heartbroken, discouraged, defeated, and lied to. It's not the inevitable talk about farmers (re)discovering organic farming; about plastic forks made from cornstarch; about solar photovoltaics; about relocalizing; about the joys of simple living; about grieving the murder of the planet; about "changing our stories"; and most especially about maintaining a positive attitude that gets me down. It's that no one, and I mean no one, ever mentions psychopathology.

Why is this important? Because those in power destroy sustainable communities—and not just sustainable indigenous communities. If people develop new ways to live on their land more sustainably, and those in power decide that land is needed for roads and shopping malls and parking lots, those in power will seize that land. This is how the dominant culture works. Everything and everyone must be sacrificed to economic production, to economic growth, to the continuation of this culture.

A few months ago I was watching a documentary on David Parker Ray, a serial killer from Truth or Consequences, New Mexico, who is suspected of killing up to sixty women. He kidnapped women and held them as rape slaves. He turned an entire tractor-trailer into a well-stocked torture chamber, where he videotaped what he did to them. In the documentary, an FBI profiler compared Ray's attitudes toward his victims to those most people have toward tissues: Once you use them, are you concerned about what happens to them? Of course not, she said. And that was how Ray perceived—or rather didn't perceive—his victims: simply as something to use and throw away.

When the profiler said this, my first thought was *passenger pigeons.* Then *chinook salmon.* Then *oceans.* How deeply do most members of this culture mourn passenger pigeons? Salmon? Oceans? This culture as a whole, and most of its members, gives no more consideration to the victims of this way of life than David Parker Ray gave to his victims. Blindness to suffering is one of this culture's central defining characteristics. And it is a central defining characteristic of sociopathology.

The New Columbia Encyclopedia states that a sociopath can be defined as one who willfully does harm without remorse: "Such individuals are impulsive, insensitive to others' needs, and unable to anticipate the consequences of their behavior, to follow long-term goals, or to tolerate frustration. The psychopathic individual is characterized by absence of the guilt feelings and anxiety that normally accompany an antisocial act."

Um, how sensitive are members of this culture, on the whole, to the needs of native forests (98 percent gone), native grasslands (99 percent gone), ocean life (90 percent of the large fish gone)? How sensitive is this culture to indigenous land claims? How clearly are members of this culture able to anticipate the consequences of destroying forests, grasslands, oceans, or denying indigenous land claims? With sea level already rising and glaciers already disappearing, how capable are this culture's decision makers of anticipating the consequences of global warming?

Dr. Robert Hare, an expert on sociopaths, states that "among the most devastating features of psychopathy are a callous disregard for the rights of others and a propensity for predatory and violent behaviors. Without remorse, psychopaths charm and exploit others for their own gain. They lack empathy and a sense of responsibility, and they manipulate, lie and con others with no regard for anyone's feelings." I'm reminded of something Red Cloud said: "They made us many promises, more than I can remember. They only kept but one. They promised they would take our land, and they took it."

Hare also says, "Too many people hold the idea that psychopaths are essentially killers or convicts. The general public hasn't been educated to see beyond the social stereotypes to understand that psychopaths can be *entrepreneurs,* politicians, CEOs and other successful individuals who may never see the inside of a prison." They can be the president, a boss, a neighbor.

Let's now consider the dominant culture in relation to the characteristics of sociopaths as listed in section F60.2 of *The ICD-10 Classification of Mental and Behavioural Disorders,* published by the World Health Organization, Geneva, 1992:

a) *callous unconcern for the feelings of others.* Where to start? Have members of this culture shown any concern for the feelings of the indigenous as they've stolen their land? How about the feelings of nonhumans being driven from their homes, or those being driven out of existence? Further, doesn't the mainstream scientific community demand that emotion be removed from all scientific study? Aren't we also told that emotions must not interfere with business decisions and economic policy? Do chickens in battery cages have feelings? What about dogs in vivisection labs? What about trees? Rain? Stones? The culture goes beyond "callous unconcern" for the feelings of these others to deny that their feelings even exist.

b) *gross and persistent attitude of irresponsibility and disregard for social norms, rules and obligations.* Is there an action more irresponsible than killing the planet? Now consider the norms, rules, and obligations of this culture. Norms: rape, abuse, destruction. Rules: a legal system created by the powerful to maintain their power. Obligations: to get as much money and power as possible.

c) *incapacity to maintain enduring relationships, though having no difficulty in establishing them.* I live on Tolowa land. The Tolowa had enduring relationships with their human and nonhuman neighbors for at least 12,500 years. When the dominant culture arrived here about 180 years ago, the place was a paradise; now the place is trashed. Exploitation is not an enduring relationship—whether with another animal or a landbase.

d) *very low tolerance to frustration and a low threshold for discharge of aggression, including violence.* The civilized have been eradicating the indigenous for ten thousand years. The United States is constantly "discharging aggression" against (i.e., invading) other countries. Individuals and corporations and governments discharge aggression daily toward coyotes, prairie dogs, sea lions, wetlands, coal-bearing mountaintops, and oil-bearing coastal plains.

e) *incapacity to experience guilt and to profit from experience, particularly punishment.* How much guilt do you believe timber company CEOs experience over the destruction of ancient forests? And the word *profit* here does not mean the financial profit they derive from killing forests, oceans, and so on, but profit in terms of hindsight. After deforesting the Middle East, all of Europe, much of the Americas, Africa, and Asia, does it seem at all plausible that those in charge are learning from their past mistakes? Are they learning anything from their decisions and policies that are altering the climate through unrestrained burning of coal, oil, and natural gas?

f) *marked proneness to blame others, or to offer plausible rationalizations, for the behaviour.* Do CEOs take responsibility for their violence? The average rapist for his? George Bush blamed forest fires for his urge to deforest. Clinton said it was all the beetles' fault. And many still rationalize their denial of our rapidly warming planet every time a winter storm slams the East Coast.

Of course we don't all act this way. But those of us who are not sociopaths, who are trying to live differently, need to step up and call out the larger culture for the way it behaves.

Sharing our finite planet with this culture is like being stuck in a room with a psychopath. There is no exit. Although the psychopath may choose other targets first, eventually it will turn to us. Eventually we'll have to fight for our lives. And so if we want access to a landbase we can inhabit, and want our descendants to be able to live there long into the future, we need to organize politically to stop this lethal culture in its tracks.

Writing Strategies

1. Analysis involves breaking something down into constituent parts. How does Jensen break down sociopathic behavior?

2. Explain how Jensen connects sociopathic traits to an entire civilization. Point to specific passages or sentences.

3. Sometimes an analytical process feeds a broader argumentative purpose. What passages in this essay seem more argumentative? In other words, where do you most sense Jensen's argument?

4. Jensen refers to a range of psychological experts and disciplinary texts. Describe how those sources help to support his point about sociopathic behavior.

5. Jensen also refers to Red Cloud, an American Indian (Oglala Lakota Chief) who fought against the advancement of military troops in the 1860s. How do Red Cloud's words support Jensen's point?

Exploring Ideas

1. Jensen seems to use psychopath and sociopath interchangeably. Briefly research these terms. Can you discover any consistent differences in the concepts?
2. No doubt, many Americans would be offended by Jensen's ideas. Why? Why are many not offended? (Are you offended?)
3. Jensen's comparison assumes that a culture can function as a whole—as a coherent identity. This is a common move for historians, sociologists, politicians, anthropologists, and literary writers. Give examples of times you've heard about cultures or countries being characterized as a unified whole.
4. Considering the specific behaviors listed in the *Classification of Mental and Behavioural Disorders* (items a through f in Jensen's essay), how are you a sociopath?
5. What does Jensen mean by "the dominant culture"?

Ideas for Writing

1. Focus on another psychological condition. Compare its specific behaviors or symptoms to an institution or public body.
2. What is *dominant culture?*

If responding to one of these ideas, go to the Analysis section of this chapter to begin developing ideas for your essay.

Black Like I Thought I Was

Erin Aubry Kaplan

Over the centuries, Americans have struggled with race and ethnicity. We have built laws, institutions, and schools of thought around widely held categories. But collectively, we have not made up our minds about difference, diversity, or sameness. As with many concepts, the more we explore, the more we re-discover our own misconceptions. In short, it seems that the concept of race keeps escaping us. In this essay, originally printed in the *LA Weekly,* Erin Aubry Kaplan shows how some deeply grounded assumptions about race may be shattering.

Wayne Joseph is a 51-year-old high school principal in Chino whose family emigrated from the segregated parishes of Louisiana to central Los Angeles in the 1950s, as did mine. Like me, he is of Creole stock and is therefore on the lighter end of the black color spectrum, a common enough circumstance in the South that predates the multicultural movement by centuries. And like most other black folk, Joseph grew up with an unequivocal sense of his heritage and of himself; he tends toward black advocacy and has published thoughtful opinion pieces on racial issues in magazines like *Newsweek*. When Joseph decided on a whim to take a new ethnic DNA test he saw described on a *60 Minutes* segment last year, it was only to indulge a casual curiosity about the exact percentage of black blood; virtually all black Americans are mixed with something, he knew, but he figured it would be interesting to make himself a guinea pig for this new testing process, which is offered by a Florida-based company called DNA Print Genomics Inc. The experience would at least be fodder for another essay for *Newsweek.* He got his kit in the mail, swabbed his mouth per the instructions and sent off the DNA samples for analysis.

Now, I have always believed that what is now widely considered one of slavery's worst legacies—the Southern "one-drop" rule that indicted anyone with black blood as a nigger and cleaved American society into black and white with a single stroke—was also slavery's only upside. Of course I deplore the motive behind the law, which was rooted not only in white paranoia about miscegenation, but in a more practical need to maintain social order by keeping privilege and property in the hands of whites. But by forcing blacks of all complexions and blood percentages into the same boat, the law ironically laid a foundation of black unity that remains in place today. It's a foundation that allows us to talk abstractly about a "black community" as concretely as we talk about a black community in Harlem or Chicago or South-Central (a liberty that's often abused or lazily applied in modern discussions of race). And it gives the lightest-skinned among us the assurance of identity that everybody needs in order to feel grounded and psychologically whole—even whites, whose public non-ethnicity is really ethnicity writ so large and influential it needs no name. Being black may still not be the most advantageous thing in the world, but being nothing or being neutral—the rallying cry of modern-day multiculturalists—has never made any emotional or real-world sense. Color marks you, but your membership in black society also gives you an indestructible house to live in and a bed to rest on. I can't imagine growing up any other way.

Wayne Joseph can't, either. But when the results of his DNA test came back, he found himself staggered by the idea that though he still qualified as a person of color, it was not the color he was raised to think he was, one with a distinct culture and definitive place in the American struggle for social equality that he'd taken for granted. Here was the unexpected and rather unwelcome truth: Joseph was 57 percent Indo-European, 39 percent Native American, 4 percent East Asian—and zero percent African. After a lifetime of assuming blackness, he was now being told that he lacked even a single drop of black blood to qualify.

"My son was flabbergasted by the results," says Joseph. "He said, 'Dad, you mean for 50 years you've been passing for black?'" Joseph admits that, strictly speaking, he has. But he's not sure if he can or wants to do anything about that at this point. For all the lingering effects of institutional racism, he's been perfectly content being a black man; it has shaped his worldview and the course of his life in ways that cannot, and probably should not, be altered. Yet Joseph struggles to balance the intellectual dishonesty of saying he's black with the unimpeachable honesty of a lifelong experience of *being* black. "What do I do with this information?" he says, sounding more than a little exasperated. "It was like finding out you're adopted. I don't want to be disingenuous with myself. But I can't conceive of living any other way. It's a question of what's logical and what's visceral."

Race, of course, has always been a far more visceral matter than a logical one. We now know that there is no such thing as race, that humans are biologically one species; we know that an African is likely to have more in common genetically with a European thousands of miles away than with a neighboring African. Yet this knowledge has not deterred the racism many Europeans continue to harbor toward Africans, nor the wariness Africans harbor toward Europeans. Such feelings may never be deterred. And despite all the loud assertions to the contrary, race is still America's bane, and its fascination; Philip Roth's widely acclaimed last novel set in the 1990s, *The Human Stain,* features a Faustian protagonist whose great moral failing is that he's a black man who's been passing most of his life for white (the book has been made into a movie due in theaters next month). [The movie was released in 2003.]

Joseph recognizes this, and while he argues for a more rational and less emotional view of race for the sake of equity, he also recognizes that rationality is not the same thing as fact. As much as he might want to, he can't simply refute his black past and declare himself white or Native American. He can acknowledge the truth but can't quite apply it, which makes it pretty much useless to other, older members of his family. An aunt whom he told about the test results only said that she wasn't surprised. "When I told my mother about the test, she said to me, 'I'm too old and too tired to be anything else,'" recalls Joseph. "It makes no difference to her. It's an easy issue."

After recovering from the initial shock, Joseph began questioning his mother about their lineage. He discovered that, unbeknownst to him, his grandparents had made a conscious decision back in Louisiana to *not* be white, claiming they didn't want to side with a people who were known oppressors. Joseph says there was another, more practical consideration: Some men in the family routinely courted black women, and they didn't want the very public hassle such a pairing entailed in the South, which included everything from dirty looks to the ignominy of a couple having to separate on buses and streetcars and in restaurants per the Jim Crow laws. I know that the laws also pointedly separated mothers from sons, uncles from nephews, simply because one happened to be lighter than the other or have straighter hair. Determinations of race were entirely subjective and imposed from without, and the one-drop rule was enforced to such divisive and schizophrenic effects that Joseph's family—and mine—fled Louisiana for the presumably less boundary-obsessed West. But we didn't flee ourselves, and didn't expect to; we simply set up a new home in Los Angeles. The South was wrong about its policies but it was right about our color. It had to be.

Joseph remains tortured by the possibility that maybe nobody is right. The essay he thought the DNA test experience would prompt became a book that he's already 150 pages into. He doesn't seem to know how it'll end. He's in a kind of limbo that he doesn't want and that I frankly wouldn't wish on anyone; when I wonder aloud about taking the $600 DNA test myself, Joseph flatly advises against it. "You don't want to know," he says. "It's like a genie coming out of a bottle. You can't put it back in." He has more empathy for the colorblind crowd than he had before, but isn't inclined to believe that the Ward Connerlys and other professed racial conservatives of the world have the best interests of colored people at heart. "I see their point, but race *does* matter, especially with things like medical research and other social trends," he says of Connerly's Proposition 54, the much-derided state measure that seeks to outlaw the collection of ethnic data that will be voted on in the recall election next Tuesday. "Problems like that can't just go away." For the moment, Joseph is compelled to try to judge individually what he knows has always been judged broadly, to reconcile two famously opposed viewpoints of race not for the sake of political argument—he has made those—but for his own peace of mind. He's wrestling with a riddle that will likely outlive him, though he doesn't worry that it will be passed on to the next generation—his ex-wife is black, enough to give his children the firm ethnic identity he had and that he embraced for most of his life. "The question ultimately is, are you who you say you are, or are you who you are genetically?" he muses. The logical—and visceral—answer is that it's not black and white.

Writing Strategies

1. What is Kaplan's main point about the concept of race?

2. This article relies heavily on the story of Wayne Joseph. Explain how his story works—how it helps Kaplan to make a complex point.

3. In ¶5, Kaplan explains that "Joseph struggles to balance the intellectual dishonesty of saying he's black with the unimpeachable honesty of a lifelong experience of *being* black." Why does Kaplan italicize *being*? What distinction is she making?

4. In ¶6, Kaplan says that race "has always been a far more visceral matter than a logical one." How does this statement work in the essay? What kind of distinction does it help readers to make?

5. Kaplan's article makes a classic academic move: It reveals the complexity in something that seems simple. In other words, she *complicates* our understanding of a concept. She shakes up common and comfortable ways of thinking. Find a passage in which you see Kaplan complicating an idea. Describe the comfortable way of thinking and how Kaplan shakes it up.

Exploring Ideas

1. What is the difference among race, ethnicity, nationality, and lineage?

2. White Americans sometimes imagine themselves as nonethnic—as having no ethnicity. Carefully reread ¶4 in Kaplan's article. What is her response to this way of thinking?

3. A close examination of identity requires debunking common sentiments or clichés. Consider, for instance, the notion that people should simply *be themselves.* What does this sentiment assume about ethnicity or identity? What does it ignore?

4. Kaplan reports that "Joseph remains tortured by the possibility that maybe nobody is right." In other words, he fears that there is no clear answer about his racial identity—about racial identity in general. Why is such a possibility so frightening?

Ideas for Writing

1. In what ethnic category have you always seen yourself? How has that category fused to your everyday life? How has it shaped the way you live?

2. Beyond race and ethnicity, what other category has determined your identity? Closely examine that label. Interrogate the assumptions that keep it in place.

If responding to one of these ideas, go to the Analysis section of this chapter to begin developing ideas for your essay.

"Have It Your Way": Consumerism Invades Education

Simon Benlow

What is a student? This might sound like a silly question, but *student* can be defined in different ways. So can *education*. And the way a person defines or understands these concepts can make a difference in the way that person—and others—acts. In the following essay, Simon Benlow explores what it means to be a student and to participate in an education. Notice how Benlow narrows his focus. He doesn't talk generally about all the characteristics of education, but instead examines the important role consumerism (another concept) plays in education. (Portions of Benlow's invention work are shown in later sections of this chapter.)

Two weeks ago, the faculty and staff received a memo regarding "National Customer Service Week." We were urged to take special efforts in serving our customers—presumably, our students. Certainly, I have no objections to extending extra efforts in helping students feel comfortable and situated in the college environment. However, I am deeply troubled (as are many, or most, instructors and professors) by use of the term "customer" to refer to students. I am concerned, in general, about the slow and subtle infiltration of consumerism into education (by companies buying access to students' brains), and I am downright hostile to the way "customer" has suddenly replaced the word (and maybe idea of) "student" in higher education. And because my concerns may seem ungrounded, I'd like to offer a brief analysis—a quick examination of the basic, and not-so-basic, differences between "customer" and "student."

"The customer is always right." We hear this hollow phrase resound through (almost) every corridor of our consumerist culture. The motive behind the phrase is painfully clear—to keep customers happy, to keep them from complaining, and most importantly, to keep them coming back. (Of course, the meaninglessness of the phrase is well known, too—for those of us who have had the displeasure of talking with Ameritech operators or "customer service" tellers at our banks.) The phrase is meant to maintain a climate in which the substance of anyone's concerns or complaints is obfuscated by friendly and diplomatic clichés—"your business means so much to us"; "we'll do everything we can to address the problem." Ultimately, then, the goal of customer service, in this sense, is to lull customers into a sense of complacency—even though their phones may not be working or their washers are throwing sparks.

"Have it your way!" Of course, we all know the song and the friendly fried food establishment associated with this slogan. It's a harmless phrase, in and of itself, and one that works particularly well for the franchise. It suggests to customers that their particular appetites can be catered to, that their specific tastes, no matter how eccentric (within the continuum of dip n' serve fried food) can be easily satisfied. It promotes the idea that the institution will shift its entire set of processes to meet the desires of the individual.

The meal deal bargain. Recently, in our hyper-drive-thru culture, we've been given a new ticket to ride—a quicker and easier way to get fast food (and a host of other things as well): the combo or meal deal. In the old days, we had to pull up to the drive-thru board, search under "Sandwiches" and THEN go through the labor of exploring "Sides" and "Beverages." It was all too much. Now, we can simply pull up, and say a number. We don't even have to trouble ourselves with uttering all the stuff we want to eat. We just say, "#1 with a diet." The meal deal craze is, of course, not limited to fast food; it is, simply, most explicitly manifested in the fast food industry. That is, in the fast food world, we can clearly see the motives of an increasingly consumerized culture: (1) to limit the interaction between the provider and the customer, (2) to limit the time the customer has to reflect on his/her wants, and (3) to limit the energy the customer has to exert.

Passivity. Customers are encouraged to be passive. We are prompted in a variety of ways not to be agents of our own making. Our needs and desires are met by the work of others. As customers, we pay for someone else's work, for someone else's acts of invention, creation, and production. And we not only hire out our activities (painting our homes, cooking our dinners); we also hire out our imaginations. We don't even have to imagine what is possible. Others have already done the imagining, created a product or service and have told us how we can use it. (They've even taken the extra step of telling us what NOT to do: "Women who are pregnant or who may become pregnant should not take, or even handle, these pills.") In short, *the world of the customer is based on intellectual inactivity;* we merely have to dial the phone, get online, say a number. We don't have to reflect, invent, produce, or research (*Consumer Reports*

John Mauk

has done it already). Nor do we have to shop: they will deliver. Being a customer means being driven by simple and personal desires . . . and ultimately demanding that those desires be met.

Contrary to the passive, personalizing, self-perpetuating, desire-driven customer, students are encouraged to be active. In college, students cannot simply consume knowledge. Even in its most packaged form, the textbook, knowledge must be regenerated, revised, reinterpreted, and remembered in order to be anything beyond an answer on a multiple-choice test. Students who read textbooks, literature, and articles passively will get nothing from them—it is a kind of paralyzing higher education illiteracy. Certainly, they will be able to read something aloud, or even to themselves, and maybe summarize a main point; however, they will not know how to imagine the implications or significance of a textbook chapter. (And this is what academics mean when they say, "Our students don't know how to *make meaning*.")

Students who come to college with a consumerist attitude are lost. Because they are anticipating their most basic desires will be stimulated (because that's how people are massaged into buying stuff they don't need), consumerist students come to college waiting to be tickled, waiting to see the big boom, waiting for the car chase or the sex scene, waiting for the french fry, waiting for the Cherry Coke. What they encounter, however, are rooms filled with ingredients. They see only black and white words—where they anticipate smashy colors and extravagant tools for getting their attention. In the face of pure ingredients (the stuff for making meaning), they will be confused . . . and ultimately, terribly bored.

Consumerist students (or those who have been tricked into thinking like consumers) will also have a difficult time understanding principles. Principles, established doctrines which are to be followed, or evaluated, in the processes of making knowledge, don't really exist in consumer culture (unless you count slogans as doctrines). Because everything is based on the eccentricities of the individual ("hold the pickle, hold the lettuce"), the individual need not ever think outside of his/her own desires and the reality that is created from projecting those desires onto everything and everyone in view. In higher education, principles establish how a discipline works. Physics works on principles of matter and energy. The goal of a physicist is to discover the principles and understand how they can be used. Composition works on principles—conventions of grammar and persuasion. This is not to say that all knowledge is prescribed. On the contrary, students in such classes are encouraged to invent, to break rules, to go beyond. But in order to do so, they need certain ground rules; they need to understand that certain principles exist in the world outside of their own desires. (One cannot do chemistry and simply dismiss algebra because it is distasteful.)

When I think back to the best teachers and professors in my education, I recall those who demanded everything contrary to the consumerist mentality. They insisted on active students; they made us read staggering amounts of material and then actively put that material to use; they prompted us into confusion and disorientation; they made us uncomfortable, and then, sometimes, offered paths to clarity. In short, they made us into critical, reflective agents of our own becoming, rather than passive bags of desire. Everything valuable about my education came from instructors and professors who were free from the ridiculous tyranny of consumerism.

There is no way higher education can counter the incredible momentum of consumerist culture. It is far more pervasive than the discourses of physics or composition studies. However, if we continue to allow the term "customer" to replace "student," I fear that students will become increasingly blind to the difference between consumerist culture and college culture. I fear they will become increasingly more confused by the expectations of college, and that in the nightmarish long run, colleges will become simply another extension of the consumerist machine in which everyone is encouraged to pre-package knowledge, to super-size grades, and to "hold" anything even slightly distasteful.

Writing Strategies

1. According to Benlow, what is the essential difference between *student* and *customer?* How does Benlow make this difference clear?
2. Explain how Benlow uses personal testimony. How does it help to support his point about students and customers?
3. Throughout his essay, Benlow alludes to pop culture. Find several allusions that you think are successful and explain why. Which, if any, of his allusions do you think fail?
4. Explain how Benlow prompts readers to consider the importance of the distinction between *student* and *customer*.
5. Explain how Benlow's use of the fast food slogan functions in his analysis. What does the slogan (and the accompanying song) help him to do in this essay?

Exploring Ideas

1. Analysis involves investigating particular parts, elements, or ideas within the whole. What are the particular parts, elements, or ideas within *consumerism?*
2. Benlow claims that consumerism "is far more pervasive than the discourses of physics or composition studies." Offer some support for this claim. How are the discourses of consumerism more dominant in your life than those of academic disciplines?
3. Benlow explains that consumerist students have difficulty with principles. Explain how a consumerist mind-set might be a hindrance to learning a particular principle that you've learned.
4. In what ways have you been addressed or labeled as a customer? Has your college tried to make you into a customer rather than a student? In what particular ways? Do you think it has worked against you?

Ideas for Writing

1. Spend the next 24 hours noticing terms used in conversation, on television, in junk mail, and so on. Are any terms defined or applied incorrectly?
2. Do members of some other group define themselves incorrectly?

If responding to one of these ideas, go to the Analysis section of this chapter to begin developing ideas for your essay.

Student Essay

The Real, the Bad, and the Ugly

Cassie Heidecker

Cassie Heidecker is an art student at Northwestern Michigan College. She developed the following essay about reality television. At first, she struggled not to defend these guilty pleasures but to analyze the concept itself. In this essay, she manages to avoid an explicit argument about the programs, instead revealing how they work on viewers. In her analysis, she discovers key differences among reality, realism, and realistic. And she discovers that reality shows contain a hint of viewers' everyday lives. (Portions of Heidecker's invention work are shown in later sections of this chapter.)

Reality television is a unique form of reality. It's not really real. (Everyone knows that, right?) After all, reality shows have theme music, background sounds, engaging hosts, narrators, sizzling graphics, and makeup artists. The shows are edited so that dialogue is framed and situated for maximum effect. Whatever the contestants say seems snappy, targeted, deliberate, or perfectly stupid. The shows have scenes with pitch-perfect tension, climax, and resolution. But real life has none of these. Real life is mostly boring, uselessly noisy, stagnant, uncertain, ill-defined, repetitive, hopelessly dumb, and sometimes it's quietly and privately beautiful. Such things can't be filmed and put on television for mass viewing. In short, it only takes a moment (or paragraph) to underscore some major differences between reality television and the mundane reality of everyday life.

Describes the obvious tension or apparent contradiction in the concept.

Shows aren't real like life. Life is contradictory—dumb, boring, beautiful.

But reality TV contains something. It draws millions of people away from the Internet and toward their television screens every night. The attraction might simply amount to what it's not: Shows like *Survivor, the Real World, Big Brother, Hell's Kitchen* are not the traditional television fakery where beautiful and two-dimensional humans live two-dimensional lives. These shows are not the plastic, soulless, and formulaic fiction of most primetime sit-coms and dramas. They are something else.

Alludes to specific shows.

Hints at the complexity in the concept—at this "something else."

My husband and I watch culinary reality shows like *Hell's Kitchen* and *Top Chef.* We're embarrassed about it. We don't tell our friends. These shows are trash TV and we don't think of ourselves as

Personal testimony—and a detailed confession.

They are self-aware reality TV junkies.

Allusions and explanations show a complexity to the shows.

They understand the rhetoric of the shows.

trash TV people. But when we watch (when we literally run down from our respective work or domestic duties and avoid the phone for that ridiculous hour), we stay glued to the situation. We laugh in all the places we're supposed to laugh. We holler at all the appropriate moments. We laugh at ourselves laughing. We are the unapologetic groundlings at a Shakespearean drama. We yell at the lecherous old men, the conniving women, the smug adolescents, the deceit, the flawed personalities, the near misses, and the moments of predictable victory. We talk about the obvious low-brow appeals of *Hell's Kitchen* and how the quick-fire editing makes the show totally gripping, hilarious, and winky. We discuss the intricate appeals that *Top Chef* makes on our sympathies and the complex character development that works over an entire season.

Outside source gives public resonance to the previous testimony.

Like Heidecker, most people are ambivalent. They watch but don't want to?

Specific allusions intensify the public resonance—and support the point about reality shows' unique quality.

And we're not alone. Despite the results of a Pew Research Center poll indicating that 63% of the American public thinks that reality TV shows signal our cultural decline, the ratings continue to climb. In fact, "What viewers say they want and what they really watch are not the same" (Carter). So what's the appeal? My husband and I know the shows aren't real. We know we're not watching realism. But we wouldn't be caught dead watching these shows if they featured actors pretending to hope they're going to win the next prize. (Imagine someone like Jennifer Aniston or Zach Braff playing socially awkward but earnest fry cooks.)

A single crucial question!

What then is the *reality* of reality TV?

A breakthrough point: The contestants are not practiced at being contestants. They are not imagined people.

Refers to the most complex aspect of the definition and explains how it sheds light on the concept.

Hoping to nail down *reality,* I made the risky move of consulting our unabridged *Webster's* dictionary. As I expected, the definition of reality is tricky—maddening even. The first definition: "The quality or state of being real." The definitions go on in a similar fashion until definition 2c, which states, "What actually exists: what has objective existence: what is not a mere idea: what is not imaginary, fictitious, or pretend." This definition clinches something important. While conventional television dramas are entirely pretend—mere ideas—the people on reality TV shows are real in the sense that they (probably) haven't spent years training to be on stage or behind a camera. In short, they're not actors in the artistic sense. They haven't studied moods and posture and tonality and craft and the thousands of other things that actors study. Instead, they've (probably) spent most of their lives like the rest of us—working day-to-day in some "objective existence" at some job we'd rather not have. They are folks who (probably) want another life—who are taking a momentary swing at something beyond their everyday lives. At least, that's the implied story of so many reality television shows. The contestants are from the world we occupy. And they'll most likely return to it when the season ends, when the show gets canceled, when they get kicked off, sent home, chopped, voted out, fired, or whatever the case may be.

Despite the ridiculous situations, the dopey and over-complicated rules (that flash by us at the end of the show), reality television has something that viewers automatically sympathize with: the reality behind the characters—not the show itself but the world that the contestants belong to, the world that is unscripted, the world that will surround the contestants again. Maybe the reality part of reality shows is the unfilmed everyday life that bookends the episodes themselves. This reality lingers in the air each week and becomes increasingly palpable, increasingly real, as the season draws to a close.

The heaviest analytical passage—which also contains the thesis of the essay.

So viewers always know, quietly, that real life awaits the contestants.

American Idol is the reigning champion of reality television. Every season, millions of callers dial in to make sure that the winners keep on winning, that losers keep on losing. The sheer number of calls gets at something critical about these shows: they're participatory. The shows are imbued with the life outside of them. Pop culture critic James Poniewozik explains, "Reality is more than a TV genre now. . . . It's everywhere. When Scott Brown won an upset Senate victory in Massachusetts, he was joined onstage by his daughter Ayla, an *American Idol* semifinalist from Season 5." He goes on to trace the trajectory of reality TV from mere entertainment to a kind of reality in itself: "In 1992, reality TV was a novelty. In 2000, it was a fad. In 2010, it's a way of life." In 2014, Charles B. Slocum, assistant executive director of the Writers Guild of America, West, explained that reality TV has spanned the whole continuum of popular entertainment—from innocent observation of family life in *Kids Say the Darndest Things* to sexual allure in *Taxicab Confessions*.

Alludes to the most popular example to support the point.

Reality TV is part of everyday life. It's as real as this building.

Uses the source to underscore the point made at the start of the passage.

In the world of high art, such as literary fiction, the writer works to create a fictive dream—a coherent and impenetrable fantasy. The hope is that readers enter the dream and forget the real world. When we read a novel, for instance, our hopes become tied to Gatsby, Frodo, Ishmael, Antonia, Anna, and so on. We suspend our disbelief. And in turn, we are suspended in an ornate web of un-reality. But in reality television, part of the experience is the interplay between the fabricated scene (the kooky kitchen challenge limited to rutabagas and pig liver) and the invisible everyday lives of the contestants. We know that Angelo, if that is his real name, has a life beyond the one in *Top Chef.*

Contrary examples (allusions to novels) show the particular nature of these shows and how they work on viewers (see page 156 for more on "contrary examples").

Reality TV isn't high art, but it's not simply trash either.

And we know that he's probably, at least a little, like the guy we're watching. We know that the same dude making dim sum will be out on the highways, at the grocery store, at the local coffee shop, at the bar, and late to work right along with us. That's a captivating idea. The real and the fabricated are dancing together in our heads.

A more figurative way of expressing the thesis.

For viewers, this is a powerful aesthetic experience. We know that the contestants are from our world. Most likely, just before shooting the show and being told how to stand, whom to complain about, and what to wear, they were living normal lives. And when the show is over, they'll come back to the non-limelight, to this side of the screen. They'll go back to their own couches and watch their fabricated and edited selves. Maybe this is the appeal. Maybe reality TV attracts so many viewers because of its crafty intermingling of fiction and reality, its tug on the distinctly American belief "that everybody should have a shot. That sometimes being real is better than being polite. That no matter where you started out, you can hit it big, get lucky and reinvent yourself" (Poniewozik), or even that you can temporarily play the game and then go home again.

In fact, it's an aesthetic experience—not just a guilty pleasure.

Yet another figurative way of expressing the complexity of the thesis.

Some people proclaim self-righteously that reality television is a big hoax—that the winners are hand-selected, that the contestants have been carefully chosen to maximize viewing pleasure, and so on. But these spoilers are focused on the obvious. They're saying, "Look! It can't possibly be real!" And they're right—of course! *The Amazing Race, Top Chef, American Idol,* and all their cousins are not real*istic.* They're not real*ism.* They are reality television—a unique and weird phenomenon that is as much about the viewers and our world as anything.

Acknowledges and then counters those who might dismiss the complexity of the concept.

We are the reality of reality TV.

Works Cited

Carter, Bill. "Tired of Reality TV, but Still Tuning In." *The New York Times*, 13 Sept. 2010, nyti.ms/1Ibjnub.

Current Decade Rates as Worst in 50 Years: Internet, Cell Phones Are Changes for the Better. Pew Research Center for the People & the Press, 21 Dec. 2009, www.people-press.org/files/legacy-pdf/573.pdf.

Poniewozik, James. "Reality TV at 10: How It's Changed Television—and Us." *Time*, 22 Feb. 2010, content.time.com/time/magazine/article/0,9171,1963739,00.html.

"Reality." *Webster's Third New International Dictionary, Unabridged*, Merriam-Webster, 1993.

Slocum, Charles B. "The Real History of Reality TV Or, How Allen Funt Won the Cold War." *Writers Guild of America, West*, www.wga.org/organizesub.aspx?id=1099. Accessed 5 Jan. 2014.

Writing Strategies

1. Explain what Heidecker reveals about reality television. What aspect of these shows does she help us understand?

2. How does Heidecker's personal testimony function in this essay?

3. Consider the paragraph about novels. How does Heidecker's point about literary fiction figure into the broader point about reality television?

4. In ¶10, Heidecker integrates a quotation by Poniewozik. Explain how the quotation helps support Heidecker's point about the "reality" of reality television.

Exploring Ideas

1. Heidecker nudges readers beyond an easy judgment of reality television shows. Instead, she prompts us to consider the nature of their appeal. What else can be said about the nature of the appeal? Why else do you think millions of viewers tune in to reality television?

2. Heidecker explains that in reality television, "the real and the fabricated are dancing together in our heads." In your own words, how does this work? How does reality "dance with" the un-real aspects of the shows?

3. Heidecker explains that she and her husband "discuss the intricate appeals that *Top Chef* makes on our sympathies and the complex character development that works over an entire season." Do you have a program that works in a similar fashion on you? What show appeals to your sympathies? How does it work?

4. Given Heidecker's points, what do you think are the differences between realism, realistic, and reality television?

5. Do you have any guilty pleasures? Why do you feel guilty about them?

Ideas for Writing

1. What concept is at the root of your favorite television show?

2. What do current reality television programs suggest about the concept *competition?*

If responding to one of these ideas, go to the Analysis section of this chapter to begin developing ideas for your essay.

Outside Reading

Analyzing concepts is common work across academic disciplines. Writers in philosophy, education, psychology, history, sociology, economics, engineering, law, and even practical fields such as nursing explore shared concepts. They break down the layers or dimensions of concepts such as *self*, *community*, *learning*, *anxiety*, *pathology*, *currency*, *trade*, *balance*, *fairness*, *equality*, *individual right*, *assistance*, *power*, and so on. The discoveries writers make about such concepts help to define the purpose of their fields.

Focus on your academic major, or one you are considering, and find a journal or magazine article that analyzes a basic disciplinary concept. To conduct an electronic search of journals and magazines, go to your library's periodical database perform and a keyword search. Experiment by typing in various concepts related to your chosen field. Avoid using phrases or articles such as *a*, *an*, *the;* instead, use nouns separated by *and*. The results will yield lists of journal and magazine articles. After you find an article, apply the following questions:

1. What is the thesis, or main insight, of the article? Try to narrow in on the most revealing point the writer offers.
2. Describe how the writer goes beyond the obvious, beyond a cursory understanding of the concept. Point to passages in which the writer tries to reveal some complexity that wouldn't otherwise be seen.
3. Identify the major rhetorical strategies (such as narration, description, or figurative language). In other words, describe how the writer defends or supports the thesis.
4. Identify any passages in which the writer attempts to create public resonance. The writer might, for instance, try to connect the concept to some broader understanding or some broader social issue.
5. Finally, consider the audience. Who reads the particular publication? Why? Does the audience know certain things or care about certain issues? How does the writer tap into or connect with that knowledge or set of concerns?

Invention

"What does it mean that success is as dangerous as failure? Whether you go up the ladder or down it, your position is shaky."

—Tao Te Ching

For the writing in this chapter, you must seek out meaning beyond your initial thoughts about a concept. The following sections are designed to help you through this process; specifically, to find a particular concept (in Point of Contact), to examine the concept closely (in Analysis), to make it relevant to a community of readers (in Public Resonance), to develop a focused point (in Thesis), and to develop support for that point (in Rhetorical Tools). The Invention Questions in each section are not meant to be answered directly in your final essay. They are meant to prompt inventive thinking and intensive writing.

Point of Contact

We carry concepts around with us and, for the most part, do not question them. But writers are willing to get underneath concepts that would otherwise go unquestioned. As you consider a possible topic, imagine the concepts that go unnoticed in your everyday life. To find a concept, investigate the world around you. Take a concept that goes unchallenged, uninspected. The following suggestions, questions, and images (Figure 5.2) may prompt a possible topic:

- **Work:** Success, employment, boss, customer, profit, hours, wage, honesty, freedom, career, experience
- **School:** Education, study, discipline, learning, science, humanities, grade, teacher, student, intelligence
- **Home:** Parent, mother, father, pet, living room, divorce, values, God, marriage, privacy, faith
- **Public Life:** Friend, recreation, commitment, travel, woman, man, patriotism, romance, trash, environment

- **Sports:** Team, entertainment, audience, fan, loser, victory, competition
- **Your Major:** Someone majoring in education could analyze a concept such as learning, success, assessment, or high school. Your major itself might be seen as a concept. For example, engineering is a concept, and how one works in that field depends upon one's concept of it.
- **Television:** What does a local news program that devotes sixty seconds to world news and several minutes to sports suggest about news? What does *American Idol* suggest about America or idolatry? What does *The Real World* suggest about reality? What does *The Late Show* suggest about entertainment? What does a cell phone commercial suggest about freedom? What does an insurance commercial suggest about neighbors?

As you reflect on the program or commercial, ask yourself if the concept is somehow oversimplified or misrepresented. Or does the program or commercial fairly represent the concept? Remember that you are not evaluating the television program but rather using it to prompt an idea, to discover a concept that may need analysis and explanation.

Activity

Imagine more concepts that define your everyday life. If this can be done in a small group, take turns offering concepts until each participant has chosen a potential topic.

Library of Congress

Caio Cassoli/StockXchng

Figure 5.2

Analysis

Analysis involves investigating particular parts, elements, or ideas within the whole. If we were to analyze an object, we might take it apart and look inside. We might, for instance, analyze a computer by opening the case and looking at the internal wires, the cards, and the connections. But when examining a concept, we cannot take off its cover and simply look inside—at least, not physically. Instead, we have to depend on intellectual inquiry. Rather than physical tools (screwdrivers or wrenches), we have to develop questions that get inside the abstraction. We have to ask questions that point to the particular elements of the concept. And the more particular we get, the more we're apt to discover. In other words, we should try to understand the concept in the most narrow terms possible. For example, consider *college*. To analyze the concept, we must break it down and look at particular issues: What does college suggest for people's lives? Is it a time and place for learning specific skills or for exploring boundless ideas? Is it a place for making choices or for generating options? Such questions are analytical; they help to shed light on specific issues inside the broader, more abstract idea. As you look closely at the concept you have chosen, use the following Invention Questions to break it down:

- Specifically, how does your chosen concept influence or change people's lives?
- What particular emotions, behaviors, or ideas are associated with it?
- What hidden role does it play in everyday life?
- Are there complexities to the concept that people overlook?

Phestus/MorgueFile

© Cengage Learning

Laura Kennedy/StockXchng

In his invention writing, Simon Benlow looks closely at the particular qualities that define student and customer. He attempts to get at root behaviors and attitudes:

How does it influence or change people's lives?

I'm dealing with two concepts: "student" and "customer." "Customer" influences people to buy things and ideas, but the concept also makes people believe certain things about themselves—that they are better off only when they have obtained some thing or some service. It makes people lazy. When people totally buy into the consumer mentality, they feel as though they should be waited on, catered to, and dealt with, no matter what the circumstances. Being a student is the opposite—or at least, being a good student is the opposite. Students have to discover meaning and to struggle through their own biases, while customers hope to have their biases fed.

What particular emotions, behaviors, or ideas are associated with it?

When consumerist students come to college, they get angry and frustrated. Their expectations about institutions have been created, in large part, from their interactions with retail. They've been advertised and sold to for most of their lives. In college when the tables are turned, when they have to do all the discovering, all the inventing, all the developing, they are often freaked out.

Benlow then develops these ideas in his essay. (See the particular development in the first half of his essay on page 139.)

Invention Workshop

As you consider the Invention Questions, avoid skimming the surface of broad ideas. Enlist the help of at least two other writers. Use one of the Invention Questions to launch a focused discussion. As you address the question, try to avoid chatting aimlessly about the topic (which is always tempting!). Instead, follow new ideas that surface. For example, in the following discussion, Cassie Heidecker discovers an important complexity to the concept *reality television:*

Are there complexities to the concept that people overlook?

DIANA: Yeah, those shows aren't real. They're not reality at all. Everything is scripted and the characters are all predictable. There's the quiet, good-looking guy, the mean bitch that no one likes, the bully with big muscles, the ditz. It's like a cast of stereotypes.

CASSIE: And it's great entertainment. People love watching. I think it's because the contestants are often rough around the edges. Some are rough in the middle too. But it's the lack of refinement that I like.

MICHAEL: And because the contestants aren't actors. They're people. They have day jobs and families back home.

CASSIE: You think people watch *American Idol* because the contestants have real lives?

MICHAEL: Exactly. That's part of it. They have real lives. That's why they show the small hometown once they start whittling down the contestants. They show the bedroom, the street, the place waiting for them at the end of the season. The point is, these people have real lives.

DIANA: Real lives. That's pretty funny. The reality is supposed to refer to the show, not the contestants.

CASSIE: Well, maybe it's like Michael says. The reality of their lives—outside of the show itself—might be the key. That's the big attraction.

Thinking Further

To explore further, writers look and listen for statements that bend away from the obvious. For example, in an Invention Workshop, Heidecker begins to realize something beyond the simple distinction, realistic versus unrealistic. She can pursue the idea further by asking more questions:

- How are reality television shows different from scripted dramas?
- If reality television is still scripted and edited heavily, why do the shows feel so different from conventional programs?

Watch what happens when Heidecker takes these questions and runs. She begins to discover something.

> **If reality television is still scripted and edited heavily, why do the shows feel essentially different from conventional programs?**
>
> On one hand, it feels like anything could happen. One of the characters might freak out or leave the show or cut her finger off. But realistically, viewers know that only a certain kind of anything will happen. Does that make sense? I mean, the shows we watch were likely filmed months beforehand and edited and tweaked. And I guess we know that at some level of thinking. (I'm trying to imagine myself watching *Top Chef* and thinking this way.) I know that a winner will be announced at a particular point, that a car chase isn't going to start up, that Jennifer isn't going to run into the room naked. In other words, the shows really are very predictable. But here's the thing: inside of that overall script are these contestants who could be the person next door. And as I'm watching the show (months after filming), most of those people have returned to their lives. They're real again. That's the catch. The people I'm watching are temporary celebrities and then full-time non-celebrities afterward. That's the weird attraction to it all. That's the "reality" of it.

Heidecker is thinking further; she's doing the work of academic writing. She avoids simple answers and easy responses. Her thinking is increasingly complex—and it yields a sophisticated analysis essay. (See page 143.) As you consider your own topic, explore your invention writing. Look for statements that seem unusual, that bend away from the obvious, and then generate probing questions of your own.

Public Resonance

It is up to the writer to make a concept relevant to readers. At some level, your concept already resonates with others, because a concept is, by definition, beyond particulars. Whether it is *reality, college,* or *student,* a concept necessarily involves others. Still, a concept is not always entirely understood—even by those who would, presumably, understand it. Consider *freedom:* As Americans, we often speak of it, sing about it, and even go to war over it, but do most Americans really understand the concept? Even though freedom is part of our collective language, we might not realize its complexities and meaning. As you consider the social significance of your own topic, use the following questions:

- Is the concept generally agreed upon?
- Why is it important that people have an appropriate understanding of this concept?
- Does the concept need to be rethought? Why?
- What is the possible connection between the topic and some public concern?

If you choose not to directly state the public resonance of your concept, answering these questions serves another goal—to help you envision the relationship between your audience and your topic. In thinking about the public resonance of your chosen concept, you may come across your *purpose*—the reason you are writing. If you believe that the concept is often misunderstood, then the purpose of your analysis might be to educate your audience. Or if your concept is overlooked, the purpose may be to elevate the status of the concept in your readers' mind.

In the following excerpt, Simon Benlow discovers why *student,* as a concept, is necessary and why people should rethink it. Benlow could have given up early in his exploration. He could have merely stopped with "education will suffer." Instead, he tries to imagine specific effects, and in doing so, he further draws out the difference between customer and student:

> **Is the concept generally agreed upon?**
>
> No! That's the whole problem. Many students don't know what it means to be a student.
>
> **Why is it important that people have an appropriate understanding of this concept?**
>
> If college students really understand what it means to be a student (and not a consumerist student), their experience at college will be defined by self-discovery and enlightenment rather than petty frustration and grumbling. If colleges across America continue to confuse "student" with "consumer," education will suffer. Much of the time spent in college will be on customer service (keeping students happy) rather than challenging their beliefs, developing their minds, and broadening their horizons. Customers ultimately do not want their ideas about themselves to change; they want products and services to support what they think. If college continues down the present path, it is not hard to imagine colleges being devoid of genuinely new ideas.

Benlow's essay grows out of this thinking—out of concern for the potential harm to students and higher education. We can see Benlow's initial thoughts most directly in the essay's conclusion (page 141):

> There is no way higher education can counter the incredible momentum of consumerist culture. It is far more pervasive than the discourses of physics or composition studies. However, if we continue to allow the term "customer" to replace "student," I fear that students will become increasingly blind to the difference between consumerist culture and college culture.

Thesis

You probably have many different things to say about your topic, but your project will gain focus and intensity with a thesis statement, a single claim that expresses your particular view on the concept. Look over your notes from the Analysis and Public Resonance sections. Find a theme or pattern running through those notes and try to articulate that idea in a sentence. Your project might:

- **Explain how particular parts or qualities make up a concept.**

  —Maturity involves both recognition of past failures and attempts to retune behavior with those failures in mind.

  —Punk rock involves an explicit and dramatic disdain for common wisdom, popular aesthetic, and accepted manners.

- **Reveal a side or layer of a concept that normally goes unnoticed.**

  —Health is not simply an internal condition but a sound relationship between body and an immediate environment.

  —Behind the common image of trees, lakes, and loose critters, *nature* is a verb—an unyielding cyclical process.

- **Show a quality that distinguishes one concept from another.**

  —Contrary to the passive, personalizing, self-perpetuating, desire-driven customer, students are encouraged to be active. (Simon Benlow)

  —Childhood is not pre-adulthood but an existence fundamentally distinct and characterized by a peculiar mixture of wonder and fear.

- **Explain the inner workings of a concept.**

  —Formal education and therefore educators function as one of the primary authorities in defining proper intellectual behavior and the path to work. (Petra Pepellashi)

  —In today's use of the term, *patriotism* demands a persistent turning away from self-evaluation.

Evolution of a Thesis

Remember that a thesis does not materialize out of thin air. It develops over time. It may involve a long process of reflection and discussion. And often, a good thesis emerges only after a writer has thoroughly analyzed the topic. Consider the example from the Analysis section, in which Cassie Heidecker's topic, reality television, is developed through a discussion. Her thesis evolves slowly as she tries to get a handle on the complexity of the idea:

- Reality television is not real in the sense that anything could happen.
- Reality television contains both highly edited fiction and some unscripted reality.

- We watch reality television because we understand that the contestants are, for the most part, real people.
- The reality part of reality shows is the unfilmed everyday life that bookends the episodes themselves.

As you consider your own thesis, remember that narrower statements yield more interesting writing. At first, you might think, "I can't possibly write more than a paragraph about something so narrow." However, the process of developing the ideas will generate content for your writing. And the more focused thesis will help you illustrate particular points rather than listing many marginally related issues.

Revising Your Thesis

After you have developed a single statement, take time to reconsider: What do people normally say or assume about the concept? How have you complicated or enriched the common way of thinking?

Rhetorical Tools

Examples

Each writer in this chapter puts forth a particular way of seeing a concept, and each must support that way of seeing with scenarios (hypothetical accounts), allusions (references to bits of public knowledge), and examples. Because analyzing concepts requires abstract thinking, writers must be extra careful to illustrate points with concrete examples. In his essay, Benlow uses a detailed scenario to illustrate his concept of *student:*

> In higher education, principles establish how a discipline works. Physics works on principles of matter and energy. The goal of a physicist is to discover the principles and understand how they can be used. Composition works on principles—conventions of grammar and persuasion. This is not to say that all knowledge is prescribed. On the contrary, students in such classes are encouraged to invent, to break rules, to go beyond. But in order to do so, they need certain ground rules; they need to understand that certain principles exist in the world outside of their own desires. (One cannot do chemistry and simply dismiss algebra because it is distasteful.)

In some cases, writers may use details to illustrate how *not* to conceptualize an idea. They use **contrary examples** (situations or accounts that show the opposite of the writer's point). For example, Benlow uses contrary examples in several paragraphs to show consumerist mentality—the opposite of his way of conceptualizing *student.* And Cassie Heidecker uses contrary examples to help her distinguish between genuine fiction and reality television:

> In the world of high art, such as literary fiction, the writer works to create a fictive dream—a coherent and impenetrable fantasy. The hope is that readers enter the dream and forget the real world. When we read a novel, for instance, our hopes become tied to Gatsby, Frodo, Ishmael, Antonia, Anna, and so on. We suspend our disbelief. And in turn, we are suspended in an ornate web of un-reality. But in reality television, part of the experience is the interplay between the fabricated scene (the kooky kitchen challenge limited to rutabagas and pig liver) and the invisible everyday lives of the contestants.

The contrary examples (which are actually allusions to literature) help her to narrow in on particular elements about her topic. They allow Heidecker to draw clear intellectual lines—to demarcate what something is and what it is not.

Often it is not enough to simply mention an example. A powerful and convincing strategy is to explain in detail *how* an example or allusion reveals something relevant. For example, Benlow does not simply mention consumerist slogans; he gives detailed explanations of their significance:

> "The customer is always right." We hear this hollow phrase resound through (almost) every corridor of our consumerist culture. The motive behind the phrase is painfully clear—to keep customers happy, to keep them from complaining, and most importantly, to keep them coming back. . . . The phrase is meant to maintain a climate in which the substance of anyone's concerns or complaints is obfuscated by friendly and diplomatic clichés. . . . Ultimately, then, the goal of customer service, in this sense, is to lull customers into a sense of complacency—even though their phones may not be working or their washers are throwing sparks.

Definitions and References

Sometimes a dictionary definition supports a writer's take on a concept. Or in Heidecker's case, a definition actually helps to make an important distinction:

> **What then is the *reality* of reality TV?**
>
> Hoping to nail down reality, I made the risky move of consulting our big Webster's dictionary. As I expected, the definition of *reality* is tricky—maddening even. The first definition: "The quality or state of being real." The definitions go on in a similar fashion until definition 2c, which states: "What actually exists: what has objective existence: what is not a mere idea: what is not imaginary, fictitious, or pretend." This definition clinches something important. While conventional television dramas are entirely pretend—ideas only—the identities on reality TV shows are real in the sense that they (probably) haven't spent years training to be on stage or behind a camera.

Derrick Jensen does not consult a common dictionary but, instead, goes to a specialized reference book, which gives him a list of particular qualities and behaviors for his topic. In fact, it is the "*Classification of Mental and Behavioural Disorders,* published by the World

Health Organization," that helps Jensen explain the real complexity of his topic. For both Heidecker and Jensen, the official definitions (of *reality* and *sociopath*) help to open up the ideas and reveal important dimensions.

As you consider your topic, apply the following rhetorical tools to help show increasingly complex dimensions of the concept:

- **Examples:** What specific examples in everyday life illustrate my point about the concept?
- **Contrary Examples:** What programs, ads, or other examples from everyday life illustrate an inappropriate or oversimplified way of understanding the concept?
- **Scenarios:** What hypothetical account could demonstrate the concept?
- **Allusions:** What person or event from history, current events, popular culture, or literature illustrates the point about the concept?

Invention Workshop

In small groups, collectively develop support for one another's projects. Each writer should announce his or her thesis to the group. Each group member then should offer at least one response to each of the following questions:

1. What specific examples in everyday life illustrate the writer's point?
2. Name something from popular culture (such as a television show, a movie, an advertising campaign) that illustrates the writer's point. Explain how the writer could allude to it.
3. Name something from history (a person, an event, a trend) that reveals or supports something about the writer's point.
4. Explain how the writer's point is different from how people normally think about the concept.

As the group members offer ideas, the writer should record the group members' responses so they can be integrated later.

Outside Sources

Writers are often surprised to find how many others have addressed their topics and explored the same intellectual pathways. On one hand, outside sources can help a writer substantiate points, and on the other, can help to add dimension—create intellectual twists and turns. Notice how Cassie Heidecker uses sources in both ways. In the first passage, she cites a Pew poll that adds public resonance to her personal reaction to reality television. In the second, she uses a quotation from a cultural critic who supports her own sophisticated claim:

> And we're not alone. Despite the results of a Pew Research Center poll indicating that 63% of the American public thinks that reality TV shows signal our cultural decline, the ratings continue to climb. In fact, "What viewers say they want and what they really watch are not the same" (Carter).

> The sheer number of calls gets at something critical about these shows: they're participatory. The shows are imbued with the life outside of them. Pop culture critic James Poniewozik explains, "Reality is more than a TV genre now. . . . It's everywhere. When Scott Brown won an upset Senate victory in Massachusetts, he was joined onstage by his daughter Ayla, an *American Idol* semifinalist from Season 5." He goes on to trace the trajectory of reality TV from mere entertainment to a kind of reality in itself: "In 1992, reality TV was a novelty. In 2000, it was a fad. In 2010, it's a way of life."

Heidecker illustrates a common move when using outside sources. She begins her paragraphs with her own assertion—her own understanding of the topic. She brings in the outside source, then, to reinforce a complex idea that she has already begun describing. (For more guidance on integrating ideas from sources, see Chapter 16: Integrating and Documenting Sources.)

Revision

Revision is the most difficult step for many writers. We have to genuinely face what we've said and analyze rigorously. We have to take apart what feels complete, finished, and sealed up. If we analyze well, we may find passages that work better than others—those that better support the thesis and those that veer away or simply repeat a bland point. Also, the closer we look, the less apt we are to make generalizations: *It all works. The whole thing is terrible.* Before you pass your draft to review, give it one last read and decide for yourself which passages are the most supportive, which are the most focused and intense, which are the least focused, the least vitalized.

Peer Review

Exchange drafts with at least one other writer. Before passing your draft to others, underline the thesis, or write it above your essay. This way, reviewers will get traction as they read. As a reviewer, use the following questions to guide your response:

1. Which words or phrases in the thesis could be more focused?
2. Point out passages or sentences that could use more specific illustration. Suggest an example from everyday life that illustrates the writer's point. For example, in an essay about athletics, you might read:

   > Athletics are the great motivator of many students. Without sports, many would not feel compelled to attend school at all.

   You might suggest that "the great motivator" could be illustrated more specifically.
3. Suggest an allusion (to popular culture, literature, or history) that illustrates the writer's point. Rather than accept claims as they are, help the writer make a connection to some other time, place, or text so that the concept (whatever it is) connects to a broader set of ideas.

4. The writer might rely on a dictionary to get started, but the ideas should extend beyond that definition. (The essay may take you beyond a definition that you could easily look up yourself.) Where do you feel that "liftoff" away from a standard definition? If there is no liftoff, where might the writer concentrate attention? If you can, offer a path beyond the definition.
5. Consider the paragraphs: Do they focus on one specific point? Point to any paragraphs that seem to stray into several ideas.
6. In which passages does the writer's voice seem most engaging? (Where do you feel yourself, as a reader, most inspired by the ideas?) Why?
7. Referring Chapter 19, Vitalizing Sentences, point to particular sentences and phrases that could gain intensity.

Questions for Research

If the writer used outside sources,

- Where must he or she include in-text citations? (See pages 508–509.)
- Are quotations blended smoothly into the argument and punctuated correctly? (See pages 495–506.)
- Where could more direct textual cues or transitions help readers? (See pages 504–506.)
- Is the Works Cited or References page formatted properly? (See Chapter 16.)

Reflection

As the chapter introduction says, "Writers are willing to get underneath concepts that would otherwise go unquestioned." In this sense, academic writers are not simply reporting information or expressing personal opinions. They are excavating, digging, sneaking into intellectual alleys, and exploring the cultural trash bins. They are revealing the quiet, or sometimes loud and obnoxious, complexities of everyday life.

Now that you've invented, written, revised, and edited a project, you probably have a much deeper understanding of the concept. To draw out that understanding, analyze your essay's rhetoric by answering the following questions:

1. How did you get beneath a concept?
2. What was the most revelatory insight? Was it your thesis?
3. What was your most powerful supporting passage? What does it accomplish?
4. How does your project explore the intellectual back roads and alleys? How does it go behind the conventional, obvious ways of thinking about the concept?
5. Given what you've written, will readers think or behave differently?
6. What might be the benefits to others? How might others be impacted?

Beyond the Essay: Conceptual Map

A conceptual map is a graphic presentation of ideas. Using words, shapes, lines, or photographs, the creator of a conceptual map attempts to depict the relationship and complexity of ideas. This strategy is well suited for illustrating the various layers of a concept. For instance, in the image that opens this chapter (see Figure 5.1), a conceptual map depicts the relationships in cyberspace:

> With the placement of each term, line, and graphic, the designer, Nathan Shedroff, suggests particular connections. Notice, for instance, that one of the outer spheres is "time," and it turns in tandem with "read." This suggests that time, in cyberspace, is dependent on the act of reading.

1. For this assignment, develop a conceptual map to accompany your writing project:

- Try to depict the complexity of your ideas using only key words or phrases from your essay.
- Graphically show how those words and phrases relate.
- Use lines, arrows, and other shapes to depict the relationship between ideas.
- Use colors (if possible) to group ideas or to distinguish between types of ideas.

Consider including your conceptual map as a visual aid within your essay.

2. Present your conceptual map to others. Explain how the map represents the complexity of the ideas in your essay. Explain where it succeeds in reinforcing, and falls short of representing, those ideas.

6

Analyzing Written Texts

Analysis is the act of breaking something down to see how it works. When doctors analyze a heart, they break it down to ventricles and valves. When critics analyze a film, they break it down to plot, characters, acting, and cinematography. And when musicians analyze a song, they break it down to melody, lyrics, chords, and ensemble. In other words, analysis involves pulling apart the subject (heart, film, song) and seeing how each element functions. But the goal is not merely dismantling. Ultimately, we are hoping to understand something about the subject, to discover its patterns, rhythms, and functions. In short, we are hoping to generate an insight, to develop a better understanding of the thing itself.

If you have worked through other chapters in this book, you have already been doing analysis. You have, for instance, broken down places, concepts, even your own memories. But this chapter focuses exclusively on written texts. The goal, here, is to discover something about the way texts work.

In academic life, analyzing written texts (or what we will call *textual analysis*) is crucial work, fundamental to all disciplines and the careers they generate: lawyers analyze court decisions, policies, and transcripts; historians analyze government documents, letters, diaries, or any text produced by the human hand; business leaders analyze sales projections and budget rationale; and when they are not examining patients, physicians analyze the latest medical research. In these examples, notice that we use the term *analyze* rather than *read*. You can probably sense the point: Textual analysis is a kind of intensive reading, a way to interact with an article, essay, book, or blog. It involves prying into the elements, operations, rhythms, and structure of a text. In other words, it requires that we understand the ideas *and* examine how they develop. It involves comprehending the points while tracing how they get made.

Textual analysis relies on (what many teachers and scholars call) *reading critically,* which is different than skimming, browsing, or reading for content. Reading critically involves a deep understanding of the text—an awareness of how it works: what it's trying to accomplish, what it asserts, how it supports ideas, what positions it pushes against, what it implies, what it asks of readers, and so on. Reading critically is reading analytically—not for the sake of judgment or criticism but simply for more insight.

This chapter will help you to find a text to analyze, examine that text closely, and then develop a written analysis. The following essays model a range of approaches to textual analysis. As you read, you will notice some obvious differences. For example, Sharon Angel takes on a historic declaration, Adrienne Carr takes on a commencement address, and our sample analysis examines a traditional academic essay. Each analysis also takes on slightly different elements. Angel focuses more on *context,* Carr focuses on the speaker's attempt to engage the audience, and our analysis focuses on argumentative *appeals*. Although different in scope, these analyses all seek to discover something. Each goes beyond breaking down the text in question and draws out insights from the analytical process. After reading the sample analyses, you can find a text to analyze in one of two ways:

1. Go to the Point of Contact section to find a topic from everyday life, or
2. Choose one of the Ideas for Writing following the essays.

After finding a text, go to the Analysis section to begin developing your thoughts.

What about Literature?

Although stories, novels, plays, and poems are, indeed, written texts, they have some unique qualities—worthy of their own study and exploration. In fact, an entire field of study known as literary criticism focuses on the analysis of literary texts. This chapter, however, focuses on nonliterary written works such as essays, articles, and blog posts.

Readings

The Default Setting: An Analysis of David Foster Wallace

Adrienne Carr

Adrienne Carr is a writer and artist. In this essay, she analyzes the now famous 2005 commencement address by David Foster Wallace. Carr explains rhetorical elements such as context and support, but she focuses most attention on Wallace's overt attempts to connect with his audience. It's in those attempts—when Wallace stops to manage the audience's reflexes—that Carr finds the most compelling insights. (For a better understanding of this analysis, you might first search for and read Wallace's address.)

In 2005, David Foster Wallace delivered the commencement address for Kenyon College. At the time, Wallace was a celebrated literary figure, a relatively young and rising star known for his scathing critiques of popular culture and fantastically dense fiction. But in the address, he is neither scathing nor dense. The David Foster Wallace speaking at Kenyon is not a heavy-hitting writer or powerhouse intellectual. Instead, he is an earnest voice, a member of an older generation trying desperately to impart a difficult and "unsexy" message.

The context of the address is key. Wallace is delivering a commencement for one of the nation's top liberal arts colleges, so his audience is postured to launch into the privilege awaiting those from an esteemed institution. But Wallace does not condemn that privilege. He is not out to hammer his audience about class issues. He is up to something else. He uses the grand occasion to highlight the opposite: the uninteresting, uncelebrated, and most forgettable moments of everyday life. And he argues that these moments, the boring and unsexy ones, provide an opportunity to apply the skills learned from a college like Kenyon. In other words, higher education, he explains, does not provide knowledge, disciplinary skills, or facts. Instead, it provides the ability to shift away from one's "default" response to tedium. This is his main point—one that he asserts, reinforces, and even insists upon throughout the address.

To support his point, Wallace depends on some unfancy rhetorical moves. His speech is not full of witty insider references or arcane allusions. It relies, instead, on some basic scenarios—imagined situations that place the audience in the unglamorous sights and sounds of everyday life:

> [L]et's say it's an average adult day. . . . You haven't had time to shop this week because of your challenging job, and so now after work you have to get in your car and drive to the supermarket. . . . And the store is hideously lit and infused with soul-killing Muzak or corporate pop and it's pretty much the last place you want to be but you can't just get in and quickly out; you have to wander all over the huge, over-lit store's confusing aisles to find the stuff you want and you have to maneuver your junky cart through all these

> other tired, hurried people with carts (et cetera, et cetera, cutting stuff out because this is a long ceremony) and eventually you get all your supper supplies, except now it turns out there aren't enough check-out lanes open even though it's the end-of-the-day rush.

The level of detail forces Wallace's point: there is no escaping everyday life—no way to diffuse the ongoing, nonstop labor of getting through the week. And the detail in this early passage sets Wallace up for more scenarios later in the address, where he dramatizes the shift out of default setting, where he explains, for instance, that people—especially those who are supposedly educated—can shift into a better mindset, one that recognizes others' struggles, others' absolute agony in getting through the day. His early scenarios come from the solipsistic

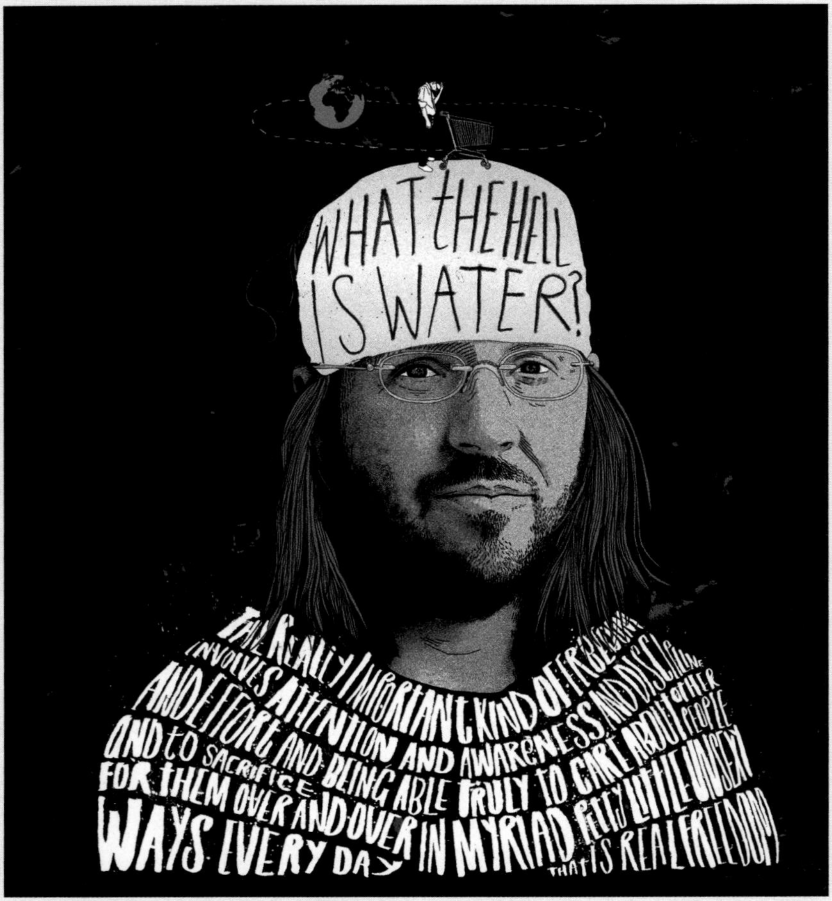

Courtesy Peter Strain

lens—the one that thinks only "about MY hungriness and MY fatigue and MY desire to just get home," while his latter scenarios project a human open to the world of others.

Wallace's address, then, embodies a kind of evolution—a movement from self-centered default thinking to intellectual freedom. That is the unmistakable structure of the address. But as he moves along, Wallace stops in mid-passage (sometimes in mid-sentence) to draw attention to his own rhetoric. In nearly every paragraph, Wallace talks directly about his own attempts to keep his audience engaged. He dances with his listeners' expectations—their anticipation of standard lines, common sayings, and conventional elements of the commencement address. He calls out and grapples with those expectations. For example, Wallace begins with an old tale of two young fish and a wise older one. The unmistakable point of the story is that the younger fish swim along oblivious to the stuff around and within them. They don't understand, as the wise fish does, that they are in water. Wallace then steps out the story—out of the speech itself—and deals with his listeners' potential reaction:

> This is a standard requirement of US commencement speeches, the deployment of didactic little parable-ish stories. The story ["thing"] turns out to be one of the better, less bullshitty conventions of the genre, but if you're worried that I plan to present myself here as the wise, older fish explaining what water is to you younger fish, please don't be. I am not the wise old fish.

Shortly after, Wallace again draws attention to the conventions of the genre—and this time, he acknowledges a cliché:

> Of course the main requirement of speeches like this is that I'm supposed to talk about your liberal arts education's meaning, to try to explain why the degree you are about to receive has actual human value instead of just a material payoff. So let's talk about the single most pervasive cliché in the commencement speech genre, which is that a liberal arts education is not so much about filling you up with knowledge as it is about quote teaching you how to think.

In effect, Wallace has bridged a gap between himself and his audience. He and his listeners now know—if they didn't already—the conventions and formulas of the rhetorical situation. They are all rolling their collective eyes at what is supposed to be said. The conventional cards are on the table. Then Wallace makes an important move: he defends the "pervasive cliché." For the remainder of his speech, he argues for the power and significance of that cliché. But even as Wallace is arguing his case (helping his listeners to imagine the full value of shifting from their default mindsets), he pauses: "Again, please don't think that I'm giving you moral advice, or that I'm saying you are supposed to think this way, or that anyone expects you to just automatically do it." And later, after laying out rationale for moving out of default, he pauses again: "But please don't just dismiss it as just some finger-wagging Dr. Laura sermon." In these overt attempts to engage listeners, Wallace shows an open desperation. So many apologies and qualifiers reveal his estimation of the immediate audience—their skepticism, their reflex toward boredom, their over-familiarity with institutional life, their unwillingness to take advice. He seems to know that his audience might tune out at any second, that his most immediate listeners are resistant to advice, to lectures, to older people handing down edicts. And so Wallace says repeatedly that he isn't one of those and isn't doing any of that—all while being one of those and doing all of that. Wallace is, in fact, the older fish. He does give sage advice. He does impart wisdom. And he does, in the end, explain what water is: the tedium of everyday life that calls out our (everyone's) default settings:

> The plain fact is that you graduating seniors do not yet have any clue what "day in day out" really means. There happen to be whole, large parts of adult American life that nobody talks about in commencement speeches. One such part involves boredom, routine, and petty frustration. The parents and older folks here will know all too well what I'm talking about.

Wallace's speech is about the invisible stuff all around and within us—the stuff that flows through people's proverbial gills and makes us breathe, think, and swim in particular ways. And what's most interesting is his own desperate strategy to manage his audience's default setting—the graduates' suspicions and reflexes in that very moment.

After Wallace's untimely death in 2008, the address attracted a huge readership. "It became a treasured piece of writing reprinted in *The Wall Street Journal* and the *London Times,* commented on endlessly in blogs, and emailed from friend to friend" ("This Is Water"). Something about this particular text generated millions of views and ultimately prompted Little, Brown, and Company to publish it as a stand-alone mini-book. Now millions of people experience the work in a different context—not only in print but also after Wallace himself is gone from the podium. It's difficult to say what ignited the immense appeal—maybe the terrible irony that Wallace committed suicide after years of depression, maybe the everyday clarity that the address provides, or maybe Wallace's recognizable struggle to reach through this foggy default life.

Work Cited

Wallace, David Foster. *This Is Water: Some Thoughts, Delivered on a Significant Occasion, about Living a Compassionate Life*. Little, Brown, 2010.

Writing Strategies

1. Identify Carr's thesis. What sentence best characterizes her main insight about the Wallace address?

2. Carr uses a significant amount of quotations from Wallace's address. Explain why those quotations are necessary in the essay. Or explain where she could have minimized the quoted passages in favor of paraphrase or summary.

3. Unsuccessful conclusions simply restate or summarize the author's thesis. But Carr's conclusion offers an idea. Explain how that idea relates to the rest of her essay.
4. Carr gets dangerously close to at least one analytical "pitfall." Where do you think this happens? Do you think she falls entirely? Or does she manage to stay on safe analytical ground? Explain your answer. (For a detailed explanation of "pitfalls," see page 192.)
5. Do you sense subtle praise or any form of evaluation in Carr's analysis? Explain how Carr either avoids evaluation or veers close to it.

Exploring Ideas

1. Writer's voice is the presence of the writer in the text. Explain Carr's voice. Where do you see (or hear) Carr's voice in this analysis?
2. If you haven't already, read the Wallace address or find the audio recording online. After you have read or listened to the address, explain why you think the address has become so popular.
3. What other rhetorical elements do you detect? What are the most significant elements that Carr does not describe here?
4. In your own words, explain default setting as it applies to people and everyday life.
5. How does Wallace's death figure into your understanding of the Kenyon address?

Ideas for Writing

1. Famous writers, politicians, artists, actors, and entrepreneurs often give commencement addresses. Search for possible addresses to analyze. (Make sure to consider the specific context—both the school and the date.)
2. Consider your favorite professional writer: a novelist, journalist, poet, or reporter. Visit that writer's website or publisher-sponsored site. Search for a speech, manifesto, open letter, or formal correspondence to analyze.

Student Essay

Declarations of Transformation

Sharon Angel

A songwriter, illustrator, and writer, Sharon Angel is currently pursuing a degree in liberal studies at Northwestern Michigan College. In the following essay, she analyzes a Declaration of Sentiments by Elizabeth Cady Stanton. In her research, she discovered striking similarities between Stanton's Declaration and Thomas Jefferson's Declaration of Independence. She uses those similarities to drive her analysis.

A declaration is more than a speech or a document. A declaration is a transformative action—like a baptism or pronouncing someone guilty. "It changes reality in accord with the proposition of the declaration" ("Illocutionary"). The Declaration of Independence, for example, absolves the thirteen colonies of the States of America from allegiance to the British Crown. Throwing off the abusive rule of King George III, it gives the American colonies "among the powers of the earth, the separate and equal station to which the Laws of Nature and Nature's God entitle them." The Declaration establishes specific charges against King George's "absolute tyranny" which aided in justifying the lengthy and hard-fought Revolutionary War. Decades after penning the Declaration of Independence, Thomas Jefferson stated that "All its authority rests . . . on the harmonizing sentiments of the day" (qtd. in "Primary Sources").

In the mid-1800s Americans were still clinging to British moral standards—having not yet solidified a separate, American identity. Men and women assumed separate spheres of conduct, a phenomenon pre-dating Great Britain ("Separate"). Distinct cultural expectations dictated that men were to occupy the public arenas of politics and law while women were to remain confined to the private/domestic realm, leaving those who were not males of European descent legally short-changed. The Constitutional legislation of the founding fathers determined who was a legal citizen, who could exercise a full vote, and therefore, who would have representation when laws were being created, abolished or amended. It was this circuit of power retention that gave birth to another American declaration—the Declaration of Sentiments.

In 1840, Elizabeth Cady Stanton and Lucretia Mott each travelled from America to London to attend the first World's Anti-Slavery convention. They were representatives for their respective abolitionist groups but were not allowed to speak or vote because they were women ("Seneca"). Bonded by this experience, Mott and Stanton decided to host their own convention for women's rights. In 1848, they held a conference in Seneca Falls, New York. The Declaration of Sentiments was drafted for this conference and was presented along with a set of resolutions to be debated and voted upon. Like the Declaration of Independence, Stanton's declaration was modified and then ratified with the signatures of those present ("Seneca"). But this similarity of function is only one of many ways that Stanton's declaration plays off of Jefferson's.

The Declaration of Sentiments adds to the discussion of oppression and "inalienable rights" put forth in the Declaration of Independence. Stanton parallels Jefferson's charges against King George's subjugation of the American colonies with charges against men who subjugate women to a male-dominated (social and legal) power structure. Stanton's strategy demonstrates intellectual prowess, dispelling the perception that women are not designed for rational thinking. Since it was immodest for a Victorian woman to embarrass male company in the slightest way, constructing a document mimicking a lawyer's language was a bold move. By doing so, Stanton steps into a cultural role primarily reserved for well-educated males and leverages the esteemed character of Jefferson as support for her own Declaration. She employs his words and format as a springboard for her argument.

Stanton appeals to the values Jefferson puts forth (equity, justice, liberty) but also exposes why and how the execution of those values fell short. She argues that women have been "oppressed and fraudulently deprived" of their liberty (and pursuit of happiness) by the very institution meant to protect these rights for all its citizens. This line of argument, then, compares King George's reign over the colonies to men's reign over women. In fact, Stanton even syncs her language with Jefferson's and describes "a history of repeated injuries and usurpations on the part of man toward woman." She implies, then, that any American glad to be freed of imperial tyranny should empathize with the plight of women.

The opening statements of both the Declaration of Independence and the Declaration of Sentiments call for a change in policy. Jefferson calls for a dissolution of political bands, and Stanton calls for "one portion of the family of man to assume among the people of the earth a position different from that which they have hitherto occupied, but one to which the laws of nature and nature's God entitle them." After their opening statements, Jefferson and Stanton support their claims with a series of grievances.

Stanton phrases the majority of her grievances against male subjugation as Jefferson phrases many of his indictments against King George's tyranny—opening with the two words "He has." For example, Stanton writes "He has compelled her to commit to laws, in the formation of which she had no voice," which refers to women being excluded from the vote. In this way, Stanton points out the connection between women being silent and women remaining silent. She illustrates the ways women's rights are violated on a daily basis—phrasing the grievances with words such as "withheld," "deprived," "monopolized," and "usurped."

The laws of marriage also served to threaten women's self-respect and well-being, confining them to the service of their husbands' household. Because a married woman was not allowed to own property, all of her assets became her husband's. It was even legal for a husband to beat his wife if he disapproved of her behavior. Evoking such conventions of the day, Stanton claims, "He has made her, if married, in the eye of the law, civilly dead. . . . In the covenant of marriage, she is compelled to promise obedience to her husband, he becoming, to all intents and purposes, her master—the law giving him power to deprive her of liberty, and to administer chastisement." The term "master" (a possible reference to the master-slave relationship) could hardly be ignored at a time in history when the abolitionist movement was highly controversial and soon to become officially lethal.

Although Stanton argues that women are excluded from public positions of status and honorable professions (such as teaching theology), she does concede that man has "allowed her in church, as well as state." But she uses the concession to expose how women were still relegated to subordinate roles.

Stanton builds her argument brick-by-brick, revealing how man established an "absolute tyranny" over woman, "oppressing her on all sides." She cites inequitable wages, a complete lack of universities that would accept women, and the cultural barring of women from professions of stature (such as law and medicine) as means of keeping them in "subordinate stations" and blocking their avenues to wealth. Stanton also points out moral double-standards such as the "false supposition of the supremacy of man" stating that man has claimed as his right "to assign for her a sphere of action, when that belongs to her conscience and to her God." After supplying proof that "He has endeavored in every way that he could, to destroy her confidence in her own powers," Stanton closes by echoing the call for action introduced in her opening statement:

> Now, in view of this entire disfranchisement of one-half the people of this country, their social and religious degradation—in view of the unjust laws above mentioned, and because women do feel themselves aggrieved, oppressed, and fraudulently deprived of their most sacred rights, we insist that they have immediate admission to all the rights and privileges which belong to them as citizens of the United States.

And with this final claim, Stanton restates the thrust of her argument, putting more momentum behind the purpose of her declaration, which is nothing short of a demand at a time when women were supposed to remain silent.

Works Cited

Cady Stanton, Elizabeth. "The Declaration of Sentiments, Seneca Falls Conference, 1848." *Internet Modern History Sourcebook*, edited by Paul Halsall, Fordham U, Nov. 1998, legacy.fordham.edu/halsall/mod/senecafalls.asp.

"The Declaration of Independence: A Transcription." *National Archives and Record Administration*, www.archives.gov/exhibits/charters/declaration_transcript.html. Accessed 30 Dec. 2013.

"Illocutionary Act." *Wikipedia*, 24 Dec. 2013, en.wikipedia.org/w/index.php?title=Illocutionary_act&oldid=705096894.

"Primary Sources: The Declaration of Independence." *The Heritage Foundation*, www.heritage.org/initiatives/first-principles/primary-sources/the-declaration-of-independence. Accessed 28 Dec. 2013.

"Seneca Falls Convention." *Wikipedia*, 12 Dec. 2013, en.wikipedia.org/w/index.php?title=Seneca_Falls_Convention&oldid=708556478.

"Separate Spheres." *Wikipedia*, 7 Jan. 2014, en.wikipedia.org/w/index.php?title=Separate_spheres&oldid=697290217.

Writing Strategies

1. Identify Angel's thesis. What sentence best characterizes her main insight about Stanton's declaration?
2. Angel spends several paragraphs on context. Explain how those paragraphs feed into or support her analysis of the text—the declaration itself.
3. In her conclusion, Angel offers a lengthy quotation from the declaration. How does this serve to conclude her essay? How does it relate to the thesis? How does it offer an insight?
4. Explain how Angel deals with the element of intertextuality.
5. Do you sense any form of evaluation (praise, blame, celebration, judgment) in Angel's analysis? Explain where any subtle evaluation may take place.

Exploring Ideas

1. Angel is analyzing a text from another century. Why might that temporal leap create some extra layer of difficulty?
2. Angel begins by focusing on the declaration as a genre—a type of text that does a specific thing in the world. In your own words, describe the difference between a *declaration* and an *essay*, between a *declaration* and a *treatise*, between a *declaration* and an *argument*.
3. Why is Stanton's Declaration of Sentiments still relevant? Why might a contemporary college student find it worthwhile, even crucial, to read closely?
4. After Stanton's Declaration, it took Congress another seventy-two years to pass the Nineteenth Amendment. Why?
5. Seek out Stanton's Declaration of Sentiments online. Compare it to the Declaration of Independence. Beyond those that Angel points out, what elements do the two texts share?

Ideas for Writing

1. Find a historic speech or declaration to analyze. Use search terms such as *historic, declaration, speeches, famous,* or *address.*
2. The Supreme Court, the White House, and Congress (all three branches of government) store and chronicle famous opinions and speeches. Search the websites of these institutions to find a text. (And make sure that you are, indeed, at a government site, which should end in *gov.*)

The Weight of Sanity: A Sample Analysis of Ann Marie Paulin

We developed the following textual analysis of Ann Marie Paulin's essay (printed in Chapter 8, page 243). Ours is only one possible approach. Someone else could write a compelling analysis of Paulin's essay and draw attention to other significant elements. Our strategy was to call out and explain the function of Paulin's purpose, thesis, and main support strategies. And along the way, we discovered an interesting layer to Paulin's essay.

In recent decades, an army of writers has condemned mass media for its fixation with slimness. Thousands of professors, physicians, psychologists, teachers, journalists, and students have argued vehemently about the emotional and physical injury caused by popular culture's parade of super-thin models. In her essay, "Cruelty, Civility, and Other Weighty Matters," Ann Marie Paulin goes a step beyond blaming mass media. She shows how incessant imagery and messaging have shaped public consciousness. Paulin is not out to blame mass media but to exorcise the value system that has taken root in everyday life.

Paulin begins with a blast of personal testimony: "I swear, if I have to sit through one more ad proclaiming that life is not worth living if you aren't thin, I'll slug somebody." Of course, the most demanding element here is Paulin's voice—her willingness to air such frustration and, of course, to slug somebody. But the opening also establishes two key points: First, the problem involves an immense volume of messages that has accumulated into something inescapable. Second, the message is not simply that being thin is better than being fat. It's that being fat is the worst fate possible. Fat people are portrayed in mass media as "sorrowful empty losers."

In her second paragraph, before she launches into a range of support strategies, Paulin heads off a potential mischaracterization of her stance: "I'm not advocating that everyone in America go out and get fat." This brief qualifier is a defense against bad thinking—the illogical extremes that drive American diets. We are a culture, Paulin explains, that consumes mass quantities of donuts along with toxic diet pills: "We may talk tofu but we gobble glazed." In other words, when it comes to eating, not eating, and all the behaviors in between, American mainstream culture is nowhere near reasonable. And in the next paragraph, she references two articles that show how often and why diets fail. The references, examples, and allusions show a culture with confused reflexes—one that "encourages obesity . . . yet breeds a prejudice against fat people."

The next point in her line of reasoning takes the majority of her essay. In fact, Paulin devotes the next eight paragraphs to the notion that normal everyday people, not the mean old media, are the agents of discrimination. She explains how a majority of respondents (79%) to two personal ads preferred to date a drug addict rather than an overweight person. She describes a university study in which men and women ranked "an obese person as the least desirable sexual partner" over those with mental or physical dis-

"The Weight of Sanity: A Sample Analysis of Ann Marie Paulin." Reprinted with permission of author.

abilities. And then Paulin moves methodically through everyday life, calling out people in charge of learning (teachers), medical care (doctors), and even growing up (parents). In each case, the bigotry is highlighted with surveys and data. And over the course of twelve packed paragraphs, the point becomes clear: the average citizen who lives, works, browses the Internet, and watches television accumulates a general bigotry about body shape: "The constant repetition of this message in various forms does the damage to the humans who watch and learn."

Throughout these passages, Paulin also describes cause and effect. She shows the harm of such persistent bigotry: lower wages, persistent loneliness, and condemnation from family members and associates. Each effect gets its own full paragraph of grim statistics. And as her essay develops, the argument comes full circle. As it turns out, Americans accept the characterization of obese people as sorrowful losers. We dutifully treat the non-skinny with as much open disdain as they can handle—and then a little more.

Much of Paulin's argument, then, is a kind of cultural analysis—an examination of how mass media creates a value system and how that value system, in turn, creates daily life. But beneath this analysis, Paulin's argument appeals to readers' sense of fairness. After all, the statistics and anecdotes show a civilization methodically discriminating against a group of people who have less power, less money, and less social mobility than their slimmer counterparts. She calls out the "harm," "insensitivity," the "virulently negative attitudes" that obese people encounter. And whenever a writer works so hard to report unfairness, she is usually—as in this case—nudging readers toward the opposite.

But the most consistent appeal—the one that begins, ends, and weaves through Paulin's argument—involves moderation. She calls on readers to think in more rational terms, to recognize (and therefore turn away from) the ridiculous, the illogical extremism, "wrongheaded notions," "nonsense," "hugely oversimplified" thinking, "less than accurate" portrayals, "fanatics," "foolish notions," and "crazy ideas" that populate mainstream thinking about obesity. In her seventh paragraph, she describes an advertisement for Slim Fast. She contrasts the ad's world (that celebrates thinness above all else) to a different world (that values family and sanity and health). This stark contrast establishes a kind of choice in readers: stay crazy or get smart; accept the unreasonable or start resisting it.

In her final passage, Paulin reinforces her main appeal. After working through all the cruelty and incivility related to body size, she nails down the main distinction of her argument. It is not fat vs. skinny, kindness vs. cruelty, or acceptance vs. shame. While those distinctions matter, and probably lurk in the subtext of every passage, Paulin's main distinction is sane vs. crazy:

> While I was watching the evening news, a story came on about a young woman who was run over by a bus. I vividly recall that as the station played the footage of the paramedics wheeling the woman away on a stretcher, I said to myself, "Yeah, but at least she's thin." I've been lucky enough to have gained some wisdom (as well as weight) with age: I may be fat, but I'm no longer crazy. There are some things more important than being thin.

Writing Strategies

1. Identify the thesis. What sentence best characterizes our main insight about Paulin's essay?
2. Paragraph seven relies on a series of brief quotations. Explain how those quoted phrases work in our analysis. What specific point are we trying to establish?
3. How does this analysis deal with context? Explain where context comes up, where it gets discussed—even indirectly.
4. We conclude with a lengthy quote from Paulin. Explain what analytical point that quote helps us to make.
5. Do you sense any form of evaluation (praise, blame, celebration, judgment) in our analysis? Can you tell if we find Paulin's claims important or valuable? Explain where any subtle evaluation may take place.

Exploring Ideas

1. In our analysis, we deal briefly with Paulin's voice. What else could we have done with Paulin's voice? Why might her voice be more important than we suggest?
2. In our opening paragraph, we claim that "an army" of writers has taken on the issue of media and body image. Why do you think so many writers have taken on the issue in recent years?
3. Despite that army of writers, mass media still rely almost exclusively on super-thin models and perfectly sculpted bodies to sell everything from phones to yogurt. Why? Does Paulin's essay hold some answer?
4. Consider our title, which is an intertextual play on Paulin's title. What are other possible titles for this analysis? How else could we have played with Paulin's language?
5. We claim that Paulin's essay is "a kind of cultural analysis." In your own words, explain the relationship between textual and cultural analysis. How do they overlap? How does one rely on the other?

Ideas for Writing

1. Find an online article that argues about mass media's impact on women's body image. Analyze that argument. Be careful not to get pulled into claims; instead, stay outside of the argument and explain how it works.
2. Find an online article about the connection between mass media and men's health. Analyze that argument—and, again, be careful not to get pulled into the argument itself.

Invention

Point of Contact

In some ways, analyzing a written text is relatively easy because the elements are, literally, printed or posted in black and white. (You don't have to imagine what is being "said" as you do with an image.) However, written texts have many elements, not just words but layers of implication and suggestion. There are subtleties lurking between, beneath, and around the text itself. So no matter what you are analyzing—a blog, magazine article, journal article, or even a book—the process involves a sizable set of questions. Your target text can be any written published document. We suggest that you choose something easily accessible—a text that you can return to often or even annotate as you read. Consider one of the following options for your analysis. And for more information on each category, see pages 472–475 in Chapter 15:

- Journal Articles: Journals are written for scholars in a specific academic field such as history, linguistics, rhetoric, engineering, nursing, or chemistry. The information is specialized—sometimes so highly specialized that following the logic proves difficult to those outside of the field. Still, not all journal articles require years of study or expertise. In fact, finding a journal related to your chosen field may generate good analytical focus. If you are studying psychology, for instance, you might find an interesting article in *Psychology Quarterly.*
- Magazine Articles: Magazines are aimed at general audiences rather than scholars in a specific discipline. The information is presented so that nonspecialized readers can easily follow the ideas and consider the claims. You might think of magazines in two—very broad—categories: the widest possible readership and special interest. The first category usually provides highly accessible articles. They are brief (less than 500 words), accompanied by photos, and come to quick conclusions. The second category offers more in-depth reporting, longer reports, and even personal essays written by specialists in a field:

  Widest Possible Readership: *Better Homes and Gardens, Cosmopolitan, Men's Health, Sports Illustrated, Women's Day*

  Special Interest: *The Economist, Forbes, National Geographic, Orion, Scientific American*
- Books: An entire book could serve as a target text—especially if the book makes a single and coherent argument or stays focused on a particular event. The upside of taking on a book is the sheer amount of material. There is plenty to consider. However, the amount of text could also pose a challenge. If you are dealing with hundreds of pages, you might find it difficult to narrow down the main idea—the thesis, the supporting premises, or even the purpose.

- Speech Transcripts: Speeches have a unique rhetorical dimension—they were delivered on a particular date, a particular occasion, to a particular audience. And even if they are centuries old, they echo the occasion. A written transcript of nearly any formal speech can be found on the Internet. Consider historic speeches such as Abraham Lincoln's Gettysburg Address or current speeches such as Barack Obama's State of the Union. (See the analysis of David Foster Wallace's commencement speech in this chapter.)
- Websites: Websites are as varied as books. They can be immense—with a huge range of contributors, individual articles, and even kinds of text. For instance, CNN's website contains news articles, government reports, blogs, and editorials. Taking on an entire website could prove challenging. We suggest narrowing your focus to a specific article or blog post. With a narrower focus, you will find it easier to trace textual elements—a coherent writer's voice, a thesis or main claim, consistent rhetorical tools, and so on.

Analysis

Textual analysis requires that we look at the whole and find smaller elements within it. And while written texts have a huge range of potential elements, the following steps are crucial for sound analysis:

Analyzing Purpose Textual analysis requires that we understand what a text is trying to accomplish. In other words, we should try to understand the purpose of the text—what it attempts to do for or to readers. Is it out to change minds, promote a service, argue for institutional change, celebrate a public figure, defend a policy, or something else? If we can determine the specific purpose, other elements come into focus. But if we misinterpret the purpose, we might get all kinds of things wrong. Consider, for instance, what happens when you misinterpret the purpose of an e-mail or text. Imagine that a friend texts you to suggest a meeting place and time.

John Mauk

John Mauk

You interpret the text as an agreement rather than a suggestion. You show up but she doesn't because her purpose was to start a conversation about, rather than to confirm, the meeting place.

There are several long-standing ways to categorize purpose. One classic approach makes three divisions: to inform, to persuade, to entertain. According to this classic view, any given rhetorical act (such as a speech, text, report) seeks to inform, persuade, or entertain an audience. Although these categories are somewhat helpful, they only get us so far. For instance, we can only understand so much if we say that a report is *informative*. There are more specific purposes that we can sense if we focus on how information is presented. The report might be warning its readers, historicizing an issue, connecting ideas that seem otherwise disconnected, filling in intellectual gaps, and so on. If we understand a more specific purpose, we will have a better understanding of the text—and be in a better position to explain other elements.

Broad Purpose: to inform

Specific Purposes: to amend, to explain, to expose, to historicize, to warn, etc.

The same goes with argumentative or persuasive texts. We might decide that an article is trying to persuade its readers, but persuasion is a broad category. If we can sense something more specific, we will understand the text better. We also stand a better chance of sensing the claims and rhetorical tools used throughout.

Broad Purpose: to persuade

Specific Purposes: to accuse, to calm, to condemn, to celebrate, to correct, to counter, to defend, to dismiss, to incite, to justify, to overturn, to praise, to provoke, to rally, to silence, to solve, etc.

Although this brief list may seem somewhat repetitive, each term—*each potential purpose*—has some important function and unique quality. Imagine the difference between two widely read articles on an international news site. Article A condemns a school loan policy. Article B counters that policy. The first makes harsh a judgment; the second explains the logic of a

competing policy. These are two very different articles that would likely have different kinds of support and effects on readers.

And to make matters more complicated, written texts often have more than one purpose. They try, for instance, to predict and solve, to amend and historicize, to defend and calm. In fact, any combination you can imagine has likely been at the heart of more than one article, essay, or blog written in the past month alone! A good analysis attempts to recognize and describe that combination.

Activity

The essays in this book have been categorized, in part, according to rhetorical purpose. Essays in Chapter 2, for instance, primarily *remember* a key experience from the past; those in Chapter 4 *analyze* a concept; those in Chapter 9 *evaluate* a place or thing. But there are two problems with our categories: (1) They are a bit too broad, and (2) they suggest that each essay has a singular purpose. Choose any essay in Chapter 2 through 13. Read the essay closely and then describe the purpose as narrowly and accurately as possible. Consider the possibility that the essay may, in fact, be more specific than the chapter title suggests and that it may have a dual or multifaceted purpose.

Analyzing the Thesis/Main Idea It may come as no surprise that academic essays are not the only written texts with thesis statements. Articles, editorials, and reports of all kinds usually have a single insight that drives the content. And if we are doing textual analysis, we should try to understand that insight. From there, we can determine how all other elements come into play. Remember, however, that thesis statements are not always—or often—at the end of the first paragraph. (That conventional placement of the main idea works in scholastic writing, but in college, professional, and popular contexts, the main idea may come in the middle of a text, in the conclusion, or anywhere at all. It might also be implied—not stated directly but suggested by all the other elements.)

Analyzing Support/Rhetorical Tools You are likely familiar with a major aspect of rhetorical analysis—the elements that writers use to support their claims. If you have written an academic essay (and chances are that you have written a number of them!), you have worked to support and develop your ideas with common *rhetorical tools*. You have likely used allusions, narration, secondary sources, definitions, examples, and so on. For the analytical work in this chapter, you will identify and explain how other writers use them. The following list contains rhetorical tools from previous chapters. Depending on the nature of your chosen text, some will be more relevant than others:

- **Allusions:** references to history, science, nature, news events, films, television shows, or literary texts (see pages 55, 123)
- **Authorities/Outside Sources:** references to published sources (see page 158)

- **Definitions:** denotative (dictionary) or connotative (commonly agreed upon) meaning for words (see page 157)
- **Description:** focused and specific detail (see page 89)
- **Dialogue:** direct discussion between two or more people (see page 56)
- **Examples:** specific cases or illustrations of a phenomenon (see page 156)
- **Facts:** agreed-upon events or truths, or conclusions drawn from investigation (see page 274)
- **Figurative language:** metaphors, similes, analogies, or any statement that changes the literal and denotative (dictionary) definition of words (see pages 90, 124)
- **Narration:** any form of storytelling (see page 88)
- **Personal Testimony/Anecdotes:** individual accounts or experiences usually in narrative form (see page 274)
- **Scenarios:** hypothetical or fictionalized accounts (see page 274)
- **Statistics:** information (often given as numerical value) collected through experimentation, surveys, polls, and research (see page 274)

And this list is only the beginning. There are other rhetorical tools to explore and identify, especially if you are analyzing an argumentative text—one that is evaluating, persuading, or taking a stand on an issue. In that case, be on the lookout for argumentative support strategies:

- **Appeal to Logic:** relates the argument to the audience's sense of reason *or* creates a line of reasoning for the audience to follow
- **Appeal to Emotion:** relates the argument to an emotional state of the audience, or attempts to create a particular emotional state in the audience
- **Appeal to Character:** relates the argument to a quality of the author/speaker
- **Appeal to Need:** relates the argument to people's needs (spiritual, economic, physical, sexual, familial, political, etc.)
- **Appeal to Value:** relates the argument to people's values (judgments about right/wrong, success, discipline, selflessness, moderation, honesty, chastity, modesty, self-expression, etc.)

Finally, argumentative texts have an additional layer: They engage opposing claims and positions directly. In fact, some argumentative texts devote significant passages to confronting the opposition. They engage what others have said about the issue at hand. Following are three common elements related to opposing or outside positions:

- **Counterargument:** anticipates and refutes claims or positions that oppose those being forwarded by the writer
- **Concession:** acknowledges the value of others' claims
- **Qualifier:** acknowledges the limitations of, or makes clear boundaries for, the writer's own argument

Activity

Read April Pedersen's article, "The Dog Delusion," in Chapter 8. In small groups, try to identify rhetorical tools from the preceding list. Seek out support strategies (such as allusions, personal testimony, and examples), as well as argumentative elements such as appeals, counterarguments, concessions, and qualifiers.

Analyzing Organization The arrangement of all these elements also matters. As you are well aware, writers consider all the ramifications of introductions, conclusions, and everything in between. A text might build from the broadest to the most specific point. It might begin with narration and then return to it in the final sentences. It might clump all counter arguments together or counter only in the conclusion. Each organizational strategy can impact the overall effect of the text. Imagine the difference between an article that starts with personal testimony and one that begins with a string of statistics. The two strategies would impact audiences differently and may also create different voices. A sound textual analysis explains how the order of elements plays into the overall effect and function of the text.

Analyzing Voice and Vitality Voice is the presence of the writer in the text—more specifically, the character or tonality of that writer. We're not talking about the real human who is off somewhere in the world (or in history) but the identity that is lurking within the elements of the text itself. As we explain in Chapter 1 and Chapter 18 all texts—even the most formulaic—have voice. From the thesis to its placement, from figurative language to popular allusions, everything that happens in a text shapes the way a writer sounds to the audience. For example, imagine an article that begins with an allusion to punk rock, specifically to the Sex Pistols, and how that article might differ from one that begins with an allusion to Beethoven. Of course, these are extreme differences, but they show how one single element can impact the overall feel of a text—and the way the author sounds in the readers' thinking.

Analyzing Context Translated directly, context means with text. In other words, context involves all the cultural, human, and physical stuff around the text itself—all the forces that motivated the writer, influenced the claims, and even shaped the nature of the audience. If we want to understand a text, we have to examine the context and its constituent parts:

- **Publication:** the journal, magazine, or website that first brought the text into public view. Focusing on the publication can tell us a great deal about text—primarily the kind of audience the writer expected to reach.
- **Intended Audience:** the type of readers most likely to read the text. An analysis of the intended audience includes some basic demographic factors such as age, gender, sex, race,

socioeconomic class, political affiliations, religion, even geographical location. Once we narrow in on these factors, we can develop an understanding of the audience's values and assumptions. For example, if we are analyzing a declaration from the Occupy movement in the United States published in a popular magazine such as *The Nation,* we can quickly draw some conclusions about the intended audience's values—that the readership supports policies that yield greater forms of social justice. If we know that, we can understand why the declaration may not spend lengthy passages trying to convince the audience of that value.

- **Exigence:** the specific provocation for the text. Exigence is a Greek term that usually translates as crisis. For example, a major winter storm, a government shutdown, and a breakdown in peace negotiations are public exigencies that may provoke a range of articles, reports, and blogs. But exigence can also be thought of as an issue or occasion. A parade, a commemoration, a solar eclipse, or an uptick in employment might spur writers into action. And if we can discern the exigence driving a text, we might better understand its claims, appeals, allusions, and examples.
- **Cultural Context:** the prevailing values and beliefs that shape everyday life around the text. Writers and readers belong to communities, cultures, and civilizations. They live within a huge network of events: political upheavals, entertainment trends, national tragedies, weather patterns, and so on. And public texts shimmer with all that collective activity. From direct references to subtle traces, a text includes elements of the culture around it. And a good analysis includes those traces.

Analyzing Intertextuality Texts often speak back to or depend on other texts to make meaning. They exist in dialogue with other written works. This dialogue is called *intertextuality*. For example, the signs shown in Figure 6.1 make meaning, and humor, by echoing or referencing some other statement:

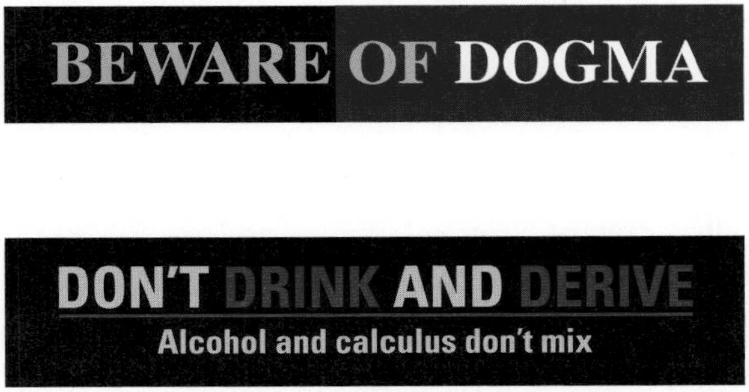

internetbumperstickers.com

Figure 6.1 These signs use intertextuality to make meaning

Although each sticker makes some sense alone, they all have more meaning if we know the references—if we know, for instance, the old saying about making lemonade when life hands you a lemon. We (as readers) participate in the meaning-making process. We bring our prior knowledge forward and create a compound text—a kind of chemical reaction (at least in our thinking) that's ignited by the two statements: one directly in front of us and one swirling around in our prior experience. In recent years, advisers have picked up on this intertextual strategy. Consider the "Got Faith" ad campaign, Figure 6.2, which echoes the famous "Got Milk" ads that came several years before. In this way, intertextuality adds layers of meaning to any text. When designers and advertisers make a text speak to other familiar texts, they tap into the public domain.

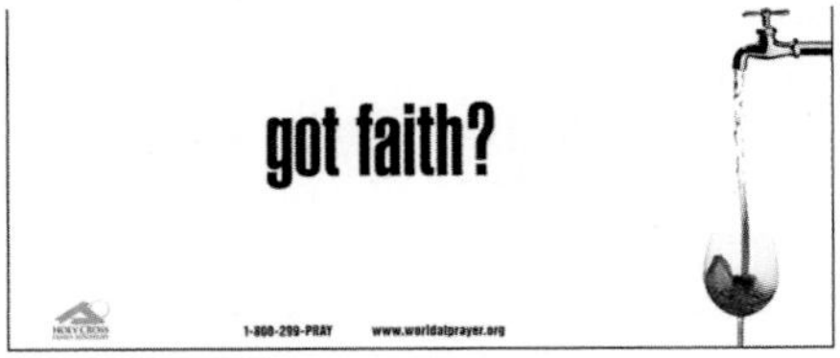

Holy Cross Family Ministries

Figure 6.2 "Got Faith" ad campaign

Analyzing Subtext If people have ever told you to "read between the lines," they were hoping you would sense a layer of implied ideas—those suggested but not directly stated or written. This layer of implication is sometimes called subtext—meaning that it is under (sub) the more visible and obvious layers. Subtext might also be thought of as a collection of assumptions and hidden values, messages that are not obvious but are present nonetheless. For example, when someone asks what you do for a living, the question involves more than your job. It involves issues of status, identity, economic situation, schedule, even personality. And if you offer a short answer ("I'm in marketing"), that answer has subtext. The same goes with a formal written text. Many of the claims, questions, and supporting statements have subtext. And a good analysis calls out that subtext.

Activity

Humor relies on subtext. We laugh at jokes because we know what's left unsaid. Laughter, in a sense, is the sound of us acknowledging what we understand but leave unexpressed. Consider, for instance, these fake state mottos. What ideas are implied in each statement?

Arizona: But It's a Dry Heat
California: As Seen on TV
Colorado: If You Don't Ski, Don't Bother
Florida: Ask Us about Our Grandkids
Indiana: 2 Billion Years Tidal Wave Free

Finally, it is important to approach your target text with a sense of discovery. Although this chapter has listed a number of important elements, your target text probably contains other crucial and interesting layers—elements that we have not considered, named, or even imagined. Perhaps your target text relies on a particular term or concept known only among a small group of readers. Or maybe your text repeats a certain phrase that helps to create a logical rhythm over the course of its argument. Or maybe it makes some elaborate move such as shifting voice to accommodate a shift in focus. The possibilities are unlimited. Anything can happen—especially if we're attentive to subtlety. Use the following questions to begin analyzing your target text:

- What is the specific purpose?
- What is the thesis—the single insight that drives the content?
- What specific rhetorical tools support the thesis?
- How does the text appeal to readers?
- How does the text engage opposing positions or claims?
- How does the organization influence the development of ideas?
- How does the writer's voice show up in the text?
- How do the contextual elements (publication, intended audience, exigence, or cultural context) figure into the text itself?
- How might the text echo or quietly reference another text to make meaning?
- What is the subtext? What implications are made?
- What other unique elements operate in the text? How do they intensify the ideas, support the thesis, or develop some other element?

Thinking Further: Although textual analysis involves identifying and explaining rhetorical elements, the goal is always discovery—to develop a better and richer understanding of the text itself. Successful analyses reveal some pattern, connection, or subtle layer of the target text that might otherwise be missed. And one of the most direct ways to make such a discovery is to combine elements—to ask how different elements work together, influence one another, or intersect in some way. The following questions can get you started. As you examine your target text, consider these and other questions that seek some connection among the elements:

- How does the context impact or shape the purpose?
- How might the context shape the subtext?
- How might opposing opinions show up quietly in the subtext?

- How does the intended audience impact the organization or voice?
- How might the audience shape the nature of the support strategies used throughout?
- What patterns or repeating elements do you detect, and how might they impact other elements?

In her invention writing, Adrienne Carr makes some important discoveries about her chosen text (a commencement speech by David Foster Wallace). In the following excerpts, you can see how Carr begins developing an idea about Wallace's voice. In the first passage, she senses a complexity in the voice. In the second passage, she follows up with the idea:

How does the writer's voice show up in the text?

Wallace begins by admitting that he'll perspire through the event. This calls attention to his own anxiety, his own effort. He is, from the start, establishing a presence, a character that is aware of the situation and maybe even humbled by it. He is not aloof or nonchalant. On the other hand, he openly condemns or dismisses the whole commencement genre and its "bullshitty" qualities. So Wallace's voice is complex. It's earnest and dismissive—hopeful and gruff. In a sense, there are at least two tones or notes at work.

How does the intended audience impact the organization or voice?

Most of that argument involves detailed scenarios—driving home from work, going to the grocery store, and so on. In or between these scenarios, Wallace consistently stops and draws attention to his own argument. These moments always involve some correction for his audience: *Don't think I'm doing this; please don't believe that I'm saying that.* It's as though Wallace is trying to get out in front of his audience's biases—as if he's imagining their worst prejudices and trying to fix them so that they can follow his next point. These correctional rest stops make up much of the speech. There are at least eleven passages (depending on how you count) in which Wallace addresses and tries to tweak his audience's assumptions. And it's these passages where Wallace is most earnest or at least most present. It's where we see him building up to his most intense and difficult points. The longer and more involved the rest stop, the more complex and taxing the point that follows. Wallace's voice works almost like a huddle between him and the audience—where he gets to call "time-out," gather his listeners, and make sure that everyone is with him.

Good invention writing often works in this fashion: The writer senses some quality, question, or even a kind of trouble—something that doesn't sit easily or fit into a simple category. And if the writer is attentive, she keeps working with that quality. As in Carr's case, she might even discover something crucial.

Thesis

Remember that this project is about your target text—about the way it works. As the previous section suggests, there are many elements and, therefore, many ideas that you can develop about the text. You can write about any, all, or some combination of the elements you have discovered. And so it helps to develop a main point, an analytical thesis that can anchor your ideas. Consider the following sample thesis statements—how they might anchor a textual analysis:

Statements that focus on one key element:

- In her article about animal rights, Marlow Henderson uses stark detail to reveal the traumatic life of stray dogs in the Detroit area.
- In his editorial "Making the Grade," Gary Mueller supports his claims primarily with statistical evidence, but the whole argument depends upon his unstated belief that students can make the right choices.
- Rosa Delmonico's article "Having It All" methodically counters a series of mainstream assumptions about successful women.

Statements that highlight the interaction of several elements:

- Chloe Holloway's "Race and Pet Patterns" relies exclusively on personal testimony to suggest—but not state directly—big questions about the gulf between white and black America.
- The subtext of Michael Krug's blog post depends on the audience's familiarity with the income tax laws.
- In his book chapter "Late Night Feeding Frenzies," Khalil Khan uses cultural context to show how food choices are tied to historical variables.

These samples are only the beginning of what's possible. So much depends upon the nature of the target text, the specific elements, and even your own understanding—your take on what's most significant among all the elements. For instance, consider the statement about Holloway's "Race and Pet Patterns." Although one writer might see unstated "big questions" as the most significant element in the article, another writer might focus more on the particular function of Holloway's voice and how it softly manages a difficult political issue.

Common Thesis Problems: As we explain in the Rhetorical Tools section, textual analysis comes with some unique problems or potential pitfalls. The two most frequent problems are summary and evaluation. In other words, writers often get caught up in summarizing too much or evaluating the target text. But there are also some more subtle traps that can settle into your project early on—even when you're developing a working thesis statement. See "Four Common Pitfalls" (page 192).

Evolution of a Thesis

A focused thesis seldom, if ever, falls from the sky or congeals instantly in our brains. Thesis statements develop over time. They become more intensive, more concentrated, as writers work through ideas. For Adrienne Carr, the thesis started with an interest in David Foster

Wallace's voice. Notice how the following statements evolve. The first acknowledges a distinct quality about the voice. The second explains how that quality works within the text—how it functions throughout the speech. The third and fourth refine the idea with narrower terms (*manage* rather than *address, default setting* rather than *assumptions*).

- Wallace's voice is complex. It's earnest and dismissive—hopeful and gruff. In a sense, there are at least two tones or notes at work.
- Throughout his speech, Wallace steps out of one voice and into another, which allows him to address his audience directly.
- The most distinct element through the speech is Wallace's strategic management of his audience's assumptions.
- Wallace strategically manages his audience's default setting—the graduates' suspicions and reflexes in that very moment.

Notice, too, that the last two statements get more focused: "manages" is more focused than "address," and "default setting" is more focused than "assumptions." Each statement gets more narrow and, therefore, more revealing about the target text.

Of course, it doesn't always work like this. Thesis statements morph in any number of ways. For Carr, the voice issue, which she discovered early in her invention work, carried over to other issues and other questions. She saw a distinct quality, explained how that quality interacted with another element (the audience), refined the nature of that interaction, and then connected it to the text as a whole. The thesis, then, shows up toward the end of Carr's analysis:

> Wallace's speech is about the invisible stuff all around and within us—the stuff that flows through people's proverbial gills and makes us breathe, think, and swim in particular ways. And what's most interesting is his own desperate strategy to manage his audience's default setting—the graduates' suspicions and reflexes in that very moment.

Rhetorical Tools

This may sound redundant, but textual analysis is all about the text. That means most of your writing will stay focused on specific elements of your target text. Only rarely should you venture away from it and describe some other issue or source.

Identifying and Explaining Textual Elements A good textual analysis identifies the text's elements and explains how they work—for instance, how they support the thesis, how they reinforce the purpose, how they correspond to the intended audience and so on. In the following passage, Carr identifies the context of Wallace's speech and explains how it works. She doesn't simply point out the element. She explains how it functions, how it figures into the purpose and main idea:

> The context of the address is key. Wallace is delivering a commencement for one of the nation's top liberal arts colleges, so his audience is postured to launch into the privilege awaiting those from an esteemed institution. But Wallace does not condemn that privilege. He is not out to hammer his audience about class issues. He is up to something else. He uses the grand occasion to highlight the opposite: the uninteresting, uncelebrated, and most forgettable moments of everyday life. And he argues that these moments, the boring and unsexy ones, provide an opportunity to apply the skills learned from a college like Kenyon.

These two moves are critical for rhetorical analysis: *identifying an element and explaining its function*. In fact, the most successful analyses develop insights from the second move. As they come to understand the function of all the elements, they discover something about the inner workings of the text. As Carr's analysis develops, she discovers an important connection among the elements in Wallace's speech: the details of the scenario and the overarching organization. In the following passage, she explains this connection:

> The level of detail forces Wallace's point: there is no escaping everyday life—no way to diffuse the ongoing, nonstop labor of getting through the week. And the detail in this early passage sets Wallace up for more scenarios later in the address, where he dramatizes the shift out of default setting, where he explains, for instance, that people—especially those who are supposedly educated—can shift into a better mindset, one that recognizes others' struggles, others' absolute agony in getting through the day. His early scenarios come from the solipsistic lens—the one that thinks only "about MY hungriness and MY fatigue and MY desire to just get home," while his latter scenarios project a human open to the world of others.

Focusing on Specifics As analysts get closer and closer to their texts, they begin to see the significance of individual sentences, phrases, and even word choices. Some of the most powerful insights, in fact, come from that close attention. In the following passage, Sharon Angel draws attention to a particular word ("master") and how it functions within the text—and in the original context:

> Because a married woman was not allowed to own property, all of her assets became her husband's. It was even legal for a husband to beat his wife if he disapproved of her behavior. Evoking such conventions of the day, Stanton claims, "He has made her, if married, in the eye of the law, civilly dead. . . . In the covenant of marriage, she is compelled to promise obedience to her husband, he becoming, to all intents and purposes, her master—the law giving him power to deprive her of liberty, and to administer chastisement." The term "master" (a possible reference to the master-slave relationship) could hardly be ignored at a time in history when the abolitionist movement was highly controversial and soon to become officially lethal.

Finding Patterns A pattern is any meaningful repetition. The presence of a recurring element may help to show something about a text. Imagine, for instance, if a text had four paragraphs that began with a similar kind of concession:

> "My opponents believe, rightly, that . . ."
> "My opponents believe in a sound theory of . . ."
> "My opponents accept a fine principle . . ."
> "My opponents also cling to an important value system . . ."

Such a pattern would be hard to ignore. And it would likely figure heavily into the voice. At the least, it would determine how other argumentative elements function. But not all patterns are as easily identifiable. For example, in his commencement speech, David Foster Wallace consistently and directly grapples with his audience's expectations. And in her analysis, Carr discovers this recurring move and explains its significance:

> In these overt attempts to engage listeners, Wallace shows an open desperation. So many apologies and qualifiers reveal his estimation of his audience—their skepticism, their reflex toward boredom, their over-familiarity with institutional life, their unwillingness to take advice.

This is an important discovery for Carr. In fact, it is, in her own words, "the most interesting" discovery about Wallace's speech:

> Wallace's speech is about the invisible stuff all around and within us—the stuff that flows through people's proverbial gills and makes us breathe, think, and swim in particular ways. And what's most interesting is his own desperate strategy to manage his audience's default setting—the graduates' suspicions and reflexes in that very moment.

Summarizing To understand how a text works (analysis), we must understand what it is saying (summary). The *how* depends upon the *what.* Usually, rhetorical analysis relies on an initial, brief summary. For instance, Angel and Carr begin their analyses with brief (one or two paragraphs) summaries of their target texts. Such an introductory summary is a conventional and effective strategy. It allows writers and readers to get a good sense of the text. Without that initial basic understanding, analysis is nearly impossible.

And even after we summarize, when we enter analytical territory, we still need summary. Even when we're doing analysis, we need to summarize briefly. For instance, notice how the following passage relies on a brief summary (highlighted). In this case, summary and analysis are working together. The power of the analysis depends upon a close and accurate summary:

> The next point in her line of reasoning takes the majority of her essay. In fact, Paulin devotes the next eight paragraphs to the simple notion that normal everyday people, not the mean old media, are the agents of discrimination. She explains how a majority of respondents (79%) to two personal ads preferred to date a drug addict rather than an overweight person. She describes a university study in which men and women

ranked "an obese person as the least desirable sexual partner" over those with mental or physical disabilities. And then Paulin moves methodically through everyday life, calling out people in charge of learning (teachers), medical care (doctors), and even growing up (parents).

Although summary is important to good analysis, it can also become a problem. It can overshadow the analytical moves. If we are doing analysis (if analysis is the goal), then we must be careful to keep summary from taking over—from eclipsing our explanation of how the argument works. This can be a difficult path. Notice the differences among the following moves: summary, almost analysis, and analysis. In the first, the writer strictly summarizes. In the second, the writer identifies Paulin's appeal to value but then shifts into summary—merely restating Paulin's points rather than analyzing the appeal. And in the third, the writer genuinely analyzes Paulin's move:

Summary

In Paulin's seventh paragraph, she explains a Slim Fast advertisement that sends a sad message—that diet products are more important than one's children or family.

Almost Analysis

In Paulin's seventh paragraph, she appeals to value by describing a Slim Fast advertisement. In the advertisement, a woman announces that Slim Fast "is the best thing that ever happened to me." Paulin explains how sad it is that the woman did not put the product at least second to her child.

Analysis

In her seventh paragraph, she describes an advertisement for Slim Fast. She contrasts the ad's world (that celebrates thinness above all else) to a different world (that values family and sanity and health). This stark contrast establishes a kind of choice in readers: stay crazy or get smart; keep on accepting the unreasonable or start resisting it.

To accomplish genuine analysis, a writer has to both identify the element and then explain how it works. For instance, if we discover an appeal to value, we have to describe what values, what cherished ideals, the writer appeals to and how that drives the argument forward or how it supports the main claim.

Quoting Strategically Most textual analyses depend on quotation. The writer narrows in on specific words, phrases, and sentences to illustrate points and develop ideas. In this sense, quotation is a type of textual evidence; it is support from the target text. For example, consider Carr's analysis of David Foster Wallace. She gives several quotations from the text, which allow her to make the following claim:

In these overt attempts to engage listeners, Wallace shows an open desperation. So many apologies and qualifiers reveal his estimation of the immediate audience—

> their skepticism, their reflex toward boredom, their over-familiarity with institutional life, their unwillingness to take advice. He seems to know that his audience might tune out at any second, that his most immediate listeners are resistant to advice, to lectures, to older people handing down edicts.

If Carr hadn't integrated Wallace's own words, her characterization would be groundless. After all, she is a drawing a conclusion about Wallace. To do so, she must rely heavily on his text. Wallace's words give credence to the way Carr understands his effort. And in her analysis of a Declaration of Sentiments, Sharon Angel makes a similar move. She also relies on textual evidence. She highlights specific sentences and even words to support her claims. In the following passage, she explains that Stanton (author of the Declaration) connects or "taps into" women's struggle:

> Stanton points out the connection between women being silent and women remaining silent. She taps into women's unspoken struggle for fair treatment by illustrating the ways women's sense of equity is violated on a daily basis—phrasing the grievances with words such as "withheld," "deprived," "monopolized," and "usurped."

Activity

Chapter 5 describes conceptual maps or graphic presentations of ideas (see page 161). Conceptual maps are often used to help writers understand abstract relationships—how ideas correspond, overlap, intersect, and so on. This practice can be especially helpful with textual analysis. Before you write a draft, make a graphic presentation of your chosen text. Use circles to categorize the text's rhetorical elements, arrows to show how the ideas develop from point to point, and other shapes to show opposing positions. You might even draw out the context—the values and assumptions swirling in the culture around the text.

Caution: Four Common Pitfalls

Rhetorical analysis comes with a few unique dangers—four pitfalls to avoid. This first pitfall is **evaluating the text**. In evaluation, we make and defend judgments about the worth of an argument. We condemn it, celebrate it, or explain that it's okay but not great. Analysis does none of that. It avoids judging the success, the worth, the soundness, or acceptability of the text. Analysis avoids taking a side for or against. In the first list that follows, the statements judge the worth of the target texts. They are evaluative statements. The second list makes analytical points:

Evaluative

Wallace does a good job of supporting his main idea.

Stanton's ideas are right on target.

Paulin convinces me that a change is definitely in order.

I don't accept these claims.

I am suspicious of Wallace's ideas because they seem ungrounded.

Analytical

Wallace relies on personal testimony to ground his most complex points.

Stanton echoes Jefferson's Declaration as a way to reinforce shared values.

Paulin develops an appeal to value with several paragraphs.

Wallace directly addresses his audience's assumptions about the situation.

Stanton appeals to emotion by connecting the power of the nationalism to the power of gender equality.

Now, let's look at the difference between evaluation and analysis in a full paragraph. In the first passage, the writer openly celebrates Wallace's speech. This passage is clearly evaluative because it judges the soundness of Wallace's points. The second passage (taken from Carr's analysis on page 189) is clearly analytical. It avoids judging Wallace's points and, instead, explains his rhetorical strategies:

Evaluative

Wallace's level of detail makes the speech successful. As he lays out the tedium and daily grind of getting to the grocery store, waiting in line, and battling one's way home, he creates a gripping scenario that a reader simply cannot ignore. The masterful scenario dramatizes the solipsistic life of the average person and makes readers, no matter who they are, ashamed to even imagine that life. And the scenarios that come later in the speech do the opposite: they create a vision of someone open to the world of others.

Analytical

The level of detail forces Wallace's point: there is no escaping everyday life—no way to diffuse the ongoing, nonstop labor of getting through the week. And the detail in this early passage sets Wallace up for more scenarios later in the speech, where he dramatizes the shift out of default setting, where he explains, for instance, that people—especially those who are supposedly educated—can, if they choose—shift into a better mindset, one that recognizes others' struggles, others' absolute agony in getting through the day. His early scenarios come from the solipsistic lens—the one that thinks only "about MY hungriness and MY fatigue and MY desire to just get home," while his latter scenarios project a human open to the world of others.

Second, some writers get lured inside the points of the text they are analyzing, and rather than remain outside of that text, on solid analytical ground, they begin **making a case**. In the first passage that follows, the writer further develops—makes a case for—Ann Marie Paulin's idea.

It's as if the writer has suddenly been possessed by Paulin. In the second passage, we stay on solid analytical ground:

> **Making a Case**
>
> Paulin shows how the average citizen, who lives, works, browses the Internet, and watches television, accumulates a general bigotry about body shape. The normal response to fat people is one of disgust and condemnation. Even drug addicts are held in higher regard than someone over the recommended weight. Landlords, dates, teachers, even parents all share the belief that fat people are inherently unworthy.
>
> **Analyzing**
>
> Paulin shows how the average citizen, who lives, works, browses the Internet, and watches television, accumulates a general bigotry about body shape. She moves methodically through everyday life and calls out people in charge of housing (landlords), learning (teachers), and even growing up (parents). In each case, the bigotry is highlighted with surveys and testimony.

The third pitfall involves **describing the effect of the original argument**. In this situation, the writer describes how the argument (or a part of it) might affect an audience. This is not inherently wrong. After all, rhetorical analysis does involve an examination of the argument's impact on an intended audience. But this quickly gets dangerous whenever the original argument (the text being analyzed) is left behind and the focus shifts to imagined audience responses. After all, we don't know exactly how an audience will respond. We cannot assume that readers or viewers will automatically laugh, think, cry, or get angry. The following passage crosses into dangerous territory because it begins to move away from Paulin and emphasizes particular audience responses:

> Readers feel Paulin's anger and desperation. They begin to understand the incredible unfairness surrounding the everyday lives of so many Americans. As they internalize the injustice, they understand exactly what drives Paulin's argument.

Again, we don't know for certain what readers feel or understand. But we do know how the text works; we know how it attempts to appeal to readers. And that is the safer analytical focus. In the following passage, we appropriately describe the relationship between Paulin's text and her readers:

> Paulin's argument appeals to readers' sense of fairness. After all, the statistics and anecdotes all show a civilization methodically discriminating against a group of people who have less power, less money, and less social mobility than their slimmer counterparts. She calls out the "harm," "insensitivity," the "virulently negative attitudes" that obese people encounter. And whenever a writer works so hard to report unfairness, she is usually—as in this case—nudging readers toward the opposite.

While the previous pitfall focuses too much on an imagined audience, the fourth pitfall involves **describing the author's intent**. This strategy is fraught with problems. Because we cannot genuinely know a writer, advertising agency, or movie director's thoughts, we must be careful not to conjure them based on one argument. In the following example, the writer leaves behind an analysis of the argument and begins imagining the interior life of the author (Paulin):

> Ann Marie Paulin was hoping to wake people up, to stop dieting, and to live a better and freer life. She didn't want people to suffer the way she has—or the way she did when she was younger. That's why she wrote the essay the way she did. She put her full force into it because she knew that's what it would take to make people listen.

Reflection

Textual analysis requires that we switch off a basic intellectual motor: skimming. When we zoom through a news website or take in a quick billboard advertisement, we skim and consume meaning as a whole. We usually don't break it down. We don't ask hard questions. Instead, we glide over the surface and accept whatever it offers. Many of the texts we encounter in mainstream consumer culture have been written with this mind. The messages, brief reports, and ads are written to provoke an automatic feeling or thought. This chapter calls on your willingness to stop skimming, to consider the textual particles and elements that might otherwise be missed. And now that you've written a text, try your hand at analyzing it as thoroughly as possible. In other words, try to analyze your own analysis!

1. Thesis: What is your single most compelling discovery about your chosen text? What single analytical statement do you make about it?
2. How do you go about breaking down your chosen text? What elements do you pull apart? What do you call them?
3. How do you deal with context? How does the publication or delivery of your chosen text figure in to your writing?
4. Do you explore intertextuality and/or subtext? How do they shape your understanding of the chosen text, and how far do you get into them?
5. How do you structure your analysis? What organizational strategies do you rely on? For instance, do you walk through your chosen text paragraph by paragraph? Do you handle rhetorical elements separately?
6. Consider your voice. Sometimes analysts adopt the tone—or just subtle echoes—of their chosen texts. (This is not necessarily bad. If anything, it shows a subtle intertextual play.) Did this happen to you? Explain any specific passages.

Revision

Peer Review

Underline your thesis or write it at the top of your essay so that reviewers will understand your focus as they read your draft. Then, exchange drafts with at least one other writer. Reviewers should use the following questions to guide a helpful response:

1. Based on the writer's summary, do you have a good sense of the text? If you can, explain the text in a brief passage.
2. Where could the writer get more specific about his or her chosen text? Check for general or vague phrases such as "appeals to readers" or "supports the thesis." If such statements are not followed up with specific descriptions, the writer can likely get more specific.
3. Has the writer fallen into any pitfalls? (See pages 192–195 for specific descriptions.) If so, point them out. Consider each separately:
   a. Evaluating (praising or condemning) the text
   b. Making a case for the text's argument or claims
   c. Describing the effect of the text on an intended audience
   d. Describing the author's intent rather than the text itself
4. Consider the writer's paragraphs. Are they coherent? Do they take on one rhetorical element and explain that element thoroughly? Point out any paragraphs that take on too much—that explain (or try to explain) too many rhetorical elements.
5. Underline any sentences or phrases that could be more readable and concise. (Hint: In textual analysis, sentences sometimes become long and cumbersome because the writer is trying to manage her own language *and* that of the text in question. Watch out for especially lengthy sentences. If you have a hard time following the logic, suggest strategies for shortening and vitalizing.)
6. Finally, check for some important conventions of textual analysis:
   a. Make sure the writer is using present tense to discuss the text (unless the writer is discussing the delivery of a speech).
   b. Make sure the writer uses "quotation marks" for direct statements, phrases, and words taken from the chosen text.
   c. Make sure the writer has explained where the chosen text was delivered or published.

Beyond the Essay

As we explain earlier in this chapter (page 184), subtext is a collection of assumptions and unstated messages that operate between the lines of a text. And every text has this layer: To some degree, your chosen text (the one that you analyzed) relies on readers to make some connections, to fill in some intellectual gaps, to understand the value of some concept and apply it to the situation at hand. In other words, texts don't say everything required of readers. Readers do much of the work. For example, consider the messages in the following passage from Ann Marie Paulin's essay (page 246):

> At the least, given the reports and studies, we can conclude that weight prejudice is not merely aesthetic judgment. It's an alarming trend, just like obesity itself, that hurts real people. When people are denied a place to live or a means of support not because of any bad behavior or lack of character or talent on their part but because of someone else's wrongheaded notions, then we need to get our minds straightened out.

Such a passage implies, but does not state, ideas such as: *Prejudice is bad. Aesthetic judgments are easier to dismiss than other forms of judgment. People should not be denied basic rights. People internalize what others think of them. Weight does not represent someone's character. Many people operate as though weight does represent character*. As readers, we pick up on these points. We formulate them and then use them to understand the nature of Paulin's argument.

Return to your chosen text and focus exclusively on all the things that are not said. This does not mean that you're looking for secret messages. It means you're looking for shared messages—ideas that are, perhaps, so widely accepted—or so finely stitched into the text—that they go unstated. After developing a list of those ideas, present them in some form other than a conventional essay. For example, chart them out in a conceptual map. If possible, clump the implied statements together according to topic. You can take this process a step further by listing other texts (articles, websites, novels, films, television programs) that are, somehow, related to each clump of statements. In other words, you might show the subtle intertextuality at work in the subtext!

7 Analyzing Images

"At the speed of light, policies and political parties yield place to the charismatic images."

—Marshall McLuhan

Mainstream life in the United States is deluged with images—not random pictures and photographs, but carefully selected images designed to influence what we think and how we feel. Drawings, computer graphics, digitized photos, and airbrushed faces surround us. The minute details of each appeal to our values, desires, needs, and assumptions. And even after the image itself is gone and its immediate appeal is behind us, it still influences how we see the rest of the world.

There is no doubt about it: The barrage of images in our culture dramatically influences how we think, how we live, what we value, what we believe. But are we victims of everything we see? Is each advertisement, poster, graphic, and illustration another intellectual demand? Can we do more than see and accept? What value is gained from seeing inside the workings of images? Living in an image-soaked culture prompts such questions. Especially since most of the images we encounter were designed to influence our thinking, such questions may be vital.

As images in consumer society become increasingly sophisticated, consumers need to become more sophisticated seers. We'll then be more able to see what things are about—and what else they are about. When we break down an image, we can better understand how it works, how it conveys meaning, how it conceals values and beliefs. And we can also better understand how that image relates to the world around it. In short, the more analytical we become, the more we see.

Analysis is the act of breaking down something to its basic elements and attempting to understand something of value in the process. Therefore, analyzing images involves breaking down the elements of an image and understanding how those elements convey

John Metz

Figure 7.1 Window display at a GNC store.

ideas and feelings, how they work on the consciousness of the viewers, how they speak to a surrounding culture, and how they resonate with surrounding values and beliefs.

At first glance, images might seem simple, coherent, and impenetrable. However, even the most simplistic image has rhetorical tools, strategies for persuading readers of some idea. For example, the advertisements in Figure 7.1 were displayed in the window of a health food store. The poster on the far left relies on the image of a young woman. She is sassy and vibrant. She asserts herself outward. The image connects the product and health with youth, vitality, and even a fashionable hairstyle and makeup. The poster on the right features a sunflower, a symbol of nature and purity. The sunflower, along with the promotion for a "new look," sits on a green background, which helps convey newness and freshness.

Such details are no accidents. They are closely scrutinized and are meant to impact consciousness in particular ways. But even if they were accidents, the particular elements impact readers. The particulars help convey ideas, assumptions, and values. Any detail, a streak of sunlight through an image or the reflection of a passing car, may also create an effect—whether or not the artist intended it. Regardless of the intent, we should be cognizant of the way details, the minute and the marginal, figure into the meaning of the image.

This chapter will help you analyze a particular image, develop a focused explanation, and communicate your ideas in writing. Specifically, the goal is to explain how the elements of an image work to impact the feelings and consciousness of viewers. The following essays will provide insight into various analytical strategies. As you read them, notice, for example, how Rebecca Hollingsworth ("An Imperfect Reality") analyzes an image by focusing on how particular visual details function to create an overall effect. Hollingsworth then explains the significance of that effect. As you read, pay attention to the details each author mentions, their effects, and the import of those effects. After reading the essays, you can find an image of your own in one of two ways:

1. Go to the Point of Contact section to find a subject from your everyday life, or
2. Choose one of the Ideas for Writing that follow the essays.

After finding a subject, go to the Analysis section to begin developing the evaluation.

READINGS

Readings

Rise of the Image Culture: Re-Imagining the American Dream

Elizabeth Thoman

Americans are so used to watching TV that they take the commercials for granted and don't consider the impact these images have on their lives. As Elizabeth Thoman, founder of *Media & Values* magazine, says, "Each commercial plays its part in selling an overall consumer lifestyle." Throughout her essay, Thoman explains how television commercials have become fused with the patterns and habits of everyday life and how that fusion might be staved off with a new critical awareness.

Like most middle-class children of the '50s, I grew up looking for the American Dream. In those days there were no cartoons in my Saturday viewing, but I distinctly remember watching, with some awe, *Industry on Parade.* I felt both pride and eager anticipation as I watched tail-finned cars rolling off assembly lines, massive dams taming mighty rivers and sleek chrome appliances making life more convenient for all.

When I heard the mellifluous voice of Ronald Reagan announce on *GE Theatre* that "Progress is our most important product," little did I realize that the big box in our living room was not just entertaining me. At a deeper level, it was stimulating an "image" in my head of how the world should work: that anything new was better than something old; that science and technology were the greatest of all human achievements and that in the near future—and certainly by the time I grew up—the power of technology would make it possible for everyone to live and work in a world free of war, poverty, drudgery, and ignorance.

I believed it because I could see it—right there on television.

The American Dream, however, was around long before television. Some believe the idea of "progress" goes back to when humankind first conceived of time as linear rather than cyclical. Certainly the Judeo-Christian heritage of a Messiah leading us to a Promised Land inspired millions to strive for a better world for generations to come.

Indeed, it was the search for the "City on the Hill" that brought the Puritans to the American colonies and two centuries later sent covered wagons across the prairies. In 1835, Alexis de Tocqueville observed that Americans "never stop thinking of the good things they have not got," creating a "restlessness in the midst of prosperity" that drives them ever onward.

Even the U.S. Constitution, remember, only promises the pursuit of happiness. It doesn't guarantee that any of us will actually achieve it.

It is this search for "something-more-than-what-we've-got-now" that is at the heart of the consumer culture we struggle with today. But the consumer culture as we know it could never have emerged without the invention of the camera and the eventual mass-production of media images it made possible.

Reproducing Pictures

In 1859 Oliver Wendell Holmes described photography as the most remarkable achievement of his time because it allowed human beings to separate an experience or a texture or an emotion or a likeness from a particular time and place—and still remain real, visible, and permanent. He described it as a "conquest over matter" and predicted it would alter the physics of perception, changing forever the way people would see and understand the world around them. Holmes precisely observed that the emergence of this new technology marked the beginning of a time when the "image would become more important than the object itself and would in fact make the object disposable." Contemporary advertising critic Stuart Ewen describes the photographic process as "skinning" the world of its visible images, then marketing those images inexpensively to the public.

But successive waves of what might be called reality-freezing technology—first the photograph, followed by the phonograph and the motion picture camera—were only some of many 19th-century transformations that paved the way to our present image culture. As the wheels of industrialization began to mass-produce more and more consumer goods, they also increased the leisure time available to use these products and the disposable income required to buy them. Soon the well-being of the economy itself became dependent on an ever-expanding cornucopia of products, goods, and services. The Sears-Roebuck catalogue and the department store emerged to showcase America's new abundance and by the turn of the century, as media critic Todd Gitlin notes, "production, packaging, marketing, advertising, and sales became functionally inseparable." The flood of commercial images also served as a rough-and-ready consumer education course for the waves of immigrants to America's shores and the thousands of rural folk lured to the city by visions of wealth. Advertising was seen as a way of educating the masses "to the cycle of the marketplace and to the imperatives of factory work and mechanized labor"—teaching them "how to behave like human beings in the machine age," according to the Boston department store magnate Edward A. Filene. In a work world where skill meant less and less, obedience and appearance took on greater importance. In a city full of strangers, advertising offered instructions on how to dress, how to behave, how to *appear* to others in order to gain approval and avoid rejection.

Granted, the American "standard of living" brought an end to drudgery for some, but it demanded a price for all: consumerism. Divorced from craft standards, work became merely the means to acquire the money to buy the goods and lifestyle that supposedly signified social acceptance, respect, even prestige. "Ads spoke less and less about the quality of the products being sold," notes Stuart Ewen, "and more about the lives of the people being addressed."

In 1934, when the Federal Communications Commission approved advertising as the economic basis of the country's fledgling radio broadcasting system, the die was cast.

Even though early broadcasters pledged to provide free time for educational programs, for coverage of religion, and for news (creating the famous phrase: the "public interest, convenience, and necessity"), it wasn't long before the industry realized that time was money—and every minute counted. Since free enterprise dictates that it's better to make money than to lose it, the American commercial broadcasting system was born. But it was not until the 1950s that the image culture came into full flower. The reason? Television.

Television was invented in the 1930s, but for many years no one thought it had any practical use. Everyone had a radio, even two or three, which brought news and sports and great entertainment right into your living room. And if you tired of the antics of *Fibber McGee and Molly* or the adventures of *Sergeant Preston of the Yukon,* you could always go to the movies, which was what most people did at least once a week.

So who needed television? No one, really. What needed television, in 1950, was the economy. The post-war economy needed television to deliver first to America—and then to the rest of the world—the vision, the image, of life in a consumer society. We didn't object because we thought it was, well, just "progress."

What Price Progress?

Kalle Lasn, a co-founder of the Canadian media criticism and environmentalist magazine *Adbusters,* explains how dependence on television first occurred and continues today each time we turn on our sets: "In the privacy of our living rooms we made a devil's bargain with the advertising industry: Give us an endless flow of free programs and we'll let you spend 12 minutes of every hour promoting consumption. For a long time, it seemed to work. The ads grated on our nerves but it was a small price to pay for 'free' television. . . . What we didn't realize when we made our pact with the advertisers was that their agenda would eventually become the heart and soul of television. We have allowed the most powerful communications tool ever invented to become the *command center of a consumer society* defining our lives and culture the way family, community and spiritual values once did."

This does not mean that when we see a new toilet paper commercial we're destined to rush down to the store to buy its new or improved brand. Most single commercials do not have such a direct impact. What happens instead is a cumulative effect. Each commercial plays its part in selling an overall *consumer lifestyle.* As advertising executive Stephen Garey noted in a recent issue of *Media & Values,* when an ad for toilet paper reaches us in combination with other TV commercials, magazine ads, radio spots, and billboards for detergents and designer jeans, new cars and cigarettes, and soft drinks and cereals and computers, the collective effect is that they all *teach us to buy.* And to feel somehow dissatisfied and inadequate unless we have the newest, the latest, the best.

Just like our relatives at the turn of the century, we learned quickly to yearn for "what we have not got" and to take our identities from what we own and purchase rather than from who we are or how we interact with others. Through consuming things, through buying more and more, we continue the quest for meaning which earlier generations sought in other ways—conquering the oceans, settling the land, building the modern society, even searching for transcendence through religious belief and action. With few places on earth left to conquer today, the one endless expanse of exploration open to us is the local shopping mall.

Transcending Materialism

Thus the modern dilemma: While few of us would turn in our automatic washing machines for a scrub board or exchange our computers for a slide rule, neither can we expect the images of the past to provide the vision for the future. We must recognize the trade-offs we have made and take responsibility for the society we have created.

For many today, the myth of "progress" is stuttering to a stop. The economic slowdown of the early '90s presents only the most recent example of the human suffering created by the boom and bust cycles of the consumer economy. But even if some magic formula could make steady economic growth attainable, we can no longer afford it. Material limits have been set by the Earth itself. Unlimited exploitation in the name of "progress" is no longer sustainable.

True progress, in fact, would be toward a materially renewable lifestyle that would fulfill the physical, spiritual and emotional needs of all—not just some—of the world's people, while allowing them to live in peace and freedom. Under such a system, communication's most important aim would be to bring people together. Selling things would be a part of its function, but not the whole.

Disasters like Chernobyl and the Alaskan oil spill raise hard questions about the long-term social impact of technological innovation. In the U.S., the loss of whole communities to the ravages of drugs, crime, and homelessness threatens the very principles which allow any humane society to flourish.

At the same time, the global events of 1991—the breakup of the Soviet Empire, the struggles for national identity, even the rise of fundamentalist governments in many parts of the Third World—bear witness to a growing desire for meaningful connections as well as material and political progress.

In many ways we are living in a new world, and around that world hungry eyes are turning toward the Western democracies' longstanding promises of freedom and abundance—the promises the media has so tantalizingly presented.

Yet behind the media culture's constantly beckoning shop window lies an ever-widening gap. West or East, North or South, the flickering images of the media remain our window on the world, but they bear less and less relationship to the circumstances of our day-to-day lives. Reality has fallen out of sync with the pictures, but still the image culture continues.

We'll never stop living in a world of images. But we can recognize and deal with the image culture's actual state, which might be characterized as a kind of mid-life crisis—a crisis of identity. As with any such personal event, three responses are typical:

1. *Denial.* Hoping that a problem will go away if we ignore it is a natural response, but business as usual is no solution.
2. *Rejection.* Some critics believe they can use their television dials to make the image culture go away, and urge others to turn it off, too. But it's impossible to turn off an entire culture. Others check out emotionally by using drugs, alcohol, addictions of all kinds to vainly mask the hunger for meaning that comes when reality and images don't converge.
3. *Resistance.* A surprisingly active counterculture exists and is working hard to point out the dangers of over-reliance on the image culture. But such criticism is negative by its very nature, and critics tend to remain voices crying in the wilderness.

A positive alternative is needed. What I have called *media awareness*—the recognition of media's role in shaping our lives and molding our deepest thoughts and feelings—is an important step. The three steps I have outlined above provide simple but effective tools for beginning to work through this process. Although they seem basic, they have their roots in the profound state of being that Buddhism calls *mindfulness:* being aware, carefully examining, asking questions, being conscious.

Even a minimal effort to be conscious can make day-to-day media use more meaningful. Being conscious allows us to appreciate the pleasure of a new CD album and then later turn it off to read a bedtime story to a child. Being conscious means enjoying a TV sitcom while challenging the commercials that bait us to buy. Being conscious allows us to turn even weekend sports events into an intergenerational get-together.

But however achieved, media awareness is only a first step. Ultimately, any truly meaningful attempt to move beyond the image culture will recognize the spiritual and emotional emptiness that the material objects it sells cannot fill.

By convincing us that happiness lies at the other end of the cash register, our society has sold us a bill of goods. To move beyond the illusions of the image culture we must begin to grapple with some deeper questions: Where is the fine line between what I want and what all in society should have? What is the common good for all?

Or to rephrase Gandhi: "How do we create a society in which there is enough for everyone's need but not everyone's greed?"

Thousands of years ago a philosopher wrote of a cave of illusion in which captive humans were enraptured by a flood of images that appeared before them while they ignored the reality outside the cave. This prophetic metaphor contained its own solutions. Once again we are summoned into the light.

Writing Strategies

1. What is Thoman's thesis?
2. How does Thoman use history to develop the main idea? What other strategies does she use?
3. What connection does Thoman make between images and lifestyle?
4. How is Thoman's essay a call to action?

Exploring Ideas

1. In ¶8, Thoman quotes Oliver Wendell Holmes as saying the "image would become more important than the object itself and would in fact make the object disposable." With others or alone, think of examples to support Holmes's point.
2. Interview others to find out how they think advertising influences them. Based on the interviews, to what degree would you say others have media awareness? (See ¶15.)
3. In her conclusion, Thoman references Plato's Allegory of the Cave. Read Plato's allegory, which can easily be found on the Internet. How does Plato's point about image and reality support Thoman's insight?
4. What is the difference between *advertising* and *education?*

Ideas for Writing

1. Explore the relationship between advertising images and the economy, education, family, health, or the environment.
2. Thoman says, "Most single commercials do not have such a direct impact. What happens instead is a cumulative effect." (¶15) Use a certain type of image to support or refute this theory.

If responding to one of these ideas, go to the Analysis section of this chapter to begin developing ideas for your essay.

The Mighty Image

Cameron Johnson

Although exposed to advertising every day, most Americans are unaware of how advertisements and commercials work in their everyday lives. Although ads and commercials seem harmless—or even absurd, as Cameron Johnson explains in the following essay—companies spend millions on advertising because it works. Johnson also explains the logic that keeps most people from seeing the effects of advertising in their lives. (Portions of Johnson's invention work are shown in later sections of this chapter.)

Begins with public resonance: by addressing a flawed way of thinking among many Americans.

To what degree are we independent, free, separate, in control?

Introduces the issue of images.

How do images influence our thinking?

Claims that most Americans don't realize the influence images have.

By the time we Americans are old enough to make hard choices (what to buy, what to wear, what to drive, where to shop, where to buy our degrees, and the like), we imagine ourselves as independent, free, separate, and in control. We like to see ourselves making our own decisions. And because we are attracted to such a self-image, we believe in it. We believe it is *true.* This belief requires us to dismiss the rhetorical power of images in our lives. In fact, most people argue adamantly that they are not influenced by advertising images, that what they purchase is the choice of their own coherent and impenetrable consciousness. Some may concede that images conjure up certain feelings. They may admit, "Those images really moved me" or "That picture brought out lots of feelings in me." But other than the occasional emotional poke, images, say most Americans, have no effect on their reasoning powers—and absolutely no effect on their behaviors.

Brief analysis of images and their role in public behavior.

Spending habits suggest that images influence the way we think.

Develops a line of reasoning: millions of products get purchased after a slick marketing campaign; mainstream thinking is that images don't make people buy things; we should explore this logic further.

This is a peculiar stance in a culture that is submerged in advertising images—ones that are highly successful at getting millions of people to wear, drive, buy, and even fight over the same things at the same time. A quick glance at America's spending habits (millions of products suddenly get purchased directly after a slick marketing campaign) reveals the tremendous power of a finely wrought image. Still, the mainstream argument against the power of advertising goes something like this: *Images do not make people buy things. They do not make kids do drugs. They do not make people buy blue jeans or tennis shoes. They do not make adults smoke cigarettes or buy cars or jewelry.*

■ Writing Strategies ■ Exploring Ideas

Such statements have an obvious logical ring to them. Of course images do not *make* anyone buy anything. Pictures alone do not *make* people do things. But wait. We should explore this logic a bit further.

Pictures alone don't make people buy things. So, how does it work?

In the mainstream perspective, humans are *either* driven by media images or they are entirely independent thinkers. They *either* see something and buy a car or they decide not to buy a car. They *either* want a certain pair of blue jeans or they don't even imagine themselves wanting them. Such a perspective ignores the complexities of desire and the power of images. Of course, people do not simply run to the car lot and buy an SUV after seeing an ad in *Time.* But they consume the image and *the apparent value of the image.* When we see an image (whether it be a hairdo, a body type, or a vehicle), we also get an assumption about its worth in the culture. And this assumption stays with us. It molds into our sense of daily life. (This is, of course, why corporations spend millions of dollars to place images everywhere—so that our ideas about daily life naturally come to include the product or the image.)

Further analyzes the way images work in everyday life—explaining the complexity of how images influence thinking (debunking the oversimplistic view).

Consuming an image means consuming "the apparent value of the image."

Contrary to popular belief, humans are gregarious. We think and act in groups, according to historical trends. About every five years in America, kids laugh at what came five years earlier: "Look at that guy's jeans!" "Hey, check out the hairdo on her!" About every decade or so, certain social behaviors become extinct or come into favor: wearing hats, not wearing hats, getting married at 18, waiting to get married, having multiple sexual partners, being monogamous, and so on. And in the bigger spectrum of history, political consciousness changes: from thinking Indians should die to forgetting they exist, from thinking women should stay home and breed to celebrating female CEOs. How do these trends occur? How can a population make such tremendous shifts in belief in relatively short periods of time? Again, human beings don't think or make decisions in isolation. They decide on their hair, clothing, cars, homes, favorite colors, favorite body types, favorite drinks, and favorite pastimes according to the huge cultural menu of their time. Every important psychologist, anthropologist, and philosopher of the twentieth century taught us this: People do make free choices only insofar as they are free from overt oppression, *but they do not make choices that are free of culture.*

Broad cultural allusions help make connections for readers.

Why do certain behaviors become extinct or come into favor?

Uses questions *(How do . . . ? How can . . . ?)* to lead readers to the next point.

People choose from a cultural menu.

Sharp analytical points help make distinctions and reveal the role of images in everyday life.

Take, for example, the SUV craze in the United States. Certainly, we can point to various causes for the increased sales of

An extended example about SUVs to illustrate the previous point.

Reasons why people should want to buy an SUV.

SUVs over the past decade: more disposable income, cheap gas prices (relative to other industrialized nations). But given the tremendous escalation of SUV sales, we might assume that significant changes have occurred: dramatic increases in snow throughout the nation, the general depletion of the highway system, rampant mudslides from coast to coast, a sudden migration from cities to mountain hideaways, a dramatic increase in family size, a sudden discovery of free and accessible oil reserves, a sudden realization that SUVs save lives.

Develops the extended example about SUVs.

Why SUVs aren't a logical choice.

Specific examples help to influence the readers' way of thinking.

None of these occurred. But the opposite in each case has: People are generally moving to warmer climates and to cities; snowfall amounts are diminishing even in "snow belts"; family size is shrinking; oil is increasingly more expensive and coated in political stickiness; SUVs are involved in deadly rollover accidents; the nation is increasingly paved—perhaps the smoothest it's ever been in its paleontological history. And more roads go more places. Generally speaking, people have fewer reasons than ever to drive trucks, fewer reasons than ever to drive big people haulers, fewer reasons than ever to have four-wheel drive, fewer reasons than ever to own humungous, extra-large carrying capacity, super-low-gas-mileage vehicles. But the average suburban family is *more* likely to drive such a vehicle—one originally conceived as a tool for ranches or military operations.

With the groundwork laid in the previous two paragraphs, Johnson emphasizes the role of the advertising image.

How prevalent is advertising in our culture? To what extent does it overcome rational thinking?

Specific details from Toyota 4Runner ad help drive home the idea.

Given the facts, we have to look at the mighty image. Given all the issues at hand (the history, the economics, the politics, the geography, the climate, the demographics), we must analyze what's most prevalent and powerful in our culture: advertising. Take, for example, a typical SUV ad, one for a Toyota 4Runner. The 4Runner descends a rocky cliff—a near-vertical drop—and rocky terrain stretches for miles into the background. The main text proclaims: "No intelligent life out here. Just you." (One wonders if Toyota's marketing executives are terribly ironic or terribly shortsighted.) At the bottom of the ad, a smaller message says, "Daily stops to the middle of nowhere." Certainly, most Americans live nowhere close to the middle of nowhere. Very few people will ever get to a place where they are surrounded by nothing but rocks, and even fewer will ever aim a truck down a cliff.

Points out the logical absurdity of the Toyota 4Runner ad, while acknowledging that the ad works.

If we were to examine this ad and then assess the demographics of the buying public, we might guess that it's a joke—or an attempt to ruin Toyota. But the ad obviously works. It conjures up an attractive un-reality for potential consumers. We also might guess that the ad appears in an outdoors magazine—perhaps *Ranchers Quarterly, Mountain Lion News,* or *Rock Slide Specialist.* But the ad appears in *Time*—a decidedly mainstream, middle-class periodical. The vast majority of its readers commute to work on urban streets and suburban highways—and descend the gradual paved slopes of parking garages. Given the distance between readers' actual lives and the ad's imagery, Toyota may have just as logically featured the landscape of Mars.

What other ads work by conjuring up "an attractive un-reality for potential customers"?

Reference to Mars points out logical absurdity.

But such an image leaves an impression. It resonates with our songs (". . . purple mountains' majesty . . ."); it appeals to our longing for escape; it captures our desire for solitude and security; it fits into our drive to scoff at nature. And when such imagery pounds the average citizen relentlessly, it begins to reside in the consciousness. It becomes familiar. Even though most Americans will never see the top of a mountain or careen down a cliff (on purpose), they can buy (into) the vehicle attached to the impression.

Advertising images appeal to our values, desires, and underlying beliefs—not our logical reasoning.

Further analysis: The repetition of advertising images has an impact on people's consciousness.

The image creates an *allure,* that is, an attractive association of the thing (ridiculously large truck) with a set of ideas (escape, individualism, America, majesty, power, etc.). That set of ideas can be entirely divorced from reality, entirely separate from the needs of everyday life. But everyday life doesn't matter, nor does the logic that it might yield. The mighty advertising image makes it all irrelevant.

Makes final connection between image and a set of ideas (values, beliefs, assumptions).

Writing Strategies

1. Describe Johnson's voice as a writer, and refer to several passages for support.

2. How does Johnson's introduction effectively lead into the rest of his essay?

3. Identify one concession Johnson makes, and explain how he uses it to further his own argument.

4. What does Johnson imagine his readers think, and how would he like to change their thinking?

5. Johnson concludes ¶8 by saying, "Given the distance between readers' actual lives and the ad's imagery, Toyota may have just as logically featured the landscape of Mars." How does (or doesn't) Johnson earn the right to make such a claim?

Exploring Ideas

1. Provide support for Johnson's claim that advertisements mold our sense of daily life.
2. In his opening sentence, Johnson lists several "hard choices" Americans have to make. What do such choices say about American culture? What do they say about Johnson?
3. In a group, explore what images Americans consume, settling on several key images. What do those images say about America?

Ideas for Writing

1. What popular image contradicts the facts (medical, scientific, historical, and so on)? What are the consequences of the contradiction?
2. How is a particular advertising image effective despite its illogical appeal?

If responding to one of these ideas, go to the Analysis section of this chapter to begin developing ideas for your essay.

Student Essay

An Imperfect Reality

Rebecca Hollingsworth

In the following essay, Rebecca Hollingsworth, who studied art at Northwestern Michigan College, goes beyond the first glance and shows readers how an image (an autism-awareness magazine ad) works on the consciousness of viewers. Through analysis, Hollingsworth breaks down the particulars of an image to show how the overall ad conveys ideas, assumptions, and values, and thus influences the viewers' thinking.

Every day we hear more and more about developmental disorders that afflict children in the United States, disorders that have been misunderstood, downplayed, or ignored. With recent advances in child development and behavior studies, and, perhaps to a large extent, with the explosion of pop psychology personalities like Dr. Phil, Americans are paying more attention than ever to children's mental health. Of course, the general public isn't necessarily any more educated about developmental disorders than it was in the past, but experts and non-experts alike are now insisting that it's okay, even fashionable, to acknowledge and address the ways in which our children aren't "perfect."

One health epidemic at the forefront of public consciousness is autism, a brain disorder that impairs a person's ability to communicate, socialize, and participate in group behavior. Often surfacing by the time a child is three years old, the symptoms of autism include stifled speech and difficulty in displaying joy or affection. According to a 2007 study by the U.S. Centers for Disease Control and Prevention, about 1 in 150 American children are autistic—a staggering number that makes autism the fastest-growing developmental disorder in the United States. Since the release of these findings, nonprofit organizations across the country have been working to raise public awareness of this national health crisis. The largest of these organizations, Autism Speaks, recently launched a multimedia campaign aimed at parents of autistic, or potentially autistic, children.

The 2006 autism awareness campaign sponsored by Autism Speaks challenges common notions of the "perfect kid" by revealing how the reality of autism crushes unrealistic ideals of young American girls and boys. The campaign features a series of television, radio, online, magazine, and billboard advertisements that emphasize the prevalence of the disorder. The campaign's magazine ads show kids doing "kid things"—that is, playing dress-up for girls and playing sports for boys. In one ad (see Figure 7.2), a young girl adorns herself with brightly colored clothes and jewelry as proud mom looks on.

The girl wears a cropped, short-sleeved, light pink jacket unzipped to reveal a billowing fuchsia-and-black striped tie and matching fuchsia beaded necklace. She commands

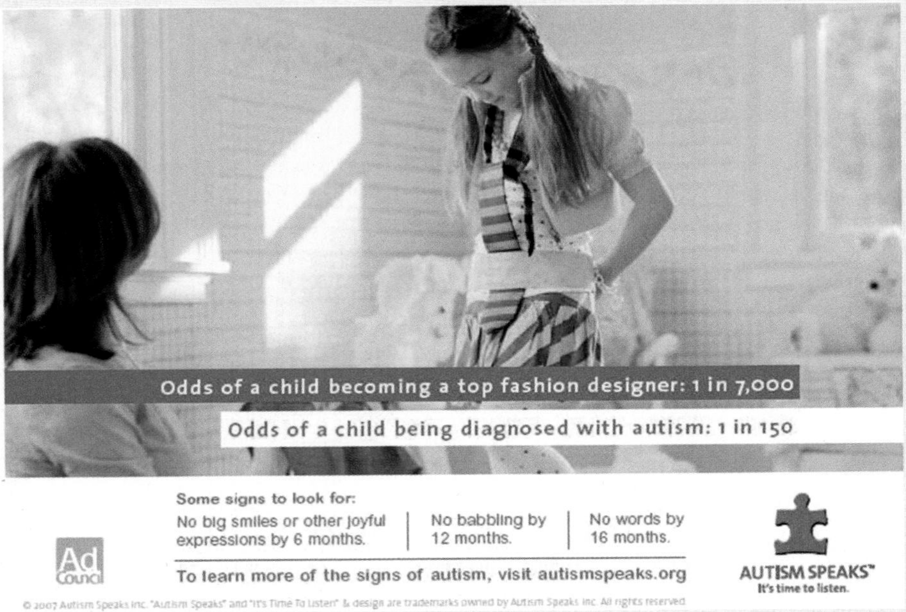

Autism Speaks

Figure 7.2 "Autism Speaks" ad

the attention of her mother and of us; she stands in a fashionable pose with one leg slightly bent as she looks down to tie a light pink belt around her waist. She towers above her mother, who sits in the lower-left corner of the ad, watching her daughter from the sidelines. The mother's gaze creates a direct line of vision to the young girl, drawing the viewer's eye to this fashionable focal point. Like mom, we look on as the young girl tries on one piece of clothing after another, suggested by the pink, white, and blue clothes draped over furniture in the background. The girl's jewelry—the chunky necklace and the dangly charm bracelet—and her sophisticated tie clash with her long, stringy pigtail braids and big white teddy bear in the background. The pink-and-white washed walls covered in a busy pastel pattern remind us that this is a child's room and that we are witnessing child's play.

The text of the ad jolts us into a reality that is discordant with the idealistic image. Bannered text across the bottom of the image reads, "Odds of a child becoming a top fashion designer: 1 in 7,000. Odds of a child being diagnosed with autism: 1 in 150." This startling statistic of the likelihood that this young girl—any young girl—is autistic turns our viewing experience upside down. As we watch the young girl over her mother's shoulder, we must confront the prevalence of this developmental disability in American children—and the very real possibility that our own child may be that 1 in 150.

The text of the ad goes on to educate parents about the warning signs of autism: a child's inability to show joy by six months, to babble by twelve months, and to talk by sixteen months. And all this text, along with the sobering 1 in 150 statistic, fences us off from the image. In fact, the text separates us from the scene. It's behind the mother's shoulder, but in front of our eyes. We know something she doesn't. In classic dramatic irony, we see the looming, or probable, reality that neither child nor mother can imagine in the ideal bedroom.

The sponsor's logo (a puzzle piece in the shape of a child) and slogan ("Autism Speaks: It's time to listen") appeal to a parent's responsibility to pay attention to her child's behavior, to monitor each developmental step or lack thereof, to hope for the best, to fear the worst. And like all such ads—those that appeal to the complex tangle of parent responsibility and fear—the message begs many questions: Does autism really speak, or does it whisper? How will I know? Once I hear it, what do I do? How could autism affect my child's chances in the world? Is it curable? Is it deadly?

In this sense, the ad does what numerous other campaigns do: it scares us. But this one aims at a particularly vulnerable place: the intersection of our idealism and our fear. It contrasts deluded notions of success—defined here as becoming a top fashion designer—with a statistically harsh truth. We can no longer bask in the old *one in a million* cliché. Like the pretty imagery in the fictional bedroom, that number has been upstaged by a more demanding probability.

Work Cited

United States, Department of Health and Human Services, Centers for Disease Control and Prevention. "Prevalence of Autism Spectrum Disorders: Autism and Developmental Disabilities Monitoring Network, Six Sites, United States, 2000." *MMWR Surveillance Summary*, vol. 56, no. SS-1, 9 Feb. 2007, www.cdc.gov/mmwr/preview/mmwrhtml/ss5601a1.htm.

Writing Strategies

1. According to Hollingsworth, what does the Autism Speaks advertisement encourage us to think?
2. Hollingsworth breaks the ad down into its basic elements. Which specific elements are most important to her analysis? How, according to Hollingsworth, do the elements work on the consciousness of readers?
3. Identify three places where Hollingsworth connects ideas for readers, where she leads readers from one idea to the next. Why is or isn't her strategy effective?
4. Hollingsworth generally avoids first-person pronouns in her essay. When she uses them (such as in her opening sentence and in ¶5), she uses the plural *we* and *us* instead of the singular *I* and *me*. What is the effect of these plural pronouns on readers? Why might Hollingsworth have decided to use the plural instead of the singular? What is the effect created when she does use the singular *I* in ¶7?
5. Study Hollingsworth's use of subjects and verbs. Choose two sentences in which the verbs are especially lively, and explain how they communicate an idea that is important to the main point.

Exploring Ideas

1. In groups or alone, decide which additional detail of the image Hollingsworth could discuss. How would the additional detail strengthen her analysis?

2. Look up "dramatic irony" and explain Hollingsworth's statement, "In classic dramatic irony, we see the looming, or probable, reality that neither child nor mother can imagine in the bedroom." How is this irony important to Hollingsworth's main point?

3. With a group of peers, examine all the details of an ad, and then decide: What is the main idea of the ad? How does it encourage viewers to think or act? How do images help readers understand and accept the ad's main idea? How do text and image work together? Seek out and explain the importance of one hidden, or less obvious, detail.

4. How are you like an ad? What visual details have you created about yourself, and what main idea do you want these details to communicate?

Ideas for Writing

1. Hollingsworth says, "In this sense, the ad does what numerous other campaigns do: It scares us." Find a particular ad and explain how it scares us. What vulnerability does it take aim at? How does it strike fear? What does the ad achieve beyond scaring viewers?

2. Find an ad that you consider to be educational. How does the ad connect with readers beyond providing educational information? How does it get the readers' attention? How does it appeal to the readers' basic values or beliefs?

If responding to one of these ideas, go to the Analysis section of this chapter to begin developing ideas for your essay.

Invention

Most of the images that constitute everyday life are meant to prompt an idea or emotion—not to be analyzed. (This, say many scholars, is all the more reason to analyze them.) In developing ideas for this project, we have to work against what most images ask of us. We have to see into them, into how they work. We have to break down the parts, and then reassemble them in our own minds to understand how they impact viewers. The following sections are designed to help you through this process, specifically, to find a particular image (in Point of Contact), to examine the image closely and understand its relationship to viewers (in Analysis), to develop a focused point (in Thesis), and to develop support for that point (in Rhetorical Tools). The Invention Questions in each section are not meant to be answered directly in your final essay, but to prompt inventive thinking and intensive writing.

Point of Contact

Images are everywhere. And every image contains more meaning than we might initially imagine. Explore the following possibilities to find a specific image for your own analysis. Consider all the elements of the image: the pictures, text, colors, placement, models, clothing, blank space, audience, and even the surrounding materials such as stories and columns.

Print Advertisements

Print ads (see Figure 7.3) range from dense collages of pictures and words to a single image with one slogan. Browse any magazine or newspaper. Also consider print advertisements that lurk in more inconspicuous places, such as your credit card bill, a public bathroom, a phone book, a calendar, and so on.

© Volkswagen of America, Inc. Image Courtesy of The Advertising Archives

Advertising Archives

Figure 7.3 Print advertisements

David Pollack/K.J. Historical/Corbis

Blue Lantern Studio/Corbis

Figure 7.4 Posters

Posters

Most often, posters work like billboards. They are designed to catch a passing eye—to shout loudly enough so that anyone in the vicinity will notice the message (see Figure 7.4).

Internet Images

Images found on the Internet range from shocking photos of war to wondrous shots of outer space. Consider sites such as Newsmap (newsmap.jp) or Buzztracker.org in which stories of the world are represented graphically (see Figure 7.5).

2005 Chin Music Press. Used with permission

Figure 7.5 Internet image

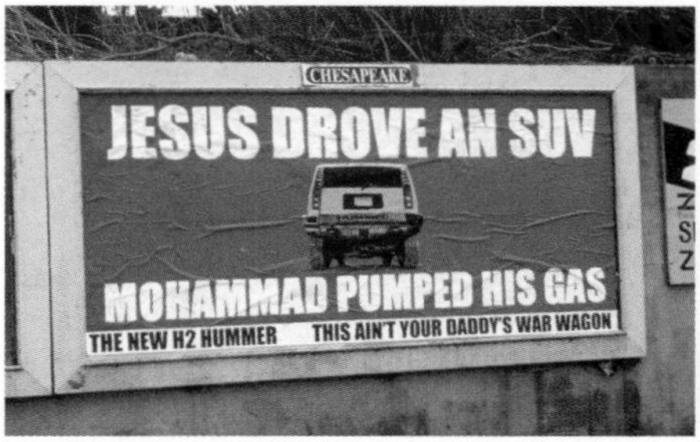

Ron English/Popaganda

Bill Aron/PhotoEdit

Figure 7.6 Billboards

Billboards

Billboards are made to distract people, to yank attention away from the road (see Figure 7.6). Examine one closely to understand how it works toward that goal.

Analysis

Analyzing an image involves looking at the content (the subject matter) of the image, and then considering the particular visual elements, such as shapes, lines, and colors. Because any image consists of various elements, it can be helpful to remember four main layers: those elements accounting for the image's visual effect, the text, the subtext, and the context. Then consider how the layers work together.

Image

Even the simplest image contains the following elements:

Content The subject, information, or objects that are pictured. Everything within an image is important—from the largest to the tiniest object or detail. They all figure into the nature of the image; they all impact the consciousness of viewers.

Framing What has been placed within the boundaries of the image. Whether by choice, by accident, or by necessity, certain objects are included in the image while other objects are left out. Whether a photographer's (or designer's) deliberate move or pure accident, the framing impacts what is seen. It closes in on a particular range of objects and closes out the rest of the world.

Composition The way the visual elements of the image are arranged within the frame. Some objects stand in the foreground, others in the background or off to the side. Objects may be crowded, touching, overlapping, far apart. The spatial relationships can be both aesthetic—that is, pleasing to the eye—and meaningful. Composition also includes matters of light and darkness, lines, shapes, focus, and so on.

Focus The degree to which some areas of the image are sharp (or clear) and other areas are blurry. The focus impacts the movement of the eye. Sharper objects automatically attract attention away from blurry or fuzzy objects, thereby prompting viewers to see and understand the image in a particular way.

Lighting The degree to which some areas of the image are brightly lit and other areas are in low light or in shadows. An entire image may be dark or light, or some parts of the image may be in shadows or in bright light. Although shadows and light may be a natural consequence of a sunny day or a tall building blocking a photographer's light, the way the elements are lit creates an effect. Like careful planning, accidents also can produce strong images.

Texture How the image, or certain objects in the image, looks like it would feel if you could touch it. Images can suggest, or appear to have, texture. Just as tree bark and a marble countertop have different textures, visual images can suggest how they might feel if touched. Even if content, framing, composition, and such are all the same in two images, a smooth or rough texture may suggest a different idea about what is being pictured.

Angle and Vantage Point The angle at which the image is presented, or the vantage point or perspective from which a photograph, for example, is taken. Every image suggests a perspective. A photograph of a politician speaking with a crowd of supporters behind him suggests one meaning, while a shot of the same politician from behind and speaking to a mere handful of people suggests something else. A low-angle shot of the politician might suggest power; a high-angle shot looking down on the politician might suggest weakness.

Significance The collective meaning or impact of all the elements. Our ultimate goal is to figure out how all these elements work together to express ideas, just as the elements of an essay, novel, poem, or movie work together. When analyzing, we focus on one element at a time, but we are always looking at more than one element. For example, when we consider how an image is framed or composed, we are also considering the image's content. When we talk about composition, we are looking at how these various formal elements work together. All elements of an image must be considered, yet some elements will have more impact than others.

Consider the image of the man playing guitar (Figure 7.7): A man, presumably a farmer, plays an acoustic guitar in an open field. The background is nearly empty except for the lower part of a distant building. The distance behind the man matters—perhaps as much as the man himself. Directly beside him sits a small electric amplifier. The man and the amplifier—adjacent, focused, well lit, in the foreground—seem like a mixed pair, like they do not belong together, especially surrounded by an open field of dirt. But all the elements of the image insist that we see them together. Even the angle—seeing both of them from the front—makes us (the viewers) feel like an audience. What do all these elements prompt us to think, to imagine, to assume? What feelings are conjured by the interplay of the elements?

Dawn M. Turner/MorgueFile

Figure 7.7

Activity

In a small group, analyze the image of the man playing guitar (Figure 7.7). Consider content, framing, composition, focus, lighting, texture, angle and vantage point, and the significance of all the elements.

Examine the image you have chosen for your project. The following questions will help you analyze how the image works to affect viewers.

- **Content**

  What content—subject or information—is presented in the image? What are the main objects in the image? Of the main elements, which appear to be most prominent? Which are less prominent?

- **Framing**

  How is the image framed? What has been placed within the boundaries of the image? What has not been included? How do the boundaries influence your focus?

- **Composition**

  How are the elements of the image arranged? Are visual elements symmetrical (distributed evenly) or asymmetrical (not distributed evenly)? Are elements touching, overlapping, close together, or far apart? Are elements above or below each other, or to the left or the right of each other? What is in the background? What might the relationship of elements encourage someone to think?

- **Focus**

  How is the image focused? That is, what objects or areas appear most clear or sharp? What objects or areas are not clear? Is anything unusual or striking about the focus? How does the focus draw your attention? How does it affect the relationship of certain elements?

- **Lighting**

  How is the image lit? That is, what objects or areas are well lit? What areas are dark, or in shadow? Is the light harsh or soft? Is there a contrast of tones from light to dark? What is darkest, and what is lightest? How does the lighting affect what is pictured? How might different lighting change the image?

- **Texture**

  What is the texture of the image? If you could touch what is pictured, how would it feel? How does the photograph's texture relate to its content?

- **Angle and Vantage Point**

  From what angle is the photograph taken? Is it straight-on? Is it exaggerated? How does the angle affect the composition of the image? That is, are some elements more in the foreground or background? Are some more prominent?

You may, in your analysis, consider other elements as well. Colors, for example, may be subdued or bright and splashy. Such details may have significance.

Text

Images—such as photographs, diagrams, and charts—often work in conjunction with written text. In advertising or on posters, meaning is often generated by an interaction of image and text. When text accompanies an image, the two fuse into a single idea. But we can pull them apart and see how they work. For instance, Cameron Johnson examines the way text gives meaning to the image of an SUV:

> The 4Runner descends a rocky cliff—a near-vertical drop—and rocky terrain stretches for miles into the background. The main text proclaims: "No intelligent life out here. Just you." (One wonders if Toyota's marketing executives are terribly ironic or terribly shortsighted.) At the bottom of the ad, a smaller message says, "Daily stops to the middle of nowhere." Certainly, most Americans live nowhere close to the middle of

> nowhere. Very few people will ever get to a place where they are surrounded by nothing but rocks, and even fewer will ever aim a truck down a cliff.

In Johnson's case, the text is a crucial part of the image. The persuasive power of the image is intensified (even generated) by the short burst of text. And to make matters a little more complicated, text often speaks back to or depends on other texts to make meaning. That is, the text exists in dialogue with other texts—a quality called *intertextuality*. As we explain in Chapter 6 (page 183), text usually generates meaning because it echoes other texts—other stories, songs, poems, declarations, and documents. This *intertextual* echoing shows up consistently in the world of advertising, where short bits of text carry as much meaning as possible.

Examine the image you have chosen for your project. If the image has accompanying text, answer the following questions:

- How does the text correlate with the significance of the image?
- How do content, framing, composition, focus, lighting, texture, angle, and vantage point help to convey the ideas?
- Does the text echo other texts? (How does the language depend on our familiarity with other texts?)

As we explain in the previous chapter (page 184), subtext is a layer of unwritten ideas that lurk beneath the written words. Just like text, images also have subtext. Even if they have no written text, they still imply ideas. In advertising, images and text often work together to suggest a layer of subtext. Subtext is invisible, so finding it is hard work. We have to look closely at all the elements of image and text and connect them with common values and assumptions. Notice Cameron Johnson's exploration of subtext:

> **Besides the obvious statements or ideas, what subtle assumptions or beliefs are suggested by (or lurking in) the image?**
>
> To accept anything in the ad as attractive, viewers must believe they are independent—that they have lives of rugged off-road exploration. Maybe it isn't so literal. That is, people might not see themselves driving a truck down a cliff, but they have to believe in the value of rugged self-determination—let's add physical in there: rugged, physical self-determination. The ad relies on that. It only makes sense (especially within the pages of *Time* magazine!) if readers are caught up in that set of beliefs. The ad implies: "Hey . . . you're the type to bust loose and you need a vehicle to get you where you're going." (Of course, most people don't bust loose—especially the people who can afford such vehicles.)

Examine the image you have chosen for your project and answer the following questions:

- What seems to be the main idea of the image?
- Besides the obvious statements or ideas, what subtle assumptions or beliefs are suggested by (or lurking in) the image?
- How do content, framing, composition, focus, lighting, texture, angle, or vantage point suggest subtle assumptions or beliefs?

Context

Analyzing an image involves examining how the image relates to its context—the things and people surrounding it. We have all seen an image of the *Mona Lisa,* but how might our response to the painting change if we saw it in the Louvre, as shown in the top image below?

Specific Context The specific context is the real physical space that surrounds the image—the building, the magazine, the neighborhood, the campus, the wall, and so on. Every image is affected by the specific context in which it appears. In the images shown in Figure 7.8, da Vinci's *Mona Lisa* (the world's most reproduced work of art) is surrounded by different contexts. In the first image, the crowded room at the Louvre influences how the *Mona Lisa* is viewed and what it means. In the other images, the *Mona Lisa* has been recontextualized (recast in different graphic surroundings, even different clothes!). The contexts change how da Vinci's original image works.

Figure 7.8 *Mona Lisa* in different contexts.

© Matthew Jacques/Shutterstock.com

Library of Congress Prints and Photographs Division Washington, D.C [LC-DIG-highsm-12441]

Robert Cross/Chicago Tribune/MCT/Getty Images

Cultural Context Nothing exists without culture. Beyond the physical space surrounding an image, the broader culture provides meaning. The values and beliefs that shape everyday life also impact the way an image works—why it gets made, how it gets received.

In his analysis of an SUV ad, Cameron Johnson relies on the specific context (the magazine that published the ad) and the cultural context (the lifestyle of *Time* readers):

> If we were to examine this ad and then assess the demographics of the buying public, we might guess that it's a joke—or an attempt to ruin Toyota. But the ad obviously works. It conjures up an attractive un-reality for potential consumers. We also might guess that the ad appears in an outdoors magazine—perhaps *Ranchers Quarterly, Mountain Lion News,* or *Rock Slide Specialist.* But the ad appears in *Time*—a decidedly mainstream, middle-class periodical. The vast majority of its readers commute to work on urban streets and suburban highways—and descend the gradual paved slopes of parking garages. Given the distance between readers' actual lives and the ad's imagery, Toyota may have just as logically featured the landscape of Mars.

Examine the image you have chosen for your project and answer the following questions:

- What beliefs, attitudes, or morals does it support or appeal to?
- What beliefs, attitudes, values, or morals does it chafe against?
- What public concern does the image speak to?
- How might people benefit by exploring the possible meanings of the image?

In his response to the Invention Questions, Cameron Johnson comes to an easy conclusion about his image, a Toyota 4Runner.

> **What beliefs, attitudes, values, or morals does it support or appeal to?**
>
> That's easy. The image [for Toyota 4Runner] appeals to the value of independence, individualism. Americans like to think of themselves "out there" alone—doing it on the edge of the frontier. It's in our history. And . . . still . . . we're all caught up in that thinking. Many of our goods are sold to us with this basic belief in mind. We are enamored with the idea of ourselves driving across the open majesty of the country with no rules, no road, no official place to be. In the ad, the truck is aiming down a cliff (a flippin' cliff!) and no sign of civilization ruins the moment. (Apparently, that's a fun thing . . . a sign of one's independence, aiming an expensive truck down a cliff.) The print in the ad says, "No intelligent life out here. Just you." Besides that being pretty funny, it reinforces the appeal to independence. Apparently independence = off the road, off the beaten path.

Johnson is just beginning to get traction with his point. He discovers the main appeal in the ad, and the particular elements that drive the appeal.

Thinking Further

Whenever a question is easy to answer, writers should use that momentum and explore further. They should revel in the ease of the answer and then keep developing nuances, asking more questions. Notice, for instance, what happens when Cameron Johnson continues thinking. He goes beyond the initial answer (that the ad appeals to the idea of independence) and discovers the irony or absurdity of the image:

> What's weird about the appeal is this: Most people aren't at all independent. They follow rules, go to work every day, drive in the correct lanes, park in garages or metered spaces or yellow-lined areas. They trim their lawns to the exact length (about 1/2 inch within the presumed correct length for the neighborhood). They dress according to the rules of their generation. They certainly don't drive their expensive (and very clean) new trucks down cliffs. This ad (and every ad like it) is totally divorced from the real life most people lead. Most Americans are rule followers. We think what the media commentators (or government propaganda) tell us. We do what we can to stay in the lines. But the world of advertising makes it seem like we're all careening down cliffs, splashing through rivers, rockin' it out on the banks of some lake. It ain't true.

This paragraph of invention writing shows Johnson exploring ideas and discovering an insight that will drive the analysis for his essay. This is not Johnson's only invention writing though. Earlier invention helped him think his way up to this discovery. Just one paragraph or page of invention writing won't usually strike gold. Exploring, discovering, and developing ideas takes time and lots of thinking.

One trick to invention writing is to make sure you write in the spirit of invention. Your purpose is to explore, discover, and develop ideas. It is not to just write down what you think, report what you know, ask (but not answer) questions, or make an outline—these are some of the mistakes students make when they are trying to figure out what their invention writing is supposed to do. Invention writing is not when you write to communicate what you think or know to readers; instead, it is when you write to explore deeper into an idea, to figure out what else you might think.

Invention Workshop

In a small group, use the Invention Questions to explore your image in depth. First, share your image with others in your group. Then apply one of the Invention Questions. Once someone in the group offers a possible answer, record the response. Someone else in the group should then continue that thinking by asking how the first responder arrived at his or her point. Remember, your goal is to examine the image closely to discover insights about how particular elements impact viewers.

Thesis

The purpose of this project is to analyze how an image (or set of images) works to impact viewers. The analysis should reveal something that readers would not otherwise see or imagine. It should show the insides, the mechanics, of the image. Consider the following examples:

- In trendy music videos, the camera looks up from the ground at the performers, which reinforces the notion that the performers have power over, and speak down to, their audiences.
- Beyond the main image of the Cadillac, the sophisticated background elements make the pitch to potential consumers.
- Presidential campaign commercials rely on the imagery of middle-class America so that candidates will be seen as normal working Joes.

Notice that each statement explains the significance, the meaning or impact, of a particular element of the image. Take, for example, the third statement. It explains how *the imagery of middle-class America* (a particular element) casts the candidates as normal working Joes (the element's significance; its meaning or impact). A good thesis for this project has two important qualities:

1. A focus on a particular element, and
2. An explanation of its significance

Look over your invention notes and focus on a particular element (something in the content, the composition, the framing, etc.). Then explain its significance—how that element works to convey meaning or impact the viewers.

Common Thesis Problems

As in most writing projects, the more specific the claims, the more intensive the ideas will be. If you can point to a particular element in an image and explain how that element works, then you are probably on your way to a focused thesis. Notice the problems in the following statement:

> Many *Sports Illustrated* ads use women as the main focus.

It lacks significance and focus. It targets "many" ads and offers a sweeping statement about them—they use women. The statement does not explain how something in those ads works, how they influence people, or how the individual elements create messages.

The following statement also lacks focus:

> *Rolling Stone* magazine makes one thing clear: sex sells.
>
> *Rolling Stone* is a good-sized magazine—with a table of contents, album lists, pictures, ads, articles about politics, music reviews, movie reviews, and so on. Of course, someone could associate all those elements with sex, but the project would

probably lack serious analysis of particular elements. A writer with such a statement needs to look more closely at something specific in *Rolling Stone.*

Activity

Rewrite the preceding two statements so they are more focused. Consider the two important qualities:

1. A focus on a particular element, and
2. An explanation of its significance

Evolution of a Thesis

Thesis statements do not always evolve in a neat fashion, progressing from a broader to a more focused insight. Sometimes (maybe most times), they wander, circle back, and jump around as the writer tries to get traction. In the following, we can see Johnson searching out meaning through single sentences. He is trying to connect two things: a particular element of the ad and the meaning of that element for viewers. All of the following statements are attempts, some better than others, at forging that connection.

- SUV ads, like that for the Toyota 4Runner, appeal to Americans through natural imagery.
- Ads like the one for Toyota 4Runner give a vision of life that many Americans strive for.
- Even though most Americans' lives do not resemble the natural imagery of SUV ads, that imagery appeals to what many people imagine about themselves.
- The scenic imagery of SUV ads appeals to a lifestyle that most Americans imagine for themselves but rarely realize.
- The ad for Toyota 4Runner relies on natural imagery that is far outside the experience of most Americans, but the ads still have strong appeal.
- The ad for Toyota 4Runner reveals a trend in SUV advertising: The background imagery connects to an illusive vision of American life—one that is contrary to the situation or needs of most potential consumers.

Revising Your Thesis

Develop a working thesis statement that includes attention to a specific element of an image and explains its significance. Then in a small group, discuss each person's statement. Apply the following:

- Does the statement focus on a specific element (something in the content, composition, framing, angle, focus, etc.)? How could the specific element be narrower?
- Beyond the writer's statement, what is the significance (possible meaning or impact) of that specific element? (What else might it suggest about people, lifestyles, nature,

America, clothing, social class, race, gender, politics, domestic life, art, music, and so on?) Be creative. Imagine that the significance is not what people initially assume!

- Make a case for the most surprising or hidden significance in the image. Make a connection that seems, at first, outrageous. Try to convince others in the group that your point is valid.

Rhetorical Tools

For analyzing images, support comes in two general categories: (1) details from the image, and (2) evidence outside of the image. The first is essential. Readers will need to see how specific claims correspond to the image itself. The second category includes a wide variety of strategies and will help provide meaningful context to your points.

Using Details from the Image

Any close analysis relies on specific details of the subject. For instance, if you are analyzing an advertisement, readers would expect to see particular features of that ad and an explanation that connects those features to your main point. In her analysis, Rebecca Hollingsworth shows readers how details make meaning:

> Like mom, we look on as the young girl tries on one piece of clothing after another, suggested by the pink, white, and blue clothes draped over furniture in the background. The girl's jewelry—the chunky necklace and the dangly charm bracelet—and her sophisticated tie clash with her long, stringy pigtail braids and big white teddy bear in the background. The pink-and-white washed walls covered in a busy pastel pattern remind us that this is a child's room and that we are witnessing child's play.

Hollingsworth's analysis shows the power of subtle details that might get overlooked:

> As we watch the young girl over her mother's shoulder, we must confront the prevalence of this developmental disability in American children—and the very real possibility that our own child may be that 1 in 150.

Because we are looking over the mother's shoulder (at the girl from her mother's vantage point), the image confronts us with a real possibility—about American children and about *our own child.* Hollingsworth's careful analysis adds up to a main point:

> In this sense, the ad does what numerous other campaigns do: It scares us. But this one aims at a particularly vulnerable place: the intersection of our idealism and our fear. It contrasts deluded notions of success—defined here as becoming a top fashion designer—with a statistically harsh truth. We can no longer bask in the old *one in a million* cliché. Like the pretty imagery in the fictional bedroom, that number has been upstaged by a more demanding probability.

Likewise, Cameron Johnson uses the details of a specific magazine ad to illustrate his thesis that advertising images are out of sync with the reality of everyday life. Notice that he does not merely mention the details; he also explains how those details illustrate his point:

> Take, for example, a typical SUV ad, one for a Toyota 4Runner. The 4Runner descends a rocky cliff—a near-vertical drop—and rocky terrain stretches for miles into the background. The main text proclaims: "No intelligent life out here. Just you." (One wonders if Toyota's marketing executives are terribly ironic or terribly shortsighted.) At the bottom of the ad, a smaller message says, "Daily stops to the middle of nowhere." Certainly, most Americans live nowhere close to the middle of nowhere. Very few people will ever get to a place where they are surrounded by nothing but rocks, and even fewer will ever aim a truck down a cliff.

Return to any notes you generated from the Analysis section of this chapter. Ask yourself the following questions about the image:

- What details (about the content, focus, composition, framing, lighting, texture, angle, and significance) best illustrate my main point?
- What specific text best illustrates my main point?
- Does subtext help to support my main point?
- Does the context help to support my main point?

Using Other Evidence

In some ways, you are attempting to convince readers that your understanding of the image is reasonable. To this end, you can go beyond the image itself and allude to any related events, images, people, or behaviors in the present or past. Some of the readings in this chapter use cultural allusions (references to other well-known texts, films, pictures, photos, or events). For example, in his analysis of ad images, Cameron Johnson refers to broader cultural trends to support the claim that people are influenced deeply by the messages around them:

> Contrary to popular belief, humans are gregarious. We think and act in groups, according to historical trends. About every five years in America, kids laugh at what came five years earlier: "Look at that guy's jeans!" "Hey, check out the hairdo on her!" About every decade or so, certain social behaviors become extinct or come into favor: wearing hats, not wearing hats, getting married at 18, waiting to get married, having multiple sexual partners, being monogamous, and so on. And in the bigger spectrum of history, political

consciousness changes: from thinking Indians should die to forgetting they exist, from thinking women should stay home and breed to celebrating female CEOs. How do these trends occur?

Consider the following questions:

- How do cultural trends or events relate to the image I am analyzing?
- Does anything in history show how the image (or type of image) has influenced people?
- Can I create a scenario (a hypothetical situation) to illustrate my point about the image?
- Can I narrate a personal experience to show something important about the image?

Research

Using a periodical database (such as InfoTrac® College Edition) or an Internet search engine (such as Google), explore how others have discussed the image you are analyzing. Most likely, you won't find sources about the specific image (unless you are analyzing a historic piece of art or popular culture). However, you'll likely find sources about the type of image—whether an automobile ad, a billboard, a rural photo, and so on. For instance, if Cameron Johnson were exploring for outside sources, he might begin a keyword search with the following combinations:

sport utility vehicle *and* advertisement

sport and utility *and* vehicles *and* advertising

automobile *and* advertisements *and* nature

Of course, keyword searches are not an exact science. (They're not a science at all.) They are always attempts—and sometimes require several restarts with substitutions and small changes. For instance, changing automobile to car or ad to advertisement may yield significantly different results. For more assistance with using databases and online catalogs for research, see Chapter 14: Finding Sources.

Activity

Before drafting your essay, write out your thesis and main support in one paragraph. Then discuss your paragraph with several peers. How could the thesis be more focused and intense? What additional support strategies could help?

Revision

Your analysis should reveal something readers would not otherwise see or imagine. This involves inventing your way to a focused and insightful thesis and then using rhetorical tools to help readers understand and accept that thesis. Before exchanging your draft for peer review, return to the questions in the Analysis, Public Resonance, and Rhetorical Tools sections, and explore further from your new perspective (the perspective you developed last time you worked through those questions). See how you can improve your focus, insight, and support before getting feedback from a peer.

Peer Review

Write down what you think your analysis reveals, and then exchange drafts with at least one other writer. After reading your draft, the other writer should write responses to the following questions:

1. What did the analysis reveal? That is, what didn't you see or imagine about the image until you read the essay?
2. How might the thesis be more specific and revealing? Offer particular rewording, or a whole new direction, even if you think the thesis is good as is.
3. What additional details from the image might be used to strengthen or refocus the analysis?
4. Are there any blueprinting passages? Can they be eliminated? Suggest a strategy that keeps readers focused on the ideas rather than on the structure of the essay.
5. What sentences can be combined through subordination? Combine two sentences in the opening paragraph, subordinating one idea to the other. Combine at least two sentences elsewhere in the essay.
6. Consider the following vitality strategies explained in Chapter 19:
   - Mark any clichés. Explain how the cliché conceals or blurs thinking, and then suggest an alternative to the cliché.
   - Note any stilted language. Suggest an alternative approach to the passage.
   - Help the writer experiment with sentence length and brevity. Reconstruct one paragraph, extending some sentences and abbreviating others. Try to create intensity with shorter sentences.
   - Change vague nouns to specific nouns.
   - Change *be* verbs (*is, are, was, were*) to active verbs.
   - Change clauses to phrases.
   - Change phrases to words.
   - Combine sentences.
   - Repeat structures.
   - Intensify verbs.
7. What grammatical or proofreading issues make reading difficult or create small distractions for readers?

Reflection

Before moving on to another writing project, reflect on this one. The following questions ask you to consider your own rhetoric. The writing you do in response to these questions is sometimes called *meta-writing*, which is when you take a step back to think and write about your writing. Getting this distance can help you see and learn new things, even after you've written your essay.

1. What is the essay's thesis?
2. How does your analysis of a particular visual element (or several elements) reveal a new way of understanding the image?
3. How does a particular reference to evidence from outside the image help readers understand and accept your thesis? If you didn't use any outside evidence, what outside evidence might you have used and why?
4. What is the essay's most intense passage and why?
5. How did the essay evolve through the process of inventing, drafting, and revising?
6. How did writing this essay help you develop as a writer and thinker?

Beyond the Essay: Video Briefing

1. "What was your analyzing images essay about?" We are often asked such questions, not only about essays we have written, but also about other aspects of our lives. A boss may ask, "What happened last night with the customer who called this morning to complain?" A professor may ask, "How is your writing project coming along?" A family member may ask, "How'd Cindy's softball game go?" In some cases we can simply answer, "Not much" or "Fine." But sometimes we must give a clear and accurate account of events or an appraisal of progress—a briefing—either verbally or in writing.

   Some briefings are impromptu, such as those called for by the previous situations: we don't have time to prepare and must answer on the spot. Other briefings are more prepared and formal: for example, each day the president's press secretary briefs the press on important issues.

   For practice with briefings, create a two-minute video briefing of your analyzing images essay. Your briefing should include your main idea (thesis), your main supporting ideas, and any important details necessary to fill in any gaps for the audience. You may decide to write out the entire text of your briefing. If you do, try not to simply read the text for your briefing. Or, you may decide to jot down key points. However you do it, record your briefing using a computer or smartphone and review and redo it until you are happy with your delivery.

   Consider including your video file as part of your essay.

2. In several paragraphs, explain how effectively your briefing communicates the ideas from your essay. For example, in what way does the video more effectively communicate your ideas? In what way is the essay more effective? How might viewing the video help someone better understand your essay, and why?

8 Making Arguments

The Kobal collection/Art Resource, NY

"Someone who makes an assertion puts forward a claim—a claim on our attention and to our belief."

—Stephen Toulmin

Argument is the art of persuading people how to think. This may sound absurd since most people, we hope, already know how to think, or at least *what* to think about particular issues. But with argument, we can change how people view things, even slightly, and so affect how they approach and process ideas.

Arguments come to us in different forms. We hear them given in speeches, debates, and informal discussions. We hear them every day on talk shows, in break rooms, college hallways, and public meeting places like restaurants and pubs. Arguments get delivered through action. They come explicitly in protests, parades, sit-ins, labor strikes, and elections. They also come in more subtle forms: People donate to charities (thereby expressing their favor of a particular cause); they patronize or boycott a particular store; they choose not to vote (thereby expressing their stance against the entire political process). Arguments get made through art in all media: sculpture, painting, music, and so on. And arguments are major elements of literature. For example, it has been said that Aldous Huxley's book *Brave New World* argues against the extremes of materialism and industrialization and that Kate Chopin's *The Awakening* argues for a new vision of women's identity. Even poems offer arguments: Walt Whitman's masterpiece *Leaves of Grass* argues for the value of common American workers and their common language.

People in all occupations make or deal with arguments. For example, a human resources manager for a packaging company argues in a report that more supervisors should be hired in the coming fiscal year; several department store sales associates collectively write a letter to store and regional managers in which they claim current scheduling practices minimize sales commissions; the public affairs director of a major automobile company argues that a new advertising campaign should not be offensive to a particular demographic group; the lawyers for a major computer software company argue in a district court that the company's business practices comply with federal antitrust laws. In academia, argument is everywhere:

- The biology faculty at a state university argues for the need to study cloning and to petition the administration for more leeway to do research.
- A historian argues about the number of Native Americans on the continent before European settlers so that people more deeply understand history.
- A psychologist argues that Freudian analysis is overused and that new strategies for exploring patients' psychological makeup should be further developed.
- College administrators argue for more state funds for their schools.
- Students in an architecture class argue that a particular structural design is more sound than competing designs.
- Students in a nursing program must convince others that a new staff management technique is valuable for large hospitals.

In any situation, those who can deliver the most sophisticated and engaging arguments tend to have the most influence. Of course, a sophisticated and engaging argument involves a great deal of strategy. For instance, in academic argument, blatant personal attacks, outright aggression, and sugar-coated language are not valued, nor are empty phrases ("don't question what's in my heart") and mean-spiritedness ("your ideas are simply idiotic"). But although academic writers are not out to squash an opponent or cuddle up to audiences, they do more than simply present their opinions. In providing a new way of thinking about a particular topic, academic writers must also analyze others' ideas and explain how their own claims relate to those of others.

This chapter will help you discover an argumentative topic, explore that topic in depth, develop a sophisticated argument, and communicate your argument in writing. The following essays will provide insight into various argumentative strategies. For example, every argument has a main claim (thesis) that can be expressed in a single sentence, and particular support strategies such as examples, scenarios, and so on, that unpack that claim. As you read, look for the main claim (it may be explicitly stated or implied) and the support strategies that help readers understand and accept it. After reading the essays, you can find a topic in one of two ways:

1. Go to the Point of Contact section to find a topic from everyday life, or
2. Choose one of the Ideas for Writing that follow the essays.

After you find a topic, go to the Analysis section to begin developing your argument.

Readings

The Dog Delusion

April Pedersen

Sometimes writers examine the behaviors and reflexes that seem most harmless. When a trend seems uncritically accepted in everyday life, writers step forward. In this essay, April Pedersen, a writer and illustrator living in Reno, Nevada, goes after a seemingly innocent behavior: dog idolization. As the argument develops, Pedersen deals with a range of opposing positions and assumptions.

There was a time when "Dog is my co-pilot" was merely a fun slap at the "God is my co-pilot" bumper sticker, and it was funny precisely *because* nobody would ever think to elevate their dog to such a height. Within the past decade, however, pets—primarily dogs—have soared in importance. ("Dog is my co-pilot" is now the slogan of *Bark*, a magazine of dog culture, and the title of an anthology—published by *Bark*'s editors—billed as essays, short stories, and expert commentaries that explore "every aspect of our life with dogs.") Canines, with their pack instincts and trainability, are by far the most likely pet to be anthropomorphized as a family member, a best friend, or a "fur baby," treated accordingly with gourmet meals, designer apparel, orthopedic beds, expensive therapy, and catered birthday parties. Some people even feel (and in some cases, demonstrate) that their dogs are worth dying for. Others say the animal lovers are going too far.

In a Pew Research Center study, 85 percent of dog owners said they consider their pet to be a member of their family. However the latest trend is to take that a step further in seeing

April Pedersen

April Pedersen, "The Dog Delusion," from *The Humanist Magazine*, November/December 2009. Reprinted with permission of the author.

the animal as a child. A company that sells pet health insurance policies has dubbed the last Sunday in April as "Pet Parents Day." Glance through magazines like *Bark, Cesar's Way* (courtesy of "Dog Whisperer" Cesar Millan), and other mainstream publications, and the term "pet parent" crops up regularly. The "my-dogs-are-my-kids" crowd isn't being tongue-in-cheek, either. They act on their beliefs, buying Christmas presents, photos with Santa, cosmetic surgery, and whatever-it-takes medical care for their animal. In fact having a puppy, claimed one "mother," is "exactly the same in all ways as having a baby." And while pushing a dog around in a stroller would have gotten you directions to a mental health facility twenty years ago, today it's de rigueur to see a canine in a stroller (or a papoose), and some passersby are downright disappointed to discover a human infant inside.

Who's to say what a pet's value is (aside from the purchase price)? Shouldn't people be free to spend whatever they want on things for their dog? What real harm is there in believing one's schnauzer is a "child who never grows up?" The implications are more ridiculous and far reaching than you might expect. Take the widely held notion that dogs give us unconditional love and nonjudgmental loyalty. Praising dogs for being incapable of acting like bad people is not only junk logic, it turns the animal into an idealized (godlike?) version of ourselves, to be rewarded with all manner of pampering. How can the comparatively complex human being compete with creatures said to exude unwavering faithfulness, forgiveness, trust, love, and innocence? Pets are pegged as more loving, more pure, more giving, more devoted. They are implied to be our moral superiors for not stealing money, starting wars, or judging people by their physical appearance. They accept us for who we are, while we come across as scheming, judgmental malcontents who love on condition only. I have quite a collection of misanthropic utterances from dog lovers, most along the lines of "I'll take dogs over humans any day," and "dogs love without having an agenda!" It's no surprise that many dog lovers would rather be stranded on an island with a dog than with their spouse (or with any other person for that matter). Then there's the CEO who said he doesn't trust clients who don't have pets. How sadly similar to the religious who say they don't trust nonbelievers.

Further undermining humans, dogs trained for various tasks are routinely referred to as soldiers, officers, actors, therapists, heroes, or athletes. But a police dog simply can't know the moral difference between a stash of cocaine and an old sock. One of the most absurd examples of anthropomorphism I've seen was a funeral for a drug-sniffing dog. The sheriff's department went all out with a motorcade, flag-draped casket, bag pipers playing "Amazing Grace," a eulogy from a pastor, and a rose-adorned easel on which the dog's portrait rested. Officers from all across the Western United States paid their respects, and the service received heavy local media coverage. All this for an animal that couldn't even grasp what a "law" was.

"Dogs are for people who can't have kids," a gay newspaper columnist told me recently. It's true that homosexual (and straight) couples who can't or don't want children of their own often migrate towards dogs as child substitutes and view the arrangement as a different kind of family, but a family nonetheless. Such dog-based "families" may at first blush seem benign or even beneficial. After all, people with a family mentality are more likely to form stable, safe neighborhoods and have a vested interest in the community. Those without children may benefit from nurturing a living creature and learning to be less self-centered. But doesn't it make more evolutionary sense to want to care for the young of your own species over another species? Couples without kids for whatever reason could still opt to be foster parents, mentors, or Big Brothers/Sisters to make a positive difference in a child's life instead of funneling all their concerns into dogs. And what about devoting one's time to saving endangered species of animals (whose survival also affects that of humans)?

Yet each day dogs gain more and more importance, protection, and access to realms once reserved for humans. Michigan is considering a bill that would allow pet care as a tax write-off. What's next? Dogs counted as residents in the U.S. Census?

This shift in the status of dogs hasn't gone unnoticed by animal rights advocates. Already thirteen U.S. cities have ordinances that ditch "pet owner" for "pet guardian." The change is intended to be merely symbolic, its fans claim. If so, why make the effort? I worry it's a foot in the door to gradually desensitize society to the outlandish idea of pets being the equals of minor children. Allowing ourselves to glance down the slippery slope, we might foresee absurd lawsuits over injuries to pets, murder charges for those suspected of negligence in a pet's death, and laws requiring guardians to strap their fur kids into car seats, or to walk them twice a day, or giving any number of rights to the animals. Recently dog owners have begun to demand off-leash beaches and trails, under the premise that dogs have a "right" to run free. What's next, making spaying or neutering a crime, because pets should have the right to reproduce? Or allowing dogs to bite people or chase livestock in order to fulfill their right to behave as predators? Where would the "pet" line for special status be drawn? At gerbils? Ferrets? Canaries? Hermit crabs? The funny part is, not even the pet industry can decide if pets are children or property. In ads hawking pet supplies, dogs and cats are promoted as family members, loved ones, and babies. Yet the defense strategy, if sued over, say tainted pet food or a defective squeaky toy, is to focus only on the economic aspect of the pet.

Viewing dogs as our children extends to risking life and limb to save them as well. What would evolutionary psychologists make of healthy people of reproductive age leaping to their deaths into scalding hot springs, icy rivers, or smoke-filled infernos in an attempt to rescue a possibly neutered animal? Among surveyed pet owners, 93 percent, which includes the young and childless, would do just that. Of course, most dog owners fully expect their pet to save them, Lassie style, should the need arise. But if not trained for rescue work, most dogs would simply stare, hide, or eat the contents of their owner's picnic basket as their master sinks under the lake's surface. Cases abound where pets happen to save people from perilous situations, but they, the pets, were acting as animals, not as humans.

One can always argue that, from an environmental perspective, the pets-as-kids thing makes sense. With the human population reaching unsustainable numbers, pets can fill our desire to nurture without adding to the surplus of humans. Even so, dogs still eat a lot and produce a lot of waste (which has to be cleaned up unless the status lift requires potty training). And don't forget that dogs have to come from somewhere, and parents will show

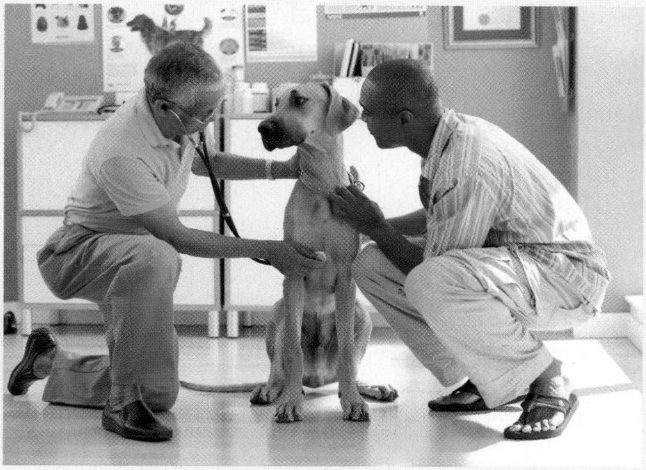

LWA-Dann Tardif/Corbis

preferences for certain breeds. Puppy mills would be happy to meet the increased demand for dogs, if it can be considered ethical in the best of circumstances to take puppies away from their mothers and litter mates and give them to another species to raise them. Interestingly, our popular pets such as the domestic dog play no balancing role in any ecosystem; they are human-developed and human-maintained. Even feral dogs prefer to hang around our villages, urban areas, and garbage dumps instead of returning to the woods to dance with wolves. And if too many people opted against having children in favor of pets, the result couldn't be good for economies; children are the future workforce, consumers, voters, tax payers, innovators, you name it.

Let's outsmart dogs a little by cutting back on the over-the-top stuff. The dogs won't notice. Funds spent on a dog's blueberry facial or in-room canine massage at a swanky hotel ($130 an hour) are about as close to setting a pile of cash on fire in front of a destitute person as I can imagine. Ditto on buying a sweater for an animal covered in fur, or a carob-coated eclair for a scat eater, or personalized cookies for the species that can't read (that would be all species except us). Certainly dogs can't visualize themselves as Homo sapiens of any age, and are becoming obese and even ill-mannered at the hands of their besotted owners. It makes no sense whatsoever to pour so much time, money, and emotion into an animal whose main "goal" in life is to leave its scent on a tree. Think about it—how would you like to be a dog? To be unable to talk, write, or question. To look upon a masterpiece of art without an ounce of admiration, to gaze at the starry night without an iota of wonder, to see a book and have not the slightest inclination to open it, or stare without comprehension at a voting booth.

It's fine to enjoy a pet. I've had several myself, including a cat that lived eighteen years. When his kidneys failed, a $12,000 kidney transplant was off the radar (a case can be made that such surgery on an animal is unethical anyway), and I didn't consider him to be my son. This need not diminish pets. We can enjoy them for what they are, without the anthropomorphic delusion.

Writing Strategies

1. Plenty of pet owners would disagree with Pedersen's claims. Explain how Pedersen takes on opposing views. Describe a particular passage and explain how she pushes back or refutes the opposition.
2. How does Pedersen concede to the opposition or qualify her points? Describe particular passages. (For information on concessions and qualifiers, see pages 279.)
3. Explain how Pedersen uses appeals to logic. (See pages 275 for an understanding of appeals.)
4. Read about logical fallacies on pages 280. How does Pedersen's use of *slippery slope* impact her argument?
5. Pedersen appeals to values throughout her argument. What particular appeals to value do you detect?

Exploring Ideas

1. Pedersen explains that "our popular pets such as the domestic dog play no balancing role in any ecosystem; they are human-developed and human-maintained." Why is this point important to her argument?
2. Explain why it would be wrong to characterize Pedersen as "anti-dog."
3. Pedersen compares some pet owners to "the religious who say they don't trust nonbelievers." Consider this comparison. How might dog ownership resemble religious belief or practice?
4. Even if you disagree vehemently with Pedersen, why might she have a sound position?

Ideas for Writing

1. Consider some other widely accepted form of ownership. How might it be undermining human development?
2. What particular aspect of dog ownership makes people more humane?

If responding to one of these ideas, go to the Analysis section of this chapter to begin developing ideas for your essay.

Cruelty, Civility, and Other Weighty Matters

Ann Marie Paulin

As with most engaging essays, Paulin's originates in personal circumstance. (See her invention writing on page 267.) Also, as with most engaging essays, the writer extends her thinking into the public sphere. As you read "Cruelty, Civility, and Other Weighty Matters," notice how Paulin puts forth an argument while keeping herself in the background, only briefly referring to herself in the essay's introduction and conclusion. As you will see, Paulin goes beyond the increasingly common argument against the media's portrayal of women; she reveals something about the subtle effects of that portrayal. Paulin, who teaches English and gender studies at Owens Community College in Toledo, Ohio, shows that a writer's voice matters—that savvy use of voice actually creates layers to an argument. That is, her voice rehumanizes the issue and the people involved. If the media have dehumanized "fat people," Paulin does more than argue against the media; she strikes back with an intense, multifaceted presence.

I swear, if I have to sit through one more ad proclaiming that life is not worth living if you aren't thin, I'll slug somebody. So much for the theory that fat people are jolly. But, contrary to what magazines, talk shows, movies, and advertisements proclaim, we aren't all a bunch of sorrowful, empty losers with no friends and no self-esteem, either. As with most complex issues—religion, politics, human relationships—most of what we see in mass media is hugely oversimplified and, therefore, wrong. So, if many of us recognize the media are notorious for getting things less than accurate, you might wonder why I let these images bother me so much. Well, if you were one of the millions of fat Americans living in a culture where you are constantly depicted as some sort of weepy loser, ill-dressed buffoon, or neutered sidekick, your good nature might wear a bit thin as well. But far more important than my ill temper is a creepy sense that these inaccurate images have shifted our vision of what is important in life way out of whack, so far out that people are being hurt. What I'm proposing here is that we need to get some perspective on this issue.

First of all, let me make it clear that I'm not advocating that everyone in America go out and get fat. According to the news media, we are doing that very handily on our own, in spite of all the messages to the contrary and the shelves of diet food in every supermarket. (One of my colleagues came by today with a newspaper article on the Krispy Kreme Donut chain; evidently, Americans eat three million Krispy Kreme donuts each day. We may talk tofu, but we gobble glazed.) Americans all need to work on eating healthier and getting some exercise. Of course, the thin fanatics claim to advocate a healthy lifestyle as well, but I question how healthy people are when they are living on low-calorie chocolate milk drinks, or taking herbal supplements containing goodness knows what, or loading up on the latest wonder diet pill. Remember Fen-phen?

And most diets don't work. An essay by Rebecca Puhl, Ph.D., and Chelsea Heuer, MPH, in the *American Journal of Public Health,* cites studies which found:

> Most weight losses are not maintained and individuals regain weight after completing treatment. Patients who have lost weight through lifestyle modification typically regain 30% to 35% of their lost weight during the year following treatment, and regain most (if not all) of their lost weight within five years. ("Obesity Stigma" 1021)

The authors go on to quote from a study by Mann, et al. "Dieters who gain back more weight than they lost may very well be the norm, rather than an unlucky minority" (qtd. in Puhl and Heuer 1021). My point here is not to argue that overweight people should not try to lose weight for health reasons. Indeed, even a modest weight loss of ten percent of a person's body weight is beneficial to one's health (Puhl and Heuer, "Obesity Stigma" 1021). But such modest weight loss, while healthy, is rarely enough to earn a person fashionably thin status. And despite what the cultural messages suggest, most of us fat folks are trying to eat more sensibly, but the environment does play a role. In a culture where most of us are rushed from

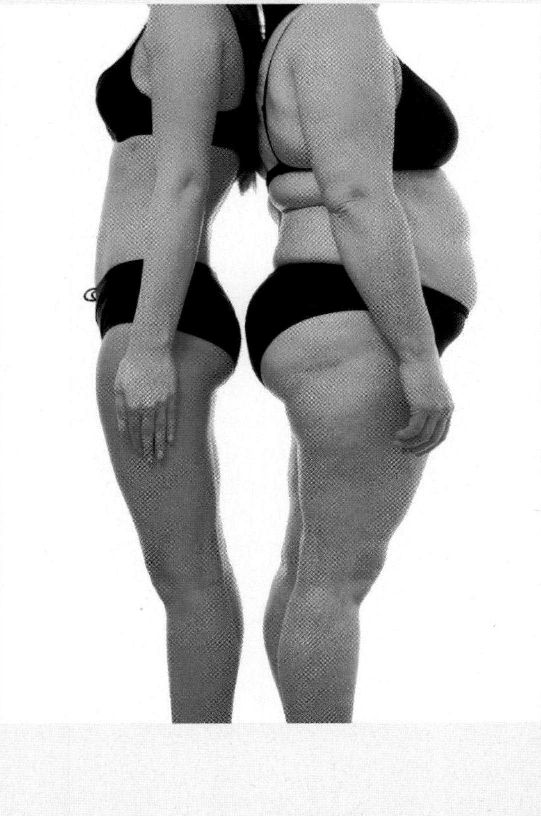

work to classes to other activities, the temptation to grab fast food is huge. Sugary or fatty foods are often available in grab and go packages that are so much easier to take to work or eat in the car than making a healthy snack. And, there is evidence to suggest we may even be wired to prefer junk food. Brownell and colleagues, in an essay in *Health Affairs,* cite studies which show: "Animals given access to food high in sugar and fat—even when healthy food is freely available—consume calorie-dense, nutrient-poor food in abundance, gain a great deal of weight, and exhibit deteriorating health" (379). I know, I know. We aren't rats. We are thinking beings, but this article goes on to point out that it is not so different for people: "Research has shown consistently that people moving from less to more obese countries gain weight, and those moving to less obese countries lose weight" (379).

So we are surrounded by a culture, even an infrastructure, that encourages obesity, yet the culture also breeds a prejudice against fat people. Various articles and news magazine programs have reported that Americans of all sizes make far more than simple aesthetic judgments when they look at a fat person. Fat people are assumed to be lazy, stupid, ugly, lacking in self-esteem and pride, devoid of self-control, and stuffed full of a host of other unpleasant qualities that have nothing to do with the size of a person's belly or thighs. But, as anyone who has ever been the victim of such prejudice can tell you, the impact such foolish notions have is real and harmful. For example, Marilyn Wann, in her book *Fat! So?,* cites an experiment in which "[r] esearchers placed two fake personal ads, one for a woman described as '50 pounds overweight' and the other for a woman described as a drug addict. The drug addict received 79 percent of the responses" (59). So, in spite of the agony addiction can cause to the addict and those who love her, people would rather get romantically involved with an addict than a fat person. And not much has changed. In a 2008 article, "The Stigma of Obesity: A Review and Update," Puhl and Heuer report:

> One study asked college students (N=449) to rank order six pictures of hypothetical sexual partners, including an obese partner, a healthy partner, and partners with various disabilities (including a partner in a wheelchair, missing an arm, with a mental illness, or described as having a history of sexually transmitted diseases. Both men and women ranked the obese person as the least desirable sexual partner compared to the others. (10)

While it is certainly good news to see that people can look beyond disabilities, such as a wheelchair or a missing arm, and see the value of the whole human being, it is distressing that Americans refuse to do the same for a person's weight. Why would anyone want to date someone who will land them in the STD clinic? How dangerous is that? And yet, such a person is clearly seen as a better romantic choice than a heavy person. Here is a case where weight prejudice is certainly more dangerous to the person with the prejudice than it is to the fat person.

5 Another area of discrimination based on weight is in employment, both in getting hired in the first place and in receiving equal pay for equal work. In 1998, Wann pointed out that the average fat woman earns about $7000 less per year than her thinner sisters (80). Today, things are still not improving. As of 2004, a study from the National Longitudinal Survey of

Youth found that obese men and women suffered a "wage penalty" for their excess weight. For men, wages ranged from 0.7–3.4% less than their slimmer coworkers, while for women the wage losses ranged from 2.3 to 6.1% (qtd. in Puhl and Heuer, "The Stigma of Obesity" 10). Here, as in other areas, we find that obese women are penalized more by society than obese men. Either way, in many jobs, a person's weight has nothing to do with the quality of their performance. In my case, I teach English at a community college. Jobs in academia require an advanced degree, so I happen to have a Ph.D., which has nothing to do with my body size, unless you want to count the weight I gained from thousands of hours sitting reading, sitting at a keyboard, sitting grading papers.

At the least, given the reports and studies, we can conclude that weight prejudice is not merely aesthetic judgment. It's an alarming trend, just like obesity itself, that hurts real people. When people are denied a place to live or a means of support not because of any bad behavior or lack of character or talent on their part but because of someone else's wrongheaded notions, then we need to get our minds straightened out.

The messages are particularly insidious when they suggest that being thin is more important than a man's or, more often, a woman's relationships with her loved ones or even than her health. The media churn the images out, but the public too often internalizes them. For example, in one commercial for Slim Fast, the woman on the ad is prattling on about how she had gained weight when she was pregnant (seems to me, if you make a person, you ought to be entitled to an extra ten pounds) and how awful she felt. Then there is a shot of this woman months later as a thin person with her toddler in her yard. She joyously proclaims that Slim Fast is "the best thing that ever happened to me!" The best thing that ever happened to her?! I thought I heard wrong. What about that little child romping by her heels? Presumably, there is a daddy somewhere for that little cherub. What about his role in her life? The thought that losing that weight is the most important thing that ever occurred in her life is sad and terrifying. It's even worse for the folks who share that life with her. I kept hoping that was not what she meant. I'm sure her family is really most important. But she didn't say, "Next to my baby, Slim Fast is the best thing that ever happened to me." Advertisers don't spend millions of dollars creating ads that don't say what they intend them to; this message was deliberate. Granted, this is only one ad, but the message is clear: The consumer is the center of the universe, and being thin is the only way to ensure that universe remains a fun place to live. The constant repetition of this message in various forms does the damage to the humans who watch and learn.

While we can shrug off advertisements as silly, when we see these attitudes reflected among real people, the hurt is far less easy to brush away. For instance, in her essay, "Bubbie, Mommy, Weight Watchers and Me," Barbara Noreen Dinnerstein recalls a time in her childhood when her mother took her to Weight Watchers to slim down and the advice the lecturer gave to the women present: "She told us to put a picture of ourselves on the 'fridgerator of us eating and looking really fat and ugly. She said remember what you look like. Remember how ugly you are" (347).

I have a problem with this advice. First, of course, it is too darn common. Fat people are constantly being told they should be ashamed of themselves, of their bodies. And here we see another of those misconceptions I mentioned earlier: the assumption that being fat is the same as being ugly. There are plenty of attractive fat people in the world, as well as a few butt-ugly thin ones, I might add. Honestly, though, the real tragedy is that while few people in this world are truly ugly, many agonize over the belief that they are. Dr. Pipher reported: "I see clients who say they would rather kill themselves than be overweight" (91). Pipher wrote of these attitudes in 1995, but there is not much evidence to suggest we have become any more reasonable or sensible. In fact, in the article "Stigma and Discrimination in Weight Management and Obesity," Brownell and Puhl cite a 2001 study which showed that "28% of teachers in one study said that becoming obese is the worst thing that can happen to a person" (21). Statements like this make me despair for my profession. We are supposed to encourage critical thinking, not mindlessly parrot nonsense and pass it on to the younger generation. And if people think being fat is the worst thing that can happen, they have not watched the world news lately. How would people feel if the attitude was reversed: *The worst thing you can be is thin. All those skinny students must be lazy and stupid. They haven't got enough sense to eat enough or to look the way we want them to. Why bother with them?* And don't think that idea doesn't apply to fat prejudice. Brownell and Puhl cite another study that shows "controlling for income and grades, parents provide less college support for their overweight children than for their thin children" (21). What is up with that? A person's weight certainly has nothing to do with his or her intellect or curiosity about the world. Plus, based on the data I've reported so far, we plus size folks need all the education we can get just to struggle up to a living wage.

10 And don't think teachers are the only educated people with crazy ideas about overweight folks. Based on my research, the medical profession is full of people who despise us. "Stigma and Discrimination in Weight Management and Obesity" reports that "24% of nurses say they are 'repulsed' by obese persons" (21). That's a virulently negative attitude to get from someone upon whom your life may depend. And according to Puhl and Heuer, things are just as depressing with the doctors: "In a study of over 620 primary care physicians, 50% viewed obese patients as awkward, unattractive, ugly, and noncompliant" ("Stigma of Obesity" 4). But how many people are willing to be compliant with someone who makes them feel awkward, unattractive, and ugly? The article goes on to explain that "one-third of the sample [of doctors] further characterized obese patients as weak-willed, sloppy, and lazy" (4). That's a lot of judgments to make after a ten-minute office visit. Shoot, my doctor is a republican, and if I'm willing to overlook that, the least he can do is overlook a few extra pounds. But, all kidding aside, this prejudice may have real and dangerous effects. Overweight people often do not seek medical care, especially preventive care. Puhl and Heuer go on to report:

> Several studies show that obese persons are less likely to undergo age-appropriate screenings for breast, cervical, and colorectal cancer. Furthermore, research shows that lower

> rates of preventive care exist independently of factors that are typically associated with reduced health care use, such as less education, lower income, lack of health insurance, and greater illness burden. ("Stigma of Obesity" 7)

This bullying of the overweight is not only coming from professional and public life. Sadly many people face the cruelest ridicule from family, those we count on most for love and support. Another example of this bullying comes from Pipher's book *Hunger Pains: The Modern Woman's Tragic Quest for Thinness.* Pipher recounts a conversation she overheard one day in a dress shop:

> I overheard a mother talking to her daughter, who was trying on party dresses. She put on each dress and then asked her mother how she looked. Time after time, her mother responded by saying, "You look just awful in that, Kathy. You're so fat nothing fits you right." The mother's voice dripped with disgust and soon Kathy was crying. (89)

Pipher goes on to suggest that Kathy's mother is a victim of the culture, too, because she realizes how hard the world will be on her fat daughter. Unfortunately, what she doesn't realize is how much better her daughter's quality of life would be if she felt loved by her mother. Puhl and Heuer cite the results of a 2006 study of 2,449 overweight and obese women. "Participants were provided with a list of 22 different individuals and asked how often each individual had stigmatized them because of their weight. Family members were the most frequent source of weight stigma, reported by 72% of participants" (qtd. in "Stigma of Obesity" 10).

And the familial insensitivity doesn't stop at adulthood. In Camryn Manheim's book *Wake Up! I'm Fat,* the actress discusses her battle with her weight. She expected many of the difficulties she encountered from people in the entertainment industry, which is notorious for its inhuman standards of thinness for women. But when she gained some weight after giving up smoking, she was stunned when her father told her she should start smoking again until she lost the weight (78). In *The Invisible Woman: Confronting Weight Prejudice in America,* W. Charisse Goodman cites a 1987 study that concluded: "When good health practices and appearance norms coincide, women benefit; but if current fashion dictated poor health practices, women might then engage in those practices for the sake of attractiveness" (30). Like taking up smoking to stay slim.

Certainly everyone is entitled to his or her own opinion of what is attractive, but no one has the right to damage another human being for fun or profit. The media and the diet industry often do just that. While no one can change an entire culture overnight, people, especially parents, need to think about what they really value in the humans they share their lives with and what values they want to pass on to their children. We need to realize that being thin will not fix all our problems, though advertisements for diets and weight loss aids suggest this. Losing weight may, indeed, give a man or woman more confidence, but it will not make a person smarter, more generous, more loving, or more nurturing. It won't automatically attract the dream job or the ideal lover. On the contrary, people who allow the drive to be thin to control them may find that many other areas of their lives suffer: They may avoid some celebrations or get-togethers because of fear they may be tempted to eat too much or the "wrong" foods. They may cut back on intellectual activities like reading or enjoying concerts or art museums because those activities cut into their exercise time too much. The mania for thinness can cause a person to lose all perspective and balance in life. I know. It happened to me. My moment of revelation came about twelve years ago. I was a size ten, dieting constantly and faithfully keeping lists of every bite I ate, trying to lose fifteen more pounds. While I was watching the evening news, a story came on about a young woman who was run over by a bus. I vividly recall that as the station played the footage of the paramedics wheeling the woman away on a stretcher, I said to myself, "Yeah, but at least she's thin." I've been lucky enough to have gained some wisdom (as well as weight) with age: I may be fat, but I'm no longer crazy. There are some things more important than being thin.

Works Cited

Brownell, Kelly D., et al. "Personal Responsibility and Obesity: A Constructive Approach to a Controversial Issue." *Health Affairs*, vol. 29, no. 3, Mar.-Apr. 2010, pp. 378–86.

Brownell, Kelly D., and Rebecca Puhl. "Stigma and Discrimination in Weight Management and Obesity." *The Permanente Journal*, vol. 7, no. 3, Summer 2003, pp. 21–23.

Dinnerstein, Barbara Noreen. "Bubbie, Mommy, Weight Watchers and Me." *Worlds in Our Words: Contemporary American Women Writers*, edited by Marilyn Kallet and Patricia Clark, Prentice Hall, 1997, pp. 347–49.

Goodman, W. Charisse. *The Invisible Woman: Confronting Weight Prejudice in America*. Gurze Books, 1995.

Manheim, Camryn. *Wake Up! I'm Fat*. Broadway Books, 1999.

Pipher, Mary. *Hunger Pains: The Modern Woman's Tragic Quest for Thinness*. Ballantine Books, 1995.

Puhl, Rebecca, and Chelsea Heuer. "Obesity Stigma: Important Considerations for Public Health." *American Journal of Public Health*, vol. 100, no. 6, June 2010, pp. 1019–28. *PubMed Central*, doi:10.2105/AJPH.2009.159491.

---. "The Stigma of Obesity: A Review and Update." *Obesity*, vol. 17, no. 5, May 2009: pp. 1–23. *Wiley Online Library*, doi:10.1038/oby.2008.636.

Wann, Marilyn. *Fat! So? Because You Don't Have to Apologize for Your Size*. Ten Speed Press, 1998.

Writing Strategies

1. Why do you think Paulin refers to "overweight" people as "fat"? What is the effect of this word on readers?

2. Paulin helps readers to understand her main ideas by stating them at the beginning of paragraphs. Find three paragraphs in this essay that begin with the main idea. Do those sentences also connect the paragraph to the previous paragraph? If so, describe how.

3. Paulin uses written sources to support her argument. In some places she directly quotes the sources; in others she paraphrases or summarizes (that is, she puts what the source says in her own words). Find an example of each (quote, paraphrase, summary). How do you know the information is from a source? Does Paulin make that clear? Notice how Paulin introduces the information and punctuates it.

4. Paulin's conclusion does not merely summarize points she has already made. Reread the conclusion and describe how it goes beyond mere summary. What does it try to do?

5. Paulin seems to know that her audience needs to be nudged along to accept her point. In your view, what particular rhetorical strategy is most effective at nudging readers to see the real harm of the media's portrayal of weight?

Exploring Ideas

1. How is weight a public issue?

2. In her opening paragraph, Paulin says that inaccurate images about weight "have shifted our vision of what is important in life way out of whack, so far out that people are being hurt." Then she calls for perspective. What support can you provide for her claim that our vision of what is important is out of whack? What support can you provide that people are being hurt?

3. Why should or shouldn't comedians refrain from making fat jokes about specific individuals?

4. In her conclusion, Paulin says, "[P]eople who allow the drive to be thin to control them may find that many other areas of their lives suffer." Apply her thinking to some other situation besides body weight, and explain how a particular drive has led to suffering.

Ideas for Writing

1. In what subtle ways are short people marginalized or dismissed in everyday life?

2. What are the quiet hardships of beauty? Focus on one particular struggle that traditionally attractive girls, boys, men, or women encounter.

If responding to one of these ideas, go to the Analysis section of this chapter to begin developing ideas for your essay.

Student Essay

Floppy Disk Fallacies

Elizabeth Bohnhorst

As computers become increasingly fused to everyday life, students and teachers may struggle to ask hard questions about the proper role of technology in the classroom. In 2005, Elizabeth Bohnhorst wrote this essay for a college class. Since then, computers have, no doubt, become more normalized in classroom teaching. As you read, consider how Bohnhorst's argument resonates with the current educational climate—if her argument has become more or less significant in recent years.

"Another boring PowerPoint," responds Jennifer when I ask about her day at school. I might not find these words so discouraging coming from a company executive after a long meeting or even a college student leaving an informative lecture. But these words of an eleven-year-old elementary school student leave me feeling slightly uneasy. PowerPoint presentations are intended to compel students to become more interested in the subject with the use of neon colors and moving graphic images. But these flashy additions to current educational strategies haven't fooled everyone. The text and material covered is still the same boring grammar and spelling lessons, but the educator has altered: It is a screen.

The personal testimony feeds into the main idea.

Even young children can see past the techno mania.

This final flat statement reinforces an obvious problem with flashy technology.

Computers can undoubtedly contribute wonders to the field of education. In fact, computer education is a must if children intend to thrive in modern society. The possibilities are endless when it comes to surfing the Web or using the thousands of educational programs currently available. These programs are capable of reading text on a computer with icons beside words that take students to a galaxy of options, icons to learn more about the era in which the text was written, fascinating facts about the author, and helpful notes about the morals of the story. But computers are being used more and more frequently as a substitute for books, blackboards, and in some cases, the teachers themselves.

A thorough concession to the educational power of technology.

Computers link kids to more and more information, more options, more data.

A turnabout paragraph—ending with a counterargument.

America leads the world in the amount and density of computers in our public schools. In 1992, the typical high school had

■ Writing Strategies ■ Exploring Ideas

The evidence shows the scope of the issue—that computer technology has become a widespread and conventional classroom tool.

one computer for every ten students, while elementary and middle schools averaged thirteen students per computer (Anderson). Compared to current numbers, the early 1990s were a time of deprivation. Some schools, such as Kent Central School in rural Connecticut, are considering funding for each student to have his or her own laptop. After visiting the school, Anne Guignon reports that "students use the computers in school, take them home each night, use the computers for homework, and soon will be able to tap into the Internet." In such situations, traditional school lingo such as "Take out a piece of paper and a number two pencil" might be replaced with "Take out your floppies and boot up your Toshibas." Unfortunately for some students, dogs cannot digest discs.

More evidence that administrative bodies across the country celebrate computers as a primary educational tool.

And the Texas Board of Education is only steps behind the Kent Central School. "The Texas Board of Education now has state officials seriously examining whether to give all public school students laptops instead of textbooks," states a *New York Times* investigator. The Board "is looking at $1.8 billion in projected costs for textbooks over the next six years, and . . . given technology improvements that have lowered the price of computers, it may be cheaper, to say nothing of innovative, to lease a laptop for each of the state's 3.7 million students" (Guignon).

So much of the school budget will go to computer retailers.

5 Now, what could possibly be wrong with such a sophisticated device for learning? In reality, "thirty years of research on educational technology has produced almost no evidence of a clear link between using computers in the early grades and improving learning," states Michael Dertouzus, director of the MIT Laboratory for Computer Science. In fact, evidence of hazardous effects of frequent use of computers in young children is overwhelming. They do little to promote a healthy childhood. "Computers are perhaps the most acute symptom of the rush to end childhood. The national drive to computerize schools, from kindergarten on up, emphasizes only one of the many human capacities, one that naturally develops quite late—analytic, abstract thinking—and aims to jump start it prematurely," continues Dertouzus.

What many people have been saying for years: a screen may not be the most interactive or nurturing form of education. In fact, it might be the opposite.

Evidence shows no causal connection between computers and better learning.

The "national drive" refers back to her previous paragraphs.

This gets into more complex, but less obvious, injuries—into the quiet layers of harm that computers do to young students.

Elementary schools are not only responsible for teaching children reading, writing, mathematics, and other basic skills; they also reinforce and indirectly establish guidelines for everyday behavior. Therefore, consistent use of computers in schools ultimately plants the idea in the developing mind that computers are safe, educational, and perhaps one of the most important tools of modern society.

All these illuminated boxes!

Thus, a child returns home from school after hours of staring into an illuminated box, flips through the channels of yet another illuminated box, and then proceeds to play "Final Fantasy Four" on the Macintosh for three more hours. A 1999 study by the Kaiser Family Foundation showed that children ages two to eighteen spent an average of four hours and forty-five minutes per day plugged into electronic media of all kinds. These numbers are excluding the time spent with such machinery during school hours (Dertouzus).

The emotional and social values learned during childhood are also disrupted by computerized education in elementary and middle schools. Students learn more than state capitals and multiplication; they develop a sense of social importance and are taught values of friendship and other relationships. Through interaction with peers, intimacy and companionship are only a few of the many principles computers are unable to relay to children. Dr. Stanley I. Greenspan, former director of the Clinical Infant Development Program, is concerned that the impersonal culture formulated by computerization has serious detrimental effects on children's emotional development: "So-called interactive, computer-based instruction that does not provide true interaction but merely a mechanistic response to the student's efforts," states Greenspan, can be directly linked to "the increasingly impersonal quality that suffuses the experience of more and more American children" (qtd. in Dertouzos). He also adds that lack of nurturing for children at home and at school can likely result in "increasing levels of violence and extremism and less collaboration and empathy" (qtd. in Dertouzos).

Here, we walk even further into those layers of harm. The writer keeps moving us into deeper dimensions.

Computers don't teach socialization—unless we count the quick blurbs and self-promotion of Facebook.

We're definitely seeing increased violence.

To go yet further into the harm and past the common assumptions, she analyzes the concept of *creativity.*

Besides affecting emotional and social development in primary students, computers can also disrupt creative thinking. Like all other electronic viewing systems (television and video games), computers leave little or no room for imagination. Of course, the virtual reality computers create is often full of fantastic images. However, because imagination involves generating one's own images and ideas, consistent exposure to ready-made images only makes it more difficult for children to summon their own creativity. The intensity of the images squashes the need for intensive creativity.

Another turnabout paragraph: a concession followed by a counterargument.

Computer software is often, then, anti-imagination. It does the imagining for students.

Educational psychologist and former school principal Jane Healy has observed that "teachers find that today's video-immersed children can't form original pictures in their mind or develop an imaginative representation. Teachers of young children lament the fact that many now have to be taught to play symbolically or pretend—previously a symptom only of mentally or emotionally disordered youngsters" (qtd. in

Dertouzus). Not only do these images affect creativity and imagination; they also have potential to diffuse the sparks of curiosity. For example, if a class is learning about regional watersheds, computerized classrooms will most likely turn to the handy diagrams so conveniently laid out on the screens before the students. In a classroom that values hands-on learning techniques, a school field trip to a local stream or swamp may be an effective strategy. In short, a successful education should not replace children's curiosity to explore the world around them with Internet Explorer.

Explore is a verb. Explorer is a product. Big difference!

10 On the other hand, technology is an effective way to get kids interested in learning, considering "that there is a passionate love affair between children and computers" (Setzer). A colorful computer screen is obviously more attractive to a child than an old novel or a textbook. But this attraction is more likely a fascination with animation and sound effects rather than a genuine exploration of ideas. Dr. Valdemar W. Setzer, a professor of computer science, wonders, "What happens to a student who gets used to learning with computers? Will she be able to tolerate a normal class without all those cosmetic and video game effects?"

A call for pause: for thinking through the implications, that have been offered throughout the essay.

Computers are another form of cosmetic!

As technology's role in American society grows, we should observe its influence in public education. It is easy to consider the benefits of computerization: simplicity, standardization, and elimination of other physical controversies. But in the same light we must also consider the hazards and how important traditional education is to children. The obvious concern with traditional education is the students being "left behind" in the rush toward increasing technological advancements.

She gives a qualifier: the distinction between teaching computer skills and more complex dimensions of human development.

Educating students in computer skills is and should be a priority in all schools. But when it comes to teaching basic skills and allowing for intellectual development, human interaction and exploration of the real world should never come second to electronic devices. In an effort to preserve the qualities of education, we should not allow ourselves to become mesmerized by teachers that require an electrical outlet and textbooks that require a point-and-click to turn the page.

The difference between computer skills and other skills.

Works Cited

Anderson, Ronald E., editor. *Computers in American Schools, 1992: An Overview*. IEA Computers in Education Study, U of Minnesota, Minneapolis, 1993.

Dertouzos, Michael. "Developmental Risks: The Hazards of Computers in Childhood." *Fool's Gold: A Critical Look at Computers in Childhood*, edited by Colleen Cordes and Edward Miller, The Alliance for Childhood, 2000, pp. 19–44.

Guignon, Anne. "Laptop Computers for Every Student!" *Education World*, 19 Jan. 1998, p. 6.

Setzer, Valdemar W. "A Review of Arguments for the Use of Computers in Elementary Education." *Southern Cross Review*, no. 4, 2000, www.southerncrossreview.org/4/review.html.

Writing Strategies

1. Bohnhorst begins with some personal testimony. How does that impact her argument? What is the effect?
2. Why does Bohnhorst's reference to PowerPoint strengthen her argument about computers?
3. Bohnhorst is tackling a common assumption in education: that more technology is inherently good. Describe her strategy for confronting and overturning this assumption. How does she do it?
4. How does Bohnhorst apply appeals to value in her argument?
5. How does Bohnhorst deal with specific opposing ideas? Where does she reveal the shortcomings of other positions? Where does she acknowledge the value of other positions?

Exploring Ideas

1. Consider the following claims made by Bohnhorst:

   Computers can undoubtedly contribute wonders to the field of education. (¶2)

   In fact, computer education is a must if children intend to thrive in modern society. (¶2)

   With others, explore these claims further, trying to discover new ways of thinking about them. Begin by discussing whether you think the claims are true, and then pinpoint and explore why people might disagree.
2. Bohnhorst explains that "the intensity of the [computer] images squashes the need for intensive creativity." Explore how this might work. Consider a specific video game or website and describe how its intensity squashes a need for creativity.
3. How might computers in the classroom prevent learning?
4. How do you define learning? How does popular educational software fit into or oppose your definition of learning?

Ideas for Writing

1. What argument might you make by taking a more extreme stance on the role of computers in education?
2. To develop your own argument, research some claim Bohnhorst makes, such as "teachers find that today's video-immersed children can't form original pictures in their mind or develop an imaginative representation." (¶9)

If responding to one of these ideas, go to the Analysis section of this chapter to begin developing ideas for your essay.

Whales R Us

Jayme Stayer

Good writers often invite, and sometimes force, us to confront ideas we would rather not examine. In his argument about SeaWorld, Jayme Stayer sheds new light on the park. His points might seem unreasonable at first. After all, why should someone target a theme park? But Stayer's essay illustrates an important move in academic writing: uncovering the layers of meaning behind the propaganda of everyday life. Stayer, a professional musician and T.S. Eliot scholar, is a Jesuit, an order of priests and brothers in the Catholic tradition. He has taught at Texas A&M–Commerce, Universidad Centroamericana in El Salvador, and John Carroll University.

Mickey Mouse scares the bejesus out of me. Shamu, on the other hand, simply makes me queasy. I'm not the first to express loathing for Mickey & Co.: a giggling rodent as mascot for a nasty, litigious, multimedia *Über*-corporation. But you don't hear too many people railing against SeaWorld, though Shamu has a dark side too.

One of the first things to irk me at a SeaWorld park happened during a bird show. A perky blonde was displaying a few parrots, and she kept up a stream of banter about their feeding habits and origins. "When our ancestors came to this continent," she breezily explained to an audience chock full of non-Europeans, "they brought with them this breed of parrot from Africa." Since I'm almost certain that slaves brutally shipped to the Americas were not allowed bird cages as carry-on luggage, what she should have said was that European—not "our"—ancestors stopped off in Africa and loaded up with parrots and slaves. One needn't be a fanatical multiculturalist to be ruffled by inaccurate history and specious assumptions about an audience's makeup.

In America, unexamined notions of history and the coercive politics of majority identity go hand in hand with boorish nationalism. (See, for example, the debate over the Confederate flag and its supposed status as symbol of a unitary "Southern" culture.) Oddly, the bird show at SeaWorld confirmed this. Her parrots now retired, the perky woman waltzed around the stage with a bald eagle while the audience was subjected to a chummy patriotic tune. So the eagle was presented not as the largest or most impressive of birds, or as indigenous to Canada, or even as another instance of the marvels of creation, but as the Bird of American Democracy—this, in spite of the fact that eagles' politics tend to the monarchist side and that their feeding habits indicate a predisposition for brutal dictatorship. The bird becomes valued, in other words, for the cultural associations "we" Americans slapped onto it, not for any of its intrinsic properties. The eagle, in SeaWorld's monistic version of the world, becomes just another happy commodity—like parrots, slaves, designer clothes sweatshops—that makes America the Great Nation It Has Always Been.

But not all employees were as chipper as the bird show people. There are two types of teenagers who work at SeaWorld the aggressively happy and the sullenly aggrieved. These two opposed mentalities are as old as the summer job itself: namely, the optimism of youths who want to change the world vs. the cynicism of kids who despise their jobs, resent their pay, and wouldn't give a hooey if they were fired because some enraged Yuppie did not get good service with a grovelling smile when he bought his Sno-Cone. I personally sided with the disaffected and wished I had brought copies of *The Communist Manifesto* to slip into their pockets.

5 The most important job at SeaWorld—and teenagers are particularly good at it—is making lots of noise. Since most Americans are terrified of being alone in a store without Muzak, SeaWorld willingly obliges its customers with rock-concert levels of decibels. All of the shows keep up a noxious patter complete with ear-splitting sound effects; the walkways have abrasively loud music piped over them; and even the exhibits have teenagers chained there with microphones in hand, droning their mantra of dull facts.

It is ironic that a park putatively designed to extol the wonders of nature is obsessed with high-tech wizardry and mega-voltage noise, noise, noise—even when it is extolling the wonders of nature's silence. Another talking point of the bird show featured how silently an owl could fly. The bird's flight began in blissful silence, but halfway through its flight the soundtrack faded back in with a shimmer of violins, followed by a cymbal crash when the owl landed. Even the absence of noise is packaged with noise: The owl's silence is first framed with amplified yakking (noise), then underlined as it happens (quiet noise), then punctuated (big noise) so the audience knows when to clap (make more noise).

One of the most ludicrous moments of the Shamu show was an assertion by another relentlessly cheerful teenager: "We here at SeaWorld believe we have the greatest jobs in the world." With its overtones of Orwellian party-speak, it was only slightly risible until she added: "We get to work with nature's most wonderful animals and contribute to the world's knowledge about them." Her jejune assumption that "world knowledge" exists as some kind of huge, accumulative spittoon—rather than a set of competing claims and shifting paradigms—was hilarious enough, particularly coming from a kid who is probably still struggling with basic algebra and who wouldn't recognize "world knowledge" if it landed on her in a heap. I imagined her logging on to a marine biology chat group and making an announcement—in all caps, no doubt—followed by an emoticon: "SHAMU DID A BACK FLIP TO-DAY!!! :)" Thus does the world's cup of knowledge runneth over.

And that insistent refrain of "We here at SeaWorld believe" was another thing that rankled me, because it was usually followed by patronizing flimflam. Some prime examples: "We here at SeaWorld believe that animals should not be taken from their natural habitat." Or: "We here at SeaWorld believe only in the use of positive reinforcement in the training of animals." The audience is supposed to believe that these are lovely sentiments. How noble that they try to find injured or orphaned animals to "befriend." How comforting to know Shamu isn't being shocked with electricity or poked in the eye when he's tired or just damned

Kamal Sellehuddin/ZUMA Press/Corbis

fed up with giving piggyback rides. Most disturbing was that these credos came mostly out of the mouths of the teenage staff, whose inexperience made their We-Believe proclamations ring even more hollowly.

Taken individually, some of these moments were only mildly unnerving, but there was one occurrence that stood out as gratuitous. Situated on a lake, the SeaWorld I visited featured a water show with ski jumps and corny skits. The theme of that year's show was *Baywatch*, which involved—predictably enough—nubile bodies in poorly choreographed dance routines, the bold rescue of someone in the water, and the odd appearances of two buffoons (fat old man with hysterical wife), all of which was irritatingly narrated by an emcee's we-havin'-fun-yet? voice-over. At one point, the old man and his wife were "accidentally" pulled into view: the man (vertical) on skis, the woman (horizontal) with her legs wrapped around his torso. They were in the unmistakable position of sex, the two actors in a flurry of feigned embarrassment at having been "caught." (Whut in tarnation cud be more funny than ol' fat folks havin' sex? Har dee har har.) The emcee and other characters on stage slyly absolved themselves of complicity in this vulgarity by shrugging their shoulders, as if to say: "Golly, what was that all about?" SeaWorld, by the way, bills itself as a place for the whole family.

10 You might think that a park that sponsors PG-13 shows would divest itself of prudishness.

Alas, there was more self-righteousness there than at a revival. Case in point: the shark exhibit. Before we could enter, we were forced to watch a short film about sharks; the doors to the exhibit were pointedly barred until after the film was over. The film gave us a hellfire-and-damnation scolding: you thought that sharks were human predators? WRONG. You thought sharks were abundant in the ocean? WRONG AGAIN. After airing its grievances with us—the ill-informed public—it asserted that much damage had been inflicted on these misunderstood fishies. Because we've all been shark-haters at heart, fishermen have felt free to kill them. Quivering with virtue, the film called "intolerable" the fishermen who "senselessly" destroyed the sharks, either because the sharks got caught in the nets or because the sharks fed on prized fish. With vast self-contentment SeaWorld then relayed how they had successfully worked to stop this great evil.

While I'm pleased to have my horror-film notions of sharks corrected, the film's smugness was unbearable. And in spite of SeaWorld's professed vigilance, I'm not convinced that sharks aren't still being arbitrarily killed somewhere in the world. Even so, I wonder if sharks, given the choice, would prefer to stay in a SeaWorld bathtub for the rest of their lives or take a chance with those fishnets.

Of the many inanities hurled at me, my favorite was an emcee's sign-off: "And remember," she intoned from a precipitously high moral ground, "before we can have peace *on* the Earth, we have to make peace *with* the Earth." Indeed. As if, in the interest of world peace, the United Nations agenda should be scuttled in favor of dotting the globe with SeaWorlds to promote feel-good vibes between humans and dolphins. Here's more glib reasoning: to make peace *with* the Earth implies the Earth was a peaceful place before we humans mucked things up. Yet the last time I looked, the Earth was full of viruses, earthquakes, predatory animals, and a survival-of-the-fittest mentality that SeaWorld has apparently never heard of.

And maybe it was petty of me to be irked when the woman narrating Shamu's activities insisted that whales scratch their backs on the pebbled shores when they're contented. There was captive Shamu scratching his back on the simulated shore. The audience oohed and aahed. Never mind that Shamu had been explicitly directed to scratch his back, and that to have disobeyed would have resulted not in a whack on the head (lucky for him) but in the withholding of food (not so lucky). Is that contentment then? With the help of an extraordinarily costly visual aid, the audience was expected to "learn" a fact of whale behavior that could be shown only at the cost of candor.

15 SeaWorld, I realized after an afternoon of learning very little, was a place that was desperately trying to present itself as a place where education occurs. And for twenty-some bucks, your educational experience goes roughly like this: You can give up an afternoon of watching vapid TV shows and take your whole family to watch a skit based on a vapid TV show. You get to ogle busty women and hirsute men. You get to have constant noise crowd out any independent thoughts that might be percolating to the surface of your brain. You get to harbor the illusion that America is a happy, white, European family, as well as a leading maker of world knowledge, and that SeaWorld is largely responsible for such happiness and

abundance. You get to imagine you hold the key to world peace (remember to give the dog a kiss when you get home). You get to indulge in patriotic goosebumps ("the *American* eagle!"), have your heart-strings jolted ("Ah—Shamu's happy to be here!"), get your sluggish sense of morality jump-started ("*baaaad* fishermen, *gooood* sharkie"). And if you're willing to invest another three bucks, you can fling a sardine at dolphins that have been petted to within an inch of their lives. Best of all, at the end of the day you get to go home with the vaguely self-congratulatory feeling that you've *learned* something, by God.

I'm an educator, and I pay close attention when someone is trying to teach me something. So on my way out of SeaWorld, I asked myself what I had learned. Like a student who has crammed for an exam, I was able to recall lots of idiocies, but could only say I had truly learned two things. (1) Thanks to the film, I learned that sharks attack humans only when provoked, and, (2) thanks to their anthropomorphizing skits, I learned that sea otters are cute little buggers. Even if these elements were judicious pedagogical objectives (which they are not), they still don't add up to anything resembling education. In fact, the entire experience of SeaWorld is suspiciously similar to the exact opposite of education: mind control.

It was only in retrospect that I realized that these annoyances were related: the high-pitched entertainment and trivial sexual jokes, the shut-up-and-listen attitude, the constant noise and verbal presence, the Big Brotherly refrains of exactly what "We here at SeaWorld believe." These are all rhetorical strategies of a government diverting its citizens, masking something it doesn't want the public to know. And what is it that SeaWorld doesn't want its customers to think about?

In a review lambasting Disney World, an author hilariously describes the ideology of the place as "benign fascism": The streets are immaculately clean; the worker bees wear impossibly happy smiles; the rides and trains run on time; and every day, the gloved hero appears on parade, where the hordes worship him and his lickspittles with songs and fireworks. The author's comparison of Mickey to Mussolini is more than just amusing: He ties it into his critique of how history is portrayed at the Epcot center. Because Disney does not want to offend any of its ethnically and racially diverse customers (SeaWorld: take note), their film on American history carefully controls the emotional barometer of its vacationers. The Disney film of American history is whitewashed to the point of banality, and such central topics as the atomic bomb, racial conflict, and imperialist genocide are entirely avoided. The point is that fascists, benign or not, always have political and economic reasons for telling history the way they do. And like Disney World and other fascist operations, SeaWorld likes to keep a tight grip on what and how its visitors think.

Take, for example, the "we-believe-animals-should-be-treated-in-this-way" gestures that continually crop up. These assertions pose as facts the audience ought to memorize in preparation for an exit quiz. Yet the nervous tic of emphasizing the politically correct means of treating animals in captivity belies SeaWorld's uneasiness with the larger, unasked question: Should we even have animals in captivity for our bourgeois amusement? Nowhere in their literature, exhibit signs, or rehearsed prattle of their miked minions is this basic question broached or answered.

20 Part of the way SeaWorld can get away with ignoring the obvious fact that these animals are there for our entertainment is that it nervously insists that it is a place of science and research, and disingenuously implies that entertainment easily meshes with education and research. While I scoff at the idea that important research gets done at SeaWorld, the problem isn't really with what kinds of knowledge SeaWorld makes, or how much, or how important it is. Rather, the problem is SeaWorld's communication of that knowledge, or to be more explicit, their refusal to level with its visitors about its real cultural role and worth. If they would fess up to the fact that SeaWorld is essentially a playground and not a classroom, that might be a start towards a real educational experience.

SeaWorld keeps up its image of itself as a classroom by propagating signs with facts and statistics on them. These factoids—and their Post-it Note ubiquity—are a peculiar manifestation of "textbook knowledge": boring chunks of data unconnected to any larger, compelling theme. There were a plethora of facts swimming around at SeaWorld and a dearth of ideas, which is why I couldn't remember anything at the end of my day. Like the eager student who has a bad teacher, I was given no complex or interesting framework inside of which ideas jostled about; so I was reduced to cramming lists of unconnected information in preparation for a never-to-be-taken exam.

I'm not suggesting that SeaWorld become a place that sponsors round-table discussions of animal rights and lets biology students present their theses during Shamu intermissions. But I do think that instead of slavishly subscribing to popular notions of science, SeaWorld might call them into question. This is what real education does.

As it stands, none of our deeply rooted cultural beliefs are explored or challenged at SeaWorld. After a trip there the visitor is likely to keep thinking that facts are equivalent to knowledge; that America is synonymous with Europe; that science and technology are the greatest goods imaginable; that education means being fed a list of facts in a condescending manner; and that sated, docile fish—who decorously eat buckets of non-cute sardines—are practically vegetarians.

A skit in which a lovably frisky sea otter has its head chomped off by a hungry predator is not the kind of bloody epiphany SeaWorld is likely to promote. Imagine the screams of the unsuspecting children. Imagine the lawsuits of offended suburbanites who like their nature sanitized and safe. But imagine, too, how such a moment would educate an audience about the dangers of humanizing certain animals at the expense of others. Such a skit might end with a question to the audience about why its government enacts laws to protect the habitat of owls but not of insects or low-income humans.

25 The only cultural assumption that was seriously challenged at SeaWorld was the premise of *Jaws*—and that was much too heavy-handed, not to mention incorrect, as events in Florida have shown. It turns out that sharks *will* attack idle swimmers. It should come as no surprise that a capitalist venture like SeaWorld can't even get its basic facts straight. Neither can the tobacco industry seem to grasp what everyone else knows about nicotine addiction. Nor is Disney equipped to navigate the treacherous waters of American history.

Surely the most real moments at SeaWorld occurred when the fascists lost control, for example, when the staff had trouble getting the animals to obey their directions. Such glitches in the program put their slapstick routines and canned jokes on hold, and forced them to talk to the audience about fixing this problem. It also gave the teenage apparatchiks an opportunity for some inspired ad-libbing, disburdening them from their less endearing lecture notes.

If the ideology of Disney is benign fascism, then the ideology of SeaWorld is exploitative spectacle masquerading as education. Too occupied with obscuring the real moral, environmental, and scientific issues at stake, SeaWorld is constitutionally incapable of teaching respect for nature. Love of nature is spiritually informed and politically assertive. It is not the kind of passive, sentimental quackery SeaWorld prefers, and it cannot be taught with the crude tools in SeaWorld's lesson plans: glib moralizing, base pandering, and clichés masquerading as insights.

But in the last analysis, SeaWorld—to paraphrase Auden—makes nothing happen. SeaWorld is a reflection of American culture: a consequence, not a cause; a mirror of consumerist desires, not a promoter of political change via education. The American traits SeaWorld reflects most clearly are its gullibility and irrationality. It's a consolation, albeit a small one, to consider that Americans are likewise gullible to the very real beauty of nature. It's that kind of openness—and not SeaWorld's preaching—that makes the connection between humans and dolphins seem worth investigating. It's less of a comfort to consider another analogy between Americans and marine life that SeaWorld leaves unexplored: America's exorbitant arms race, its rape of the environment, its valorization of guns and violence, its giddy, media-fueled acclamation of the death sentence that disproportionately murders minorities: Are these not strikingly similar to the fierce logic of the food chain? Screw the little guy; I'm hungry and more powerful.

So my advice is to go to SeaWorld anyway. Even inside the ideological frame where they are forced, the creatures there—including the teenagers—are amazing, hilarious, and terrifying. Who can remain unimpressed when a mammal the size of a Mack truck lifts itself out of the water? As for SeaWorld itself: If, aided by earplugs and skepticism, you can ignore what they're trying to teach you, you just might learn something.

Work Cited

Alexander, Maxwell. "Promise Redeemed: At Long Last Mickey." *Johns Hopkins Magazine*, vol. 47, no. 2, Apr. 1995, p. 5.

Writing Strategies

1. What word would you use to describe the voice of this essay—humorous, serious, urgent, angry, light, or something else? Identify several passages to support your description.
2. Stayer is trying to call SeaWorld out—to reveal something disingenuous or fake about the park's rhetoric. In your own words, what is Stayer trying to reveal?
3. How does counterargument function in this essay? Point to particular passages in which Stayer is countering some opposing claim and explain how that passage figures into the overall point of the essay.

4. How does Stayer use SeaWorld to make broader points about American culture?

5. How does Stayer's conclusion work on the audience? Describe what the conclusion does for readers—how it reinforces or develops a kind of relationship between Stayer and the readers.

Exploring Ideas

1. What new way of thinking does Stayer introduce? (Consider his points about education, entertainment, theme parks, even American popular culture.)

2. Based on this essay, how are Stayer's thoughts, values, beliefs, or feelings similar to or different from yours?

3. Stayer argues, "If the ideology of Disney is benign fascism, then the ideology of SeaWorld is exploitative spectacle masquerading as education." In small groups, paraphrase this sentence. How does this point work in Stayer's overall argument?

4. How does Stayer's thinking go beyond one's initial ideas about entertainment parks?

5. Research the documentary *Blackfish*, which was released in 2013, long after Stayer's visit to SeaWorld. What part of Stayer's argument seems to resonate most with the claims made in the documentary?

Ideas for Writing

1. What public place—such as SeaWorld—presents itself in a way that is different from what you know (or suspect) about that place?

2. What public place presents itself honestly and accurately?

If responding to one of these ideas, go to the Analysis section of this chapter to begin developing ideas for your essay.

Invention

Academic audiences demand more than "three reasons why I believe X" arguments. They want to experience more in an argument than a writer's personal beliefs; they want to learn a new way of thinking. So academic writers often look for a way to make people rethink an issue. They try to create a new position on a familiar topic or assert a position on an entirely fresh topic. And good writers do not merely *choose* topics; instead, they *build* topics from the novel and surprising moments of everyday life.

The following sections are designed to help you develop ideas for your argument: specifically, to discover a topic (in Point of Contact), develop particular points about the topic (in Analysis), make it relevant to a community of readers (in Public Resonance), focus your position (in Thesis), and create support for that position (in Rhetorical Tools). The questions in each section will help you generate intense ideas and start writing. Your responses to the Invention Questions may take you in various directions, and some of your responses may get left behind. That is to be expected in academic work—or in any work that seeks to discover something valuable.

Point of Contact

Some situations in everyday life are obviously significant—what they mean for our lives, or for the lives of others, is apparent. When our country goes to war or when a new president is elected, for example, most Americans understand the significance. Many situations, however, are far more subtle; their potential meaning is hidden by life's hustle and bustle. To understand their meaning, we must stop in our tracks and focus on them. Use the following suggestions, questions, and images (Figure 8.1) to explore possible topics. If a question seems engaging to you, or if you associate some emotion or idea with the question, start writing. Ask yourself: "Can I change someone's mind about this situation or issue?"

School

What lurking attitude is ruining the learning process? If we're a country of progress, why should history be taught anyway? How is mainstream fashion brainwashing even the smart kids? Will football be the end of serious public education? How was *Napoleon Dynamite*'s portrayal of high school right on target? How are high schools destroying students' ability to cope with the first year of college? How is high school its own form of religion?

Work

What doesn't the public understand or appreciate about my work? Are the work expectations fair? Are the hours fair to workers? What hidden forces or assumptions work against productivity? Why don't people in my line of work get paid more? Are they paid way too much?

Figure 8.1

Home

What does my neighborhood layout suggest about being a human? How does the layout of my house or apartment or dorm help me to be a better person? What is the central appliance in my living space and how does that affect my thought process? Should more people have gardens? What do cathedral ceilings (or some other architectural feature of our homes) make people think about themselves?

Community

Does my town know what to do with teenagers? Does the water taste funny? Does my town offer ample mass transit? How does the police force function—as keepers of the peace or something else? How important are trees?

Pop Culture

How does *American Idol* impact popular music? Can a democracy seriously thrive without a good punk scene? What is a culture without a vibrant funk subculture? Should we be leery or supportive of a whole channel dedicated to food? What does the Discovery Channel do for science? Should there be a fun show about language and writing? Calculus?

Your Major

Look through a current journal in your field to find controversial issues: Are entry-level personnel in my field treated fairly? Is some research in my field or major controversial? Is my field undervalued by the public? Has my field changed any of its practices, for better or worse, in recent years? Should my field be more diverse (in gender and/or ethnicity)?

Activity

Make a list of other questions that draw attention to troubling situations in the world around you. What attitude or basic assumption lies beneath some troubling behavior or policy?

Analysis

Analysis cracks open the layers of a topic—and helps writers to see more than their initial thoughts about it. Without analysis, writers may find themselves with little new to say. As you answer the Invention Questions, avoid answering too quickly. Instead, use the questions to search for deeper understanding, which will then translate into more intensive writing. Allow time and space for your own thinking to develop:

- What is the particular point of crisis or tension?
- How has the situation (or condition, behavior, policy) come about, and why does it continue?

- What are the effects of the situation (or condition, behavior, policy)?
- Why do I have an opinion on this topic?
- Why is my belief valuable?

Ann Marie Paulin looks beneath the initial tension or problem and discovers a hidden layer. She goes beyond being "angry" and discovers that media trends indirectly support, even "encourage," mistreatment and incivility:

> **Why do I have an opinion on this topic?**
>
> I have been fat since I was a kid. For about two days in my twenties I starved my way down to a size ten, thereby earning this head-turning compliment from the guy I was then dating: "You'd be a real fox if you'd just lose a few more pounds." I've had complete strangers say the most astonishing things to me on the street. For example, on my way through a parking lot to get to my car, I passed a young man who looked over at me and shouted: "I don't !,#$ fat chicks!" Who was asking? While these behaviors have sometimes hurt me, they mostly make me angry. And when I look around at the society in which I live, I don't see any signs that this kind of behavior is discouraged. Indeed, the media seems to suggest that fat people, by their very existence, seem to deserve contempt and abuse.
>
> **How has this situation come about?**
>
> Where it gets tricky is that by the media's definition, damn near everyone is fat. How has this situation come about? I'm not sure, but I've watched it develop. When my mother was young, a size ten or twelve was a respectable dress size. When I was in my twenties, a size eight was a respectable size. Now, you must be a size four, two, or even better, a zero to be considered thin. Now, a six-foot-tall model who wears a size twelve dress is considered plus size. She only gets her photo in Lane Bryant ads and such. It's as if society has completely forgotten the concept of "normal size," and so a person is either thin (if you can count all her bones when she appears in a bathing suit) or she's fat. And that leaves the majority of women believing they are fat and hating themselves for it).

Paulin's thinking shows how writers work: In the process of analyzing ideas, they create various possible writing directions. However, as they begin to develop their projects, they become more focused and revelatory; they grab onto one point and take it somewhere. They go beyond the common complaints and reveal a particular quality, effect, or layer of the issue.

Invention Workshop

Enlist the help of another writer in answering one of the Invention Questions. Use the question to initiate a discussion. Explore further by questioning one another's responses to the questions. For example, Jack is focusing on his high school education. Notice how the discussion with Marcus goes beyond Jack's initial response:

What is the particular point of crisis or tension?

JACK: My high school education was inadequate. I graduated with a B average, and I came to college having to take developmental courses before I could even begin taking credit courses.

MARCUS: But is that the high school's fault?

JACK:	Well, if I couldn't cut the mustard in entry-level college courses, why did I get mostly Bs in high school? It seems like something's out of whack.
MARCUS:	OK. So the standards are too low in high school?
JACK:	Yeah, I think so.
MARCUS:	Were you ever warned about the standards in college?
JACK:	Sure. All the time, teachers would scare us with things like, "Wait 'til you get in college; you've got to work constantly to keep your grades up."
MARCUS:	But did anyone ever share specifics with you? Did you know what kinds of writing, for instance, you would be doing in college?
JACK:	Not really. It's all been a big surprise.
MARCUS:	Maybe that's the issue: high school students (and maybe teachers and administrators) don't really know what kinds of things go on in entry-level college courses.
JACK:	Yes—and so there's this huge gap in between, and some students fall right into it.

It would be easy to reinforce Jack's initial idea—the inadequacy of high school—by sharing examples of bad teachers or rotten classes, but Marcus and Jack do better. They develop the initial idea into something more specific and revealing: the gap between high school and college standards.

Thinking Further

Analysis is not about answering a question and finding an answer. The real insights lie beneath the answers. Return to your responses to the Invention Questions and try to find the most valuable ideas:

- What statements reveal something specific?
- Which statements or phrases seem new to you?
- Which statements or phrases make a new connection, one that you had not considered before?

Now, you can take the statements or phrases forward and use them to develop increasingly intense ideas for your argument. If nothing stands out at this point, consider re-approaching the Invention Questions and invite another person to join your exploration. And this time, deliberately take the ideas further:

- What behavior, policy, or quality is at the heart of the topic? (What is beneath the tension you initially discovered?)
- What attitude, value system, or assumption rests beneath the actions of people who are involved?

Public Resonance

Writers transform issues or personal concerns into arguable topics, issues that matter in some way to other people. Making a personal concern resonate with a public issue is simply a process of extension. To this end, the following Invention Questions can be used as springboards from personal concerns to public issues. For example, examine the following question: *Is my living situation conducive to my goals as a student?* You may have answered: "Yes. I live at home with my parents and commute to school." Your situation is not unique. Many college students struggle with their living situations—with the decision of living on campus, in a nearby apartment complex, or at home with their parents, away from the campus altogether. This decision involves more than a simple personal choice. It has something to do with college funding, with the success of college students, with the entire college experience. In this sense, your situation resonates with a more public issue. The initial (more personal) question might evolve into a more public question: *Is it beneficial for college students to live at home while going to school?* As you consider your own topic, use the following questions to move from a personal concern to a public issue.

- Who might care about this issue? Why?
- Who *should* care about this issue? Why?
- How are my readers involved in this issue? How *could* they be involved?
- What group of people might understand or sympathize with my situation?
- Is this issue an example of some trend?
- Why is it important that others hear my opinion about this issue?
- What else has been said about this issue, and how are my ideas different?

Public resonance is key in Ann Marie Paulin's project. Her essay shows that the more a topic affects people, the more attention it may deserve. In her responses to the Invention Questions, she explores the hidden messages in ads and the unstated assumptions lurking in the public domain. Paulin's responses show her making connections between her own situation and many others. By extending her thinking outward, she is developing the public dimensions of her idea:

Who might care about this issue? Why?

This is certainly a very public issue because it is almost impossible to escape the media: magazines, newspaper ads, billboards, radio, TV, movies, ads plastered in public restrooms and on the walls of buses, ads in your e-mail every day. And every one of those images that deals with weight or beauty makes it clear that to be fat is completely unacceptable and completely fixable if only a person tries hard enough and buys the right products.

Now, if this were just an issue of vanity, it might be something that could be shrugged off. But it goes much deeper than that. If you really pay attention to those ads, their real message is often that if you are fat, no one will love you. Your husband will leave you (if you ever manage to get one to begin with). Your children will be ashamed of you. Your friends will give up on you. You will be alone and unloved because you are fat. That is the message that really hits us where we live. Who wants to be some lonely outcast? We must conform to whatever it takes.

> And so, most of us try the diets, the pills, the exercise classes, the wonder machines, and sometimes even more extreme measures like stomach stapling surgery. But in spite of all the time, money, and effort we expend, most of us are still fat. If you look at the studies done, the results are all about the same: Anywhere from 90% to 98% of the people who lose weight gain it all back within five years.

Sometimes writers need to go beyond the *actual* effects or consequences of an issue and *imagine* the possible ways others are involved. Consider the following: A writer is arguing about college students living at home. The issue seemingly affects only college students, and maybe their parents. But the writer makes the issue resonate with many other potential readers by transforming a personal issue into a more public one:

> How college students live is not simply a matter of personal choice and comfort. It is a public issue, a public education issue. At the federal, state, and local levels, Americans are increasingly focused on the out-of-school living conditions of elementary and secondary students. Whenever people talk about the quality of education, invariably they end up discussing the living situation of students—the stability of their homes, the qualities of the neighborhoods. Why? Because people are beginning to realize that education does not occur in a vacuum, that how and where students live impact how they learn. But for some reason, we don't seem to be concerned once students are in college. Consequently, millions of college students swarm off to school every fall, often without deeply considering the implications of where they will live. And when millions of dollars of loans and grants go down the drain when students fail out their first year, we don't seem to ask the same questions we ask about elementary and secondary students.

Research

Consider using outside sources to help you invent—to help you imagine the hidden values, assumptions, and attitudes people have about the topic. Discover what has been said about your topic, what people have argued, why they have taken certain positions, or why they have ignored it altogether. (See Chapter 14 for help with finding sources.)

Going from Private to Public

Private Concern:

Where should I live during my first year in college?

Public Concern:

What is the relationship between college failure rates and student living conditions?

Thesis

An argumentative thesis invites debate or suggests that opposing claims exist. For example:

> But far more important than my ill temper is a creepy sense that these inaccurate images [about body type] have shifted our vision of what is important in life way out of whack, so far out that people are being hurt.

The process of narrowing down an argument to an intensive single sentence helps writers to understand the heart of their idea. At an early stage in your project, you need not settle into an exact wording, but trying to generate a focused statement can help your ideas gain intensity.

An argumentative thesis should have four qualities:

Arguability

It should be arguable. That is, an arguable thesis should take a stand on an issue that has two or more possible positions. If you can conceive of other possible positions on the topic, you are probably in arguable territory.

Scope

It should be appropriately narrow. Scope can be addressed by asking narrow enough questions. Be careful of broad questions: *Is my town boring?* To answer such a question, one would have to consider all of the town's complexities, all of its goings-on, all of its people, all of its places, and so on. However, the question *Does my town offer sufficient activities for teens?* is more easily answerable—and ultimately arguable.

Public Resonance

It should address an issue that resonates with the readers. A good argument addresses a concern that others have *or that a writer thinks they should have.* In other words, a thesis should express something that matters (that has some significance) to readers. It should involve others.

Revelation

Academic writers attempt to do more than argue for their own opinions. They try to *reveal* an unfamiliar topic or reveal a new layer to a familiar topic. *Revelatory* thesis statements change readers' (and the writer's) thinking because they show something new. They clear away the mundane thinking and reveal the roots of an issue. Often, revelatory thesis statements:

- Include a reference to the opposition.
- Overturn or contradict popular opinion.
- Show a particular effect or relationship.
- Uncover a hidden layer.

Activities

1. Transform the following into revelatory thesis statements:
    - The Internet has changed the world.
    - Video games are bad for kids.
    - Sixteen-year-olds who commit crimes should be punished as adults.

2. In a small group, choose one of the following topics and develop at least one revelatory argumentative statement:
   - Leash laws in your town
   - The process for choosing presidential nominees
   - Product placement in movies
   - The cost of college textbooks
   - High school English courses

Evolution of a Thesis

Writers can always increase the focus and revelation of a thesis. The following idea evolves into an increasingly sophisticated point:

- College students benefit from living at home.
- Traditional college students still need the support structure of their home lives to deal with the new challenges of college.
- Because college culture demands intense intellectual and social change from high school culture, traditional college students need the support structure of home.

The first statement announces a simple opinion. The second narrows in on a specific tension: "the new challenges of college." But the statement is still a bit vague, and the idea will intensify with even more focus on that tension. The third statement brings us up close to the primary tension and shows us something that might otherwise escape our awareness: the "intense intellectual and social change" between high school and college culture. Readers of the last two theses, especially the third, has been given a novel insight about schooling. In this way, revelatory thesis statements are more than personal opinion; they are particular and persuasive insights.

Common Thesis Problems

The Question Problem A question is not a thesis, because it offers no stance. People sometimes use questions to imply a stance: *Isn't that the point of college? Why can't you be like your sister?* But this is generally an informal strategy—something people do in everyday talk. A formal argumentative stance should suggest a particular position amid a realm of many others.

The Obvious Fact Problem An argument that simply announces a commonly known condition is no argument at all. Imagine someone arguing: *Many people go to college for their futures; Americans love cars;* or *Space exploration is expensive.* Such statements do not invite opposition because they are widely held beliefs. They are safe statements about the condition of our civilization. But the statement *Space exploration is too expensive to continue at its present pace* invites opposition.

The Personal Response Problem Argument depends upon the presence of several other perspectives peering at the same topic. However, when people proclaim a personal response (about their tastes, likes, dislikes, or desires), they merely make public their own state of mind. "I really liked the movie" is not an argumentative stance. It is a statement about a person's tastes. But the statement, "Johnny Depp's portrayal of a wayward pirate illustrates his superior range as an actor" invites opposition. Other positions can engage the point critically.

Revising Your Thesis

Before moving on, try to express the main point of your argument in a single sentence. Then evaluate the statement using the following questions:

- How is the statement arguable? (What other positions might be taken?)
- Can the statement be narrower? (What words are too vague or broad?)
- With what public issue or concern does the statement resonate?
- How does the statement reveal a unique insight or hidden layer of the issue?

You might also exchange your working thesis statement with two or three peers and use these questions to generate helpful responses.

Rhetorical Tools

Crafting an essay, or any written text, is a recursive process: Writers move back and forth, drafting, rethinking, redrafting. It is not a simple step-by-step journey that looks the same for everyone. But all writers benefit from a large collection of strategies, various tools they can use according to their particular needs, situations, and voices. The strategies in this section will help you build a sophisticated and engaging text—one that emerges from your particular ideas. Academic argument involves four basic ingredients or elements:

- Main claim/thesis
- Support
- Counterargument
- Concession

Support

Support gives substance and legitimacy to an argumentative claim and comes in a variety of forms. Consider the following as a collection of usable support strategies, a toolbox for persuading readers of your position, despite the particular topic.

Examples Specific cases or illustrations of a phenomenon. (See Pedersen ¶4 and 6, Paulin ¶7, Stayer ¶6 and 7.)

Allusions References to history, science, nature, news events, films, television shows, or literary texts. (See Paulin ¶2, Stayer ¶1–4 and 9.)

Personal Testimonies/Anecdotes Individual accounts or experiences. While testimony comes from an eyewitness ("I saw the train coming around the mountain ..."), an anecdote is told by the arguer as though he or she is an objective reporter of events ("The incident on the train tracks started with the train coming around the mountain ..."). (See Pedersen ¶11, Paulin ¶1 and 2, Bohnhorst ¶1.)

Scenarios Hypothetical or fictionalized accounts. (See Pedersen ¶7.)

Statistics Information (often given as numerical value) collected through experimentation, surveys, polls, and research. (See Pedersen ¶2, Paulin ¶4, Bohnhorst ¶3.)

Authorities References to published (most often written) sources. When using authorities, writers must formally document the use of any information, ideas, and expressions taken from sources. For an extended explanation of formal documentation and integration of sources, see Chapter 14: Integrating and Documenting Sources. (See Paulin ¶2, Bohnhorst ¶5.)

Facts Agreed-upon events or truths, or conclusions drawn from investigation. (See Stayer ¶1 and 2, Bohnhort ¶2.)

Additionally, arguments depend on appeals, which make a connection between the topic and the audience's thought process. In fact, appeals have such rhetorical force that they give meaning to and can even dominate over other forms of evidence. The first three appeals that follow (to logic, emotion, and character) are often discussed using three classical Greek terms: *logos* (for logic), *pathos* (for emotion), and *ethos* (for character). These are sometimes referred to as the Classical appeals.

Appeal to Logic Relates the argument to the audience's sense of reason or creates a line of reasoning for the audience to follow. (See Pedersen ¶7, Paulin's conclusion, Stayer ¶14 and 15 and 19, Bohnhorst ¶10 and 11.)

Appeal to Emotion Relates the argument to an emotional state of the audience, or attempts to create a particular emotional state in the audience. (See Paulin ¶1 and conclusion.)

Appeal of Character Relates the argument to a quality of the author/speaker. (See Pedersen ¶11, Stayer ¶15.)

Appeal to Need Relates the argument to people's needs (spiritual, economic, physical, sexual, familial, political, etc.). (See Bohnhorst ¶8 and 9.)

Appeal to Value Relates the argument to people's values (judgments about right/wrong, success, discipline, selflessness, moderation, honesty, chastity, modesty, self-expression, etc.). (See, Bohnhorst ¶7 and 8.)

The appeal to logic, or *logos,* is the most valued appeal in formal argument. It requires the arguer to establish premises—claims that must be accepted in order for the main claim (or conclusion) to be acceptable. One example is the *syllogism,* which asserts two premises and a conclusion: A is true and B is true; therefore, C must also be true.

Too often, writers limit themselves by assuming that facts and statistics are the primary support tools for a good argument, when the truth is that facts and statistics are merely a fragment of what's possible—and what's most valuable. Writers have the whole world of culture and history within reach. They can make connections (allusions) to historical or current events, literary texts, science, nature, and their personal lives. For example, perhaps you see a connection between your topic and a recent news event. You could briefly explain details of the event and then describe what it means for your topic—how it reveals something significant and ultimately validates your opinion. The same thing goes for a movie, an ad, or a historical event. For instance, imagine a writer developing the argument about college residence policies. He might bring popular culture to his aid:

> In movies and popular television shows, college is nearly always portrayed as a raucous social engagement. The typical movie college student (like those in *American Pie* or *Animal House*) is a dormitory, apartment, or frat or sorority house dweller who thrives or suffers in the family-free environment. The whole point of college in mainstream movies is to create a living situation in which the students just tread the line between responsible participation in society and utter immersion in bohemian life. It's no wonder that going to college seems synonymous with "going away" to college. When students long to avoid living in the chaotic social climate of campus life, they are working against more than some college policies. They are working against popular culture.

If you see a connection, especially one that others might not see, it can create a new way of thinking about the topic. Use the following questions to develop allusions, testimony, and scenarios for your argument:

- Does a historical situation or trend (say, the rise of a particular fashion, organization, or individual) illustrate something about my topic?
- How has popular culture treated my topic? Does it show up in television shows, movies, or commercials? If so, how is it characterized, mishandled, or celebrated?
- Have fictional characters illustrated something important about the topic or some behavior related to it?
- How does nature (animals, life cycles, plants, biological processes, and so on) demonstrate something about my topic?
- What has science taught people about my topic?
- Do any news events illustrate my point or stance?
- What have I witnessed or experienced that illustrates my point?
- What hypothetical situation could illustrate my point?
- What do other writers or authorities on the matter say about the topic?

Now, imagine how using appeals can help your argument. The various appeals can be applied to nearly any topic. Notice how a writer might tie an argument about college students to broader values—family intimacy and self-determination:

> Going to college should not have to mean going away to college. The intellectual commitment required of a student should not necessarily require a domestic commitment. Coming into an institution should not necessarily mean abandoning the intimacy of family. And entering college should not mean entering a compulsory social climate. But policies that require first-year students to live on campus impose a domestic and social arrangement onto students.

The most valued strategy in formal academic argument is the appeal to logic—or what is often called a *line of reasoning.* When writers create a line of reasoning, they create an intellectual path for readers—several steps (sometimes called premises) that lead to the writer's thesis. Consider the topic from the previous section: college students living at home. If we want to convince readers to believe that colleges should not require students to live on campus, we might create the following line of reasoning:

1. The shift from high school to college culture is significant.
2. Many students experience a kind of culture shock in the transition.
3. This culture shock negatively impacts their academic performance.

Each of these statements requires further explanation, examples, illustration, evidence, and appeal. In other words, this line of reasoning might require several lengthy passages of text. But if the readers could accept each claim, then they would be led directly to the main point—that college policies should not require on-campus residence for all first-year students.

As you consider your own topic, use the following questions to develop appeals:

- What line of reasoning can I create for readers to follow? What premises do readers have to accept before they accept my thesis?
- How can I connect the topic to people's values (sense of right and wrong, success, discipline, selflessness, moderation, honesty, chastity, modesty, self-expression, etc.)?
- How can I connect the topic to people's basic needs (spiritual, economic, physical, sexual, familial, political, etc.)?
- How can I connect the topic to people's emotions (fear, hope, sadness, happiness, etc.)?
- Does my life (my role in a relationship, on a job, in school, on a team, etc.) lend credibility to my position on this topic?

Activity

Generate a variety of appeals for each of the following claims:

- Although war illustrates human cruelty and malice, it also illustrates human compassion and sympathy.
- Most proponents of capital punishment fail to consider the impact on the executed person's loved ones.
- Democracy cannot thrive in a two-party system.
- Excessive marketing leads to a lack of civility and respect among citizens.

Counterargument

Counterarguments anticipate and refute claims or positions that oppose those being forwarded by the writer. Writers must anticipate and account for positions outside of or opposed to their own claims(s) and include reasoning to offset that potential opposition. For example, a savvy teenager who wants to attend a party will imagine his parents' concerns and work them into his argument about why he should be allowed to go. A politician will anticipate her opponent's position on an issue and formulate her speech accordingly.

The most successful arguers are good counterarguers. They address and even dismantle the specifics of opposing claims. In her essay, Ann Marie Paulin counterargues by summing up advice given to Barbara Dinnerstein: "She told us to put a picture of ourselves on the 'fridgerator of us eating and looking really fat and ugly. She said remember what you look like. Remember how ugly you are." In the paragraph that follows this advice, Paulin explains why she disagrees:

> I have a problem with this advice. First, of course, it is too darn common. Fat people are constantly being told they should be ashamed of themselves, of their bodies. And here we see another of those misconceptions I mentioned earlier: the assumption that being fat is the same as being ugly. There are plenty of attractive fat people in the world, as well as a few butt-ugly thin ones, I might add. Honestly, though, the real tragedy is that while few people in this world are truly ugly, many agonize over the belief that they are. Dr. Pipher reported: "I see clients who say they would rather kill themselves than be overweight" (91). I never have figured out how trashing a fellow being's self-esteem is going to help that person be healthier.

In academic argument, opposing claims are vital. Instead of ignoring or fearing them, good writers *use* them to develop points. In developing your argument, try to address opposing claims. Doing so will make your own argument more complex, more developed, and more persuasive.

In fact, some writers anticipate the opposition and integrate a counterargument directly into their thesis statements. For example, let's examine the working thesis: *College students benefit from living at home while attending school.* This thesis is somewhat focused, but it could be better if we imagine the opposition: Someone might argue that the college experience depends on moving away from home, that intellectual growth requires leaving one's family and familiar turf. This opposing position might be supported with personal testimony and stories in literature that tell of heroes leaving their homeland to seek knowledge or wisdom in the world. We would do well to consider these points, and perhaps work against some of them directly. We might even work part of the logic into our own thesis: *Despite the attraction of living away from home and experiencing life in unfamiliar territory, college students benefit from living at home while attending school.* This thesis now contains a counterargument. It is both an assertion and a response to a primary opposing point.

Invention Workshop

This activity is designed to generate counterarguments. The process involves an intensive group exchange. Follow these steps:

- Assemble writers into small groups (three or four per group works best).
- Each writer should have his or her thesis statement (main argumentative claim) written down.
- The first writer should read his or her thesis statement aloud to the group.
- Taking turns, each group member then should attempt to refute the position given in the statement. The idea is to play devil's advocate, to complicate the writer's ideas.

- The writer should record each opposing claim that is offered.
- After everyone in the group has given an opposing claim to the first writer, the second writer should recite his or her thesis, and the process begins again.

Concession and Qualifier

Although counterarguments refute objections, concessions acknowledge the value of others' claims. Put another way, if the writer says that an objection or alternative is wrong, the response is a counterargument; but if the writer says that the objection or alternative is right, that response is a concession.

Concession is a vital aspect of academic argument. In her argument, Elizabeth Bohnhorst offers a thorough concession to the value of computers before she begins her powerful argument against their role in the classroom:

> Computers can undoubtedly contribute wonders to the field of education. In fact, computer education is a must if children intend to thrive in modern society. The possibilities are endless when it comes to surfing the Web or using the thousands of educational programs currently available. These programs are capable of reading text on a computer with icons beside words that take students to a galaxy of options, icons to learn more about the era in which the text was written, fascinating facts about the author, and helpful notes about the morals of the story.

Conceding in academic argument does not make an argument wishy-washy. In fact, a good concession, such as Bohnhorst's, shows that a writer understands the broader context—other opinions, values, hopes, and perspectives. A good writer might discuss the logic of another position and show, *to some degree,* how that position has validity. This does not mean that the writer's own point is weak; on the contrary, it means that his or her point is so strong and valid that it can even acknowledge the soundness of other positions.

Qualifiers are closely related to concessions. They acknowledge the limitations of, or make clear boundaries for, the writer's own argument. For example, when giving a speech on the evils of corporate tax evasion, a senator qualifies her statements: "Granted, most companies in America pay taxes responsibly, but we must focus on those few rogue and politically powerful companies." When arguing for a salary increase, a union leader acknowledges a point made by the opposition: "We understand that economic times ahead could be perilous and that a salary increase could make the company more financially vulnerable to outside forces, but the future of the company certainly depends upon the well-being of its loyal employees." And in her argument, Paulin makes an explicit qualifier, which may keep readers from mischaracterizing her position:

> First of all, let me make it clear that I'm not advocating that everyone in America go out and get fat. According to the news media, we are doing that very handily on our own, in spite of all the messages to the contrary and the shelves of diet food in every supermarket.

Activity

Before drafting an essay, plan out your main elements. Write out your working thesis and then, below it, create five headings:

- Personal testimony
- Examples, allusions, or scenarios
- Evidence from sources or reference to authorities
- Opposing positions
- Counterarguments, concessions, or qualifiers

Under each heading, list the ideas or information you've generated so far. This plan, or informal outline, can help you to move forward.

Caution: Logical Fallacies

Logical fallacies are flaws in the structure of an argument that make the claims invalid. A fallacy is a falsehood, so a logical fallacy is a logical falsehood that makes no sense within a given situation. For example, consider this familiar line:

> If you break a mirror, you'll have seven years of bad luck.

We may recognize this as superstition. In academic terms, it is called *faulty cause/effect.* That is, the broken mirror does not actually cause misfortune in one's life. The statement seems categorically faulty. However, the success (or logic) of any argument depends on the particular situation. All argumentative statements exist in situations that give those statements credibility. (If someone's entire fortune were tied to a mirror, then the previous statement would be more logical!) Statements are logical or illogical based on the situation.

In academia, recognizing logical fallacies is part of being a critical thinker in all disciplines. There is no quicker way to make readers of your own work suspicious than committing any of the following fallacies when making an argument:

Ad hominem (Latin for *to the person*) Attacks a person directly rather than examining the logic of the argument:

- We cannot possibly consider Ms. Smith's proposal because she is a Catholic.
- Mr. Mann's argument is suspicious because he is a socialist.

Strawperson Exaggerates a characteristic of a person or group of people and then uses the exaggeration to dismiss an argument:

- Islamic fundamentalists are crazy. They only want to destroy Americans. We cannot accept their claims about imperialism.
- Environmentalists are radical. They want to end everyone's fun by taking cars and boats away.

Faulty Cause/Effect Confuses a sequential relationship with a causal one. Assumes that event A caused event B because A occurred first:

- Since the construction of the new baseball stadium, homelessness in the downtown area has decreased.
- The tax cut made energy rates drop.

Either/or Reasoning Offers only two choices when more exist:

- Either we destroy Russia or it will destroy us.
- The American people will choose to control their own lives or give away their wills to socialist candidates.

Hasty Generalization Draws a conclusion about a group of people, events, or things based on insufficient examples (often, the logical flaw behind racist, sexist, or bigoted statements):

- Men are too possessive. My ex-boyfriend would never let me go out alone.
- French people are rude. When I went to France, the civilians grunted French statements when I asked for help.

Non sequitur (Latin for *it does not follow*) Skips several logical steps in drawing a conclusion:

- If we do not trash the entire tax code, the downtown area will slowly deteriorate.
- A new baseball stadium downtown will help with the homelessness problem.

Oversimplification Does not acknowledge the true complexity of a situation or offers easy solutions to complicated problems:

- If we could give kids something to do, they wouldn't get depressed.
- This credit card will end all of my financial problems.

Slippery Slope Assumes that a certain way of thinking or acting will necessarily continue or extend in that direction (like a domino effect). Such an argument suggests that once we begin down a path, we will inevitably slip all the way down, and so the effects of a particular action or idea are exaggerated:

- If the college makes students take more mathematics, the next thing we know, advanced calculus and quantum physics will be requirements for all graduates.
- If North Vietnam succeeds in making South Vietnam communist, it will eventually threaten the shores of the United States of America.

False Analogy Makes a comparison between two things that are ultimately more unlike than alike. The differences between the things make the comparison ineffective or unfair, or the comparison misrepresents one or both of the things involved:

- Writing is like breathing: you just do what comes naturally.
- Like Galileo, Bill Clinton was breaking new ground, but no one understood him.

Begging the Question Attempts to prove a claim by using an alternative wording of the claim itself:

- Girls should not be allowed into the Boys' Military Academy because it is for boys only.
- I believe that all cigarette smoking should be banned from public places because I truly believe in smoking bans.

Activities

1. What logical fallacies might you overhear in everyday situations? Consider the following scenarios: a customer trying to return an item; a store clerk trying to sell an extended warranty; a teacher explaining why a student cannot receive credit for a late assignment; a student arguing that he or she should receive a better grade; two politicians debating a tax cut; a husband explaining why he should go fishing with his cousin all weekend.
2. In groups, write an example for each of the fallacies listed in this chapter.
3. In groups, write short argumentative essays loaded with logical blunders. Someone in each group should read the completed essay aloud, and the class should attempt to point out and name the fallacies.

Revision

Sometimes, argumentative essays take on too much. Their focus is too broad. A broad thesis prompts writers to make vague, often unsupportable, points. Take one last look at your thesis—the main argumentative assertion of your essay. Does it focus on a particular tension, a particular aspect of an issue, a specific element or dimension of a broader topic? What words or phrases (*things, people, society*) can be substituted for something more specific? How might you focus on one aspect of an issue rather than the whole issue?

Peer Review

Underline your thesis, or write it at the top of your essay so that reviewers will get traction as they read. Then, exchange drafts with at least one other writer. Reviewers should use the following questions to guide a helpful response:

1. How well can you follow the writer's line of reasoning? (See appeal to logic, pages 275.) Imagine the line of reasoning as though it is a stone path. If the path is well laid out, you should feel a stone at every step. If it is not, you might miss a step; you might feel like some intellectual step is missing.
2. Can you think of another cultural, literary, historical, or political allusion that relates to the writer's position?
3. Suggest specific points that the writer should concede or qualify. For instance, the writer's position might seem too extreme; the claims might include too many people or a large, diverse group without making any distinctions. Point out such claims, and help the writer to see the need to acknowledge subtlety, complexity, and exceptions.
4. Can you imagine another opposing point that the writer could address in a counterargument? Although the writer may have dealt with several opposing positions, you might think of an additional issue that should be addressed.
5. Consider the writer's voice. Circle passages or sentences that shift mood and speak *at,* rather than *with,* readers. Suggest an alternative strategy or phrasing.
6. Do paragraphs focus on one main point? Point to sentences in paragraphs that stray from the initial idea put forth in the paragraph.
7. What is the most engaging passage in the draft so far? Why?
8. Check for sentence vitality.
    - Where can the writer change linking verbs to active verbs?
    - Where can the writer avoid drawing attention to *I* and *you?*
    - Consider vitality strategies from other chapters:

      —Help the writer change unnecessary clauses to phrases.

      —Help the writer change unnecessary phrases to words.

      —Point to expletives (such as *there are* and *it is*).

      —Help the writer change passive verbs to active verbs for more vitality.

      —Help the writer avoid common grammatical errors: comma splices, sentence fragments, or pronoun/antecedent agreement.

Questions for Research

If the writer used outside sources,

- Where must he or she include in-text citations? (See pages 508–509.)
- Are quotations blended smoothly into the argument and punctuated correctly? (See pages 495–506.)
- Where could more direct textual cues or transitions help readers? (See pages 504–506.)
- Is the Works Cited or References page formatted properly? (See Chapter 16.)

Reflection

Academic essays are not merely vehicles for communicating thought. They are intellectual playing fields—places for writers and readers to discover something. Those discoveries do not exist in the vacuum of an essay; they resonate outward through the lives of the writers and readers. An argument essay in particular sets out to assert something about the world, and that assertion is bound to impact reality—because people live according to the arguments they accept. Now that you have written an argumentative essay, consider its rhetorical layers:

1. How does your thesis reveal something about everyday life?
2. How does your essay challenge something about the way most people live and think?
3. How important are appeals to your argument?
4. How do you engage opposing positions? How do they make your argument more complex?
5. How do you concede or qualify?

Beyond the Essay: The Open Letter

Argumentative essays have changed the world. They've started revolutions, supported religious movements, initiated new scientific organizations, spotlighted atrocities, and prompted a broad range of political events. But sophisticated arguments can impact the world through other genres too.

The open letter is closely related to the essay. It is aimed at a particular audience, a particular reader or set of readers, but it also resonates with a broader audience. An open letter draws both writer and readers, and an otherwise private discussion, into a public setting. For example, Martin Luther King, Jr.'s "Letter from Birmingham Jail" was originally aimed at nine fellow clergy members, but the letter also speaks to millions of others. In effect, King's response to a particular audience is also for a broader audience. The conversation occurs among a few particular people, but the issues and claims involve many. Or consider the apostle Paul's letters to the Romans that now constitute part of the New Testament. They have become known to millions of readers, but they were originally aimed at a particular group of people. Or more currently, newspapers and magazines often print open letters to the president, to an editor, or to corporate heads. Hundreds, thousands, or millions of others read and are influenced by these letters. And one might argue that these others are really the main audience.

Because letters are written with a particular audience in mind, they may draw attention to specifics about the readers' lives, such as specific behaviors, policies, attitudes, or events. The writer may then draw out the significance, explaining the impact on or meaning for others (the public resonance).

Return to your essay and imagine a particular person or group of people who should read and accept your claims. Then develop an open letter addressed to that particular audience. But don't just make a few simple changes in your essay and call that a letter. Instead, *take a big step back*: Imagine a different rhetorical situation, this one having a different audience, a different method of delivery, and a different purpose. Although you may end up using some especially nice strategies from the essay, approach the letter as if writing from scratch.

The following questions may help shape your ideas:

- Who is the primary audience? Who is being explicitly addressed in the letter?
- What other audience is there? Who else might read the letter and what might their response be? Can they take action based on the letter? How might they think or act differently because of reading it?
- How can you appeal to the primary audience? How can you make a specific connection between them and the issue? How might the letter also appeal to others reading it?
- What pieces (phrases, sentences, ideas, strategies) can you take from the essay and include in the letter? Why these pieces? What pieces should you leave behind? What new pieces should you create for the letter?

9 Responding to Arguments

Carlos Cazalis/Corbis

"We hold these truths to be self-evident, that all men are created equal, that they are endowed by their Creator with certain inalienable rights, that among these are life, liberty, and the pursuit of happiness."

—The Declaration of Independence

Arguments are all around us. They lurk in nearly every situation—public or private—and we often respond to arguments that hover but are not stated directly. Some situations generate a huge range of arguments. Like magnets, they attract a storm of claims, facts, testimony, appeals, counterarguments, concessions, and qualifiers. Consider, for instance, the border between US and Mexico. In recent years, it has created a litany of arguments about federal and state budgets, immigration, race, national identity, drug use, poverty, labor, minimum wage, taxes, healthcare, education, and human rights. As with many political issues, the border has developed its own argumentative cosmos, filled with radical new claims, traditional platforms, and competing interpretations of founding national documents. The positions get bantered around on radio talk shows, blogs, and of course political campaign ads. Entering that cosmos can be tricky. With so many issues and positions swirling around, it can be difficult to find a particular point of contact.

In academia, writers understand the power and peril of big argumentative issues. Rather than take on a huge swirl of claims, they often focus and respond to specific texts:

- A psychologist responds to Freud's theory of ego development, explaining that such a theory is not valuable in treating female patients.

- A political science student supports a revised historical account of U.S. foreign policy that holds Henry Kissinger partly responsible for atrocities in Chile during the 1970s.
- Law students respond to a Supreme Court ruling that upholds the rights of law enforcement officers to detain citizens for traffic violations. They argue that the ruling erodes protections against "unreasonable search and seizure."
- An English professor reviews a controversial new book and defends its claims against rampant consumerism.

As these examples suggest, responding to an argument does not necessarily mean disagreement. The initial argument (whether a court ruling, a book, an essay, or a historical account) provides the position on a topic. A writer has many options beyond agreement or disagreement. For instance, he or she might agree with the initial argument and extend the ideas with additional points, disagree with a particular point, redefine the issue, or point out some logical flaws.

As you can imagine, this is a somewhat more sophisticated task than what we examined in Chapter 8, Making Arguments. However, responding to arguments is an engaging activity, one that is not only vital to and valued in academia, but also necessary for maintaining a democracy.

Although a writer can respond to many different kinds of argument, this chapter focuses primarily on arguments that are formally delivered. The chapter will help you discover and analyze an argument, develop a sophisticated argumentative response, and communicate your position in writing.

Read the following essays, which illustrate a variety of strategies for responding. Early in each essay (each argument), the author refers to a particular aspect of the original argument, and this reference provides a purpose and traction for the response. As you read, notice how this reference to the original argument is made. After reading the essays, you can find an argument in one of several ways:

1. Go to the Point of Contact section to find an argument from everyday life,
2. Choose one of the Ideas for Writing that follow the essays, or
3. Respond to any argumentative essay from another chapter in this book.

After you find a topic, go to the Analysis section to begin developing your response.

Readings

What Orwell Didn't Know

George Lakoff

George Orwell, the pen name of Eric Arthur Blair (1903–1950), was a journalist, novelist, and political commentator famous for his most popular works, *Animal Farm* (1945) and *1984* (1949), two influential novels that have been required reading in many high school and college courses. Like *Animal Farm* and *1984,* Orwell's essay "Politics and the English Language" (1946) has been required reading for many college students. As George Lakoff (1941–), a professor of cognitive linguistics at the University of California, Berkeley, explains in the following essay, Orwell argues that inaccurate language leads to "political propaganda and its effects." While Lakoff commends Orwell's essay for its important contribution, his response labels it an anachronism because, as Lakoff explains, those in his profession have "learned a lot about the brain, the mind, and language since then."

George Orwell will forever be a hero of mine. When I read *1984* in high school, I became sensitized to the workings of propaganda. After more than forty years as a linguist and cognitive scientist, I remain sensitized.

When I first read "Politics and the English Language" as an undergraduate in the late 1950s, I loved it. Nearly fifty years later I find it an anachronism. Why? I, and those in my profession, have learned a lot about the brain, the mind and language since then. Orwell's essay belongs to an earlier time, a time that lacked our deepening understanding of how the human brain works.

Orwell suffered from what we might now call the "Editor's Fallacy": Bad habits of "foolish thought" and inaccurate, slovenly, dull, pretentious, ungraceful, and meaningless language—the "decay of language"—lead to political propaganda and its effects. If we just "let the meaning choose the word," he claimed, we would all be saved. This is not only false, it is dangerously naïve.

Orwell fell into traps—false views of language: *Meanings are truth conditions. Words have unitary meanings. If people are told the truth, they will reason to the right conclusions—unless they are stupid or ignorant. And ignorance can be cured by truths conveyed in good prose.*

All of that is false. Yet progressives still fall into those traps. Even you, dear reader, may have fallen into them. And even *I* am trying to cure ignorance via truths conveyed in good prose. I am banking on cognitive dissonance—yours! Dissonance between the real brain and the apparent mind. Intellectuals are confident they know their own minds, though they realize they don't know their own brains. But their brains betray their confidence in their minds. Neuroscience and cognitive science reveal a far more interesting picture than Orwell could have guessed.

Probably 98 percent of your reasoning is *un*conscious—what your brain is doing behind the scenes. Reason is inherently emotional. You can't even choose a goal, much less form a plan and carry it out, without a sense that it will satisfy you, not disgust you. Fear and anxiety will affect your plans and your actions. You act differently, and plan differently, out of hope and joy than out of fear and anxiety.

Thought is physical. Learning requires a physical brain change: Receptors for neurotransmitters change at the synapses, which changes neural circuitry. Since thinking is the activation of such circuitry, somewhat different thinking requires a somewhat different brain. Brains change as you use them—even unconsciously. It's as if your car changed as you drove it, say from a stick shift gradually to an automatic.

Thought is physical in another way. It uses the brain's sensory-motor system. Imagining moving uses the same regions of the brain as moving; imagining seeing uses the same regions of the brain as seeing. Meaning is mental simulation, activating those regions of the brain. Reasoning from A to B is the neural activation of the mental simulation of B, given the mental simulation of A. Mental simulation, like most thought, is mostly unconscious.

Thought is structured, in large measure, in terms of "frames"—brain structures that control mental simulation and hence reasoning.

You think metaphorically, perhaps most of the time. Just by functioning with your body in the world as a child, you learn at least hundreds of simple "conceptual metaphors"—metaphors you think with and live by. For example, Quantity is understood in terms of Verticality (More is Up), and the words follow along: *prices rise and fall, skyrocket and hit bottom.* Why? Because every day of your life, if you pour water into a glass, the level rises. You experience a correlation between quantity and verticality. In your brain, regions for registering verticality and quantity are activated together during such experiences. As a result, activation spreads, and circuits linking Verticality to Quantity are formed. Those circuits constitute the metaphor More is Up in your brain. As a child lives in the world, his or her brain acquires hundreds of such "primary" conceptual metaphors that are just there waiting to be used in everyday thought.

We have high-level moral worldviews—modes of reasoning about what's right and wrong—that govern whole areas of reason, both conscious and unconscious, and link up whole networks of frames and metaphors.

Cultural narratives are special cases of such frames. They stretch over time and define protagonists and antagonists—and heroes, victims, and villains. They define right and wrong, and come with emotional content. And most important, we all live out cultural narratives—with all their emotionality and moral sensibility. We even define our identities by the narratives we live by.

What are words? Words are neural links between spoken and written expressions and frames, metaphors, and narratives. When we hear the words, not only their immediate frames and metaphors are activated, but also all the high-level worldviews and associated narratives—with their emotions—are activated. Words are not just words—they activate a huge range of brain mechanisms. Moreover, words don't just activate neutral meanings; they are often defined relative to conservative framings. And our most important political words—*freedom, equality, fairness, opportunity, security, accountability*—name "contested concepts," concepts with a common shared core that is unspecified, which is then extended to most of its cases based on your values. Thus conservative "freedom" is utterly different than progressive "freedom," as I showed in detail in *Whose Freedom.* Liberals such as Paul Starr, in *Freedom's Power,* unselfconsciously use their own version of freedom, as if there were no other version. Not understanding conservative "freedom" and pointing out its problematic nature greatly weakens one's effect.

A few words in political language can activate large portions of the brain: *War on Terror, tax relief, illegal immigration, entitlements* (turned to conservative use by Ronald Reagan), *death tax, property rights, abortion on demand, cut and run, flip-flop, school choice, intelligent design, spending programs, partial birth abortion, surge, spreading freedom, private accounts, individual responsibility, energy independence.*

When they are repeated every day, extensive areas of the brain are activated over and over, and this leads to brain change. Unerasable brain change. Once learned, the new neural structure cannot just be erased: *War on Terror* be gone! It doesn't work. And every time the words are repeated, all the frames and metaphors and worldview structures are activated again and strengthened—because recurring activation strengthens neural connections. Negation doesn't help. "I'm against the War on Terror" just activates the *War on Terror* metaphor and strengthens what you're against. Accepting the language of issue and arguing the other side just hurts your own cause.

Can you counter such brain change? There are two possibilities. First, you can try to mark the idea—as silly, immoral, stupid, and so on—by having lots of people say so over a long period of time. That's what conservatives did with "liberal," starting back in the 1960s when most people wanted to be liberals. *Tax and spend liberal, liberal elite, liberal media, limousine liberal,* and so on repeated over and over slowly got across the idea to lower- and middle-class Republicans that liberals were elite, financially irresponsible, and oppressing poor conservatives. And it undermined liberals' confidence in themselves.

The second strategy is to provide an alternative honest framing—either by inhibiting what is in the brain or by bypassing it. Done honestly, it is righting history. Done dishonestly, it is "rewriting history." Conservatives have done this with the Vietnam War: We lost because we didn't use enough force—"*We had one hand tied behind our backs.*"

Neither is quick or easy.

Today, sophisticated right-wing propaganda is very well-written—the editor in Orwell would love David Brooks's prose. Mind control works via brain change, through the effective use of well-written language to activate not just frames, conceptual metaphors, and emotions, but whole worldviews. When the language is repeated and the words become just "the normal way you express the idea," then even the best people in the media get sucked in. Journalists have to use words people understand, and they have to use the words most people normally use to express the ideas they are writing about. As a result, they often have no idea that they are using conservative language, which activates a conservative view of the world as well as the conservative perspective on the given issue. They are rarely aware that in doing so, they are helping conservatives by strengthening the conservative worldview in the public's mind, and thereby accelerating brain change.

Once a member of the public has undergone brain change, he or she then thinks as a conservative on the issue. Not convinced rationally, just subject to the techniques every marketer uses. Is free will being exercised? The very idea of "free will" has been changed.

Orwell wasn't aware of how brains, minds, and language really work, nor was anyone else in 1947. But we don't have that excuse today. Yet even the very best of our news media are stuck in the same traps. Every now and then a result about the brain will leak out into the *Science Times* or *Discover,* only to be forgotten the next week. But what we know about the brain, the mind, and language barely ever makes it to the front page or opinion pages where politics is discussed. The ghost of Orwell still haunts our very best news and political opinion media.

Orwell's old-fashioned views about reason and language also haunt the Democratic Party. But there are promising developments. Presidential candidate John Edwards has rejected the very term *War on Terror* as an inappropriate metaphor and a means to grab power. In the Democratic debate in New Hampshire in June 2007, the questions Wolf Blitzer of CNN asked were all framed from a conservative viewpoint. Democratic candidate Barack Obama stepped forward and rejected *one* of the conservatively framed questions as "specifically designed to divide us."

In another positive development, progressives have been saying out loud that conservatism itself is the problem. Robert Borosage, in the *The American Prospect,* staunchly argues from a progressive worldview, "Conservatives cannot be trusted to guide the government they scorn. Not because they are incompetent or corrupt (although corruption and incompetence abound), but because they get the world wrong."

This is half right. But it ignores the thousands of conservative "successes" from *their* point of view, which Borosage cites as "failures." In hundreds of cases (excepting Iraq—a big exception), conservatives would say that George W. Bush got the world right—because he changed the world as he wanted to.

If Democrats think that those who voted for Bush will consider all those "successes" as failures, they might just find a way to lose the next election. Moral: To counter conservatism, you have to understand, and publicly discuss the problems with, the conservative moral worldview. And to do that, you need to know how largely unconscious worldviews work.

Conservative think tanks, over thirty-five years, started with the conservative worldview and showed how to apply it everywhere on every issue, and even beyond issues in the acts of governance—cutting regulating budgets, reassigning regulators, using the courts to redefine the laws, changing the facts on Web sites, eliminating libraries. New Democratic think tanks haven't helped much. The problem is that they are *policy* think tanks. They mistakenly think that "rational" programs and policies constitute political ideas. They don't understand unconscious thought. It's the unspoken ideas behind the programs and the policies—the worldviews, deep frames, metaphors, and cultural narratives—that need to be changed in the public mind. Only one progressive think tank, the Rockridge Institute, is even working in this direction. Its handbook for progressives, *Thinking Points,* applies the study of mind to the cause of truth.

Is it legitimate to use the real mechanisms of mind—worldviews, frames, metaphors, emotions, images, personal stories, and cultural narratives—to tell important truths? Hell, yes!

It is usually the only way that works. Al Gore's movie, *An Inconvenient Truth,* uses all those mechanisms of mind and heart—and it works. Had it just given facts and figures unframed, it would have flopped.

It is time to exorcise Orwell's ghost. We all need to understand how the brain, mind, and language really work. We need to apply that knowledge effectively to make truths meaningful and give *truths* the power to change brains. Our democracy depends on a clear and open understanding of the political mind.

Writing Strategies

1. Describe Lakoff's opening strategy. How does it set the tone for the essay?
2. What does Lakoff disagree with George Orwell about? To Lakoff, why is the disagreement important?
3. Lakoff says, "Thought is physical." Summarize his explanation and then explain how this idea is important to Lakoff's main point.
4. As part of his response, Lakoff defines *words.* How is his definition important in helping readers understand and accept his main idea?
5. According to Lakoff, what are the real mechanisms of mind, and why should they be used to tell important truths?

Exploring Ideas

1. Lakoff says, "You think metaphorically, perhaps most of the time." Summarize Lakoff's explanation, and then come up with an original example of metaphorical thinking that supports Lakoff's point.
2. Explain Lakoff's idea that cultural narratives are frames.
3. With a group of classmates, come up with an original example to illustrate Lakoff's claim that "[a]ccepting the language of issue and arguing the other side just hurts your own cause."
4. Why does Lakoff think "[o]nce a member of the public has undergone brain change, he or she then thinks as a conservative on the issue"?
5. Do some research on think tanks to become more informed about what they are. What is the purpose of a think tank? Why are think tanks important to Lakoff's response?

Ideas for Writing

1. Respond to an older way of thinking that has played an important role in your development, but that now needs to be revised in some important way.
2. In groups or alone, generate ideas for an essay by creating five titles, filling in the blanks: What ______________ Didn't Know About ______________.

If responding to one of these ideas, go to the Analysis section of this chapter to begin developing ideas for your essay.

Entitlement Education

Daniel Bruno

We often respond to the people (and arguments) that we agree with the most. In the following essay, Daniel Bruno agrees with most of Peter Sacks's original argument. His introduction explains: "But he fails, it seems, to emphasize enough a most harmful effect of this sense of entitlement." Bruno's response does not disagree but rather *emphasizes* a crucial point in an attempt to make *readers* more aware of it. (Portions of Bruno's invention work are shown in later sections of this chapter.)

Overall summary of original argument.

Entitlement: expecting to get good grades for little effort.

Main response to the original argument.

(Attention to "I") Bruno's thesis, and distinction between his argument and the original.

In his book *Generation X Goes to College,* Peter Sacks describes, among other things, the sense of entitlement that some students in today's consumerist culture have toward a college education. One entire chapter explores this issue alone, providing examples of this "sense" and looking into its "humble beginnings." Sacks shows how consumerism has invaded education, leading some students to expect good grades for little effort. But he fails, it seems, to emphasize enough a most harmful effect of this sense of entitlement. The biggest problem, as I see it, is that although students are able to graduate from high school (and even some colleges) with minimal effort, those students may find themselves cheated in the long run.

How might they be cheated? One might argue that students get cheated because entitlement doesn't go on forever. At some point it stops. For example, a college graduate with a marketing degree, but especially weak thinking or writing skills, may find himself disadvantaged on the job. It is not that his boss puts her foot down; instead, the job does. Our student finds himself not well prepared for it. He gets cheated because he is disadvantaged at his job—a job that he paid money to learn how to do. Of course the point isn't about marketing majors. The same is true of students in any field. (Marketing is just what came to mind.)

Cheated out of quality of life.

Analysis of several possible arguments about the results of student entitlement.

One might also claim that students will be cheated because their lives will somehow *be less.* This argument claims that a person's intelligence contributes to his quality of life. Here we must remember that "intelligence" is not just "knowledge." Instead, it is being able to use knowledge, to make connections and figure things out, to see

■ Writing Strategies ■ Exploring Ideas

causes and solve problems. A person may have much knowledge—that is, he may have accumulated a lot of facts—but not have much intelligence . . . or so the argument goes. As one goes from first grade to twelfth, from twelfth grade to college, and from freshman to senior, education shifts focus from mere accumulation of information (knowledge) to application of information (intelligence). And while we may accumulate more knowledge as a senior in college than we did as a senior in high school, the focus in college has (or should have) shifted from mere knowledge to intelligence—that is, to the ability to make good use of one's knowledge.

Intelligence = being able to use knowledge.

Other standard arguments claim other ways students might be cheated. For example, we might feel sorry for someone who doesn't get a joke—or a reference. Allusions to literature, history, philosophy, and so on allow us to say much in few words. But does the listener understand? If a person is unaware of common references—the Battle of the Bulge, Normandy, Existentialism, T. S. Eliot, World War I, Rasputin, John the Baptist, Gandhi, apartheid, Jonas Salk, Johnny Appleseed, Lewis and Clark, the Trail of Tears, slavery, the Donner Party, and so on—he misses out on conversations, on meaning, on *connecting with his fellow inmates.* Of course, here one might counter that you don't need to know all of these things. And, I agree, you don't. People tend to hang out with people who have similar interests and tastes.

Transition.

Cheated out of standard cultural knowledge.

Uses historical and other allusions to prove his point about allusions.

Concession.

One more argument claims that because we live in a democracy, we must be well-educated. Since all the citizens are responsible for the government, our forefathers promoted public education so that all citizens—not just the wealthy and elite—would know how to read and write. Thomas Jefferson wrote,

This gives the topic extra public resonance (since the democratic process is at stake).

Cheating the whole democracy.

> I know no safe depository of the ultimate powers of society but the people themselves; and if we think them not enlightened enough to exercise their control with a wholesome discretion, the remedy is not to take it from them, but to inform their discretion by education. This is the true corrective of abuses of constitutional power. (278)

In what ways can educated citizens correct abuses in a democracy? A person's way of life, his purchases and activities—not just a person's vote or protest march—is part of the responsibility. Thus, consumers and neighbors and co-workers and so on should behave responsibly and think intelligently. It is our responsibility as citizens of a democracy.

Transition paragraph that leads us to Bruno's particular stance.

True enough, these are all ways that students who are allowed to just slide by end up getting cheated. But another way (and one less talked about) strikes me as being far more offensive. This reason hinges on the fact that many students are not just sliding by.

Return to the original argument.

Modern = marked by distinctions between lowbrow and highbrow thought. Postmodern = marked by chaos and blurring of boundaries.

Quotations illustrate particular points of the original. A properly used colon—to introduce a quote with words that could be punctuated as a sentence—provides coherence. Readers know immediately the relationship of the words on the left and right of the colon. Quotation marks provide coherence by making clear that the words inside them are from a source.

1/4 students feel entitled.

3/4 students do not.

More summary of the original argument.

Diversity in skill and attitude.

In *Generation X Goes to College,* Peter Sacks illustrates that all of today's college students cannot just be thrown in the same big barrel. In describing the modern/post modern clash in education, he spends the majority of his time talking about those students who are underprepared, who lack the basic study skills required in academic work, and who demonstrate little real commitment to their own education. Yet, he does not discuss this problem in isolation. He also mentions another type of student. For example, he introduces the reader to Marissa and Carol: "As very good students, [their views] were virtually excluded by The College in order to accommodate the whiners and complainers" (61). And he says they "suffered not only educationally" (63). In addition to discussing specific good students, an entire chapter presents survey results about students' attitudes toward education. While he makes claims such as "nearly a quarter of the students . . . harbored a disproportionate sense of entitlement," this very statement tells the reader that a full three-quarters (that is, three out of four) students *do not* "harbor a disproportionate sense of entitlement" (54–59). He wraps up the book by focusing on another student, Andie, who he describes as "a good student, constantly picking [his] brain for information and feedback on her work" (186–87). His final paragraph, before the Epilogue, says, "Let's create a system that encourages people like Andie at least as much as the ones who don't give a damn" (187). Thus, Sacks shows that today's students are a more diverse group—in skill level, background, and attitude toward education—than has ever before been gathered together in the college classroom.

Transition paragraph.

Now when we connect two things—the present grade-inflated, entitlement-driven education system that has got a foothold in most of America's high schools and colleges AND the diversity in skill and attitude toward education of today's college students—two problems appear.

Motivated students are cheated.

One problem is that the motivated students are not being as challenged as they could be. Although their situation is not ideal, it is far from hopeless. They have at least three options: (1) take advantage of the easy system and learn a little along the way; (2) motivate themselves, working harder (and learning more) than the system requires them to; and (3) attend a more academically rigorous school (of course such schools still exist, though they are likely to cost more to attend).

While motivated students suffer in our too-lax system, so do the un- (or under-) motivated ones. And these students, who need our help the most, are the ones most cheated. As Sacks says, "I now believe the students are the real victims of this systematic failure of the entitlement mindset" (189). The students who are allowed to slide by, who are content to slide by, who perhaps don't even realize that they are sliding by because sliding by is all they know—those students find themselves arriving at college less prepared and less motivated than the "better students." And what happens next? Sadly, the gap between these two groups grows even wider.

Undermotivated students are cheated.

Sacks's quotation supports Bruno's argument.

Gap between students grows bigger.

The motivated student with good study skills (the one who has had at least an adequate high school education) attends class, takes notes, understands reading assignments, follows instructions, develops even better habits of mind, gains even more knowledge, and learns ways of making that knowledge work for her and her fellow humans. But in a system where B's are average and C's might indicate that although a student "tried" she did not demonstrate understanding or skill, the poorer students continue to advance through the system while remaining trapped at the bottom. Their level of thinking does not change much, while that of their better-prepared peers does.

Scenarios are the main support tool.

The injustice, then, has been done to the students (as Sacks says, the students are the victims). While the student has happily skipped (or unhappily slogged) along through sixteen years of formal education, she is allowed, if she wants, to come away with very little in terms of education. She is allowed, unfortunately, to escape practically unscathed by learning. The problem, of course, is that the two students have entered college on different academic levels and the one on the higher level has graduated on an *even higher* level while the one on the lower level has remained pretty much the same.

Sacks and Bruno argue the same point.

Students would do well to look around them, at the room full of fellow classmates. They should imagine that many of those students will be graduating one day. And they should imagine the students in the classroom next door and across the hall and in all the other buildings on campus. They will be graduating, too. They should also imagine all those students at the more than 4,000 other colleges throughout the country: Ohio State, Michigan, Michigan State, Findlay College, Iowa State, Oklahoma A&M, The University of

They do not even realize they are being cheated.

The statistic creates some alarm for student readers.

Utah, California This or That. (*The Chronicle of Higher Education*'s 2000–2001 "Almanac" lists 4,096 colleges in the United States.) Many of those students are well-prepared, working hard, and developing even better habits and thinking skills.

Competition for jobs and status.

Qualifier.

The "I" draws attention to Bruno's personal concern.

It's too late for many!

In our competitive world, the sad truth is that even some of the very good students, though their college dreams were to be doctors and lawyers and pharmacists and engineers, will be waiting tables. Don't get me wrong: There is no shame in that. The point is, that's not why they went to college. The truth is that for some students, college will be a tough uphill climb (a climb that could have been avoided with a more adequate high school education). A sadder truth, I am afraid, is that because of skills and attitudes developed in high school, for some students the reality of genuine learning (as opposed to just getting by) might already be too late.

Works Cited

"The Nation." *The Chronicle of Higher Education: Almanac Issue 2000-01*. 1 Sept. 2000, p. 6.

Sacks, Peter. *Generation X Goes to College*. Open Court Publishing, 1996.

Writing Strategies

1. Are you able to understand Bruno's response to Peter Sacks, even if you have not read *Generation X Goes to College?* What helpful background information does Bruno provide? What other information might have been helpful?
2. Bruno defines "intelligence" in his essay. How is this definition important? Might he have deleted this definition without damaging his essay?
3. What is Bruno's thesis?
4. Explain how Bruno's essay has public resonance. That is, how is what he says important to others besides himself?
5. What evidence does Bruno provide to support his thesis? What other kind of evidence might he have provided?

Exploring Ideas

1. With a group of peers, explore how the education system you have experienced is or is not "too lax." Provide specific examples.
2. What is the purpose of education in elementary school? High school? College? After you write out responses, explore further with a group of peers: what else might be the purpose, or *a* purpose, of education?

3. How might high school better prepare students for college? How might it better prepare them for life?
4. Bruno says, "[academically] poorer students continue to advance through the system while remaining trapped at the bottom" (¶12). Explore Bruno's claim further: Is it true? Can you provide examples for support? Why do some students get trapped at the bottom? Is it okay for them to be trapped there? What, if anything, should be done about this?

Ideas for Writing

1. What does Bruno get wrong?
2. If you agree with Bruno, what new and important point might you add?

If responding to one of these ideas, go to the Analysis section of this chapter to begin developing ideas for your essay.

Student Essay

Reality Check

Alison Hester

Although some responses point out how an argument is wrong, others spotlight the particular value of an argument. Do Americans ignore reality? In the following essay, Alison Hester illuminates Jayme Stayer's claim that they do. Stayer's challenging essay (256–263) uncovers layers of meaning that readers at first might have difficulty accepting. Our initial response might be, Why criticize an amusement park? How can such criticism be worthwhile? Shaping an essay from her responses to the Invention Questions in this chapter, Hester helps readers understand and accept Stayer's claims.

SeaWorld is a place where humans can come to a better understanding of animals and experience the tranquility and magnificence of nature. To some, this is a valid and heartfelt statement about SeaWorld. But to others, such as author Jayme Stayer, it is not only a false statement, but one that masks a perilous underscoring issue of American culture. In his essay "Whales R Us," Jayme Stayer bravely exposes the truth behind SeaWorld's lofty statements and divulges the well-hidden realities of SeaWorld. Stayer steps apart from the crowd to reveal that what is deemed normal and satisfactory in society is actually the opposite, which, in turn, compels his readers to come to terms with reality.

In America we have produced a society that allows its citizens to ignore reality. We buy designer clothing made by children in sweatshops, drive cars that are impractical but stylish and status-setting, and permit the majority of the our population to pay little to no attention to other countries' governments or issues. Living in a country without reality is easy and pleasant and upholds our American way of life. Stayer discusses ignoring reality, shows us its destructiveness, and divulges underlying dangers in his darkly humorous analysis of SeaWorld.

Jayme Stayer reveals the multitude of falsehoods in SeaWorld. He shows how SeaWorld is not a representation of nature's tranquility but a bombardment of noise and underdeveloped factoid presentations. Throughout his essay, Stayer accuses SeaWorld of a plethora of inexcusable blunders. He turns their lofty statements about contributing to "world knowledge" (257) and making "peace with the earth" (259) against themselves to expose their blatant hypocrisy and lack of knowledgeable statements. Stayer chuckles at the idea of world knowledge being something fixed, an "accumulative spittoon" (257), and corrects this hasty, generalized outlook by explaining that world knowledge is in actuality "a set of competing claims and shifting paradigms" (257). Stayer challenges the idea that we can prospectively make peace with the earth by reminding us the world isn't innately peaceful but a place of "viruses, earthquakes, predatory animals, and a survival-of-the-fittest mentality" (259). He criticizes their mindless skits while suggesting that sex is a reality that family viewers should not have to face at

---

SeaWorld. As the essay continues, it takes on a more serious nature. Stayer decides to dig even deeper into the design of SeaWorld to reveal its true intentions.

Stayer brings his reader's attention to the issue of SeaWorld's focus on education. After a thorough analysis and discussion of SeaWorld's "education," Stayer concludes that what takes place isn't education at all, but a form of "mind control" (260). Stayer has discovered that all of the microphones, manipulated applauding, and silly skits are there for no other purpose than to distract viewers from the reality of what they are witnessing. SeaWorld has decided what their audience needs to see, hear, and think in order to enjoy their visit. They make sure to keep bad thoughts out by replacing them with noise, "heartfelt" slogans, and the conjured proof of the captive animal's happiness and contentment. SeaWorld carefully sidesteps another harsh reality, which Stayer brings to the surface.

5 The animals at SeaWorld are there solely for our entertainment. In order for SeaWorld to hide this reality, they inform their audience of all the education that occurs at SeaWorld. The problem is, as Stayer points out, that "SeaWorld's communication of that knowledge, or to be more explicit, their refusal to level with its visitors about its real cultural role and worth" (261)

Mike Theiss/Ultimate Chase/Corbis

is the most pressing issue of all. SeaWorld has decided for the better of the audience's entertainment to conceal the truth behind why SeaWorld even exists and instead base everything on education that doesn't even take place. What does this say about Americans and entertainment?

Through all of his examples, clever quips, and harsh accusations, Stayer's essay evolves into the real issue at hand. Stayer has discovered that SeaWorld is a "consequence" (262) of American culture: a result of Americans creating a world where a person may never have to face reality. SeaWorld is a perfect example of an ever-increasing problem in America. At SeaWorld, Americans are privileged to enjoy a show while avoiding harsh realities of potentially miserable animals or our abuse of nature in general. We have placed our entertainment above accepting reality and being able to believe what we see and hear. Those who believe that SeaWorld truly does support education and living harmoniously with the earth's creatures inevitably disagree with Stayer's arguments and disdainful outlook on SeaWorld.

Some might argue that SeaWorld is really a place of education. This would mean that there is no mind control and Stayer's argument falls. If SeaWorld really is based around teaching, learning, and the transfer of knowledge, then Stayer must have made countless inaccurate observations. That would mean that all the whale's back flips and the dolphin's synchronized jumps were not the point of the show, but rather the actual facts about the whales and dolphins were. This is obviously not so. People go to SeaWorld to see these sea creatures perform magnificent shows and create presumed warm connections between humans and nature. SeaWorld is not about the animal's vanishing habitats, or their family dynamics, or even how we can help these animals. Although these subjects might be footnotes at SeaWorld, the real purpose is undeniably entertainment.

We would like to believe that SeaWorld is simply a fabulous way to learn. But after reading Stayer's essay, having the realities of SeaWorld revealed, one cannot deny that he makes a strong case. Stayer daringly commits the unspeakable crime of exposing a carefully masked reality of American culture. Stayer suggests that perhaps SeaWorld is another product of American desires, that we place our hunger for agreeable entertainment above individual opinion and being able to realize the truth behind something. A world has been created where animals are in synthetic environments, are hassled all day long, and if they could, would trade the security and comfort for true freedom. Acknowledging the truth of these creatures' existence at SeaWorld makes one realize that there can be no true education or productivity at the expense of captive creatures. But there is no reason to face these realities at SeaWorld if you don't wish to.

Yes, it's true, reality is an ugly portrait. It's no wonder, as advanced as our culture is, that we would create a world without reality. A world without reality is undeniably more pleasant and unrestrained. But to ignore reality is like ignoring a covered pot full of boiling water. Eventually the water will spill over the sides and create an unnecessary mess. That is exactly what reality is in America. We cover and ignore it, but it still exists. Hopefully, as a collective culture we can come to terms with the danger of denial and face the ugliness of reality. It's frightening to realize that continuing to live in a bubble without reality will eventually lead to a boiling-over that at one point was controllable.

Work Cited

Stayer, Jayme. "Whales R Us." *The Composition of Everyday Life*, edited by John Mauk and John Metz, 5th ed., Wadsworth, 2014, pp. 256–62.

Writing Strategies

1. To what argument does Hester respond? Based on Hester's response, summarize Jayme Stayer's argument.

2. How does Hester respond to those who think SeaWorld might be a place of education? What specific support strategies are important in her response?

3. Notice how Hester guides readers through her response. Identify several sentences in which she uses pronouns or introductory phrases to connect one idea to the next.

4. What support does Hester provide for the claim that "there can be no true education or productivity at the expense of captive creatures?"

5. Describe Hester's voice as a writer. Refer to two sentences as support for your description.

Exploring Ideas

1. Hester says, "Stayer steps apart from the crowd to reveal [that] what is deemed normal and satisfactory in society is actually the opposite, which, in turn, compels his readers to come to terms with reality." What about SeaWorld is deemed normal and satisfactory? Why isn't this normal or satisfactory? According to Hester, how does Stayer compel readers to come to terms with reality?

2. In your view, what, like SeaWorld, claims to be a place of education but isn't?

3. Based on Hester's thinking, how might reality spill over and create an unnecessary mess, as Hester suggests in her conclusion? Do you agree or disagree with her fears?

4. What other reality of American culture is masked?

5. How does the image on this page support or refute Stayer's argument?

Ideas for Writing

1. Write an argument that further develops Hester's claim that "there can be no true education . . . at the expense of captive creatures."

2. Respond by providing more and stronger support that American culture creates "a world without reality."

If responding to one of these ideas, go to the Analysis section of this chapter to begin developing ideas for your essay.

Invention

Responding to an argument involves sophisticated thinking and planning. In a sense, this project is an argument^2, an argument to the second power. You are not only taking on another argument (with its own layers and nuances), but you are also developing a layered argument of your own. The following sections are designed to help you through the invention process, specifically, to find an argument (in Point of Contact), to discover the mechanics of that argument (in Analysis), to understand how the points relate to a community of readers (in Public Resonance), to invent a focused stance of your own (in Thesis), and to develop your own support (in Rhetorical Tools).

Point of Contact

In this chapter, the point of contact is an actual argument. You will be responding to an explicit argument that someone else has formulated or to an argument expressed by many people. Remember that an argument need not be an essay; arguments are also made by advertisements, posters, and billboards. To find an argument that may relate directly to the goings-on of your life and community, examine the following options and the images in Figure 9.1:

- **Local/City/Campus Newspapers:** Search the editorial pages and letters to the editor for arguments.
- **National Newspapers:** Publications such as the *New York Times, USA Today,* and *The Wall Street Journal* have editorial pages and columnists who offer arguments on various political and social issues.
- **Magazines:** Popular weeklies (such as *Newsweek, The Nation, Time,* and *US News and World Report*) and monthly or quarterly magazines (such as *Utne Reader* or *The New Republic*) are filled with argumentative articles and personal columns on social and political issues.
- **A Publication from Your Major** (such as *Education Journal, Nursing, Applied Science and Engineering*): Examine not only main articles but also reviews and personal columns.
- **Disciplinary Databases** (databases that focus on specific disciplines): Go to your library and check the electronic databases for your major or a closely related one.
- **Websites:** Go to your favorite search engine and enter topical keywords (*dogs, skateboards, economy,* etc.). You might find argumentative sites or pages more quickly if you combine potential topics with words such as *law, policy, argument, crisis,* or *debate.*

You can also focus your search on arguments made by bloggers by using blog searchers such as Google Blog Search (blogsearch.google.com), or a blog directory such as the one found at technorati.com.

Choose an argument that interests you and that you can address with some authority. Once you have found a potentially interesting argument, answer the following question:

- Why does the argument interest me?
  —Because something or someone has been omitted?
  —Because something or someone has been misrepresented?
  —Because I disagree or agree with it?
  —Because it raises an important issue that should be further discussed?
  —Because it changed my mind on a topic?
  —Because it is potentially important (helpful or dangerous)?

Figure 9.1

Analysis

To analyze the argument in front of you, it may help to think of that argument as having two layers: (1) the four elements of argument and (2) the underlying warranting assumptions.

The First Layer: The Four Elements of Argument

Thesis Before we can respond to an argument, we must know *exactly* what is being argued. That is, we must figure out the thesis, the particular stance the writer takes on the topic. Finding the thesis for a written argument can be trickier than it seems. Although some essays have explicit theses (stated directly), others are implied (not stated, but suggested by the supporting points). Once we locate the thesis (or understand it based on the details of the argument), we can then see how it is supported.

Support Initially, the thesis might seem outlandish, but good support strategies will invite readers to accept even the most extreme thesis statements. Remember that support comes in a variety of forms:

Statistics	Scenarios
Authorities	Appeal to Logic
Facts	Appeal to Emotion
Examples	Appeal of Character
Allusions	Appeal to Need
Personal Testimonies/Anecdotes	Appeal to Value

Depending on the medium of the argument (essay, poster, etc.), the support may be varied. Or the writer may depend on a single key support strategy. We might ask: *How well does the support strategy connect to the thesis?* Or, *Given this argument, how appropriate is the support strategy?* For a detailed explanation of support strategies, see pages 273–277 in Chapter 8.

Counterargument Sophisticated arguments anticipate and refute opposing claims. In fact, the success of an argument may depend on its counterarguments—on the ability of the writer to fend off opposing claims. A key counterargument strategy is the turnabout paragraph, in which a writer explains an opposing perspective and then responds directly.

Concession Concessions acknowledge the value of opposing claims. Writers who concede acknowledge that others' positions may offer some insight outside of the writers' own claims. When writers concede points, their arguments do not lose force; instead, they appear more fair-minded. A writer who concedes shows that he or she has considered a range of other ideas.

To fully understand the first layer of the argument, answer the following questions for the argument to which you are responding.

- What is the main claim/thesis?
- What are the means of support for the main claim?
- Do the support strategies sufficiently prove the thesis?
- How does the argument address opposing claims? Are those claims sufficiently refuted?
- Does the argument concede to outside positions? What is the effect of those concessions?
- Does the writer define the issue correctly?

Daniel Bruno uses one of these Invention Questions as a springboard to discover a specific shortcoming in Sacks's book:

> **Does the writer define the issue correctly?**
>
> Sacks defines the issue correctly as far as he defines it. Entitlement education has the negative effect that he says it does, but he fails, it seems, to discuss or focus on an important aspect of the issue, which is that some students, who don't have an entitlement mentality, learn a great deal in school while others, who do, don't learn a great deal, or very much at all. The students who have the entitlement mentality slide by while their classmates are learning more and more. The gap between the two groups widens. So, what does this mean to those students who feel entitled to good grades because they showed up (high school) or paid the tuition (college)? They get grades, but did they learn anything? Did they get an education?

Rogerian Argument

Rogerian argument is based on the work of Carl Rogers (1902–1987), who is best known for his contributions to clinical psychology and psychotherapy. Rogers's ideas about mutual understanding, trust, and supportive rather than competitive rhetoric have become key concepts in argument.

According to Rogerian argument, arguers should first try to understand opposing views. In "Communication: Its Blocking and Its Facilitation" (1952), he writes, "The next time you get into an argument . . . stop the discussion for a moment and for an experiment, institute this rule. 'Each person can speak up for himself only after he has first restated the ideas and feelings of the previous speaker accurately, and to that speaker's satisfaction.'" This means that "before presenting your own point of view, it would be necessary for you to really achieve the other speaker's frame of reference—to understand his thoughts and feelings so well that you could summarize them for him."

This sounds simple, but it isn't. Rogers says, "But if you try it you will discover it one of the most difficult things you have ever tried to do. However, once you have been able to see the other's point view, your own comments will have to be drastically revised." According to Rogers, doing this takes courage: "If I enter, as fully as I am able, into the private world of a neurotic or psychotic individual, isn't there a risk that I might become lost in that world?"

As you respond to an argument for this chapter, first accurately summarize it. For help, ask a group of classmates to suggest where you might be misrepresenting the original argument.

The Second Layer: Warranting Assumptions

Beneath the first, most visible, layer of an argument lurk warranting assumptions: the beliefs that connect points in an argument. Warranting assumptions are the root system of an argument; although they most often go unstated, they are as important as the most directly worded points. When we dig up warranting assumptions and investigate them closely, we can decide for ourselves if they are reasonable.

Philosopher Stephen Toulmin developed a powerful analytical system for digging up assumptions. In his perspective, every argument has a structure with interrelated parts. Using this, we can see how those parts relate and how well they function. Here are the three basic elements:

Claim: The main argumentative position (or thesis) being put forward

Grounds: The support for the position (evidence, examples, illustrations, etc.)

Warranting Assumption: The idea, often unstated, that connects the claim and the grounds—or that justifies the use of the grounds for the claim

The warranting assumption lies (often hidden) between the claim and the grounds. See how the elements work in the following example:

Claim:	Sport utility vehicles are dangerous.
Grounds:	Many models roll over easily.
Warranting Assumption:	Vehicles that roll over easily are dangerous.

The assumption lies between the claim and the grounds, connecting them logically.

In this example, the rollover frequency of SUVs supports the claim that they are dangerous. The warranting assumption (vehicles that roll over easily are dangerous) lies between the claim and the grounds. The assumption is entirely acceptable; few people would challenge it. But consider a different argument:

Claim:	Sport utility vehicles are valuable to the average American driver.
Grounds:	The extra-large carrying capacity and four-wheel drive capability meet traveling needs.
Warranting Assumption:	Extra-large carrying capacity and four-wheel drive are valuable for the average American driver's traveling needs.

The assumption here is less acceptable. Someone might argue against this warranting assumption on the grounds that the average American driver does not need extra-large carrying capacity and four-wheel drive, and that these aspects are actually unnecessary for most drivers. Stating the assumption thus reveals a particular weakness in the argument and provides an opportunity to respond.

Dissecting arguments in this fashion allows for various critical opportunities. Writers can focus attention on (take exception or agree with) two different layers of an argument: grounds and/or assumptions. Consider, for example, the first claim: *Sport utility vehicles are dangerous.* Although the assumption *vehicles that roll over easily are dangerous* is acceptable, the grounds for the claim *many models roll over easily* can be challenged. Someone might agree with the assumption but cite statistics showing that only a few models are prone to rollover accidents.

Claim:	Sport utility vehicles are dangerous.	
Grounds:	Many models roll over easily.	(Questionable)
Warranting Assumption:	Vehicles that roll over easily are dangerous.	(Acceptable)

Responding with such statistics could help a writer challenge the original argument. In this case, the responding writer would be challenging the grounds. For other arguments, both the grounds and assumption might be arguable:

Claim:	The environment is not in danger from human influence.

Grounds:	The environment is supporting the Earth's population today.	(Questionable)
Warranting Assumption:	The present human population directly illustrates the health of the environment.	(Questionable)

Here, both the grounds and the warranting assumption are questionable. Although the grounds could be refuted on their own terms (by illustrating the vast numbers of people starving throughout the world), the more interesting response might point to the warranting assumption. The mere presence of people, of course, does not indicate the health of the environment. Someone, for instance, might point to dramatic increases in skin and other cancers to illustrate the effects of greenhouse gases and environmental contamination. In this case, discovering the warranting assumption would allow a responding writer to point out a flaw in the logic.

The following questions can help you develop a response to the argument you have chosen to examine.

- What is the warranting assumption?
- Is the assumption acceptable or arguable?
- Can I prove that the assumption is incorrect?
- What else does the author of the argument assume (about life, identity, society, people's behavior, time, politics, human nature, etc.)?

Public Resonance

Public resonance refers to the way in which a topic (or argument) relates to a community. In most cases, any published argument that you find will already have public resonance, especially if it comes from a newspaper, magazine, or journal. Your job, however, is not complete. As a responding writer, you can draw attention to the effects of the original argument on its readers and on the community at large.

To develop public resonance, examine the argument to which you will respond, and answer the following questions:

- Has the argument had an impact on readers? Any specific person or people?
- How *could* the argument affect people (negatively or positively)?
- What other issues or situations does the argument relate to or address?
- How can I relate the argument to the needs/wants of my audience (or anyone who is involved in the topic)?

Invention Workshop

In a small group of writers, use one of the Invention Questions to start a discussion about your topic. First, briefly explain the original argument (the argument to which you are responding) to your group members. Then pose the question. (It may be helpful to write the question on a board or have all group members focus on this page so the question does not get lost in the discussion.)

In the following excerpt, Daniel Bruno explores *what* and *how* people might think about the topic of student entitlement. Here, Bruno has narrowed in on a particular issue from the original argument (Peter Sacks's book about college students). It's not merely that students shouldn't feel entitled to high grades. Bruno goes further and discovers the double jeopardy of entitlement: Those who feel entitled are "missing out" on their own educations:

How can I relate the argument to the needs/wants of my audience (or anyone who is involved in the topic)?

Some students feel entitled, which means expecting a good grade automatically, without working or learning anything. Some don't. The wants of the entitlement students are different than their needs. They want a grade or degree but need to learn and work. Interestingly, the students who feel entitled are the ones missing out, while the ones who don't feel entitled benefit. Maybe the students who believe they are entitled would benefit from thinking about the students who think differently, the ones who they will be competing against in the future, the ones who perhaps will be better prepared and have a better work ethic. The entitlement-minded students may find out too late that others are working hard and developing good skills and attitudes.

Research

What have others said about your topic? If you are responding to a specific text (like an article or a book), go beyond that author's views and seek out other perspectives. Examine your invention writing and seek out keywords. Enter them into a periodical database search. (Remember that periodical databases, such as InfoTrac® College Edition, rely on keywords rather than phrases.) Enter main nouns linked together with *and.* If you have no luck, keep changing the nouns; try replacing them with synonyms. For instance, Bruno might enter: *students and college and entitlement.* Then, he might try: *students and college and attitude.* He might replace *attitude* with *achievement, success, study skills, apathy,* or a combination of these.

Thesis

Responding to arguments is complicated because another set of claims must be engaged. But do not let those other claims confuse you. Resist chasing ideas throughout the original argument, and instead focus on a particular issue and then springboard into your own reasoning. Your argument might do one or more of the following:

- Redefine the issue according to your understanding.

  Sacks shows how consumerism has invaded education, leading some students to expect good grades for little effort. But he fails, it seems, to emphasize enough a most harmful effect of this sense of entitlement. (page 294)

- Argue for the value of a particular point or assumption in the original text.

  In "Technology, Movement, and Sound," Ed Bell argues against our culture's increasing love affair with technology. The real value of his argument is its focus on the relationship between personal technology and public effects.

- Argue against a particular point or assumption in the original text.

  Simon Benlow insists that students are increasingly more consumerist in their approach to education, but consumption is not inherently passive or anti-educational.

- Extend the original argument to include a broader set of ideas.

  April Pedersen concludes, "When his kidneys failed, a $12,000 kidney transplant was off the radar (a case can be made that surgery on an animal is unethical anyway), and I didn't consider him to be my son." Although it might be hard to argue that $12,000 is too much to spend on saving a human life, Pedersen's point can be applied to humans as well as dogs: Far too many receive medical care that is unnecessary and arguably unethical, even if it is life-saving.

- Narrow the argument and suggest an important emphasis.

  As Jayme Stayer argues in "Whales R Us," theme parks such as SeaWorld are a "reflection of American culture . . . not a promoter of political change." His argument shows us that mainstream American culture may entirely lack a language for political change.

As you can see in these statements, it is not enough to say "I disagree" or "I agree." Instead, a project such as this benefits from a more focused point—one that shows something (important, harmful, inaccurate, valuable, etc.) in the original argument. The following questions can help generate the thesis of your argumentative response.

- With what *particular* point do I agree or disagree?
- How are my assumptions different from or similar to those of the writer?
- How is the original argument too narrow or too exclusive?
- What particular point in the original argument might readers fail to see? Why is it so important?
- How can I extend or broaden the original argument?

Evolution of a Thesis

Notice how the following idea evolves from summary, to gut reaction, to analytical insight:

- In "Crimes Against Humanity," Ward Churchill argues that the use of Native American symbols for sports teams is racist. **Summary**
- Churchill's argument made me mad, and I think it may do the same to a lot of people. It basically suggests that everyone who supports certain professional sports teams is somehow tied to genocide. **Gut reaction**
- Mainstream America might need to be pushed before it will accept new ideas. **Analytical insight**
- Churchill's "Crimes Against Humanity" reminds us that mainstream opinions often do not change unless people encounter shocking, even offensive, claims. **Focused statement**

Throughout this intellectual journey, the writer, by discovering something specific about Churchill's argument and its potential effect on readers, moves from dismissing the argument to revealing a quality in it.

Thinking Further

Although gut reactions can get a writer started, they are often too vague. The following statements show what someone might feel directly after reading an argument. While these initial feelings are valuable, they are only the beginning:

- Ann Marie Paulin's argument is right on target.
- April Pedersen's argument is important for dog lovers to hear.
- In "Crimes Against Humanity," Ward Churchill is just making a mountain out of a molehill.

These initial reactions must be explored. The writers might ask:

- What particular idea or assumption of Paulin's argument is insightful or valuable? Why is it insightful or valuable?
- Why is Pedersen's argument important? What particular aspect is valuable to animal lovers?
- Why might the issue really be a mountain?

In asking such questions, the writers can take their gut reaction to the next level—to more focused ideas:

- Ann Marie Paulin reveals the quiet everyday prejudices against overweight people.
- April Pedersen's argument correctly challenges the common misconception that caring for pets as one would care for humans is harmless.
- Churchill describes a view of American history and sports that most people do not consider.

Revising Your Thesis

With a group of peers, explore your thesis statements. Each group member should share his or her thesis. Then the group should collectively attempt to narrow it by asking questions such as the preceding ones. Go after broad adjectives (*valuable, wrong, irresponsible, good, intense,* etc.). Prompt the writer to give specific descriptors or explanations. Also, check out the Common Thesis Problems in Chapter 8 on pages 272–273. The same problems may lurk in this project as well.

Rhetorical Tools

Even though you are responding to someone else's argument, you are still creating your own argument. Consider all the argumentative strategies introduced in Chapter 8.

Using Support

Remember you have the whole world beyond the original argument to support your points. You can use various forms of evidence (such as personal testimony, examples, and facts, as well as allusions to history, popular culture, and news events) and appeals.

- What particular examples from everyday life show my point?
- Does a historical situation or trend (say, the rise of a particular fashion, organization, or individual) illustrate something about my topic?
- How has popular culture treated my topic? Does it show up in television shows, movies, or commercials? If so, how is it characterized, mishandled, or celebrated?

- How has literature (novels, poetry, drama, short stories) dealt with my topic? Have fictional characters illustrated something important about the topic or some behavior related to it?
- How does nature (animals, life cycles, plants, biological processes, and so on) demonstrate something about my topic?
- How can this topic relate to people's sense of logic? What line of reasoning can I create for readers to follow?

(See pages 273–277 in Chapter 8: Making Arguments, for more help in developing evidence and appeals for your argument.)

Counterarguing

Good writers address opposing claims. Notice how Alison Hester responds to an opposing position:

> Those who believe that SeaWorld truly does support education and living harmoniously with the earth's creatures inevitably disagree with Stayer's arguments and disdainful outlook on SeaWorld.
>
> Some might argue that SeaWorld is really a place of education. This would mean that there is no mind control and Stayer's argument falls. If SeaWorld really is based around teaching, learning, and the transfer of knowledge then Stayer must have made countless inaccurate observations. That would mean that all the whale's back flips and the dolphin's synchronized jumps were not the point of the show, but rather the actual facts about the whales and the dolphins were. This is obviously not so. People go to SeaWorld to see these sea creatures perform magnificent shows and create presumed warm connections between humans and nature. SeaWorld is not about the animal's vanishing habitats, or their family dynamics, or even how we can help these animals. Although these subjects might be footnotes at SeaWorld, the real purpose is undeniably entertainment.

As you develop your own argument, ask yourself the following questions:

- Apart from the author of the original argument, who might disagree with my position? Why?
- What reasons do people have for disagreeing with me?
- What evidence would support an opposing argument?

Conceding and Qualifying Points

When responding to an argument, a writer should be especially mindful of giving credit to others' points. For example, in Bruno's response to Peter Sacks's book, he acknowledges several important elements of Sacks's argument:

> His final paragraph, before the Epilogue, says, "Let's create a system that encourages people like Andie at least as much as the ones who don't give a damn" (296). Thus, Sacks shows that today's students are a more diverse group—in skill level, background, and attitude toward education—than has ever before been gathered together in the college classroom.

Exploring the following questions will help you to see possible concessions for your own argument.

- Does the original argument make any valid points?
- Does my argument make any large, but necessary, leaps? (Should I acknowledge them?)
- Do I ask my audience to imagine a fictional situation? (Should I acknowledge the potential shortcomings of a fictional or hypothetical situation?)
- Do I ask my audience to accept generalizations? (Should I acknowledge those generalizations?)

Activity

After responding to the preceding questions, discuss with peers the extent to which you should concede and qualify each point you discovered. For example, if you discovered that your argument made a large but necessary leap, should you acknowledge the leap in a phrase, a sentence, or an entire paragraph?

Remembering Logical Fallacies

Logical fallacies are logical stumbles—gaps or shortcomings in reasoning. Examine the original argument closely to determine if it is free of fallacies. Finding logical fallacies in an argument can help you generate a response. For example, in the following passage, the writer points to a logical shortcoming in the original argument:

> Smith argues that incoming college students cannot handle the intellectual rigors of academia. He characterizes an entire generation as "undisciplined and whimsical." But like all arguments about entire generations, Smith's depends upon a hasty generalization. The truth about today's college students is far more complex than Smith's assertions, and any statement that seeks to characterize them as a whole should be looked upon with suspicion.

See a list and examples of logical fallacies in Chapter 8, pages 280–282.

Activity

Write a one-paragraph summary of the essay you plan to write, stating your thesis and main supporting ideas. Share your summary with several peers and look for logical fallacies such as ad hominem, strawperson, faulty cause/effect, either/or reasoning, hasty generalization, non sequitur, oversimplification, slippery slope, false analogy, and begging the question. (See pages 280–282.) Although such fallacies are common in one's early thinking about an issue, they can be hard to spot. To find them, you may have to discuss the summaries and examine ideas carefully.

Revision

The Invention Questions in this chapter are not meant to be answered just once. The value of these questions is in responding to them as a way of discovering and developing new ideas, then returning to them and exploring further from your new perspective. Before you exchange drafts with a peer, revisit the questions in the Analysis, Public Resonance, Thesis, and Rhetorical Tools sections of this chapter. Try to ratchet up your thinking even further.

Peer Review

Exchange drafts with at least one other writer. Before exchanging, underline your thesis (or write it at the top of the first page) so that others will more quickly get a sense of your main idea. Use the following questions to respond to specific issues in the drafts:

1. Can any phrases or terms in the thesis be narrowed? If so, circle them and make some suggestions for more focus.
2. Is the main idea of the original argument sufficiently summarized? (Could the summary be shorter? How?)
3. Where could the writer support broad statements with specific evidence (allusions, examples, facts, personal testimony, scenario)? Writers often fall into the habit of making broad claims that should be illustrated. For instance, someone might argue, "All students learn differently." But such a statement needs to be supported with specifics. Otherwise, readers have no reason to accept it, no reason to see it as true.
4. Where might the writer oversimplify the original argument/issue or mischaracterize the original author's position? (Look especially for ad hominem or strawperson logical fallacies. See pages 280–282.)
5. What paragraphs shift focus? Where do you sense gaps in the lines of reasoning? How could the writer fill those gaps?
6. Circle any clichés or overly broad statements that could be transformed into specific and revelatory insights.

7. Consider sentence vitality:
   - What sentences are over-embedded? (Point to any clauses that overlap with other clauses, causing a disconnect between ideas.)
   - Examine attributive phrases. Point out unnecessary phrases or sentences that could be boiled down.
   - Consider other vitality strategies explained in Chapter 19.

     —Where can the writer change linking verbs to active verbs?

     —Where can the writer avoid drawing attention to *I* and *you*?

     —Help the writer change unnecessary clauses to phrases.

     —Help the writer change unnecessary phrases to words.

     —Point to expletives (such as *there are* and *it is*).

     —Help the writer change passive verbs to active verbs for more vitality.

     —Help the writer avoid common grammatical errors: comma splices, sentence fragments, or pronoun/antecedent agreement.

Questions for Research

If the writer used outside sources,

- Where must he or she include in-text citations? (See pages 508–509.)
- Are quotations blended smoothly into the argument and punctuated correctly? (See pages 495–506.)
- Where could more direct textual cues or transitions help readers? (See pages 504–506.)
- Is the Works Cited or References page formatted properly? (See Chapter 16.)

Reflection

Consider this: Just as we discuss ideas with others as part of the invention process, we also play out discussions in our own minds. We have both external and internal dialogues. For example, to invent for this essay, you may have written responses to Invention Questions, discussed publicly (with others), and created internal dialogues (imaginary discussions inside your head). We create internal dialogues while driving, walking the dog, working out, and so on. These dialogues—like invention writing and public discussions with others—use rhetorical tools to explore and develop new ways of thinking.

1. Which did you rely on most for invention: written responses to Invention Questions, public dialogue, or internal dialogue? Which might you have utilized more and why?

2. List two key points in your essay.
   a. For each point, did you invent the point through written responses to Invention Questions in the text, public dialogue, internal dialogue, a combination of the three, or some other way? Explain.
   b. How did each key point function in the essay? Was it the thesis? A support strategy? An opening (introduction) strategy? Part of the conclusion?
3. If you can recall any internal dialogue from your invention process, describe how it worked:
   a. Who was your imaginary discussion partner?
   b. What was the nature of the discussion? Was it cooperative, combative, or something else?
4. How was your essay a response to an ongoing public discussion? What specific ideas from that public discussion was your invention (writing as well as public and private dialogues) a response to?

Beyond the Essay: Tattoo Design

If designing a tattoo for a college writing class sounds crazy, consider the rhetoric of the tattoo and the prevalence of tattoos in the United States, in the world, on your college campus, in your classroom, on TV, and so on. Tattoos (body art)—like essays, letters, videos, or speeches—do rhetoric; they communicate ideas through particular strategies (colors, images, words, placement, and so on). Given their prevalence, tattoos must be communicating something important.

1. Design a tattoo that expresses the main idea of the essay you've written for this chapter. Whether you design your tattoo on paper or on the computer, consider both the idea you want to communicate and the visual elements that will present that idea. What image or images might you use? What words? What font size or style? Where on one's body should the tattoo go, and how does the location affect the message?
2. In several paragraphs, explain the rhetoric of the tattoo you designed.

10 Evaluating

Wilfried Heider/StockXchng

"The trouble with normal is it always gets worse."

—Bruce Cockburn

Evaluating is the act of judging the value or worth of a given subject. We make informal judgments constantly throughout our daily lives: We decide that we like a particular car more than another, or that one song on the radio is better than another. Such evaluations are informal because they involve little analysis; that is, we do not usually take the time to thoroughly analyze each song we hear on the radio as we are sweeping through stations. We also take part in formal evaluation, a process that goes beyond an expression of likes and dislikes: Teachers must evaluate student performance; jury members must evaluate events, people, and testimony; voters must evaluate political candidates; members of unions must evaluate contracts; managers must evaluate employees; executives must evaluate business proposals; citizens must evaluate laws and lawmakers. In such situations, mere personal tastes cannot dictate evaluative decisions. Instead, a formal process—sometimes entirely intellectual, sometimes organized in visible steps—is necessary for sound evaluation.

The ability to make formal evaluations is essential to academic thinking and writing:

- Biologists at a national conference evaluate the success of a particular molecular research process.
- Law enforcement students are assigned to evaluate a new highway safety program.
- Crime lab scientists evaluate a particular procedure for gathering evidence.
- University civil engineers evaluate a downtown rezoning plan.
- English professors evaluate a new textbook for the department literature courses.
- Education faculty members and graduate students evaluate the state's controversial new standardized tests.
- Art students evaluate a set of paintings from the early Modernist era.

Much literary work is also evaluative. Barbara Kingsolver's *Poisonwood Bible,* for example, condemns twentieth-century missionary work in Africa. Yann Martel's *Life of Pi* critiques scientific rationality. Ralph Ellison's *Invisible Man* reveals a range of racist assumptions and practices. And Jonathan Swift's *Gulliver's Travels,* perhaps one of the most famous examples of evaluative literature, critiques (or satirizes) political and economic institutions of eighteenth-century England.

Whether one is an author, jury member, civil engineer, or voting citizen, the person who can evaluate well and make judgments outside of his or her personal tastes is able to make valuable decisions, to help distinguish the best course of action, to clarify options when many seem available. And in a culture that is increasingly filled with choices (among political candidates, retirement plans, religious paths, and lifestyles, to name just a few), it is increasingly important for literate citizens to evaluate well.

The essays in this chapter all make judgments and, in doing so, present their subjects to readers in a particular light. In other words, each writer gives an opinion about a subject (be it a video game, a television show, etc.) and then supports that opinion by showing selected details of the subject. Although the writers give some form of overview (some general summary about the subject), they also focus the readers' attention on the details that support their judgments. This is fair play. In drawing attention to certain details (and ignoring others), they are simply creating argumentative positions—the positions they want readers to accept. Notice, also, that the writers tend to draw on support outside their subjects; that is, they refer to other similar subjects to show particular points, which gives credibility to their judgments.

This chapter will help you develop a formal evaluation of a particular subject and communicate your evaluation in writing. The following essays will provide insight to various evaluation strategies, for example, the application of criteria (standards of judgment) to determine the value of the subject. In "*The Andy Griffith Show:* Return to Normal," Ed Bell evaluates the show based on a particular criterion: that the show is comforting. As you read this chapter's essays, notice how the claim, support, and organization are shaped by one or more criteria. After reading the essays, you can find a subject in one of two ways:

1. Go to the Point of Contact section to find a topic from your everyday life, or
2. Choose one of the Ideas for Writing that follow the essays.

After finding a subject, go to the Analysis section to begin developing the evaluation.

Readings

Talibanned

Benjamin Busch

Benjamin Busch is an actor, poet, essayist, photographer, film producer, and former Marine major. As an actor, he played memorable characters on programs such as *Homicide, The Wire,* and *Generation Kill.* As a Marine, he served two tours in Iraq and was awarded the Bronze Star. He has, then, an acute understanding of the tension between reality and fiction. In this article, Busch uses one particular criterion to evaluate a video game: realism. This essay was recorded in an edited form as "A Video Game Does Not a Soldier Make" on National Public Radio's *All Things Considered.*

My Grandfather fought the Nazis and was wounded. For years afterward, my father re-created that war in games in his Brooklyn neighborhood, where some of the children playing had lost their fathers overseas. But war games require two sides, and someone in Brooklyn always had to play the Germans.

When I was a boy, I was given plastic army men. They were posed already fighting. I arranged them in the sandbox behind our house, and I killed them. I voiced their commands and made the sounds of their suffering. I was every one of them, and I was their enemy. I imagined their war—and I controlled it. I was a child. But I lost those magical powers as a Marine in Iraq.

We know children are immersed in digital interactivity now, and the soldier of today has grown up on video games. It is becoming a new literacy of sorts. Playing and risking your life are different things, of course. In the video war, there may be some manipulation of anxiety, some adrenaline to the heart, but absolutely nothing is at stake.

The military has recognized the attraction of trigger based combat games and has incorporated them into recruitment and training. There is an official U.S. Army Game called *America's Army.* Gamers are encouraged to download a free video game where they can "play *America's Army 3* on Steam and earn Steam Achievements, ranking up among your friends as you earn distinguished status, badges, medals, and ribbons." Without leaving home, players can comfortably attain rank and recognition online as imaginary soldiers on a game platform designed to transform their entertainment into military service. On the same site the U.S. Army places ads picturing members in uniform. One says:

> Meet PVT Alaniz. He joined the Army to pay for a college education and is proud to follow in his grandfather's footsteps. Free room, board and laundry allow him to put money toward some of the important things in life: like treating his girlfriend and buying a plasma TV to play Xbox 360. Check out the opportunities the Army created for PVT Alaniz.

The truth is that there are two ways out of Afghanistan: wounds or luck. Proficiency is only part of surviving the randomness of death, and playing games will not protect or endanger soldiers or governments. If gamers are inspired to join the Taliban, they should talk to John Walker Lindh first. And for those who truly want to play for a Medal of Honor, recruiters are standing by. Only eight have been awarded since we invaded Afghanistan. All but one have been posthumous.

Writing Strategies

1. Busch begins his essay with some family history and personal testimony. Explain how these two introductory paragraphs help to launch his evaluation.
2. What is the essay's most powerful statement against *Medal of Honor?*
3. In ¶9, Busch says, "We can only hope that business values social decency, and respects essential humanism but a gaming company is only truly concerned with market reception in the form of product sales." How does this subtle appeal to decency help with his evaluation of the video game?
4. How does Busch counterargue or concede to opposing positions? Describe particular passages.
5. Explain how Busch's conclusion reinforces his position on *Medal of Honor.*

Exploring Ideas

1. Consider Busch's point: that *Medal of Honor* "equates war with the leisure of games." Why might that equation be something to evaluate, even if (or especially if) you are an avid gamer?
2. Busch explains that the U.S. military works closely with private corporations to develop software. Why might that interaction be a concern for both soldiers and citizens?
3. Busch describes gaming as "sedentary adventurism in need of a subject." How is this phrase an indictment of gaming? How is *sedentary adventurism* negative?
4. In his conclusion, Busch alludes to John Walker Lindh—a U.S. citizen who traveled to Afghanistan in 2001, trained with Taliban forces, and fought against the U.S. military. He was captured that year, detained as an enemy combatant, and is currently serving a twenty-year prison sentence. How does Lindh's story figure into the argument about games such as *Medal of Honor?*

Ideas for Writing

1. Video games are often condemned for their levels of violence. Choose a particular game and develop an evaluation. Avoid simply attacking or defending the portrayal of violence. Consider other criteria.
2. Focus on an advertisement for military recruiting. Evaluate its moves, its strategies, its realism, or even its parallels to popular video games.

If responding to one of these ideas, go to the Analysis section of this chapter to begin developing ideas for your essay.

The Andy Griffith Show: Return to Normal

Ed Bell

Evaluations invite readers to see why something is valuable or deficient. To do this, a writer may propose a new standard of judgment (a criterion) upon which the evaluation is based. For example, a writer might *suggest* that a television show should not only entertain but also *comfort* its audience. In this essay, Ed Bell, a writing instructor, does just that, first establishing comfort as a potential criterion for a prime-time television sitcom, then arguing how well *The Andy Griffith Show* meets that criterion. Portions of Bell's invention work are shown later in this chapter.

From those early days of Lucy and Ricky to our own Dharma and Greg, situation comedies have been part of American culture. And for all the advançements, it still seems like the plots of most of them are something cooked up by Lucy who dragged along Ethel and got caught (and ultimately forgiven) by Fred and Barney . . . uh . . . Fred and Ricky, I mean. Whether or not these shows instruct is, I suppose, debatable. But what is not debatable is that over the past 50 years they have entertained millions. And, I would suggest, through that very act of entertaining us, they have comforted us—the most comforting of them all being *The Andy Griffith Show.*

Introduction discusses what sit-commgno2s do (their purpose): instruct, entertain, comfort. Evaluation of show can be based on how well the shows do this.

Connects to life of viewer: Do sitcoms instruct? How?

More than any other sitcom, *The Andy Griffith Show* leaves its viewers with a sense that everything is all right. While *Three's Company* or *Dharma and Greg* or *MASH* may also wind things up happily after 30 minutes, there is—even though the complication of that particular week's crisis has been worked out—always a sense on those shows that things are not quite right. Yet *The Andy Griffith Show* leaves us with the feeling that, even though our friends sometimes get big-headed ideas or strangers from Raleigh come driving or dancing or swindling their mixed-up way into our peacefulness, life will eventually return to normal, all warm and wonderful.

Main claim: "More than any other sitcom . . ."

Okay, but there must be "other" shows like *Andy*—such as *Leave It to Beaver*.

Criteria for evaluation. How *Andy Griffith* differs from other shows—it's more comforting because things return to normal.

On *Three's Company* or *Seinfeld* or *Friends,* things work out in the end. The friends are getting along just fine, but we can see that they are bound for another conflict in a week or so. Though this week's crisis has worked itself out, the pace of their lives or their natural temperaments or

Develops argument by discussing what happens in other shows: Things work out okay, but we can tell a new crisis will loom.

■ Writing Strategies ■ Exploring Ideas

their complicated living conditions are still spinning wildly and we know next week they're in for trouble again. On *Dharma and Greg* or *Green Acres* or *I Love Lucy* (even on *The Dick Van Dyke Show*), the family has once again survived, but as with the shows about friends, on the shows about families there seems to be only temporary comfort in the happy ending. Dharma and Greg are still bound for a divorce. Lisa, on *Green Acres,* is only putting up with the farm life a little while longer and Oliver loves it so much that he is never going back to the city. Though she is ironically more suited to the place than he is, she longs always to live elsewhere. No one could possibly put up with all Lucy's scheming. And as for Richard and Laura Petrie, the most stable of our sample couples, to the average American they seem only a step away from falling into the New York swinger crowd. On *MASH* or *Hogan's Heroes* or *Gomer Pyle,* they are either at war or could be. There's little real and lasting comfort in these folks who are gathered together out of necessity so far from home. Yes, they're buddies and that's nice, but it's all so temporary.

This seems to go beyond initial thinking. (I've never thought about it.)

This doesn't exhaust all the sitcoms or all the types, but it does set up the reasons that *The Andy Griffith Show* comforts us more than the others. The show's main character, Andy, is full of southern wisdom. He is quiet and listens and makes better decisions in the midst of all the madness than we could have. That is comfort number one: Someone—the general, the man in charge, *the sheriff*—has things under control. All the madness results from one of three things: either intruders, but Andy gets rid of them after they have caused only a little trouble; or just

Author concedes that there are other sitcoms and other types of sitcoms.

Goes beyond initial thinking here. Gets specific. Show provides comfort because someone's wise. Madness because of (1) intruders; (2) natural growing up; (3) ego, ambition, pride.

CBS/Landov

boys (Opie and sometimes his friends) going through what is natural to go through growing up, but Andy deals with this expertly, too; or ego, ambition, and pride—usually Barney is having the trouble here, though it could be Aunt Bea or one of the others. Andy understands all of this, though not so well or right away that the show isn't a little bit interesting. The plot is better than most sitcoms: There is always a solution that takes a little while to get to, and we believe it when we finally do.

Develops argument through specific analysis of *The Andy Griffith Show.* Shows specifically why/how *Andy Griffith* comforts us.

What's most comforting about this show, however, is that things return to normal. That is, *The Andy Griffith Show* offers us a normal that can be returned to. With *Andy Griffith* we get a sense that the complication has blown through like a summer thunderstorm, instead of us getting the sense that a little blue sky has blown through a place where it is otherwise always thunderstorming. The characters are at home. They're not strangers thrown together, and they haven't been transplanted in some strange land (such as Hooterville, New York City, or Postmodern America). They are familiar with their surroundings and like (both "similar to" and "fond of") each other. The zaniness on *Andy Griffith* could just as well not ensue . . . but it does. On all those other shows, it must ensue. How couldn't it?

Main idea: says what is most comforting about the show (relates to title of essay).

This seems to go beyond initial thinking: Things are normal and get wacky, instead of things generally just being wacky.

The situation itself—small-town people in a small town—is comforting. The show develops this sense with Andy's quiet wisdom, but also with the integrity of the wacky supporting characters. All of them to some degree are like Barney—a liability and an asset all at once. They are, like us, good people flawed. We are all familiar with the show's gentle theme song, whistled as Andy and Opie walk along with fishing poles. And the black and white camera shots are always perfectly composed, like a photo we'd see in *Life* magazine. The dialog is quiet, engaging, funny, real. For 30 minutes we are practically back in the womb of Mayberry—a place that doesn't exist, but does. It is a place that, whether we ever felt it as a child or not, as adults we feel that we once knew. We can feel it now, and *The Andy Griffith Show* captures what we all now think that we once felt back then.

Connects to readers (public resonance): They are, like us, good people flawed. The use of "we" (though not required) helps make this connection.

The situation itself (small-town life) contributes to comforting.

Not all sitcoms set out to comfort, though all do set out to entertain. Some, such as *All in the Family* or *Soap* or *Will and Grace,* might even set out to challenge us, to make us think. But *The Andy Griffith Show,* I believe, sets out to entertain and comfort and it succeeds as no other show ever has . . . or ever will. *The Cosby Show* could only circle in *Andy's* orbit. The reason is, I suppose, because the times have changed. Today an attempt to create the comfort of Mayberry (an attempt to say your small-town life is idyllic) would somehow

Concession/qualifier: Not all sitcoms set out to comfort. Some may even do the opposite.

The show captures something. What is it?

Concludes by providing a possible reason why *The Andy Griffith Show* is more comforting than today's shows.

fail. It would seem a lie without any of the twenty-first-century issues (drugs, pregnancy, homosexual kissing), without any of the edgy technology, the music, the rapid-fire slick wit, the self-aware writing and directing. Mayberry exists, cliché as it sounds, in our hearts. The show, like no other, captured what we want to remember, whether it happened or not. It tells us that blue skies are normal.

Connects to viewers because it is comforting. Assures viewers that blue skies, not storms, are normal. (Even if this is not true? Is it?)

Writing Strategies

1. What criteria (standards of judgment) does Bell use to evaluate *The Andy Griffith Show?*
2. Highlight any background or summary information necessary to understand Bell's evaluation. Where does such information appear? Why is it helpful?
3. Evaluations are forms of argument. Describe how Bell makes some conventional argumentative moves: How does he use appeals? How does he counterargue?
4. Describe how Bell's allusions to other television shows support his main idea. How are those other shows used?

Exploring Ideas

1. How does Bell's essay encourage readers to think differently about TV sitcoms—or entertainment in general?
2. *The Andy Griffith Show* originally aired through the 1960s—over forty years ago. How is Bell's evaluation still relevant? How does he work to make it relevant?
3. Think of three television shows that might impact the quality of a viewer's life. Explain how each show might influence the way that people think or act.
4. How do popular television shows relate to popular sentiments or values? Do they, for instance, reflect what we imagine about ourselves, what we hope for, what we fear? Explain the relationship between what we watch and who we are.

Ideas for Writing

1. What television show is overestimated or underestimated? Why do audiences have the wrong take on it?
2. Examine a popular website and try to discover an element of the design that people may not usually consider—font use, spatial arrangement, color scheme, and so on. How does that particular aspect positively or negatively impact the overall effect of the site?

If responding to one of these ideas, go to the Analysis section of this chapter to begin developing ideas for your essay.

Student Essay

Star Trek: Where No Man Has Gone Before

Jaren Provo

Most people have a favorite television program, but few of us consider how that program resonates with broader cultural trends—how it speaks to, addresses, or challenges common biases and prejudices. In this essay, Jaren Provo takes a close look at *Star Trek*. She goes beyond merely celebrating its attributes; she evaluates *Star Trek* according to the role it has played in shaping attitudes about and within popular culture. Provo wrote this essay for her first-semester college writing course.

> "The greatest danger facing us is ourselves, and irrational fear of the unknown. But there's no such thing as 'the unknown,' only things temporarily hidden, temporarily not understood." —Captain James T. Kirk

Since its stunning and innovative debut in 1966, *Star Trek* has given modern culture a new promise for the future, one of peace, cooperation, and tolerance not seen in such tenacity or splendor before or since. Yet, despite the significant cultural contribution *Star Trek* has made, many see this legendary universe as unreachable, non-applicable, influencing only the stereotypical Klingon-quoting, uniform-donning, convention-going fan. However, this view is false. *Star Trek* empowers mainstream America to imagine a future of hope-filled opportunity rather than horrific obliteration.

Each of us is familiar with *Star Trek* in some manner, whether it be the phrase "Beam me up, Scotty" (which, actually, was never said verbatim in the series), the *USS Enterprise,* the . . . very . . . long pauses . . . of William Shatner's portrayal of Captain Kirk, or its groovy theme music. *Star Trek* is best described, by Roddenberry himself, as the 1960's television show set "close enough to our own time for continuing characters to be fully identifiable as people like us, but far enough into the future for galaxy travel to be fully established" ("*Star Trek* Is"). It is not until much later in the franchise that we realize *Star Trek* is set in the 2260s AD, focusing on the crew and voyages of the starship *Enterprise* as it carries out its five-year mission of peaceful exploration. As the *Enterprise* travels through space, it encounters various worlds with attributes reminiscent of Earth, and discusses numerous issues of political, social, and human nature. *Star Trek* shows us, through a cast of recurring dynamic characters and a space-oriented view, a reflection of humanity and its possibilities.

The specific focus here is Roddenberry's first series, the original series (or what Trekkies refer to as TOS). There have been five television spin-off series and ten movies deriving their roots from TOS, but each successive reiteration of *Star Trek* brings an even more commercialized version of Roddenberry's standard-defying innovation. In these new series, special effects have

---

replaced meaningful plots; de rigueur characters have replaced dynamic ones. Roddenberry's vision rose above the need for believable explosions, unrecognizable aliens, and shoot-em-up alien-invader plots, such that *Star Trek* struggled to remain on the air during its short (but syndicate-able) three-year stint; it was a vision that broadcasting officials placed little promise in, as it was most certainly not a mainstream science fiction show.

But this vision was so powerful and so magnificent that it opened an avenue to engage humans in their own universe. While popular culture at the time focused on the individual and his or her worldly place in society, *Star Trek* expanded the horizons of the human mind toward the furthermost reaches of space. In the *Star Trek* future, there are no physical boundaries or burdens, for the greatest, most inaccessible reaches of the universe are merely a warp speed away, the unknown cultures of a million worlds much like Earth are open for communication and exploration. Indeed, one of the core principles of *Star Trek* is the "parallel worlds concept"—that there are billions of planets with conditions comparable to Earth that could harbor similar social, ecological, and humanlike development ("*Star Trek* Is"). It is this principle that shapes the core mission of the *USS Enterprise* herself: "to boldly go where no man has gone before."

And in so doing, the humans of the twenty-third century do not have to face a decimated, physically and culturally broken world similar to those in many recognizable pop culture realms, such as *Terminator* or *The Matrix.* Instead, they are a functioning global culture. These individuals are able to realize their own humanity by exploring and relating to alien cultures in the depths of the universe, offering aid and relief to struggling civilizations, but willing to observe and maintain the customs of the native peoples. This core idea constitutes the Prime Directive, a predominant theme throughout *Star Trek.* The Prime Directive advocates involvement with, but not indoctrination of, other cultures (unless there is a lack of a progressing, stable culture). To each world the *Enterprise* travels, it promotes a mission of peace and negotiation, rather than conquest.

Through this process, humans become increasingly tolerant of groups within their own species. Bigotry or intolerance in any form is seen as a horrendous trait and a mark of low character. On the bridge of the *Enterprise,* such individuals as an African woman, Asian American man, Scottish engineer, pointed-eared alien without emotions, nationalistic Russian youngster, and even an Iowan hunk with a rhythmically related speech deficiency are regular residents, each respected for his or her own talents and merit as a member of the crew. Even representatives of such backgrounds as German, French, Irish, Indian, British, Native American, and more are seen frequently on the *Enterprise.* Jeff Greenwald, author of *Future Perfect: How "Star Trek" Conquered Planet Earth,* echoes this idea: "[*Star Trek*] has given us a model of a truly multicultural world, where all races and creeds are afforded equal respect and rights" (qtd. in Schrof 8). Together, this diverse and accepting group explores the human condition, such items as the role of good and evil (in such episodes as "The Savage Curtain" and "The Enemy Within"), maturity and age (in the episodes "Miri," "Charlie X," and "The Deadly Years"), and an ambition-free life ("This Side of Paradise").

However, some feel that *Star Trek*'s diverse cast is not as accepting and multicultural as it appears. In his piece, "Carved From the Rock Experiences of Our Daily Lives: Reality and *Star Trek*'s Multiple Histories," Lincoln Geraghty concedes that TOS casts "token" minority members as crew and is deficient because of its lack of an openly homosexual crewmember (161). In this way, he argues, *Star Trek* repeats the "mistakes other popular television series made" (161). However, it is important to observe the cultural climate of the 1960s, especially in popular media. If indeed minority groups were portrayed, they were often playing roles of servants (Asian Americans), slaves (African Americans), or senseless and vicious warriors on the Western plains (Native Americans). The latter was not often represented by those from this culture; often, individuals of Italian descent were given the roles of Native Americans. Though perhaps not main characters with substantial parts (with the exception of Spock, who is an alien and would in a sense be considered a member of a "minority" group), these individuals are not degraded, but are respected on the merit of their performance and contributions to the ship itself. These individuals also took on a more active role as *Star Trek* progressed; in the third season, *Star Trek* was even so bold as to portray the first interracial kiss on television ("Plato's Stepchildren"). Given the exclusive nature of the times, *Star Trek*'s role was an advanced platform (unlike other pop culture outlets) upon which racial, ethnic, and gender acceptance could be built.

Together, these humans learn from past mistakes, attempting to avoid their occurrence in other cultures developing in similar manners (as in the episodes "Patterns of Force" and "A Taste of Armageddon"). Indeed, as William Blake Tyrrell states in his 1977 article (around the peak of *Star Trek*'s syndication-led revival), "*Star Trek* creates a future world where the glories of the past are pristine and the failures and doubts of the present have been overcome. It gives us our past as our future, while making our present the past, which . . . is safely over and forgotten" (qtd. in Geraghty 167). But in *Star Trek,* the past is not so much forgotten as it is no longer dwelled upon; it is often revisited for comparative and developmental purposes. Humanity in the future does not degrade; it matures and refines itself toward a more ideal form.

Notably absent from *Star Trek*'s list of qualities is the predominant science fiction theme regarding space aliens: "When they come, they'll destroy us all." This permeated view is reflected in numerous locales, such as *Independence Day, Invasion of the Body Snatchers,* and H.G. Wells' *War of the Worlds.* Yet in *Star Trek,* the first contact with aliens is a diplomatic one, in which logical, peaceful Vulcan representatives come to Earth to note their presence and encourage future technological development. After this contact, more connections are forged with other alien worlds, such that the United Federation of Planets develops (with a flag suspiciously reminiscent of that of the United Nations) to promote peaceable cooperation among these cultures. Alien cultures are not (generally) out to conquer Earth and all of humanity in a blazing inferno of death and destruction, but are civilized, developing worlds willing to forge ties with others in the universe to assure mutual survival.

Also uncharacteristic of *Star Trek* but common in the sci-fi realm is the element portraying humans as slaves of technology, hopelessly existent only in body. This concept is perhaps most prevalent in the *Matrix* trilogy. Yet *Star Trek* foretells humans as harnessing the resources of technology to propel themselves outward into space, to explore, to contact, to impact in a positive way. The transporter and warp drive allow for expedient, efficient movement among planets and realms; the communicator (predecessor to the flip-phone?) and universal translator aid in interpersonal and intercultural contact; the scientific tricorder (a handheld programmable scanning device) and ship's scanners enhance exploration purposes; and medical tricorders and unknown, but apparently technical, whirring devices devised from salt 'n' pepper shakers exist for medical purposes. True, some matters of technology are dangerous and destroy human independence, such as the M-5 Multitronic Computer in the episode "The Ultimate Computer." Essentially, this device is meant to save lives by replacing the human presence on a starship, yet it manages to entirely control the ship and destroy hundreds of innocent lives in the process. However, this technology is not typical, and ends up being destroyed. M-5 reminds us to maintain a fine balance between technology serving and subverting humankind.

Some, however, disagree with the assertion that *Star Trek* promotes a palate of peace, tolerance, and diplomacy, pointing to the predominant enemy throughout the series: the Klingon Empire. They observe the constant conflict between the Klingons and the Federation, between their opposing interests of complete colonization and diplomatic cooperation. Certainly the Federation is not peaceful toward or tolerant of this group of aliens. Yet, the Klingon Empire is an imperialistic, dictatorial force of conquest interested in destroying the diplomatic network of the Federation and its promotion of freedom and democracy. Actions taken against the Klingons are in matters of defense, not of aggression, and peace negotiations between the Klingons and Federation persist throughout and beyond the series. Eventually, internal political movements bring the dictatorial regime to its knees, and even the Klingons themselves are incorporated into the Federation.

Many also claim that *Star Trek* is merely a scripted TV show, unrealistic and inaccessible to all but the most obsessive fans. However, *Star Trek* has reached and influenced some of the leaders of technology and society, including individuals such as Bill Gates, several NASA scientists and engineers, and even the late Dr. Martin Luther King, Jr. The message of *Star Trek* resonates through these and other individuals familiar with *Star Trek*'s ideals, such that all in society are influenced by this series. Many outlets in society and the media also carry *Star Trek*'s concepts into their settings on an entertainment level. Considering entertainment's pivotal role in our society (take, for instance, the large number of individuals who gain current events knowledge from comedy shows such as *The Daily Show, The Tonight Show with Jay Leno,* and *Saturday Night Live*), the sheer entertainment quality of *Star Trek* brings it into our everyday lives. Furthermore, the core concepts of *Star Trek* are not fictional and far-reaching, but are based on events and themes within the Vietnam War era and relating to the human condition.

Imagine a world in which *Star Trek* is absent. We would miss more than the phrases "He's dead, Jim" and "Beam me up, Scotty," more than warp drive and the same men in red shirts dying before the introductory theme each week. Our culture would be void of a revolutionary promise, a promise of tolerance, peace, exploration, and humanity in our future. Without *Star Trek,* modern pop culture would be filled only with bleak visions for tomorrow, of aliens ruthlessly invading and destroying Earth, of a humanity decimated and barely clinging to the edge of existence, of survival depending upon backstabbing and cruelty. *Star Trek* is one of the few (perhaps the only) candles flickering in the darkness of popular apocalypticism, a guarantee of a secure future where tomorrow may not be such a horrible thing after all.

We must be sure not to violate the magnitude of *Star Trek* and its whispers of truth for the days ahead. We must not be intolerant of that which heralds a tolerant tomorrow, doubtful of a harbinger of hope, or disparaging toward a beacon of peace or humanity. The zeitgeist bestowed upon our culture by *Star Trek* must be appreciated for its complexities and considered in its hopeful message to the people of today.

Works Cited

Geraghty, Lincoln. "Carved from the Rock Experiences of Our Daily Lives: Reality and *Star Trek's* Multiple Histories." *European Journal of American Culture*, vol. 21, no. 3, Nov. 2002, pp. 160–76. *Academic Search Elite*, doi:10.1386/ejac.21.3.160.

Schrof, Joannie M. "A World of Trekkies." *U.S. News and World Report*, 29 June 1998, p. 8.

"*Star Trek* Is." *Memory Alpha*, memory-alpha.wikia.com/wiki/Star_Trek_is. . . . Accessed 8 Apr. 2014.

Writing Strategies

1. How does Provo address the common dismissal about "Trekkies"?

2. Although she does not state them directly in the essay, what can you infer about Provo's criteria (standards of judgment)? In other words, in her view, what makes a good television program? Why does *Star Trek* meet those standards?

3. How does Provo counterargue? Describe how particular counterarguments add dimension and value to her essay.

4. Provo's points often sound extremely positive—as though she cannot imagine a downside to the topic. Where does Provo qualify or concede to some other point of view? Why might she be justified in such glowing praise of the program?

5. How does Provo's sentence structure influence her voice? Focus on a particular paragraph and explain how the sentences impact the "sound" of the argument.

Exploring Ideas

1. Provo argues that television programs are more than entertainment—that they deal with important culture issues within a given era. What current television dramas attempt to deal with the political and cultural tensions of our era? How do they succeed or fail?

2. Provo celebrates *Star Trek* because it challenged racial prejudices of the 1960s. Do you think television can genuinely challenge or overturn common assumptions about race or gender? Why or why not?

3. Provo argues that most science fiction in popular culture, other than *Star Trek,* predicts a future of "horrific obliteration." What recent movies or television programs reinforce Provo's point? Do any challenge her notion?

4. From ancient times to the present, civilizations imagine other nations, tribes, people, or species as inherently wicked or debased. Oral stories, religious traditions, novels, and popular movies often characterize some faraway, unknown group as hostile, weird, or even corrupt. How does *Star Trek* fit into that long tradition?

Ideas for Writing

1. What particular program works to break down common prejudices or stereotypes? How does it succeed or fall short?

2. Consider a current commercial or ad campaign. How does it subtly reinforce negative stereotypes about people? Why don't viewers tend to acknowledge such stereotypes?

If responding to one of these ideas, go to the Analysis section of this chapter to begin developing ideas for your essay.

Invention
"I criticize by creation . . . not by finding fault."

—Marcus Tullius Cicero

Invention is the primary strategy for generating new ideas. As you work through the following sections, imagine possibilities beyond your initial thoughts. The Point of Contact section will help you to find a subject for the evaluation; Analysis will help you to develop particular points about the subject; and Public Resonance will help you to make it relevant to a community of readers. The Thesis and Rhetorical Tools sections will help you develop a specific claim and support it appropriately. As in the other chapters, the Invention Questions in each section are not meant to be answered directly in your final written assignment. They are meant to prompt reflection and discovery; however, your answers may translate directly into your drafts.

Point of Contact

Evaluators need to have particular insight into their subject, so choose something that you can examine carefully. Your instructor may provide subjects, or you can use the following suggestions and questions to seek out and focus on a particular subject. Once you've focused on a subject, take notes. Record as much information about the subject as possible.

Attend an Event (A carnival, circus, beauty pageant, dance, tractor pull, art show, concert, poetry reading, company meeting, college class, etc.). What happens before the event? What is the mood? How are the participants treated during the event? What kinds of interaction occur during the event? Where does the event take place? What impact does the location have on the event?

Investigate a Person (A government official, doctor, religious leader, talk show host, roommate, professional athlete, work supervisor or manager, work associate, etc.). Evaluating a person can be tricky because it is easy to fall into an explanation of one's likes and dislikes. Instead, focus on the qualities or actions of the person in terms of his or her particular position or title. Is he or she willing to listen to people? For how long? What does he or she do while listening to someone? How do people respond or react to this person? Are people comfortable around this person? Is this person entertaining, enlightening, engaging, comforting, informative, energizing (or the opposite of any of these)?

Visit a Place (A restaurant, movie theater, night club, amusement park, college classroom or campus, shopping mall, grocery store, etc.). Gather information about the place. How do people behave? What behavior is tolerated, supported, ignored? What is on the walls? How does this influence the mood of the place? How much open space is available? Is the place empty, crowded, stuffy, clean, lonely, isolated, intense?

John Mauk

Watch a Movie or Show (A motion picture, sitcom, documentary, television drama, music video). Gather information and details, going beyond simple likes and dislikes. Does the dialogue reveal something about the characters that their actions do not? What kinds of graphic or sexually explicit images appear? Is the movie/show humorous or frightening in some way? How? What message(s) does the movie/show offer? Does the movie/show have stereotypes (of rich people, poor people, women, men, racial groups, children, the elderly)?

Read a Text (A book, article, poster, letter, website, etc.). Consider texts from your major. In this case, go to one of the journals for your major, or to a database in your library. In some ways, evaluating a text is easy because it can be examined closely without having to rewind or travel somewhere. However, a written text can be a complicated mass of elements. What is the main idea or main argument of the text? What kind of evidence or support is used? How formal is the language? What is the tone of the text? If the text is an argument, does it address counterarguments? Does it use concession? What strategies are used to draw readers into the ideas of the text?

Analysis

Imagine taking your car to a mechanic because you hear a strange knocking sound when you accelerate. As you pull into the garage, the mechanic smiles and exclaims, "Hey, nice car! I love Ford Mustangs! There's nothing wrong with *that* car." Obviously, you'd be a bit disoriented, and maybe a little grumpy. You'd also probably complain: "Hey, I want you to tell me what's wrong with the car—tell me why it's making that sound!" The problem with this scenario is that the mechanic does no analysis and uses no *criteria* (the standards on which judgments are based). The evaluation of the car is based on the mechanic's own likes and dislikes.

Or imagine reading a review of a fine Italian restaurant. While ignoring the wine list, entrees, and presentation of the food, the reviewer gives the restaurant a very low rating because of a limited number of ice cream flavors. In this scenario, the reviewer uses the *wrong* criteria. The reviewer evaluates a fine dining establishment with criteria for judging an ice cream shop. This would be similar to judging a historical drama negatively because it is not funny: historical dramas are not, usually, supposed to be funny, nor are fine Italian restaurants supposed to have wide varieties of ice cream.

Discovering the Purpose of the Subject

The first analytical step is to discover the subject's purpose or goal—to understand, in other words, what the subject is attempting to achieve. We can only develop criteria and then evaluate a subject if we know the subject's purpose and audience. For example, we can evaluate a movie only if we understand what the movie is attempting to do: to succeed as a comedy for teens, to maintain high action for adults, or to retell a classic fairy tale for children. Evaluating something means understanding what that subject is attempting to do.

- What does your subject try to achieve? (Be specific. For example, an Italian restaurant may be attempting to provide an elegant dining experience with a particular ethnic cuisine. This is different from the goal of a general chain restaurant such as Denny's, which attempts to provide economically priced food from a general menu.)
- What do other like subjects try to achieve? (Think about subjects similar to yours—other teachers, other comedic movies, other restaurants, and so on.)
- Who is your subject's audience? (Whom does your subject attempt to engage or attract?) If you have not already considered the audience, imagine who might use, benefit from, and interact with the subject.
- What goals *should* your subject, or all subjects like it, have? (It might be argued, for instance, that a restaurant should attempt to elevate the dining experience, to transform the mundane act of eating into a cultural and social event. Once this criterion is established, someone might then use it to judge a particular restaurant.)

In Ed Bell's invention writing, he grapples with the idea of entertainment—what it does and should do for its audience:

> **What does this subject try to achieve?**
>
> The *Andy Griffith Show* is a sitcom (situational comedy). It tries to entertain people. If people are entertained, they will continue watching the show. That's the basic idea. But entertain how? Some shows entertain through violence, others drama, some through sex, and so on. Sitcoms try to entertain through comedy, but not just comedy. There has to be something even more specific than just comedy. Comedy how? What kind of comedy? *The Andy Griffith Show* has a particularly comfortable, slow pace to it. One might say that the show tries to entertain, but in a relaxing, maybe even comforting, way.
>
> **What is the subject's audience?**
>
> The original audience for this show was the general American public in the 1960s, I imagine. Perhaps the show's producers had some more specific demographic in mind. But at the time, most people got three stations—NBC, CBS, and ABC. Americans tuned in to watch one of three shows. Looking back, it may be difficult, yet interesting, to imagine the audience. I imagine it being a simpler time. I wonder if such a show could even be created today, or if it would seem unrealistic, fake, insincere. The audience today is different but still likes the show. For some reason, the show has maintained its appeal (perhaps because it's just pleasant, comforting). Maybe there's something valuable about creations from the past.

Applying Criteria to the Subject

Now that you have a sense of the subject's purpose, you can begin making specific evaluative points. Refer to your notes from the Point of Contact section and answer the following:

- In what particular ways does the subject achieve its goal? What specific parts, tools, or strategies help the subject to achieve its goal?
- In what particular ways does the subject fall short of achieving its goal?
- What goals does the subject ignore?

- How does the subject compare to and contrast with other similar subjects?
- What is unique about your subject's approach or strategy to achieving its goal?

In his exploration of *The Andy Griffith Show,* Bell discovers the main point of his essay:

> **How does the subject compare to and contrast with other similar subjects?**
> More recent sitcoms take on issues. *All in the Family* comes to mind. That sitcom changed things a little. It opened up the range of what a situational comedy can be or do. As for shows more like it that do not attempt to take on cultural issues as *All in the Family* did, they are all pretty much the same: standard situations, basic character types, and so on. It seems that these shows always begin with some normal, comfortable scene; then something happens to create confusion or turmoil; then it gets sorted out in the end. If it's different at all, maybe *The Andy Griffith Show* returns to normal. Or, said another way, maybe the normal that it returns to is a different kind of normal—a normal that is more comfortable and lasting. (We might call this type of normal "Mayberry.") That is to say, other sitcoms of the time such as *Hogan's Heroes* or *Gomer Pyle* (and later ones like *MASH* or *Three's Company*) don't really start or end with a "normal" situation. Instead, with those shows you have inevitable trouble always bound to emerge.

Public Resonance

A meaningful evaluation considers how the subject affects or influences people—how it resonates with people's lives and concerns. For example, a movie critic might argue that children's movies carry the responsibility of developing notions of right and wrong. Or someone might suggest that a restaurant affects the health and well-being of a community and influences the image of a neighborhood. Ultimately, it is up to the writer to reveal the influence of a subject.

Each of the writers featured in this chapter (Busch, Provo, and Bell) develops public resonance by connecting the specific subject to broader social issues. In her essay, Jaren Provo makes an explicit case about *Star Trek*. She, in fact, argues about the show's influence on American pop culture:

> Imagine a world in which *Star Trek* is absent. We would miss more than the phrases "He's dead, Jim" and "Beam me up, Scotty," more than warp drive and the same men in red shirts dying before the introductory theme each week. Our culture would be void of a revolutionary promise, a promise of tolerance, peace, exploration, and humanity in our future. Without *Star Trek*, modern pop culture would be filled only with bleak visions for tomorrow, of aliens ruthlessly invading and destroying Earth, of a humanity decimated and barely clinging to the edge of existence, of survival depending upon backstabbing and cruelty. *Star Trek* is one of the few (perhaps the only) candles flickering in the darkness of popular apocalypticism, a guarantee of a secure future where tomorrow may not be such a horrible thing after all.

In his article, Benjamin Busch also deals explicitly with public resonance. In the following passage, he transitions from his own objections to broader, and murkier, problems associated with video games and the portrayal of war. The paragraph begins with a kind of concession about legal responsibilities but then ends with some larger (social or humanistic) layers of responsibility:

> Despite my objections to certain aspects of the video war game, I don't know that game makers have any particular responsibilities to any of us. They are a market based entertainment business. Their sales are subject to mature audience restrictions like film and pornography, but game ratings are not enforced by any government agency in the United States. We can only hope that business values social decency, and respects essential humanism but a gaming company is only truly concerned with market reception in the form of product sales. The responsibility is placed on the consumer and parents. At the age of 18, an American citizen can vote, and can enlist in the armed services without parental consent. We should assume that they can also choose their entertainment for better or for worse. Issues of responsibility arise when our military develops war games with private companies and then allows them to be sold publicly. The game then partially becomes a governmental, even military, product and its messages are unable to speak free of politics or real war.

As Busch and Provo illustrate, public resonance can become an integral part—maybe the most critical part—of your argument. Use the following questions to help develop public resonance for your own evaluation:

- How does the subject influence people's lives (their health, attitudes, living conditions, etc.)?
- Why is this subject important in people's lives?
- What do people expect from the subject?

Invention Workshop

With at least one other writer, use one of the Invention Questions to launch an intensive and focused discussion about your subject. Try to go beyond your first thoughts on the subject. For example, Linda, who is evaluating a new restaurant in her town, transcends her initial thoughts. Her discussion leads to a more complicated understanding of the subject and its relationship to people's lives:

Why is this subject important in people's lives?

LINDA:	That's easy . . . a restaurant serves people food. And people need food.
MARCUS:	But do restaurants just provide food?
JACK:	No, they also provide service—someone bringing you the food. And they also make eating a social event.
LINDA:	But that isn't the important part.
MARCUS:	Well, it isn't the main part, but I'd say people need that social aspect in their lives, and eating is naturally a social activity. That's what's so enjoyable about eating out—you get to feel social.
LINDA:	But eating is also a personal thing, right? It's about the home and family, too.

JACK: I would say that restaurants are important because they provide a place where people can feel slightly special—like they're somewhere besides their living room with a bowl of cereal. They make eating feel elevated.

LINDA: If that's the case, what's the deal with all these restaurants saying they're "just like home"?

MARCUS: Well, that's the goal of those chain restaurants, which really aren't like home at all. They're trying to make people feel close to home.

LINDA: So these restaurants provide something psychologically to people. I guess that's why restaurants spend so much on atmosphere and advertising.

MARCUS: So what about the particular restaurant Chunky's? Does it make people feel "at home"?

LINDA: Not really. It feels like a chain restaurant that's attempting to not feel like a chain restaurant.

Linda has discovered something beyond the obvious about the subject's purpose: Restaurants aren't simply about food; they are also about familiarity. (There's an important psychology to food service!) This discovery could impact how she evaluates the particular restaurant.

In Bell's invention writing, the public resonance is tied to the main discovery he makes in Analysis. In the following excerpt, he narrows in on the actual thesis of the essay:

Why is this subject important in people's lives?

It is some people's favorite TV show, a show that they grew up watching and that gives them a certain feeling. It makes them feel good. It makes them feel at home. The same could be said about *Star Trek* or *Will and Grace* or other shows. Specifically, *The Andy Griffith Show* goes beyond being funny in the way that it presents what people might like to think of as "normal." Life is full of all sorts of characters (some wacky, some annoying) and all sorts of situations or complications arise, and in all sitcoms (maybe not all, but probably) the conflict is resolved. But *The Andy Griffith Show* seems to suggest that the resolution is normal, whereas other shows suggest that conflict or tension is normal.

Research

Consider using outside sources to help you figure out what others have said about the subject. Do not expect to find writers who share your perspective. Instead, explore for various perspectives. Have people generally found the subject valuable, worthy, deficient, dangerous, helpful? If your subject is very specific (such as a local diner) you might search for evaluations in that general category (local diners). See Chapter 14 for help with finding sources.

Thesis

An evaluation makes a judgment about a subject. An evaluative thesis statement gives focus to that judgment: The thesis sheds light on a particular element of the subject. For instance, a movie has many elements, such as characters, plot, cinematography, themes, special effects, and dialogue. A thesis can help create focus, telling readers that the evaluation will deal primarily with plot, not character development and costumes:

> The movie's plot is unnecessarily confusing.

An evaluative thesis need not be completely positive or completely negative. It need not, for example, claim that a particular movie is absolutely great or downright rotten. Many evaluative thesis statements are a mixture of judgments. A statement might concede some value but focus primarily on a shortcoming as in the following:

> While the movie's cinematography is engaging, the plot is unnecessarily confusing.
>
> Although the student government has been more public than in previous years, it has still failed to address the student body's most significant concerns.
>
> Even with the new ensemble tricks, which provide an interesting layer of ear candy, Ebenezer Typhoon's new collection of songs still lacks any substantive message.
>
> The menu at Robinson's Grill may lack diversity, but it does what so many other restaurants cannot: deliver a genuinely local dining experience.

Evolution of a Thesis

A good thesis gives focus to an entire project. Linda's evaluation of a restaurant (in the Public Resonance section) gains focus as she works to craft a thesis. First, she discovers the subject's purpose. Then, while exploring public resonance, she discovers another, less obvious, layer. From there, she refines the idea into an evaluative claim:

- Chunky's attempts to give people a variety of good food and friendly service.
- People like to feel attached to their surroundings, to the places they shop and eat. Therefore, restaurants such as Chunky's try to create the illusion that diners are patronizing a friendly neighborhood grill.
- Although Chunky's attempts to make people feel comfortable in a small neighborhood grill, it doesn't work very well.
- Although Chunky's attempts to make people feel comfortable in a small neighborhood grill, the atmosphere and food still seem prepared by a distant corporate chef.

Linda's thesis evolved as she worked through the complexities of the subject. She discovered a subtle gap between the restaurant's purpose and the actual dining experience. This insight reveals something that might otherwise go unnoticed.

Common Thesis Problems

The Blurry Focus Problem A sufficiently narrow focus can mean all the difference between intensive and bland writing. First, a writer needs to home in on a particular subject, such as a particular band, a particular college campus or program. But that is often not enough. As in the following examples, the specific subjects still do not provide intensive points:

- Green Day is a great punk band.
- Big River Community College is a good school.

These statements need more focus. The writers could examine more particular elements (such as the themes of Green Day's songs or the accessible class times at Big River). Or the writers could develop more vital statements by avoiding the broad predicates "is a great . . ." and "is a good. . . ."

The Obvious Fact Problem The goal of evaluative writing is to help readers see the subject in a new light—to help them see some particular value or shortcoming. But writers sometimes fall into the trap of stating the obvious:

- Howard Stern offends people.
- Although some purists did not like it, the *Lord of the Rings* trilogy made a lot of money at the box office.

Both of these statements announce common knowledge, facts about the radio shock jock and the Peter Jackson movies. But neither statement offers an evaluation. The stated facts say nothing about the value or shortcoming of the subjects. Offending people, for instance, may be a good thing. And making lots of money may not mean much about the movies' artistic success.

The Noncommittal Problem An evaluation is an argument; therefore, the writer should put forth a position. But it may be tempting to back away from the evaluation and to let readers make up their own mind about the subject. The following examples back away; they lack a committed stance:

- The new building will please some and offend others.
- It's up to individual readers to decide whether or not they appreciate Kingsolver's *Poisonwood Bible*.

The noncommittal problem is related to a broader issue: Some writers are afraid of pushing too hard. They want to avoid forcing readers into a perspective. Although this seems like a legitimate concern, we should remember that readers need not be *forced* into an opinion or new perspective. Instead, they can be invited, lulled, guided, nudged, or attracted. Writers should seek to make their opinions so attractive, reasonable, enlightened, and compelling that readers feel as though they must adopt them. In short, don't fear commitment! Readers are waiting around for their minds to be changed.

Revising Your Thesis

Develop a thesis by asking a basic question: On what particular value or shortcoming do I want to focus? Try various wordings for your thesis. Let the idea evolve, tighten, over several attempts. Then, share the thesis statement with two other writers. As you look over their statements, look for all three common problems: blurry focus, obvious fact, and noncommittal. Suggest strategies for narrowing and intensifying the statements.

Rhetorical Tools

Using Support

Most of the claims made in evaluations are supported with specific information about the subject itself. The writer points out particular details that illustrate the main idea and show the value or shortcoming of the subject. For example, Ed Bell describes particular features of *The Andy Griffith Show:*

> The show's main character, Andy, is full of southern wisdom. He is quiet and listens and makes better decisions in the midst of all the madness than we could have. That is comfort number one: Someone—the general, the man in charge, *the sheriff*—has things under control. All the madness results from one of three things: either intruders, but Andy gets rid of them after they have caused only a little trouble; or just boys (Opie and sometimes his friends) going through what is natural to go through growing up, but Andy deals with this expertly, too; or ego, ambition, and pride—usually Barney is having the trouble here, though it could be Aunt Bea or one of the others. Andy understands all of this, though not so well or right away that the show isn't a little bit interesting. The plot is better than most sitcoms: There is always a solution that takes a little while to get to, and we believe it when we finally do.

Beware of Too Much Summary

A writer should present some basic facts about, or summarize, the subject as part of the evaluation. The presentation or summary of the subject should *not* constitute the majority of an evaluation, but should offer only the relevant details about the subject. For example, an evaluation using the thesis *While the movie's cinematography is engaging, the plot is unnecessarily confusing* would not devote long passages to the dress or appearance of the characters. Such information would be unnecessary and irrelevant to the evaluation.

You might also go beyond the subject itself—beyond your particular text, show, person, place. As explained in Chapter 8, writers have the world of history and culture at their disposal. This applies to evaluation as well. To prove a point about the subject, you can borrow from other moments in history, from science, nature, popular culture, or merely point out other like subjects. For example, Jaren Provo goes beyond her topic, *Star Trek,* to reinforce her thesis:

> Many also claim that *Star Trek* is merely a scripted TV show, unrealistic and inaccessible to all but the most obsessive fans. However, *Star Trek* has reached and influenced some of the leaders of technology and society, including individuals such as Bill Gates, several NASA scientists and engineers, and even the late Dr. Martin Luther King, Jr. The message of *Star Trek* resonates through these and other individuals familiar with *Star Trek*'s ideals, such that all in society are influenced by this series. Many outlets in society and the media also carry *Star Trek*'s concepts into their settings on an entertainment level. Considering entertainment's pivotal role in our society (take, for instance, the large number of individuals who gain current events knowledge from comedy shows such as *The Daily Show, The Tonight Show with Jay Leno,* and *Saturday Night Live*), the sheer entertainment quality of Star Trek brings it into our everyday lives. Furthermore, the core concepts of *Star Trek* are not fictional and far-reaching, but are based on events and themes within the Vietnam War era and relating to the human condition.

To develop claims using outside support, consider the following questions:

- Does a historical situation or trend (such as the rise of a particular fashion, organization, or individual) illustrate something about my topic?
- Does my topic or situation appear in any movies or television shows? If so, how is it handled?
- Does my topic appear in any works of literature? If so, how is it handled?
- Has science taught us anything about my topic?
- Have I witnessed or experienced someone or something that illustrates my point?
- Can I construct a scenario to illustrate my point?

Counterarguments and Concessions

Evaluations can also involve counterarguments and concessions (see Chapter 8, pages 277–280). Because evaluations are argumentative, they must acknowledge that other opinions (other judgments about the subject) are possible. In another passage from Provo's essay, she explains an opposing position, and then in a classic turnabout paragraph, she counters:

> However, some feel that *Star Trek's* diverse cast is not as accepting and multicultural as it appears. In his piece, "Carved From the Rock Experiences of Our Daily Lives: Reality and *Star Trek's* Multiple Histories," Lincoln Geraghty concedes that TOS casts "token" minority members as crew and is deficient because of its lack of an openly homosexual crewmember (161). In this way, he argues, *Star Trek* repeats the "mistakes other popular television series made" (161). However, it is important to observe the cultural climate of the 1960s, especially in popular media. If indeed minority groups were portrayed, they were often playing roles of servants (Asian Americans), slaves (African Americans), or senseless and vicious warriors on the Western plains (Native Americans). The latter was not often represented by those from this culture; often, individuals of Italian descent were given the roles of Native Americans. Though perhaps not main characters with substantial parts (with the exception of Spock, who is an alien and would in a sense be considered a member of a "minority" group), these individuals are not degraded, but are respected on the merit of their performance and contributions to the ship itself.

Invention Workshop

This activity is designed to generate counterarguments. The process involves an intensive group exchange. Follow these steps:

- Assemble writers into small groups (three or four per group work best).
- Each writer should have his or her thesis statement (main evaluative claim about the subject) written down.
- The first writer should read his or her thesis statement aloud to the group.
- Taking turns, each group member then should attempt to refute the position given in the statement. The idea is to play devil's advocate, to complicate the writer's ideas.
- The writer should record each opposing claim that is offered.
- After everyone in the group has given an opposing claim to the first writer, the second writer should recite his or her thesis, and the process begins again.

Revision

Revision requires sound evaluation. As with all forms of evaluation, writers should judge their work according to particular criteria—standards beyond the writers' own likes and dislikes. In a college writing course, these standard are often made explicit on syllabi, assignment prompts, or rubrics. The criteria often come in some of the following broad categories: *focus, support, depth, development, organization, documentation, grammar,* and *mechanics.* Like the sections of this chapter, common criteria often begin with the more difficult or abstract issues, such as *focus* or *depth,* and work toward more concrete or rule-based issues such as *grammar.* Look carefully through your course materials for these standards so that your revision is guided by shared criteria.

Peer Review

Exchange drafts with at least one other writer. Use the following questions to respond to specific issues in the drafts:

1. Can any phrases or terms in the thesis be narrowed? If so, circle them and make some suggestions for more focus. Does the thesis avoid the common problems? (See pages 345–346.)
2. Does the evaluation summarize or describe the subject thoroughly? (Where might the summary or description be unnecessary or unrelated to the main idea?)
3. Where could the writer support broad evaluative claims with specific details about the subject? For instance, someone might argue "the plot is unnecessarily complicated" but avoid pointing to specific points in the plot. (This is a critical omission for an evaluative argument, so examine the claims closely.)
4. Where might the writer go beyond the specific subject (the place, text, person, etc.) and allude to some other like subject? How could other like subjects help readers to see the main idea?
5. What other evaluative claims could be made about the subject? How could the writer address other, perhaps opposing, opinions?
6. Do any paragraphs shift focus from one point about the subject to another? Write "shifts focus" in the margins.
7. Identify any passages of harsh description. (See page 570.)
8. As a reviewer, point to particular sentences and phrases that could gain vitality and intensity. Use the following:

    a. Look for unnecessary interrupting clauses and phrases. Underline them and/or draw an arrow to show where the phrase or clause can be moved.

    b. Rewrite a sentence to create more intensity with a repeating pattern.

c. Cross out wordy phrases, and write in more concise options.

d. Consider other vitality strategies explained in Chapter 19.

- What sentences are over-embedded? (Point to any clauses that overlap with other clauses, causing a disconnect between ideas.)
- Examine attributive phrases. Point out unnecessary phrases or sentences that could be boiled down.
- Where can the writer change linking verbs to active verbs?
- Where can the writer avoid drawing attention to *I* and *you*?
- Help the writer change unnecessary clauses to phrases.
- Help the writer change unnecessary phrases to words.
- Point to expletives (such as *there are* and *it is*).
- Help the writer change passive verbs to active verbs for more vitality.
- Help the writer avoid common grammatical errors: comma splices, sentence fragments, or pronoun/antecedent agreement.

Reflection

Writers of all stripes struggle to evaluate their own work. We often fall on one side of a perilous fence: either celebrating our ideas too enthusiastically or cutting ourselves down too quickly. Quite often, those extremes (*I did a great job* verses *I'm a terrible writer*) keep us from understanding what we've accomplished. But good writers try to look honestly at their own rhetoric. They apply some criteria beyond their own likes, fears, and hang-ups. Now that you've written an evaluation, evaluate *it.* (That's right. Evaluate your performance as an evaluator.) Avoid the extremes: exuberant enthusiasm and self-deprecation. Instead, consider the following questions that focus on the essay's rhetoric, and let these questions guide you to an honest look at your work:

1. How did you do more than express a personal opinion? How did you help readers to genuinely resee the subject?
2. Could you have better engaged opposing positions? Did you do more than dismiss or refute the opposition? How could you have more genuinely dealt with other perspectives, values, or assumptions?
3. How inventive were your allusions? How well did you use support outside of the subject itself?
4. How did your voice engage readers? Was it boring? Did it do something other than speak in academic monotone?

Beyond the Essay: Evaluation Form

Student course evaluations, those forms that you fill out at the end of every semester, are a topic of debate in higher education. Although evaluations are meant to measure the success of a course, some administrators and professors argue that course evaluations are too prone to bias—that students who do well give good evaluations and students who do poorly give poor evaluations, or that many students through no fault of their own cannot really understand the goals and the value of the course. Others argue that student evaluations are popularity contests that encourage professors to inflate grades. All these arguments *evaluate* evaluations.

An important part of the conversation about course evaluations involves *criteria*—the standards that should be used to make the evaluation. These criteria might include rigor of the material, convenience for students, entertainment (enjoyment), entertainment (motivation), the students' interests, the instructor's appearance, instructor personality, grading policies, academic standards, quality of the syllabus, schedule of assignments, clarity, adherence to course or departmental objectives, individual student needs, and acknowledgment of a student's personal life and complications that occur throughout the semester. (More issues than these exist, and as a student you may have a quite different list than your professor. Why?)

1. As a class, discuss what criteria you think should be used to create a course evaluation. Then, with a group of peers, create a course evaluation form for a college class. Ask yourselves: What criteria should be used in a college classroom evaluation? Then create the form and discuss its pros and cons with the class.
2. In several paragraphs, argue for the criteria you used in creating a college writing classroom evaluation.

11 Searching for Causes

KELD NAVNTOFT/epa/Corbis

"One great cause of failure is lack of concentration."

—Bruce Lee

When something happens in a community, everyone wants to know why. Why did the apartment building catch on fire? Why did the incumbent mayor's campaign lose momentum? Why are so many kids absent from school? What causes the traffic jam on I-95 every day? Why did the stock market suddenly drop? Why did the terrorists attack? Of course, everybody has guesses, but it takes a close analysis to discover the possible causes of such phenomena. Fire officials inspect the ashes of a burned apartment building; political scientists examine candidates' speeches and poll results; civil engineers look closely at travel patterns and highway capacity; economists deliberate over consumption trends and overseas markets. In all these cases, the people searching for causes are detectives attempting to find answers amid a dizzying array of possibilities.

The search for causes constitutes much of the workload in many occupations. Doctors, of course, diagnose patients (looking for the cause of particular symptoms). Psychologists try to understand the causes of personality disorders or behavioral problems. Business executives hold weekly meetings and discuss the causes of production failures. Education specialists work with children to find the cause of scholastic problems.

As you can imagine (or as you may have witnessed), the search for such causes is not easy. Any number of factors can contribute to an effect. Take, for example, low proficiency test scores in public schools: school administrators might argue that poor teaching is the cause; teachers may point to poor parenting and discipline problems in the classroom; parents may point to bullying on school grounds or drug abuse; others might point to the tests themselves as the cause. The search for this cause, as it turns out, is a heated debate.

In academia, students spend much of their time studying causes:

- In an engineering class, students try to discover what causes one generator to produce more energy than another.
- Educational psychology students discuss why a particular student has lost all motivation.
- In history and economics seminars, students study economic conditions of the nineteenth century and debate the causes of the American Civil War.
- A class of physics students tries to determine the cause of black holes.

It might even be said that academia prepares people to understand causes in different fields—that is, that the study of a particular discipline gives students the critical perspectives necessary for asking the right questions (to find the right answers) within their fields. But despite the particular field or discipline, the process of discovery (of focusing and analyzing) is much the same, and the act of communicating one's discoveries is key in every situation.

This chapter will help you focus on a particular topic (a behavior, event, trend), discover a possible cause, and then develop an argument in favor of that cause. The following essays will provide insight into necessary writing strategies. For example, each essay in this chapter puts forth a particular claim about what caused or causes something—about *why* something happens. The author might not state it this way, but readers could write down the main claim as *X causes Y*, filling in X with the *cause* and Y with the *behavior, event, or trend*. The entire essay then helps readers understand and possibly accept that claim. As you read, identify the X and Y parts of the main claim and the particular support strategies (examples, explanations, facts, statistics, and so on) that help readers accept it. After reading the essays, you can begin looking for a particular relationship in one of two ways:

1. Go to the Point of Contact section to find a problem from your everyday life, or
2. Read the following essays and choose one of the Ideas for Writing that follow.

After finding a subject, go to the Analysis section to begin developing the evaluation.

Readings

Is Google Making Us Stupid? What the Internet Is Doing to Our Brains

Nicholas Carr

The following essay appeared in the July/August 2008 issue of *The Atlantic*. While the title asks if Google is making us stupid, the essay examines how not just Google, but technology (typewriters, clocks, the Internet) changes the way we think. Nicholas Carr is author of *The Shallows: What the Internet Is Doing to Our Brains*.

"Dave, stop. Stop, will you? Stop, Dave. Will you stop, Dave?" So the supercomputer HAL pleads with the implacable astronaut Dave Bowman in a famous and weirdly poignant scene toward the end of Stanley Kubrick's *2001: A Space Odyssey.* Bowman, having nearly been sent to a deep-space death by the malfunctioning machine, is calmly, coldly disconnecting the memory circuits that control its artificial brain. "Dave, my mind is going," HAL says, forlornly. "I can feel it. I can feel it."

I can feel it, too. Over the past few years I've had an uncomfortable sense that someone, or something, has been tinkering with my brain, remapping the neural circuitry, reprogramming the memory. My mind isn't going—so far as I can tell—but it's changing. I'm not thinking the way I used to think. I can feel it most strongly when I'm reading. Immersing myself in a book or a lengthy article used to be easy. My mind would get caught up in the narrative or the turns of the argument, and I'd spend hours strolling through long stretches of prose. That's rarely the case anymore. Now my concentration often starts to drift after two or three pages. I get fidgety, lose the thread, begin looking for something else to do. I feel as if I'm always dragging my wayward brain back to the text. The deep reading that used to come naturally has become a struggle.

I think I know what's going on. For more than a decade now, I've been spending a lot of time online, searching and surfing and sometimes adding to the great databases of the Internet. The Web has been a godsend to me as a writer. Research that once required days in the stacks or periodical rooms of libraries can now be done in minutes. A few Google searches, some quick clicks on hyperlinks, and I've got the telltale fact or pithy quote I was after. Even when I'm not working, I'm as likely as not to be foraging in the Web's info-thickets, reading and writing e-mails, scanning headlines and blog posts, watching videos and listening to podcasts, or just tripping from link to link to link. (Unlike footnotes, to which they're sometimes likened, hyperlinks don't merely point to related works; they propel you toward them.)

For me, as for others, the Net is becoming a universal medium, the conduit for most of the information that flows through my eyes and ears and into my mind. The advantages of having immediate access to such an incredibly rich store of information are many, and they've been widely described and duly applauded. "The perfect recall of silicon memory," *Wired*'s

---

Clive Thompson has written, "can be an enormous boon to thinking." But that boon comes at a price. As the media theorist Marshall McLuhan pointed out in the 1960s, media are not just passive channels of information. They supply the stuff of thought, but they also shape the process of thought. And what the Net seems to be doing is chipping away my capacity for concentration and contemplation. My mind now expects to take in information the way the Net distributes it: in a swiftly moving stream of particles. Once I was a scuba diver in the sea of words. Now I zip along the surface like a guy on a Jet Ski.

I'm not the only one. When I mention my troubles with reading to friends and acquaintances—literary types, most of them—many say they're having similar experiences. The more they use the Web, the more they have to fight to stay focused on long pieces of writing. Some of the bloggers I follow have also begun mentioning the phenomenon. Scott Karp, who writes a blog about online media, recently confessed that he has stopped reading books altogether. "I was a lit major in college, and used to be [a] voracious book reader," he wrote. "What happened?" He speculates on the answer: "What if I do all my reading on the web not so much because the way I read has changed, i.e., I'm just seeking convenience, but because the way I THINK has changed?"

Bruce Friedman, who blogs regularly about the use of computers in medicine, also has described how the Internet has altered his mental habits. "I now have almost totally lost the ability to read and absorb a longish article on the web or in print," he wrote earlier this year. A pathologist who has long been on the faculty of the University of Michigan Medical School, Friedman elaborated on his comment in a telephone conversation with me. His thinking, he said, has taken on a "staccato" quality, reflecting the way he quickly scans short passages of text from many sources online. "I can't read *War and Peace* anymore," he admitted. "I've lost the ability to do that. Even a blog post of more than three or four paragraphs is too much to absorb. I skim it."

Anecdotes alone don't prove much. And we still await the long-term neurological and psychological experiments that will provide a definitive picture of how Internet use affects cognition. But a recently published study of online research habits, conducted by scholars from University College London, suggests that we may well be in the midst of a sea change in the way we read and think. As part of the five-year research program, the scholars examined computer logs documenting the behavior of visitors to two popular research sites, one operated by the British Library and one by a U.K. educational consortium, that provide access to journal articles, e-books, and other sources of written information. They found that people using the sites exhibited "a form of skimming activity," hopping from one source to another and rarely returning to any source they'd already visited. They typically read no more than one or two pages of an article or book before they would "bounce" out to another site. Sometimes they'd save a long article, but there's no evidence that they ever went back and actually read it. The authors of the study report:

> It is clear that users are not reading online in the traditional sense; indeed there are signs that new forms of "reading" are emerging as users "power browse" horizontally through titles, contents pages and abstracts going for quick wins. It almost seems that they go online to avoid reading in the traditional sense.

Thanks to the ubiquity of text on the Internet, not to mention the popularity of text-messaging on cell phones, we may well be reading more today than we did in the 1970s or 1980s, when television was our medium of choice. But it's a different kind of reading, and behind it lies a different kind of thinking—perhaps even a new sense of the self. "We are not only *what* we read," says Maryanne Wolf, a developmental psychologist at Tufts University and the author of *Proust and the Squid: The Story and Science of the Reading Brain,* "We are *how* we read." Wolf worries that the style of reading promoted by the Net, a style that puts "efficiency" and "immediacy" above all else, may be weakening our capacity for the kind of deep reading that emerged when an earlier technology, the printing press, made long and complex works of prose commonplace. When we read online, she says, we tend to become "mere decoders of information." Our ability to interpret text, to make the rich mental connections that form when we read deeply and without distraction, remains largely disengaged.

Reading, explains Wolf, is not an instinctive skill for human beings. It's not etched into our genes the way speech is. We have to teach our minds how to translate the symbolic characters we see into the language we understand. And the media or other technologies we use in learning and practicing the craft of reading play an important part in shaping the neural circuits inside our brains. Experiments demonstrate that readers of ideograms, such as the Chinese, develop a mental circuitry for reading that is very different from the circuitry found in those of us whose written language employs an alphabet. The variations extend across many regions of the brain, including those that govern such essential cognitive functions as memory and the interpretation of visual and auditory stimuli. We can expect as well that the circuits woven by our use of the Net will be different from those woven by our reading of books and other printed works.

Sometime in 1882, Friedrich Nietzsche bought a typewriter—a Malling-Hansen Writing Ball, to be precise. His vision was failing, and keeping his eyes focused on a page had become exhausting and painful, often bringing on crushing headaches. He had been forced to curtail his writing, and he feared that he would soon have to give it up. The typewriter rescued him, at least for a time. Once he had mastered touch-typing, he was able to write with his eyes closed, using only the tips of his fingers. Words could once again flow from his mind to the page.

But the machine had a subtler effect on his work. One of Nietzsche's friends, a composer, noticed a change in the style of his writing. His already terse prose had become even tighter, more telegraphic. "Perhaps you will through this instrument even take to a new idiom," the friend wrote in a letter, noting that, in his own work, his "'thoughts' in music and language often depend on the quality of pen and paper."

"You are right," Nietzsche replied, "our writing equipment takes part in the forming of our thoughts." Under the sway of the machine, writes the German media scholar Friedrich A. Kittler, Nietzsche's prose "changed from arguments to aphorisms, from thoughts to puns, from rhetoric to telegram style."

The human brain is almost infinitely malleable. People used to think that our mental meshwork, the dense connections formed among the 100 billion or so neurons inside our skulls, was largely fixed by the time we reached adulthood. But brain researchers have discovered that that's not the case. James Olds, a professor of neuroscience who directs the Krasnow Institute for Advanced Study at George Mason University, says that even the adult mind "is very plastic." Nerve cells routinely break old connections and form new ones. "The brain," according to Olds, "has the ability to reprogram itself on the fly, altering the way it functions."

As we use what the sociologist Daniel Bell has called our "intellectual technologies"—the tools that extend our mental rather than our physical capacities—we inevitably begin to take on the qualities of those technologies. The mechanical clock, which came into common use in the 14th century, provides a compelling example. In *Technics and Civilization,* the historian and cultural critic Lewis Mumford described how the clock "disassociated time from human events and helped create the belief in an independent world of mathematically measurable sequences." The "abstract framework of divided time" became "the point of reference for both action and thought."

The clock's methodical ticking helped bring into being the scientific mind and the scientific man. But it also took something away. As the late MIT computer scientist Joseph Weizenbaum observed in his 1976 book, *Computer Power and Human Reason: From Judgment to Calculation,* the conception of the world that emerged from the widespread use of timekeeping instruments "remains an impoverished version of the older one, for it rests on a rejection of those direct experiences that formed the basis for, and indeed constituted, the old reality." In deciding when to eat, to work, to sleep, to rise, we stopped listening to our senses and started obeying the clock.

The process of adapting to new intellectual technologies is reflected in the changing metaphors we use to explain ourselves to ourselves. When the mechanical clock arrived, people began thinking of their brains as operating "like clockwork." Today, in the age of software, we have come to think of them as operating "like computers." But the changes, neuroscience tells us, go much deeper than metaphor. Thanks to our brain's plasticity, the adaptation occurs also at a biological level.

The Internet promises to have particularly far-reaching effects on cognition. In a paper published in 1936, the British mathematician Alan Turing proved that a digital computer, which at the time existed only as a theoretical machine, could be programmed to perform the function of any other information-processing device. And that's what we're seeing today. The Internet, an immeasurably powerful computing system, is subsuming most of our other intellectual technologies. It's becoming our map and our clock, our printing press and our typewriter, our calculator and our telephone, and our radio and TV.

When the Net absorbs a medium, that medium is re-created in the Net's image. It injects the medium's content with hyperlinks, blinking ads, and other digital gewgaws, and it surrounds the content with the content of all the other media it has absorbed. A new e-mail message, for instance, may announce its arrival as we're glancing over the latest headlines at a newspaper's site. The result is to scatter our attention and diffuse our concentration.

The Net's influence doesn't end at the edges of a computer screen, either. As people's minds become attuned to the crazy quilt of Internet media, traditional media have to adapt to the audience's new expectations. Television programs add text crawls and pop-up ads, and magazines and newspapers shorten their articles, introduce capsule summaries, and crowd their pages with easy-to-browse info-snippets. When, in March of this year, *The New York Times* decided to devote the second and third pages of every edition to article abstracts, its design director, Tom Bodkin, explained that the "shortcuts" would give harried readers a quick "taste" of the day's news, sparing them the "less efficient" method of actually turning the pages and reading the articles. Old media have little choice but to play by the new-media rules.

Never has a communications system played so many roles in our lives—or exerted such broad influence over our thoughts—as the Internet does today. Yet, for all that's been written about the Net, there's been little consideration of how, exactly, it's reprogramming us. The Net's intellectual ethic remains obscure.

About the same time that Nietzsche started using his typewriter, an earnest young man named Frederick Winslow Taylor carried a stopwatch into the Midvale Steel plant in Philadelphia and began a historic series of experiments aimed at improving the efficiency of the plant's machinists. With the approval of Midvale's owners, he recruited a group of factory hands, set them to work on various metalworking machines, and recorded and timed their every movement as well as the operations of the machines. By breaking down every job into a sequence of small, discrete steps and then testing different ways of performing each one, Taylor created a set of precise instructions—an "algorithm," we might say today—for how each worker should work. Midvale's employees grumbled about the strict new regime, claiming that it turned them into little more than automatons, but the factory's productivity soared.

More than a hundred years after the invention of the steam engine, the Industrial Revolution had at last found its philosophy and its philosopher. Taylor's tight industrial choreography—his "system," as he liked to call it—was embraced by manufacturers throughout the country and, in time, around the world. Seeking maximum speed, maximum efficiency, and maximum output, factory owners used time-and-motion studies to organize their work and configure the jobs of their workers. The goal, as Taylor defined it in his celebrated 1911 treatise, *The Principles of Scientific Management,* was to identify and adopt, for every job, the "one best method" of work and thereby to effect "the gradual substitution of science for rule of thumb throughout the mechanic arts." Once his system was applied to all acts of manual labor, Taylor assured his followers, it would bring about a restructuring not only of industry but of society, creating a utopia of perfect efficiency. "In the past the man has been first," he declared; "in the future the system must be first."

Taylor's system is still very much with us; it remains the ethic of industrial manufacturing. And now, thanks to the growing power that computer engineers and software coders wield over our intellectual lives, Taylor's ethic is beginning to govern the realm of the mind as well. The Internet is a machine designed for the efficient and automated collection, transmission, and manipulation of information, and its legions of programmers are intent on finding the "one best method"—the perfect algorithm—to carry out every mental movement of what we've come to describe as "knowledge work."

Google's headquarters, in Mountain View, California—the Googleplex—is the Internet's high church, and the religion practiced inside its walls is Taylorism. Google, says its chief executive, Eric Schmidt, is "a company that's founded around the science of measurement," and it is striving to "systematize everything" it does. Drawing on the terabytes of behavioral data it collects through its search engine and other sites, it carries out thousands of experiments a day, according to the *Harvard Business Review,* and it uses the results to refine the algorithms that increasingly control how people find information and extract meaning from it. What Taylor did for the work of the hand, Google is doing for the work of the mind.

The company has declared that its mission is "to organize the world's information and make it universally accessible and useful." It seeks to develop "the perfect search engine," which it defines as something that "understands exactly what you mean and gives you back exactly what you want." In Google's view, information is a kind of commodity, a utilitarian resource that can be mined and processed with industrial efficiency. The more pieces of information we can "access" and the faster we can extract their gist, the more productive we become as thinkers.

Where does it end? Sergey Brin and Larry Page, the gifted young men who founded Google while pursuing doctoral degrees in computer science at Stanford, speak frequently of their desire to turn their search engine into an artificial intelligence, a HAL-like machine that might be connected directly to our brains. "The ultimate search engine is something as smart as people—or smarter," Page said in a speech a few years back. "For us, working on search is a way to work on artificial intelligence." In a 2004 interview with *Newsweek,* Brin said, "Certainly if you had all the world's information directly attached to your brain, or an artificial brain that was smarter than your brain, you'd be better off." Last year, Page told a convention of scientists that Google is "really trying to build artificial intelligence and to do it on a large scale."

Such an ambition is a natural one, even an admirable one, for a pair of math whizzes with vast quantities of cash at their disposal and a small army of computer scientists in their employ. A fundamentally scientific enterprise, Google is motivated by a desire to use technology, in Eric Schmidt's words, "to solve problems that have never been solved before," and artificial intelligence is the hardest problem out there. Why wouldn't Brin and Page want to be the ones to crack it?

Still, their easy assumption that we'd all "be better off" if our brains were supplemented, or even replaced, by an artificial intelligence is unsettling. It suggests a belief that intelligence is the output of a mechanical process, a series of discrete steps that can be isolated, measured, and optimized. In Google's world, the world we enter when we go online, there's little place for the fuzziness of contemplation. Ambiguity is not an opening for insight but a bug to be fixed. The human brain is just an outdated computer that needs a faster processor and a bigger hard drive.

The idea that our minds should operate as high-speed data-processing machines is not only built into the workings of the Internet, it is the network's reigning business model as well. The faster we surf across the Web—the more links we click and pages we view—the more opportunities Google and other companies gain to collect information about us and to feed us advertisements. Most of the proprietors of the commercial Internet have a financial stake in collecting the crumbs of data we leave behind as we flit from link to link—the more crumbs, the better. The last thing these companies want is to encourage leisurely reading or slow, concentrated thought. It's in their economic interest to drive us to distraction.

Maybe I'm just a worrywart. Just as there's a tendency to glorify technological progress, there's a countertendency to expect the worst of every new tool or machine. In Plato's *Phaedrus,* Socrates bemoaned the development of writing. He feared that, as people came to rely on the written word as a substitute for the knowledge they used to carry inside their heads, they would, in the words of one of the dialogue's characters, "cease to exercise their memory and become forgetful." And because they would be able to "receive a quantity of information without proper instruction," they would "be thought very knowledgeable when they are for the most part quite ignorant." They would be "filled with the conceit of wisdom instead of real wisdom." Socrates wasn't wrong—the new technology did often have the effects he feared—but he was shortsighted. He couldn't foresee the many ways that writing and reading would serve to spread information, spur fresh ideas, and expand human knowledge (if not wisdom).

The arrival of Gutenberg's printing press, in the 15th century, set off another round of teeth gnashing. The Italian humanist Hieronimo Squarciafico worried that the easy availability of books would lead to intellectual laziness, making men "less studious" and weakening their minds. Others argued that cheaply printed books and broadsheets would undermine religious authority, demean the work of scholars and scribes, and spread sedition and debauchery. As New York University professor Clay Shirky notes, "Most of the arguments made against the printing press were correct, even prescient." But, again, the doomsayers were unable to imagine the myriad blessings that the printed word would deliver.

So, yes, you should be skeptical of my skepticism. Perhaps those who dismiss critics of the Internet as Luddites or nostalgists will be proved correct, and from our hyperactive, data-stoked minds will spring a golden age of intellectual discovery and universal wisdom. Then again, the Net isn't the alphabet, and although it may replace the printing press, it produces something altogether different. The kind of deep reading that a sequence of printed pages promotes is valuable not just for the knowledge we acquire from the author's words but for the intellectual vibrations those words set off within our own minds. In the quiet spaces opened up by the sustained, undistracted reading of a book, or by any other act of contemplation, for that matter, we make our own associations, draw our own inferences and analogies, foster our own ideas. Deep reading, as Maryanne Wolf argues, is indistinguishable from deep thinking.

If we lose those quiet spaces, or fill them up with "content," we will sacrifice something important not only in our selves but in our culture. In a recent essay, the playwright Richard Foreman eloquently described what's at stake:

> I come from a tradition of Western culture, in which the ideal (my ideal) was the complex, dense and "cathedral-like" structure of the highly educated and articulate personality—a man or woman who carried inside themselves a personally constructed and unique version of the entire heritage of the West. [But now] I see within us all (myself included) the replacement of complex inner density with a new kind of self—evolving under the pressure of information overload and the technology of the "instantly available."

As we are drained of our "inner repertory of dense cultural inheritance," Foreman concluded, we risk turning into "'pancake people'—spread wide and thin as we connect with that vast network of information accessed by the mere touch of a button."

I'm haunted by that scene in *2001.* What makes it so poignant, and so weird, is the computer's emotional response to the disassembly of its mind: its despair as one circuit after another goes dark, its childlike pleading with the astronaut—"I can feel it. I can feel it. I'm afraid"—and its final reversion to what can only be called a state of innocence. HAL's outpouring of feeling contrasts with the emotionlessness that characterizes the human figures in the film, who go about their business with an almost robotic efficiency. Their thoughts and actions feel scripted, as if they're following the steps of an algorithm. In the world of *2001,* people have become so machinelike that the most human character turns out to be a machine. That's the essence of Kubrick's dark prophecy: as we come to rely on computers to mediate our understanding of the world, it is our own intelligence that flattens into artificial intelligence.

Writing Strategies

1. What is the essay's thesis?
2. Explain how Carr uses a combination of support strategies to help readers understand and accept the thesis.
3. Describe the essay's opening strategy.
4. Carr draws attention to an assumption of Sergey Brin and Larry Page—that we'd all "be better off" if our brains were supplemented, or even replaced, by an artificial intelligence. Why does Carr think this assumption is unsettling? How is questioning the assumption important to Carr's point?
5. Identify a concession Carr makes and explain how it is important to his argument.

Exploring Ideas

1. Explain how you have taken on certain qualities of an intellectual technology (a tool that extends one's mental capacities).
2. What is Taylor's ethic, and how is it beginning to govern the mind?
3. What does Carr think we will sacrifice if we lose the "quiet spaces opened up by the sustained, undistracted reading of a book, or by any other act of contemplation . . ."? Do you agree or disagree? What evidence can you provide to support your position?

Ideas for Writing

1. What besides technology has caused people's minds to function differently?
2. What particular aspect of the media has changed the way people's minds work?

If responding to one of these ideas, go to the Analysis section of this chapter to begin developing ideas for your essay.

Throwing Up Childhood

Leonard Kress

The most personal or intimate exploration can have significance for others. Even the contents of one's stomach can have public resonance. Good writers can make a personal search for causes resonate with the lives of others. In this essay, Leonard Kress tries to pinpoint the cause of his bulimic childhood behavior. In that search, he realizes that his own understanding runs contrary to expert opinion and the official positions of published research. But he focuses on, even seeks out, the tension between his own understanding and the answers he finds. In this sense, Kress's essay illustrates thinking further—exploring the cracks and crevices of what he knows and what others know.

I remember standing breathless and exhilarated in the hotel lobby, the rest of my family still in the dining room finishing their evening meal. I'm not sure whether or not they can see what I see—the thin gray broken line on the carpet, leading all the way to the back entrance. This time I don't make it out to the patio, the swimming pool, down to the beach, inundated this summer with jellyfish and jelly lichen, Portuguese Man O'War. If only they would leave their table, they could easily find me by following the half-digested dinner rolls and the masticated but intact sirloin morsels, the bitter tomato-broth they soak in. Hansel, whom I imagine to be about my age (seven and a half), couldn't have left a better trail for him and his sister to follow back to their woodland cottage. Even if the birds had pecked it clean, that bile-stain would still remain, like a stripe dividing a country highway. We are here in Miami Beach to visit my grandparents, Ada and Max, and since they live in a tiny apartment, we are staying in this beachfront hotel, more luxurious than we are used to. It occurs to me that only the desk clerk has been following my whole grand performance with any interest. Whatever others there might be carefully and kindly turn away their gaze. But the desk clerk glances over to me and across the lobby, as if surveying both the damage and the cause of it. I recognize that smirk and wonder, was he a vomiter too? I don't have a clue and don't really care; he assiduously computes the cleaning bill.

Begins with personal narrative.

Very detailed description.

Allusion to Hansel and Gretel.

More public resonance: the behavior is not new or even that unusual.

He is a type of child—a "vomiter."

This isn't the first time. As far back as I can remember, meals out with my parents were capped with similar grand gestures. It didn't

New paragraph pulls readers out of the details.

■ Writing Strategies ■ Exploring Ideas

matter whether it was a Howard Johnson's, a deli, a steakhouse—sometimes I'd conveniently make it to the bathroom sink or toilet; other times I'd leave a pile on the floor, splatter the door, the parking lot, the car. I don't know how it happened; I can't make sense of the progression that leads up to it. I ordered from the menu like my brother and sister—appetizer, entrée, dessert. I didn't steal from anyone's plate, stabbing a slab of beef or spearing a soggy fry while they tied a shoe or fidgeted over a response to some parental inquiry. I didn't pick their dregs, dumping half-gnawed bones onto my own fully gnawed pile, I didn't reach across plates and setting to grab a soppy crust of bread or buttered roll. We were all healthy eaters in my family, and we were all well within the recommended weight guidelines. Granted, I was a fast eater; my father and brother were also fast eaters—we lacked the patience to chew, always anxious to move on to something new. I certainly didn't deliberate over the plate like my younger sister did, who always ate like a bird. She'd barely be attending to her main course while the rest of us scraped up the last of our desserts. Compared to her, I wolfed my food, scarfed it, inhaled it, terms I heard over and over again much later. I was a healthy, active second-grader; dinner meant disjuncture, interruption, tactic of delay constructed by mothers to keep their sons from the real work of childhood—hide and seek, wiffle ball, bikes, backyard Olympiad.

No obvious reason for his vomiting.

He was not an overeater. He was not obese or unhealthy.

Intensive details.

Active and energetic—otherwise "normal"?

I often wonder now what led me to such disgusting behavior—what might lead any child to such disgusting behavior. Like any good 21st-century questioner/researcher, I go to the Internet, hopeful that a search of current medical literature will provide answers and understanding. So I begin my search, seated in front of my computer. I find a gopher (its name is OVID—aptly named for the ancient Roman writer of *Metamorphoses* or *Transformations*), and it's as versatile as a left-handed shortstop, a triple-threat, able to simultaneously search pediatric, psychology, anthropology, and other allied health databases. I'm confident that with the right *keyword search,* the exact *cross-referencing* or *Boolean limitation,* I will be able to call up some insight. This should be a breeze, I think, *childhood bulimia,* thousands of hits, hundreds of studies from millions of research dollars. After all, anorexia/bulimia was, arguably, *the disease* of the 1990s. I do find something. In *The International Journal of Eating Disorders* (1995) there's an article titled, "Premorbid Onset of Psychopathology in Long-term Recovered Anorexia Patients." And the abstract tells me that 58% of anorexics reported "childhood anxiety

Paragraph shift indicates the new focus: from describing the behavior to searching for causes.

An allusion to the writer. Are the titles significant?

Narrating the actual searching process.

Anorexia and bulimia are the same type of disease? ("the disease of the '90s")

Eating disorders associated with psychological problems.

disorders at age ten (plus or minus five years)." The most common is childhood depression beginning well before the eating disorder. I also locate "Determinants of Adolescent Obesity: A Comparison with Anorexia Nervosa," in *Adolescence* (1988), which claims that "both anorexics and the obese are characterized by overprotectedness and enmeshment, resulting from a poor sense of identity and effectiveness." After a whole week of research, this seems to be the extent of my findings. I can find nothing to urge me to go beyond the abstracts, nothing at all, though I type in "eating disorder," "vomiting," "obesity," "abnormal psychology," "gluttony," "disgusting and destructive behavior"—always cross-referenced with "childhood."

Outside source.

The literature does not describe his case.

I was a happy child. I really was. And not only in my parents' estimation. I see it now in old snapshots and projected slides. When I was two, the neighbors nicknamed me "Smiley." It stuck. Nothing fazed me—not even the most traumatic incident of my early life, driving my trike over the sides of that same neighbor's screened-in porch, the screens removed for spring cleaning. The tumble left a pus-filled bruise, two weeks in draining. My parents said that I never flinched or lost that smile, even as that neighbor dug and poked and pressed and guiltily reapplied her expert pity dressings, the whole time boasting incessantly about her favorite nephew, a fighter pilot almost blasted out of the Korean sky a few years back. "Praise God," I remember her saying, "that he wasn't tortured or starved." Thank God he returned, intact, and (my parents informed me years later) in time to be chosen as one of the original Mercury 7 astronauts. Somehow it seems that this might have been right about the time that I began my career as a public barfer.

Paragraph shifts from the search back to describing the past.

Details to show he was healthy and energetic.

Could this be a connection or a cause?

Only once do I remember doing it in secret. It was at my grandparents' golden wedding anniversary celebration, a feast my grandmother herself with the help of her Kovno and Litwak sisters, Bronx nieces, and Jersey City daughters prepared. I am not one, however, to gorge on a sumptuous catalogued recitation of the feast (more scrumptious than the feast itself?). For the food itself never seemed to matter. For the most part, I ate whatever was cast in front of me. The party took place at my aunt's apartment in Stuyvesant Town on the East Side, where the shouts of roller skaters and stickball players rose up from the playground, mixing with the shrill stab of ambulance, police car, fire truck, and the play-by-play of the Yankees . . . and it is this final detail that I most vividly recall—not the carp swimming all night in the bathtub, walloped against the porcelain

Why is this the most vivid detail for him? Is there a connection?

The details show the culinary tradition of his family.

Here's the first connection between the search and his experience: it's pleasurable.

The outside source integrated (colliding with?) his experiences.

New paragraph: focus on others around him.

Allusion to the ant and grasshopper story.

Public resonance: Does everyone have a technique for releasing tension?

Catharsis = relief/release of tension.

The main cause is need for catharsis?

Draconian = code of extreme severity or rigor.

rim in the morning, then beheaded and sopped in a bucket of brine. Not the pickled tongue or brisket or pot roast, and kasha, knishes, blintzes served up beneath gobs of sour cream, like Chekhov's "crisp bleenies, lacy and plump as the shoulder of a merchant's daughter." There was a full week of food preparation that I gobbled down and then disposed of with great ease and easing. I didn't even have to stick my finger down my throat; I could simply will the partially chewed hearty chunks of meat and potato up from their sour churning stock. It felt so good! *The Encyclopedia of Pediatric Psychology* (1979) reports that children who vomit, farfetched as it sounds, even "those who have learned society's aversions . . . can overcome such scruples and experience vomiting as cathartic, even orgasmic."

I still find it odd that my parents never questioned why I did it. They never seemed to mind, though I'm sure they did, privately. They must have been embarrassed, if not mortified, by my behavior. In spite of that, we went out to dinner often, several times a month. Not once did they ask me to modify my order, limit my portion. They never motioned the waitress aside, and with the promise of a bigger tip, asked her to go easy on the fries. My brother and sister were silent, too, as though my barfing were a perfectly acceptable alternative to an after-dinner mint, a toothpick, a wet-wipe wrapped like a condom. Perhaps they were too busy stashing away the details of the affront, safekeeping for a time of need—like Aesop's despicable, self-righteous ant. I can only imagine the hay they might have later made by simple melodramatic evocations of the sounds of my gagging, as it echoed in tiny bathrooms. The deep, throaty sound of plosively expelling vomit. "Well, whatever I did can't be as gross and disgusting as THAT," I can hear them repeating over and over till they got what they wanted. Or did they have their own equally disgusting but self-customized techniques of catharsis and orgasm back then—I wondered. Does everyone, I still wonder? And how could a "D" in French or a detention or a missed meal or a dent in the car compare with what I did, over and over and over?

It couldn't, of course, it would pale in comparison to that cathartic act of throwing up (knowing that others could hear my retching) that left my face bloodless and pale, my extremities tingling, my chest heaving with giddiness. Perhaps earlier generations of parents and child psychologists had a better understanding of its power and attraction. And that's why older writings on the subject, rare but not unheard of, prescribe such drastic, almost Draconian treatment to stop the behavior. *The Encyclopedia of Pediatric Psychology* (1970) lacks entries for either anorexia or bulimia and refers to it as "psychogenic vomiting." It predates the public and medical concern over the condition, and takes a stern, almost Victorian approach to treatment:

His situation, again, seems slightly different than the literature suggests.

> Karo syrup, Phenobarbital, anticonvulsants, chlorpromazine, antihistamines, chin straps, esophageal blocks, thickened feedings, removal of normal appendix, electric shock therapy, and even intensive prayer are all reported to have been used successfully to resolve the problem.

In some cases, and in my case, I suppose, the patient simply outgrows it.

Writing Strategies

1. How does the essay's introduction grab readers' interest? How does it establish a tone for the essay?
2. Identify a particular sentence and explain how it helps bring the essay to life.
3. Though Kress deals with a very personal issue, how might his essay resonate with others? What sentences in the essay are most likely to reach out and connect with others, and why?
4. Identify an allusion, using it to explain how allusions convey meaning.

Exploring Ideas

1. Explore a past behavior of your own, searching for its cause. Research the behavior by reading about it and/or talking to others. Your goal is to arrive not at *the* cause, but at several possible causes. List the possible causes.
2. Evaluate each of the possible causes you discovered for #1. Which ones seem most likely to be the cause of your behavior? Provide convincing evidence to support your conclusion.
3. If you were Kress's parent, what would you do?
4. What does your response to #3 say about your basic values or beliefs?
5. Why is the essay's ending effective? What is its effect?

Ideas for Writing

1. Reflect as an adult on a puzzling childhood experience. What might be the cause of a certain behavior that you have not yet understood?
2. Kress considers his family's reaction to his vomiting. What is the cause of someone else's puzzling reaction to you?

If responding to one of these ideas, go to the Analysis section of this chapter to begin developing ideas for your essay.

Student Essay

American Consumerism

Jamie Bentley

Writers often agree with an argument, yet see value in redirecting attention to some other aspect of the issue *(agree and redirect).* In the following essay, Jamie Bentley, a first-year student at Umpqua Community College, responds to Simon Benlow's "An Apology to Future Generations" (pages 428–433). First she acknowledges Benlow's idea about the harmful effect a consumerist culture has on the environment, and then she argues about the *more* harmful effect it has on the American family.

Contemporary American culture has a well-documented obsession with consuming things. According to Simon Benlow, "You know how opulently we lived, how we gorged ourselves daily, how we lived beyond the means of ourselves and of the following generations" (428). Benlow states that we have "irreparably harmed the world for those beyond [our time]" (428). There is no doubt that we are harming the environment somewhat; however, more than harming the environment, this consumerist culture is causing individual economic problems and contributes to the breakdown of the family.

While we are individually causing economic distress for ourselves, we are helping to better the economy of the nation. From 1950 to 2000, the gross domestic product (GDP) per capita tripled to $35,970 (Cox). This incredible gain in wealth for our nation supposedly helped us all. Sixty-eight percent of American families own a home, 98% own color televisions, 94% own VCRs, 90% own microwaves, and 83% own washing machines (Cox). I say "supposedly helped" because, while these things greatly increase our comfort and entertainment, they also greatly increase personal debt. The average American household has $18,700 of debt, not including mortgages ("Introduction"). In 2000, the average American's consumer debt was 96% of his disposable income; by 2004, that consumer debt increased to 113% of his disposable income ("Introduction").

One cause of such increased debt is that "[a]ccording to the *San Antonio Business Journal,* there are over 785 million credit cards currently in circulation, used to charge $1.5 trillion each year" ("Introduction"). Jennifer Errick says, "Americans like to shop. We like big stuff and we like lots of it. Everything in our lives is getting bigger, from vehicles and houses to TV screens and bathtubs" (qtd. in "Introduction"). Everything is getting bigger, including debt. Credit cards allow instantaneous purchases. Our society is one of instant gratification, and that is part of what makes credit cards so popular. We no longer have to wait to buy something we want until we have enough money; we can just charge it now and pay for it later. In fact, the "[a]verage increase in consumer spending when credit cards are used instead of cash [is] 23%" (New Road Map Foundation). This idea of "buy now, pay

---

later" is largely responsible for our debt. People charge much, much more than they can afford because they think they can always pay later. They do not take into account that all those purchases add up very quickly, and so does the interest that is charged.

Because such massive debt is being accrued by consumers, 1.6 million personal bankruptcy filings took place in the year 2004, up from only 900,000 in 1995 ("Introduction"). "'The U.S. Chamber of Commerce estimates businesses lose about $40 billion annually to bankruptcies,' notes the *Arizona Daily Star,* 'passing much of the cost on to consumers'" ("Introduction"). This causes a vicious cycle, because when the businesses pass on costs to consumers, they increase prices, which costs the consumer more money, which can lead to more debt, which can lead to more bankruptcy.

American consumerism is not only causing more debt, but it is also causing a sharp decrease in savings. In 1973, the average amount of disposable income put into savings was 8.6%; in 1994 it was 4.2%; by November 2005, it was negative 0.2% (New Road Map Foundation; "Introduction").

This consumerist mentality is also contributing to the breakdown of the family unit. When the average family is in debt by $18,700 ("Introduction"), it increases the likelihood that both parents will need to work, and work more hours, in order to pay off this debt. With both parents working, the children will need to be in daycare or have some sort of childcare provided for them. When families don't spend time together, they tend to drift apart.

According to a survey done by the New Road Map Foundation, the average parent spends 6 hours a week shopping, but only 40 minutes a week playing with their children. What kind of message does this send to our children? While there is no doubt that these parents love their children, it is subtly sending the message that things are more important than time spent together. This same survey by the New Road Map Foundation showed that "American parents spent 40% less time with their children in 1991 than they did in 1965." That is so incredibly sad, and unfortunately, it will more than likely just get worse. Even sadder still is the fact that only 34% of Americans said they were "willing to forgo raises and promotions to devote more time to their families" (New Road Map Foundation). Children will grow up thinking this is normal, and they will try to provide the same "quality" of life for their children as they had growing up. They will try to accomplish this by working more hours to earn more money so they can buy more things for their families.

The constant shopping and having more material possessions is not making us happier. Ed Diener and Martin Seligman, psychologists, did more than 150 studies on the links between happiness and wealth and found "that there has been no appreciable rise in life satisfaction over the past decades, despite our increased material wealth" (Dalton). When parents spend the majority of their time shopping or working, the family unit is placed under stress, and relationships start to suffer (Dalton). It's very difficult to have a relationship with someone who's never there, and as the New Road Map Foundation study shows, parents are spending less and less time with their children.

John Metz

Joseph Beckenbach, a software consultant from San Jose, CA, has joined the anti-consumerist movement in order to put less emphasis on consuming (shopping in particular) so that he can "keep . . . focus on what's more important in life, like spending time with my daughter" (qtd. in Emert). The anti-consumerist movement has created what's called Buy Nothing Day in order to encourage more people to put less emphasis on shopping, as Joseph Beckenbach has. Buy Nothing Day takes place on the day after Thanksgiving, the day that begins the mad rush of holiday shopping for many people. The editor of *Adbusters* magazine thinks that only 1 million people participated in Buy Nothing Day in the year 1999, and that was globally. With 6 billion people on the planet, that was only .0001% (Emert). More people need to take action and get involved with activities such as Buy Nothing Day, or simply just spend more time together as a family.

All of our consuming is also causing damage to the environment. "For packaging (cans, bottles, cartons, etc.) alone, the U.S. uses approximately: 50% of its paper, 75% of its glass, 40% of its aluminum, and 30% of its plastics" (New Road Map Foundation). Every year, the amount of waste in the U.S. is equivalent to filling "a convoy of 10-ton garbage trucks

145,000 miles long" (New Road Map Foundation). If we would just buy less, we would waste less. Most everything we buy comes in some sort of packaging; if our nation as a whole would buy less, manufacturers would produce less, which would equate to less of our resources being used for packaging and ultimately less waste.

A 1991 survey found that "8 out of 10 Americans regarded themselves as 'environmentalists' and half of those said they were 'strong' ones"; 78% of Americans "believed that a 'major national effort' [is] needed to improve the environment" (New Road Map Foundation). However, only 22% of Americans were found to be "actively working toward solutions" (New Road Map Foundation). This seems to be a classic example of the saying "do as I say, not as I do."

Oisin Coghlan, from Friends of the Earth, "believes about 5 per cent of the population are willing to change their behaviour [sic] with minimal pushing, but many more belong to the 'I will if you will' contingent" (qtd. in Cullen). Because our culture is one that is focused on popularity, and what is cool to do at the moment, many people will only do something if "everyone else is doing it." Coghlan also believes that people need incentives in order to become more "green" (Cullen). This plays off of our society's selfish attitude. Many people will only do something if it has something in it for them. Why should they drive out of their way to spend more money on a product that may or may not have an impact on the earth if there is nothing in it for them? Joel Makower, president of Green Business Network, asks if people will choose the green product over the non-green product, and the answer he comes up with is very true, and a perfect reflection of most people's attitudes:

> . . . if you probe deeper into consumer attitudes, the real answer is that consumers will choose the greener product—IF it doesn't cost more, comes from a brand they know and trust . . . can be purchased at stores where they already shop . . . doesn't require a significant change of habits to use . . . and has at least the same level of quality, performance, and endurance as the less-green alternative.

This just goes to show how selfish most people are. We say we care about the environment, but we don't really want to do anything about saving it if it is inconvenient for us in any way, shape, or form.

People keep saying we need to improve the environment, but we are so focused on consuming things that we would rather keep up our current lifestyle than actually do something to prevent further damage to the environment and further loss of resources. One way to improve the environment would be to start spending less money! "Every time we spend money we consume resources, so saving money links directly to saving forests, other species, mineral resources, water and ultimately the earth. For ourselves, and for all of life, we must return to financial sanity" (New Road Map Foundation). By consuming less, we wouldn't have to work as much with the intent to earn more money in order to pay off our debts. That would free us up to spend more time with our families.

By consuming less, we would waste less because there would be less to throw away. By consuming less, manufacturers would be forced to produce less, which would save more resources. By consuming less, we are helping the environment, but we are ultimately helping ourselves by reducing our debts and allowing us to become more family-oriented instead of "stuff"-oriented.

Works Cited

Benlow, Simon. "Apology to Future Generations." *The Composition of Everyday Life*, 5th ed., edited by John Mauk and John Metz, Wadsworth, 2014, pp. 428–33.

Cox, W. Michael, and Richard Alm. "Consumerism Creates a Healthy Economy." *Is American Society Too Materialistic*? Edited by Ronnie D. Lankford, Greenhaven Press, 2006. At Issue. *Opposing Viewpoints In Context*, ic.galegroup.com/ic/ovic/ViewpointsDetailsPage/ViewpointsDetailsWindow?failOverType=&query=&prodId=OVIC&windowstate=normal&contentModules=&display-query=&mode=view&displayGroupName=Viewpoints&limiter=&currPage=&disableHighlighting=false&displayGroups=&sortBy=&search_within_results=&p=OVIC&action=e&catId=&activityType=&scanId=&documentId=GALE|EJ3010413203&source=Bookmark&u=nysl_me_wls&jsid=76fa7bcc066d57d6689bdba8e24febfe.

Cullen, Paul. "Landfill and Lightbulbs: Are We Ready to Abandon Our Destructive Past?" *The Irish Times*, 14 Jan. 2008, www.irishtimes.com/business/landfill-and-lightbulbs-are-we-ready-to-abandon-our-destructive-past-1.928517.

Dalton, Patricia. "Materialism Undermines the Family." *Is American Society Too Materialistic*? Edited by Ronnie D. Lankford, Greenhaven Press, 2006. At Issue. *Opposing Viewpoints in Context*, ic.galegroup.com/ic/ovic/ViewpointsDetailsPage/ViewpointsDetailsWindow?failOverType=&query=&windowstate=normal&contentModules=&mode=view&currPage=&zid=&action=e&prodId=OVIC&display-query=&limiter=&dviSelectedPage=&displayGroupName=Viewpoints&displayGroups=&disableHighlighting=&sortBy=&search_within_results=&p=OVIC&catId=&activityType=&scanId=&documentId=GALE|EJ3010413213&source=Bookmark&u=nysl_me_wls&jsid=ea7b3b9c0fbb0398b9c501a4571d3ec0.

Emert, Carol. "Anti-Consumerism Movement Urges Less Shopping/Less Can Be More—Buy Nothing Campaign Gains Strength." *San Francisco Chronicle*, 26 Nov. 2000, www.sfchronicle.com/business/article/Anti-Consumerism-Movement-Urges-Less-Shopping-3236919.php.

"Introduction" *Is American Society Too Materialistic*? Edited by Ronnie D. Lankford, Greenhaven Press, 2006. At Issue. *Opposing Viewpoints in Context*, ic.galegroup.com/ic/ovic/ReferenceDetailsPage/ReferenceDetailsWindow?failOverType=&query=&prodId=OVIC&windowstate=normal&contentModules=&display-query=&mode=view&displayGroupName=Reference&limiter=&currPage=&disableHighlighting=false&displayGroups=&sortBy=&search_within_results=&p=OVIC&action=e&catId=&activityType=&scanId=&documentId=GALE|EJ3010413101&source=Bookmark&u=nysl_me_wls&jsid=2f4853685dad6584a561a8fa5474417e.

Makower, Joel. "Whatever Happened to Green Consumers?" *Satya Magazine*, Sept. 2000, www.satyamag.com/sept00/makower.html.

New Road Map Foundation. "All Consuming Passion: Waking Up from the American Dream." *EcoFuture*, 17 Jan. 2002, www.ecofuture.org/pk/pkar9506.html.

Writing Strategies

1. According to Bentley, what impact does consumerist culture have on the American family?
2. What support strategies does Bentley use to help readers understand what she means by "consumerist culture"?
3. Describe Bentley's voice as a writer and provide two sentences that support your description.
4. Based on her essay, what does Bentley value? Provide two ideas from her essay that support your response.

Exploring Ideas

1. What might be the benefits of people consuming less? What might be the drawbacks?
2. What evidence can you provide that shopping and having more material possessions are not making us happier?
3. Bentley's essay speaks to two issues: the environment and the family. What other issue is seriously impacted by consumerism, and how?
4. With a group of peers, explore some reasons for credit card debt. Generate a list of reasons that people get into debt, and then group the reasons into three to five categories.

Ideas for Writing

1. Why is American society obsessed with consuming things?
2. What is the root cause of the increase in individual debt?

If responding to one of these ideas, go to the Analysis section of this chapter to begin developing ideas for your essay.

Invention

"All human beings should try to learn before they die what they are running from, and to, and why."

—James Thurber

Invention is an act of discovery. It involves opening all the intellectual cases we have closed in everyday life. It involves asking questions where we had assumed we knew the answers. For this chapter, invention involves asking why something occurs (or has occurred) and going beyond the first (and second) guess. In Point of Contact, ask adventurous questions to find a topic. In Analysis, imagine unseen causes. In Public Resonance, consider the ways your topic extends outward and affects the public. In Thesis, focus your ideas to a particular insight, and in Rhetorical Tools, explore a range of possible support strategies. The Invention Questions in each section are not meant to be answered directly in your final written assignment. In fact, as you work through the sections, avoid simply answering them and then moving on. Instead, use them to explore and to develop revelatory ideas.

Point of Contact

The search for a cause begins with a question: Why did something happen? Why does something continue? What causes some phenomenon? The following questions can help you to explore possible topics. After you have decided on a particular topic, go to the Analysis section to continue your search for causes.

Work

- Why are some sections/groups/teams more successful than others?
- Why is workplace efficiency up or down?
- Why are profits for the company or organization up or down?
- Why are some workers more content or fulfilled than others?

Local Events

- Why is urban sprawl taking place in your community?
- Why is a local sports team winning or losing?

- What makes one school perform better than others?
- Why are some areas of town more policed than others?
- Why do so many yards look the same?

Social Trends

- What causes road rage? Teenage rebellion? Conformity to fashion trends?
- Why are the elderly isolated?
- Why is depression on the rise in the United States?
- Why do Americans love sport utility vehicles?
- Why does the condition of streets change throughout a city?
- Why doesn't anyone care about the future?

Campus Issues

- Why do college students binge drink?
- Why do some students cheat? Procrastinate?
- What causes boredom?
- Why are some classes more difficult for large numbers of students?

Politics

- Why do younger generations tend not to vote?
- Why does a certain community consistently vote Democratic or Republican?
- What has made political discourse so uncivil?

Your Major

- What has caused the field to thrive (or deteriorate) in recent years?
- What has fueled a recent debate in the field? Why has the debate continued?
- Find the cause of a phenomenon in your field, for example:

  —*History:* a revolution, a military victory or loss

  —*Art:* a style (such as impressionism), an artistic revolution

  —*Biology:* an organism's short life span

  —*Criminal Justice:* a jury decision, a Supreme Court decision to hear a case

  —*Business Marketing:* the success or failure of a marketing campaign

JACK: But wouldn't you say that joining a cult is a little more extreme than buying a car or having an affair?

DIANA: Sure, but remember that a lot of people long for something more than sex and fast cars. They wonder what's out there, what their purpose is, what's beyond this life.

JACK: And religious cults have all those answers—well, at least that's the argument.

DIANA: Yeah, so the whole issue may be related to loneliness and longing rather than sickness.

Thinking Further

Invention is not simply answering a few questions. Instead, it is a process of exploring, discovering, and developing ideas. Ideas that emerge from initial responses should be explored even further. For example, in his dialogue with Diana and Marcus, Jack's thinking evolves:

Beginning of the dialogue:	Sick people join cults.
End of the dialogue:	Loneliness and longing, which run rampant in mainstream culture, drive people to wonder what they're missing. This is where cults come in.

With this new understanding, Jack might come to more insightful conclusions about the perspective of people who join cults:

> I guess in the eyes of a potential cult member, a cult doesn't look like a cult. I mean, a group doesn't hang a "Cult" sign on the door. They don't say, "Hey!! Join our cult!! We'll all kill ourselves next year! It'll be great!!" No. A cult is merely a group of people who offer a web of relationships and a clear purpose in life. Isn't that why people go to college even though they hate it?! Isn't that why people join the Army?? A clear sense of purpose?!! Is college a kind of cult? Is the Army?!! Here's the message of both institutions: "Leave behind everything—your family, etc. Come here. Stay with us. And . . . you have to follow our strict schedule of events. But in the end, you'll be way better off." Holy crap! We're a culture of . . . cults.

Jack's continued exploration of why people join cults has taken him into new intellectual territory. He is exploring the relationship between something he thinks is dangerous (cults) and something he thinks is normal (college, the army).

Use the following questions to further explore your topic:

- How has your understanding of the cause developed? What new idea has entered your thinking?
- Why didn't you think about this before?

Research

Find an outside source (a website, article, or book) about your concept. (Consult Chapter 14: Finding Sources to help you explore.) The author(s) of the source may have a different understanding of the causes. Summarize the main points of the source, then answer the following questions:

- Does the source suggest a cause for the phenomenon?
- If not, does the source imply or assume a cause?
- Does the source account for the most direct cause?
- Does the source account for indirect or multiple causes? Hidden causes?

Public Resonance

Some topics automatically resonate with public concerns. For example, Jamie Bentley's essay discusses how our love of consumption harms the environment, causes individual economic problems, and contributes to the breakdown of the family. But other topics may seem more difficult to connect with. Local or intensely personal topics, for instance, may seem less linked to broader concerns. Who would think that childhood vomiting could be an interesting topic or make for a valuable essay? But Leonard Kress makes his own vomiting experience resonate (in more than one way) with readers:

> My brother and sister were silent, too, as though my barfing were a perfectly acceptable alternative to an after-dinner mint, a toothpick, a wet-wipe wrapped like a condom. Perhaps they were too busy stashing away the details of the affront, safekeeping for a time of need—like Aesop's despicable, self-righteous ant. I can only imagine the hay they might have later made by simple melodramatic evocations of the sounds of my gagging, as it echoed in tiny bathrooms. The deep, throaty sound of plosively expelling vomit. "Well, whatever I did can't be as gross and disgusting as THAT," I can hear them repeating over and over till they got what they wanted. Or did they have their own equally disgusting but self-customized techniques of catharsis and orgasm back then—I wondered. Does everyone, I still wonder? And how could a "D" in French or a detention or a missed meal or a dent in the car compare with what I did, over and over and over?

In this paragraph, Kress broadens the scope, including his siblings and "everyone." He makes the connection for us: Not everyone throws up for catharsis, but, he supposes, everyone may have some technique for experiencing relief, release, or comfort. This broader scope does not mean that Kress is losing focus—he is bringing others into the issue. As a writer, he knows that his job is to invite others into his exploration, into his search for causes. Imagine how your topic involves others who are not directly associated with it. Use the following questions to help generate a sense of public resonance for your topic:

- What are the effects of this phenomenon?
- Whom does it affect? How does it affect them?
- How does it affect people indirectly?
- How does my position or understanding relate to popular perspectives on the topic?

In his exploration, Leonard Kress looks outward and compares his personal search with "pop psychology." He decides that his personal experience (and intellectual response) is different from what he sees in the media. But he doesn't therefore decide that his topic has no public resonance. Instead, he decides to explore the contrast between his experience and common characterizations.

> **How does your position or understanding relate to popular perspectives on the topic?**
>
> In writing this, I guess I am caught in the popular mania of confession. I consider myself to be a fairly private person, but all around I see people (in books, articles, on TV, etc.) revealing the most personal and embarrassing details about their lives. And doing so with relish. The fact that this piece deals with childhood makes it somewhat easier, of course. This is as close as I came to a taboo subject—and it intrigues me that my experience was so different from the media and pop psychology take on eating disorders and adolescent girls.

Kress's move here is vital to academic writing: When a writer discovers contrast or tension between his own experience and that of others, he has discovered something worth exploring more—something worth writing about.

Like Kress's topic, Jack's topic of cult membership might seem to affect only specific people—cult members, their families, maybe the communities surrounding a cult. But Jack goes further than that and imagines the broader and subtler factors:

> **How does it affect people indirectly?**
>
> If people are drawn to cults through deep loneliness, then cults potentially relate to everyone—that is, anyone who cares about family, friends, the quiet neighbor, etc. Our days are filled with constant inattention to others. Most people choose their narrow paths (their jobs and their small circle of friends) and leave everyone else. Many of us will go weeks without truly acknowledging anyone outside of our little circles. Rarely do we invite the quiet guy from work out with us; rarely do we call our cousin to see how she's doing. We leave lonely people behind us every day.

Jack discovers that cults might relate to everyone. He can now explore this idea even further, examining the messages that popular culture sends to people: that we must have intense social engagement to achieve happiness and fulfillment, that solitude should be avoided, that excitement and purpose should define every minute of our lives. Jack would then be exploring the culture surrounding cults. He would be thinking like a sociologist and assuming that any one behavior is linked to a broad system of attitudes, messages, and group behaviors.

While searching for public resonance, writers might find not only public resonance but new angles on the topic. For example, if Jack's exploration of public resonance raises ideas about pop culture and social engagement, these discoveries could lead Jack to think about social networking and then about Facebook and its relationship (or similarity) to cults.

Activities

1. Present your ideas to a small group of peers, explaining the phenomenon's cause and its public resonance. Ask group members how the phenomenon affects their lives.
2. Explain how the group discussion helped you discover and develop ideas regarding public resonance and the topic in general. What new ideas emerged, and how might they help shape your essay?

Thesis

The kind of writing done in this chapter is both analytical and argumentative. Each author offers an analysis of the topic and an argument for his or her understanding of the cause. Each has a thesis that focuses on the causes or set of causes most responsible for the phenomenon. As you consider your main point, examine all possible avenues. (You may even begin writing and drafting before your ideas take shape.) Your thesis might do any of the following:

- Argue for a particular cause.

  Professional sports have gotten more violent because of the intensity of sports coverage in the media.

- Argue that several factors equally cause the phenomenon.

  Writing proficiency among American high school students continues to diminish because of a broader cultural disinterest in reading and a fundamental misunderstanding of language.

- Argue against an apparent cause or widely held belief and for a less obvious or more complicated cause.

  People drive gas guzzlers not because they are selfish and insensitive but because they are uneducated about their real choices.

> The music industry is losing profits not because college kids are insatiable thieves but because the industry has not evolved with the listening habits of the new generation.

As you consider your topic, decide on your emphasis: Will it be important to thoroughly describe several causes or to focus on one?

Evolution of a Thesis

Your main idea may not come into focus immediately. Notice how Jack's thesis evolves from his initial thoughts into a sophisticated point.

Jack focuses on a particular phenomenon:

- What makes people leave everything and everyone behind and join cults?

He uses the Invention Questions on page 377 to probe for causes:

- *What state of mind or psychological need may have led to the phenomenon?* Some form of mental disease makes people join cults.

He works through his initial thoughts and discovers a less obvious cause:

- Deep loneliness and lack of purpose in life cause people to leave their families and join cults.

Jack struggles to integrate public resonance into his understanding of the cause:

- The deep loneliness and loss fostered by our hurried society create desperate searches for belonging and purpose, and cults sometimes fulfill those needs.

Activity

Reflect on how your main idea, like Jack's, came into focus:

- What phenomenon did you focus on?
- What Invention Question(s) did you use to probe for causes?
- What less obvious cause did you discover?
- How did you integrate public resonance into your understanding of the cause?

Common Thesis Problems

Perhaps the two most common thesis problems are psychological, striking before the writer ever touches a key or marks a paper:

1. **Fear of Ongoing Invention:** Some writers assume that thesis statements are fixed, unchangeable structures that must be strictly adhered to throughout a writing project. As they draft ideas and generate support for their initial point, they avoid asking hard questions and making new connections; that is, they fear continued invention once they've

started drafting. But thesis statements are not traps. They are merely statements that help writers focus and intensify their thinking *as they are writing.* The human brain functions in new ways once serious writing and shaping begin; therefore, writers should allow their own writing to help them with new ideas.

2. **Fear of Commitment:** In contrast to the first fear, some writers avoid committing to a focused statement. They wander around without attempting to establish a particular idea, without digging in to a specific intellectual place. Such wandering, if it goes on for too long, often leads to shallow ideas (saying lots of different things about lots of different things). Although invention is key throughout the process, invention is not general wandering. Better ideas come when writers dig in their intellectual heels.

For more related common thesis problems, see Chapter 8, pages 272–273.

Revising Your Thesis

Write out responses to these questions: *Am I afraid of ongoing invention? Why? Am I afraid of commitment? Why?* Then discuss your responses with a group of classmates:

1. How many people in your group have a fear of, or resistance to, ongoing invention or commitment?
    - What reasons do group members give for their fear of, or resistance to, ongoing invention? (What caused their fear or resistance?)
    - What reasons do group members give for their fear of, or resistance to, commitment? (What caused it?)
2. Discuss how each group member arrived at his or her thesis for this chapter's essay. Which group members might have committed to a rigid thesis too early? Choose an Invention Question from earlier in the chapter that they should explore further for ongoing invention.
3. For group members who have trouble committing to one idea, help them focus their statement. Choose an Invention Question they should explore to help narrow and deepen their thoughts.

Rhetorical Tools

Remember that you are not simply explaining a cause. You are arguing that a particular cause (or set of causes) could be responsible for a phenomenon, and you also are arguing that your understanding of the cause/effect relationship is worth considering. Therefore, consider the support strategies of argument (from Chapter 8: Making Arguments).

The writers in this chapter use a broad range of support strategies. To support his argument, Kress depends on information from his own life. And while personal experience in the form of narration is his primary support, he also uses authorities (outside sources). Nicholas

Carr also uses personal testimony (in his second paragraph, for example), then relies on various authorities to support his claims. Use the following questions to develop support for your thesis:

- How can I illustrate the relationship between the cause and the effect? (What line of reasoning can I use?)
- Does a historical event or figure help to show the cause?
- Can I allude to a similar phenomenon (with a similar cause) to support my point?
- Does a literary work (novel, poem, drama) or popular culture text (movie, television program, song) support my point?
- How do other writers discuss this cause?
- Does something in nature (in animal or plant life) support my point?
- Has anyone done scientific study on this phenomenon? Does it support my point?
- Have I witnessed or experienced someone or something that illustrates my point?
- Can I construct a hypothetical situation that illustrates my point?

Integrating Authorities (Outside Sources)

Outside sources must be integral to your own points and carefully integrated into your argument, not just inserted. For example, notice how Carr integrates an outside source to support his personal testimony about having trouble reading:

> I'm not the only one. When I mention my troubles with reading to friends and acquaintances—literary types, most of them—many say they're having similar experiences. The more they use the Web, the more they have to fight to stay focused on long pieces of writing. Some of the bloggers I follow have also begun mentioning the phenomenon. Scott Karp, who writes a blog about online media, recently confessed that he has stopped reading books altogether. "I was a lit major in college, and used to be [a] voracious book reader," he wrote. "What happened?" He speculates on the answer: What if I do all my reading on the web not so much because the way I read has changed, i.e., I'm just seeking convenience, but because the way I THINK has changed?"

Carr introduces his main point in his own words, and then he introduces an outside source, Scott Karp, as support. Notice that Carr provides Karp's credentials: "Scott Karp, who writes a blog about online media, . . ." When using authorities as support, it is important to provide readers with information about the source:

> Bruce Friedman, **who blogs regularly about the use of computers in medicine,** also has described how the Internet has altered his mental habits.

> But a recently published study of online research habits, **conducted by scholars from University College London,** suggests that we may well be in the midst of a sea change in the way we read and think.
>
> But it's a different kind of reading, and behind it lies a different kind of thinking—perhaps even a new sense of the self. "We are not only *what* we read," says Maryanne Wolf, **a developmental psychologist at Tufts University and the author of** *Proust and the Squid: The Story and Science of the Reading Brain*. "We are *how* we read."

For more help with this support strategy, see Chapter 16: Integrating and Documenting Sources.

Counterarguing

Counterarguments defend against opposing claims. Writers must anticipate and account for positions outside of or opposed to their own claims(s) and include reasoning to offset that potential opposition. In many cases, writers must contend directly with arguments that forward another cause. Leonard Kress, for example, argues against common views and explains the way his position differs from others'. Here, Kress points to authorities who seem to miss the mark:

> I also locate "Determinants of Adolescent Obesity: A Comparison with Anorexia Nervosa," in *Adolescence* (1988), which claims that "both anorexics and the obese are characterized by overprotectedness and enmeshment, resulting from a poor sense of identity and effectiveness." After a whole week of research, this seems to be the extent of my findings. I can find nothing to urge me to go beyond the abstracts, nothing at all, though I type in "eating disorder," "vomiting," "obesity," "abnormal psychology," "gluttony," "disgusting and destructive behavior"—always cross-referenced with "childhood."

Because Kress mentions these other causes (or other takes on the phenomenon), we get the sense that he has a broad understanding of the topic—he is not simply guessing at a cause, but has explored other possibilities. The following questions can help you develop counterarguments:

- What other causes could be attributed to this phenomenon? (Why are these other causes less acceptable or less valid?)
- What other reasons do people have for disagreeing with me?
- What support will most effectively respond to opposing positions?

Conceding

Concessions acknowledge the value of positions or claims other than those being forwarded by the writer. Remember that good writers (with a broad understanding of the topic) are able to concede the value of some points or qualify their own points well. As you consider your own argument, your own position about a cause, use the following questions to develop concessions and qualifiers:

- Are there legitimate reasons for taking another position on this topic?
- Does the argument make any large, but necessary, leaps?
- Do I ask my audience to accept generalizations?

Invention Workshop

For this workshop, generate opposing positions for each project. The goal here is to play devil's advocate—to imagine causes that the writer has not yet imagined. Each writer should announce his or her thesis. Group members should then take turns offering responses. Use the following questions:

- What other causes (different from the one forwarded by the writer) could be attributed to this phenomenon?
- Are there legitimate reasons for taking another position (different from the writer) on this topic?

Revision

Now get help from other writers. Before exchanging drafts with at least one other writer, underline your main idea (your thesis) or write it at the top of your draft.

Peer Review

Use the following questions to respond to specific issues in the draft:

1. Can any phrases or terms in the thesis be narrowed? If so, circle them and make some suggestions for more focus. Does the thesis avoid the common problems? (See pages 382–383.)
2. Can you follow the writer's line of reasoning? Do you accept the cause the writer asserts? Why or why not?
3. What other support strategies could the writer employ? (Consider examples, allusions, scenarios, and so on. See pages 383–386.)

4. Mark any paragraphs that shift focus from one point about the subject to another.
5. If the writer uses outside sources, are they integrated smoothly into the argument? (See pages 497–506 in Chapter 16: Integrating and Documenting Sources, for specific strategies.)
6. Consider the writer's voice.
   a. Identify any passages that seem preachy.
   b. Does the writer seem credible? What passages support your decision?
   c. Identify a passage that seems flat, without intensity. Suggest a strategy for the writer to create a sense of wonder.
7. As a reviewer, point to particular sentences and phrases that could gain vitality and intensity. Use the following:
   a. Look for confusing strings of phrases. Suggest a revision.
   b. Rewrite a passage of the draft, and use a series of phrases or clauses to intensify an idea.
   c. Consider other vitality strategies explained in Chapter 19.
      - Look for unnecessary, interrupting clauses and phrases. Underline them and/or draw an arrow to show where the phrase or clause can be moved.
      - Rewrite a sentence and create more intensity with a repeating pattern.
      - Cross out wordy phrases and write in more concise options.
      - What sentences are over-embedded? (Point to any clauses that overlap with other clauses, causing a disconnect between ideas.)
      - Examine attributive phrases. Point out unnecessary phrases or sentences that could be boiled down.
      - Where can the writer change linking verbs to action verbs?
      - Where can the writer avoid drawing attention to *I* and *you*?
      - Help the writer change unnecessary clauses to phrases and phrases to words.
      - Point to expletives (such as *there are* and *it is*).
      - Help the writer change passive verbs to active verbs for more vitality.

Reflection

Writing about a cause can have consequences for readers, the writer, and a community as a whole. To consider the possible consequences of the essay you wrote for this chapter, step back now and reflect on the essay's rhetoric:

1. The chapter introduction states that "people searching for causes are detectives attempting to find answers amid a dizzying array of possibilities." As a detective, what answer did you find?
2. What rhetorical tools most help readers understand and accept the answer you found?

3. Based on their new understanding, how might readers think and behave differently? How might this behavior affect others?
4. What particular paragraph or sentence might have the strongest impact on readers and why?
5. How does your essay contribute to an ongoing discussion, and how might it prompt readers to make a further contribution?

Figure 11.1 "Road Salt," a photo essay

Beyond the Essay: Photo Essay

A photo essay is an essay built not of paragraphs but of photographs. Consider Figure 11.1. In some parts of the country, salt is put on the roads to melt snow and ice. This salt rusts cars. The photo essay makes a point about the economics of road salt and its cost to average drivers: Drivers pay by washing the salt off their cars, getting their cars repaired, and ultimately by purchasing new vehicles.

1. Now that you have invented ideas for your essay, look for images that communicate the same way of thinking about the topic, and arrange them into a photo essay. Consider using the photo essay within your written essay to help readers understand and accept your thesis.
2. Explain in several paragraphs how the images work together to make your point.

12 Proposing Solutions

Ron Haviv/VII/Corbis

"I believe that if you show people the problems and you show them the solutions, they will be moved to act."

—Bill Gates

In everyday life, crisis is a constant. Problems emerge in every facet of our existence: In professional life, problems arise in working conditions, policy implementation, coworker relations, labor/management relations, and government standards; our communities face problems such as homelessness, pollution, school violence, terrorism, and urban sprawl; at home, the list of possible problems can seem endless. Although many of us have the privilege of ignoring such problems, someone in some capacity has to address them. Whether elected official, shift supervisor, environmental scientist, department chair, or scout leader, someone ultimately has to address daily crises and propose solutions.

In academia, people in all disciplines have to propose solutions:

- In an engineering class, students propose solutions to structural problems in a building designed before earthquake construction codes.
- In a business class, students must convince their peers that a particular strategy for solving a company's financial problems is the most efficient.
- In a calculus class, students explore several ways to solve a problem and then convince their peers and instructor that one particular way is the best.
- For a national conference on employment trends, graduate students and faculty members propose strategies to counter the increasing demand for low-salary instructors.

When writers propose solutions to problems, they are involved in many layers of analysis. They must analyze the problem to discover its causes—some of which may lie hidden in abstraction. They must also consider all the possible ways for addressing the problem and then come to some conclusion about the most appropriate solution. Proposing solutions also involves argument: writers have to convince readers that the problem must be addressed, that action is necessary. They also must argue for the value of their particular solution. This is what politicians do for a living; members of Congress, after all, spend much of their time arguing, first, that particular problems deserve allocated funds and, second, that those funds should be used in particular ways.

You might think of proposing a solution as a double-layered argument: First, you must argue that a problem worthy of attention or action exists and, second, that a particular solution will best solve it. Proposing a solution involves all the elements of an argument (thesis, support, counterargument, and concession). And as the following essays illustrate, writers who acknowledge the true complexities of their problems and solutions will better engage their readers and will meet with less opposition. Some solutions are not necessarily complicated physical solutions, but rather simple reconsiderations—that is, new ways of thinking about familiar problems.

This chapter will help you develop an argument that proposes a solution. As you read the following essays, notice how each first helps readers understand the problem. Once the problem is explained, look for these parts of the solution: the author's main claim (or proposal); support for the main claim; counterarguments that anticipate and respond to possible objections; and concessions that acknowledge weaknesses in the proposed solution. After reading the essays, you can uncover a problem to write about in one of two ways:

1. Go to the Point of Contact section to find a problem from your everyday life, or
2. Choose one of the Ideas for Writing that follow each essay.

After finding a subject, go to the Analysis section to begin developing ideas for your essay.

Readings

Where Anonymity Breeds Contempt

Julie Zhuo

As a project design manager for Facebook, Julie Zhuo studies social behavior on the Web. In this article, first published in the *New York Times,* November 29, 2010, Zhuo describes the problem of trolling and how both legal bodies and corporate entities are moving to address it. Zhuo's solution emerges from a causal analysis. In other words, she first names the primary cause of the problem before she offers sound solutions.

There you are, peacefully reading an article or watching a video on the Internet. You finish, find it thought-provoking, and scroll down to the comments section to see what other people thought. And there, lurking among dozens of well-intentioned opinions, is a troll.

"How much longer is the media going to milk this beyond tired story?" "These guys are frauds." "Your idiocy is disturbing." "We're just trying to make the world a better place one brainwashed, ignorant idiot at a time." These are the trollish comments, all from anonymous sources, that you could have found after reading a CNN article on the rescue of the Chilean miners.

Trolling, defined as the act of posting inflammatory, derogatory or provocative messages in public forums, is a problem as old as the Internet itself, although its roots go much farther back. Even in the fourth century B.C., Plato touched upon the subject of anonymity and morality in his parable of the ring of Gyges.

That mythical ring gave its owner the power of invisibility, and Plato observed that even a habitually just man who possessed such a ring would become a thief, knowing that he couldn't be caught. Morality, Plato argues, comes from full disclosure; without accountability for our actions we would all behave unjustly.

5 This certainly seems to be true for the anonymous trolls today. After Alexis Pilkington, a 17-year-old Long Island girl, committed suicide earlier this year, trolls descended on her online tribute page to post pictures of nooses, references to hangings and other hateful comments. A better-known example involves Nicole Catsouras, an 18-year-old who died in a car crash in California in 2006. Photographs of her badly disfigured body were posted on the Internet, where anonymous trolls set up fake tribute pages and in some cases e-mailed the photos to her parents with subject lines like "Hey, Daddy, I'm still alive."

Psychological research has proven again and again that anonymity increases unethical behavior. Road rage bubbles up in the relative anonymity of one's car. And in the online world, which can offer total anonymity, the effect is even more pronounced. People—even ordinary, good people—often change their behavior in radical ways. There's even a term for it: the online disinhibition effect.

Many forums and online communities are looking for ways to strike back. Back in February, Engadget, a popular technology review blog, shut down its commenting system for a few days after it received a barrage of trollish comments on its iPad coverage.

Many victims are turning to legislation. All 50 states now have stalking, bullying or harassment laws that explicitly include electronic forms of communication. Last year, Liskula Cohen, a former model, persuaded a New York judge to require Google to reveal the identity of an anonymous blogger who she felt had defamed her, and she has now filed a suit against the blogger. Last month, another former model, Carla Franklin, persuaded a judge to force YouTube to reveal the identity of a troll who made a disparaging comment about her on the video-sharing site.

But the law by itself cannot do enough to disarm the Internet's trolls. Content providers, social networking platforms and community sites must also do their part by rethinking the systems they have in place for user commentary so as to discourage—or disallow—anonymity. Reuters, for example, announced that it would start to block anonymous comments and require users to register with their names and e-mail addresses in an effort to curb "uncivil behavior."

10 Some may argue that denying Internet users the ability to post anonymously is a breach of their privacy and freedom of expression. But until the age of the Internet, anonymity was a rare thing. When someone spoke in public, his audience would naturally be able to see who was talking.

Others point out that there's no way to truly rid the Internet of anonymity. After all, names and e-mail addresses can be faked. And in any case many commenters write things that are rude or inflammatory under their real names.

But raising barriers to posting bad comments is still a smart first step. Well-designed commenting systems should also aim to highlight thoughtful and valuable opinions while letting trollish ones sink into oblivion.

The technology blog Gizmodo is trying an audition system for new commenters, under which their first few comments would be approved by a moderator or a trusted commenter to ensure quality before anybody else could see them. After a successful audition, commenters can freely post. If over time they impress other trusted commenters with their contributions, they'd be promoted to trusted commenters, too, and their comments would henceforth be featured.

Disqus, a comments platform for bloggers, has experimented with allowing users to rate one another's comments and feed those ratings into a global reputation system called Clout. Moderators can use a commenter's Clout score to "help separate top commenters from trolls."

15 At Facebook, where I've worked on the design of the public commenting widget, the approach is to try to replicate real-world social norms by emphasizing the human qualities of conversation. People's faces, real names and brief biographies ("John Doe from Lexington") are placed next to their public comments, to establish a baseline of responsibility.

© Adchariyaphoto/Shutterstock.com

Facebook also encourages you to share your comments with your friends. Though you're free to opt out, the knowledge that what you say may be seen by the people you know is a big deterrent to trollish behavior.

This kind of social pressure works because, at the end of the day, most trolls wouldn't have the gall to say to another person's face half the things they anonymously post on the Internet.

Instead of waiting around for human nature to change, let's start to rein in bad behavior by promoting accountability. Content providers, stop allowing anonymous comments. Moderate your comments and forums. Look into using comment services to improve the quality of engagement on your site. Ask your users to report trolls and call them out for polluting the conversation.

In slowly lifting the veil of anonymity, perhaps we can see the troll not as the frightening monster of lore, but as what we all really are: human.

Writing Strategies

1. Explain how anonymity figures into the problem of trolling.

2. In ¶3 and 4, Zhuo alludes to the ring of Gyges. Explain how that allusion helps to support Zhuo's main claim about anonymity.

3. How do the model's lawsuits (referenced in ¶8) help to establish the nature of the problem—and the nature of Zhuo's solution?

4. Zhuo engages opposing positions in quick fashion. Explain the particular opposing positions that Zhuo anticipates. How does she counter or concede to these positions?

5. Zhuo's conclusion suggests that the problem emerges from something fundamental in human nature. Explain how her conclusion makes you rethink the problem.

Exploring Ideas

1. Zhuo says that Facebook is attempting to "establish a baseline of responsibility." Explain how Facebook's solution directly addresses the cause of trolling.

2. Trolling has become a significant trend. In other words, it's not just a few bad people. Are Plato and Zhuo correct about the immense power of anonymity? Are there other causes behind this trend?

3. How is trolling a social problem? In other words, how does it affect us all—beyond the specific victims?

4. What is the closest you've come to trolling or cyberbullying? Are you willing to explain your behavior?

5. Reread ¶5. What should happen to people who torture the parents of dead children?

Ideas for Writing

1. Can you think of another strategy for solving trolling and cyberbullying? Make a case for a specific solution to these behaviors.

2. What other, perhaps more subtle, behaviors have you witnessed on social networking sites? Consider a particular problematic behavior and its effects on users.

If responding to one of these ideas, go to the Analysis section of this chapter to begin developing ideas for your essay.

Attending to the Word

Deirdre Mahoney

Our culture's response to illiteracy and low academic performance has involved sweeping proposals: more standardized testing, more teacher accountability, required master's degrees for all K–12 teachers, better buildings, newer textbooks, more administrators, no more art and music classes, and so on. But writing instructor Deirdre Mahoney invites us to look very closely at reading. In this argument, we are invited to analyze the act of reading, to understand the intellectual nuances of engaging text. And then, we might more readily accept a less sweeping, more elegantly basic solution. Portions of Mahoney's invention work are shown throughout this chapter.

Today's college students are suffering, and unnecessarily so. I see them arrive in my writing classes each semester eager and determined, but all too often the motivation and passion dissipate when they come face-to-face with—well—words on the page. This is distressing for both them and me. My students are not illiterate by any means, as they successfully broke the code of sound-to-symbol in the earliest elementary years. Since that time, they've continued to learn in public and private school systems or they've been home-schooled. They're educated and plenty adept at moving through the system. But I'm not convinced any of this means they are capable of truly committing to a book, an essay, or any document requiring sustained focus and labor-intensive thinking and doing. And what interferes most with their abilities to focus and commit? Lack of a pencil in hand while attempting to read, contemplate, and retain the text on the page.

When I tell my students the only way to read a book is with pencil gliding freely across the page (no highlighters please), they look stymied. Selected passages ought to be underlined, I maintain, and tricky vocabulary circled. Further, I suggest that handwritten symbols in the form of stars, asterisks, squiggly lines, question marks, brackets, and the like warrant placement alongside their personal comments posted in the margins. After all, the white space on the printed page could use the company. My students offer good enough reasons, however, for *not* writing in their books: (1) Writing in books during the K–12 years is absolutely taboo, they tell me, and they've been successfully trained to do as told; (2) Some college bookstores won't buy back textbooks with extensive personalized annotations and markings. Students need cash at semester's end, so they dutifully comply. But how is any of this non-writing good for thinking and learning? I'm pretty sure it's not. We might find the current state of affairs particularly worrisome if we frame the problem this way: In an attempt to educate, it seems that educators and a whole lot of other well-meaning adults have worked successfully to ensure disengagement with the printed word, often during the most formative and critical years of literacy acquisition.

"Don't write in the book." Even though I remain convinced this is perfectly awful advice, the mantra remains standard, announcing itself from every corner of our culture.

A few years back Kathie Coblentz, New York Public Library cataloger and author of *The New York Public Library Guide to Organizing a Home Library,* disclosed to a *New York Times* reporter her penchant for scribbling notes on the pages of books in her *private* collection. My elation was short-lived when the reporter amiably cautioned readers *not* to do the same (Braden). But why not, especially if the scribbler is also the owner? Think about this (mis)guiding principle for a moment and you too may share my distress and bewilderment.

I've been scribbling in books for years (lightly and in pencil, I might add) but I'm not nearly as self-disciplined as bibliophile Kathie Coblentz, as I write in books I borrow from libraries. There. I've said it. At a later date, I sometimes borrow the book again and am greeted by my previously penciled notes still etched softly in the margins. Two important things seem to occur in this moment. First, I'm promptly reacquainted with my previous thoughts and, second, I'm often surprised at how much my thinking has shifted since the previous visit to the page, a sure sign that the human mind is in a constant state of making meaning as it constructs and then reconstructs itself.

5 So, I think the problem is clear. Our system of educating, parenting, and nurturing unwittingly conspires to ensure students' disciplined detachment from words on the page. In other words, creating disengaged adults begins early. My proposal is simple and not particularly original, but I'll reiterate it nonetheless. Those of us committed to raising and teaching need to raise and teach differently. For starters, we need to insist that from the earliest stages of literacy acquisition all humans—especially the tiniest in size and age—be invited to scribble fervently as they explore books. If we take into account the opening statement in Maryanne Wolf's *Proust and the Squid: The Story and Science of the Reading Brain,* it becomes apparent that humans could use an assist. Wolf avows forebodingly, "We were never born to read" (3). Ditto for writing. Out of necessity, it seems, resourceful adults looking for ways to enhance overtaxed memories found their way to literate practices. In doing so, the human brain began to evolve in ways probably not intended in the original blueprint. That is, in the process of teaching oneself to read and write, the brain began to reinvent itself, thus enhancing human development and evolution. Experts concur that coding and decoding symbols enhances thought and consciousness, which in turn literally alters brain matter. In other words, what we do with our brains determines what our minds are or what they might become.

We are born with the capacity for language built into our genetic code. It's simple enough. People aim to foster human connection, and speech makes itself apparent in children eager to converse soon after birth. Without any overt instruction, the youngest of tots uses speech to assert needs and preferences, often doing so in the form of the familiar toddler command: "More cookie" or "Me hold you." In short order, the toddler strings phrases together and begins to verbalize incessantly with anyone willing to stop and chat a bit. So the advent of spoken language seems straightforward enough, but literacy acquisition, or the ability to read and write, remains a stellar unintended achievement and a considerable cognitive coup if there ever were one. Depending on how we do the math, our ability to pen language goes back five thousand years or so, half that if we're talking specifically about the creation of the Roman alphabet. If we consider that humans were vocalizing perhaps as far back as one hundred thousand years before stumbling on to technologies for capturing memory in print, we recognize the veritable brevity of the written word. And although a relatively recent human innovation, the written word has enhanced the mind's cognitive prowess.

Again, in *Proust and the Squid,* Wolf writes, "Reading can be learned only because of the brain's plastic design, and when reading takes place, that individual brain is forever changed, both physiologically and intellectually" (5). In his essay "Writing Is a Technology that Restructures Thought," esteemed twentieth-century theorist Walter Ong informs the reader, "[W]riting is utterly invaluable and indeed essential for the realization of fuller, interior, human potentials. Technologies are not mere exterior aids but also interior transformation of consciousness . . ." (23). Neuroscientist and Nobel Prize winner Eric R. Kandel confirms in his memoir *In Search of Memory: The Emergence of a New Science and Mind* that "Today, most philosophers of mind agree that what we call consciousness derives from the physical brain . . ." (378). Kandel cautions, however, that all this business of consciousness is "more complicated than any property of the brain we understand" (379). Current neuroscience, complete with functional magnetic resonance imaging (fMRI) and other fancy tools, seems to substantiate Ong's and Kandel's claims. So if the specialists are correct in their collective assertion that literate acts transform consciousness (we might call it "knowingness") and brain construction, why would anyone choose to read a text *without* a pencil grasped firmly in hand? Why not enthusiastically dot the text with penciled symbols and words as matter of habit? More importantly, why wouldn't the "pencil to page" mantra become the preferred teaching strategy of parents and educators everywhere?

I'm passionate about penciling, but this doesn't mean I disapprove of today's sophisticated technologies. Not at all. Like most, I often wonder how we functioned effectively before the arrival of the word processor, cable television, fancy phones, and the Internet. No doubt about it: Current technologies provide us with unprecedented speed and convenience, perfectly timed supports for life in the twenty-first century. I'm grateful every day for their availability; however, the loyal pencil, an archaic invention if there ever were one, continues to garner my full support. The graphite-enhanced wooden stick offers definite advantages. It slows my reading and thinking, allowing opportunity to interact more purposefully with words on the page. Additionally, I'm sure the sensual aspect of sharpened graphite pressing softly against textured paper plays a key role in arousing the neurons. The pencil draws me into the text and invites my active participation, and when my voice appears as light markings on the page it becomes clear that I've assumed my required role in the conversation. The bright yellow #2 meandering along the page ushers me from passivity to activity. Call me sentimental or just demanding, but I want my students to join me in leaving traces on pages. After all, what might be lost in the process? Certainly not enhanced brain development, sustained focus, or heightened awareness. Let the scribbling begin.

Works Cited

Braden, Carole. "A Bibliophile, 3,600 Friends, and a System." *The New York Times*, 10 Feb. 2005, nyti.ms/1Rxb6tL.

Kandel, Eric R. *In Search of Memory: The Emergence of the New Science of Mind.* W. W. Norton, 2006.

Ong, Walter. "Writing Is a Technology That Restructures Thought." *Literacy: A Critical Sourcebook*, edited by Ellen Cushman et al., Bedford/St. Martin's, 2001, pp. 19–31.

Wolf, Maryanne. *Proust and the Squid: The Story and Science of the Reading Brain.* HarperCollins Publishers, 2007.

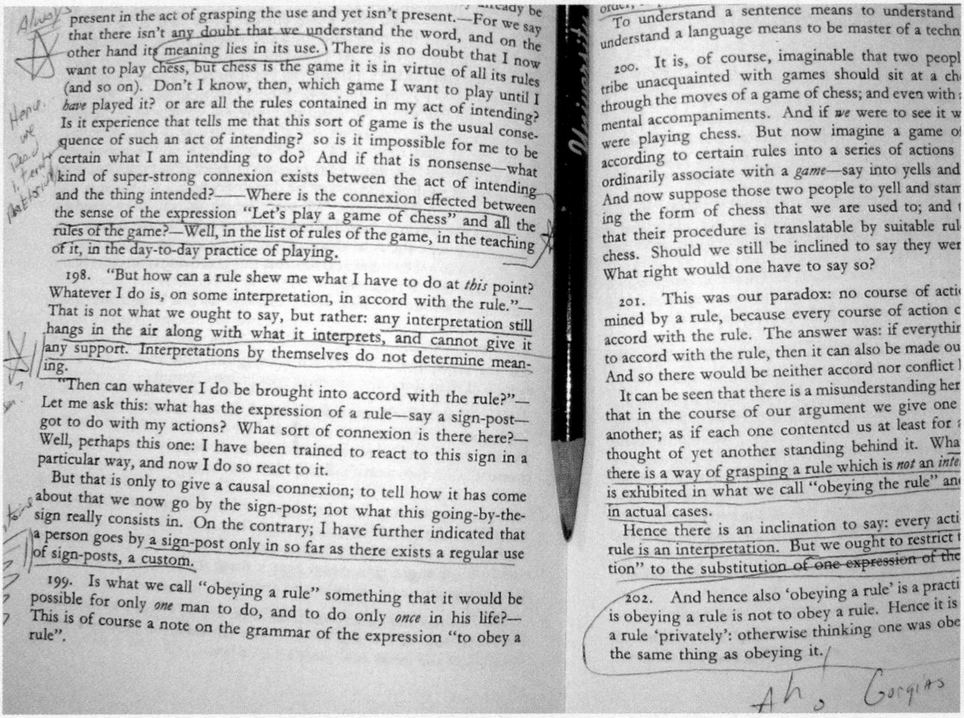

...already be present in the act of grasping the use and yet isn't present.—For we say that there isn't any doubt that we understand the word, and on the other hand its meaning lies in its use. There is no doubt that I now want to play chess, but chess is the game it is in virtue of all its rules (and so on). Don't I know, then, which game I want to play until I *have* played it? or are all the rules contained in my act of intending? Is it experience that tells me that this sort of game is the usual consequence of such an act of intending? so is it impossible for me to be certain what I am intending to do? And if that is nonsense—what kind of super-strong connexion exists between the act of intending and the thing intended?——Where is the connexion effected between the sense of the expression "Let's play a game of chess" and all the rules of the game?—Well, in the list of rules of the game, in the teaching of it, in the day-to-day practice of playing.

198. "But how can a rule shew me what I have to do at *this* point? Whatever I do is, on some interpretation, in accord with the rule."—That is not what we ought to say, but rather: any interpretation still hangs in the air along with what it interprets, and cannot give it any support. Interpretations by themselves do not determine meaning.

"Then can whatever I do be brought into accord with the rule?"—Let me ask this: what has the expression of a rule—say a sign-post—got to do with my actions? What sort of connexion is there here?—Well, perhaps this one: I have been trained to react to this sign in a particular way, and now I do so react to it.

But that is only to give a causal connexion; to tell how it has come about that we now go by the sign-post; not what this going-by-the-sign really consists in. On the contrary; I have further indicated that a person goes by a sign-post only in so far as there exists a regular use of sign-posts, a custom.

199. Is what we call "obeying a rule" something that it would be possible for only *one* man to do, and to do only *once* in his life?—This is of course a note on the grammar of the expression "to obey a rule".

To understand a sentence means to understand
understand a language means to be master of a techn

200. It is, of course, imaginable that two peopl
tribe unacquainted with games should sit at a ch
through the moves of a game of chess; and even with
mental accompaniments. And if *we* were to see it w
were playing chess. But now imagine a game o
according to certain rules into a series of actions
ordinarily associate with a *game*—say into yells and
And now suppose those two people to yell and stam
ing the form of chess that we are used to; and
that their procedure is translatable by suitable rul
chess. Should we still be inclined to say they wer
What right would one have to say so?

201. This was our paradox: no course of acti
mined by a rule, because every course of action c
accord with the rule. The answer was: if everythir
to accord with the rule, then it can also be made ou
And so there would be neither accord nor conflict
It can be seen that there is a misunderstanding her
that in the course of our argument we give one
another; as if each one contented us at least for
thought of yet another standing behind it. Wha
there is a way of grasping a rule which is *not* an inte
is exhibited in what we call "obeying the rule" an
in actual cases.
Hence there is an inclination to say: every acti
rule is an interpretation. But we ought to restrict
tion" to the substitution of one expression of the

202. And hence also 'obeying a rule' is a practi
is obeying a rule is not to obey a rule. Hence it is
a rule 'privately': otherwise thinking one was obe
the same thing as obeying it.

John Mauk

Writing Strategies

1. Closely examine Mahoney's introduction. How does the first paragraph focus our attention on a particular aspect of a broader problem? In your own words, explain how this problem is more specific than illiteracy.

2. Trace the logic of the essay (the line of reasoning) and explain each intellectual step leading to the solution.

3. In ¶5, Mahoney refers to a source (Wolf) and then extends the point: "Wolf avows forebodingly, 'We were never born to read' (3). Ditto for writing." Why is this step critical to Mahoney's line of reasoning?

4. How does Mahoney's use of personal testimony fit into the argument? (Could the argument function without that testimony?)

5. Focus on particular passages in which Mahoney deals with some opposing position or concern. Describe her tactic. How does she deal with that opposition? Does she deflect, take apart, destroy, neutralize, calm, or something else?

Exploring Ideas

1. Mahoney claims that most of her students have learned how to "move through the system" of education without really attending to language. How does this resonate with your own experience? Why is simply "moving through the system" a bad thing?

2. In Mahoney's words, "Our system of educating, parenting, and nurturing unwittingly conspires to ensure students' disciplined detachment from words on the page. In other words, creating disengaged adults begins early." Give a specific example of a practice or scholastic behavior that encourages students to be detached "from words on the page."

3. After walking us through her line of reasoning, Mahoney wonders: "So if the specialists are correct in their collective assertion that literate acts transform consciousness (we might call it 'knowingness') and brain construction, why would anyone choose to read a text *without* a pencil grasped firmly in hand?" Try to imagine why people would choose to read without a pencil in hand. What reasons, besides those Mahoney counters, might people have for ignoring her solution?

4. Mahoney argues that reading with a pencil "slows [her] reading and thinking, allowing opportunity to interact more purposefully with words on the page." What type of opportunity is this? What is *opportunity* during the reading process?

5. Describe the specific way that you attend to text. Do you skim, occasionally skim, or read closely? How would you characterize your interaction with words on the page? Are they strangers passing by? Are they people you're desperately trying to know?

Ideas for Writing

1. Point out and attempt to solve another particular layer or aspect of illiteracy in the United States.

2. What other problem could be solved with something elegantly simple—like a pencil?

If responding to one of these ideas, go to the Analysis section of this chapter to begin developing ideas for your essay.

Student Essay

Reverence for Food

Rachel Schofield

Writers, thinkers, activists, parents, and some politicians have argued about America's bad diet for years. Thousands of voices jeer junk food, fast food, and fake food. So Rachel Schofield, who wrote the following essay for her first-year college writing course, works to show a new dimension to a common argument. She does not simply reinforce what readers likely know about junk food; instead, she reveals a problem with the way mainstream culture views and obsesses over food.

Acknowledges and then goes beyond the usual arguments about obesity and diet.

It's more than obesity and bad diets. It's disconnection from the earth.

The typical American meal today is fast and convenient. Microwave dinners, frozen pizza, Hot Pockets™ fast food, soda. It's mostly fake food, even though our waistlines seem to say otherwise. Economists and historians agree that the advent of processed foods after World War II contributed to the downfall of the family farm and rise of the factory farm. And many argue that it has also contributed, if not outright caused, America's current obesity epidemic. But we've heard these arguments before. Aside from the obvious health and economic concerns, what are the deeper consequences of eating such processed foods? America's food system, with its fast convenience foods, disconnects us from food's source, resulting in less reverence for food and decreased respect for nature itself.

Appeal to tradition: Our ancestors may have had the right relationship to the earth.

Historically, humans have worshipped the earth and gods of agriculture and fertility. There is a common myth among many cultures that the earth is the giver of life, and in a very literal sense, it is true. Food comes from the earth, and we require it for sustenance. Many great civilizations flourished under these gods, recognizing their connection to the earth and giving thanks for its sacred bounty. In the past, we revered the earth, nature, and food because we could directly see that our lives depended on them. Most of the population worked the fields and witnessed the divinity of the soil as it miraculously produced their daily bread. Today our lives still depend on nature's produce, but most of us have lost our connection. In losing our reverence, we have allowed for the birth of Frankenfoods.

Jump forward (or should I say backward?), and today's food is fast, cheap, and easy. The prostitute of processed food has replaced

---

■ Writing Strategies ■ Exploring Ideas

the revered goddesses who once nurtured our crops. Our blind faith in science has led us to a world where humans re-create in the lab what already exists in nature. We mutilate the natural into virtually unrecognizable forms. Enter high-fructose corn syrup—a highly processed, unnatural liquid. A complicated and convoluted method of chemical alchemy is utilized to create this all-too-artificial sweetener:

Prostitute vs. goddess (the powerless versus the powerful).

The writer builds up the point with her own line of reasoning before giving the info from the source.

> First, cornstarch is treated with alpha-amylase to produce shorter chains of sugars called polysaccharides. Alpha-amylase is industrially produced by a bacterium, usually *Bacillus sp.* Next, an enzyme called glucoamylase breaks the sugar chains down even further to yield the simple sugar glucose. Unlike alpha-amylase, glucoamylase is produced by *Aspergillus,* a fungus, in a fermentation vat where one would likely see little balls of *Aspergillus* floating on the top. The third enzyme, glucose-isomerase . . . converts glucose to a mixture of about 42 percent fructose and 50–52 percent glucose with some other sugars mixed in . . . liquid chromatography takes the mixture to 90 percent fructose. Finally, this is back-blended with the original mixture to yield a final concentration of about 55 percent fructose. . . . (Forristal)

If we literally are what we eat, then we're all full of junk.

Brings the info from the source to a crescendo.

As unappetizing as vats of floating fungus and bacterial enzymes may sound, Americans are blissfully consuming more and more of this revolting substance. "Since its introduction in the early 1970s, the cheap sweetener's use has jumped 4,000 percent; it's now showing up in everything from sodas to steak sauce" (Callahan). Our food comes more and more from chemical concoctions rather than the earth; we have lost our sense of connection with the very thing that sustains us. We make the distance between life-giving nature and ourselves greater through over-processing our food. In some kind of strange twist of logic, we actually make our food less nutritious.

Our food choices are increasingly illogical . . . and weird.

Again, the paragraph builds to a climactic statement.

5 Food still enables us to survive, but we no longer revere it. Some would disagree, citing the weight problems engorging our country. We see food 24/7 on TV, hear about it on the radio, see it advertised on billboards, and even in Internet pop-ups. Advertising works. We buy what we see, yet the low nutrition levels in our highly processed foods leave our bodies starving for more, and we only give them more junk. We can see the preeminence of food in the dedication of temples to food all along our highways; fast food chains are more popular than ever. However, there is a difference between obsession

A turnabout paragraph of sorts!

Obsession with fake food ≠ reverence for the real thing.

with food and reverence for it. Our fast food restaurants and freezer aisles are brothels where impure, chemically altered food is bought and sold. Almost gone are the days when honest, unadulterated food can be purchased by the American family.

The quote supports this step in the line of reasoning: Americans are stuck in our obsession with fake food.

How can Americans have reverence for food when we have so many artificial consumables surrounding us? And to complicate the problem, "Compare the price of a grapefruit to that of a pack of strawberry-flavored Twizzlers" (Zinczenko). It seems that processed food is almost always cheaper and more accessible than wholesome fresh foods. What can a struggling American family do when the only thing they can afford is cheap processed food?

Turnabout paragraph: an alternative solution and its potential shortcoming.

A new tax won't solve the problem.

David Zinczenko of *Men's Health* proposes that we put a sin tax on unhealthy and unnatural foods. What if "OJ cost less than that *high-fructose* horror known as Sunny Delight? Wouldn't America be a little bit healthier?" (Zinczenko) But a tax on the powerful agribusiness industry, with its already entrenched team of lobbyists in Washington, seems a long way off. Eric Roston of *Time* magazine states: "Although U.S. taxpayers subsidize American farmers generously—to the tune of $20 billion a year—that's not likely to change anytime soon. Besides, corn is so cheap that even a farm policy that doubled the crop's price might make only a marginal difference in grocery-store prices."

Another turnabout paragraph: an alternative solution and its shortcoming.

A real solution has to go to the root of the problem.

Another solution comes from Arkansas governor Mike Huckabee. He has proposed "a plan whereby food stamps would be worth more when they're applied to healthy foods" (Zinczenko). This is a great idea, and I commend the governor for doing so. But this is just a superficial jab. It does not address the origin of the problem: lack of reverence for nature and food.

Another turnabout: explains the ideal and why it won't work.

The ideal never seems to work out.

The ultimate cure for our lack of connection to nature would be for each person to grow his or her own food. We would be in the fields, dealing directly with the earth itself. We would relearn the lost art of cultivation: how to care for the earth and provide for its needs so it can do likewise for us. One-on-one interaction with nature herself would be the best way of rejuvenating our reverence for food. However, this ideal is neither practical nor possible for the vast majority of people. Why is that so? Because we would have to drastically alter our consumer lifestyles. We would have to take time out of our busy day and spend it at what many see as the mundane task of digging in the dirt.

10 Before we can begin, we must change the way that we think about the earth. It is not some dead mass of matter, but rather a complex interconnection of life. Far from being boring, farming is an entrance into life itself. We can begin to take baby steps toward the ideal. Americans can buy food from their local organic stores. Better yet, they could get to know the people who grow their food. And, whenever possible, Americans should start their own gardens. Once we experience its creation firsthand, it is almost impossible not to have a healthy respect for all the time, effort, and hope embodied in the art of farming.

The solution to our food problem: Change our thinking about the earth itself!

The solution is qualified—in "baby steps." This is more acceptable than a grand recalibration of all food items.

Works Cited

Callahan, Maureen. "Sugar Smack." *Health*, Oct. 2006, p. 150. *Academic OneFile*, go.galegroup.com/ps/i.do?id=GALE%7CA191065577&v=2.1&u=nysl_me_wls&it=r&p=AONE&sw=w&asid=d13a0e03c00bd6411c016705c1a31798.

Forristal, Linda Joyce. "The Murky World of High Fructose Corn Syrup." *Wise Traditions in Food, Farming and the Healing*, Weston A. Price Foundation, 3 Dec. 2003, www.westonaprice.org/health-topics/the-murky-world-of-high-fructose-corn-syrup/.

Roston, Eric. "America's Obesity Crisis: Agriculture: The Corn Connection." *Time*, 7 June 2004, p. 83. *Academic OneFile*, go.galegroup.com/ps/i.do?id=GALE%7CA246543137&v=2.1&u=nysl_me_wls&it=r&p=AONE&sw=w&asid=00aab925d2a4b72c3cc8dd16df644502.

Zinczenko, David. "Food Fight!" *Men's Health*, June 2006, p. 22. *Academic OneFile*, go.galegroup.com/ps/i.do?id=GALE%7CA148650891&v=2.1&u=nysl_me_wls&it=r&p=AONE&sw=w&asid=f3855222f915f06f54240b44467935fc.

Writing Strategies

1. How does Schofield get us to see something beyond the obvious: that junk food is bad?

2. How are appeals to value operating in Schofield's argument?

3. What is Schofield's line of reasoning? Trace the backbone of the argument—its basic steps—through the paragraphs, and characterize each step in one sentence.

4. What is Schofield's solution? How does it address the cause of the problem?

5. How does Schofield deal with opposing positions? Point to particular passages in which she counters or concedes.

Exploring Ideas

1. Schofield argues that other solutions, such as Governor Huckabee's, are "superficial." Why is it important to discover the origin, the root cause, of a problem before proposing a solution?
2. Schofield argues that the solution begins with an intellectual change: "Before we can begin, we must change the way that we think about the earth." How is such a change possible?
3. Why do you suppose "we" (mainstream Americans) have lost reverence for the earth, for nature, for real food? What particular cultural, economic, or political forces caused this?
4. In everyday life, we are invited to revere flags, sports heroes, politicians, our alma maters, and sometimes religious figures. What would it mean to revere food? And who might take offense at this notion?
5. Schofield makes a distinction between obsession and reverence. In your own words, how would you describe that distinction? What is the fundamental difference between *obsessing* and *revering?*

Ideas for Writing

1. Schofield argues that mainstream American culture has forsaken food. What other basic or fundamental thing has mainstream American culture forsaken? What problem has this created? How do we solve it?
2. What other specific social problem can we solve simply by readjusting our perspective?

If responding to one of these ideas, go to the Analysis section of this chapter to begin developing ideas for your essay.

Invention

"No problem can withstand the assault of sustained thinking."

—Voltaire

For this chapter, your topic will be a particular problem—some situation that needs to be changed or an idea that needs to be rethought. Be wary of global problems like hunger, poverty, or racism. They are not unapproachable or unsolvable, but such big problems usually have local or particular expressions, and it is the local or particular that is often the most appropriate place to start. Focusing on a particular problem also sets the ground for a manageable solution. For example, solving financial difficulty for single-parent students is more manageable than solving poverty in general.

The following sections are designed to help you through the invention process: specifically, to discover a problem (in Point of Contact), to develop an understanding of its causes and develop a possible solution (in Analysis), to make it relevant to a community of readers (in Public Resonance), to develop a focused statement about the problem and solution (in Thesis), and to develop support for your argument (in Rhetorical Tools). The Invention Questions in each section are not meant to be answered directly in your final written assignment. They will, however, help you to think further into your topic, to develop intense claims and insightful points.

Point of Contact

Social problems are not necessarily physical or material; they can be intellectual, spiritual, or psychological. Consider problems related to bad policies (all first-year students must live on campus), narrow thinking (a government administration that assumes energy must come from fossil fuels), or troubled systems (a bureaucracy in which all decisions must be made at the executive level before action can be taken).

Writers often do best with topics with which they are familiar, or with which they can become familiar. To discover particular problems, consider the different circles of your life. Use the following suggestions and questions to help dig up a problem that you, as a writer, witness or experience, and attempt to see problems that others might disregard. See the problems that lurk behind the obvious. If one of the suggestions prompts you to see a problem, begin by recording details—that is, try to explain the particulars of the problem:

School

- Are students missing too many classes?
- Do my instructors communicate poorly with students?
- Are my peers lazy?
- Are enough courses offered to students?
- Do instructors give enough or too many exams?
- Did my high school education adequately prepare me for college?
- Is the curricular gap between high school and college too wide?

Government

- Does the city government do enough for children? For senior citizens?
- Does state government overlook the particular needs of my community?
- Are citizens sufficiently involved in local government?
- Do average citizens know how tax dollars are spent?
- Are there enough minorities in public office?

Television

- Is prime-time television too adolescent?
- Are sports televised too often?
- Is there something wrong with the way sports are televised?
- Are talk shows tasteless, moronic, or disrespectful?
- Has art been abandoned by popular culture?

Your Major

- What are the problems related to employment in my field?
- What about job security? Safety for the workers? Safety for the public?
- Do people enter the major or career field for the wrong reasons?

Community

- Are the elderly people in my family or community isolated?
- Do people in my neighborhood ignore one another?
- Are there too few animals in people's lives? (Too many?)

Ronnie Bergeron/MorgueFile/ Rich Stern/StockXchng

- Does traffic in my community interfere with daily life?
- Are billboards tasteless or boring?
- Are there too many chain stores or strip malls in my community?

Activity

Now go beyond these suggestions. In groups or alone, develop more strategies for encountering and exploring social problems. Imagine what might be wrong, or what can be better than it is.

Analysis

Problems

Any solution must address the causes of a problem. Therefore, analyzing a problem to discover all possible causes is essential to developing a good solution. Often the causes of a problem are not clear, however. A problem may originate from an abstract source, such as a long tradition, a widely held attitude, or a flawed assumption. And writers must search through such abstractions to find the possible causes. To understand the full complexities of your problem, respond to the following questions:

- What are the causes of the problem?
- What are the most troubling or alarming images associated with the problem?
- What are its short-term effects? Long-term effects?
- What other situation (event, attitude) does this problem resemble?

In her invention writing, Deirdre Mahoney explores her topic: students' inability to read intensively and critically. Her own language takes her somewhere. Here, she discovers that the problem is one of commitment—or even the relationship her students have with text:

What are the most troubling or alarming images associated with the problem?

Here's what's troubling and distressing: Each semester I meet many college students who mean well and want to succeed but who are entirely removed from the printed word. That is, they know how to read . . . to a point. These students often associate reading with glancing or skimming and that's it. Sometimes they skip the reading assignments entirely. So here we have it—adults who really don't understand what it means at all to commit to a text. These are students who don't fully realize that decoding sophisticated texts (or even somewhat sophisticated texts or even just slightly sophisticated texts) will take focus and self-discipline and perhaps, even, a whole lot of time. They don't seem to fully understand that engaging in literate practices, especially on the college level, requires all kinds of ongoing, serious application and hard work. Really hard work.

What are its short-term effects? Long-term effects?

The effects are complicated. Often it takes students weeks into a semester before they come to terms with (glancing and skimming), hoping for a different outcome—that of the easily earned revelation. But, of course, success doesn't work that way. Significant challenges most often require commitment to a task not easily begun or completed. So, what are the short-term effects? Failure, decimated confidence, learned helplessness, and hopelessness.

Generally speaking, college students who commit—who are willing to attend to words on the page and to embrace the challenge of analyzing a text seriously and laboriously—can begin to train their minds to function differently and more effectively. They might begin to experience access to ideas that they've previously not had the abilities to know or retain. They might discover liberation, confidence, and their own abilities—they might come to understand that the human mind can be trained.

Research

You may respond to the Invention Questions on different levels, first providing your own initial responses and then gathering information from outside sources. Such sources may include friends, coworkers, family members, websites, articles, and books. (Consult Chapters 14 and 15 to help you explore.) As you research, look not just for ideas that support your initial responses but, more importantly, for ideas that might change the way you think.

Solutions

Before settling on a solution, consider how the solution will work, how it will address the causes of the problem, and how it might fail. Answers to the following questions will be vital to developing your solution and to making it persuasive to readers. While you will benefit from understanding all of the following issues, your readers may need some points emphasized over others. Ask yourself what points seem least obvious, or most debatable, to your audience. Respond to the following questions to develop your solution:

- What action (solution) will best address the causes of the problem?
- What might stand in the way of this solution?
- How will the solution change the situation?
- Does this solution have potential shortcomings or limitations?

Again, Mahoney's invention writing takes her thinking into the complexities. She begins with the most fundamental acts of learning to read:

What action will best address the causes of the problem?

We need a culture shift. We need to think differently about the printed word and our relationship to it. We need to assume that we are always teaching reading and learning how to read throughout our lives—just as we do in the earliest stages of development. Three-year-olds read the same book over and over. They request we read it to them over and over. They want to retell it over and over. They read it (in their own way) to themselves over and over. Three-year-olds seem to understand the notion of tenacity and commitment. We need to do a better job of teaching students that reading and thinking are labor-intensive, by design.

We must allow students the right to underline and scribble in books.

What might stand in the way of this solution?

Students, often to their credit, are managing too much at once. Where I teach, many must earn money to put themselves through school and pay the bills. Their academic schedules are full, and they allot themselves so much time for this course and that course. So it's important to point out that students are not afraid to take on significant challenges, but I think what they don't fully understand is that they have to adopt a different vision for themselves—they must begin to imagine themselves as capable readers of complex texts.

At this point, Mahoney is thinking in brave terms: a cultural shift! She's imagining that people could begin *thinking* differently (which is certainly more difficult than implementing a policy or action).

In analyzing the specific problem, Mahoney is also exploring broader cultural trends. She's exploring public resonance! It is important to realize that insights about public resonance may come at any time during the invention process. Because the process of exploration and discovery cannot be divided simply into separate steps or stages (analysis, public resonance), one must always be on the lookout for insights.

Public Resonance

Some topics may seem difficult to connect to a broad public concern, but good writers bring *seemingly* marginal topics into the center of public consciousness. The problem you have chosen may obviously affect (or potentially affect) a community or society at large. However, no matter how much your problem involves or affects people, you still must make it known. As you consider your own topic, respond to the following questions:

- Who should care about this issue? Why?
- What particular community, place, or group does this issue affect?
- How might my reader(s) be involved in this issue?
- Why is it important that others hear my opinion about this issue?

In Mahoney's invention writing, she picks up on a point from her Analysis responses. Some core ideas are gaining momentum: Children and adults alike must develop *intellectual tenacity* as part of literacy.

Who should care about this issue? Why?

Parents, educators, and anyone who cares about books and ideas should care, especially all of us who want to see our kids succeed in school.

How might my reader(s) be involved in this issue?

Parents who save and save for their kids' college education and who think they are preparing their kids for college and beyond might most need to hear this message, as they might be the ones who are not seeing how important it is to help their children fall in love with words—from the earliest years—and then to continue to foster that relationship throughout the school years. All too often, I sense that parents believe we are off the hook once we've created literacy in our children, but that's actually just the beginning. Without fostering the relationship or constantly celebrating intellectual tenacity, we fall short in our jobs.

Invention Workshop

The public resonance may not be clear at first, but working through all the possibilities can help your topic to expand in interesting ways. Enlist the help of other writers, and in a small group, answer one of the questions for your topic. As a group, work at collectively building a sophisticated answer to the question.

In the following, Marcus has discovered a problem in his community: Elderly people in nursing homes and senior living centers are isolated from others. In a discussion with peers, Marcus develops his initial thinking:

"What particular community, place, or group does this issue affect?"

MARCUS: Primarily the elderly. Senior citizens are primarily concerned about this issue, and as medical advances allow people to live longer, it seems like we all should be worried—because we'll all be old someday.

LINDA: But shouldn't the younger generations be concerned about the isolation of the elderly, too—I mean beyond just caring about themselves as they age?

DIANA: Yeah . . . even if they don't care, it seems like stuffing the elderly away from mainstream society can't be a good thing, for anybody.

MARCUS: It's like we are ignoring a huge group of people—the group that probably has the most insight and experience about big social problems.

LINDA: And I would even say personal and family problems. I know in my family, it was always my grandmother who understood everyone's problems and could talk through them without getting angry or mean. She was the one who gave everyone a sense of direction.

MARCUS: So when society shuts away its elderly, maybe the biggest victims are the younger generations. Of course, it's bad for the elderly, but in a more indirect and long-term way, maybe their absence from mainstream society is an even bigger wrong. Maybe the younger generations feel the effects in the long term without their patience, insights, and experience.

Thesis

A thesis for this project should offer a specific strategy for addressing a specific problem. The following examples show a range of possible strategies:

- If the sales associates at Dalworth's had more discretion over break time, the management/employee tension would decrease significantly.
- The budget crisis at Midland State College can only be addressed with a tuition increase.
- Small-group work can help writers get beyond their frustration with invention.
- The degradation of rural areas cannot be stopped with peaceful public rhetoric. Significantly higher gasoline taxes would, however, keep people from building homes farther away from their jobs.
- If the country could begin to take back the airwaves from corporate interests, democracy might then begin to flourish.
- When America's hunters and fishermen see their shared interests with strong environmental groups, their combined political force will help counter the unchecked movement into wildlife areas.

Thesis statements tend to go off track for a few consistent reasons. Before committing to a statement (to something that may impact everything hereafter!), see the Common Thesis Problems in Chapter 8 (pages 272–273), which overlap with this chapter.

Evolution of a Thesis

Notice how a thesis might evolve out of the invention process. Marcus's topic (isolation of the elderly) can be developed into a focused and sophisticated point. He begins by articulating the problem. Then he tries to make the problem more specific. Finally, he works to integrate the solution:

- In the long run, younger generations may feel the effects of the elderly's isolation.
- Older generations are isolated—their experiences, insights, and wisdom cut off from the people who need it most: everyone else.
- We have to make our grandparents the center of our families, not the marginal human satellites they are presently.
- Because older generations are isolated, their experiences, insights, and wisdom cut off from those who need them most, families should rethink how grandparents figure into everyday life.
- The lost experiences, insight, and wisdom of the older generations can be reintegrated into culture only through families; therefore, each family should work to place its grandparents at the center of everyday life.

Try to express your own problem and your solution in a sentence or two before moving on.

Revising Your Thesis

Could your thesis be narrower? Writers sometimes seek out problems that are simply too big: hunger, racism, sexism, political deceit, and so on. But such giant problems have too many causes and too many forms. Writers are more apt to create a focused argument and offer an important insight if they take on a specific problem—one that can be located in a particular place and time. Before moving on, make certain that your problem is narrow—as narrow as possible.

Rhetorical Tools

Remember that proposing a solution is a form of arguing. In fact, the process may involve two layers of argument: (1) persuading readers about the nature or degree of the problem and (2) showing the value of a particular solution. The goal is not necessarily to convince readers that only one solution is possible but that a particular solution to an important problem has merit.

Although the act of proposing solutions can vary greatly, good proposal essays have certain key elements (which you have already begun to develop):

- **Problem:** Includes illustrations or examples, an explanation of causes, and a picture of short- and long-term effects.
- **Solution:** Includes an explanation of how that solution will address, confront, or stop the causes of the problem.

- **Counterargument:** Addresses concerns about or opposing claims to the solution or the articulation of the problem.
- **Alternative Solutions:** Include any other potential strategies for addressing the problem. Articulating alternative solutions requires an explanation of why these are less desirable than the main solution being offered.
- **Concession/Qualifier:** Acknowledges any possible shortcomings of the solution or concedes value to some opposing claim or alternative solution.

The development of these elements depends upon your particular problem and solution. Some problems, for instance, require significant explanation; that is, you might need to work hard just to make readers aware of the complexities of the problem. Or perhaps you have a problem that is rather apparent (such as abandoned buildings plaguing an entire section of town). Consider how your audience may view the problem, and make certain to convince your readers to see the problem as you do.

Also, remember the strategies from Chapter 8: Making Arguments. Writers have the whole world of culture, history, and science within reach. By alluding to key historical moments, relevant literary texts, news events, or popular culture figures, you can make claims more persuasive to readers or show that your position is shared by others. Use the following questions to help construct supporting points for your argument (and see the examples in the chapter readings):

- ▶ Does a historical situation or trend (the rise of a particular fashion, organization, or individual) illustrate something about my topic? (See Schofield ¶4 and 5.)
- ▶ Has science taught us anything about my topic? (See Mahoney ¶5–7.)
- ▶ Have I witnessed or experienced someone or something that illustrates my point? (See Mahoney ¶1 and 4.)
- ▶ Can I construct a hypothetical situation that illustrates my point or dramatizes my solution? (See Schofield ¶9 and 10.)

Discovering Counterarguments and Alternative Solutions

In proposing a solution, you are arguing that a problem exists *and* that a particular solution will address it. But someone might argue with you about several points: that the problem is no problem at all, that your solution will not work, that your solution is inappropriate—too costly, inhumane, unmanageable, and so on. A good arguer addresses those possible objections and may even dig into opponents' assumptions. (See Mahoney ¶2 and 3.)

Every problem has many possible solutions, and a good writer acknowledges other possibilities. But acknowledging solutions other than your own involves explaining their shortcomings. That is, as you mention other solutions, you must also make it clear that they are not as valuable as yours for some reason. Other solutions, for instance, might be less efficient, more dangerous, less ethical, less manageable, or simply inadequate. (See Schofield ¶7 and 8.)

Considering other solutions can also help you understand the strengths and shortcomings of the solution you are promoting. For instance, a solution to Marcus's problem (from the Public Resonance section), isolation of the elderly, might involve refiguring the concept of the nuclear family to include grandparents, uncles, aunts, and cousins. Only in reconceptualizing the basic family unit, he might argue, will elderly members of society find more genuine social engagement. But he might also address other solutions, such as programs that bring together schoolchildren and nursing home residents. According to his argument, such solutions might fall short of creating deep and lasting relationships for the elderly.

As you consider your own topic, apply the following questions:

- Who might not see this as a problem? Why?
- Why might my solution not work?
- What other solutions could be (or have been) attempted?
- Why is the solution I am proposing better or more effective?

Avoiding Logical Fallacies

Logical fallacies are flaws in the structure of an argument that can make readers call the claims into question. (See further explanation of logical fallacies in Chapter 8, pages 280–282.) In proposing solutions, be especially cautious of the following fallacies: faulty cause/effect, non sequitur, and slippery slope. When considering the possible long-term effects of a solution, writers may make any of several logical errors:

- Imagining an effect unrelated to present causes **(faulty cause/effect)**
- Skipping several logical steps between a cause and a possible effect **(non sequitur)**
- Extending present circumstances to their most dramatic or disastrous conclusion without sufficient logical cause **(slippery slope)**

Consider Marcus's topic: *Mainstream society isolates the elderly.* It might be valuable for Marcus to project the long-term effects of this problem. However, he should be cautious and not overstate the effects.

Logically Sound

- Without the insight of older generations, mainstream society may continuously forget the social crises of the past and have to relive many burdens.
- As older generations are further isolated, the difficulties they have lived through are isolated with them. And without constant real-life reminders in our midst, younger generations are likely to ignore a past that is not written by official voices of history.

Logically Unsound

- The United States will have to go through another two world wars because it has completely forgotten the past.
- Everyone will eventually think like children without the elderly in everyday life.
- Society will eventually keep everyone over fifty years old locked away.

Revision

Academic audiences value directness and intensity. They do not want to struggle through overly wordy phrases and jumbled sentences. And they don't like boredom any more than anyone else. In short, academic audiences are people too. They want to stay awake and be engaged. Examine your draft. Focus specifically on the following issues:

- **Delete the Obvious:** Consider statements or passages that argue for or detail what you and your peers already assume. Although you might use some common assumptions or common knowledge to build an idea, avoid telling readers what they already accept.
- **Intensify the Least Obvious:** Think about your essay as a declaration of new ideas. What is the most uncommon or fresh idea? Even if it's a description of the problem or a slightly different take on solving it, develop it further. Draw more attention to it.

Peer Review

Exchange drafts with at least one other writer. Before passing your draft to others, underline the thesis or write it at the top of your essay. This way, reviewers will get traction as they read.

As a Reviewer, Use the Following Questions to Guide Your Response

1. After reading the draft, do you believe that the problem the writer describes is worthy of attention? Do you think it's a problem worth solving? If not, what might the writer do to make the problem more significant?
2. Do you think the writer's solution is appropriate for the problem? Will it address specific causes? Is it manageable? Realistic? Humane?
3. Try to imagine a reason why the writer's solution will not work. What unforeseen forces or variables should the writer consider?
4. What other solutions might be as or more productive in solving the problem?
5. Consider the organization of the essay. Do any paragraphs shift focus without sufficient cues? Do you feel like any paragraphs move away from their initial points without taking you along? Point to specific places in the essay that move too abruptly from one idea to another.
6. How would you describe the writer's tone? (See page 573.) Do you feel invited into the topic, or do you have to work at keeping your attention focused? (Is the writer's voice too

flat, too uninteresting, too typical?) Rewrite a short passage of the draft using a different voice. Help the writer to imagine how a different voice might sound.

7. Consider sentence vitality:
   a. Help the writer to avoid obvious content. Circle any sentences or passages that seem obvious to you.
   b. Help the writer to avoid padding. Underline phrases that inflate simple ideas and draw out sentences unnecessarily.
   c. Help the writer to "call a fool a fool." Rewrite any phrases or sentences that seem to hedge, that circle around a more direct and intense wording.
   d. Consider other strategies from Chapter 19, Vitalizing Sentences.

Reflection

One powerful way to better understand your own work is to analyze its basic elements or perform what is often called *rhetorical analysis.* In rhetorical analysis, writers describe how arguments work. Looking at the proposal you've written, develop a final analytical statement:

1. How does the essay confront a problem and offer a solution?
2. How does the essay go beyond the common intellectual reflexes related to the problem? For instance, does it show things in a different light? Does it assert something that others don't see? Does it call for a solution that has not been attempted?
3. How does the essay take on opposition? How does it counterargue or concede? Or why doesn't it?

Consider this final statement more of a report than an evaluation. Imagine that you are explaining the mechanics of your argument rather than defending your point of view. For instance, you might explain how your essay provides specific examples of the problem and how those examples reveal layers of difficulty. You might explain how your solution directly connects to the original cause of the problem. You can also describe how outside sources figure in—as support for your proposed solution, as background about the problem, as opposition to your ideas.

Beyond the Essay: Comic Strips and Other Media

The comic strip in Figure 12.1 encourages you to express the idea from your essay in some other form: a letter, speech, and so on. Why? Students sometimes see education—or certain college courses such as this one—as separate from their actual lives. However, the course is not only related to your major; it is directly related to your major, and it is, more importantly, related to your *life.*

Writing courses such as this one look at what really goes on in everyday life, and they present what goes on (invention strategies, rhetorical strategies, and so on) in an organized way.

John Metz

Figure 12.1 Comic Strip assignment

Admittedly, a college writing course can be a confusing and seemingly irrelevant place. But if you can remember that the invention strategies in this book are a description (not a prescription) of how everyday people think and communicate effectively, you can more successfully fuse schoolwork and real life.

Now that you have written a proposing solutions essay, communicate your solution in some other form such as a letter, speech, poster, bumper sticker, website, photo essay, T-shirt, poem, song, performance, or comic strip.

13 Thinking Radically: Reseeing the World

Ingo Arndt/Minden Pictures/Getty Images

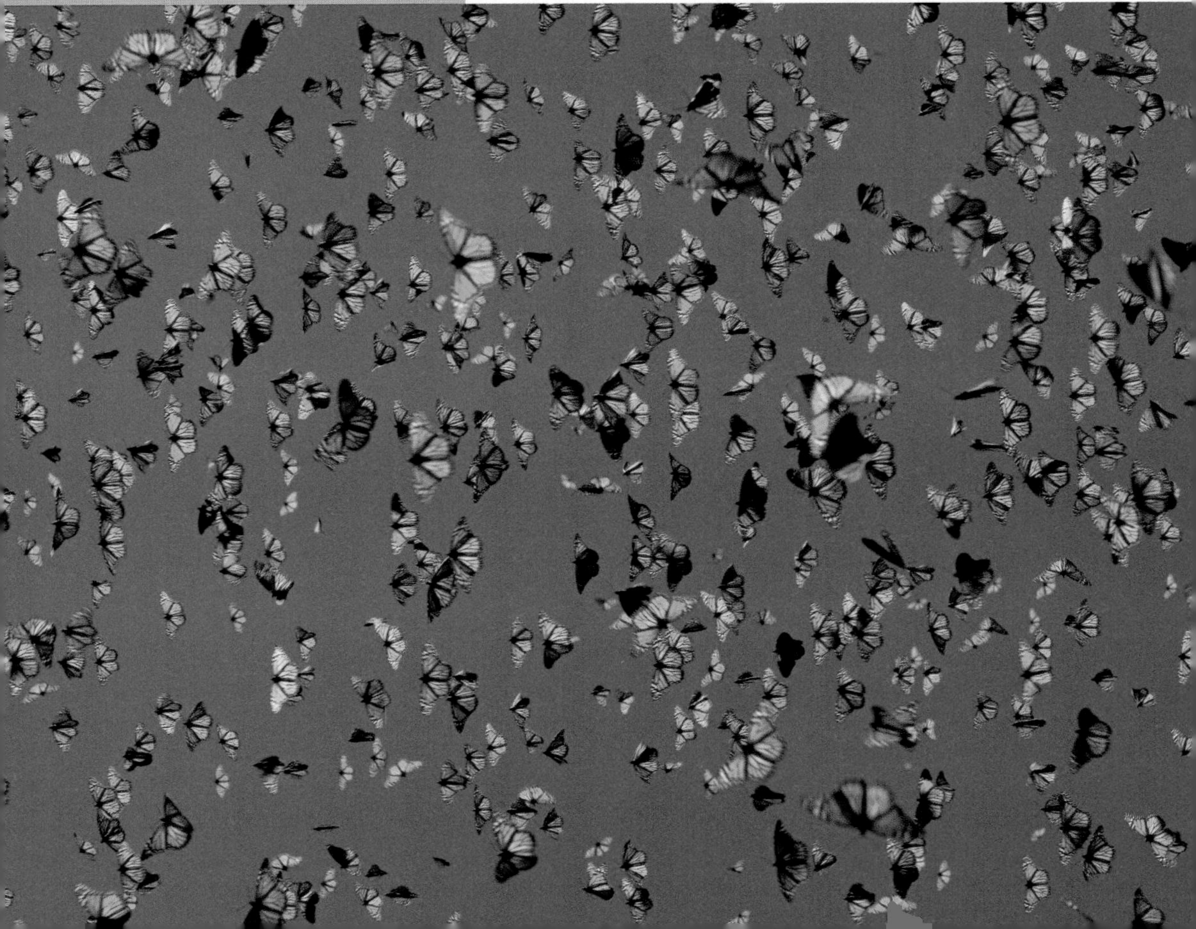

"We must therefore look in the obscurest corners and summon up courage to shock the prejudices of our age if we want to broaden the basis of our understanding of nature."

—Carl Jung

Living in a society demands a certain degree of conformity. As individuals in a society, we conform to laws, clothing styles, hairstyles, and even culinary tastes (most Americans like french fries but not raw oysters). We also conform to ways of thinking; we learn to follow intellectual conventions. This is not to say that we all think alike, not by a long shot, but we do buy into conventional modes or patterns of thought that, on the one hand, allow us to participate in shared knowledge but, on the other hand, limit intellectual possibilities.

Mainstream thought invites us to accept a particular view of reality, and with it, certain assumptions. Consider the following:

- Progress involves technological advancement.
- The past is behind us.
- People who make lots of money are successful.
- Poor people are worse off than rich people.
- We make individual choices.
- Time is constant.

Such ideas are what we might call *common sense,* in that they represent widely held, and largely unexamined, beliefs. But some people have examined and even challenged such common ideas. For example, thinkers such as Wendell Berry challenge the idea that human progress necessarily involves increased dependence on technology; several important religious figures (Jesus, Buddha, Muhammad) overturned the inherent value of monetary riches; and Albert Einstein showed the world that time is not constant but relative. We might say that such figures transcend and challenge commonsense thinking. They call into question those beliefs that rest beneath layers of intellectual practice and everyday life. They show us questions where we may have assumed solid answers.

People who transcend conventional thinking are not *radical* in the sense that they want to destroy mainstream life. (We are not talking here about anarchists, religious zealots, or specific political positions.) Rather, they are radical *thinkers:* They escape conventional thought patterns. Although convention calls on us to think within the lines, radical thinkers work to see beyond those lines and then communicate what ideas are possible. Their writing seeks to reform conventional thinking.

Radical thinking is not necessarily a matter of topic choice; in fact, topics are not, in themselves, radical. Radical thinking involves an adventurous *approach* to a topic and offers a new way to think. For example, in 1784, Benjamin Franklin first put forth the idea of daylight savings time. After waking at an unusually early hour in the morning and finding that the sun had risen, he imagined that people could change their clocks to coincide with sunrise throughout the seasons.

In 1543, Nicolaus Copernicus challenged the conventional theory that the Earth is the center of the universe. He defied church law and common sense of the day and claimed that the Earth rotates around the sun. History is filled with such intellectual adventurers, those who transcended norms to see relationships beyond the obvious, to find meaning outside of cultural norms, and to imagine perspectives beyond the present:

- W. E. B. DuBois argued against mainstream thinking about African Americans' place in society. Although most politicians, educators, and civic leaders walked a moderate line, assuming that black people in the United States could thrive in subservient positions, DuBois imagined that African Americans should act as leaders for national and global change.
- Psychologist Carl Jung broke away from his colleague Sigmund Freud (and the conventional wisdom of the psychological community) to argue that human unconscious is, in part, a collective rather than an individual phenomenon.

Questioning Common Sense Living in a society means participating in common practices and beliefs. But a common belief is not always the best belief. Imagine possibilities for the following and fill in the blanks:

Most people in my community want _______ without examining the underlying meaning.

I have always been taught to think _______ but now see a different way.

Exploring the Past and Future A radical vision sees beyond the confines of the present. A radical thinker might imagine what the world would be like if the American Revolution had not occurred, or how work in the United States will be defined in fifty years. As you imagine time beyond the present, fill in the blanks for the following:

In the past, people's perspective of _______ was fundamentally different from our present understanding.

In the future, people will probably understand _______ differently than we do.

Going to the Root The term *radical* comes from the Latin *radix,* which means *root* or *source.* Radical thinking might be seen as a process of finding the root or essence. For example, someone might explore the essence of womanhood or manhood, the true meaning of growing old, or the essence of education. Fill in the blanks in the following questions:

What is the essence of _______?

What is the most fundamental quality of _______?

Activity

In a small group, use the categories in this section to ask more questions. After generating more questions within these categories, try to create more categories, and then create several questions for each category. Do not stop generating questions until everyone participating has encountered a potential topic.

Analysis

The intellectual activity in this chapter involves *theory*—reasoning that is divorced from practical or physical particulars. When people theorize, they explore the realm of ideas and assumptions and make generalized claims. For example, when Sigmund Freud theorized about the nature of the unconscious, he was not making guesses about his own mind, but that of the *human* mind. He theorized that psychological ailments emerge from childhood crises. His theory, like all theories, could be applied to particular situations; he used the general notion to help cure problems within specific patients.

Everyone has theories (general accounts or concepts that inform how we receive ideas and act on the world), but theories are usually not discussed openly. They most often lie undetected in our minds. For instance, people may have a theory about knowledge acquisition; that is, they may have a general account of how people come to know things. This theory may be fairly complicated and may involve memory, experience, and language use—but rarely do people examine such theories closely and ask hard questions: *How does language acquisition relate to knowledge acquisition?* Doing theory, then, is the act of examining and developing our concepts. As you can imagine, theorists take little for granted. They are not willing to accept the answers they have been given, but rather look around them and imagine what other answers may be possible.

Activity

Doing theory requires a degree of intellectual play, as well as some deliberate and constructive probing. With several peers, choose one of the following topics:

- The difference between men and women
- When a child becomes an adult
- The relationship between individual and community
- The relationship between humans and nature

Each participant should explain his or her theory about the topic in one minute—or one paragraph if using e-mail or instant messaging. After each participant has a turn, start again: Everyone should take another turn and build upon or speak back to particular points made in the previous round. After the second round, start again. After several rounds, each participant should write a brief paragraph explaining how the theory session changed, developed, confirmed, expanded, or highlighted his or her ideas.

Now, *theorize* about your topic: Explore freely, beyond prior assumptions or quick answers. Ponder your topic for as long as possible before coming to any conclusions. Keep a notepad with you for a day or for several days while you rethink your ideas. Record even the most off-beat or seemingly irrelevant notions. The following questions will help you make connections and discover meaning:

- What is the basic or essential quality of the topic?
- How does the topic affect or influence thinking?
- How does conventional thought or practice keep people from a radical perspective on this topic?
- What is the origin of the topic?
- What do people normally not consider about the topic?

Use these questions to begin a process of exploration that you will continue through writing. For example, Linda, a business major, has chosen to explore the *essence of business*. In a discussion with peers, she begins to explore the topic:

What is the basic or essential quality of the topic?

LINDA:	Well, I wonder if this topic can even be thought about radically, but let's try it: I think the basic quality of business is competition.
MARCUS:	Competition with other people?
LINDA:	Yes . . . I think so. Other people or companies—or even countries.
MARCUS:	For that matter, what about towns and communities?
LINDA:	Yeah, I guess so. Towns and communities do compete for customers, for market, for tourism dollars.
DIANA:	So are all these people and communities competing for money?
LINDA:	Ultimately, yes. But at first, they are competing for more customers or clients.
MARCUS:	So . . . is it always about more customers? More money?
LINDA:	Well, I'd think so. Certainly, for retail stores, the daily goal is getting more people through the doors and to the cash register than the store across the street.
DIANA:	What if we looked at it like the companies are living organisms? I just saw something about bears on the Discovery Channel: Every summer and fall, before hibernation, the bears try to consume as much food as possible. But they also need to conserve their strength. They don't want to exert a lot of energy while trying to eat all this food. The ultimate goal isn't the amount of food. It's survival. The bears are competing for food, like salmon, but the essence of their competing is survival.
LINDA:	So . . . back to business . . . companies are not necessarily competing for just money; they're competing for survival, for life.
MARCUS:	That makes a lot of sense. Surviving in business involves making a lot of money (more than others), but it also involves conserving. Think about it: Companies that are out just to make a lot of money go down quickly because they didn't conserve.

The important moment here is Diana's brave reference to the Discovery Channel. Although bears and business have little in common, Diana is thinking about the essence of things—how entities stay alive. Her inventive connection makes the group rethink the essence of business. And now Linda's thoughts on the essence of business are beginning to take flight. She is going beyond the quick, easy response and exploring some hidden dynamics of business. If she continues developing these ideas, she could transcend conventional wisdom and make valuable discoveries.

Thinking Further

Everyday language is filled with sayings that suggest indisputable truths. Widely used yet unexamined, these sayings, sometimes called *clichés,* conceal more truth than they communicate. They might even misguide our thinking. Consider the following: *What doesn't hurt you only makes you stronger. Bigger is better. Back to the basics. Boys will be boys.* Such clichés might get in the way of exploring your own topic, but they can also mark the exact spot where radical thinking is most needed. The following questions may help you explore beyond conventional thinking:

- Can you think of any clichés related to your topic?
- How do they limit thinking?
- Might the opposite of the cliché be true?

Activity

In a small group, share topic ideas. Then list the common sayings, assertions, and opinions related to each topic. Capture all the conventional wisdom associated with each topic. What do people normally think, feel, and say about each? What are the common opinions, complaints, and hopes? The goal is to give each writer a clear sense of the conventional so that he or she can think beyond it.

In his invention writing about the future, Simon Benlow explores the present:

What do people normally not consider about the topic?

People do not normally consider pollution and the future because nothing in our popular culture invites us to, unless it's some silly movie inviting us to imagine a post–world war future, or a not-so-silly documentary that we forget about as soon as the lights come back up. In general, we're not asked to consider how our present wants will influence anyone beyond ourselves. The presiding language of our culture is filled with provocations to be fulfilled, to be happy (i.e., buy lots of things and drive a new car). We keep building/buying bigger and bigger vehicles, and consider our actions only (only!) when gas prices go up. In other words, the general trend in buying goods is to wrap ourselves in as much luxury as our wallets allow.

Benlow then goes further when he thinks about the language we use in everyday life. He tries to get beyond the common phrases (such as "the future") that hide complexity:

Can you think of any clichés related to your topic?

Maybe "the future" itself is a cliché. If a cliché hides or glosses over complexity, that phrase ("the future") hides something. It hides the people out there in the distance . . . the real people who'll no doubt have to deal with our wants! When we say "the future" or "posterity" or "our children," we're just glossing over the real people who'll be living with policies and laws and practices that emerge from our overindulgence. "Make sure to wear your air mask, Connor." "Oh, I left it at school yesterday." And then, of course, if anyone today brings up things like breathing nontoxic air or drinking clean water, they get deemed "environmentalists," "tree huggers," "liberals," etc. These terms are ways of dismissing the present and the future . . . real humans with real lungs and kidneys. We've become a culture of lunatics.

Public Resonance

In one sense, your topic may already have public resonance. Because you are theorizing (exploring general ideas rather than particular situations), your topic may easily connect to others. However, radical thinking runs the risk of alienating others. When writers transcend conventional wisdom, they must invite others into the new vision, which is no small task (consider Galileo's fate!). Use the following questions to help connect your ideas to readers' concerns:

- What is conventional thought on the topic?
- What nonconventional claims have been made about the topic?
- What keeps people from understanding the thing/idea in nonconventional ways?
- How would a new understanding of the topic help people? (Who, particularly, would a new understanding help?)

In his invention writing, Simon Benlow goes beyond naming "conventional thought." He tries to explain the nature of present thinking, how it works, how it is limited:

What is conventional thought on the topic?

The thing is . . . there is no conventional thought on this matter. People do not genuinely think about the future—in the specific and local sense. They don't imagine their lives affecting their grandchildren's world. People have been lulled into a present-tense-only mentality. Sure, most parents try to provide for their children . . . but they don't imagine how their lives (outside of creating a savings account) will affect the world that their children (and their children's children's children) will inhabit. In general, people in America spend most of their time thinking about their own financial existence, and the future earning power of their children. But they do not think about the air, the land, the water of the world 50 years, or 100 years, from now . . . and they don't imagine how present global politics might impact the future.

Writers who make radical (or new) claims cannot simply dismiss the beliefs of others; they must build an intellectual bridge between conventional thought and new thought. In a sense, this is the primary objective of the writing in this chapter. When making adventurous claims, it is especially important to make these connections, so your ideas have genuine significance and are more than vague abstractions. Simon Wykoff begins and ends his essay with a connection to readers' beliefs:

> A common stereotype in today's society is that of the lazy bum. People see a homeless man on the side of the road, waiting for handouts, and assume that's all he ever does. In reality, this couldn't be farther from the truth. As the painter Willem de Kooning once said, "The trouble with being poor is that it takes up all of your time." This is absolutely true, and I think you'll find that homeless people are incredibly busy doing the most important job to all of us: surviving.

Wykoff immediately speaks to what many people believe: "A common stereotype in today's society. . . ." He helps readers see that stereotype: "People see a homeless man on the side of the road, waiting for handouts, and assume that's all he ever does." Then he offers an alternate way of thinking: "I think you'll find that homeless people are incredibly busy doing the most important job to all of us: surviving." The details throughout the essay help readers understand and accept an alternate viewpoint to the common stereotype. Then in his conclusion, Wykoff makes an explicit connection between this alternative and others' beliefs:

> As you can see, my father's day was far from that simplistic stereotype of the bum who sits on street corners all day and waits for people to help him out. What people don't seem to realize is that to survive on the streets, you have to take things into your own hands. You need to have perseverance, stamina, and a little bit of luck. Though it may seem outlandish, I think you'll find that many homeless people work just as much, or more, than you.

Thesis

A thesis provides focus. Because the ideas for a Thinking Radically essay are potentially abstract and far-reaching, a focused thesis will help keep the text from wandering. Notice how the following thesis statements focus on a particular topic, acknowledge a conventional view, and offer an alternative way of seeing. For example,

> Behind our desire to drive bigger vehicles and own bigger homes lurks more than an attraction to symbols of personal success; it is, rather, a deep hostility toward other people and the environment.

This thesis focuses on a particular topic: the desire to drive bigger vehicles and own bigger homes. It acknowledges a conventional view: This desire is related to one's personal success. And it offers an alternative way of seeing: The desire actually has more to do with one's hostility toward other people and the environment. Consider the focused topic, conventional view, and alternative way of seeing in the following thesis statements:

- Although a glass ceiling may prevent women from climbing the ladder of success, women and men both would have a better quality of life if they participated on the lower rungs only.
- Though *Jeopardy* is often perceived as a test of intelligence, it is really a test of knowledge. A better test of intelligence is *Survivor* or *The Amazing Race,* which requires more analytical thinking skills.
- More gunfights and car crashes actually make a movie duller, not more exciting.
- Because people have come to believe it is the ultimate power, modern medicine has ironically done more harm than good in most people's lives.
- It is commonly thought that the North defeated the South in the Civil War. In fact, the South now controls the American government.
- Even just a cursory look at one's own life will turn up evidence that every American's primary function these days is to consume.

- Although the American school system prepares citizens for employment, it allows (and perhaps encourages) them to be helpless against propaganda.
- Farmers or dogcatchers as politicians would serve the people better than professional politicians do.
- A president who doesn't understand why terrorists might fly planes into buildings is ultimately far more dangerous than the terrorists.
- The poor are better off than the wealthy.
- Had the electric guitar not been invented, the accordion would have continued its reign as the most popular instrument among American youth.
- Although students should feel comfortable in a college classroom, the uneasiness some students feel is necessary to learning.
- All animals, not just humans, should be given the right to life, liberty, and the pursuit of happiness.
- Because of credit and debt, most Americans today are unknowing slaves to the wealthy.
- College professors aren't any smarter than the average Joe.
- Eggs are more valuable than gold.
- Mundane tasks, like weeding a garden or doing the dishes, are a form of meditation that most Americans should indulge in more often and more earnestly.
- The way that Americans communicate with each other is a bigger threat than terrorism.

Activity

Choose one of the sample thesis statements in this section. Describe how it is or is not radical. Does it transcend or speak back to some particular conventional way of thinking? Does it reveal something usually overlooked or dismissed? How does the wording and construction of the sentence help readers see something new?

Evolution of a Thesis

Do not be in a hurry to solidify your thesis. As you write and think, ideas will evolve, and this *evolution* of ideas is the goal of academic writers. In the previous example, when Linda explored the topic of business, her ideas transformed over time. She started by trying to discover the essence or root of business. In her early discussion with peers (see the Analysis section, page 443), she discovered an alternative way of thinking, as illustrated in the move from the first and second statements. More focused and inventive thinking led her to the final statement.

Linda begins with a widely held understanding of her topic:

- The essence of business is making money.

  She develops a position different from conventional thinking:

- Like any organism, the essence of business is survival.

  She shapes the idea as she writes:

- Beneath the everyday affairs of making money, the essence of business is survival, which involves consuming and conserving.

Because this chapter invites you beyond your initial opinion, you might be wondering: *Am I supposed to give my opinion, or what?* This is a fair question. A radical statement is an opinion insofar as a single writer is offering a new way to see a topic. But it is more than a personal opinion. It is a writer's attempt at rethinking something, and an invitation to others to rethink.

Although you may begin your exploration with an opinion, your thinking will evolve. When a writer provides support for an opinion, the opinion becomes a claim. By supporting a claim, the writer is now making an argument, not just expressing an opinion or saying what he or she thinks.

Revising Your Thesis

How do you know that your opinion is speaking back to conventional views? How do you know that you've gone far enough in your thinking? To answer these questions, you might enlist the help of others in reevaluating your thesis. In a small group, present your topic. Have the group members describe all the conventional opinions they can imagine. Then present your thesis and explain why you think it responds to or transcends conventional thinking. The group should then ask:

- Does the thesis uncover something new?
- Does it offer a new way of seeing the topic?
- If not, what is holding it back?

Rhetorical Tools

It will take various rhetorical tools to help readers understand and possibly accept an entirely new vision. In addition to the ones mentioned here, consider the strategies discussed in other chapters, particularly Chapter 8.

Using Narration

Narration draws readers into a set of events. A narrative or story can help writers illustrate a broader point; when making adventurous claims, a narrative can help bridge the gap between conventional and radical ideas. Throughout his essay, Simon Wykoff uses narration to help readers understand his broader point about how hard some homeless people work:

> Once he had some food in his belly, he usually tried to locate a current paper. This often meant waiting around in coffee shops until someone left one on the table after their breakfast. Sometimes this step could take him hours, but he was determined not to waste the precious money on a newspaper when he could get it for free with patience.
>
> As soon as he had the paper, he thumbed through it, looking for jobs he could feasibly apply to. Due to his particular circumstances, he was without official identification. This, of course, made the search much more difficult. If he found something, he would tear off the piece of the paper and store it to refer to later.

Using Description

Writers making adventurous or radical claims must consider the intellectual positions of their audience. Because readers may have no mental pictures of the ideas being put forth, it is up to the writer to sufficiently describe or characterize ideas. Notice Benlow's description, which helps readers to see evidence of his claims:

> Nearly every person of every town had his or her own internal combustion engine lawn mower, leaf blower, snow blower, hedge trimmer. Nearly every home and vehicle had air conditioners. And beyond these "utilities," we had hordes of trinkets, recreational instruments, and pleasure devices that all, eventually, had to lie in waste somewhere when our fickle appetites refocused on the new faster-smoother-quicker-shinier-more-interactive-more-believable-gadget.

Using Figurative Language

Literal description is sometimes insufficient to communicate the depth of an idea. This is when writers turn to figurative language, such as similes and metaphors, which help to represent complex or particularly abstract ideas. Notice Benlow's simile, which develops into a metaphor:

> Like a mass of delirious adolescents, we made ourselves increasingly giddy, posing for ourselves and for one another, posing in every aspect of our lives: our homes, travel,

> clothes, food, water, and vacations. It was a mammoth parade of teenage delirium that began in New York, wormed through every tiny town of the Midwest, and wrapped around itself in dizzying perpetual circles on the beaches of California. As it came through every town, no one could resist it. It banged and clamored and woke everyone from dreamy isolation, and so even the most ascetic types found themselves playing along in some small way.

Counterarguments and Concessions

Especially when their claims are unconventional, writers must anticipate and account for positions opposed to their own. Counterarguments anticipate and refute opposing positions while concessions acknowledge their value. In one sense, a Thinking Radically essay, or any essay that makes an argument, is like one big counterargument to a more conventional way of thinking. Notice how Wykoff frames his entire essay as a counterargument, or response, to another position:

> A common stereotype in today's society is that of the lazy bum. People see a homeless man on the side of the road, waiting for handouts, and assume that's all he ever does. In reality, this couldn't be further from the truth. . . .

Kathleen Norris's essay illustrates the same point. After explaining a certain way of thinking about celibacy, Norris responds, framing the rest of her essay as a sort of counterargument:

> One could well assume that this is celibacy, impure and simple. And this is unfortunate, because celibacy practiced rightly is not at all a hatred of sex; in fact it has the potential to address the troubling sexual idolatry of our culture.

Although it can help to think of one's entire essay as a counterargument, it's also important to make smaller counterarguments at key points throughout the essay, taking on particular opposing points within the broader, overall argument.

Whereas counterarguments refute, concessions acknowledge the value of others' positions. Even though a text making radical claims may not be openly argumentative, by definition it seeks to overturn conventional ideas. For this reason, concessions can be essential to engaging potentially apprehensive readers. Notice Benlow's concession in the following example. Most of his essay condemns his own generation, but he offers this small note, suggesting that people were more weak than evil. Without such a concession, readers would be more apt to reject Benlow's ideas as purely antagonistic:

> Although it is probably impossible, I hope you do not look back and characterize us as purely self-serving and wicked, but as trapped in our own enterprise. We were a young culture with no parents.

Outside Sources

Radical or adventurous claims do not exist in a vacuum; they exist alongside other similar claims and discoveries. While Wykoff develops his argument primarily through a personal narrative about his father, notice how he reinforces this position with an outside source:

> The next thing he did after looking for job opportunities was to get money in order to buy food for the rest of the day. While you may see many homeless panhandling, I think people don't realize that a large number of homeless actually do small-time work for their daily bread. As mentioned in an online editorial, the homeless these days are increasingly working menial tasks for extra cash, or just to survive (Hilton). For all the people you see standing outside of stores with signs, others are playing instruments on street corners, gathering cans for recycling, or washing windows.

Research versus Mesearch

Finding outside sources that confirm our positions and support our worldviews is usually easy. But such work, what we might call *mesearch,* misses the spirit and goal of *research,* which is to explore beyond our own initial suppositions, to read and rethink topics. Researching can be an inventive process—one that catapults us beyond initial ideas.

Avoid:

- Collecting statistics without questioning them, reflecting on them, and evaluating their significance.
- Limiting your exploration to sources that share your opinion or perspective.
- Merely "proving" your position with others' words.

Try:

- Gathering perspectives from a variety of sources.
- Closely examining writers who oppose your perspective or who see the world differently.
- Directly addressing the unstated assumptions and values in the sources. Try to discover what the writers value, hope for, or dismiss. What is their basic view of the world, and how does that influence their approach to the topic?

Revision

Because you are asking readers to resee an idea so completely, you must first participate in that reseeing by revising carefully. Before exchanging drafts with another writer, revisit the Invention Questions in the Analysis and Public Resonance sections to see how they might help you write an even more focused, more revealing thesis. Then revisit the Rhetorical Tools section to see how else you might help readers understand and accept your thesis.

Peer Review

Exchange drafts with at least one other writer. First underline the thesis or write it at the top of your essay. This way, reviewers will get traction as they read.

As a reviewer, use the following questions to guide your response

1. Does the thesis offer a new way of thinking about the topic? Why or why not?
2. In what sense does this essay transcend or speak back to conventional thinking?
3. Where is the writing most descriptive and specific? Where could the writer be more specific? Remember that it is easy, but less valuable, to remain entirely abstract and general. If the writer makes a general statement (about business, students, women, and so on), it must be exemplified. As a reader, you should come away from the essay with some specific image or impression imprinted on your thoughts. Have you?
4. Where does the writer use appeals to logic? Can you follow the line of reasoning? If not, at what point does it break down? (See the discussion of logos in Chapter 8, page 275.)
5. Play devil's advocate for a moment: What points seem entirely ungrounded or unreasonable? Why? What could the writer do to make the point more reasonable?
6. Suggest specific points that the writer should concede or qualify. For instance, the writer's position might seem too extreme; the claims might include too many people or include a large, diverse group without making any distinctions. Point out such claims, and help the writer to see the need to acknowledge subtlety, complexity, and exceptions.
7. Does the writer do anything unconventional or especially engaging with the organization? Is the introduction especially intense? The conclusion? Where does the writer seem to rely on old standard strategies?
8. Consider the writer's voice:

   a. Describe how it engages you with the ideas. Do any passages seem unengaging? Why?

   b. Describe the level of formality. Is it appropriate for the topic, the writer's approach, the assignment?

9. What is the most engaging passage in the draft so far? Why?
10. Check for sentence vitality:

   a. Offer a strategy for a stylistic fragment.

   b. Consider other strategies from Chapter 19, Vitalizing Sentences.

   - If you encounter any noun clusters, suggest a revision of the sentence.
   - When possible, change nouns (such as in *make a decision*) to verbs *(decide).*
   - Circle any unnecessary modifiers (*very, really, certainly,* and so on).
   - Where can the writer avoid drawing attention to *I* and *you?*
   - Where can the writer change linking verbs to active verbs?
   - Point to expletives (such as *there are* and *it is*).
   - Help the writer change passive verbs to active verbs for more vitality.

Questions for Research

If the writer used outside sources:

- Where must he or she include in-text citations? (See pages 508–509.)
- Are quotations blended smoothly into the argument and punctuated correctly? (See pages 495–506.)
- Where could more direct textual cues or transitions help readers? (See pages 504–506.)
- Is the Works Cited or References page formatted properly? (See Chapter 16.)

Reflection

Now that you have challenged conventional thinking and explored new possibilities, step back and analyze your essay's rhetoric. As you respond to the following questions, write well, crafting complete sentences and supporting your claims:

1. How does your essay transcend the intellectual norm and reveal a new pattern of thinking?
2. How did you use rhetoric to discover and develop a new way of thinking through your response to a particular invention question in this chapter?
3. What particular support strategy (or rhetorical tool) was most important in helping readers understand the essay's main idea?
4. Why is your writer's voice effective for this particular essay? Describe your voice, and refer to several sentences from your essay as examples.
5. How did you use grammatical and sentence-level strategies to intensify your points?

Beyond the Essay: Visual Essay/Collage/Poster

Conventional thinking gets challenged in different ways. We have all seen posters, photographs, videos, movies, letters, speeches, and even bumper stickers that question conventional thinking and offer alternatives. Now that you've written an essay that challenges a conventional way of thinking, combine several images (as the collage in Figure 13.1 does) to create a visual essay that challenges common thinking.

1. On paper or on a computer, select and arrange images and words that make the point of your Thinking Radically essay. Consider including your collage as part of your essay.
2. In several paragraphs, explain how the different images of your collage combine to put forth a unified main claim about the topic.

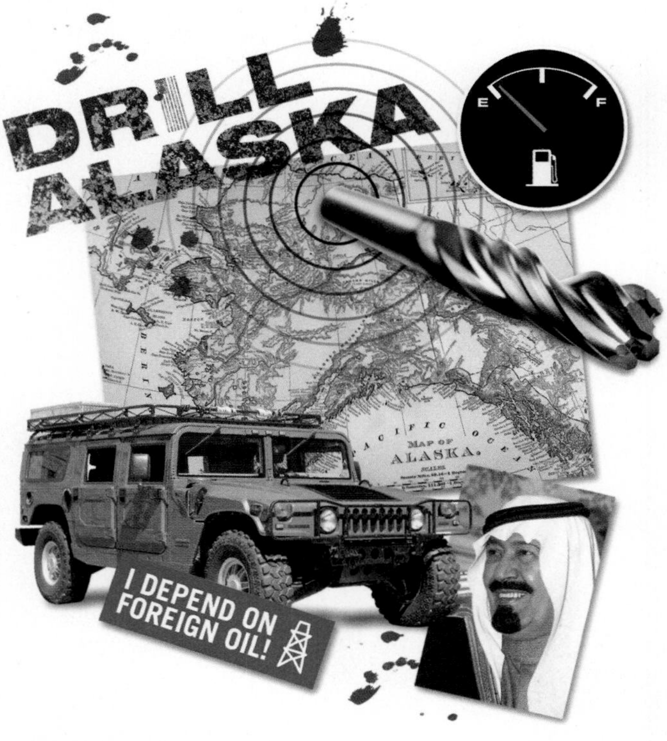

Figure 13.1 A visual collage.

14 Finding Sources

Yvain Genevay/Geologos/Corbis

Using Catalogs and Databases

When writing instructors refer to sources, they most often mean nonfiction published works: books, periodicals (journals, magazines, and newspapers), government documents, reference texts, audio recordings, video recordings, and digital texts like blogs and e-mails. In short, a source is anything that has been written, reported, recorded, or performed—everything from a blog to a formal academic study. In many ways, the process of finding, reading, and analyzing sources is a process of invention. It involves not simply gathering information but also engaging the theories, assumptions, perspectives, and outright arguments of others. For this reason, researchers should not see themselves as *finding and consuming information* but rather *building ideas* with the help of (many) others.

Online Catalogs

Almost universally, libraries use online catalogs for their book and government document collections. A few simple moves can streamline the search process: Adding words narrows a search, while using fewer words broadens the scope. For instance, "economics" by itself tells the catalog to find any and all works with "economics" in the title or description. (At Northwestern Michigan College, this search yielded 1,387 works.) "Economics and consumers" narrows the search (and yielded nine works—a much more reasonable number to browse).

Most catalogs give search options: *an author search, a title search, a subject search,* or *a keyword search.* Author and title searches are appropriate only if you are seeking out a particular source or author by name. Subject searches, which are organized by common headings such as *agriculture, government,* or *gender,* may be valuable for early stages of research—before writers have begun narrowing their insights. Keyword searches are most helpful after you have generated a list of possible words and phrases related to your topic.

Periodical Databases

Newspapers and magazines most often have their own websites. But researchers can rely on electronic databases such as Academic Search Elite, JSTOR, or Academic One File to navigate through the millions of available articles. Like online catalogs, periodical databases give a range of search options: author, title, subject, and keyword searches. Adding words to a search tends to narrow the focus (and limit the number of returns). For example, the keyword search for "weight" on one database produced 804 entries. Narrowing the search by typing "weight and body" produced only 146 entries. Thus, if you are seeking sources about weight and the body, "weight and body" would narrow the results to more relevant sources.

Database searches can be made more efficient by using the following words (called *Boolean operators*):

- Using *and* between words narrows a search by finding documents containing multiple words—*weight and body.*
- Using *or* between words broadens a search by finding documents with either word in a multiword search—*weight or body.*
- Using *and not* between words finds documents excluding the word or phrase following "and not"—*weight and not body* (that is, *weight* only, without any references to *body*).
- Using *near* between words finds documents containing both words or phrases that are near, but not necessarily next to, each other—*weight near body.*

Also, remember that a simple keyword search can turn up thousands of returns. Narrowing one's focus by typing "weight and body and media," for example, will eliminate irrelevant returns found by typing just "weight."

Sources themselves can also lead the way to more sources. If an article, for instance, seems particularly helpful or in tune with your claims, examine its works cited or references list. Chances are, the author has already made some connections or used sources that are directly relevant to your topic and position.

In the old days of walking through library stacks and looking for a particular book, researchers would invariably scan adjacent titles—and often find a number of similar sources. That still happens today! People *still* find important sources in print form. Also, many databases and online catalogs have added tools that connect researchers to related material. For example, after a researcher has clicked on a source, the database may give a list of related search words or subjects. In other words, the database may "know" what you want. (Databases are smart—and getting smarter.) In Figure 14.1, the database offers a link, in the left margin, that connects users to similar sources. Once you have found a key article, this "SmartText" feature connects you to sources that are often directly related.

Where Are We? The Web or a Database?

Periodical databases are not necessarily on the web. They are their own special island. Although they are accessible via an Internet service, they are not websites. Databases such as Academic Search Elite function like resource centers. They collect and categorize articles—most of which have been published in print prior to being uploaded in the electronic format. In other words, database administrators and editors have already done significant work for you. They have compiled sources, created abstracts, and uploaded them into searchable categories and sub-categories. And some have even created the formal citations (MLA, APA, Chicago, and so on) for each source. Such databases are usually not open to everyone on the Internet. They are for subscribers only—or for students who attend a school that has paid the subscription fee.

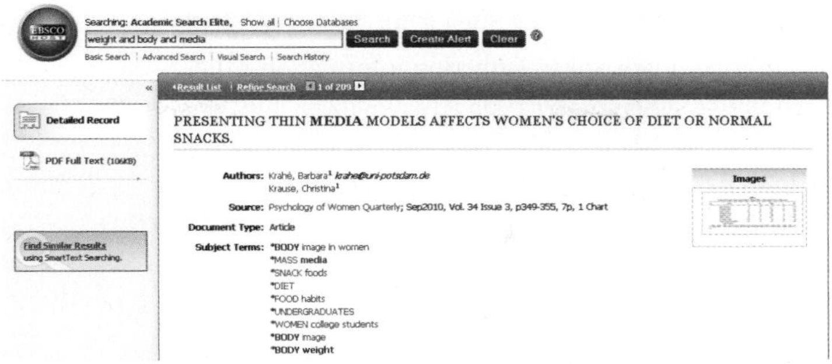

Figure 14.1 Periodical database of the kind you might find at your school's library

Activities

1. In a periodical database, try several keyword approaches for each of the following questions: In what ways might organized sports harm the young children who participate in them? What is the impact on the environment of people relocating to western states? What novel written in the last half of the twentieth century has been most influential?
2. List the different types of sponsors for websites that you found. For example, did you find government-sponsored websites? Websites created and maintained by businesses? Individuals? Nonprofit organizations?

Conducting Interviews

At a basic level, interviewing involves gathering information from a single person. But it can mean a great deal more. Good interviewers seek to engage interviewees in intensive conversations. They probe for knowledge and ideas, but they also allow interviewees to explore and develop ideas. A good interview, like a good essay, goes beyond basic knowledge; it provides insight.

Asking the Right Questions

Good interview questions create focus, yet allow interviewees to explore. Although they may seek out specific information (data, facts, dates), interview questions should go beyond collecting basic knowledge. (In fact, asking interviewees basic information that can be retrieved through print sources undermines the interview process.) A more valuable strategy is to prompt interviewees to reflect on the meaning of issues or to make connections between ideas. Notice the difference between the following:

> What's it like being a doctor?
>
> How has working in the medical field influenced your personal life?

The first question does not focus attention on any particular issue; the interviewee could talk about anything related to the profession. The second question, however, draws attention to a particular issue, asking the interviewee to consider a particular relationship. It is more specific than the first question but still calls for a certain degree of exploration.

Effective questions can come from good planning, but good interviewers also depart from their scripted questions when they see an opportunity to further engage the interviewee. Following up on an interviewee's answers, in fact, is the interviewer's most powerful research tool. Although a survey can only ask a list of preformulated questions, an interview can follow a line of thought that comes from an interviewee's response.

Imagine the following scenario, in which a researcher is interviewing a civil engineer:

INTERVIEWER:	Is being a civil engineer interesting?
ENGINEER:	Sure. I get to deal with all kinds of people and very real situations.
INTERVIEWER:	Is being a civil engineer hard?
ENGINEER:	Well, some of the work can be difficult. Trying to figure in all the variables in a given project can be a mathematical nightmare.
INTERVIEWER:	What would you tell someone who wants to become a civil engineer?

Here, the interviewer comes up short in several ways. First, the questions are mundane. As worded here, such questions would probably not yield focused and insightful answers; they prompt the engineer to respond in general terms. They are surface questions (the kind one might ask at a party), which yield short and uncomplicated answers. Also, the interviewer ignores opportunities to follow up. After the engineer's first responses, the interviewer could have asked about the "very real situations" or the "mathematical nightmare" but leaves both ideas and, instead, moves to the next question. This interview does not probe for insight or engage the thoughts of the interviewee, but merely poses a list of unrelated questions. The following example, however, shows a different approach:

INTERVIEWER: How is a civil engineer important to society?

ENGINEER: Well, civil engineers conceptualize living space for the public. They envision what it might be like to live in particular place, say, a downtown area, and then lay out plans to make a park, an intersection, even an entire downtown livable—and they do it all while considering how an area will grow and how people's needs may change.

INTERVIEWER: So civil engineers have to be visionaries?

ENGINEER: Yes! They are not simply figuring formulas about buildings and zones and land; they are imagining what it might be like to live and work within a given area in the present and future.

INTERVIEWER: And they do all this while accommodating the demands of city officials?

Here, the interviewer starts with a more insightful question. Although the first interviewer depends on a vague concept ("interesting"), the second interviewer seeks out the meaning of a potential relationship (between civil engineers and society) and consequently receives an insightful response. Also, the interviewer in the second scenario springboards from the engineer's answers ("So civil engineers have to be visionaries?"), thereby extending initial thoughts. The second interview evolves, even within a short amount of time.

Integrating Interviews into Your Writing

Ideas from an interview can be incorporated into various writing situations and purposes. An interview can be used to support claims made in argument, to help explain an idea, or even to help explain the history or significance of some topic. In the following example, notice how the information helps support an idea:

> Most often the water sewers can withstand the runoff from storms, but the past season has illustrated the inadequacy of the current sewer system. According to Harold Johnston, director of utilities, the sewer system was overwhelmed twice in the past three and a half months, and the result was that untreated sewage flowed out into Silver Lake. When an overflow occurs and untreated water spills into the natural water system, the high amounts of bacteria affect the wildlife and jeopardize the health of swimmers and water enthusiasts. In essence, anyone or anything in the lake for days after an overflow is swimming in sewage.

Here, the writer is trying to persuade readers that the water treatment system in her town is inadequate. The claim made by the director of utilities supports the idea. Although the writer probably collected extensive information about the treatment system, she used only one particular point in this paragraph because it directly supports the main idea. (Other information might be used in different passages.)

Planning an Interview

When setting up an interview, be sure to respect the interviewee's position and accommodate his or her schedule. Researchers should never impose themselves on potential interviewees. Use the following hints and strategies:

- Always request an interview well in advance of your own deadlines.
- When making a request, introduce yourself and the reason for the interview: Explain the nature of your research and how the interview will be integrated.
- Beforehand, negotiate a reasonable amount of time for the interview (such as thirty minutes)—and stick to it so as not to impinge on the interviewee's time.
- Plan out the method of recording responses—writing, audiotaping, or videotaping. Ask the interviewee if his or her answers can be recorded, and if his or her name can be used in the research.
- At the end of the interview, thank the interviewee for his or her time, and leave promptly.

Field Research

Interviews are one type of field research, which is often referred to as *primary* research because the researcher interacts directly with the subject(s) and is engaged in the activities and behavior of the thing being studied. Other kinds of field research include experiments, observations, and surveys.

Creating Surveys

Although an interview is based on an individual's knowledge, a survey attempts to find public opinion on a topic. An interview is driven, in part, by the interviewee; his or her insights may influence the direction or emphasis of the interview. But with surveys, the researcher prearranges the direction and emphasis with carefully formulated questions.

Generating Questions

In generating survey questions, a researcher should consider three points:

1. Questions should not lead the respondent to a particular answer. Good survey questions avoid influencing the respondents' thinking about the issue. For instance, a question that asks *Is our current president completely out of touch with public opinion?* leads the respondent toward a negative evaluation of the president. Such questions prompt respondents to take up a certain position even before answering. A better approach is to state the question without leading the respondent, such as: *Is the current president in touch with labor issues in the United States?*
2. Questions should narrow the focus of the respondents on a specific topic. Although good survey questions should not influence the respondents' thinking on an issue, questions should create a particular focus. For instance, a question that asks *Has the president taken an appropriate stance on international trade?* is more focused than *Do you like our current president?*
3. Questions should use common or unspecialized language. Because survey respondents may come from different walks of life, survey questions should avoid technical jargon or specialized terminology.

Choosing Respondents

Surveyors must consider the demographics (or particular characteristics) of their potential respondents.

What is the age range in the respondent group?

What is the racial makeup of the respondent group?

What is the gender makeup of the respondent group?

What is the occupational makeup of the respondent group?

What is the geographical origin of the respondent group?

People's occupations, gender, ethnicity, age, and geography impact their understanding of the world—and how they are likely to respond to any particular issue. For instance, imagine a survey about college life: If all the respondents are college instructors, the answers will probably reflect certain biases and assumptions—which may be entirely different from those of students or people not associated with college life.

Recording and Using Responses

Responses can be recorded in various ways. Perhaps the easiest means is to elicit written responses by asking the respondents to write or check off their answers. But if that is not possible, the researcher must do the recording by writing or taping. (If you plan to record answers, either with video or audio equipment, you must always ask the respondents' permission.)

Survey responses are most often used to show public opinion about a topic or to illustrate common trends in everyday life. A writer researching work issues among students at her college might discover important trends:

> Although many students take a full course load, they also work late on weeknights and throughout the weekends. In an informal survey, 24 of 35 respondents reported that they work at least 25 hours each week—and 21 of those 35 work over 30 hours each week. One student explained her situation bluntly: "No one told me that a full load of classes would compete with my work schedule. I thought I could do both, but it's nearly impossible."

Notice that the writer uses the information from the survey to enhance the significance, or the public resonance, of her topic. She sets up the idea in her first sentence and then plugs in the information from the survey.

The sample survey "that follows" offers room for the respondents to write in answers and to develop their thoughts. You could imagine someone responding to this survey fairly quickly because the questions are limited in number and fairly simple. Although it could offer some valuable insights about working hours, it is also limited in its scope, like all surveys. Because this survey does not ask for personal information from the respondents (age, sex, education, etc.), the researcher should be careful not to make broad statements about salary and job satisfaction in the United States, but to stay focused on the amount of time people dedicate to their jobs.

Sample Survey: Working Hours

Please respond to the following questions. Use the back of the page if you need more space.

1. Do you currently hold a full-time or part-time job? If so, what is the nature of the work?
2. If you work part time, how many hours per week?
3. How many hours per week are you contracted to work? (Or how many hours per week are you supposed to work, according to the job description?)
4. How many hours per week do you normally work (at or away from the job site)? Do you work on weekends?
5. How much time do you spend preparing for and/or traveling to and from work? (Feel free to give specifics.)
6. Is overtime mandatory or voluntary at your job? (What kinds of incentive are offered for overtime?)
7. Do you feel sufficiently compensated for the work you do? Why or why not?

---

15 Analyzing, Synthesizing, and Evaluating Sources

John Metz

Developing Critical Literacy

In the age of digital information, researchers have to make constant decisions about the nature and use of sources. They have to decide how a Wikipedia entry, for instance, may differ from a journal article or a historic document. They have to *analyze* the intended audience of sources, *evaluate* sources according to standard criteria, and *synthesize* sometimes contradictory voices. The process can be dizzying. Researchers must develop the ability to sift through the mountains of opinions, reports, images, theories, and data—and to make sound judgments about the nature of all that information. Scholars and teachers across the disciplines often refer to this ability as *critical literacy.*

"Just the Facts, Please"—Or Maybe Not

In a world saturated with information (news reports, breaking news reports, blogs, tweets, documentaries, and talk shows for every political persuasion), people sometimes long for simple facts. They want to read or hear something without an overt opinion attached to it. But this can be a naïve and even dangerous hope. Facts are tricky. They can *appear* unbiased, but they often emerge from a particular worldview, from a specific way of interpreting a situation. For instance, consider the following two reports about the same event:

> A. Today in Milford, rush hour traffic was slowed when over two thousand protesters gathered around the town square to challenge a new city ordinance that will allow Pemblebrook Industries to open another facility in the city limits. The new facility will bring thirty to forty new jobs into Milford. Construction is to begin by early fall.
>
> B. Today in Milford, over two thousand people gathered downtown in a peaceful protest against a new city ordinance that will change zoning of the Stark's wetland area. The ordinance, passed in an unpublicized overnight council meeting, was celebrated by Pemblebrook Industries, which hopes to drain and pave the wetland and make way for a new bottling facility.

Both passages report facts, and the facts themselves may seem unbiased. However, the selection of facts in each portrays a particular slant on the situation. In passage A, the situation itself is framed by traffic. In passage B, the situation is framed by the cause of the protest. In A, we learn about new jobs but do not learn about the destruction of wetlands. In B, we learn about an overnight meeting but not the jobs. Each report invites us to see the Milford protest in a particular light. If these passages were published in a newspaper, the headlines might read:

Headlines for A:

New Bottling Facility Coming to Town

Forty New Jobs for Milfordians

City Council Paves the Way for New Facility

Outraged Environmentalists Hit the Streets

Headlines for B:

Backroom Deal Dooms Stark's Wetlands

Quiet Zoning Change Concerns Milford Citizens

Public Outrage at Overnight Rezoning

The End of Milford's Wetlands

These headlines seem factual—like they are beyond opinion. But they all select and emphasize a single dimension of the situation. And that selection supports a way of valuing, devaluing, supporting, or ignoring a set of concerns. Both selections, both sets of headlines, are biased *and* factual.

Collectively held opinions can also parade around as facts. When an entire community (or civilization!) believes something without question—as every community does—the idea functions as a fact. Here are some commonplace beliefs that were, at one time, considered facts:

- Women cannot make rational decisions but can only mimic the decision-making process of men.
- If she doesn't drown, she's a witch.
- People of African descent are naturally prone to criminality.
- People of Mediterranean descent are naturally more passionate than northern Europeans and Asians.
- We can determine personality traits by feeling the shape of an individual's skull.
- The Earth is flat.
- Mental disorders are caused by an unacknowledged sin.
- Bleeding supports good health.
- Jews are the root cause of economic hardship in Europe.
- The Iraqi government was involved in the 9/11 attacks.

Of course, most people in the United States now look on these beliefs as terribly sexist, racist, tragic, or just wrongheaded. But at given points in the past, these were collectively asserted as uncontested truths. In some cases, they were taken for granted. They were "facts."

"Numbers Don't Lie"—Or Do They?

Sometimes we can be convinced that numbers are beyond opinion—that they simply represent a truth about the world. Again, this is a dangerous assumption. Numbers, like any text or symbol system, can be used for a range of purposes. We should see statistics as argumentative statements based on various assumptions and variables. As readers, we rarely have access to the assumptions and variables. Most often, about 78 percent of the time, we see only the conclusion—only the number. We are not invited to understand the research situation or the reasoning behind the numbers. For this reason, statistics can be more difficult to evaluate than a well-developed argument.

Of course, plenty of statistics are generated in a careful and sound manner, but many are produced under questionable circumstances or through flawed procedures. If the procedure is flawed, then the numerical conclusions are flawed—and they can distort the reality and urge people to accept ideas that simply are not true. The following flaws or misuses occur frequently, and they may even support some popular claims about medicine, health, and politics:

- Biased sampling
- Data dredging
- Data manipulation
- Discarding of unfavorable data
- Misapplication
- Overgeneralization

When we see statistics in an argument (or used as evidence to support an argumentative statement), we should think through the reasoning. Without a sound line of reasoning, an argument does not benefit from all the statistics in the world. In the following passage, the numbers might distract us from the logical fallacies (such as *begging the question* and *non sequitur*):

> According to the Learning Styles Institute, three out of five students are visual learners. That means 60 percent of all students learn best from pictures and charts. Therefore, teachers should use more visuals. If teachers use more visuals, students will get better grades and perform better on standardized tests.

The percentage has a kind of automatic persuasive power to it. But the overall line of reasoning is fraught with problems. The Learning Styles Institute provides nothing in this passage that explains how it defines *visual learner.* Does the study show how a person responds consistently—over weeks, months, years, or decades—to the same stimuli? If not, how can the Learning Styles Institute justify the label? Furthermore, we don't know what *learning* means in this situation. Does it mean consuming and remembering the content of a picture? Does it mean developing increasingly sophisticated insights? We simply do not know. And the answer would certainly change how we accept the argument. Furthermore, we don't know the demographics of the sample—who was involved in the 60 percent. Were there 10, 100, 1,000 students? Were they tested under a variety of situations, seasons, times of day? The problem with statistics in this case is clear: They can eclipse critical questions and prompt uncritical readers to be persuaded by flawed reasoning. Like a fancy paint job on a bad car, they can keep us from looking under the hood—or even starting the engine.

Summarizing and Analyzing Sources

Research requires an understanding of the content and context of sources. We have to understand not only what is being said (content) but also who is being addressed and where the conversation takes place (context). Every source—from book to article to blog—exists in a context of other voices and assertions. And if we don't understand that broader conversation, deciphering a source can be like walking into a dark cave and hearing nothing but weird echoes. For more on analyzing written texts, see Chapter 6, page 178.

Content

To understand the content of a source, we have to understand the source on its own terms. In other words, we have to understand its typical qualities. In the same way that a good traveler enters another country and tunes into its sensibilities, good researchers tune into their sources' sensibilities. For instance, we cannot hope that a sophisticated essay will loudly announce its main idea or give a bullet list of solutions. Academic essays simply do not behave like breaking news updates.

Each type of source has unique purposes and functions. A newspaper article, for instance, updates readers on a current event; an academic essay walks carefully through a focused and sophisticated idea; a blog expresses the opinions or experiences of an individual; a scholarly book takes on the assumptions or collective knowledge of a discipline. Obviously, such generalizations do not hold true for every source, but researchers gain more insight when we can shift our own readerly expectations according to the specific text in front of us. An academic essay, for instance, might build slowly to the main idea. A newspaper article may announce the main idea in the first passage or the headline. In a book, the main idea may come at the end of the introduction—after the author has explained a range of other opinions. If we know such patterns (and don't expect an essay to function like a report), we'll likely understand far more.

A key strategy for understanding content is summarizing the source—reading and then explaining the main idea as accurately as possible. This can be a challenge. We have to avoid skimming the surface and blurring away a source's specific insight. For instance, notice how the first statement in the following examples vaguely characterizes John Steinbeck's essay (from Chapter 3) while the second statement gives a more focused characterization of his *insight:*

> **Blurred Summary:** In "Americans and the Land," John Steinbeck describes early Americans' treatment of the land.
>
> **Focused Summary:** In "Americans and the Land," John Steinbeck describes the American settlers' disdain for the frontier and their "childlike" aggression, which destroyed the early forests, extinguished species, and diminished the continent's fertility.

This section introduces summary as a strategy for better understanding a source. Chapter 16 (pages 498–500) goes further and explains how to use summary inside of a research essay. In other words, this chapter introduces summary as a tool for understanding content, and Chapter 16 explains summary as a tool for integrating others' ideas into your own work.

Context

To understand context, we should consider two aspects of a source: audience and publication cycle. *Audience* refers to the intended readership—to the particular people inclined to read, study, or purchase the source. Are they from an academic discipline? Do they know a particular set of terms and issues that the general population does not? Are they hobbyists? What about their cultural sensibilities? Are they mad at the government or minorities? Do they believe in a god? Are they suspicious of organized religion? Are they older or younger? What is their overall level of literacy? Can they follow a complex line of reasoning for thirty pages? Do they like NASCAR or fine art? Such questions are figured into publication decisions about the source. For instance, *Forbes* magazine, which is pro-corporate and politically conservative, will likely not publish a lengthy treatise against the banking industry, nor will a scholarly journal in chemistry publish an article on how to make a can of soda explode.

As you can probably detect, writers and publishers make an important distinction between academic and popular audiences. Academic readers have different expectations than popular audiences. For instance, a scholar reading *Philosophy of Science* expects a certain level of analytical rigor that will likely be absent in a magazine such as *Newsweek*. And although general distinctions are difficult to maintain for all sources, it may be helpful to understand the following:

Readers of Academic Sources Expect

- Appeals to logic
- Rigorous analyses
- Evidence or theoretical backing for claims
- Formal documentation (such as MLA)

Readers of Popular Sources Often Expect

- Familiar characterizations and descriptions
- Appeals to value and emotion
- References to popular issues, places, and people

Researchers also should consider the publication cycle of their sources. Does the source get updated weekly? Monthly? Every three years? Has it been reprinted from an original publication? If it's an online source, has anyone taken responsibility for updating the information? Have updates attempted to address changes in the issue? Such questions point to the way information is handled—and what is published. Book publishers, for instance, are less apt to print ideas that are bound to fluctuate on a daily, weekly, or monthly basis. Instead, they publish work that will remain relevant through time. If the source does deal with issues that fluctuate (the stock market, important political figures, fashion trends, health care legislation), then researchers should expect sources to monitor those changes and deal with them accordingly. (These issues also correspond to timeliness, one of the criteria for evaluating sources. See page 486.)

Activity

In a small group, develop a list of imaginary publication failures—instances when the source does not match the audience's expectations; for instance:

- An article about lowering one's cholesterol in a punk rock magazine
- A report on best deals among L.A. marijuana distributors published in *Time* magazine
- A lengthy article about shifting epistemological assumptions in literary criticism published in *Sports Illustrated*

Understanding Common Source Types

Books and e-books come in a huge variety: fiction (novels, short story collections) and nonfiction (everything else), textbooks (like *The Composition of Everyday Life*) and trade books (everything sold outside of college curricula), and single-authored books and edited collections. One need only browse a bookstore to understand the immense number of subject categories. For academic research, it's important to remember that books generally take years to write, revise, and publish, so they are not the timeliest source of information. People don't value books for their timeliness but for their depth and richness, for their potential to reveal complexity, history, and the subtle nuances within a topic. Writers sometimes use the phrase *book-length project* to characterize work that involves a careful exploration of a complex issue.

Like all sources, books do exist in a conversation, but it may take place over years, decades, even centuries. In other words, with a book, the context may be more difficult to detect than with a tweet, blog, or article. The author(s) may be responding to a claim made long ago. Authors and publishers know this, and they have created some tools to help readers get a sense of the context. For instance, on the back cover and inside sleeve of print books, publishers often tell readers about the nature of the broader conversation. They explain how the work responds to a trend, how it engages a problem or debate, and how it contributes something new. In print and e-books, authors (or editors) use the preface and introduction to explain how their work fits into or responds to a tradition.

Periodicals include magazines (for a general audience), journals (for a specialized audience), and newspapers (both local and national). Popular magazines, such as *People* or *Newsweek,* offer information about mainstream news but rarely provide in-depth analysis of issues, and even more rarely deal with issues outside of major social and political topics. However, some magazines support in-depth reporting. *Harper's* magazine and *The New Yorker,* for instance, are well known for publishing incisive articles that go beyond common perspectives. Even entertainment magazines such as *Rolling Stone* often publish lengthy analytical articles on current issues or significant political figures.

Scholarly journals, which are usually specific to one discipline (such as English, engineering, nursing, business, or marketing), offer very detailed analyses and well-developed opinions on an endless range of topics. The writing in academic journals is most often well researched and documented, so it tends to be more reliable than that of popular magazines. It may also use discipline-specific jargon that could confuse nonexperts.

At first glance, journals and magazines may look a lot alike, but closer inspection will reveal significant differences. Generally, journals are written for academic or highly specialized readers. The articles put forward new theories or practices in a particular field of study (sociology, psychology, nursing, English, chemistry, history, etc.). The goal of academic articles is not necessarily to communicate an opinion but to explain a new idea—and thereby help the discipline, as a whole, to evolve. Magazines are written for general readers, who may have a particular interest (politics, mountain climbing, hunting). If you are not certain what kind of periodical you have, use the following criteria:

Journals

- Seek to advance knowledge in a *field of study*
- Deal with principles, theories, or core practices in an academic discipline
- Are associated with a particular discipline or field of academic study

- Have few advertisements, which usually appear only at the beginning and end (not between or among articles)
- Have few colors and flashy pictures (unless they are related to a study or article)

Magazines

- Report information/news or offer how-to advice
- Offer the latest technique in a hobby or sport
- May appeal to readers with a particular *interest*
- Have advertisements throughout the pages, even interrupting articles
- Tend to have more colors and pictures

Newspapers are most valuable for highly publicized topics—those that are or have been visible to the public eye: political events, public figures, national or local disasters, and significant cultural events. For this reason, the context of a newspaper article is fairly easy to detect. The headlines alone help readers to understand the issue, the rhetorical or political tension, and the people involved. For instance, we don't have to think much to understand the context of the *USA Today* headline:

> Obama to Birthers: "I Was Born in Hawaii"

For the most part, newspapers give the latest updates on current issues but refrain from giving lengthy background information. There are exceptions. For instance, *The New York Times* still funds, supports, and features lengthy analyses of political and cultural issues. But generally, newspapers are records of daily or weekly events more than tools of deep exploration.

Although the move to electronic publication has shrunk the number of printed newspapers, researchers still have access to a staggering number of local and national titles, such as the following, that are increasingly available online: *Afro American, American Banker, Amsterdam News, Atlanta Journal-Constitution, Boston Globe, Chicago Tribune, Christian Science Monitor, Denver Post, Detroit News, Houston Chronicle, Los Angeles Sentinel, Los Angeles Times, Muslim Journal, The New York Times, San Francisco Chronicle, St. Louis Post-Dispatch, Times-Picayune [New Orleans], USA Today, Wall Street Journal, Washington Post.*

Government documents include reports, transcripts, pamphlets, articles, speeches, books, maps, and films. State, local, and federal government bodies have accumulated huge amounts of information about everyday life. Government websites may be the best sources for researching general behavioral trends: what we purchase, how we live, how we get sick, how we heal, what we drink, what we eat, how we vote. Although the U.S. government is the nation's largest publisher, state and city governments publish as well. Such documents, which can be of great value in one's research, can be found online with keyword searches or by going directly to the Government Printing Office (GPO) website at www.access.gpo.gov.

Reference works such as dictionaries, encyclopedias, and almanacs can be seen as sources about sources. In other words, reference works give a general overview about the scholarship on a given topic. They explain what has been thought and said about key issues in a field. Particularly helpful reference works are topic-specific encyclopedia. Consider, for instance, the following titles, which represent a huge number of specialized reference books:

Encyclopedia of Popular Culture
Catholic Encyclopedia
Encyclopedia of Occultism and Parapsychology
Encyclopedia of Literary and Cultural Theory
Encyclopedia of Counseling
Encyclopedia of Chemical Technology
The Encyclopedia of Phobias
The Encyclopedia of Fantasy
Encyclopedia of Popular Music
The Encyclopedia of Quantum Physics

Researchers often consult reference works early in the process—as a way of gathering keywords or concepts that they use for further searches.

Audiovisual materials include videos, CDs, DVDs, films, photographs, and any type of recording. As organizations and governmental bodies increasingly move to digital storage, researchers can access a growing body of online recordings. For example, the Academy of American Poets offers videos of poets reciting their work; organizations such as Amnesty International offer video reports; and many governmental sites now include recorded speeches and video updates.

Synthesizing Sources

As we explained in the previous section, information does not come free of biases and worldviews. Information usually comes in the form of theories, arguments, and hypotheses. In other words, research often involves swimming in others' opinions. Good researchers swim well. They understand how to read, question, and accept the ideas around them. Bad researchers grasp at chunks of statistical and factual debris.

It is also important to remember that writers rarely find sources that neatly overlap, or completely agree with, their own positions. In fact, research should not be seen as a process of seeking out agreement, but as a process of bringing together various kinds of information, viewpoints, and arguments. Sometimes, writers do not find any sources that share their position on a specific topic. Instead, they discover sources that partially overlap in some way. All of these sources, then, help give dimension to the writer's ideas. In Figure 15.1, notice that supporting evidence (for instance, some fact or statistic that backs up the writer's stance) is only one possibility.

For example, consider the topic *light pollution.* Imagine that a writer begins the research process with a vague sense of her position—that too much light hinders most people from seeing the night sky. A quick search of the web and periodical databases will likely yield some sources that share her position.

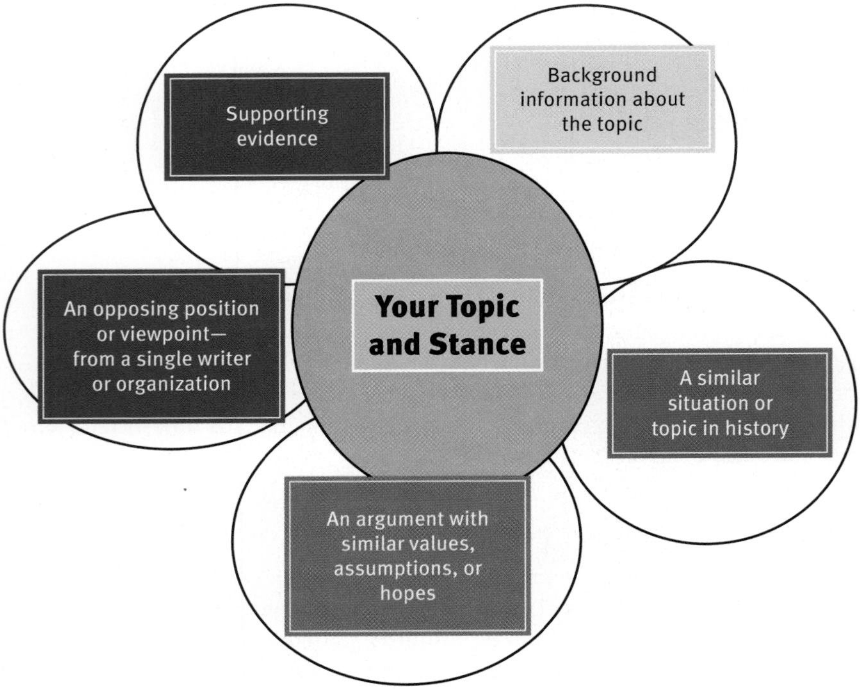

John Metz

Figure 15.1

She might find statistics on the number of Americans who cannot see constellations other than the Big Dipper. And she might also find background information about the topic: when it became a concern for astronomers, or how much it impacts plant life. But then she can go further. In some invention work, the writer may discover that the night sky is important because it bestows a sense of wonder and humility in people. In her research, she could seek out sources that celebrate the power of wonder—a sociologist who argues that civilizations without a deep sense of wonder quickly fade from history, or a religious scholar who argues for the value of humility. Perhaps she even finds some rationale for parking lots that are lit all night from a major retailer. She then develops a counterargument to address that rationale. In her reading, she might also discover a similar but related issue—noise pollution and its effects on agriculture. Although this information about noise pollution may not directly support her main claim, it may show a trend in history—that people have always battled the slow invasion of technology into the natural world. All of these sources could help develop an insightful and rich argument. Figure 15.2 represents these sources in relation to the main topic, light pollution.

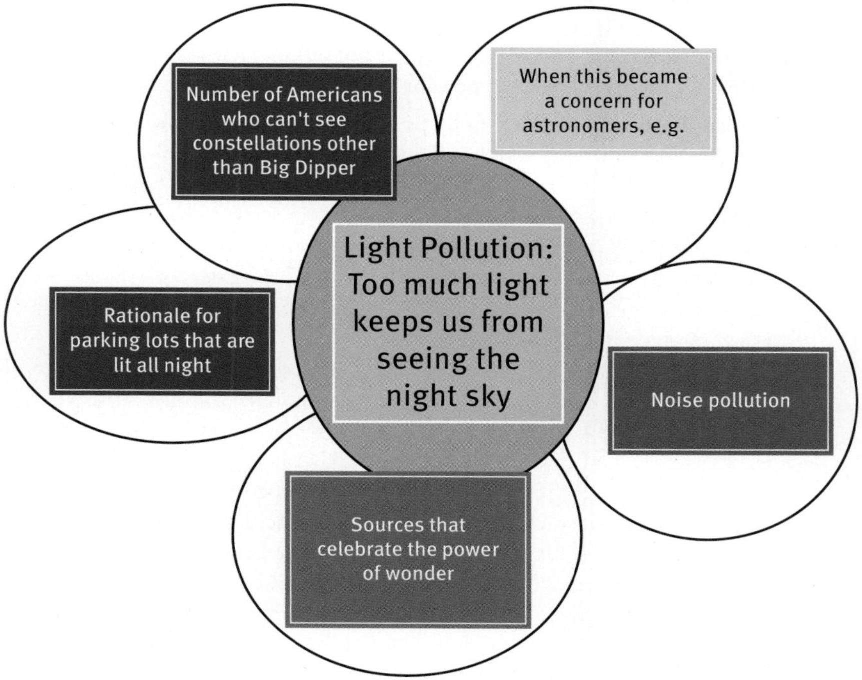

Figure 15.2

Synthesis literally means *bringing together.* So synthesizing sources involves bringing a range of voices and texts together. Academic researchers know they may find closely related sources—for instance, three articles on the local effects of light pollution. But they also know they may find no closely related sources or merely a smattering of texts that are distantly related. In this common scenario, the researcher has to bridge gaps between and among sources. And bridging those gaps often creates exciting insights. When researchers begin writing—formulating the relationships among sources—they often create nuances in their own thinking and discover dimensions of the topic itself.

In the following passage from her essay "Cruelty, Civility, and Other Weighty Matters" (page 243), Ann Marie Paulin assembles a range of sources. Notice how the shaded passages help establish connections among her sources. Paulin does the work of bringing the sources into her own line of reasoning:

> And most diets don't work. An essay by Rebecca Puhl, Ph.D. and Chelsea Heuer, MPH, in the *American Journal of Public Health,* cites studies which found:
>
> > Most weight losses are not maintained and individuals regain weight after completing treatment. Patients who have lost weight through lifestyle modification typically regain 30% to 35% of their lost weight during the year following treatment, and regain most (if not all) of their lost weight within five years. ("Obesity Stigma: Important Considerations" 1021)
>
> The authors go on to quote from a study by Mann, et al: "Dieters who gain back more weight than they lost may very well be the norm, rather than an unlucky minority" (qtd. in Puhl and Heuer 1021). My point here is not to argue that overweight people should not try to lose weight for health reasons. Indeed, even a modest weight loss of ten percent of a person's body weight is beneficial to one's health (Puhl and Heuer, "Obesity Stigma: Important Consideration" 1021). But such modest weight loss, while healthy, is rarely enough to earn a person fashionably thin status. And despite what the cultural messages suggest, most of us fat folks are trying to eat more sensibly, but the environment does play a role. In a culture where most of us are rushed from work to classes to other activities, the temptation to grab fast food is huge. Sugary or fatty foods are often available in grab and go packages that are so much easier to take to work or eat in the car than making a healthy snack. And, there is evidence to suggest we may even be wired to prefer junk food. Brownell and colleagues, in an essay in *Health Affairs,* cite studies which show: "Animals given access to food high in sugar and fat—even when healthy food is freely available—consume calorie-dense, nutrient-poor food in abundance, gain a great deal of weight, and exhibit deteriorating health" (379). I know, I know. We aren't rats. We are thinking beings, but this article goes on to point out that it is not so different for people: "Research has shown consistently that people moving from less to more obese countries gain weight, and those moving to less obese countries lose weight" (379).

So we are surrounded by a culture, even an infrastructure, that encourages obesity, yet the culture also breeds a prejudice against fat people. Various articles and news magazine programs have reported that Americans of all sizes make far more than simple aesthetic judgments when they look at a fat person. Fat people are assumed to be lazy, stupid, ugly, lacking in self-esteem and pride, devoid of self-control, and stuffed full of a host of other unpleasant qualities that have nothing to do with the size of a person's belly or thighs. But, as anyone who has ever been the victim of such prejudice can tell you, the impact such foolish notions have is real and harmful. For example, Marilyn Wann, in her book *Fat! So?,* cites an experiment in which "[r]esearchers placed two fake personal ads, one for a woman described as '50 pounds overweight' and the other for a woman described as a drug addict. The drug addict received 79 percent of the responses" (59). So, in spite of the agony addiction can cause to the addict and those who love her, people would rather get romantically involved with an addict than a fat person. And not much has changed. In a 2008 article, "The Stigma of Obesity: A Review and Update," Puhl and Heuer report:

> One study asked college students (N=449) to rank order six pictures of hypothetical sexual partners, including an obese partner, a healthy partner, and partners with various disabilities (including a partner in a wheelchair, missing an arm, with a mental illness, or described as having a history of sexually transmitted diseases. Both men and women ranked the obese person as the least desirable sexual partner compared to the others (10).

While it is certainly good news to see that people can look beyond disabilities, such as a wheelchair or a missing arm, and see the value of the whole human being, it is distressing that Americans refuse to do the same for a person's weight. Why would anyone want to date someone who will land them in the STD clinic? How dangerous is that? And yet, such a person is clearly seen as a better romantic choice than a heavy person. Here is a case where weight prejudice is certainly more dangerous to the person with the prejudice than it is to the fat person.

Assignment: Summarizing, Analyzing, and Synthesizing Sources

Much academic research is driven by a need to understand what others think—to know how scholars are debating and probing a topic. In others words, academic researchers are not always (or even often!) driven by the desire to find proof for their own convictions. They are, instead, out to discover the tensions and curiosities about a topic. This assignment focuses on that discovery process. It is designed to help writers explore the boundaries of a topic, to find multiple sources, bring them together, and develop new insights. The goal is not to prove a point or reinforce one's own opinion but to explore how other writers have addressed a topic—what others believe, assume, or imagine. The following steps will help guide you through that process:

1. **Search for Sources:** First, consider a topic—perhaps one that you have already written about. Draw a circle in the middle of a page with your topic and stance (if you have one). Then, in separate circles, write out possibilities for the following: background information; supporting evidence for your position; similar situations or topics in history; the values, assumptions, and hopes underlying your position; and opposing positions and the people or groups that might hold them. Use those circles, then, to generate keywords for searching databases or the Internet.
2. **Summarize the Content:** After finding two or more sources, summarize each. Briefly describe the main idea, or thesis, of the sources. (Be careful not to blur away the particular insight of the source.)
3. **Analyze the Context:** Next, analyze the content and context of the sources. Avoid evaluating the worth or value. In other words, avoid arguing that the sources are good, bad, credible, agreeable, and so forth. Instead, explain how the sources fit into a broader conversation about the topic. Consider the following questions:
   - Who is the intended audience? Scholars? The general public? Any particular group?
   - How do the sources speak to the audience? How do the sources address the values of their audience?
   - What do the writers seem to value? What ideas or principles or hopes do you detect?
   - How do the sources deal with the audience's potential questions, concerns, or doubts? Do they ever address potential concerns or doubts directly?
4. **Synthesize Ideas:** Synthesis involves explaining all the ways sources relate to one another—how they support, inform, or oppose one another. Synthesis can also involve the relationship between sources and the writer's own thinking about the topic. In other words, you might explain how the sources respond to, rub against, undermine, extend, challenge, or reinforce your own ideas. Consider the following questions:
   - How do the sources overlap or contradict? How do they approach the topic differently? Beyond the obvious claims and opinions, what assumptions or unstated values seem to overlap or conflict?
   - How do the sources contribute to your understanding of the topic or your ability to engage in this conversation?
   - What further questions do the sources provoke?
   - How do the sources reveal some layer of the topic that you did not imagine or discuss prior to researching?
   - What perspective do the sources offer to you? For instance, do they address some psychological or philosophical layer that you did not imagine?

Sample Synthesis

Exploring Caffeine Views

Jim Crockett

In his essay, "Mugged" (Chapter 3, page 72), Jim Crockett explores the relationship between himself and his coffee mug. As he explores the meaning of that relationship, he suggests in one passage that he may be addicted to caffeine. Although that is not the main assertion in his essay, it gave him a springboard into research. In the following essay, Crockett illustrates three critical moves in academic research: (1) He briefly summarizes two sources related to his topic; (2) he analyzes the content and context of each source; and (3) he synthesizes the sources and his own prior thoughts on the topic. In other words, he marries sources and his own understanding of the topic. This marriage of ideas generates new insights. Notice that Crockett does not use the sources to uphold his own initial thoughts. In fact, in the final section of this essay, he corrects part of his prior thinking.

In his magazine article "Caffeine Addiction Is a Mental Disorder, Doctors Say," George Studeville explains that caffeine withdrawal may be officially classified as a psychological disorder. Studeville describes how Roland Griffith, a professor at Johns Hopkins, makes the case for the "syndrome" of caffeine withdrawal. In her article, "Is Caffeine Addictive?—A Review of Literature," Sally Satel concludes that caffeine does not meet the criteria for an addictive drug. While people commonly use the term *addiction* for heavy caffeine use, Satel argues that mild and temporary withdrawal symptoms do not warrant equating the drug with others, like heroin, that are harmful, even ruinous, to individuals and society.

These articles, then, seem to oppose one another: Griffith assumes that caffeine should be considered an addictive drug, while Satel argues that consistent use and mild temporary withdrawal symptoms do not meet the DSM (Diagnostic and Statistical Manual of Mental Disorders) standards for genuine chemical addiction.

Studeville writes for a popular magazine. His readers, then, are not familiar with the jargon of the discipline or its ongoing professional debates. And Studeville himself is a reporter rather than a doctor or professor. His purpose is to inform readers about ongoing research—and a particular argument from Griffith, a professor of behavioral biology and neuroscience. His voice is informal and even a bit dramatic. The title offers the most absurd or extreme characterization of Griffith's argument. "Mental disorder," for common readers, suggests a kind of pathology, a chronic condition. The article offers Griffith's position on caffeine addiction and withdrawal, but it offers no opposing claims. The argument goes unchallenged, uncontested. And according to the title, "doctors" (all or most?) seem to say that Griffith's argument is correct.

Satel is an MD and researcher. She takes on the opposition directly—explaining why some people classify caffeine as an addictive drug. Her section on "methodological problems" reveals some of the flaws and hiccups in this type of research.

The researchers in both articles (Griffith and Satel) seem to value accuracy and a scientific method. Griffith says that he launched his study because "doctors and other health professionals have had no scientifically based framework for diagnosing the syndrome." Satel calls for her colleagues to make fine distinctions in previous studies—and to discount conclusions drawn from studies that lack reliability and credibility. But they differ in an important way—Griffith's argument calls for the collapse of categories: If one cup of coffee creates "physical dependence" (or anything like it), then coffee contains a dependent drug. Satel wants to make distinctions: Some drugs are ruinous to the individual's life, while other drugs (like caffeine) merely create a mild form habituation. Griffith wants to erase degree and difference. Satel suggests that degree of dependence is all the difference in the world.

When We Talk About Drugs and Addictions and Habits, What is the Battle?

As Satel explains, dependence on a drug comes from a need to acquire "physiological homeostasis"—or physical stability. This is, perhaps, different from my acknowledgement about coffee: that drinking it is a daily grounding ritual, a practice that works against the social forces. I suggest that our culture, our *econoculture,* pulls us away from ourselves—that it has left behind its roots in the wilderness. Instead of intimacy and simplicity, we have to blast through everyday life. (The other drivers looked at me angrily—*get the hell out of my way!*—while I meekly tried to rescue my helpless little mug at the busy intersection.) The two sources, and particularly Satel, raise this question: When we talk about drugs and addictions and habits, what is the battle? In my "Mugged" essay, I suggest that the battle might be psychological or philosophical rather than chemical. I focus on the act of drinking, the ritual of carrying my old familiar mug in a society that invites me to buy something new every time I turn around. That's a big battle! Sure, it's not physiologically addictive . . . and maybe I'm not really addicted to caffeine. Maybe that's just a common way of putting it. If Satel's right, after all, I'd just get a headache if I quit. But if I left my mug behind, if I bought (into) the plastic/paper cup world around me, maybe I'd be joining another realm of addiction—a bigger and more ruinous one.

And I don't mean this metaphorically. I mean it for real. I'm thinking, on this morning, of the recent government bailouts: $750 billion to keep the world of super-consumption chugging along. Rather than put serious resources into education, into health care, into the crumbling infrastructure, into alternative energy, we have to inject huge amounts into a habit. And the Treasury Secretary says that the injection will likely create more bad behavior and that we shouldn't monitor it too closely. (The main thing: Get the junkies their fix! And hurry!) There's nothing we can do. We're stuck in a violent cycle. And this resonates with my point about *econoculture.* We're all now working to support the addicts on Wall Street and their political mules in Congress. If the addicts don't get their fix, they'll crumble and the whole economy will shake.

Maybe this is going too far. But Satel's essay makes me think about addiction in social terms. She says that it's not enough for us to simply think about the withdrawal. Instead, we have to think about *harm.* Do the drug and withdrawal hurt the individual and the society? This is where Satel and I overlap, and where I end up wondering: What kinds of addiction am I participating in? What kinds of withdrawal? What addictive behavior does my life encourage? How do I get out of those behaviors? Can I? What personal choices can I make if I am not in control of the drug and its effects?

Works Cited

Satel, Sally. "Is Caffeine Addictive?—A Review of Literature." *The American Journal of Drug and Alcohol Abuse*, vol. 32, no. 4, 2006, pp. 493–502. *Academic Search Premier*, doi: 10.1080/00952990600918965.

Studeville, George. "Caffeine Addiction Is a Mental Disorder, Doctors Say." *National Geographic*, 19 Jan. 2005, news.nationalgeographic.com/news/2005/01/0119_050119_ngm_caffeine.html.

Evaluating Sources

Sources should be relevant, reliable, credible, timely, and diverse. Sources that do not adhere to these criteria can diminish an academic project and even damage an author's credibility.

Relevance

A relevant source is appropriately related to the writer's topic. A writer's first inclination may be to find those sources that directly support his or her thesis statement; that is, sources that speak directly about the writer's particular subject and that espouse his or her particular stance on it. However, such an approach limits the intellectual possibilities—especially because the research process might develop or change how a writer thinks about a subject. Sources do much more than back up someone's opinion. They might help to explain the complexities of the subject, the history of the subject, the writer's position, or even opposition to the writer's position.

Because sources can be used in various ways, one that seems only remotely related to your project might, in fact, be extremely valuable in the long run. Consider the following example: A writer is researching voting practices in his community and wants to make a claim about low voter turnouts in recent elections. He finds a newspaper article about a local school scheduled for demolition that had previously been used as a voting location. This article at first might seem unhelpful. After all, how does this particular school relate to voting trends in the community? It may, in fact, suggest a great deal about voting. That is, one of the factors in voter turnout is proximity to voting locations. This article might, therefore, show a trend in a declining number of voting locations. The same writer might find a government web page about the history of voting in his state. At first this source may not seem valuable because the writer is primarily concerned with recent voter activity. However, the history may provide some clues about the system itself, about the reasons for establishing Tuesdays as election days, about the number of constituents in a given area—all potentially valuable factors in understanding the complexities of recent voter turnout.

Reliability

Reliability refers to the quality of information in the source. A reliable source uses verifiable information and helps readers trace the sources of information. The most reliable sources document the information they offer. (That's why academic audiences value some type of formal documentation, such as in-text citations and a bibliographical list.) In effect, formal documentation says to readers, "Here is the path to relevant research."

For published books and academic journal articles, reliability may not be an issue because such sources endure a process of critical peer review. However, many publications do not have peer reviews. Most magazines and newspapers also do not have room to include formal documentation. Their editorial policies exclude in-text documentation and Works Cited lists.

But there are other ways for writers to signal reliability, such as an appositive phrase. In the following examples, the underlined appositive phrases lend some reliability to the information. Even though the passages lack formal documentation (a formal link to a particular text), they give readers specific cues about the nature of the source:

> Kalle Lasn, a cofounder of the Canadian media criticism and environmentalist magazine *Adbusters*, explains how dependence on television first occurred and continues today each time we turn on our sets.

> Deirdre Mahoney, a professor of writing at Northwestern Michigan College and a scholar of rhetoric, argues that online courses are significantly more challenging for college students than traditional face-to-face courses.

Notice that the information after the name indicates the source's credentials. When a formal Works Cited list is not possible, writers in many publications use such phrases to document the reliability of their information.

Remember that most popular magazines are guided by a primary force: money. Editorial policies are driven by the need to make information attractive to consumers. Therefore, claims may be inflated, mitigating details may be played down, and generalizations are common. Also remember that magazines are funded in large part by corporate advertising and so are not apt to publish articles that might compromise relationships with those advertisers. For these reasons, researchers should always be cautious about quoting popular magazines (or even news magazines) as unbiased truth.

Credibility

Credibility refers to the internal logic of the information presented in the source. A credible source does not attempt to hide its biases or its argument. It makes logical claims and helps readers follow its logic. If the source offers an argument, it makes its position clear and reveals its biases. (Of course, it is free of logical fallacies.) If the source attempts to inform rather than persuade, it does not spin information or conceal its biases.

The question of credibility may also involve the source's author. Some authors have more credentials than others. However, a book or article by a well-known author should not necessarily outweigh one by a less familiar writer. Many academic and professional writers are not necessarily big names in popular media but are well respected within small communities because they have spent years researching a particularly focused issue. For instance, Patricia Limerick, a highly respected historian, has written a great deal about the American West. Although her name is not recognizable to the general public, it is often noted in history scholarship.

But how would a researcher know this? For instance, if you were not a historian, how would you know about Patricia Limerick's scholarly status? Fortunately, online search engines and databases have made many authors and their bodies of work instantaneously accessible.

First, most periodicals and online news outlets hyperlink author names. If you click on the name, you'll see other works by the same author in that publication. Second, scholarly databases such as Academic Search Complete hyperlink author names as well. If you click on the name, you'll see other works by the same author from *any publication* in the database. Third, you can always Google an author—and here is where plenty of scholars do, in fact, rely on Wikipedia and other open-access sites. Cross-referencing an author name can turn up a list of her works, the sources of publication (magazines, journals, or presses that published her work), and even debates surrounding her works. In short, an online search can show how an author has been received, celebrated, or even condemned by a particular readership. (For more guidelines on such searches, see the next section, "Evaluating Online Sources.")

Timeliness

A significant concern in academic research is the date of the sources. It is important that claims are supported with sources that are not obsolete or behind the times. But this criterion depends upon the issue and the claim being made. Some claims require very current sources. For example, a writer making a claim about the marriage laws would be wise to consider sources published only within two to three years of her research. (Because the laws have changed and continue to create significant public debate, sources that are ten years old may be antiquated.) However, that same writer might also want to discuss the concept or development of equality in the United States and discover a valuable text by a nineteenth-century philosopher. In this case, the writer would use current texts to support claims about time-sensitive topics and would refer to an older source to express an issue that stretches beyond a particular era.

Diversity

Diversity refers to the variety of sources a writer uses. Good writers seek to develop their projects and their perspectives with different voices and media. Writers develop their views on a subject from a range of sources—much in the same way that we develop our views on religion or marriage or education from taking in and making sense of information from various sources. For example, our religious beliefs may have been influenced primarily by our parents, but other sources, such as childhood friends, books, movies, and music, also influence us. Even views that oppose our own are important, because they help us to define the borders of our beliefs.

Writers should hope to read and synthesize various sources about their topics; otherwise, their perspectives, and ultimately their positions, can be limited. This means that writers should explore *different perspectives.* They should not seek out conformity of opinion but diversity of thought. For this reason, writers often attempt to seek out different types of sources. They hope to view their topics from as many angles as possible—from different scholarly communities and from popular or mainstream perspectives.

Evaluating Online Sources

Back in the 1990s, when the Internet was first getting traction, teachers and scholars made a clean distinction between print and online sources. That was an important distinction: Although most conventional content (books, journals, academic studies, and so on) was still printed and distributed by hand, the Internet was home to any kind of content whatsoever. Because it was mostly ungoverned, the Internet had no conventional ways to filter information. Anyone with a mouse and a little know-how could publish. (A bored seventh-grader could create a homepage that resembled—at least on the surface—a NASA site.) But twenty years have made a big difference. Now, almost everything that counts as a published source in academic writing is—or will soon be—digital and online. So it is increasingly irrelevant to make a distinction between print and online sources—at least when it comes to evaluation. In other words, an article published by *Time, Nursing Science Quarterly*, or *The New Yorker* is no different in terms of credibility or reliability whether you retrieve it in print or online. However, the shift to online sources has created issues that academic researchers must understand:

1. **Authorless-ness:** Some information on the Internet is *unattributed*. In other words, it has no author. Passages, charts, even entire articles are passed around, forwarded, and reforwarded, with no reference to their origin. Anyone could have generated the information for whatever purpose. This creates a credibility problem. And if the information cannot be cross-referenced, it also creates a reliability problem.

   What to do: Most librarians, researchers, and instructors suggest using only texts (whether they are articles, blogs, reports, or tweets) that can be traced to an author or publisher. In other words, you should be able to identify the author: the individual, company, group, or organization responsible for generating the information.

2. **Misinformation Blitz:** Misinformation is nothing new. Textbooks, history books, television news channels, and even government reports have fumbled facts, mischaracterized situations, and skewed numbers. But with the invention of social media, the speed of misinformation has dramatically increased. Now, erroneous information can spread across the globe in a matter of minutes. And once false information has been widely distributed, it becomes its own kind of reality that is difficult or impossible to counter. In fact, a number of studies have shown that corrections to misinformation—if they do get published and distributed via social media—reach *less than half* of the original audience. For instance, imagine that someone tweets erroneous information about a murder trial. That tweet may reach 100,000 people within a few hours. And if the original tweeter discovered that his information was wrong, the correction may only reach 40,000 people—and at a slower pace. In short, misinformation often travels more quickly and more widely than corrections.

   What to do: Avoid using information that comes via social media—such as Twitter or Facebook. If something seems compelling, scan the Internet for competing, corrected, or simply different information about the topic in hand.

3. **Marketplace Bias:** Bias also must be considered. Because the purpose of many sites is to sell something, they may provide information that is slanted. Of course, bias in itself is not bad. Bias is only negative when it is concealed. If a source is trying to sell something, its claims should not be accepted as unbiased truth. And if the source asks for personal information, it may have an alternative agenda. Although some online sources (such as newspapers) require you to register to enter the site, many other sources may ask for personal information so they can market products or services to you.

   What to do: First, always determine the author and publisher of information. If the publisher is a for-profit business (for instance, a website ending in .com), ask yourself if money may have influenced the nature of the information. Second, try to cross-reference claims, facts, or data. If possible, seek out information in not-for-profit publications, such as academic journals. Finally, do not give a website your personal information if you simply want an article. Instead, visit your institution's library and request the article through a database.

4. **Source Confusion:** Now more than ever, it is important for researchers to understand the differences among source types. A blog post, for instance, is different from a traditional article. The two sources come to publication through different processes: Although an article may go through several drafts, with input from various staff writers, and get clearance from at least one or two editors, a blog post may go straight from the writer's screen to the Internet. Even a blog published by an esteemed news organization might go through very little editing or fact-checking. In short, the two sources might be entirely different but look entirely the same.

   This is not to say that a blog—by definition—is less reliable or credible. It may simply offer the kind of argument, interpretation, or angle that a report or journalistic article does not. Imagine the following statement appearing on a news site: "The situation in Fallujah is a catastrophe." Such a claim could come from an unnamed blogger, a journalist in Iraq, the Joint Chief of Staff, or a retired general. Good readers/researchers will always know the origin of such a statement, but even good researchers have to keep their radar on high. If they know the type of source, they can better trace where the information comes from, who's saying what, and for what reasons.

   What to do: Know your sources. In fact, use labels in your own notes—and try to avoid broad terms such as *website*. Instead, try to determine if you are reading a blog, a feature article from a news site, a report on a government site, and so on.

5. **Abandoned Sites:** In a typical scenario, a student group develops an advocacy website. Over the course of a semester, the site gets loaded with data, statistics, and stories about a key issue. The site stays active for a semester while individuals from the group continue to update the information. Over the summer, the group disintegrates and the site is forgotten, but it stays on the university server. Three years go by and the site still stands. Although it looks interesting and vibrant, the information is outdated.

   As we explain on page 486, timeliness depends upon the nature of the information. Some ideas, assertions, concepts, and theories stay relevant for years or even centuries. But other information can quickly change. If a website deals with time-sensitive topics and does not stay current, it may as well be a dead link.

What to do: If you use information from a website, simply make sure that you can find a date when the site or page itself was last updated. If you cannot find a date, consider cross-referencing the information or even try to contact the site's administrator.

To evaluate the content of websites, ask the following questions:

- Who sponsors this site, and what credibility do they have?
- Is the site attempting to sell something? If so, how might that impact the nature of the information?
- Does the site ask for personal information? (Does it state the purpose of this request?)
- Are statistics/data supported with appropriately documented sources? If not, how can you trace the information and cross-reference it with another source?
- Is the information presented up to date? (When was the site last updated?)

Assignment: Evaluating a Source

Evaluating literally means calling out the value of something. When we evaluate sources, we draw attention to their value—not according to how much we agree with them but according to specific criteria. In other words, evaluating is not about praising sources that support our biases but explaining how sources stack up according to categorical standards: relevance, reliability, credibility, timeliness, and diversity (pages 484–486). For this assignment, find and save a particular source—one that you can read closely. Develop a brief formal evaluation. For each criterion, consider the following key questions:

Relevance

- Does the source speak directly to my specific topic?
- How does the source help to clarify some broader or related point?
- How does the source help to explain the history or complexities of the topic?

Reliability

- Does the source offer formal documentation? Do other sources check out? Are they available?
- If there is no formal documentation, does the source acknowledge authorities with related credentials or qualifications?
- What about the source itself? Is it published by a reputable organization?

Credibility

- Does the source make an argument? If so, are the claims well supported and well reasoned? Do you sense any logical fallacies?
- Does the source attempt to conceal its biases?
- Do you have reason to question the author's credibility? (If so, do a quick web or database search to see if the author has written for or is referenced in other publications.) Is your reason for questioning the author's credibility reasonable? (Are you unnecessarily suspicious?)

Timeliness

- Is this a time-sensitive topic?
- If this is a time-sensitive topic, why might the information in the source be either timely or out of date?

Diversity

- Do my sources represent a variety of viewpoints?
- How do the sources represent different value or belief systems?

"Drink Earlier, Drink Less": A Source Evaluation

The following essay evaluates a source—in this case, a magazine article by Bond Pittman, published in June 2013. The first paragraph explains the topic and argumentative approach: We're searching for the cause of binge drinking. The second paragraph summarizes Pittman's article and explains its relevance to our project. The next five paragraphs deal primarily with credibility because that is the most complex criterion for an argumentative article that relies primarily on appeals and examples. More importantly, credibility generates the most concerns or questions when it comes to Pittman's article. The final paragraph deals with timeliness and even reinforces Pittman's relevance. Of course, not every essay that evaluates a source should be organized in this fashion. So much depends upon the topic and the source in question. But this essay illustrates one common and sound way to generate an initial draft.

Binge drinking among college students won't seem to go away. Despite a range of initiatives and campus policies, college students keep on consuming alcohol in dangerous spasms of excess. Plenty of policies, parent groups, and laws aim to manage the behavior by managing alcohol—i.e., trying to keep it as far away from campuses and underage students as possible. But alcohol itself is not the cause of excess. There's something else—something before the alcohol even becomes available—that causes such widespread and persistent binging.

In June of 2013, *The American Spectator* published an essay on binge drinking by Bond Pittman, a senior at Hillsdale College in Michigan. His was the winning entry in the magazine's writing contest: "Each semester, *The American Spectator* holds its college essay contest, an opportunity for undergraduates to show their writing skills and sound off on a pressing issue. Our most recent topic, 'The pros and cons of binge drinking,' elicited this essay by an up-and-coming student from Hillsdale College."

Pittman certainly comes down against binge drinking. He offers some not-so-surprising information about physical effects: weight gain, anxiety, alcohol poisoning, and death. And he argues, in his final passages, for moderation—for restraint even when the surrounding social forces urge indulgence and abandon. But what's most relevant (for this project) is Pittman's analysis of cause. He spends much of his essay exploring the social and institutional forces that cultivate excess. Even though he doesn't enumerate them, he names three: First, he explains the general mainstream attraction to excess:

> We live in a civilization of bingers. Teenagers commonly indulge in irregular and excessive sleeping hiatuses. Credit card companies make fortunes on people's inability to curtail shopping splurges. And it's rare to find victors of the one-potato-chip challenge. I down at least two bowl-sized mugs of Dunkin' every morning, and I waited to watch nine hours of *Downton Abbey* in one sitting because I couldn't bear the week-long wait between episodes.

In other words, the culture at large supports super-consumption—and Pittman, himself, is in the crowd. Second, he argues that the federally stipulated drinking age (twenty-one) "removed

The American Spectator, June 2013, http://spectator.org/articles/55591/drink-earlier-drink-less

[alcohol] from the civic domain and unintentionally given it a clandestine appeal." Third, he blames a lack of role models. His generation, he says, admires no one for his or her noble restraint.

Pittman's credibility depends on his own experience—more specifically, on *the way he explains* his own experience. After all, Pittman is a senior at a midwestern college. He is literally in the middle of this phenomenon, and so his testimony is crucial. Fortunately, the most detailed and coherent passage of the essay focuses on his experience:

> I discovered just how accessible the partying scene was to underage students only hours after my parents dropped me off for freshman orientation. My first night as a college student, I found myself at an off-campus house party packed with upperclassmen and a handful of other freshmen. We were told that free alcohol was available for us. I stood in the middle of the room, squashed between a girl's sequined back and a football player's sweaty arm. I knew I could throw myself into this sea of reckless abandon, or I could stay on solid ground. It was tempting to jump, but after I found my way out of the middle of the crowd, I turned and looked at the spectacle around me. The faces were all those of strangers (no one cared so much as to ask me my name). Everyone was either already drunk or intending to be, and soon.

This passage, even standing on its own, sheds light on binge drinking. It is a kind of exposé about student life. And much of its power comes from what isn't said: the smooth transition from orientation to party. The passage is persuasive not only because of the "reckless abandon" it describes but also for the simple facts of the narrative: Within hours of arriving at college, Pittman is surrounded by free alcohol and serious drinking.

Throughout the essay, Pittman makes some broad claims against his generation and mainstream culture at large, but those claims seem, at the least, in line with his experiences. If he's opinionated, he's not trying to hide it, nor is he trying to scorn his peers. But his credibility does take a hit—not because he's a mere college student or novice writer. (In fact, his writing is clever, engaging, and often careful in its reach.) His credibility diminishes because of his political allegiance.

The American Spectator is openly conservative. Not that there's anything wrong with conservatism, but this conservatism often borders on prejudice and bigotry. In the June issue, along with Pittman's article, writers and longtime contributors rail against gay marriage (that will be, according to George Neumayr, "imposed" on all Americans), openly make fun of President Obama, and offer goofy caricatures of anyone they can deem a liberal. In short, the June 2013 issue upholds a tradition of excessive bias that fills mainstream news magazines across the political continuum. So it is difficult to attribute credibility to *any* text published on its site or in its pages. As with so many similar magazines, its audience expects pot shots and gross portrayals of those who might disagree.

Bond does come out, in his first line, as an adherent to political conservatism. He begins with reigning queen of the American right:

> "You gotta be thinking Sam Adams, not drinking Sam Adams." Sarah Palin gave this advice to the college students attending this year's Conservative Political Action Conference. Just another round fired from her stockpile of one-liners, but her remark was well aimed: College students drink. A lot.

Palin is, then, left behind for the remainder of the essay, and so her presence serves only to announce political allegiance. From there, Pittman's political conservatism shows up in his not-so-veiled hostility toward the federal government:

> If all parents and children followed the letter of the law, most Americans coming of age after 1984 (when the federal government blackmailed the states by withholding federal highway funds if they refused to raise the drinking age to 21) would have their first experience drinking alcohol not in the controlled, safe environment of a home, but in a bar with other freshly turned 21-year-olds.

This is conservative boilerplate: Laws from the federal government are heavy-handed and always against the sanctity of home life. In a more moderate magazine—perhaps one not so comfortable with the shared notion that federal government is always bad—such an historical reference may have been qualified or characterized in less biased terms. And there's one other instance when Pittman seems careless or at least deaf to a broader audience. It happens in his description of the party: "Some girls," he says, "had mascara streaked across their faces, whether due to the hot, sticky atmosphere or from crying, I don't know." Certainly, responsible readers can imagine how sorrow and injury go swirling about a drunken college party, but it's difficult to imagine, from an informed and careful understanding, a roomful of college-age women both crying and dancing. (In short, there's a terrifically naïve argument about women lurking in the off-hand guess at their smeared makeup.)

But the good news for Pittman is that he is not a consistent contributor to *The American Spectator*. He does not make a living fanning the flames of political hostility. Unlike the usual contributors (such as Ben Stein, William Tucker, George Neumayr), Bond does not swing at his political enemies. In fact, he may not even have them yet. More importantly, Pittman does offer insight on the topic. He knows something about "those angsty years" of college. Despite some sloppy characterizations (of women and governments), his insights are often lucid—as in the following passage where he reaches beyond the clichés of his peers:

> I have asked people who regularly drink in order to get drunk why they do so, and the answer is generally the same: "It relaxes me to have more fun and helps me to express myself more freely in social situations." But the modern partying scene is the antithesis of community. It involves "dancing" in which human persons are not the essential participants; certain attached body parts are. It presses drinking to the point where the cognitive person behind the red Solo cup is blotted out, and the best nights are often considered to be those that cannot be remembered.

Such passages reveal layers beyond unhealthy behavior. They show something about an unhealthy worldview—more so than a mountain of statistics and legal references. In short, Pittman's firsthand and wide-eyed observation of his peers offers serious insights that more distant (older) writers may not willingly conjure.

Finally, it's easy to say that Pittman's essay is timely. But what's interesting and unfortunate is that it will stay timely for years to come. While binge drinking may find new tools and fashionable avenues on social media (such as the recent NekNominate game), it seems to be firmly rooted in college culture.

16 Integrating and Documenting Sources

Rob Howard/CORBIS

Integrating Sources

Sources can add dimension, insight, and depth to your own ideas. They can also add a layer of difficulty. As sources are integrated, sound organizational principles must still apply: Ideas should remain focused, paragraphs must be coherent, and your own line of reasoning should be apparent to readers. Also, information from sources should be blended smoothly into the text so that readers (1) understand its relationship to the writer's own ideas, and (2) know where the information came from. The challenge is to maintain coherence and flow while integrating other voices and opinions. The best way to achieve coherence is to develop an overall plan for your essay before drafting. That is, develop a general strategy for your organization and decide how the sources will function in that plan.

Source Functions

This section explains four common functions for sources in an essay. As you examine the following passages, notice how the writers set up the source's ideas and even provide further commentary on the source.

Sources That Support Your Thesis Writers won't always find sources that directly support their thesis statements. But when it happens, they often select the most powerful statements and quote directly. For example, in her argument against intensive computer use in elementary school classrooms, Elizabeth Bohnhorst (from Chapter 8) integrates several quotations from a source:

> Now, what could possibly be wrong with such a sophisticated device for learning?
>
> In reality, "thirty years of research on educational technology has produced almost no evidence of a clear link between using computers in the early grades and improving learning," states Michael Dertouzus, director of the MIT Laboratory for Computer Science. In fact, evidence of hazardous effects of frequent use of computers in young children is overwhelming. They do little to promote a healthy childhood. "Computers are perhaps the most acute symptom of the rush to end childhood. The national drive to computerize schools, from kindergarten on up, emphasizes only one of the many human capacities, one that naturally develops quite late—analytic, abstract thinking—and aims to jump start it prematurely," continues Dertouzus.

Sources That Support a Premise A premise is one step in your line of reasoning—one logical progression toward your main idea (or thesis). Often writers find a source that supports only a single step. That source may not be related at all to your overall topic, but it may provide some key backing—at a key moment. For example, in her essay (from Chapter 12), Deirdre Mahoney argues that students should learn how to write in the margins of books while they read. In the following passage, Mahoney develops a particular point in her line of reasoning, and she uses a source, Maryanne Wolf, to back up this particular point:

> So, I think the problem is clear. Our system of educating, parenting, and nurturing unwittingly conspires to ensure students' disciplined detachment from words on the page. In other words, creating disengaged adults begins early. My proposal is simple and not particularly original, but I'll reiterate it nonetheless. Those of us committed to raising and teaching need to raise and teach differently. For starters, we need to insist that from the earliest stages of literacy acquisition all humans—especially the tiniest in size and age—be invited to scribble fervently as they explore books. If we take into account the opening statement in Maryanne Wolf's *Proust and the Squid: The Story and Science of the Reading Brain,* it becomes apparent that humans could use an assist. Wolf avows forebodingly, "We were never born to read" (3). Ditto for writing. Out of necessity, it seems, resourceful adults looking for ways to enhance overtaxed memories found their way to literate practices. In doing so, the human brain began to evolve in ways probably not intended in the original blueprint. That is, in the process of teaching oneself to read and write, the brain began to reinvent itself, thus enhancing human development and evolution. Experts concur that coding and decoding symbols enhances thought and consciousness, which in turn literally alters brain matter. In other words, what we do with our brains determines what our minds are or what they might become.

Sources That Oppose Your Claims In argumentative writing, writers have to take on opposition. They have to counterargue and concede to contrary perspectives and claims. Often, this means making a generalization, for example:

> Some people may argue that children ought to develop an intimate connection with computers. But they ignore the subtle effects on cognitive development.

But it may also mean countering or conceding to a particular source—to specific language. In the following passage, Elizabeth Bohnhorst uses a quotation from a source to set up her counterargument:

> On the other hand, technology is an effective way to get kids interested in learning, considering "that there is a passionate love affair between children and computers" (Setzer). A colorful computer screen is obviously more attractive to a child than an old novel or a textbook. But this attraction is more likely a fascination with animation and sound effects rather than a genuine exploration of ideas.

And in her essay, Ann Marie Paulin (from Chapter 8) uses a passage from a source to launch her own objections:

While we can shrug off advertisements as silly, when we see these attitudes reflected among real people, the hurt is far less easy to brush away. For instance, in her essay, "Bubbie, Mommy, Weight Watchers and Me," Barbara Noreen Dinnerstein recalls a time in her childhood when her mother took her to Weight Watchers to slim down and the advice the lecturer gave to the women present: "She told us to put a picture of ourselves on the 'fridgerator of us eating and looking really fat and ugly. She said remember what you look like. Remember how ugly you are" (347).

I have a problem with this advice. First, of course, it is too darn common. Fat people are constantly being told they should be ashamed of themselves, of their bodies. And here we see another of those misconceptions I mentioned earlier: the assumption that being fat is the same as being ugly.

Sources That Juxtapose Your Claims Sometimes writers find sources that make similar but not necessarily supporting points. In other words, the sources may juxtapose the writer's own thinking. In these cases, the juxtaposing source might help to explain or draw boundaries around the writer's point. In his essay (from Chapter 11), Leonard Kress uses a source to show the difference between his experiences and others. His own point about the treatments for childhood bulimia comes into better view when it is placed next to a medical encyclopedia:

> Perhaps earlier generations of parents and child psychologists had a better understanding of its power and attraction. And that's why older writings on the subject, rare but not unheard of, prescribe such drastic, almost Draconian treatment to stop the behavior. *The Encyclopedia of Pediatric Psychology* (1970) lacks entries for either anorexia or bulimia and refers to it as "psychogenic vomiting." It predates the public and medical concern over the condition, and takes a stern, almost Victorian approach to treatment:
>
> > Karo syrup, Phenobarbital, anticonvulsants, chlorpromazine, antihistamines, chin straps, esophageal blocks, thickened feedings, removal of normal appendix, electric shock therapy, and even intensive prayer are all reported to have been used successfully to resolve the problem.
>
> In some cases, and in my case, I suppose, the patient simply outgrows it.

Integration Strategies: Paraphrase, Summary, Quotation

As you can see from the preceding examples, writers often quote sources directly. But paraphrase and summary are equally important moves. Imagine a writer is doing research on political action. She discovers the following passage from Martin Luther King, Jr.:

> Human progress never rolls in on wheels of inevitability; it comes through the tireless efforts of men willing to be co-workers with God, and without this hard work, time itself becomes an ally of the forces of stagnation. We must use time creatively, in the knowledge that the time is always ripe to do right. Now is the time to make real the promise of democracy and transform our pending national elegy into a creative psalm of brotherhood. Now is the time to lift our national policy from the quicksand of racial injustice to the solid rock of human dignity.

The writer decides that this information is valuable because it adds complexity to her ideas. It may be *paraphrased, summarized,* or directly *quoted.*

Paraphrase is a rewording of the original source using your own words and expressions. It conveys the detail and complexity of the original text. A paraphrase of the King passage might read as follows:

> Humanity doesn't progress without constant struggle of pious and committed individuals. Absence of such struggle means the lack of social and spiritual development. We have to use time to do what is right, to realize the idea of democracy, to change national sorrow into community and collaboration. We have to try to raise the nation up from racist practices into a place of shared honor and respect (King 130).

The paraphrase restates King's ideas, but does so without his particularly figurative language. The writer might find paraphrase valuable because she wants to share the nuances of the idea but does not want the tone of the original text (such as King's poetic voice) to interfere with or take over her own text.

Paraphrasing does not involve merely changing a word or two, or shifting around sentence parts. Inappropriate or lazy paraphrasing leads to *plagiarism:* taking others' ideas or words without attributing proper credit. In the following example, the writer does not rephrase the ideas, but merely shifts some words around and replaces others. If the following appeared in a text, it would be plagiarism:

> Human progress never rolls in on tires of inevitability; it comes by way of the tireless efforts of men willing to be co-workers with God, and without this hard work, time itself becomes an ally of the forces of stagnation. In the knowledge that the time is always ripe to do right, we must use time creatively (King 130).

Notice that in the first sentence, the writer has only substituted one word for another here and there. In the second sentence, the writer has just shifted sentence parts around. This is plagiarism rather than paraphrasing because the passage retains the original flavor and expression of the author. (See more about plagiarism on page 506.)

Summary also involves expressing a source's ideas in your own words instead of using the words of the source. But unlike paraphrasing, summary often removes much of the detail while still dealing with the complexity of the source's idea. A writer may summarize because he or she wants to illustrate a point (made by the original text) and then move on to another idea. In other words, a summary is often used to support a broader claim. For example, consider this brief summary of the original King passage. Notice that King's idea has been entirely reworded, abbreviated, and used as a supporting point:

> Even liberal-minded people believe that minority rights, somehow, evolve quietly through the decades. But Martin Luther King, Jr. made the opposite point: that humanity progresses only by the struggle of spiritually motivated people, and those people must use time for social change (130).

Because summary leaves out detail while capturing the main idea, accuracy is essential. Writers should be careful not to misinterpret the source, as in the following summary:

> According to King, only people who go to church regularly can make the world a better place. Racism will thrive without their timely efforts (130).

Summaries can be any length, depending on the writer's purpose. For instance, imagine that a writer is building a line of reasoning about justice. She wants to borrow an idea explained in King's "Letter from Birmingham Jail." She quickly summarizes King's distinction between just and unjust laws without dwelling on specifics:

> But something is not right simply because it is legal. As Martin Luther King, Jr. reminds us in "Letter from Birmingham Jail," we must appeal to some principle beyond the law. Because so many laws through history have been unjust and downright oppressive to minority groups, we cannot simply accept legality as the ultimate criterion for righteousness (132–33). In the current debate about gay marriage, we must go beyond legality and explore what is just.

Here, the writer has summarized several lengthy passages from King's text. Rather than get bogged down in the details of King's argument, she abbreviates his ideas in one sentence and then continues developing her own point. A lengthier summary might be appropriate if the writer wanted to carefully detail the difference between a just and an unjust law. She might summarize but offer slightly more detail from King's argument. In effect, she would be summarizing and paraphrasing:

> It is difficult for a population to weigh the justice of its own laws. After all, the laws seem just by virtue of their place in social structures and institutions. But as Martin Luther King, Jr., argues, there is a clean and clear distinction between just and unjust laws. First, an unjust law contradicts or opposes moral law—that set of principles above and beyond any particular society. Second, an unjust law diminishes and objectifies people. Segregation, the set of laws that maintained formal racial separation, treated

> minorities as fundamentally inferior beings—as a group to be removed from the center of society. It was, therefore, unjust. Finally, an unjust law burdens one group of people while passing over another group. In other words, it is not uniformly enacted. And unjust conditions will always come when one group develops a law that targets another group. For instance, the laws in Alabama to keep African Americans from voting were developed by white politicians and their constituents. Such laws maintained oppression, separation, and inequality (132–33). Although the people of the time did not recognize their actions as unjust, they were out of sync with moral law, with God's law.

This lengthier summary of King's argument helps the writer make a point. And if the writer were developing an extensive argument about the distinction between just and unjust laws, she might go even further with her summary. She might take several paragraphs to detail King's logic. But she would have to walk carefully—not allowing King's ideas to take over or push her own ideas aside.

Activity

In groups, summarize the following passage from Ann Marie Paulin's essay (from Chapter 8). Try to develop two different summaries—one that abbreviates Paulin's point into a single sentence and another that makes the point in a single short paragraph:

> So we are surrounded by a culture, even an infrastructure, that encourages obesity, yet the culture also breeds a prejudice against fat people. Various articles and news magazine programs have reported that Americans of all sizes make far more than simple aesthetic judgments when they look at a fat person. Fat people are assumed to be lazy, stupid, ugly, lacking in self-esteem and pride, devoid of self-control, and stuffed full of a host of other unpleasant qualities that have nothing to do with the size of a person's belly or thighs. But, as anyone who has ever been the victim of such prejudice can tell you, the impact such foolish notions have is real and harmful. For example, Marilyn Wann, in her book *Fat! So?,* cites an experiment in which "[r]esearchers placed two fake personal ads, one for a woman described as '50 pounds overweight' and the other for a woman described as a drug addict. The drug addict received 79 percent of the responses" (59).

Quotation involves using the exact words of a source. It puts a spotlight on another writer's language and allows writers to integrate especially important phrasing or passages. The key, however, is to carefully select what ideas and manners of expression are *worth* quoting. When writing down quotes, keep in mind two points:

1. Quote sparingly. Quote only when a passage is particularly striking, AND quote only the striking part. For example, do not quote an entire paragraph if you can quote just a sentence; do not quote an entire sentence if you can quote only three words from that sentence.
2. Put others' words within quotation marks. Consider the following well-chosen quotation from the original King passage:

> According to Martin Luther King Jr., "Human progress never rolls in on wheels of inevitability; it comes through the tireless efforts of men willing to be co-workers with God, and without this hard work, time itself becomes an ally of the forces of stagnation" (130).

Writers can use various strategies for punctuating quotations:

Quotation marks only When the quoted matter blends directly into your sentence without a speaking verb (such as *say, says, said, exclaims, proclaims,* or *states*) indicating a change in voice, no punctuation is required before the quotation. The sentence may be punctuated just as it would be if there were no quotation marks:

> According to Anderson's records, before the end of the decade, there were "eighteen million people involved in the crisis" (177).
>
> Emphasizing her point, Miller demands that "it is now time for something drastic to change here on campus" (43).

Speaking verb followed by a comma Speaking verbs (such as *say, says, suggests, exclaims,* or *states*) indicate a shift in voice from your voice to the voice of your source. A comma separates the speaking verb and the quotation:

> His final paragraph, before the epilogue, says, "Let's create a system that encourages people like Andie at least as much as the ones who don't give a damn" (Sacks 187).
>
> Emphasizing her point, Miller suggests, "It is now time for something drastic to change here on campus" (43).

Helpful Verbs for Attributing Quotes

says	describes
considers	insists
argues	tells
shows	offers
explains	informs
demands	claims
suggests	instructs
teaches	points out
emphasizes	

> As Martin Luther King Jr. explains, in his "Letter from Birmingham Jail," "One day the South will know that when these disinherited children of God sat down at lunch counters, they were in reality standing up for what is best in the American dream" (130).

A speaking verb combined with a noun creates an attributive phrase that can be placed at the beginning, in the middle, or at the end of a sentence. Quoting involves crafting sentences carefully to create clear and natural-sounding connections between the writer's own ideas and the words of the source. Here are some standard strategies:

> **Quotation at the Beginning of a Sentence**
> "All voting is a sort of gaming, like checkers or backgammon, with a slight moral tinge to it," explains Henry David Thoreau (56).
>
> **Quotation in the Middle of a Sentence**
> As Thoreau points out, "All voting is a sort of gaming, like checkers or backgammon, with a slight moral tinge to it" (56), and it is this moral issue that is often overemphasized on ballots.
>
> **Quotation at the End of a Sentence**
> Henry David Thoreau claims that "voting is a sort of gaming, like checkers or backgammon, with a slight moral tinge to it" (56).
>
> **Quotation Divided by Your Own Words**
> "All voting," explains Thoreau, "is a sort of gaming" (56).

Sentence followed by a colon Sometimes writers use a whole sentence to set up, or explain, the quotation. In this case, they use a colon between their own sentence and the quotation. The colon, in effect, says, "and now, here comes the other person's words":

> For example, he introduced the reader to Marissa and Carol: "As very good students, [their views] were virtually excluded by The College in order to accommodate the whiners and complainers" (Sacks 61).
>
> As George Williams notes, protection of white privilege is critical to patterns of discrimination: "Whenever a number of persons within a society have enjoyed for a considerable period of time certain opportunities for getting wealth, for exercising power and authority, and for successfully claiming prestige and social deference, there is strong tendency for these people to feel that these benefits are theirs by 'right'" (727).

If an entire sentence is a quotation—that is, if it begins and ends with a quotation mark and contains no reference to the source in between—consider the following approaches: (1) connect the quote, if appropriate, to the preceding sentence with a colon, or (2) add a cue, or transition, as an introduction to the quote.

Special Conditions in Quoting To integrate quotes smoothly into a text, writers sometimes find it helpful to omit or add certain words for clarity or cohesion. Standard guidelines exist for letting readers know how the writer has altered a quotation. Of course, the writer must be certain that he or she has not changed the source's intended meaning. Note also the standard approach to using long quotations:

Omitting Words Occasionally, writers want to leave out words or phrases of a passage they are quoting. This is done with ellipses (. . .). They tell readers that words have been taken out of the original passage. Notice how one might quote the following passage from an essay by David Crabtree:

> **Original:** The world is changing at a bewildering pace. Anyone who owns a computer and tries to keep up with the developments in hardware, software, and the accompanying incompatibilities is all too aware of the speed of change. This rapid change, especially technological change, has extremely important implications for the job market. In the past, it was possible to look at the nation's workforce, determine which of the existing occupations was most desirable in terms of pay and working conditions, and pick one to prepare for. But the rapid rate of change is clouding the crystal ball. How do we know that a high-paying job today will be high-paying tomorrow?

> **Quotation:** According to David Crabtree, "The world is changing at a bewildering pace. . . . This rapid change, especially technological change, has extremely important implications for the job market."

The ellipses indicate the missing sentence from the quotation. The same strategy can be applied to cut any amount of text from a passage. For instance, in the following sentence, a few words have been cut from Crabtree's passage:

> **Quotation:** According to David Crabtree, "This rapid change . . . has extremely important implications for the job market."

Adding Words Sometimes it is valuable to add a note or comment within a quote. In this case, writers use square brackets to set off their own words. For example, a writer may insert a word in a quoted passage to clarify a vague pronoun or to give a brief explanation:

> **Original:** After months of exhausting research, they had finally come to understand the problem with their design.

> **Quotation:** "After months of exhausting research, [the nuclear scientists] had finally come to understand the problem with their design" (Smith 82).

> Here, the writer substitutes the actual noun for the pronoun *they.* Without the noun, readers may not understand the meaning of the quotation. As in this example,

inserting bracketed comments within quotes can clear up any potentially confusing information within a quote while maintaining the flow of the sentence.

Noting an Error If a quotation is grammatically or syntactically flawed, a writer cannot simply change it. In such cases, the quotation must remain intact, and the writer must use square brackets and the three-letter word *sic* directly after the error. Otherwise, readers might assume that the error is on the part of the writer:

> In his letter to the editor, Jeremy Miller argues that "Obama should not of [sic] bailed out the auto industry or the banks." He goes on to argue against bailouts in any form.

Using Lengthy Quotes When writers quote more than four lines, they must use a block quote. As in this passage from Ann Marie Paulin's essay, writers often use a colon before block quotes:

> Another example of this bullying someone thin comes from Pipher's book *Hunger Pains: The Modern Woman's Tragic Quest for Thinness.* Pipher recounts a conversation she overheard one day in a dress shop:
>
>> I overheard a mother talking to her daughter, who was trying on party dresses. She put on each dress and then asked her mother how she looked. Time after time, her mother responded by saying, "You look just awful in that, Kathy. You're so fat nothing fits you right." The mother's voice dripped with disgust and soon Kathy was crying. (89)
>
> Pipher goes on to suggest that Kathy's mother is a victim of the culture, too, because she realizes how hard the world will be on her fat daughter. Unfortunately, what she doesn't realize is how much better her daughter's quality of life would be if she felt loved by her mother. Any person surrounded by loving family members at home is much better equipped to deal with whatever the cruel world outside throws at her or him.

Double Quotes Occasionally, writers quote a passage that contains a quotation or is itself a quotation. In this case, single quotation marks are used inside the double quotation marks:

> As Maria Gallagher has argued, "It is time that we turn the corner on the road of national energy policies and begin to take 'alternative energy' seriously" (23).

Coherence Strategies

Outside sources can make a text more sophisticated, but they can also create confusion if the writer does not make explicit connections between points. Because outside sources often increase the complexity of a text, writers have to employ *textual cues:* sentences, words, and phrases that explain the relationship between ideas and sources. Textual cues are like the road signs of an essay. They help readers keep track of who's saying what within paragraphs and throughout the essay. For example, the following textual cue helps readers keep track of previously mentioned names:

> Most music critics, *such as Smith, Castella, and Sanchez,* see the latest alternative genre as a collective response to the grunge scene of the early '90s.

Here, the critics listed have been discussed prior to this sentence, and the writer simply reminds readers about these voices and how they relate to the present point being made. Simple phrases (such as *for example*) cue readers to make connections between passages in the text:

> Jones's ideas are often seen as radical. Alberta Slavik, *for example,* casts Jones aside as a "hyper-liberal" journalist: "William Jones has gone too far, simply parading his politics at the cost of facts" (76).

In the following paragraph, notice how Daniel Bruno uses a range of textual cues. He blends together, or integrates, what he thinks and what his source says by (1) stating his main idea *(Sacks illustrates that all of today's college students cannot just be thrown in the same big barrel);* (2) directing readers to the source *(he spends, he says, he mentions);* (3) providing the information from the source that supports or explains his idea; and (4) concluding by commenting on the information:

> In *Generation X Goes to College,* Peter Sacks illustrates that all of today's college students cannot just be thrown in the same big barrel. In describing the modern/postmodern clash in education, he spends the majority of his time talking about those students who are underprepared, who lack the basic study skills required in academic work, and who demonstrate little real commitment to their own education. Yet, he does not discuss this problem in isolation. He also mentions another type of student. For example, he introduces the reader to Marissa and Carol: "As very good students, [their views] were virtually excluded by The College in order to accommodate the whiners and complainers" (61). And he says they "suffered not only educationally" (63). In addition to discussing specific good students, an entire chapter presents survey results about students' attitudes toward education. While he makes claims such as "nearly a quarter of the students . . . harbored a disproportionate sense of entitlement," this very statement tells the reader that a full three quarters (that is, three out of four) students *do not* "harbor a disproportionate sense of entitlement" (54–59). He wraps up the book by focusing on another student, Andie, who he describes as "a good student, constantly picking [his] brain for information and feedback on her work" (186–87). His final paragraph, before the Epilogue, says, "Let's create a system that encourages people like Andie at least as much as the ones who don't give a damn" (187). Thus, Sacks shows that today's students are a more diverse group—in skill level, background, and attitude toward education—than has ever before been gathered together in the college classroom.

Writers often rely on Bruno's four steps:

1. Explaining the main idea
2. Referencing the source
3. Giving information from the source
4. Commenting on that information

You might think of integrating sources as planting a tree. First, the hole should be dug. (One cannot simply plop a tree onto the ground.) Then, after the hole is prepared, the tree can be dropped into place. But the job is not done! The planter must fill in the hole, pack good dirt back into that space, and water it, making certain that the roots of the tree are nestled into the new soil. Likewise, a writer must first set up the idea—not simply plop the ideas from a source into a paragraph. Then, the information (summary, paraphrase, quotation) can be integrated smoothly into the writer's own language. Finally, the writer should then consider how to fill in and reinforce the connectedness of the source and his or her own points.

Essays that rely on outside sources also require good *paragraph transitions* (sentences and phrases that join the content of paragraphs and show the logical connections). Because sources create more dimensions in an essay project, readers require explicit intellectual help as they walk through a line of reasoning. Transition statements usually begin paragraphs and help readers to bridge from one paragraph to the next. The following sentences, which all begin paragraphs, act as bridges from previous points:

- Not all farmers, however, agree with Johnson's strategy.
- Despite this overwhelming amount of evidence, some teachers refuse to acknowledge the way gender and race figure into the classroom.
- But all of the discussion on war distracts voters from significant domestic issues that will impact everyday life in the present and future.
- Because of Smith's recent book, many researchers have begun focusing their attention on the ways technology will change our ability to communicate.

What Is Plagiarism?

Plagiarism—failing to acknowledge, or give credit to, a source of information—is intellectual theft. It involves using either (1) an idea or (2) the manner of expression of another person as if it is the writer's own idea or manner of expression. Plagiarism can take many forms and may be either intentional or unintentional. For example, knowingly turning in another person's paper and claiming it as one's own work is a serious form of academic dishonesty likely to have a severe consequence, such as damage to one's reputation and expulsion from school. Other times, however, writers plagiarize accidentally because they are unaware of the rules. They do not know, for example, that the ideas taken from a source, even if not quoted directly, must be documented.

Just as it is every driver's responsibility to know and obey the rules of the road (for his or her own benefit as well as for the benefit of others), it is every writer's responsibility to know the rules of documentation. To avoid plagiarism, you must acknowledge your source (also referred to as "citing" or "crediting" the source) whenever you express someone else's idea, opinion, or theory, or whenever you provide information such as a fact or statistic that is not common knowledge.

If you use the exact words of the source, you must indicate that by putting them within quotation marks—and also by crediting the source (using quotation marks alone does not count as crediting the source). If you use information from a source but express it in your own words (through paraphrase or summary), you should not put the information inside quotation marks, but you still must credit the source.

Most often, plagiarism occurs because writers are simply not going far enough in their paraphrasing. That is, they are not sufficiently rewording the ideas from the original source. A good paraphrase avoids using the same subjects and verbs as in the original text. To avoid this, read the original passage closely, but rather than writing down the ideas immediately, talk through them first. Remember that any one idea can be phrased in infinite ways.

Writers sometimes plagiarize intentionally because they are desperate to complete an assignment or pass a class. They set out to steal (or buy) others' ideas. In this age of technology, students can easily download text from an online source, and they can even buy college essays from websites and online databases. However, such essays are prepackaged, the topics are generalized, and the writing mundane—essentially, they are the opposite of what most college instructors want, and are contrary to the invention strategies suggested throughout this book. Also, as websites featuring prewritten essays increase, so does the ability of instructors to detect plagiarism.

The consequences of plagiarism are more far-reaching and destructive than what some students may assume. Besides failing an assignment, failing an entire class, or being expelled, students who plagiarize fail to learn essential writing and thinking skills—or even when and how to ask for help. They also establish a low standard for themselves, which is perhaps the worst result of plagiarizing.

Documenting Sources

Why document sources? There are at least three good reasons:

- **To be honest.** When presenting others' opinions, research, or manner of expression, writers give credit to, or acknowledge, their sources.
- **To gain credibility.** If a source is credible (see "Evaluating Sources" in Chapter 15, page 484), then the writer's claims gain credibility. Many times writers are not experts

on their subject matter; however, they can write confidently about their subjects as a result of sources. Also, writers are taken more seriously if they appear well informed, having "done their research."

- **To provide readers with more information.** Listing sources provides readers with access to more information. This allows readers to explore the subject matter further.

Different disciplines rely on different styles of documentation. The two most common styles are MLA (Modern Language Association) and APA (American Psychological Association).

MLA Style

English and humanities use MLA style. Like other documentation styles, MLA depends on two basic components: (1) an in-text citation of a work and (2) a list of works cited at the end of the text. These two components function in the following ways:

- In-text citations let readers know that particular ideas come from a particular source.
- In-text documentation corresponds to the complete bibliographic information provided at the end of the text.
- In-text citations lead readers directly to the corresponding Works Cited page.
- Done correctly, the in-text reference lists the first word(s)—whether it be the author's last name or the article title—plus the page reference of the citation on the alphabetized Works Cited page. This allows readers to easily locate the source in the list of works.
- The Works Cited page provides complete information for finding all formal sources. This complete information is provided only once and comes at the end of the entire text so that it doesn't interfere with ease of reading.

In-Text Citation

In-text documentation involves referencing the original text in parentheses within the actual sentences of your text; because it uses parentheses, it is sometimes called *parenthetical citation.*

An in-text citation must occur when a writer does any of the following:

- Quotes directly from a source
- Paraphrases ideas from a source
- Summarizes ideas from a source
- References statistics or data from a source

In general, for MLA style, in-text citations should include the author's last name (unless it is given within the sentence) and page number of the source from which the cited material is taken (unless the source is electronic and lacks page numbers).

"After months of exhausting research, they had finally come to understand the problem with their design" (Smith 82).

A space separates the name and the page number.

The end punctuation comes after the citation.

If the author is referred to in the sentence, his or her name can be omitted from the citation.

> Emphasizing her point, Miller demands that "it is now time for something drastic to change here on campus" (43).

If the source has no author, use the first word or phrase of the source's title and punctuate accordingly (quotation marks for an article and italics for a book).

> The oil had spread over much of the shoreline and had "already begun its death grip on a vast array of wildlife" ("Black Death" 54).

If the source has two authors, use the last name of both authors.

> (Lunsford and Ede 158)

If you have more than one work by the same author, insert the title of the work after the author name, followed by the page number.

> (Faigley, *Fragments of Rationality* 43)

If you are citing material that is already quoted in the source, cite the source in which you found the quotation and add "qtd. in" before the author's name or title.

> (qtd. in Smith 82)

If you want to acknowledge more than one source for the same information, use a semi-colon between citations within one set of parentheses.

> (Lunsford and Ede 78; Smith 82)

If you have an electronic source with no page numbers, simply exclude the page number from the citation. Do not add page numbers, and do not use those that a computer printer assigns.

> According to Martha Smith, "untold numbers of children are negatively affected by the proficiency test craze."

Works Cited

Works Cited pages list the sources that are directly cited in the text. In general, the first piece of information in the Works Cited entry should correspond directly with the first piece of information in the in-text citation. For example, notice the relationship between the in-text citation for Patricia Hampl, below, and the entire bibliographic information in the Works Cited page:

> The difference between those who write memoirs and those who write fiction is that "memoirists wish to tell their mind, not their story" (**Hampl** 330).

Works Cited

Hampl, Patricia. "Red Sky in the Morning." *Reading Culture: Contexts for Critical Reading and Writing,* edited by Diana George and John Trimbur, 7th ed., Longman, 2010, pp. 329–31.

Entries in Works Cited pages must follow strict formatting guidelines, but the process is easy if you remember the basic elements and these key rules:

- The most essential elements of any Works Cited entry are: *Author, Title*, and *Publication information*. For many sources, an important fourth element is *Location*, meaning an exact page number or URL or even a physical place where a source can be found.
- **Authors**
  - The author is the person or people who wrote or otherwise created the source.
  - The author name(s) comes first in the citation and is inverted (last name first), with a comma between last and first names.
- **Titles**
  - All words in titles are capitalized except prepositions (such as *on, in, between*), articles (*a, an, the*), coordinating conjunctions (*and, but, for, nor, or, so, yet*), and *to* in infinitives (such as *to run, to go*).
  - The titles of shorter works or works that are part of a larger whole (like an article in a magazine) are set in quotation marks, while the titles of longer or stand-alone works (books, magazines, newspapers, films, websites) are set in italics.
  - If no author is listed for a source, then your citation will start with the title of your source.
- **Publication Information**
  - Publication information will usually include the name of the publisher or sponsoring organization and the copyright or publication date.

- Publishers should be listed for books, films, television shows, and similar sources. Use complete names for publishers, but omit business words and abbreviations such as *Company* (*Co.*), *Incorporated* (*Inc.*), and *Corp.* from publisher names in your Works Cited entries. Use the abbreviation *UP* for the words University Press in the names of college publishers (Yale UP, for example).
- Publisher names should ***not*** be included in citations for periodicals or articles, for works published directly by authors or editors, for websites for which the publisher's name is the same as the title of the site, or for websites that do not produce the works they house (examples: *YouTube*, *Hulu*, or databases such as *Academic Search Premier*).
- If a month is part of the publication date, then abbreviate the names of all months in your Works Cited entries, except for the months of May, June, and July.

- **Location information**
  - For print sources that are part of a larger whole, such as an article in magazine or an essay in an anthology, provide the specific page number(s) on which the selection appears.
  - For online sources, you will need to include a URL or web address instead of page numbers. If available, it is preferable to provide a permalink or stable URL, rather than copying a URL from your browser. Also, if your source has a DOI (or digital object identifier), then you should use that identifier number in your citation (preceded by *doi*:) rather than a URL.

- **Access dates for online sources**

  An access date should be added to the end of a citation when you are citing an online source that does not have a publication date or date when the site was last modified, or when you are citing an online source that is frequently revised or updated or otherwise changed. If you include a date of access in your citation, that element comes last and is set per this example: Accessed 30 Mar. 2016.

Books

Bibliographic information for books is contained on the title page and the copyright page (the back side of the title page). The title page contains the full title of the book, the author(s), and the publishing company. The copyright page contains date(s) and any edition numbers.

Single Author Print Book

Author Name
As for all sources in MLA format, the first author name is inverted (last name first).

Title of the Source
Titles of longer or stand-alone works (books, magazines, newspapers, films, websites) are set in italics.

Palmeri, Jason. *Remixing Composition: A History of Multimodal Writing Pedagogy*. Southern Illinois UP, 2012.

Publisher
Publisher names are always found on the title page of a book. Give complete publisher names, but omit business words and abbreviations like *Company* (*Co.*) and *Inc.* from publisher names. Use the abbreviation *UP* for university presses. Cities or places of publication do not usually need to be included.

Publication Date
The date usually appears on the copyright page of a book, which is the back side of the title page. Always use the most recent date listed. Use a comma between the publisher and the date of publication.

Book with Two Authors

McKee, Heidi A., and James E. Porter. *The Ethics of Internet Research: A Rhetorical, Case-based Approach*. Peter Lang International Academic Publishers, 2009.

Book with Three or More Authors

Kargon, Robert, et al. *World's Fairs on the Eve of War: Science, Technology, and Modernity, 1937–1942*. U of Pittsburgh P, 2015.

Corporate Author or Government Publication

MLA Handbook. 8th ed., Modern Language Association of America, 2016.

United States, Office of Consumer Affairs. *2003 Consumer's Resource Handbook.* Government Publishing Office, 2003.

If an organization or company is both the author and the publisher of the source you are using (as in the *MLA Handbook* example above), then start your citation with the title of the source and list the organization only as the publisher. For government publications, if no specific person is listed as the author, then your citation should list the government as the author; start with the name of the government (United States), followed by the agency (Office of Consumer Affairs, in the example above). Many federal publications are published by the Government Publishing Office (GPO).

Subsequent Editions

Wicks-Nelson, Rita, and Allen C. Israel. *Behavior Disorders of Childhood.* 6th ed., Prentice Hall, 2005.

When a source has an edition number, find the edition information on the title page of the book. Place the edition number in the Works Cited entry directly after the title or the editor, if there is one. Use the abbreviations *2nd ed., 3rd ed.,* and so on, or *Revised ed.,* depending on what the title page says.

Republished Book

Tolkien, J. R. R. *The Hobbit.* 1937. Ballantine Books, 2003.

Older books may be published by a company other than the original publishers, or a hardcover book may be republished in paperback. In such cases, insert the original publication date after the title, and then give the recent publisher and date.

Edited Book

Busch, Frederick. *The Stories of Frederick Busch*. Edited by Elizabeth Strout, W. W. Norton, 2014.

When a source has an editor, add *edited by* after the title of the book, followed by the editor's name, not inverted. Use *edited by* even if there is more than one editor.

Translated Book

Bakhtin, Mikhail. *Problems of Dostoevsky's Poetics.* Translated by Caryl Emerson, U of Minnesota P, 1984.

When a source has a translator, add *translated by* after the title of the book followed by the translator's name, not inverted.

Online Book

Shaw, Bernard. *Pygmalion.* Brentano, 1916. *Bartleby.com*, www.bartleby.com/138/.

Start by providing complete source information for the print version of the book. Then list the title of the website (italicized) where you found the online book and the URL. If the book is part of an online scholarly project, which is often the case, include information on the sponsoring institution in your citation.

E-book

Doerr, Anthony. *All The Light We Cannot See.* Kindle ed., Scribner, 2014.

Again, provide complete source details as you would for a print version of the book. Include the type of e-reader device you used to view the book and treat that information as you would a subsequent edition. In the example above, *Kindle ed.* here stands for *Kindle edition.*

Articles

Articles appear in newspapers and periodicals (journals or magazines). Although newspapers are usually published daily, magazines are usually published weekly or monthly, and journals are published quarterly or even biannually.

Activity

Decide which type of periodical (magazine or journal) may have published the following articles, and in groups or as a class, discuss the reasoning behind your decisions:

"Heading for the Mountains: An Exciting Getaway for the Whole Family"

"Climatic Shifts in the Mountain Region"

"Coach Fired, Team Responds"

"Enzymes, Nutrition, and Aging: A Twenty-Year Study"

"The Latest in Deep Water Bait"

"Re-inventing the Microscope"

"The Epistemology of Literature: Reading and Knowing"

Article in a Magazine, Accessed Online

Author Name
Regardless of the type of source, the first author name is inverted.

Title of Article
The titles of shorter works or works that are part of a larger whole (like an article in a magazine, or an individual song) are set in quotation marks.

Paumbarten, Nick. "Food Fighter: Does Whole Foods' C.E.O. Know What's Best for You?" *The New Yorker*, 4 Jan. 2010, www.newyorker.com/magazine/2010/01/04/food-fighter.

Title of Source
The title of the magazine, journal, or newspaper is italicized.

Publication date
Include month and year directly after the title of the container. For weekly or biweekly magazines, include the full date (day, month, and year). Remember to abbreviate the names of all months except May, June, and July.

Location
For an article accessed online, include a URL (but leave *http://* and *https://* out of the link address) or a permalink or a DOI (digital object identifier) depending upon what is available for your source. If accessing an article in print, include page numbers instead of a URL.

Article in a Print Journal

Leonard, Rebecca Lorimer. "Multilingual Writing as Rhetorical Attunement." *College English*, vol. 76, no. 3, Jan. 2014, pp. 227–47.

Academic or scholarly journals often have a volume number and an issue number, and if available, these need to be included in your citation. The volume number is preceded by *vol.* and the issue number is preceded by *no*. The volume and/or issue number are followed by the publication date (month or season [if available] and year), then inclusive page numbers.

Article in Online Journal

Kingma, Mireille. "Nurses on the Move: Historical Perspective and Current Issues." *OJIN: Online Journal of Issues in Nursing,* vol. 13, no. 2, May 2008, doi:10.3912/OJIN.Vol13No02Man01.

Follow the format for print articles; however, instead of page numbers, you will include a URL or DOI (digital object identifier). Many academic journal articles have a permanent DOI assigned to them by the publisher or have an otherwise stable URL that you can include in your citation.

Journal Article Retrieved from a Database

Glenberg, Arthur M., and Thomas Grimes. "Memory and Faces: Pictures Help You Remember Who Said What." *Personality and Social Psychology Bulletin*, vol. 21, no. 3, Mar. 1995, pp. 196–206. *Academic Search Complete*, doi:10.1177/0146167295213001.

First provide full citation information for the original source, including the volume, issue, year, and page numbers. Then include the name of the database (italicized) and either a DOI or a URL to indicate where the article is located in the database. Remember that academic journal articles in a database often have a specific DOI assigned to them and it is preferable to use a DOI rather than a URL if one is available.

Article in a Print Newspaper

Swartz, Jon. "Market Won't Friend Social Media." *USA Today*, 5 May 2014, p. B1.

For a local newspaper, when the name of the city of publication is not already part of the title of the newspaper, add the city name in square brackets after the title of the newspaper (*The Star Ledger* [Newark]). National newspapers (such as *The Washington Post* or *The New York Times*) do not need any city name included. Add section letters before the page numbers if appropriate. If the page numbers are not consecutive, then list the first page number, immediately followed by a plus sign.

Newspaper or Magazine Article Retrieved from a Database

Turkle, Sherry. "The Flight from Conversation." *The New York Times*, 22 Apr. 2012, p. 1. *Academic OneFile*, go.galegroup.com/ps/i.do?id=GALE%7CA287213303&v=2.1&u=nysl_me_wls&it=r&p=AONE&sw=w&asid=e70139ddee4d97ee8aa08c5bc06d7342.

First provide full citation information for the original source, including the publication date and page numbers (if available). Then list the name of the database (italicized), and the URL address (or the permalink if available) for the article in the database.

Essay, Story, or Poem in an Anthology (such as a college textbook)

Paulin, Ann Marie. "Cruelty, Civility, and Other Weighty Matters." *The Composition of Everyday Life*, edited by John Mauk and John Metz, 5th ed., Wadsworth, 2014, pp. 243-49.

Begin with the author, followed by the title of the work (essay, story, or poem). Then give the title of the book, the editors, and the publication information. End with the page numbers on which the article or essay appears.

Encyclopedia Article

Esposito, Vincent J. "World War II: The Diplomatic History of the War and Post-War Period." *Encyclopedia Americana*, Intl. ed., 2000.

Begin with an author name if one is given. (Check for author names at the beginning or end of the article.) Put the title of the article in quotation marks and italicize the encyclopedia title. End with edition and year. If the encyclopedia or reference text is organized alphabetically (like the example above), then you don't need a page number. However, if the encyclopedia is not organized alphabetically, then include a page number for the article after the publication year.

Online-Only Sources

Official Website

Pinsker, Sarah, editor. *Robin Flies Again: Letters Written by Women of Goucher College, Class of 1903.* Goucher College, 1999, meyerhoff.goucher.edu/library/robin/.

Game of Thrones. Home Box Office, www.hbo.com/game-of-thrones. Accessed 23 Mar. 2016.

Begin with the name of the site's editor or author (if available) and the title of the site (italicized). Next, give the name of the publisher of the site or organization that sponsors the site (if available), and the date of online publication or the date of the latest update to the site (if available), followed by the URL.

For websites that do not offer a last modified or other publication date, or that change and are updated often (such as the *Game of Thrones* site), it may be helpful to include an access date at the end of your citation.

Personal or Professional Home Page

McNair, Patricia. *Patricia Ann McNair: Things Writerly and Readerly.* 23 Mar. 2016, patriciaannmcnair.com/.

Begin with the creator's name, followed by the title (or *Home page* if no title is given), publisher or sponsor (if available), the most recent date that the site was updated or revised (if available), and the URL.

Document or Page from Website

Seligson, Hannah. "High Manxiety: Thirtysomething Men Are the New Neurotic Singles." *The Daily Beast*, 4 May 2014, www.thedailybeast.com/articles/2014/05/04/high-manxiety-thirtysomething-men-are-the-new-neurotic-singles.html.

"SCA Equestrian Handbook." *The Society for Creative Anachronism*, 2012, www.sca.org/officers/equestrian/pdf/equestrian_handbook.pdf.

Begin with the author's name (if available), followed by the title of the document or page (in quotation marks), the title of the website (italicized), the sponsor or publisher, the date of publication or last update (if given), and the URL. If the web page has no title, then offer a description, such as *Home page* (not italicized) in its place. If the publisher and the title of the website are essentially the same (as in the two examples above), then the publisher name can be omitted from the citation.

Government Website

"Asteroids." *Solar System Exploration.* National Aeronautics and Space Administration, solarsystem.nasa.gov/planets/asteroids.

If a government agency (like NASA) or other type of organization is both the author and the publisher for a work, then start your citation with the title of the source and list the government agency only as the publisher.

Online Presentation

Groshelle, Zane. "Visualizing Your Pitch." *Prezi*, 19 Feb. 2015, prezi.com/oerqtrj5ie3y/visualizing-your-pitch/.

Give the author name, the title of presentation (in quotation marks), the title of the website (italicized), the publisher/sponsor of the site (if it is different from the title of the website), and the date of publication or date that the presentation was last modified. End your citation with a URL.

E-mail

Wells, Carson. "Questionable Behavior." Received by Anton Chigurh, 23 Nov. 2013.

Begin with the name of the author/sender of the e-mail, and then treat the subject of the e-mail as the title of the source, setting it in quotation marks. Include the recipient's name; if you were the e-mail's recipient, insert *Received by author* (but not in italics). End with the e-mail's date.

Online Posting

McNair, Patricia Ann. "Shake Things Out and Dance – On Endings." *Things Writerly and Readerly*, 20 July 2011, patriciaannmcnair.com/category/why-the-short-story-a-conversation-among-writers/.

List the author of the posting and the title of the posting (in quotation marks). Then give the name of the website, the date of the posting, and the URL for the posting.

Untitled Online Posting

@USPTO. "At 2pm ET, Dr. @FrancesArnold chats with us abt the Natl Medal of #Tech & #Innovation. Ask your Qs w/ #USPTOChat." *Twitter*, 24 Mar. 2016, 12:35 p.m., twitter.com/uspto/status/713056559169945604.

For a short untitled post like a tweet, include the entire message in your citation and treat the message as the title of the source (enclosed in quotations). Then give the name of the website, the date and time of the posting, and the specific URL for the posting.

Entry in an Online Encyclopedia or Dictionary

"India." *Encyclopædia Britannica Online*, 6 May 2016, www.britannica.com/place/India. Accessed 21 May 2016.

Begin with the title of the entry in the dictionary or encyclopedia, if no author is available. Then list the title of the encyclopedia, the publication or last modified date, and the URL. If you are citing an online dictionary or encyclopedia where the entries are changed and updated regularly (such as *Wikipedia*), then you may also want to include an access date at the end of your citation.

Other Sources

Abstract

Barton, Ellen. "Resources for Discourse Analysis in Composition Studies." *Style,* vol. 36, no. 4, Winter 2002, pp. 575–95. Abstract. *JSTOR*, www.jstor.org/stable/10.5325/style.36.4.575.

Use the format appropriate for the type of source (book, article, etc.) and add the descriptor *Abstract* after the page numbers. In the case of an abstract found online like this example, include the database title and URL for the article. Note that *JSTOR* provides stable URLs for sources.

Television Episode

"Lisa the Veterinarian." *The Simpsons*, season 27, episode 15, Twentieth Century Fox Television, 2016.

Provide the title of the episode or segment, the title of the series, the season and episode numbers. Include either the main production company with the year the episode was produced (as in the example above), or include the main distribution company with the original broadcast date (as in the example below).

"Lisa the Veterinarian." *The Simpsons*, created by Matt Groening, performance by Yeardley Smith, season 27, episode 15, Fox Network, 6 Mar. 2016.

If your paper is discussing the work of a particular character or other person connected with the episode, then you should include that person's name with a description in your citation. In the example above, the series creator and the actor who performs the character of Lisa Simpson, Yeardley Smith, are being emphasized.

Film

True Grit. Paramount Pictures, 2010.

If your paper is discussing a film in a general way, then your citation needs only the title of the film, the main or primary distributing company, and the year of release (or re-release, if relevant).

True Grit. Directed by Ethan Coen and Joel Coen, performance by Jeff Bridges, Paramount Pictures, 2010.

If your paper is focused on the work of a particular person connected with the film, then you should include that person's name with a description in your citation. The example above highlights the film's directors and an actor in the film.

Film or Television Episode, Accessed Online

"Unraveling." *The Killing*, season 4, episode 2, AMC, 1 Aug. 2014. *Netflix*, www.netflix.com/watch/70306003. Accessed 12 May 2016.

Start by providing complete original broadcast information (for a tv episode) or original release information (for a film). Next give the name of the online site or service (set in italics) where you accessed the tv episode or film, and then the URL. Because streaming services like *Netflix* and *Hulu* change their content often, you may also want to include an access date in the citation.

Audio Recording

Tragically Hip. "Morning Moon." *We Are the Same*, Zoe Records, 2009.

Begin with the artist's name. Then list the title of a particular song or section (in quotation marks), the title of the collection or album (italicized), the recording company, and the year of release. If you accessed the recording online, then as with a film or tv episode accessed online, you would provide the name of the site or service where you accessed the recording (like *Spotify*), set in italics, and then the URL for the recording.

Personal Interview

Mossbacher, Delaney. Personal interview. 4 Mar. 2013.

Begin with the name of the interviewee, inverted. End with the interview date.

Published Letter

Tolkien, J. R. R. "To Christopher Tolkien." 18 Jan. 1944. *The Letters of J. R. R. Tolkien*, edited by Humphrey Carpenter and Christopher Tolkien, Houghton Mifflin, 2000, pp. 67–68.

After the date of the letter, give the number of the letter, if available. List the information of the source in which the letter was published, according to the correct format for the source. (In other words, if the letter is published in a book, as above, follow the book format.)

Print brochure

A Response to Critics of Freemasonry. Brochure. The Masonic Services Association, 2004.

Give information in the same format as a book. Include as much publication information as you can locate on the brochure.

Print advertisement

"Horseshoe Casino." Advertisement. *Cincinnati Magazine*, Sept. 2013, p. 19.

Begin with the company or product name, followed by *Advertisement.* Then list the relevant publication information. For instance, if the ad appears in a periodical, list the information in the appropriate format and end with the page number where the advertisement appeared.

Work of Art (painting, sculpture, photograph)

O'Keeffe, Georgia. *Evening Star No. VI.* 1917, Georgia O'Keeffe Museum, Santa Fe.

Include the artist's name (inverted), the title of the work (italicized), the date of composition (if available), the collector or institution that houses it, and the city where it is held.

Lecture or Speech

Obama, Barack. "Remarks by the President on Osama Bin Laden." White House, 1 May 2011, East Room, Washington. Speech.

Begin with the speaker's name, and then list the title of the speech or presentation (in quotation marks). Include the name of the meeting and sponsoring organization (if applicable), the date of the event, the venue of the lecture or speech (*East Room*, in this example), and the city. It can be helpful to include a description of the event (such as *lecture* or *address*) at the end of the citation, particularly if it is a live event that you attended in person.

Performance

Shakespeare, William. *Twelfth Night.* Directed by William Church, Harvey Theater, 28 June 2008, Interlochen. Performance.

Start with the name of the person who wrote or created the work being performed (Shakespeare in the example above), and then give the title of the work being performed. Include the director, the performers (if available), the site or venue of the performance, the date, and the city where the performance was held. It can be helpful to include an additional description of the event (such as *Performance*) at the end of the citation, particularly if it is a performance you attended in person.

Sample Research Essay

Francesca Peck wrote this argument for her first-semester college writing course. Throughout the argument, she brings together, or *synthesizes,* print and online sources to support her case. As you read, take note of documentation strategies, textual cues, coherence devices, and even Peck's voice. She manages to make a formal argument while maintaining an engaging presence in the essay.

Peck 1

Francesca Peck

Professor Mauk

English 111

8 November 2013

A World Made of Pixels

Some art historians argue that America's manifest destiny started with the flash of a camera. In mid-nineteenth century, the government began distributing photographs to endorse tourism, westward expansion, and ultimately, nation building (Stetler). Photography's initial purpose in the United States was intended to *build* American culture, and over time it has *become* our culture, overexposing society to visual representations and compromising the human experience. The crunch of a shuttering aperture marks an incomplete experience, and though the photo *optically* embodies a specific moment in time, the genuine memory subtly fades into the faint distance of our past.

She uses the source (Stetler) to help set up an important distinction that operates throughout the essay.

Daughter to an airline pilot, I have flown around the world. By the time I grew mature enough to appreciate

Personal testimony helps to ground and focus the broader points about American culture and history.

Peck 2

my travel opportunities, I had already become intoxicated with an ardent passion for photography. At this young age, excessive photographing had skewed my priorities: documentation first, experience second. For years I traveled the world without fully participating in the journey because I lurked behind the viewfinder of a camera.

At the age of fifteen, I was introduced to the lush grasses of the Ecuadorian countryside. Arriving at the village of Otavalo, I learned my flashy digital camera was not accepted by the indigenous people. Here, in this town, I recognized the irrelevance of documenting my every blink when real life occurred just beyond my tripod; I realized society's obsession with photography has substituted the human eye for a camera lens, minimizing colossal memories to the 8 × 10 perimeter of experience-thieving photographs.

The personal testimony gets specific and, therefore, more supportive and helpul.

The overexposure to photography compromises our experience in other ways as well. Its excessive presence in American culture limits the connection we have with our own lives. Ever since the *real* world was introduced to the world of visual representation, specifically photography, the two have been easily mistaken. French philosopher Jean Baudrillard argued that the human mind can mistakenly replace reality with its representation—or

The new paragraph signals a shift back to general points.

The paragraph builds to Baudrillard's complex theory.

Peck uses the Felluga quotations to explain the theory of simulacrum. The quotations come at a critical point when the audience must understand a complex idea.

She makes a thorough concession to the use and power of photography. The source (Glenberg) supports the concession.

simulacrum. Simulacrum has flourished since the trends of social networks and new technology have urged their users to share photos on the web. As many now "approach each other and the world through the lens of these media images" (Felluga), our perception of life has begun its descent into two dimensions. We live in what many philosophers call the postmodern age, when "the representation proceeds and determines the real," when "there is only the simulacrum" (Felluga).

Photography itself is not to blame. In fact, photos liberate us from naturally imperfect memory. Studies show a positive relationship between pictures and short-term recollection as they allow us to return to a previous experience. A visual stimulus promotes basic memory, supporting face-to-name recall as well as other details the photo provides (Glenberg). And the value of photography extends far beyond personal use. Advertising, journalism, social media, the arts, and many other industries integrate photos in their work. Photography itself can be considered an industry by the technological advancements it has inspired; for example, funding has already begun to enable mass production of the latest memory assistant, Memoto. This device snaps a picture every thirty seconds, records time, and even tracks its location. The collected data are then organized into a timeline, accessible on computers and smartphones. Casually clipped on a jacket or shirt pocket, Memoto can capture our entire lives on camera for future viewing (Bass).

The paraphrased source (Bass) supports the broader point about the power of photography.

Memoto and its social media predecessors are to blame for the public's overexposure to visual representations. After five minutes on Facebook, we suddenly become world travelers, seeing places we have never physically been. We attended countless parties we were never a part of and gaze at people we have never personally met. This unnatural association between reality and photos has become *normal* in our society; and sadder than it is strange, the places we *actually* go, events we *actually* attend, and people we *actually* meet often fail to live up to our pre-decided expectations.

Here, Peck returns to her concern about overexposure. The previous paragraph, then, was a setup for this pointed evaluative claim.

I cannot doubt the data from scientific studies that imply the human brain has considerably reliable photo-recall ability. Images of real people, landscapes, and even diagrams seem far easier to remember than text; but if we continue with this obsession, there will no longer be a reason to remember an experience without the use of memory aids. The human body is easily manipulated: Overuse of drugs leads to dependency, excessive sugar consumption induces persistent cravings, and contact lenses can worsen natural vision. Clearly overexposure to any form of aid is dangerous to our overall well-being, and photography is no exception.

An appeal to logic: Peck develops a small line of reasoning about the impact of images on brain development.

She uses a company slogan to suggest a downside--an otherwise unstated harm.

Here's another brief appeal to logic. The question itself implies an entire line of reasoning.

She returns to personal testimony, which implicates her own actions in the harm, and then concludes with public resonance.

Peck 5

For the sake of our already imperfect memory and healthy grasp on reality, I am haunted by the dehumanization of future photographic technologies. They encourage the overuse of memory aids, increasing our dependency on technology. Memoto's slogan, "Remember Every Moment" (Bass), eclipses the difference between *memory* and *memory aids*. Memoto supports the simulacrum and disconnects us from the real world. If we rely on visual documentations, would we have any memories at all in their absence?

As a practicing photographer and aspiring photojournalist, I can admit that I too fell to the temptation of over-photographing in the hopes of revisiting my past; but with time, I grew unsatisfied with watching life through the 16.2 megapixels of my beloved Nikon. I learned that what is being experienced outside of the camera is far more important than a documentation of it. As such, we must pick our moments. We must know the more pictures taken, the less valuable each becomes. Fighting against our overexposure to photography allows us to take full advantage of the human experience, always remembering the resolution in which we view our world appears far clearer when we set our cameras down.

Peck 6

Works Cited

Bass, Noel. "Photography, A Crutch for Poor Memory Capacity?" *Noel Bass Photo/Video*, Apr. 2013, www.noelbass.com/photography-vs-memory/.

Felluga, Dino. "Modules on Baudrillard: On Simulation." *Introductory Guide to Critical Theory*, Purdue U, 31 Jan. 2011, www.purdue.edu/guidetotheory/postmodernism/modules/baudrillardsimulation.html.

Glenberg, Arthur M., and Thomas Grimes. "Memory and Faces: Pictures Help You Remember Who Said What." *Personality and Social Psychology Bulletin*, vol. 21, no. 3, Mar. 1995, pp. 196–206. *Academic Search Complete*, doi:10.1177/0146167295213001.

Stetler, Pepper. "History of Photography." ART 389, 10 Oct. 2013, Miami U, Oxford. Lecture.

Sources are listed in alphabetical order according to the first element—in this case, author last names. The first source is a posting from a personal blog. The next two online sources are from credible, stable sources (a university website and an academic journal in a database). The last source is a lecture that the student writer attended in person.

APA Style

The American Psychological Association documentation style is used in psychology, nursing, education, and related fields. But although the format is somewhat different from MLA, the strategies for finding, evaluating, and integrating sources remain the same. And even the basic principles of documentation remain the same across styles: The information in the in-text citation should correspond directly with the References page (the APA equivalent of a Works Cited page).

- In-text (or parenthetical) citations provide unobtrusive documentation of specific information.
- In-text citation lets readers know that particular ideas come from a particular source.
- In-text citation corresponds to the complete bibliographic information provided at the end of the text.
- In-text citations lead readers directly to the corresponding References page.
- Done correctly, the in-text citation lists the first word(s)—whether the author's last name or the article title—plus year of publication and the page number of the citation on the alphabetized References page. This allows readers to easily find the appropriate source on the References page.
- The References page provides complete information for finding the source easily.
- This complete information is provided only once and comes at the end of the entire text so that it doesn't interfere with ease of reading.

In-Text Citation

Like MLA style, in-text documentation for APA involves referencing the original text in parentheses within the actual sentences of your text. An in-text citation must occur whenever a writer:

- Quotes directly from a source
- Paraphrases ideas from a source
- Summarizes ideas from a source
- References statistics or data from a source

For direct quotes, APA in-text citations should include the author name, date (year only) of the source, and page number from which the cited material is taken. If the author name is given within the sentence, however, it does not need to be included in the in-text citation.

"After months of exhausting research, they had finally come to understand the problem with their design" (Smith, 2008, p. 82).

p. or pp. comes before the actual page number(s).

End punctuation comes after the parenthetical citation.

Commas separate elements within the parentheses.

Writers using APA style often include the date directly after the author's name in the sentence.

Emphasizing her point, Miller (2000) demands that "it is now time for something drastic to change here on campus" (p. 43).

If the source has no author, use the first word or phrase of the source title and punctuate the title accordingly (either with quotation marks or italics).

"Even though most of the nation's coastal shorelines can no longer sustain a full range of sea life, the vast majority of Americans seem unconcerned" ("Dead Seas," 2001, p. 27).

If the source has two authors, use the last name of both authors. (Notice that APA style uses &, an ampersand, for in-text citations and the References page.)

(Lunsford & Ede, 2004, p. 158)

If the cited material is quoted in another source, cite the source in which you found the quotation and add *as cited in* before the author name or title.

(as cited in Smith, 2008)

If you want to acknowledge more than one source for the same information, use a semicolon between citations within one set of parentheses. The sources should be listed in alphabetical order.

(Lunsford & Ede, 1984; Smith, 2008)

Electronic Sources Many electronic sources (web pages, for instance) do not have page numbers, but page numbers may appear on the hard copy. Unless the original source has page numbers, omit them from the in-text citation. Instead, either use the paragraph number (after the abbreviation *para.*), if provided, or, if the source has headings, use the heading plus the paragraph number of the source. Electronic texts (especially web pages) may lack authors; in that case, follow the same formula as with print sources, and use the title of the source in the citation.

(Vince, 2010, Blood to Brain section, para. 2)

References

The References list gives sources that are directly cited in the text. Bibliographies, on the other hand, list all the sources that a writer may have read and digested in the process of researching the project. Entries in a References list must follow strict formatting guidelines. As in MLA documentation, the guidelines may change depending on the type of source, but there are some consistent rules. For instance, the first bit of information in the reference entry should always correspond directly with the in-text citation. In the following example, from Angel's essay (page 534), the entry begins with Price—as does the in-text citation within her essay:

> Drowsiness while driving on the job is the largest contributor to occupational fatalities (Price, 2011).
>
> Price, M. (2011, January). The risks of night work. *Monitor on Psychology, 42*(1). Retrieved from https://www.apa.org/monitor

The following rules also apply to all sources:

- Author names come first. Last name first, followed by first initial of first name (and first initial of middle name, if given).
- The date comes in parentheses directly after the author names.
- Title of the work comes directly after the date. Article titles are always in regular type, while the sources in which they appear—newspapers, magazines, and journals—are italicized. (Only the first letter of the article title or subtitle is capitalized unless there are proper nouns.)
- If no author appears, the title comes first.
- Publication information follows the title of the source.
- If the source is an article, page numbers come last. If the source is electronic, the retrieval information comes last.

Printed Books

All of the necessary information for books can usually be found on the title page, which is one of the first pages.

General Format for Books

Publication Date: Comes directly after the author name, in parentheses.

Title: The first word of the title or subtitle is capitalized, as are any proper nouns. The title is italicized.

> Palmeri, J. (2012). *Remixing composition: A history of multimodal writing pedagogy*. Carbondale, IL: Southern Illinois University Press.

Author Name: Give author last name and initials of first and (if available) middle names.

Location of Publisher: Provide city and an abbreviation for the state. If the publisher is outside of the United States, give the city and country.

Publishing Company: Place a colon between the state and publishing company. End with the publisher's name.

Two or More Authors

McKee, H. A., & Porter, J. E. (2009). *The ethics of Internet research: A rhetorical, case-based approach.* New York, NY: Peter Lang Press.

Vasta, R., Haith, M. M., & Miller, S. A. (2005). *Child psychology: The modern science.* New York, NY: Wiley.

Add all additional author names, also inverted, before the title. Use an ampersand (&), not *and*, between the names.

Corporate Author

American Automobile Association. (2007). *Tour book: New Jersey and Pennsylvania.* Heathrow, FL: Author.

Use the name of the corporation for the author name. If the corporate author also published the text, write *Author* for the publisher.

Subsequent Editions

Lauwers, J., & Shinskie, D. (2004). *Counseling the nursing mother* (4th ed.). Sudbury, MA: Jones & Bartlett.

Find the edition information on the title page of the book and place the information in parentheses directly after the title. Use abbreviations: *2nd ed., 3rd ed.*, etc., or use *Rev. ed.* for "Revised edition."

Edited Book

Alarcon, D. (Ed.). (2010). *The secret miracle.* New York, NY: Holt.

If referencing an entire edited book, begin with the editor's name and *Ed.* (for "editor"). Use *Eds.* (for "editors") if the book has more than one editor. Then give the date, the title, the publisher location, and the publisher name.

Translated Book

Bakhtin, M. (2004). *Problems of Dostoevsky's poetics* (C. Emerson, Trans.). Minneapolis, MN: University of Minnesota Press.

Add the translator's name (first and middle initials and last name) and *Trans.* (all in parentheses) after the title of the book.

Printed Articles

Articles appear in newspapers and periodicals (journals or magazines). Although newspapers are usually published daily, magazines are usually published weekly or monthly, and journals are published quarterly or even biannually.

Article in a Magazine

Paumbarten, N. (2010, January 4). Food fighter: Does Whole Foods' C.E.O. know what's best for you? *New Yorker*, 35+.

Include the date (year, month, day) directly after the author name. Do not abbreviate months. If available, give the volume number in italics after the magazine title, followed by issue number in parenthesis.

Article in a Newspaper

Swartz, J. (2014, May 5). Market won't friend social media. *USA Today*, B1.

If one is listed, give the author first, followed by the date and the title of the article. After the title of the newspaper, add section letters before the page numbers.

Article in a Journal

Leonard, R. L. (2014). Multilingual writing as rhetorical attunement. *College English*, *76*, 227–247.

Most academic journals number the pages of each issue continuously through a volume. The second issue does not begin with page 1, but with the number after the last page of the previous issue. For these journal articles, place the volume number in italics directly after the journal title, and before the page numbers. If each issue starts over with page 1, provide the issue number in parenthesis after the volume number, not in italics. Finally, if the article has been assigned a *digital object identifier* (DOI), place that after the period that follows the page number, even if you accessed the article in print. (See information on DOIs, page 531.)

Article or Chapter in an Edited Book

Mickelson, R. A., & Smith, S. S. (1991). Education and the struggle against race, class, and gender inequality. In E. Disch (Ed.), *Reconstructing gender: A multicultural anthology* (pp. 303–317). Mountain View, CA: Mayfield.

After the author and date, give the title of the article or chapter. Then write *In* and the first initial and last name of the editor(s). The abbreviation *Ed.* or *Eds.* (in parentheses) should follow the editor(s). End with the title of the book, the page numbers in which the article appears, and the publication information.

Encyclopedia Article

Esposito, V. J. (2000). World War II: The diplomatic history of the war and post-war period. In *Encyclopedia Americana* (9th ed., Vol. 29, pp. 364–367). Danbury, CT: Grolier.

Begin with the author (if given) and date. Then give the title of the article. The name of the encyclopedia (after *In*) should be in italics. The edition number, volume number, and page number(s) should be in parentheses. If an editor is also named, list the first initial and last name before the title (after *In*).

Electronic Sources

As with print sources, citations for electronic sources require author(s), date, title, and publication information. Authors and titles are formatted in the same manner as print sources. The difference occurs with publication information: Publishers of electronic work sometimes assign a *digital object identifier* (DOI), which is a kind of persistent virtual address. The DOI is sometimes, not always, located at the top of the article. If a source has a DOI, you need not include a retrieval date or URL. If no DOI was assigned, however, provide a URL. (When adding the URL to your citation, break it only before slashes [/] or other punctuation and do not add hyphens.) The *Publication Manual of the American Psychological Association* (APA) says, "No retrieval date is necessary for content that is not likely to be changed or updated, such as a journal article or book." In other words, if the content is likely to stay unchanged, no retrieval date is needed. Especially with electronic sources, remember the basic principle behind citing sources: to provide a guide for finding the sources you used. Therefore, the most direct route to the source should always be used in the entry.

Website

Pinsker, S. (Ed.). (1999). *Robin flies again: Letters written by women of Goucher College, class of 1903.* Retrieved from http://meyerhoff.goucher.edu/library/robin

Sierra Club. (2011, March). Retrieved March 10, 2011, from http://www.sierraclub.org

As with all sources in APA format, begin with the author's or editor's name(s) (inverted), if available, and the date of electronic publication. Give the title of the site (italicized). Write *Retrieved* and then the date of access (if the information is likely to get edited or revised), followed by *from* and the URL (no final period).

Document from Website (Author and Date Stated)

Brennan, M. J. (2014, February 6). *Chef and farmer summit.* Retrieved from http://forsyth .cc/ces

Begin with the author name (normal APA format), followed by the date (in parentheses), the title of the specific document, the word *Retrieved* and the access date if necessary, and finally *from* and the URL.

Document from Website (No Author or Date Stated)

Equestrian handbook. (n.d.) Retrieved April 28, 2014 from http://www.sca.org/

Begin with the title. In place of the date, write n.d. in parentheses for "no date." Then, give the title of the specific document (if applicable), *Retrieved* and the access date if necessary, and finally *from* and the URL.

Personal or Professional Home Page

McNair, P. (2014, May 4) *Patricia Ann McNair: On all things writerly and readerly*. Retrieved May 6, 2014, from patriciaannmcnair.com/

Begin with the creator's name, followed by the date of the most recent update, the title, *Retrieved*, the date of access if needed, and *from* and the URL.

Journal or Magazine Article Retrieved from a Database

Ryu, D. (2013). Play to learn, learn to play: Language learning through gaming culture. *Recall, 25*(1), 286–301. doi:10.1017/S0958344013000050

Follow guidelines for a print journal. After the page number, add *Retrieved* and the home page URL of the journal if there is no DOI for the article. If there is a DOI, list it after *doi*: following the page numbers. Whether you provide a URL or DOI, do not include the name of the database.

Journal Article Online

If the online journal is exactly the same as the print version (which is most common for academic journals), then follow the format for print articles, but conclude the entry with *Retrieved from* and the URL of the journal's homepage if no DOI is assigned. If a DOI is given, list it after *doi:*

Crow, A. (2000). What's age got to do with it? Teaching older students in computer-aided classrooms. *Teaching English in the Two-Year College, 27*(4), 400–415. Retrieved from http://www.ncte.org

Birmingham, P. (2008). Elated citizenry: Deception and the democratic task of bearing witness. *Research in Phenomenology 83*(2), 198–215. doi: 10.1163/156916408x286969

Online Presentation

Groshelle, Z. (2014, April 23). *Visualizing your pitch* [Prezi slides]. Retrieved from prezi .com/oerqtrj5ie3y/visualizing-your-pitch/

Give the author name, date of publication, and the title of presentation in italics. Then give the digital file format in brackets, *Retrieved from*, and the URL.

Online Book

Shaw, B. (1916). *Pygmalion.* Retrieved from http://bartleby.com/138/index.html

Follow the format for print books, but exclude the original print publication information. End with the URL.

Abstract

Bailey, K.D. Towards unifying science: Applying concepts across disciplinary boundaries. *Systems Research and Behavioral Science*, 18(1), 41-62. Abstract retrieved from http:// onlinelibrary.wiley.com/

Include either the database name or the database URL, but not both.

Other Sources

Brochure

Masonic Information Center. (n.d.). *A response to critics of freemasonry* [Brochure]. Silver Spring, MD: Masonic Services Association.

Use *n.d.* to indicate no date, which is often necessary for brochures. After the title, add the descriptor *Brochure* in brackets before the publication information.

Personal Interview or Letter

(A. Shimerda, personal communication, March 4, 2014)

APA style recommends citing personal communications only with an in-text citation—not in the References list. In the in-text citation, give the name of the interviewee, the title *personal communication*, and the date.

Television Program

Martin, J. (Writer), & Moore, R. (Director). (1992). A streetcar named Marge [Television series episode]. In A. Jean & M. Reiss (Producers), *The Simpsons.* Los Angeles, CA: Twentieth Century Fox.

Begin with the name and title of the scriptwriter, then the name and title of the director and the date. Give the title of the episode or segment followed by the producer and the title of the program (italicized). End with the location of the broadcasting company and the company name.

Government Publication

U.S. Census Bureau. (2007). *Statistical abstract of the United States.* Washington, DC: U.S. Government Printing Office.

If no author is given, use the government agency as the author, followed by the date, the title (in italics), and the publication information that appears on the title page.

Sample Research Essay

Sharon Angel's essay, written for her second-semester English course, is part ethnography and part argument: It reveals the language and social practices of a particular group (third-shift workers) and makes a case for supporting them. Angel also illustrates some important moves for research essays: She brings together, or *synthesizes,* a range of sources and explains how they relate to her own experience. Angel also provides textual cues (see page 505) so that readers understand the relationships among sources. Finally, despite the different sources operating throughout the essay, Angel manages to keep an incisive focus.

Angel provides a separate title page, which is required for APA format.

Running head: GRAVEYARD SHIFTS 1

Graveyard Shifts

Sharon Angel

Northwestern Michigan College

Graveyard Shifts

En route to the dumpster with trash bag in tow, I'm working the graveyard shift. Tonight, rogue electrons are brewing a midnight storm. My hair stands on end as if under the spell of a snake charmer. With my empty left hand, I pry open the dumpster enough to sling in the trash with my right. The bag slips into the darkness, and I wonder "just how much pressurized-plankton polyethylene *is* required to make a trash bag?" My wonder is quashed by the sound of dumpster-lid thunder. I know this sound well but it still gives me a start. I return to the building, and the fluorescent light blinds my peripheral vision. I should feel solid, but I funnel, like liquid, into the double glass doors.

Her personal testimony shows that even heavily researched projects can begin with the writer's own experience.

Third-shift custodians know all too well how sleep deprivation affects the senses. We know the constant longing for a good day's sleep. And we know that part of our job will always involve managing a kind of persistent "jet lag."

The second paragraph connects the writer's experience to others'. It creates public resonance.

The Bureau of Labor Statistics reports that approximately 85% of America's labor force works during the day, 15% perform shift work, and only 3% do overnight shift work (*Economic news release*, 2005). The 3% who work overnight, or graveyard, shift form a subculture of little renown. When we think of a subculture (or co-culture), we often imagine a distinct group of people exercising/asserting their freedoms of choice and expression—like hipsters or hackers. As defined by the *Oxford English Dictionary* (1998), a subculture is "A group

Angel begins with statistics and then uses them to build an interesting point about group identity.

Two entirely different sources, BLS and OED, help to build a line of reasoning.

or class of lesser importance or size sharing specific beliefs, interests, or values which may be at variance with those of the general culture of which it forms part" (p. 19). Third-shift workers are definitely a "group of lesser size," and they do share interests that are "at variance with those of the general culture." But the third-shift subculture is so integrated with the daylight perspective of our 24/7 society that they may not even acknowledge their own night-shift community. Their dual existence seems invisible or at least arguable. So what does distinguish graveyard shift workers from the day-shift majority, and what bonds overnight workers in a unique way?

She goes even further into the nature of the subculture. She's exploring what's not obvious, what's otherwise hidden from plain thinking.

Typically, a subculture makes its presence known through dress, speech, musical preference, political statements, or social movements—invoking a credo or some external symbolism. But the distinction between daylight workers and overnight workers is more internal than external. What solidifies the midnight subculture is the inherent inclusion of those who have experienced the adjustment of their day/night biological clock (more precisely, the "circadian rhythm"). Yet even graveyard workers may fail to realize the consequences of adjusting one's circadian rhythm.

Angel first explains circadian rhythm and then integrates the quotation to further detail its function.

The circadian rhythm is the internal clock that determines a person's natural sleep cycle within a twenty-four hour period. It is heavily influenced by nature's day/night cycle (with daylight and darkness as external stimuli). But this internal clock affects far more than just a person's sleep. Michael Price (2011) of the APA *Monitor* summarizes Charmane Eastman, PhD, (a physiological psychologist a Rush University in Chicago) as follows: "The circadian clock is essentially a timer that lets various glands know when to release hormones and also controls mood, alertness, body temperature and other aspects of the body's daily cycle" (para. 5). The American College of Emergency Physicians (2003) adds that:

> Many bodily functions exhibit circadian rhythms, from the best known sleep/wake cycle to all of the vital signs. As we become capable of more precise measurements, more and more circadian cycles are being recognized. Even bone length has been found to exhibit a circadian periodicity. Most circadian rhythms have both an endogenous component (regulated by an internal clock located in the suprachiasmatic nucleus of the hypothalamus) and an exogenous component. The exogenous component is composed of various time clues called zeitgebers. One of the most powerful zeitgebers is the light/dark cycle. (para. 3)

The lengthy quotation is well contextualized by the previous source and Angel's language.

Recognized or not, these physiological factors dramatically affect the well-being of night-shift workers who must reestablish a circadian rhythm that is not cued by nature's daylight/darkness cycle.

If a steady sleep routine is established, overnight employees can successfully shift their circadian clock to a nocturnal schedule.

Angel follows the lengthy quotation with a thorough connection to her topic. (*The source, then, is made increasingly relevant as the essay continues.*)

But the schedule may only be adjusted a certain amount to suit weekend activities, or it will fall out of the established rhythm. This produces, at best, a feeling of jet lag—familiar to most third-shift workers. Enough time for sleep must be set aside, and spent with eyes closed to bright light, in order to establish the "dark" part of the light/dark cycle.

Again, Angel integrates sources only after she introduces the broader point, in this case: the link between sleep patterns and illness.

Extended time spent out of sync with one's circadian rhythm can not only create sleep disorders, but it can increase the risk of stress, diabetes, obesity, heart disease—and even breast cancer. Researchers have also found a direct link between the disruption of circadian rhythm and depression (Gouin, 2010). This is not to mention the fact that night-shift employees working against their circadian rhythm also put others at risk. Hypersomnia and cognitive lapses can be especially hazardous. Drowsiness while driving on the job is the largest contributor to occupational fatalities (Price, 2011). The Exxon Valdez and Chernobyl disasters were attributed in part to the fatigue of overnight workers. And the air traffic controller scandal is a perfect example of what can happen when the scheduling of night-shift employees is handled without regard for the increased risks of overnight employment. The management responsible for scheduling employees may never have worked the overnight shift. That is why support offered by a fellow third-shifter is especially meaningful—because it comes from a place of mutual empathy.

We fellow third-shifters remind each other to drive safely, offer rides and accompany each other as needed when walking outside in risky areas. When we arrive at work, we often discuss who's gotten enough sleep to function well, as if we're talking about weather conditions. At the end of our shift, there are discussions about who's craving what for their 6 a.m. dinner—or the fact that picking up a pizza on the way home is not an option. And we always know there's a listening ear when it comes to the disappointments and frustrations of missing—or being too "out of it" to enjoy social activities with our diurnal friends and family.

The paragraph returns to personal experience.

Mainstream culture's social life revolves around a diurnal existence. It is often assumed that one who works nights has their entire day available—and can simply work their sleep schedule around social activities. But one's circadian clock can only be finessed to a certain point. For example, I sleep from 8:00 a.m. to 4:00 p.m. when I'm in sync with my weekday sleep cycle. So attending a meeting scheduled for noon is equivalent to a diurnal worker attending a meeting at 3:00 a.m.

Here begins the more explicit argument about mainstream culture's inattention to the third-shift subculture.

The expectation of overnight workers to function well in the middle of their sleep cycle is an unrecognized denial of the overnight subculture. Albeit unintentional, this denial is a symptom of our failure to recognize overnight workers as a subculture, to begin with. As a third-shift worker of eight years, I can testify to the following: It would be of great advantage to third-shift employees if we were able to pop out of bed at any hour, function well, and return to quality sleep—at will. We would be able to accommodate any schedule as long as we could piece together seven hours of intermittent, deep sleep—remaining ever chipper. But that would, in turn, require humans in general to redefine themselves by taking control of their "CLOCK gene" which is "critical to the generation of circadian rhythms" (*CLOCK*, 2014, para. 1). Of course, if we altered the CLOCK gene we would be surrendering an aspect of our physiology in favor of a superhuman mechanism. That is one more reason why the bond among third-shift workers is so important. We must remind each other of our connection with the natural world because we spend so much time living under an artificial sun.

The CLOCK source is used within a mini line of reasoning about mainstream culture's "failure to recognize."

I remember one stressful evening at work when I was racing against the clock, my pupils retracted against the florescent lighting and lungs tightly bound with caffeine. A couple of co-workers rescued me at break time, leading me outside into the fresh air and pointing upward. We spent our break time taking in a sliver of a lunar eclipse. Though we did not fully escape the orange haze of street lamps, we were able to share a bit of nocturnal calm. And though it was left unspoken, it strengthened our camaraderie, and adjusted my priorities. Darkness can not only be soothing, but uplifting. Holly Wren Spaulding (2013) addresses

After more supportive testimony, Angel integrates another source (Spaulding) that speaks to a broader premise about mainstream culture's failure to recognize—or see in the dark.

this notion with insight: "When we are estranged from the dark, we lose access to vital human emotions and sensual experiences including wonder, awe and humility" (p. 83). It may be a quirky confession that I look forward to a trip to the dumpster on a blustery night, but it's a chance to briefly navigate away from the realm of artificial light. It's refreshing to spend my break lunching with co-workers at the employee picnic table (as weather permits) rather than squeeze in a trip to the neighborhood 7-Eleven. Third-shift workers stare the neon-lit, 24-7 global economy in the eye.

No longer does a lighted, 7-Eleven sign shine like an oasis in the dark of night. It has been crowded out by competing overnight gas stations, well-lit Wall-Marts and the omnipresent McDonald's drive-thru. In fact there is irony in the name "7-Eleven." It was adopted in 1947 "to reflect the store's new, *extended* hours (of) 7 a.m. to 11 p.m., seven days a week" (*History*, 2012 "Toting Away Your Purchases," para. 2). But apparently, those hours weren't enough. Consumerism keeps us manufacturing, shipping, and selling goods all night long. After all, being deprived of a multi-cow, preformed, rewarmed hamburger at three in the morning would simply be un-American. But the fact that we can measure time by an atomic clock and Skype around the globe at all hours does not mean that being "always open" is the best idea. Still, we light up the outdoors like a circus and

Angel is careful not to leave her broader points hanging. She supports them with specific background information. Here, the source supports a premise about the mainstream culture.

spend hours of both day and night basking in the blue glow of television, cell phone, and computer screens.

The lightbulb allusion helps her to build up to Tillett's point at the end of the paragraph.

Initially, the invention of the lightbulb allowed Americans to extend their day for work and pleasure. But who'd have guessed that artificial light might one day *disrupt* how well we function? Even for those who work during the day, lengthening their waking hours into the night with artificial light may result in an unhealthy overexposure. "Ocular exposure (the eye, exposed) to bright, artificial light inhibits the production of melatonin . . . which helps regulate the body's circadian rhythm and immune function, and also suppresses (breast cancer) tumor growth" (Tillett, 2006, p. A99). With all of the associated risks, one might wonder, "Why would someone *choose* to join a nocturnal co-culture?"

The BLS source returns now—at the end of the essay—to help support her argument.

It may seem surprising that "not being able to find other employment" was ranked in fifth place as a reason to work overnight. According to two articles published by the Bureau of Labor Statistics (based on their monthly Current Population Surveys CPS), one from 1997 and one from 2004, the top four reasons people chose to work the graveyard shift include "The nature of the job, personal preference, better arrangements for family or child care, and better pay" (Beers, 2000). For some, it is a career choice. In other words, the type of work they want to do happens to require working at night.

GRAVEYARD SHIFTS 10

For example, firefighters, police officers, and emergency medical staff. Individuals who have little or no problem adjusting their sleep rhythm may simply prefer to work in solitude, with less interruptions or perhaps just enjoy less traffic during their commute. The high cost of hospice and day care may also explain why one spouse may choose a night shift—so that his or her partner is always available to care for family members.

We come to work at night in order to serve the priorities we hold for ourselves or share with our diurnal loved ones. Although the meaning of "work family" takes on special significance for graveyard shift workers, it is mutually understood that our social life with the diurnal is no less important. In fact, it is especially important for the graveyard shift to remind itself that its existence extends beyond a largely, artificial environment.There is no substitute for the penetrating experience of circadian misalignment in combination with an upside-down social life. Empathizing with others who have shared this experience forms a unique camaraderie. This camaraderie validates our uncommon appreciation for the soothing side of darkness and our longing to connect with the inherent rhythm of our biological world. Graveyard shift workers rely on each other to affirm the existence of these gifts while we toil under artificial light. As we do so, we unwittingly solidify our co-cultural bond.

We now better understand the power of the camaraderie dramatized earlier in the essay.

References are listed in alphabetical order according to the first element in the entry. Publication dates, in APA format, come directly after the title or author names.

References

American College of Emergency Physicians. (2003, September). *Circadian rhythms and shift work*. Retrieved from https://www.acep.org/

Beers, T. M. (2000, June). Flexible schedules and shift work: Replacing the "9-to-5" workday? *Monthly Labor Review*. Retrieved from http://www.bls.gov/opub/mlr/2000/06/art3full.pdf

CLOCK. (2014, April 1). Retrieved April 25, 2014, from http://en.wikipedia.org/wiki/CLOCK

Economic news release: Table 5. (2005, July 1). Retrieved from http://www.bls.gov/news.release/flex.t05.htm

Gouin, J-P., Connors, J., Kiecolt-Glaser, J. K., Glaser, R., Malarkey, W. B., Atkinson, C., . . . Quan, N. (2010). Altered expression of circadian rhythm genes among individuals with a history of depression. *Journal of Affective Disorders, 126*(1), 161–166. doi:10.1016/j.jad.2010.04.002

History. (2012). Retrieved April 25, 2014, from http://corp.7-eleven.com/aboutus/history/tabid/75/default.aspx

Price, M. (2011, January). The risks of night work. *Monitor on Psychology, 42*(1). Retrieved from https://www.apa.org/monitor

Spaulding, H. W. (2013). In defense of darkness. In J. Mauk & J. Metz (Eds.), *Inventing arguments* (brief 3rd ed., pp. 83–87). Boston, MA: Cengage Learning.

Subculture. (1998). In J. A. Simpson (Ed.), *Oxford English dictionary* (2nd ed., Vol. 17, p. 19). Oxford, England: Oxford University Press.

Tillett, T. (2006, February). Headliners: Breast cancer. *Environmental Health Perspectives, 114*(2), A99. Retrieved from http://www.ncbi.nlm.nih.gov/pmc/articles/PMC1367861/

Frequently Asked Questions

What If I Don't Know What Type of Source I Have?

This question often comes up when researching electronic sources. Most online research methods lead to either periodicals (journals, magazines, and newspapers) or websites. (Online books are generally not in the same search paths as periodicals.) If you have an electronic source and are not sure if it is a website or a periodical, check the top of the first page for publication information. If the text has a volume or issue number, or date information, it is most likely a periodical. Also, an electronic article most often lists the title of the magazine or journal at the top of the first page.

How Do I Tell the Difference between a Journal and a Magazine?

In general, a magazine is published more often than a journal. Magazines are published every week *(Time, Newsweek),* every other week, or every month. Magazines are written for nonspecialized, or *general,* readership, whereas journals are written for readers with a specialized field of knowledge (such as nursing, engineering, or pharmacology). Although magazines attempt to inform or entertain the public about various (sometimes even eccentric) topics, journals attempt to investigate particular ideas, theories, or situations within a discipline or field of study. Check the publication information to see how often the periodical is published, and look at the table of contents to see if the articles are written for general or specialized readers. (See pages 474–475.)

How Do I Find the Publication Information?

Publication information for books can be found on the title page. The front of the title page has the full title, the publisher, and the city of publication, and the reverse (or copyright) page includes the copyright dates and any edition information. For periodicals, the volume and issue number usually appear at the bottom of each page and are often printed on the first page inside the cover along with the table of contents. (However, some periodicals fill the first few pages with advertisements.) Websites can be trickier. If the author, last update, or sponsoring institution does not appear on the opening (or home) page, scroll down to the bottom of the page (or look on the menu for *Information* or *About Us*).

How Do I Know the Page Numbers of an Electronic Source?

Generally, electronic sources do not have page numbers—and documentation styles do not require page numbers for websites or online journal articles. Sometimes, however, a print source will republish its contents electronically and retain page numbers. (In other words, the source appears online exactly as it does in print.) In that case, simply use the page numbers as they appear.

Should I Use APA, MLA, or Something Else?

MLA (or Modern Language Association) style is used by writers in the humanities and literature (such as English and communications). APA style is used by writers in the medical field, education, and, of course, psychology. CMS (or Chicago Manual of Style) is used by writers in humanities fields such as religion, history, and philosophy. The sciences (such as physics and chemistry) have particular styles as well. When writing for an academic audience, you should always ask what style to use. Some instructors want their students to use a particular style, regardless of their major or field of study.

Why Are There Different Documentation Styles?

The different styles have emerged over the course of years. They have developed because different research techniques sometimes call for a particular type of documentation. As academic fields grow, they develop and reward particular research strategies—and one documentation style cannot always account for those strategies.

Why Don't Some Articles Have Works Cited or Reference Pages?

Writers in magazines and newspapers use an informal strategy for referencing their sources. They use *attributive phrases* to link statements or information to particular sources (for example: *According to the English department chair at Pennsylvania State,* grades in first-year college courses have remained relatively stable). However, in scholarly work, writers document sources formally—according to MLA or APA guidelines. These shared guidelines provide a way for readers from other schools, states, countries, or centuries to follow the writer's research trail. In other words, the conventions serve an important purpose: to make certain that others beyond our particular social spheres can participate in our work.

Standard Abbreviations

MLA	APA	
ed.	**Ed.**	= Editor or Edited by
eds.	**Eds.**	= Editors
ed.	**ed.**	= Edition, usually associated with a number (4th ed.)
Rev. ed.	**Rev. ed.**	= Revised edition
n.d.	**n.d.**	= No date
n.p.	**n.p.**	= No publisher or no place
n. pag.	**n. pag.**	= No page numbers
trans.	**Trans.**	= Translator
p.	**p.**	= Page number
pp.	**pp.**	= Page numbers
no.	**No.**	= Number
pars.	**para.**	= Paragraphs
vol.	**Vol.**	= Volume

17 Organizing Ideas

John Metz

A completed text should read like a coherent journey: Readers begin with a sense of direction (a good introduction), pass through various locations (paragraphs), encounter different terrain (foreign concepts or ideas from outside sources), all while following road signs and cues (transitional words, phrases, and sentences). Having traveled an intellectual route, readers arrive somewhere unique and valuable (a good conclusion). This chapter presents strategies for shaping that journey.

Beginning

Introductions create focus and establish tone. They are the invitation to *start* thinking. But if an introduction is flat or vague, it can *stop* thinking. Notice this vague introduction:

> There are many critical issues facing today's public schools. They have to consider violence, financial constraints, teacher training, drugs, and student apathy, just to name a few. But in this difficult era, educators have become enamored with a saving grace: technology. Computers are everywhere in our public schools. But the problem is that the technology isn't the saving grace that it seems. Schools should rethink their allegiance to computers.

This introduction illustrates a few mistakes.

- The writer begins with an obvious statement, not an invitation to think or explore an issue.
- Because the introduction begins so broadly, it makes big intellectual leaps to get to the thesis at the end of the paragraph.
- The placement of the thesis at the end of the paragraph makes the earlier information seem contrived and formulaic.

In her essay, Elizabeth Bohnhorst (page 251) avoids these mistakes. She takes us directly to the critical issue. She does not need to rush through several vague statements to suggest her position on the issue. She makes it indirectly from the outset:

> "Another boring PowerPoint," responds Jennifer when I ask about her day at school. I might not find these words so discouraging coming from a company executive after a long meeting or even a college student leaving an informative lecture. But these words of an eleven-year-old elementary school student leave me feeling slightly uneasy. PowerPoint presentations are intended to compel students to become more interested in the subject with the use of neon colors and moving graphic images. But these flashy additions to current educational strategies haven't fooled everyone. The text and material covered is still the same boring grammar and spelling lessons but the educator has altered: It is a screen.

The possibilities for introductions are boundless. And the strategy always depends on the voice, the topic, and the assignment itself. Here are some conventional and sound strategies:

- Begin with a specific assertion about the topic. In his essay, John Steinbeck (page 66) begins with a general statement about American settlers and the land:

  I have often wondered at the savagery and thoughtlessness with which our early settlers approached this rich continent. They came at it as though it were an enemy, which of course it was. They burned the forests and changed the rainfall; they swept the buffalo from the plains, blasted the streams, set fire to the grass, and ran a reckless scythe through the virgin and noble timber.

- Begin with a typical belief or stereotype about the topic, and then turn to your particular insight:

  Most people assume they have no relationship with their local police departments. Other than in an emergency situation, most are even reluctant to acknowledge police officers. They often treat them as uniformed specters lurking on the roads of their towns. But the police of any community are deeply connected to the everyday patterns of life. They are serving their communities and participating in daily routines at all levels.

- Begin with a fictional account, or scenario:

  Imagine a community in which the police only appeared for emergencies, in which people had to make a 911 call simply to get a police car to visit the area. Imagine the streets of a crowded city without the occasional police cruiser. Imagine the downtown stores without the presence of a city officer.

- Begin in the past, taking readers back in time from the first sentence. Cindy Bosley (page 33) begins narrating and waits until later in her essay to characterize or give meaning to the events:

  Every evening of the annual broadcast of the Miss America Pageant, I, from the age of seven or so, carefully laid out an elaborate chart so that I might also participate as an independent judge of the most important beauty contest in the world.

- Re-create the point of contact. Explain how you first encountered the idea. This is often more informal, because it requires some personal narration, as in Derrick Jensen's (page 131) introduction:

  I don't know about you, but whenever I attend some "green" conference, I know I'm supposed to leave feeling inspired and energized, but instead I feel heartbroken, discouraged, defeated, and lied to. It's not the inevitable talk about farmers (re)discovering organic farming; about plastic forks made from cornstarch; about solar photovoltaics; about relocalizing; about the joys of simple living; about grieving the murder of the planet; about "changing our stories"; and most especially about maintaining a positive attitude that gets me down. It's that no one, and I mean no one, ever mentions psychopathology. Why is this important? Because those in power destroy sustainable communities—and not just sustainable indigenous communities.

- Begin with a popular reference. Writers often invite readers into their ideas by alluding to something in popular culture, such as a television program, an advertisement, a song, or a current event. This strategy allows readers to enter the world of the essay through a familiar door. In his article, Nicholas Carr (page 355) begins with an allusion to *2001: A Space Odyssey* moves:

> "Dave, stop. Stop, will you? Stop, Dave. Will you stop, Dave?" So the computer HAL pleads with the implacable astronaut Dave Bowman in a famous and weirdly poignant scene toward the end of Stanley Kubrick's *2001: A Space Odyssey*. Bowman, having nearly been sent to a deep-space death by the malfunctioning machine, is calmly, coldly disconnecting the memory circuits that control its artificial brain. "Dave, my mind is going," HAL says, forlornly. "I can feel it. I can feel it."
>
> I can feel it, too. Over the past few years I've had an uncomfortable sense that someone, or something, has been tinkering with my brain, remapping the neural circuitry, reprogramming the memory. . . .

- Begin with the personal and then move to the public. For example, notice how Elizabeth Thoman (page 202) starts with personal reflection but moves steadily toward the public relevance of her topic:

> Like most middle-class children of the '50s, I grew up looking for the American Dream. In those days there were no cartoons in my Saturday viewing, but I distinctly remember watching, with some awe, *Industry on Parade*. I felt both pride and eager anticipation as I watched tail-finned cars rolling off assembly lines, massive dams taming mighty rivers and sleek chrome appliances making life more convenient for all.
>
> When I heard the mellifluous voice of Ronald Reagan announce on *GE Theatre* that "Progress is our most important product," little did I realize that the big box in our living room was not just entertaining me. At a deeper level, it was stimulating an "image" in my head of how the world should work: that anything new was better than something old; that science and technology were the greatest of all human achievements and that in the near future—and certainly by the time I grew up—the power of technology would make it possible for everyone to live and work in a world free of war, poverty, drudgery and ignorance.

- Create a shared experience between reader and writer. In short, this strategy is all about public resonance: It makes an explicit intellectual bond among the writer, the issue,

Notice how Hollingsworth begins with a main idea, then introduces the source, paraphrases the supporting information, provides in-text documentation, and then comments on the paraphrased information:

> One health epidemic at the forefront of public consciousness is autism, a brain disorder that impairs a person's ability to communicate, socialize, and participate in group behavior. Often surfacing by the time a child is three years old, the symptoms of autism include stifled speech and difficulty in displaying joy or affection. According to a 2007 study by the U.S. Centers for Disease Control and Prevention, about 1 in 150 American children are autistic—a staggering number that makes autism the fastest-growing developmental disorder in the United States (Rice). Since the release of these findings, nonprofit organizations across the country have been working to raise public awareness of this national health crisis. The largest of these organizations, Autism Speaks, recently launched a multimedia campaign aimed at parents of autistic, or potentially autistic, children.

(For more on integrating sources and documentation, see Chapter 16.)

Counterarguing

Engaging other people's ideas in an essay involves making counterarguments. Counterarguments (responses formed when writers anticipate possible opposition to their claims) are often arranged in separate paragraphs. For example, you might summarize an opposing point in a paragraph, and then in a new paragraph, explain why your understanding is most appropriate, correct, or valuable. The process can be repeated as often as necessary. For example, if you have anticipated three opposing points, you might develop six paragraphs:

> Opposing Point A
>
> Your counterargument
>
> Opposing Point B
>
> Your counterargument
>
> Opposing Point C
>
> Your counterargument

Some writers use the *turnabout paragraph* for counterarguments. A turnabout paragraph begins with an opposing position and then includes the writer's counterargument. In other words, the opposing point and the writer's counter are in the same paragraph—usually separated by some explicit change in direction (such as *however, but,* or *on the other hand*). In the following example, the opposing claim (that global warming is not a real problem) is addressed within the paragraph. The paragraph also includes the change of direction:

> Some people argue that global warming is not a problem at all. They suggest that all the discussion about the ozone layer is merely fear-mongering by left-wing political

> activists. This argument, however, ignores the volumes of evidence compiled by scientists (many of whom are Nobel Prize winners) from around the world—scientists from different cultures, from different religious contexts, from different political systems, and with different political agendas. The amount of data they have collected and the sheer din of their collective voices ought to be enough to convince people that global warming is much more than the delusions of a few environmental groups.

In her essay, Rachel Schofield (page 403) makes a similar move. She directly explains the opposing position ("some would disagree") and then shifts to her way of thinking:

> Food still enables us to survive, but we no longer revere it. Some would disagree, citing the weight problems engorging our country. We see food 24/7 on TV, hear about it on the radio, see it advertised on billboards, and even in Internet pop-ups. Advertising works. We buy what we see, yet the low nutrition levels in our highly processed foods leave our bodies starving for more, and we only give them more junk. We can see the preeminence of food in the dedication of temples to food all along our highways; fast food chains are more popular than ever. However, there is a difference between obsession with food and reverence for it. Our fast food restaurants and freezer aisles are brothels where impure, chemically altered food is bought and sold. Almost gone are the days when honest, unadulterated food can be purchased by the American family.

Counterarguments can also be addressed in a subtler manner. In the following paragraph, Mahoney creates a kind of back and forth between her position (using a pencil to read) and resistance to it:

> When I tell my students the only way to read a book is with pencil gliding freely across the page (no highlighters please), they look stymied. Selected passages ought to be underlined, I maintain, and tricky vocabulary circled. Further, I suggest that handwritten symbols in the form of stars, asterisks, squiggly lines, question marks, brackets, and the like warrant placement alongside their personal comments posted in the margins. After all, the white space on the printed page could use the company. My students offer good enough reasons, however, for *not* writing in their books: (1) Writing in books during the K–12 years is absolutely taboo, they tell me, and they've been successfully trained to do as told; (2) Some college bookstores won't buy back textbooks with extensive personalized annotations and markings. Students need cash at semester's end, so they dutifully comply. But how is any of this non-writing good for thinking and learning? I'm pretty sure it's not. We might find the current state of affairs particularly worrisome if we frame the problem this way: In an attempt to educate, it seems that educators and a whole lot of other well-meaning adults have worked successfully to ensure disengagement with the printed word, often during the most formative and critical years of literacy acquisition.

You might decide that the opposing position requires significant explanation, and that it would be best to group opposing points together before giving your counter. Therefore, you might devote several paragraphs before countering:

Opposing Point A

Opposing Point B

Opposing Point C

Your counterargument to A

Your counterargument to B

Your counterargument to C

Regardless of your general organization strategy, make certain to cue readers when giving a counterargument. Readers need to understand when the focus shifts from the counterargument to the main argument. You might begin a paragraph with an opposing viewpoint: "Some opponents might argue that. . . ." If so, you will need to shift readers back to your logic: "But they do not understand that. . . ." Here is a list of some helpful transitions when doing counterargument:

On the other hand,

Contrary to this idea,

Although many people take this stance,

However, (; however,)

Despite the evidence for this position,

But

Separating Problems and Solutions

When writers propose solutions, they have to manage a range of rhetorical elements: the problem, illustrations or support for the problem, the solution, support for the solution, previously attempted or alternative solutions, shortcomings of those solutions, counterarguments, and concessions. These can be arranged in any order. Here are two standard strategies:

- Problem

  Examples/Illustrations
- My Solution to the Problem

  Examples/Illustrations
- Attempted or Alternative Solution

Explanation

Shortcoming

- Attempted or Alternative Solution

  Explanation

  Shortcoming

OR

- Problem
- Attempted/Alternative Solution A and the Shortcoming
- How My Solution Avoids This Shortcoming
- Attempted/Alternative Solution B and the Shortcoming
- How My Solution Avoids This Shortcoming
- Attempted/Alternative Solution C and the Shortcoming
- How My Solution Avoids This Shortcoming

The arrangement of elements depends on the topic. Some problems demand more attention; others less. Some solutions need significant explanation and support; others less. If the problem is fairly obvious—if readers already see it as a problem—then it will not require lengthy supporting passages, counterarguments, concessions, and so on. But if the problem is subtle—if readers don't see it as a problem—then a longer explanation is required. Writers must ask themselves two questions: First, *will readers easily accept this as a problem? If not, I'll have to persuade them.* Second, *will readers easily accept the solution? If not, I'll have to persuade them.* For example, if the problem is a violent elementary school playground, the writer may not have to work diligently to make a case. Readers are not apt to dismiss such a problem. But if the problem is a quiet form of institutional racism, then the writer might need to take more time (more paragraphs) to reveal the problem.

Concluding

As with introductions, the possibilities for conclusions are limitless, but some principles and strategies apply. First, academic writers rarely waste time summarizing or "wrapping up" points they have just made. Instead, they use their conclusions to extend points into the readers' world or to suggest the significance of their ideas. Consider the following strategies:

- End with public resonance. In his article, Derrick Jensen (page 133) creates public resonance and even calls for action:

  > Sharing our finite planet with this culture is like being stuck in a room with a psychopath. There is no exit. Although the psychopath may choose other targets first,

> eventually it will turn to us. Eventually we'll have to fight for our lives. And so if we want access to a landbase we can inhabit, and want our descendants to be able to live there long into the future, we need to organize politically to stop this lethal culture in its tracks.

Simon Benlow makes a similar, but slightly more subtle, move in his essay (page 141):

> However, if we continue to allow the term "customer" to replace "student," I fear that students will become increasingly blind to the difference between consumerist culture and college culture. I fear they will become increasingly more confused by the expectations of college, and that in the nightmarish long run, colleges will become simply another extension of the consumerist machine in which everyone is encouraged to pre-package knowledge, to super-size grades, and to "hold" anything even slightly distasteful.

Caution: The explicit call to action can move a text into overt argumentation. Of course, that is fine if the assignment is focused on argumentation. But if the assignment calls for more analytical writing, then calls to action should be limited.

- Return to an introductory image or scene. This strategy is often called "framing." Having gone through the complexities of the essay, the readers know something special and different about the opening idea or image. Returning to it does not merely restate the point; instead, it helps the readers understand just how far they've come. They understand a new poignancy, a new sticking point, about the topic. In his article, Nicholas Carr (page 362) returns to his initial allusion:

> I'm haunted by that scene in *2001*. What makes it so poignant, and so weird, is the computer's emotional response to the disassembly of its mind. . . . HAL's outpouring of feeling contrasts with the emotionlessness that characterizes the human figures in the film, who go about their business with an almost robotic efficiency. . . .

- Allude to something well known to the readers. An allusion can be a powerful conclusion strategy because it projects the point of the essay onto some other subject or idea. It extends the essay's reach outward. In his essay, John Steinbeck (page 70) makes a powerful historical allusion:

> But we are an exuberant people, careless and destructive as active children. We make strong and potent tools and then have to use them to prove that they exist. Under the pressure of war we finally made the atom bomb, and for reasons which seemed justifiable at the time we dropped it on two Japanese cities—and I think we finally frightened ourselves. In such things, one must consult himself because there is no other point of reference. I did not know about the bomb, and certainly I had nothing to do with its

use, but I am horrified and ashamed; and nearly everyone I know feels the same thing. And those who loudly and angrily justify Hiroshima and Nagasaki—why, they must be the most ashamed of all.

Questions for Organizing Your Projects

There is no secret formula for good academic writing. But there are some helpful concepts and questions. As you consider your own projects, apply the following questions, which correspond to the strategies explained throughout this chapter:

- What introductory strategy will yield the most momentum and intensity?
- What individual points should be developed separately in paragraphs?
- How should I take on opposing positions? In turnabout paragraphs or some back-and-forth strategy?
- Do I have a range of distinct support strategies? Does each warrant its own paragraph?
- Where will outside sources (if applicable) be most helpful? What specific points or passages could use the help of other voices?
- How can a conclusion go beyond summarizing? How can the final paragraph(s) leave readers with a sense that they have traveled through an important idea?

18 Developing Voice

John Metz

When we talk, we project a character or mood by choosing certain words and changing the sound, pitch, and pace of our voices. (Some people talk with dramatic ups and downs; others blab at us in a single-note dirge.) We use physical gestures, too: waving our hands, bowing our heads, opening our eyes wide or closing them. As writers, we don't use our hands or eyes to gesture to readers, but we have plenty of writerly strategies. Because we write in different contexts, for different audiences, and on different occasions, we need to be flexible, adapting our writer's voice to suit the conventions and expectations of each situation. This is one of the most valuable skills for a writer, and it's one you can hone through experiment.

Establishing Presence

When we write, we enter words, phrases, clauses, and punctuation into a document. That document, in turn, creates a voice. Whether the writer is present (still at the keyboard), far away, or long since gone, the language still has a quality that readers hear in their heads. In other words, voice is *the presence created by the writing itself.* This section explains some common strategies for controlling the nature and power of that presence.

Choosing Details

When writers stay abstract and general, when they do not commit to particulars, their voices remain less visible. Abstraction often hides a writer's voice. But when writers characterize their subjects by using particular and focused words, their voices become recognizable. For instance, throughout her essay, Jaren Provo makes some grand claims about *Star Trek,* but she grounds those claims in details. In the following, Provo's voice becomes more and more pronounced as the details increase:

> Also uncharacteristic of *Star Trek* but common in the sci-fi realm is the element portraying humans as slaves of technology, hopelessly existent only in body. This concept is perhaps most prevalent in the *Matrix* trilogy. Yet *Star Trek* foretells humans as harnessing the resources of technology to propel themselves outward into space, to explore, to contact, to impact in a positive way. The transporter and warp drive allow for expedient, efficient movement among planets and realms; the communicator (predecessor to the flip-phone?) and universal translator aid in interpersonal and intercultural contact; the scientific tricorder (a handheld programmable scanning device) and ship's scanners enhance exploration purposes; and medical tricorders and unknown, but apparently technical, whirring devices devised from salt 'n' pepper shakers exist for medical purposes.

The nature of details helps to shape voice. In other words, the particulars that writers offer influence how they are heard. In her essay, the details Cindy Bosley (page 36) shares about her hometown help shape her voice, or how she *sounds* to readers. Of the many details Bosley could offer, she chooses ones that help establish a confessional tone:

> Clearly, I lacked the save-the-whales-and-rainforest civic-mindedness required not only of Miss America, but of Junior Miss America, too. Even, although one wouldn't think it, in Ottumwa, Iowa, where my mother would go on to work in a bathtub factory, and then a glue factory, and then an electrical connectors factory (the factory worker's version of upward mobility), and finally, a watch factory where they shipped and received not just watches but cocaine in our town that at that time had more FBI agents in it than railroad engineers. And even in this town where my sister would go to work the kill floor of the pork plant where, for fun, the workers shot inspection dye at each other and threatened each other's throats with hack-knives. And even in this town where my cousin, age 13, would bring a bomb to seventh grade for show-and-tell, and get caught and evacuated, and be given community service to do because the public-school-as-terrorist-ground phenomena hadn't yet been born.

The same goes with less personal writing. In her essay, Anne-Marie Oomen (page 98) describes a sand dune. Her descriptions create a vivid picture for readers and shape the way Oomen sounds in our heads:

> A blowout is a dune summit or ridge that may have once looked like a lush foliage-covered hilltop. But because of the lightness and fragility of the soil—almost dust—and the death, due to drought or other weather conditions, of that vegetation, plus exposure to the constant westerlies, the dune sand erodes away from the roots, especially at the crest of these hills. After years of enduring this relentless wind, the vegetation blows away, and the dune begins to hollow itself out, like a bowl, weathered down from the high point, leaving the lower, less exposed sides to rise like a rim. Dune walkers commonly stumble on blowouts all over the open duneland, but this one is startling for its immensity and grandeur, a huge basin carved by wind.

Controlling Speed and Time

Having more details slows down time for readers. Like in a film, time slows down when a writer (or producer) focuses in on many particular details. Steinbeck uses details throughout his essay to focus on particular moments in history:

> Quite a few years ago when I was living in my little town on the coast of California a stranger came in and bought a small valley where the Sempervirens redwoods grew, some of them three hundred feet high. We used to walk among these trees, and the light colored as though the great glass of the Cathedral at Chartres had strained and

> sanctified the sunlight. The emotion we felt in this grove was one of awe and humility and joy; and then one day it was gone, slaughtered, and the sad wreckage of boughs and broken saplings left like nonsensical spoilage of the battle-ruined countryside.

Having fewer details speeds up time for readers. The fewer details readers get, the more quickly they move through the text. Writers decide which ideas they want readers to slow down for—and which ideas they want readers to move through quickly. For instance, Lauren Jackson (page 75) wants us to linger in a particular memory from her childhood, so she gives details to the scene, but she moves quickly out of the situation (in one final sentence), which shoos readers (along with the kids) to the next idea:

> My mother smoked Marlboro Light 100s in a box and only in the kitchen when it was cold. She was courteous to the rest of the house: keeping the children out, always emptying the ashtray right away, and spraying air freshener. I used to sit in the dining room around the corner of the wall, to be out of view, and listen to her gossip and smoke while she danced around the linoleum with the telephone cord. When her girlfriends would come over, they would drink coffee, smoke, and talk about any and everything—usually discourse unsuitable for innocent ears. They would shoo the kids out of the kitchen and explain we couldn't be around the smoke.

Managing the "I"

Some writers make themselves visible in the text. They refer to themselves and their interactions with the subject. In other words, the writerly "I" shows up in the text. But the "I" must be managed, showing up for good cause—for instance, to help create a sense of location or personal experience. In his essay, Chester McCovey (page 102) includes himself in his observations and refers to his own presence in the scenes or situations. But he does not inject the "I" without good cause. His presence helps to show the lack of front porches in a particular area, and his recollections of his grandparents help make a point about changes that have occurred in American society. His use of "I" gives support to his more general claims:

> My grandparents' garages were small, just enough for one car and a few tools—not much of a garage for today's homeowner. In those days the garage kept a car and a small lawnmower, some rakes, and so on. The garage today must keep much more. One can see, then, how the exchange occurred. Like an old-fashioned trade in baseball, gone is the home team's beloved front porch, replaced by a big, new garage. Of course the trade is much more interesting than that. And a look at how it occurred enlightens us a little about the world in which we live. More importantly, it tells us not so much about how life is now but about how it came to be. And, I would argue, it shows us the way in which things will continue to change.

Anne-Marie Oomen's present "I" (page 97) is even more important to her observation. Her own quest to understand the Sleeping Bear legend is part of her observation: "As I move over the drifts of glacial debris, walking absorbs my attention. I watch my feet, notice snail shells in abundance, along with small stony fossils."

Contrarily, some writers stay invisible. The writerly "I" never appears. Instead, their texts focus entirely on the subject. In his essay, Justin Scott (page 106) remains invisible in his observation, yet his essay still projects a particular voice:

> One thing is immediately obvious in this cemetery: Those laden with the gifts of life often choose to utilize them in death, and those less fortunate make do with what they must. Class warfare spills into the afterworld: Business owner is segregated from bricklayer, clergy is separated from atheist. There are large domineering crypts bearing the surnames of the wealthy dead inside, branch-scraping obelisks with ornate script, tombs carefully sculpted to resemble tree stumps, small temples dedicated to their dead in ancient Greek style, and inevitably, the sunken, flat, and nondescript markers of the poor or humble. . . .

Scott's passage illustrates how a voice can be projected not through "I" but through careful word choice and sentence structure. Many writers opt for Scott's strategy. They create powerful, engaging, and intimate voices without drawing direct attention to their own experiences.

Using Allusions

Allusions are references to some public bit of knowledge (such as a historical event, a political situation, or a popular culture figure). An allusion can give a personal essay a broader and more public feeling while also helping to create a particular voice. For example, the following allusion helps to characterize Benlow's voice—especially early in the essay when he sounds intolerant of consumer life. The nature of the allusion (to a seemingly unimportant matter like fast food) helps Benlow to trivialize consumer culture and appear slightly above it:

> "Have it your way!" Of course, we all know the song and the friendly fried food establishment associated with this slogan. It's a harmless phrase, in and of itself, and one that works particularly well for the franchise. It suggests to customers that their particular appetites can be catered to, that their specific tastes, no matter how eccentric (within the continuum of dip n' serve fried food) can be easily satisfied.

Heidecker uses a range of allusions. The references to popular and lowbrow television programs impact how readers hear her. Toward the end of her essay, Heidecker adds dimension to her voice when she alludes to a series of novels—such as *The Great Gatsby, Lord of the Rings, Moby Dick, My Antonia,* and *Anna Karenina:*

> In the world of high art, such as literary fiction, the writer works to create a fictive dream—a coherent and impenetrable fantasy. The hope is that readers enter the dream and forget the real world. When we read a novel, for instance, our hopes become tied to Gatsby, Frodo, Ishmael, Antonia, Anna, and so on. We suspend our disbelief. And in

> turn, we are suspended in an ornate web of un-reality. But in reality television, part of the experience is the interplay between the fabricated scene (the kooky kitchen challenge limited to rutabagas and pig liver) and the invisible everyday lives of the contestants.

Promoting Curiosity

One of the primary jobs of a writer is to pique curiosity in readers. Very rarely does a writer (in any situation) seek only to tell readers what they are already thinking. Instead, writers seek to light a small fire in readers' minds, to make them want to *consider* an issue. Perhaps the most important strategy for promoting curiosity is to embody it, that is, to be curious as a writer. Curious writers make curious readers. In the following passage, Kathleen Norris (page 425) begins making a case for celibacy, and rather than come right out of the gate celebrating the celibate life, she adopts a posture of wonder:

> But celibate people have taught me that celibacy, practiced rightly, does indeed have something valuable to say to the rest of us. Specifically, they have helped me better appreciate both the nature of friendship and what it means to be married. They have also helped me recognize that celibacy, like monogamy, is not a matter of the will disdaining and conquering the desires of the flesh, but a discipline requiring what many people think of as undesirable, if not impossible—a conscious form of sublimation. Like many people who came into adulthood during the sexually permissive 1960s, I've tended to equate sublimation with repression. But my celibate friends have made me see the light; accepting sublimation as a normal part of adulthood makes me more realistic about human sexual capacities and expression. It helps me better respect the bonds and boundaries of marriage.

The person we detect through the language seems full of wonder. And it is not only the content of the passage; also notice the sentence structure. She uses long sentences to keep the reader in her perspective.

Asking questions can also make a reader curious about the subject: *Why are the computer labs at University Hall a problem? How safe is the drinking water in our community?* In her essay, Rachel Schofield (page 404) invites readers to consider hard questions that bring them into the center of the problem:

> How can Americans have reverence for food when we have so many artificial consumables surrounding us? And to complicate the problem, "Compare the price of a grapefruit to that of a pack of strawberry-flavored Twizzlers" (Zinczenko). It seems that processed food is almost always cheaper and more accessible than wholesome fresh foods. What can a struggling American family do when the only thing they can afford is cheap processed food?

Writers must be careful though not to slow the pace of the writing too much or frustrate readers with series of questions or a tedious question/answer, question/answer approach that makes the essay drag. This technique also becomes ineffective if the questions are used as a substitute for putting forth the writer's own interesting claims and support.

Using Figurative Language

Figurative language is any phrasing that deliberately bends or changes the literal meaning or dictionary definitions of words. The following figures commonly appear in college and professional writing:

Metaphor: a comparison in which one thing is made to share the characteristics of another

Her home was a sanctuary where we felt healed spiritually and psychologically.

Simile: a comparison of two seemingly unrelated things using *like* or *as*

Life is like a box of chocolates.

Understatement: a claim that is deliberately less forceful or dramatic than reality

Hurricanes tend to create a little wind.

Hyperbole: a deliberate exaggeration

I'm so hungry, I could eat a horse.

Figurative language does more than support an idea. It also adds tonality to a writer's voice. And because figurative language transforms or bends the usual meaning of words and phrases, it should bend toward the nature of the writer's voice: sobering, comic, condemning, hopeful, absurd. For example, Forrest Gump's simile in the previous example fits with his uncomplicated and easygoing character. A box of chocolates is a simple, pleasant surprise, and so it equates with his character. (It certainly would not be fitting for Gump to say, "Life is like a raging volcanic explosion bursting forth from the fires of the earth.") In other words, the nature of a simile or metaphor directly impacts how the writer's voice sounds to readers. For instance, the first simile that follows would likely create a casual or even slightly humorous tone and the second, a more sophisticated or lofty tone:

> Hardcore punk singers are like public belchers—guys, primarily, with digestion problems and microphones.

> Hardcore punk singers are like angry court jesters, calling attention to their own raucous behavior while slipping in serious social commentary.

Whispering (Drawing Readers in Close)

Writers often use parentheses or dashes to make an aside comment or ask a rhetorical question. The material separated by parentheses or dashes is often a more intimate or personal note (something one might share only with the person sitting closest at the table). These often help create a particular voice because they reveal insights that are less public, or even less directly related to the main idea, than other information. In the following passage, Jaren Provo (page 333) makes two asides:

> After this contact, more connections are forged with other alien worlds, such that the United Federation of Planets develops (with a flag suspiciously reminiscent of that of the United Nations) to promote peaceable cooperation among these cultures. Alien cultures are not (generally) out to conquer Earth and all of humanity in a blazing inferno of death and destruction, but are civilized, developing worlds willing to forge ties with others in the universe to assure mutual survival.

Provo's first, longer aside effectively winks at the readers. It nudges us in the shoulder as if to say, "On the down-low, we know what that's all about, eh?" The second offers a slight qualifier. Because *generally* is set apart from the main part of the sentence (in parentheses), it slows readers down a bit and makes Provo's voice feel slightly more cautious, more present, more aware of us—her readers. In fact, we might say that all asides function in this way: to make the writer feel more in touch, more in cahoots, with readers. In his essay, Jayme Stayer (page 257) drops in some quick parenthetical phrases that act like small winks to readers. In other words, the parentheticals help us to feel more in the know with Stayer:

> It is ironic that a park putatively designed to extol the wonders of nature is obsessed with high-tech wizardry and mega-voltage noise, noise, noise—even when it is extolling the wonders of nature's silence. Another talking point of the bird show featured how silently an owl could fly. The bird's flight began in blissful silence, but halfway through its flight the soundtrack faded back in with a shimmer of violins, followed by a cymbal crash when the owl landed. Even the absence of noise is packaged with noise: The owl's silence is first framed with amplified yakking (noise), then underlined as it happens (quiet noise), then punctuated (big noise) so the audience knows when to clap (make more noise).

Longer sentences with long phrases can also create a sense of delicacy and can bring readers into the subtleties of a thought. In Jim Crockett's concluding paragraph, the intricacy of his long sentences brings readers into the quiet complexities of the relationship:

> Because, even though my mug is always nearby, whether on the lectern or table in front of the classroom, in the cup holder on the dashboard of my truck, on the desk where I am writing this essay, or just dangling from my hand, all it really signifies is an addiction to caffeine and the need, because I am human, for some small and securing daily grounding ritual.

Yelling (Emphasizing Points)

One way to amp up the volume of a statement is to use an exclamation mark at the end. But other strategies, such as interrupting the natural flow of a sentence with a phrase or clause, can draw attention to an idea. This does not mean that the writer is angry or shouting at readers; rather, it allows the writer to guide the readers' attention to particular ideas. This is often done, as in Jim Crockett's essay (page 72), with interrupting words, phrases, or even clauses set off by commas:

> The relationship, or mugging, that has developed with my coffee mug is one-sided and is, because a mug's needs are simple, an easy relationship to maintain.

Repeating words, phrases, or clauses can also highlight an idea. John Steinbeck repeats *us* to highlight the collective nature of the issue:

> No longer do we Americans want to destroy wantonly, but our new-found sources of power—to take the burden of work from our shoulders, to warm us, and cool us, and give us light, to transport us quickly, and to make the things we use and wear and eat—these power sources spew pollution on our country, so that the rivers and streams are becoming poisonous and lifeless.

Short sentences can work as whispers or as yells, depending on content and context. They sometimes create emphasis because of their placement after longer sentences or after questions, such as in Lauren Jackson's essay (page 75):

> At school, smoking garnered status. After some bragging and showing off the goods, I quickly joined up with "The Bad Girls." I was someone.

Using Sentence Length

Sentence length has a powerful impact on voice. Long, winding sentences that travel in and out of various ideas before returning readers to the original path can create a self-reflective and sophisticated voice, one that considers complexities. Short sentences can create a determined voice. Notice the difference between the following:

> Childhood was a gas.

> Childhood was a raucous journey of twists and turns in which each moment was its own forever and every day a monument.

Although the metaphors here impact the sound of the sentences, the length matters. The sheer time that readers spend inside of a sentence shapes how they hear it. In her essay, Cindy Bosley (page 33) uses sentence length to tug and pull at readers. The first sentence of the following passage is short, and because of the content, it is almost a whisper. The rest of the paragraph, consisting of longer sentences, takes readers further into the idea. The movement between long and short sentences creates the sensation of a living person telling a story, and the content of those sentences helps communicate the feelings and emotional complexities of that human:

> My mother had secret hopes. Finally divorced for the second time from the same man, my father, she sat with me and gave her own running commentary about who was

> cute, who smiled too much, who would find a handsome husband. My mother, having always been a little to a lot overweight, excelled at swimming, and she told me much later that she chose swimming because she didn't feel fat in the water. Her sister was the cheerleader, but she was a swimmer, too heavy for a short skirt of her own, she said.

(For more on sentence length, see Chapter 19: Vitalizing Sentences, page 578.)

Building Credibility

Good writers are inviting and curious; they avoid preachiness and hostility. They also create a sense of credibility, the quality that makes points believable. In argumentative writing, credibility is especially important for readers to understand and accept claims. This section explains some common ways that writers build or threaten their own credibility.

Drawing on Experience

A credible voice is not necessarily commanding or domineering. It might just be logical or insightful. Writers such as Leonard Kress (page 366) use personal experience to build credibility. In his essay, we get the sense that experience has taught him more than many of the supposed experts. Although his reference to *The Encyclopedia of Pediatric Psychology* is helpful, the way he uses that information to highlight his own understanding adds real credibility to his voice. By the time Kress discovers the important passage in the encyclopedia, he has established his own credibility:

> . . . I could simply will the partially chewed hearty chunks of meat and potato up from their sour churning stock. It felt so good! *The Encyclopedia of Pediatric Psychology* (1979) reports that children who vomit, farfetched as it sounds, even "those who have learned society's aversions . . . can overcome such scruples and experience vomiting as cathartic, even orgasmic."

Arguing, Conceding, and Qualifying

Argument need not be cast as an act of aggression or belligerence. Although arguments are sometimes heated and intense, they need not belittle others. In fact, the fastest way to alienate, or turn off, a reader is to sound narrow-minded, mean, arrogant, or intimidating. A good argument attracts readers and engages those who might oppose the claims being made. A bad or unsuccessful argument loses readers.

Conceding or qualifying a point can make an argument seem more controlled and more inviting; therefore, even when writers have a strong conviction, they can acknowledge the value of some other point or the limits of their own. Imagine the following argument:

> First-year college students are not mature enough to live on their own, without the guidance of parents and the familiarity of home turf. Dorm life is a celebration of

> self-destruction and disorientation. The social distractions draw students away from the real purpose of college and defeat even the most focused and determined students. Colleges should rethink the requirements for first-year students to live on campus.

Although these claims unfairly generalize college students (see *logical fallacies*) and therefore threaten the logical soundness of the argument, they also project a hasty or pushy voice. But with a concession, the same argument can be cast with a different voice. The following paragraph acknowledges some value in dorm life and, as a result, seems fairer and less alienating:

> Dorm life does hold some value for young students. It can create a climate of inquiry and academic engagement. However, many young college students are overcome by the utter freedom, lack of genuine guidance, and constant social distractions. And too many students who would otherwise succeed in their first years at college are suffering or failing because they are forced to live on campus. Colleges should, at least, begin to reevaluate requirements for on-campus living.

Conceding can create a more engaging voice, but conceding unnecessarily or too often can have negative results. Imagine the same argument, but with a distracting degree of concession:

> Living in dorms can be the best thing possible for a college student; however, dorm life can also defeat many students. Sometimes, even the brightest and most determined students can be overcome by the social distractions. Although it all depends on the individual student's personality and upbringing, college dorm life can actually work against the whole purpose of going to college. Certainly, each college should consider the characteristics of its own student body, but policies that require students to live on campus should be reevaluated.

All the concessions and qualifiers undermine the importance of the argument. The voice behind the text seems concerned about offending potential readers. But, ironically, such writing makes readers feel distant or detached from the ideas. Because the writer seems uncommitted, readers have no reason to engage the ideas. (Be cautious not to concede away your level of commitment—and your argument.)

Avoiding Harsh Description

It is tempting to use emotionally loaded terms or to proclaim an opposing view as "dumb" or "evil," but such language suggests that the writer has not fully investigated the subject. In the following, Ann Marie Paulin (page 248) does not attack the media and the diet industry with aggressive adjectives, but argues that they damage people's lives. This is a far more sophisticated and useful strategy than merely dismissing them with a negative word or phrase:

> Certainly everyone is entitled to his or her own opinions of what is attractive, but no one has the right to damage another human being for fun or profit. The media and the

> diet industry often do just that. While no one can change an entire culture overnight, people, especially parents, need to think about what they really value in the humans they share their lives with and what values they want to pass on to their children.

Be cautious of dismissing a subject by using harsh words. Imagine the following passage, in which a writer evaluates a government official:

> Mayor G. is out of his mind. He has no understanding of the political spectrum and no concept of city governance. He is just some crazy, power-hungry man looking for a soapbox to stand on. If the city really understood the depth of his insanity, it would kick him out of office immediately.

This passage echoes some of the combative language in mainstream politics, which keeps voters from looking closely at a subject. Such language is rife with logical fallacies. Instead of investigating the subject closely, it portrays a writer's unfocused aggression. In the following passage, Benjamin Busch (page 325) comes down hard against *Medal of Honor,* but his voice is sober, intense, and without nasty condemnation:

> The power of controlling your situation, to be able to stop the war and rest, is something that our soldiers are quietly desperate for. For those who patrol the valleys of Helmand, it is a way to impose limits on the uncertainty of war, and the constancy of vulnerability. A video game can produce no wounds, and take no friends away. The soldier understands the difference.

Talking with, Not Arguing at, Readers

An academic argument is not an argument with readers. It is a *conversation with readers about an argumentative position.* And if that conversation is compelling, readers may find that position valuable. In other words, argumentative writing speaks with readers about a particular position or set of positions and attempts to make one position more logical and/or valuable than others.

To help visualize the roles of a writer and readers, imagine the following: The writer sits beside a reader, pointing at and directing attention to a set of claims. The writer does not sit in front of and point his or her finger at the reader. This may seem like a subtle difference, but notice how it may change a passage. In the following example, Elizabeth Bohnhorst (page 254) urges readers to consider computers in the classroom:

> Educating students in computer skills is and should be a priority in all schools. But when it comes to teaching basic skills and allowing for intellectual development, human interaction and exploration of the real world should never come second to electronic devices. In an effort to preserve the qualities of education, we should not allow ourselves to become mesmerized by teachers that require an electrical outlet and textbooks that require a point-and-click to turn the page.

But imagine if Bohnhorst had talked at us directly. In the following, the writer tries to convince readers ("you") to change their behavior. This passage is more shrill and probably would be less engaging to readers:

> Educating students in computer skills is and should be a priority in all schools. But when it comes to teaching basic skills and allowing for intellectual development, you cannot put human interaction and exploration of the real world second to electronic devices. In an effort to preserve the qualities of education, do not allow yourself to become mesmerized by electrical wizardry.

Applying Rogerian Argument

Because argument can create hostility and turn people away from each other, Carl Rogers developed an argumentative perspective that emphasizes building connections between different positions. People who use *Rogerian* argument look for similarities rather than differences between argumentative positions. Such a strategy creates an engaging voice—one that invites exploration of ideas rather than harsh dismissals. Even though George Lakoff (page 289) argues that George Orwell was wrong about language, Lakoff begins by acknowledging the value of Orwell's ideas:

> George Orwell will forever be a hero of mine. When I read *1984* in high school, I became sensitized to the workings of propaganda. After more than forty years as a linguist and cognitive scientist, I remain sensitized.
>
> When I first read "Politics and the English Language" as an undergraduate in the late 1950s, I loved it. Nearly fifty years later I find it an anachronism. Why? I, and those in my profession, have learned a lot about the brain, the mind, and language since then. Orwell's essay belongs to an earlier time, a time that lacked our deepening understanding of how the human brain works.

In his essay, Daniel Bruno (page 294) takes a similar approach. He begins by explaining the value of a text to which he later responds:

> In his book *Generation X Goes to College*, Peter Sacks describes, among other things, the sense of entitlement that some students in today's consumerist culture have toward a college education. One entire chapter explores this issue alone, providing examples of this "sense" and looking into its "humble beginnings."
>
> Sacks shows how consumerism has invaded education, leading some students to expect good grades for little effort. But he fails, it seems, to emphasize enough a most harmful effect of this entitlement. The biggest problem, as I see it, is that although students are able to graduate from high school (and even some colleges) with minimal effort, those students may find themselves cheated in the long run.

Creating Reasonable Tone

Tone, the color or mood of a writer's voice, is vital to maintaining the readers' interest. Tone that is too emotional can overwhelm; one that is condescending can alienate. For example, when proposing solutions, writers must be careful not to force problems *at* readers. Instead, the writer's job is to present a problem and illustrate its significance *for* readers. For example, in her essay, Deirdre Mahoney (page 397) carefully presents the significance of a problem:

> Today's college students are suffering, and unnecessarily so. I see them arrive in my writing classes each semester eager and determined, but all too often the motivation and passion dissipate when they come face-to-face with—well—words on the page. This is distressing for both them and me. My students are not illiterate by any means, as they successfully broke the code of sound-to-symbol in the earliest elementary years. Since that time, they've continued to learn in public and private school systems or they've been home-schooled. They're educated and plenty adept at moving through the system. But I'm not convinced any of this means they are capable of truly committing to a book, an essay, or any document requiring sustained focus and labor-intensive thinking and doing.

It would be easy, and tempting, for Mahoney to scream and shout at her readers about students' disengagement from the written word. Imagine the following:

> Today's college students cannot read closely or intensively. They might want to perform well in their classes, but their hopes have been dashed by a careless educational system. They are victims in the worst sense. By the time they've reached my classes, very few of them will be able to learn how to read at the college level. The rest will be left behind. We've forgotten our most vulnerable population—our children.

This passage is over the top. It forces the problem at its readers and demands that they feel a particular emotion. Mahoney's passage is less confrontational, while still intense. She does not make emotional demands on readers; instead, she presents the strengths and weaknesses she sees in her students and leaves readers to reflect on them.

Following Conventions

In most academic situations, writers must follow a range of grammatical, syntactical, and formatting rules. But attending to one's voice is not so much about rules as conventions: a set of expectations shared among many readers and writers. This section explains how writers might work within and sometimes beyond the conventions.

Considering Verb Mood

The three verb moods in English are indicative, subjunctive, and imperative:

- Indicative mood makes statements or asserts facts.

  The diners are sitting at the table.

- Subjunctive mood expresses what could or should happen.

  If it were lunchtime, the diners would be sitting at the table.

- Imperative mood issues commands or suggestions.

  For lunch, sit at the table.

Most sentences in this text (and in an essay, article, e-mail, and so on) are in the indicative mood. They make statements about writing. Others are in the subjunctive; they inform readers about possible ways to act, think, or write. And others are in the imperative mood; they order, or command, readers to act, think, or write a certain way.

Imperative mood is rare in academic essays and formal proposals because it tells readers what to do or think. And when done inappropriately, imperative mood seems to boss readers around. Of course, exceptions exist. Imperative can be appropriate in the final passages of an essay. For instance, Julie Zhuo's article (page 395) is primarily in the indicative mood, as are most of the essays in this book, but to urge readers to take a particular action, she shifts to imperative in her conclusion:

> Instead of waiting around for human nature to change, let's start to rein in bad behavior by promoting accountability. Content providers, stop allowing anonymous comments. Moderate your comments and forums. Look into using comment services to improve the quality of engagement on your site. Ask your users to report trolls and call them out for polluting the conversation.

But be careful with imperative mood. It can diminish the intensity of a good argument. Because imperative mood draws attention to readers, it must necessarily draw less attention to the topic. The goal of most academic writing is to keep intensive focus on the topic, to build a compelling idea for would-be readers, not to go after the particular person holding the essay. In the following, notice how the first sentence focuses on readers rather than the topic. In other words, the energy of the sentence goes toward a nameless and invisible "you," while the second and third sentences draw more attention to the topic:

- **Imperative Mood:** While reading, use a pencil to better engage the nuances of a text.
- **Indicative Mood:** Reading with a pencil helps students to engage the nuances of a text.
- **Subjunctive Mood:** If students would use a pencil while reading, they could better engage the nuances of a text.

The differences may seem subtle, but the three sentences radically change the role of a reader. In an imperative sentence, readers are called upon—insisted upon. In indicative and subjunctive sentences, readers join the writer in a mutual examination of the topic. And because academic writing celebrates that mutual examination, indicative and subjunctive are used most often.

Adjusting Formality

Formality is adherence to an established convention. A formal text follows certain expectations and avoids slipping out of conventional language and organizational patterns. Because essays are used in a number of situations and academic disciplines, the conventions vary, and so does the expected level of formality. Generally, writing that draws no attention to the writer's presence is considered more formal. (Of course, this is a general rule, and it does not apply to all writing situations.)

A writer's voice can make the reading experience formal or relaxed, rigorous or casual. Remember that a casual voice does not necessarily mean casual thinking. A very sophisticated analysis can be presented in a casual manner. For instance, Simon Benlow (page 140) approaches the fast food/customer service issue on its own terms. He borrows the phrases and the lowbrow tone of drive-through culture:

> In the old days, we had to pull up to the drive-thru board, search under "Sandwiches" and THEN go through the labor of exploring "Sides" and "Beverages." It was all too much. Now, we can simply pull up, and say a number. We don't even have to trouble ourselves with uttering all the stuff we want to eat. We just say, "#1 with a diet." The meal deal craze is, of course, not limited to fast food; it is, simply, most explicitly manifested in the fast food industry.

You may detect a slight shift in the last sentence—where Benlow pulls away from the drive-through language and makes a broader point about society. In this sense, Benlow's voice ebbs and flows. It adopts the casual language of consumption and then snaps at those same casual-sounding phrases. (This raises an important aspect of voice, or voicing: It is far more complex than discovering a single, personal, or genuine sound. In our everyday lives, as in speech, we often shift in subtle ways, borrowing tones and phrases from popular culture, academic culture, business, entertainment, and politics. We fuse those elements into our own tongues—and it all ends up sounding like us, like the single person speaking. But don't be fooled! Voice is often, or always, filled with the subtle tones of others.)

Although some writers tend toward a formal, sober tone, others use comedy or informality to connect with readers. For example, Simon Wykoff speaks directly to readers: He is not overly casual, nor is he overly formal or elaborate. Wykoff's language can be described as conversational:

> I should interject here and explain how he got around the city. While my father was homeless, he was lucky enough to have a bicycle, which he treasured beyond everything else. It's not uncommon in a larger city to have the place you get food, the place you sleep, and the place you go to try and earn money be miles and miles apart. Because of this, even on a bike my father spent a considerable amount of time traveling. He would often ride from one end of the city to the other several times a day. This takes an incredible amount of endurance, especially when you are doing it on an empty stomach, as he often was. Many times, just a trip from the place he was sleeping to the closest bakery in the morning was a marathon.

Exploring the Boundaries

Some writers perform. Their language suggests, "Look at what I'm saying and how I'm saying it!" Some writers lay low. Their language says, "I'm here, but only to give you some information." Some writers hide. Their language says, "I hope no one sees me in this essay." Every writer has a comfort zone, the place where he or she feels most at ease. The problem is that *our most comfortable voices are not always the most appropriate* for the situation, and they do not allow us to explore language. In some situations, the intensely performative writer may need to be invisible and understated. And the writer hiding behind sentences may occasionally need to step forward and be noticed.

The best writers in all disciplines, occupations, and walks of life are not locked into a voice. They can work with various voices, depending on the writing situation. For that reason alone, it's good to recognize—and remember—the range of possibilities available. Take, for instance, three different passages from three different writers: April Pedersen (page 238), Ann Marie Paulin (page 248), and Jayme Stayer (page 258), who all appear in the same chapter:

> In a Pew Research Center study, 85 percent of dog owners said they consider their pet to be a member of their family. However the latest trend is to take that a step further in seeing the animal as a child. A company that sells pet health insurance policies has dubbed the last Sunday in April as "Pet Parents Day." Glance through magazines like *Bark, Cesar's Way* (courtesy of "Dog Whisperer" Cesar Millan), and other mainstream publications, and the term "pet parent" crops up regularly. The "my-dogs-are-my-kids" crowd isn't being tongue-in-cheek, either. They act on their beliefs, buying Christmas presents, photos with Santa, cosmetic surgery, and whatever-it-takes medical care for their animal. In fact having a puppy, claimed one "mother," is "exactly the same in all ways as having a baby." And while pushing a dog around in a stroller would have gotten you directions to a mental health facility twenty years ago, today it's de rigueur to see a canine in a stroller (or a papoose), and some passersby are downright disappointed to discover a human infant inside. —April Pedersen

> Certainly everyone is entitled to his or her own opinion of what is attractive, but no one has the right to damage another human being for fun or profit. The media and the diet industry often do just that. While no one can change an entire culture overnight, people, especially parents, need to think about what they really value in the humans they share their lives with and what values they want to pass on to their children. We need to realize that being thin will not fix all our problems, though advertisements for diets and weight loss aids suggest this. Losing weight may, indeed, give a man or woman more confidence, but it will not make a person smarter, more generous, more loving, or more nurturing. It won't automatically attract the dream job or the ideal lover. On the contrary, people who allow the drive to be thin to control them may find that many other areas of their lives suffer: They may avoid some celebrations or get-togethers because of fear they may be tempted to eat too much or the "wrong" foods. They may cut back on intellectual activities like reading or enjoying concerts or art museums because those activities cut

Vitalized writing is lively. It involves a broad range of strategies and patterns—from winding clauses that bring readers through intellectual nuances to brief phrases that pop in the reader's mind. The important principle is that sentences account for the whole reading experience: If your sentences are full of empty phrases, stiffened by dull patterns, or slowed by jumbled clauses, they won't call on readers' attention. Your writing will lie flat on the page or computer screen. But if your sentences are lively, they will pull readers along and through whatever dense concept or difficult argument you've developed.

This chapter includes strategies for ratcheting up your writing. Some call for pruning phrases, some call for substituting words, and others call for more radical changes. Throughout the chapter, we assume you have a completed draft—that your work is somewhat developed and ready for close editing. Although the examples belong to specific essays and articles, the strategies themselves can be applied widely—not only to different assignments but also to different genres of writing.

Controlling the Pace

Even the most patient and attentive readers want to move through a text. They want to experience the flow of one idea to another. So good writers manage the pace of their language. Like film directors, they move their audiences along from scene (idea) to scene (idea). This process usually involves tightening sentences as much as possible—so that longer sentences, when they do come along, mean more to the reading experience. The following strategies focus on controlling the speed of your readers' thoughts.

Turn Clauses to Phrases

A clause (which includes both a subject and verb) can often be shortened to a phrase, which makes the sentence more concise and lively. Notice how the clause in the first sentence below can be reduced to a phrase (that is, to a group of two or more words that do not include both a subject and verb). The second sentence, from John Steinbeck's essay, avoids the unnecessary "that were":

> On the East coast, and particularly in New England, the colonists farmed lands *that were* meager and close to their communities and to safety.
>
> On the East coast, particularly in New England, colonists farmed meager lands close to their communities and to safety.

The same goes for the following sentence. Notice how the second version, from John Steinbeck's essay (page 70), trims the clauses into phrases:

> When a super-highway was proposed in California which would trample the redwood trees in its path, an outcry arose all over the land *that was* so strident and fierce that the plan was put aside. And we no longer believe that a man, *because he owns* a piece of America, is free to outrage it.

> When a super-highway was proposed in California which would trample the redwood trees in its path, an outcry arose all over the land, so strident and fierce that the plan was put aside. And we no longer believe that a man, by owning a piece of America, is free to outrage it.

Although these differences are slight, the phrases (rather than the clauses) increase the sentences' vitality. And if the strategy is spread out over several pages of text, the benefits are easy to see. The paragraphs read more smoothly. (Often, when writers are concerned about "the flow" of their essays, this is the strategy to apply.)

Turn Phrases to Words

The same principle can be applied to phrases: They can often be boiled down to single words. Consider the following two sentences. The second, also from Steinbeck's essay, boils down a common phrase to a more succinct word:

> Almost every day, the pressure of outrage among Americans grows.

> Almost daily, the pressure of outrage among Americans grows.

The differences are slight, but small transformations build up throughout an essay, creating the difference between droopy and intensive writing. This strategy also makes writers search for more intense or powerful words, as in the following:

> The decision was not very smart.

> The decision was illogical.

> Back in the day, people did not assume that all communication should be instantaneous.

> Historically, people have not assumed that all communication should be instantaneous.

Combine Sentences

Sentences cue the readers. A period says, "Stop." A new sentence says, "Go." This stopping and starting creates life. But too many starts and stops keep readers from settling into ideas, so writers combine sentences to keep readers gliding along. Sentences can be combined with *coordination* (adding together clauses of equal importance). The underlined conjunctions in the following sentences show where the writers joined ideas together. The ideas before and after the conjunctions are grammatically equal. The grammar cues readers to give them equal intellectual weight:

> My father did not believe in such things for girls as shoes, clothes, haircuts, college, or photographs for Junior Miss, and so there was no way he was going to give a penny for a pageant-worthy dress or a professional photographer's 10-minutes-plus-proofs. (Cindy Bosley)

> Mrs. Rath had an ability to recognize the kids that actually wanted to read and learn and, often times, would send a few of us down to the library where it was quiet and we could have some sanctuary from the usual classroom shenanigans. (Steve Mockensturm)

Sentences also can be combined with *subordination* (making an idea less important than the main part of a sentence). Subordination involves tucking some ideas into others, creating the critical overlapping quality of good writing. The following examples show a variety of possibilities. Each sentence has a main clause (underlined), and other subordinated parts:

> For years it sat empty, the massive entrance looking out on Upton Avenue with no expression.

> As hoped for and expected, a figure appeared out of nowhere.

> Almost half a day later, around midnight, the train crunched into Chicago, where I hopped off, exhausted and exhilarated.

Notice how the third sentence, from Leonard Kress's "A Beat Education," would read differently if the ideas were separated into full sentences:

> Almost half a day later, around midnight, the train crunched into Chicago. I hopped off, and I felt exhausted and exhilarated.

Although the difference is small, this version creates more stops and starts for readers. Those shorter, separated ideas can be valuable, but good writers subordinate less important information. Hopping off the train is necessary information for Kress's narrative, but it's not the main idea, so Kress subordinates it.

Subordinate Less Important Ideas

Vitalized writing establishes a primary intellectual current—an undeniable forward momentum that allows readers to distinguish between dominant and supporting ideas. The following sentence from Rebecca Hollingsworth's essay (page 213) conveys two ideas: a main idea (that autism is a health epidemic at the forefront of public consciousness) and a subordinate idea (the definition of autism):

> One health epidemic at the forefront of public consciousness is autism, a brain disorder that impairs a person's ability to communicate, socialize, and participate in group behavior.

Consider another example from Hollingsworth. She conveys two important ideas (when autism surfaces and what its symptoms are). The first idea is subordinate to the second one because the second idea is expressed in the main, or independent, clause. Subordinating one idea to the other helps to keep the essay moving:

> Often surfacing by the time a child is three years old, the symptoms of autism include stifled speech and difficulty in displaying joy or affection.

But notice how the pace would slow if neither of the sentences included subordination:

> One health epidemic at the forefront of public consciousness is autism. Autism is a brain disorder that impairs a person's ability to communicate, socialize, and participate in group behavior. It often surfaces by the time a child is three years old. The symptoms of autism include stifled speech and difficulty in displaying joy or affection.

Experiment with Length

If writers aren't careful, their language can turn robotic: every sentence having about the same number of words, the same number of clauses, and the same types of phrases. Just as good speakers vary the sound of their voices, good writers vary the length of their sentences. Notice how Justin Scott (page 106) varies sentence length in the following passage:

> One thing is immediately obvious in this cemetery: those laden with the gifts of life often choose to utilize them in death, and those less fortunate make do with what they must. Class warfare spills into the afterworld: business owner is segregated from bricklayer, clergy is separated from atheist. There are large overbearing crypts bearing the surnames of the wealthy dead inside, branch-scraping obelisks with ornate script, tombs carefully sculpted to resemble tree stumps, small temples dedicated to their dead in ancient Greek style, and inevitably the sunken, flat and nondescript markers of the poor or humble.

In his first two sentences, Scott uses a colon to connect an explanation to the preceding sentence part, an independent clause. The colons help to break up the ideas and create a rhythm and voice. By following these shorter sentences with a longer one that expresses the different ways people are segregated in a cemetery, Scott helps give readers a sense that many ways exist. Although Scott's final sentence is lengthy, because it is grammatically correct readers will not become lost in the ideas.

Short sentences keep readers alert and moving—but only when they are interspersed with longer ones. Short sentences can also help dramatize thought, as in this passage from Chester McCovey (page 104):

> I am not saying there are no front porches. Obviously there are. And I am not saying everyone has a two-car garage instead. In my neighborhood, small garages not connected to the house still reign.

Anne-Marie Oomen (page 98) uses short sentences as well, even as single paragraphs:

> [. . .] There are tracks everywhere in this part of the dunes—deer, raccoon, mice, gulls and small birds—though I see no animals and hear little except the alarm of the crows, the distant roar of waves below the bluffs. The wind picks up, slams sand against my jeans.
>
> I think I may be lost.
>
> Deep swales. I cannot see the lake or the distant reference point of the dune. I stop disoriented, pull my hood back. . . .

Avoid Unnecessary Interruption

Sometimes writers will inject a phrase or clause between the main parts of a sentence (between a subject and its verb or between verbs and direct objects). A modifying clause or phrase, like this one, comes between main parts of a sentence. Interrupting elements can be appropriate when the subject needs explaining. For example, in the following, the interrupting element, *Bart's distempered father,* helps explain the subject. It does not slow down the reading significantly:

Homer Simpson, <u>Bart's distempered father,</u> consistently leads his family through a campaign of treacherous buffoonery.	**Appropriate interruption**

But writers sometimes unnecessarily interrupt the flow of a sentence:

Nothing, <u>in the animated town of Springfield</u>, is worthy of the praise it wants.	**Unnecessary interruption**
So I asked myself, <u>on my way out of SeaWorld,</u> what I had learned.	

In many cases, the interrupting element can be moved to the front of the sentence, which keeps the main parts of the sentence together:

> <u>In the animated town of Springfield,</u> nothing is worthy of the praise it wants.
>
> <u>So on my way out of SeaWorld,</u> I asked myself what I had learned.

Avoid Over-Embedding

Although a well-placed clause between the subject and verb can help create a clear and lively sentence, too many loose clauses can slow or even derail readers. In the following sentence, two overlapping dependent clauses (both beginning with *that*) interfere with the pace. They embed themselves between the two most important elements of the sentence: the subject (*problem*) and verb (*is*).

> The problem that Thoreau has with the government that depends upon the majority is that the majority often fails to think of what is right and what is wrong.

For better pace, the sentence might be rewritten:

> According to Thoreau, a government of the majority has a key problem: Majorities often fail to distinguish between right and wrong.

As you can see, it's easy to fix over-embedded sentences. The tricky part is seeing them in the first place. As you consider your own writing, remember that over-embedding often happens in the drafting phase when writers are shaping ideas.

Avoid Pileups

Prepositional phrases sometimes pile up and create a dense wall of unreadable words. (A prepositional phrase begins with a preposition, such as <u>in,</u> <u>of,</u> <u>between,</u> <u>on,</u> <u>beside,</u> <u>behind,</u> or <u>for.</u>) Too many prepositional phrases (even two in a row) can slow down or stop readers. You might think of it as momentum: Verbs propel readers through sentences. So when too many phrases pile up, the sentence slows down. Without verbs, the reading gets thick, sentences get muddy, and readers bog down. Good writers avoid too many phrases. The following sentence begins with three prepositional phrases:

> <u>The celebration of the holiday at the end of the month</u> will attract many tourists to the town.

If the sentence has fewer prepositional phrases, the verb (*will attract*) moves closer to the subject (*celebration*), and the sentence becomes less muddy:

> At the end of the month, the holiday celebration will attract many tourists to the town.

Avoid Vague Pronouns

Pronouns such as *these, this, those,* and *it* are often used to refer back to previous ideas so readers feel a sense of familiarity as they move forward. In short, such pronouns help to keep momentum going between sentences and paragraphs. Notice how Elizabeth Thoman (page 202) uses *this* to bring readers from one paragraph to another:

> Even the U.S. Constitution, remember, only promises the pursuit of happiness. It doesn't guarantee that any of us will actually achieve it.

> It is <u>this</u> search for "something-more-than-what-we've-got-now" that is at the heart of the consumer culture we struggle with today.

But she also gives us more information, so the transition between paragraphs is smooth: "this search for 'something-more-than-what-we've-got-now.'" The additional information keeps readers in tow. In such a passage, the pronoun offers extra glue between ideas. But imagine if the pronoun had to act alone:

> Even the U.S. Constitution, remember, only promises the pursuit of happiness. It doesn't guarantee that any of us will actually achieve it.
>
> <u>This</u> is at the heart of the consumer culture we struggle with today.

Now the pronoun carries all the burden of the transition between paragraphs. If readers are not entirely certain what *this* is, the transition is unsuccessful. For better vitality and pace, writers make pronouns refer directly to specific nouns.

Cleaning the Language

It is easy to fill up pages with useless phrases and clauses. (Perhaps you even know some tried-and-true tactics for adding five words where you might need only one, two, or three. Perhaps you recognize those moves here!) Good writers prune their language. They get comfortable with the delete key. The following strategies will help you to cut the useless stuff from your drafts and to make the remaining words mean more.

Avoid Clichés

Clichés are tired, worn-out phrases. We hear them constantly in everyday life—on greeting cards, in popular songs or political speeches, and in casual conversations. Think of all the times you have heard these phrases:

> You don't know what you have until it's gone.
>
> We should expand our horizons.
>
> Follow your dreams.
>
> Anything is possible.
>
> Children are the future.
>
> I believe in my heart that . . .
>
> Hang in there.
>
> Discover who you are as a person.
>
> People are entitled to their own opinions.
>
> Whatever will be will be.

Reach for the stars.

Think outside the box.

Everyone is different.

Different strokes for different folks.

It's all just water under the bridge.

Fight the good fight.

Or even consider smaller phrases that are plugged into sentences but are rarely inspected:

the real world

hard work

the good life

family values

the American people

today's society

common sense

The list goes on. Such common phrases are not tools for thinking—they are substitutes for thinking. Because they have been used repeatedly and in so many different contexts, their meaning has been emptied. We use clichés when there is nothing left to say—or to make it seem like there is nothing else to say. Clichés blur complex thinking. They hide the possibility of further thought. For instance, notice the thinking that might go on behind this cliché: We should expand our horizons.

> What are horizons? How do they form? Are horizons imposed on us, or do we adopt them ourselves? If they are imposed by others, can we simply choose to expand them or do we have to break some rule? How do we know when a horizon expands? What experiences or voices or situations make them expand? Are we just as likely to shrink our horizons? Isn't that human nature? What kind of action broadens our understanding? Is it just a new experience or something else?

All of these questions suggest the complexity behind the idea. But rather than promote hard thinking, clichés invite both writers and readers into quiet, unreflective agreement. In a sense, clichés are strategies for quieting the mind, which is the opposite goal of academic writing.

Avoid Stilted Language

If clichés are the common, overused phrases of the day, stilted language is the opposite—an overly elaborate jungle of pretentious clauses and phrases. Stilted language is unnecessarily elevated. Instead of communicating complex and interesting ideas clearly, it buries ideas in a jungle of language, making readers work hard to sift through a basic, yet overly written, idea.

For example, in Writer A's passage, the ideas are vague because they are stretched out over unnecessary, but pretty, phrases:

> ***Writer A:***
>
> People, in every walk of this big life, should query themselves about the direction of their occupational goals. And they should do this persistently, both before entering into a projected career path and while enduring the veritable ins and outs of said career path. Is it not fitting to examine the very essence of such matters, which would otherwise remain beyond our consciousness in the mundane existence of work? Certainly, we should endeavor to explore the cracks and folds of our lives and thereby free ourselves of any unknown shackles.

Writer A injects strings of needless constructions ("in every walk of this big life," "the very essence of such matters") and elaborate language ("their occupational goals," "mundane existence of work") that inflate the importance of the ideas. Writer A also mingles two competing metaphors at the end of the passage. As readers, we are left exploring the "cracks and folds" while also freeing ourselves from "unknown shackles." Notice a less stilted approach:

> ***Writer B:***
>
> Before entering a job, people should ask themselves if it fits their broader career plans. Even after working at a job for months or years, people should return to this question. Otherwise, the workaday lifestyle can prompt us to believe that a present career path is the best—the one that we should continue to walk.

Writer B uses a metaphor at the end, but it works here because it does not compete with other figurative language in the sentence. Now that the ideas are less ornate, they seem less overwhelming. In fact, stated more plainly, the ideas appear ordinary (which should prompt a writer to explore the ideas further). These passages reveal two major problems with stilted language: (1) It jumbles ideas so that readers are left guessing or wondering, and (2) it inflates ideas so that they seem beyond exploration. Writers and readers should not be impressed with ornate language but rather with intense ideas expressed clearly.

Avoid Unnecessary Attention to *I*

Most writers are naturally drawn to use the first-person pronouns *I, me,* and *my.* But personal pronouns can distract readers from the ideas and bog down the sentences:

> I think that social security ought to be tied to the marketplace.
>
> It is my personal belief that social security should not be a gamble.

In each of these sentences, the main idea is subordinated in a *that* clause. *I* statements such as these are unnecessary in most academic writing because the claims are already attributed to the writer. By attaching his or her name to an essay, the writer has already implied "I believe,"

"I think," "I feel," "it seems." Saying it again is redundant. However, personal pronouns are sometimes helpful or necessary. When dealing with several claims or outside sources, writers may insert the first-person pronoun to make a clear distinction between their own thoughts and others', as Paulin does here:

> For instance, in her essay, "Bubbie, Mommy, Weight Watchers and Me," Barbara Noreen Dinnerstein recalls a time in her childhood when her mother took her to Weight Watchers to slim down and the advice the lecturer gave to the women present: "She told us to put a picture of ourselves on the 'fridgerator of us eating and looking really fat and ugly. She said remember what you look like. Remember how ugly you are."
>
> I have a problem with this advice. First, of course, it is too darn common.

Paulin could have avoided the first-person pronoun: "But this advice is dangerous to young women." But she chose the first-person pronoun, perhaps because it is less formal and coincides with the voice she has established in her essay. Although writers should generally avoid first-person pronouns, writers like Paulin can make effective, occasional use of them.

Writers also use *I* for personal narratives—telling a story or anecdote involving their own experiences. Such uses are legitimate and important. Narratives draw attention to the relevant experience of the writer, which requires use of the first-person pronoun.

Unnecessary I Statement

I think that history should be taught with more attention to the lives of everyday people.

Appropriate Personal Narrative

When I was in high school, my history courses focused almost exclusively on big battles and big governmental moments.

Avoid Unnecessary Attention to *You*

The second-person pronoun *you* refers directly to readers—the people reading the text. Because academic essays are invitations to a broad audience (to instructors, peers, and even the broader community of thinkers that they represent), *you* is generally avoided. Like the first-person singular pronouns *(I, me, my), you* distracts readers from the issue at hand. But *you* is especially hazardous in academic writing because it makes writers shift into the imperative mood—the mood of commands. Here, the writer shifts focus and mood:

> Political parties do their best to keep people from closely examining issues. Instead, they wash over complexities and invite voters to stand on one side or another. You should consider your allegiance to any political party.

The first two sentences focus on political parties, people, and voters. But the final sentence shifts and suddenly speaks at the readers, telling them what to do. To most academic audiences, this shift is unacceptable.

Clean Up Attributive Phrases

When writers refer to another text, they need to introduce the author's words with attributive phrases. These phrases connect an author to his or her ideas: *According to Biff Harrison; in Jergerson's argument; as Jacobs points out;* and so on. But clumsy phrasing can get in the way:

1. In "Letter from Birmingham Jail," by Martin Luther King, Jr., King writes about how society can be unjust.
2. In Jayme Stayer's perspective, SeaWorld reveals the shallowest qualities of American culture. He believes that "[t]he American traits that SeaWorld reflects most clearly are its gullibility and irrationality."
3. Ann Marie Paulin wrote an essay about incivility and obesity. It is called "Cruelty, Civility, and Other Weighty Matters."

Each of these sentences makes a similar error: Each draws unnecessary attention to the act of writing or to the author's thoughts. Each could be boiled down:

1. In "Letter from Birmingham Jail," Martin Luther King Jr. writes about injustice.
2. In Jayme Stayer's perspective, SeaWorld reveals the shallowest qualities of American culture: "The American traits that SeaWorld reflects most clearly are its gullibility and irrationality."
3. Ann Marie Paulin's essay "Cruelty, Civility, and Other Weighty Matters" shows the deeply personal impact of media images.

Avoid Blueprinting

Sometimes writers draw attention to their own plans. That is, they tell readers what they are doing or what they are about to do. This strategy can be called *blueprinting* because it informs readers of the writer's plan (like the blueprints for a house). Blueprinting is not inherently wrong, but it draws attention away from the ideas and toward the writer's processes, and this can distract readers. Rather than announcing plans, writers can simply state the points. Consider this blueprinting passage:

> In the following pages, I will explain how the advertising images on MTV influence the present generation.

Removing the blueprinting leaves a relatively vague sentence:

> Advertising images on MTV influence the present generation.

So the writer might develop a more focused point:

> Advertising images on MTV promote the belief that clothes create identity.

When the blueprinting is removed, sentences have more potential because important content can be added. In fact, it must be added. As the previous example shows, blueprinting can fool a writer into thinking that sentences are saying more than they are. And, blueprinting can be subtle:

> Next is the composition.
>
> Now, after examining the content, we should explore composition.

These more subtle forms are common because writers use them as paragraph transitions. Although they are generally more accepted, ideas can be connected more effectively:

> Closely related to content, composition influences how viewers come to an image.

Condense Wordy Phrases

In everyday life, we use lots of phrases that contain unnecessary words. But in writing, we can clean out the filler:

black in color	condense to	black
square in shape	condense to	square
try and explain	condense to	explain
due to the fact that	condense to	because
in this day and age	condense to	today (or now)
back in the day	condense to	then
at the present time	condense to	now
for the most part	condense to	mostly (or most)
in the final analysis	condense to	finally
in the event that	condense to	if
frank and honest	condense to	honest
revert back to	condense to	revert

Notice the wordy and condensed phrases in action:

> **Wordy:** In the event that your sentences are more vital, your grades will likely improve due to the fact that instructors, for the most part, want intense ideas rather than bloated sentences.

Condensed: If your sentences are more vital, your grades will likely improve because most instructors want intense ideas rather than bloated sentences.

Avoid Expletives

To help keep things lively, writers delete unnecessary words, such as expletive constructions. Expletives begin with there or it and are followed by a form of to be, such as is, are, was, or were. (Note: Not every expletive construction must be replaced, and not every there or it followed by a form of to be functions as an expletive.) Notice how the following sentences can be revised to remove the expletive and make the writing more clean and intense:

> There were many students who voiced the need for more evening courses.
>
> Many students voiced the need for more evening courses.
>
> It is this long list of problems that made the community suspicious of the mayor's speech.
>
> This long list of problems made the community suspicious of the mayor's speech.

Throw Away the Obvious

Imagine a protester holding a sign that says, "No More Bank Bailouts!" Given the situation (a protest) and the general state of the economy (a slow recovery), most people can infer—or quietly fill in—the unstated layers of the argument. We know that the protester is against government money supporting bad behavior among bankers. Now imagine another sign that says, "No More Bank Bailouts! I Think They Are Wrong and I Don't Support Them!" The second sign says too much. Everything after the first sentence is obvious. Of course, an academic essay and a protest sign are different. But they are the same in this respect: Too many obvious statements diminish their effectiveness.

As we have argued in previous chapters, college writing is about generating new ideas—not expressing the same old opinions. This point applies even to individual paragraphs and sentences. Good writers learn to throw away obvious statements, those that readers will infer on their own. For example, in the following passage, the second and third sentences are obvious:

> When the company executives cheated thousands of employees out of their pensions, they ruined retirement for many families. It is wrong when people cheat others. And the executives should have known better than to do such a thing.

In this case, the first sentence has already done the important work. The words *cheated* and *ruined* make a powerful point. The second and third sentences, however, simply pound out what is already implied. In short, more than half of the words in the above passage can, and probably should, be thrown away.

Getting Specific

Many of the strategies in this chapter involve cutting and pruning. But when writers cut, they notice their drafts shrinking, and a shrinking draft creates its own problem: meeting the required word count of an assignment. So what can be done? How can writers develop sufficient drafts while deleting unnecessary or vague phrases? One answer is to get specific—to narrow in on particular actions, situations, people, and ideas. The more particular writers get, the more incisive their ideas become. Potentially bland statements turn into sharper insights and often into more detailed passages.

Vitalize with Verbs

Verbs are the engine of a sentence. And they are the agent of motion for a reader's mind: They move a reader's thoughts. Weak verbs make for little movement. In the following, the first sentence depends on a weak verb:

> Handheld video games are bad for kids to have in the car.
>
> Handheld video games have destroyed the family road trip.

The verb of the first sentence, *are,* is often called a *linking verb.* When linking verbs act as the main engine of a sentence, they limit what's possible. Often, they corner the writer into using a vague adjective, in this case *bad.* The second sentence uses an active and more intensive verb: *destroyed.* The second sentence creates a more engaging image. In the following sentences, linking verbs create unnecessary layers and clauses. Notice how each can be tightened and vitalized with an *active verb:*

> The problem with this *is* that the house is too expensive for our budget.
>
> Here's the problem: The cost of the house exceeds our budget.

> The committee *is* not prone to allowing everyone *to be* as free with their money as they want.
>
> The committee will probably not allow everyone to spend resources freely.

Using active verbs rather than linking verbs vitalizes writing. This is not to say that using linking verbs is always a mistake. (Sometimes, they are necessary.) However, changing to more active verbs can dramatically impact your writing, creating more focused statements, more intensive ideas, and more revelatory thinking.

Avoid *Be* Verbs When Possible

Be verbs—*is, am, are, was, were, being, been,* etc.—are a type of linking verb. They link the subject of a sentence to a noun or a quality.

> The kittens are cute.
>
> The government is out of control.
>
> Sentences are cues for readers.

Although such verbs are often necessary and valuable, they are often overused—hanging around in a sentence that would benefit from a more active verb. With a small, but important, change to the final example sentence above, we can make the verb active—and shorten the sentence:

> Sentences cue readers.

Changing *be* verbs to active verbs throughout an essay can have dramatic effects. For instance, in John Steinbeck's essay (page 69), verbs pull readers through the ideas:

> The great redwood forests of the western mountains early attracted attention. These ancient trees, which once grew everywhere, now exist only where the last Ice Age did not wipe them out. And they were found to have value. The Sempervirens and the Gigantea, the two remaining species, make soft, straight-grained timber. They are easy to split into planks, shakes, fenceposts, and railroad ties, and they have a unique virtue: they resist decay, both wet and dry rot, and an inherent acid in them repels termites. The loggers went through the great groves like a barrage, toppling the trees—some of which were two thousand years old—and leaving no maidens, no seedlings or saplings on the denuded hills.

Specify the Nouns

Vague nouns refer to nothing in particular: *people, society, things, everyone,* and so on. It is often tempting to rely on vague nouns to float ideas past readers, but vague nouns have at least two negative effects: (1) They keep readers from focusing, and (2) they signal that the writer has not committed to a statement. Vague nouns plague college writing (and instructors everywhere dislike them). Although they are not inherently evil (sometimes writers need to use words such as *things* and *people*), they generally make for vague statements.

Good writers home in on particular events and actions. They get up close to processes. For example, in her essay (page 398), Deirdre Mahoney proposes that people scribble on pages while reading. She uses personal testimony and narrows in on some important nuances. In the following passage, we see a particular thing happening to a particular person—which is usually more intense than an essay full of broad and obvious statements:

> I've been scribbling in books for years (lightly and in pencil, I might add). . . . At a later date, I sometimes borrow the book again and am greeted by my previously penciled notes still etched softly in the margins. Two important things seem to occur in this moment. First, I'm promptly reacquainted with my previous thoughts and, second, I'm often surprised at how much my thinking has shifted since the previous visit to the page, a sure sign that the human mind is in a constant state of making meaning as it constructs and then reconstructs itself.

Experimenting with Patterns

Written language is not simply linguistic. Once it enters a reader's thinking, it becomes sonic and rhythmic. Whether it is being read aloud or quietly, language moves along in pulses. It includes pauses, dips, repetition, and stops. Good writers tune in to the way their language works—and to the sound it might create in readers' minds. The following strategies will help you to tune your phrases and sentences and to maximize rhythm and movement.

Repeat Clause or Phrase Patterns

When writers don't invent, they find themselves unnecessarily repeating the same claims throughout their essay. However, repetition is not always bad. In fact, skillful repetition can add vitality and intensity to sentences. When writers re-create a sentence pattern, they create familiar linguistic territory for readers, and drive points home. For example, Jaren Provo (page 331) repeats modifiers—and even replicates the syllable patterns:

> Yet, despite the significant cultural contribution *Star Trek* has made, many see this legendary universe as unreachable, non-applicable, influencing only the stereotypical Klingon-quoting, uniform-donning, convention-going fan. However, this view is false. *Star Trek* empowers mainstream America to imagine a future of hope-filled opportunity rather than horrific obliteration.

Later in her essay, Provo repeats both clause patterns and verb structure to create a powerful conclusion:

> We must be sure not to violate the magnitude of *Star Trek* and its whispers of truth for the days ahead. We must not be intolerant of that which heralds a tolerant tomorrow, doubtful of a harbinger of hope, or disparaging toward a beacon of peace or humanity. The zeitgeist bestowed upon our culture by *Star Trek* must be appreciated for its complexities and considered in its hopeful message to the people of today.

In his essay, Benjamin Busch (page 323) uses short declarative sentences to create a rhythm, a beat that leads to a powerful idea:

> When I was a boy, I was given plastic army men. They were posed already fighting. I arranged them in the sandbox behind our house, and I killed them. I voiced their commands and made the sounds of their suffering. I was every one of them, and I was their enemy. I imagined their war—and I controlled it. I was a child. But I lost those magical powers as a Marine in Iraq.

As in these examples, repetition can make sentences feel more deliberate and intense, more dramatic and lively. Readers can actually feel the word patterns insisting on attention.

Intensify with a Series

A series of words creates a pattern for readers. When a chain of words is lined up, readers make an automatic intellectual connection. We most often see single words in a series:

> The land flattens itself out and creates a sense of <u>openness</u>, <u>emptiness</u>, and <u>space</u>.

But phrases can also be put in a series:

> The land flattens itself out and creates <u>a feeling of openness</u>, <u>a sense of emptiness</u>, and <u>an eyeful of space.</u>

Skillful writers can put entire clauses in a series. Here, the repeating clauses create an intellectual pattern, set up a way of thinking, and pull readers briskly through the images:

> They live in a place <u>where the fields lie uninterrupted, where the houses take the full brunt of the wind, where the horizon simply evaporates.</u>

Try Absolutes!

Absolute phrases—which consist of a noun, modifiers, and often a participle—modify an entire clause or sentence, not just a word or phrase. Absolutes can help intensify ideas—weaving them together to create a more sophisticated, yet concise, sentence. Consider the following sentences:

> The beauty pageant had finally concluded and the whole ordeal had finally come to an end. Cindy Bosley could now escape the desperate feelings around her.

Although these sentences are correct and functional, they can be combined with an absolute phrase. The verbs of the first sentence will be omitted and the ideas slightly compressed into an absolute phrase attached to the clause:

> The beauty pageant concluded and the whole ordeal finally over, Cindy Bosley could escape the desperate feelings around her.

If used sparingly, absolute phrases can add subtle variety, helping readers escape the march of subject/verb, subject/verb, subject/verb sentence patterns.

Try the Stylistic Fragment

Sentence fragments are grammatical errors. They occur when a writer punctuates a phrase or dependent clause as though it were a full sentence. Here are some examples of sentence fragments:

Fragment Errors

> By writing on the sidewalk in colored chalk and then hiring an airplane to write the message in the sky.

> Because the grand opening of the hotel coincided with the holiday parade and the community's main fundraising festival.

> Just when Marvin flummoxed the toss and flailed wildly at Herdie's aunt, who was then experiencing an intestinal expression.

None of the preceding examples can stand alone as full sentences. This is not because of the content, but because of the grammatical structure. None of them is an independent clause. But some writers venture into fragments intentionally. They deliberately craft fragments because breaking the conventions calls readers out of a comfortable intellectual pattern. Notice the (italicized) stylistic fragments in the following passages. They are technically incorrect. But the writers decided to use the unconventional to help create vitality and intensity.

Stylistic Fragments

> At some point in its life cycle, business must conserve. Like a lion or a bear. Like any organism.
>
> Sooner, rather than later, evaluating performance will not be the enterprise of faculty. It'll be the work of outside corporations. Profit hounds. Performance peddlers.
>
> When everything seems broken. When nothing seems fixable. When persistent crisis looms. These are the conditions that make political parties comfortable. Then, they can further etch their agendas into the masses by detailing the wrongs of the other party.

Deliberately Break a Rule!

Grammar is a set of conventions—a code agreed upon and supported by institutions within a culture. But all codes are toyed with. People who know the codes of a culture intentionally tamper for one of several reasons: They want to explore the limits of language and not simply use it; they want to assert some sense of individuality, something beyond their complicity in rules; they want readers to share in a brief moment of nonconformity.

Believe it or not, academia is a perfect place for intellectual rule breaking. In fact, many would argue that the job of academia is to make certain that students know the rules so well that they can break them with grace and purpose. Playing with the conventions of language helps us understand what's possible, intellectually speaking. Keep in mind that rule breaking should not be a mere game of self-indulgence. It should increase the vitality of the text and the readers' understanding of your ideas.

Questions for Vitalizing Your Writing

Even for the most attentive readers, lifeless, wordy, and monotone language is easy to ignore. But vibrant and lively language draws in readers. It calls them away from the other thoughts and issues vying for their attention. Once you have developed a focused draft, apply the following questions to create more lively sentences:

Controlling Pace

- Where can I increase the pace of the sentences? Where should readers move along more quickly? (For these passages, apply any of the following strategies: turn clauses to phrases, turn phrases to words, combine sentences, subordinate less important ideas, avoid unnecessary interruption, avoid over-embedding, avoid pileups, and avoid vague pronouns.)
- Where can I slow down the pace? Where should readers experience more immersion in the ideas? For these passages, try to combine sentences and experiment with length.

Cleaning the Language

- What passages contain unnecessary phrases and terms?
- What passages draw unnecessary attention to the writer (*I*), the reader (*you*), or the essay/project itself?
- What overused terms (clichés) could be substituted with more precise or descriptive words?
- What obvious statements and wordy phrases could be omitted?

Getting Specific

- What nouns could be made more specific? (Scan for broad and unhelpful terms such as *people, technology, society, things, today, children, men, women, adults, students*, and so on.)
- What verbs could be more active? (Scan for linking verbs such as *is, am, are, was, were, be*, or *being*.)

Experimenting with Patterns

- Where might a series of phrases or clauses help to intensify an idea?
- How could a repeating pattern (in a concluding or introductory paragraph, for instance) intensify the reading experience?
- Where might I try an absolute phrase or stylistic fragment?

20 Anthology: Everyday Rhetoric

The Nth Degree. Used with permission.

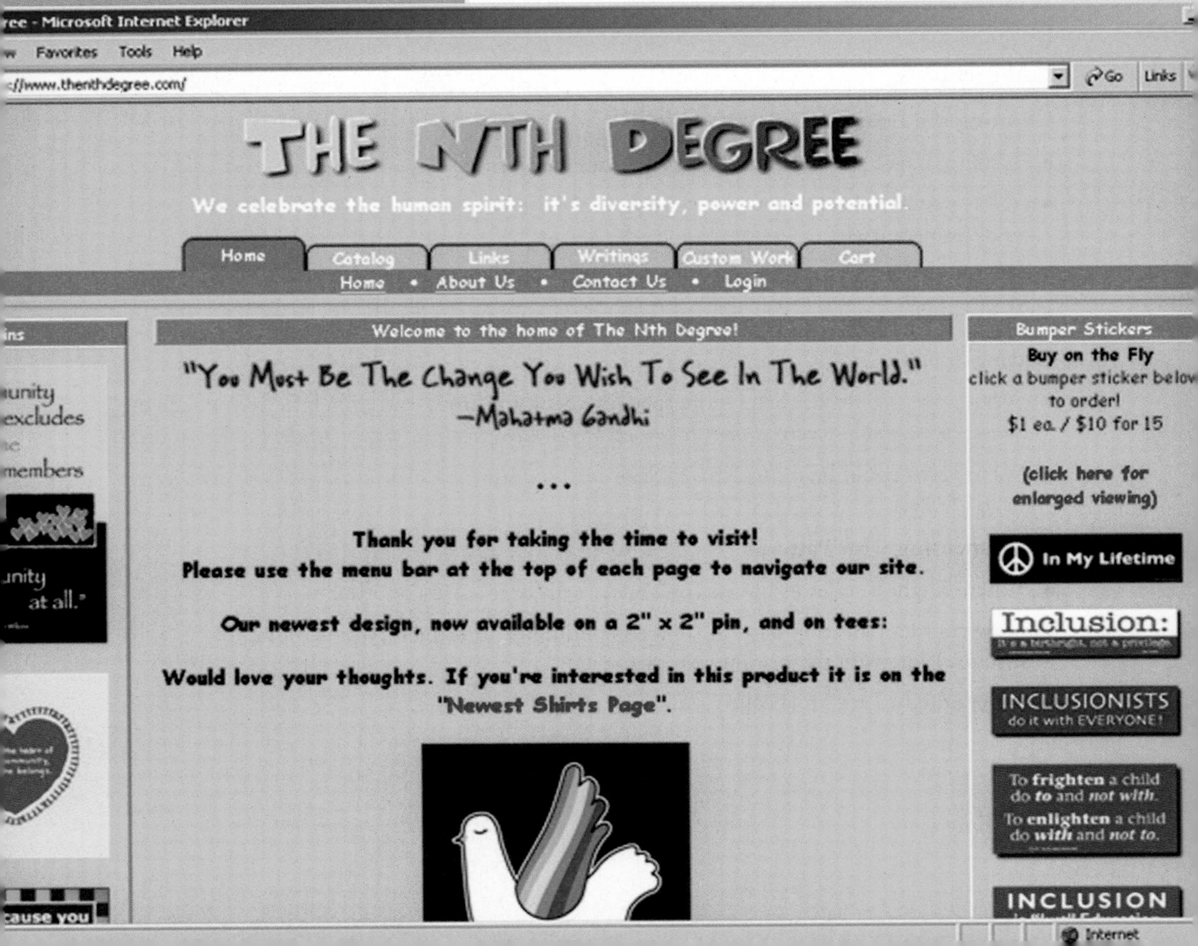

Remembering Who You Were

A Beat Education

Leonard Kress

It's easy to list the things we know. But it's impossible to list the things we do not know. Occasionally, people get a direct glimpse of the gaps in their learning and come face to face with the huge, dangerous, unruly reality beyond their knowing. For Leonard Kress, a poet and professor at Owens Community College in Toledo, Ohio, this moment came on a hobo-like trip to Chicago. As you read this essay, notice his allusion to the Beats—a group of influential writers and thinkers from the mid-twentieth century who lived hard and traveled throughout the United States, who dramatized freedom and intellectual revolution. Like Kress, many writers, musicians, artists, and scholars were influenced by the Beats and the world they imagined. (Kress's writing also appears in Chapter 11.)

At 20 I was convinced that the single most important experience, without which my education would remain shamefully incomplete, was that of hopping a freight. Doubtless, my sense of education at that time (as well as my sense of what constituted good writing) was more than mildly seasoned by huge doses of the Beats—Allen Ginsberg, Gregory Corso, William Burroughs, Kenneth Patchen, LeRoi Jones, and, of course, Jack Kerouac. That these writers were at the time considered non-scholarly, marginal, and were all but vilified by my literature teachers made them, I'm sure, that much more irresistible. I would merely open a page at random—a short story, say Kerouac's "Railroad Earth"—and find myself filled with wonder and admiration and conviction: this was sacramental:

> Remembering my wonder at the slow grinding movement and squee of gigantic boxcars and flats and gons rolling by with that overpowering steel and dust clenching closh and clack of steel on steel, the shudder of the whole steely proposition, a car going by . . . the frightening fog nights in California when you can see thru the mists the monsters slowly passing . . . when those wheels go over your leg they don't care about you.

I did manage, once at least, to imitate the Beats. I was staying with some friends in Grand Rapids, Michigan, when I decided, receiving little or no discouragement from them, to seek out the local freight yard. I figured I would ride the rails in whichever direction they took me—unconcerned as I was with notions of destination and arrival. Unable to summon up any practical or procedural advice on how to begin from Kerouac's disjointed and out-of-control prose, I simply searched for a site full of boxcars and cabooses and lanes upon lanes of tracks.

It was early morning and the yard seemed deserted, so I brazenly set forth. I had no fear of the dreaded railway dicks, no sense of the danger of heavy machinery, but I did carry with me a bright blue rucksack, a sense that all would go well if I only abandoned myself to the open road. As hoped for and expected, a figure appeared out of nowhere. I assumed he was something of a tramp or hobo—I had the sense at least not to ask him about his vocation—

and he quickly took me under his grimy wing. With no exchange of words, we managed to cross over several tracks, duck out of sight of the hollering switchers, and second-guess the direction of cars clanking over shuntings. He knew which trains were already made up and ready to pull out, and which might sit for hours filling up with unbearable heat from the morning sun. He led me to one, sitting on the outer tracks, mostly a string of lime-dusty hoppers interspersed with empty boxcars—doors flung invitingly wide open! I rushed in front of him, tossed my rucksack in, and was about to hoist myself inside, when he grabbed my leg and tackled me down to the rails. I was too shocked to resist; he pinned me to the railroad ties and moved his head in real close to mine. Just when I was sure that he was about to slit my throat, he released his grip and delivered what seemed to be a prepared speech about hopping freights. "Don't never board a still train," I remember him saying, "they shut them doors when the train's pulling out. You get stuck in there, you roast, you just roast, that's all there is to it."

Although I was a bit chastened from the stern warning, which at the time didn't seem to be warranted, and covered with brush and gravel burns from the take-down, I felt that I had just participated in some arcane initiation rite and passed through it successfully, the bearer of some sort of *tramp-gnosis.* If I were to characterize it now, I might say that it seemed to be a particular mix of the medieval Franciscan ideal, International Workers of the World notions of brotherhood and solidarity . . . and my own middle class suburban naïveté.

We strode together—in some sort of unacknowledged sync—farther down the line, to a spot beyond the cluster of workers' shacks and railroad paraphernalia. Ducking in a trackside ravine almost as if we were kids playing backyard war, we waited until the freight began its slow grinding movement, almost overwhelmed by what Kerouac called that *overpowering steel dust and clenching closh and clack of steel on steel, the shudder of the whole steely proposition. . . .* We waited, nodding as each car rolled past, until a boxcar with unshut doors presented itself to us. Then we sprung up, tossed our packs inside and scissor-jumped our way in.

While I was making myself comfortable, shifting around on a sift of rust and pebbles, dangling my legs over the side, my companion leaped off, barely losing his footing, and rushed off. I didn't know why he left. I thought at first that he had forgotten something, later that he was trying to set me up—for what, though, I couldn't imagine. He just disappeared, and though the train was barely snailing along, I was afraid to jump down after him. As it picked up speed, however, I regretted not taking that chance, as my dangling legs were almost sheared off by a switching signal the boxcar curved past.

The ride itself was unbelievably jittery and uncomfortable. I couldn't open the can of beans I'd brought along, and the slices of bread I'd stuffed into my rucksack fell onto the floor and coated themselves in rust-flecked grease. The freight did, however, grant me a spectacular view of the setting sun as it ambled ever so slowly along the banks of Lake Michigan. And it did ease through innumerable small town backyards where children ran alongside, not easily winded, cheering both the train and me on. Even young mothers waved shyly while they pinned banner-like sheets onto their clotheslines.

Almost half a day later, around midnight, the train crunched into Chicago, where I hopped off, exhausted and exhilarated. As my shaky train-legs hit the gravel of the roadbed, I thought I heard a threatening shout, so I ran, tripped mostly, over the 50 or so tracks and platforms and switchings, down a steep embankment. Right into the middle of some rundown neon-shod shopping strip near 95th Street on the South Side—bars and liquor stores and boarded-up groceries, card readers, barber colleges, and storefront churches, groups of men hanging on the corners drinking from passed-around rumpled paper bags. Here was a whole gallery of street life like nothing I'd ever seen. Somehow the rickety freight ride and all that drama and lure of the past two days quickly dissipated, replaced by an urgent sense of new gaps in my learning, of new educational possibilities.

Writing Strategies

1. Through his use of vivid language, Kress shows himself riding the rails. Identify several fresh expressions, such as "shifting around on a sift of rust and pebbles" (¶6) or "he grabbed my leg and tackled me down to the rails?" (¶3) Explain how several expressions bring his experience to life.
2. How else might Kress have vividly described his experience for readers? Write two or three additional sentences of description and explain why each one is successful at describing the scene.
3. Describe Kress's voice as a writer. What does he sound like? Provide several examples from the essay (particular word choices, for example) that support your description. How is, or isn't, Kress's voice appropriate for an essay about hopping a freight train?
4. Kress refers (or alludes) to several poets and writers in the essay. Explain the effect of these allusions, how they help to illustrate a point.

Exploring Ideas

1. How does the way Kress talks about education invite readers to think differently about the subject?
2. How is Kress's essay part of a larger discussion? What is the general subject matter—or issue—of that larger discussion?
3. What educational experiences can you remember that might help you think further, and differently, about this topic?
4. Interview several people about an important learning experience of their own. How many people's experiences included formal education settings? How many didn't? How were others' experiences similar to or different from yours or Kress's? How might these responses help you better understand and write about an educational experience of your own?

Pass It On

Molli Wallen

A current experience often reminds us of an earlier one, and from our current perspective, we discover a value of the earlier experience that we couldn't see at the time. For example, in the following essay, reading to her siblings (and then reflecting on that experience to write this essay) helps Molli Wallen find meaning in her own childhood reading experience. Wallen, a student at Kent State University at Geauga, wrote "Pass It On," a literacy narrative, for her College Writing I class in the fall semester of 2013. A literacy narrative, as explained in Chapter 2, is a type of remembering essay that focuses on a significant experience that contributed to the writer's relationship with literacy—with reading and writing (and ultimately with ideas). As you read, notice the layers of Wallen's narrative—beginning with reading to her siblings, connecting that to her own childhood reading experience, and extending her ideas outward into the public.

"Bedtime!" declares Mom from the kitchen. Immediately there is an uproar. Four five-year-olds whine as they climb the stairs to bed. "Oh great it's my turn again," I think to myself. It had been a long day of school, dance, and babysitting, and I felt like whining too. I followed the noisy out-of-tune parade up the stairs. Right and left bedroom doors close in my face as my two little brothers and two little sisters reluctantly put on their pajamas. I sit in the carpeted hallway waiting. I peek in once or twice to see if they are playing or changing. Beside me is our bag of bedtime storybooks, a hand-me-down collection given to us by a family friend. Many of the books have ripped pages from favored use but some are brand-new. Pajamas take forever but teeth are brushed quickly because after teeth comes the best part of the evening: story time and prayer time.

Everyone scrambles to find a seat on the carpet forming a circle around me. Books are eagerly shoved into my arms. I open the first book and place my finger to my lips, "shhh." All eyes are on me as we turn the page and find a man in a big yellow hat with his pal Curious George. They laugh and try to tell the next part of the story before I can read it. Again I must quiet them down in order to continue. Each page is filled with simple words and colorful pages. They giggle at the silly monkey's adventures. Often we play a letter or word game while we are reading, and they proudly point out letters and sight words that they are learning. My little brother and sisters were all born profoundly deaf. Almost two years ago, they received cochlear implants. Story time is a whole different experience for them. Because they had been born deaf, they have a disadvantage at language learning. It is important to note that "the human brain develops more rapidly between birth and age five than during any other subsequent periods" (Edie 1). Especially for deaf kids, "literacy has its foundation in auditory neural development from spoken language exposure and spoken communication practice" (Flexer 7). Seeing the excitement on their faces made me excited as well. After a while, I started to get into it too, making facial expressions and funny sounds.

Suddenly in my mind, I'm five years old sitting at my desk in my Chinese kindergarten classroom. Our concrete block classroom holds thirty of us bundled in three or more layers to stay warm. A tall, stern, black-haired lady with intense almond black eyes stares at me. I drop my head and return to my work. We sit quietly filling out page after page of the Chinese alphabet, first writing them pinyin and traditional Chinese. After hours of copying letters, we are rewarded with playground time, but before long we return to copying more Chinese characters. I don't remember story time, but I sure knew how to use the abacus by the time I finished kindergarten. After my adoption, I was home educated in the Classical model of education. During the grammar stage, my parents read and sang to me. We would sing our science, history, geography, and even our grammar. Language was more than marks on a page. It had a rhythm, meaning, and was comforting. How different life was back in China compared to life in America.

Comforting. That is exactly what story time is for my four little brothers and sisters. Putting on pajamas isn't fun, but story time is comforting and relational. The repetition and tone of voice used in story time is developing their brain and language skills. Sources state that early childhood is a critical period for language development, and in that window, certain experiences must be present in order for the child's brain to develop properly ("The Brain"). Some of those include physical, emotional, and social experiences. Reading books to my siblings every night provides these experiences and gives them the repetition they need to develop language and eventually literacy.

Little kids love to mimic adults, and because of this, adults have power to influence a child for life through reading. I ended up reading many books that night. Story time lasted for twenty minutes or so instead of the two that I usually aimed for. I now mimic my parents in the way they read to me and hope that my little siblings will one day mimic me. It is important to cherish these moments and use them as opportunities to teach and bond with your family. The next generation's education and development depends on what we pass on to them.

Works Cited

"The Brain: How Children Develop." *KBYU Eleven*, 2010, www.kbyutv.org/kidsandfamily/readytolearn/file.axd?file=2011%2F3%2F5+The+Brain.pdf.

Flexer, Carol. "The Auditory Brain: Conversations for Pediatric Audiologists." *Audiology-Online*, 25 July 2011, www.audiologyonline.com/articles/auditory-brain-conversations-for-pediatric-817. Transcript.

Edie, David, and Deborah Schmid. "Brain Development and Early Learning: Research on Brain Development." *Quality Matters*, vol. 1, Winter 2007, pp. 1–4. *ERIC*, files.eric.ed.gov/fulltext/ED526797.pdf.

Writing Strategies

1. What is the essay's thesis?
2. Identify at least three details from the essay that help readers understand and accept the thesis.
3. Describe Wallen's writer's voice using two passages from the essay to support your description.
4. Midway through the second paragraph, Wallen says, "My little brother and sisters were all born profoundly deaf." Why might Wallen have placed this sentence in the middle of the paragraph instead of starting a new paragraph here? What subtle difference might beginning a new paragraph with the sentence have created?

Exploring Ideas

1. Write a paragraph in which you describe the joy, fun, excitement, pleasure, or comfort of having been read to. Try providing a few vivid details about the experience. Can you discover and explain the underlying reason for the feeling you experienced?

2. In her third paragraph, Wallen describes two early literacy experiences—one before and one after adoption. Recall your own early literacy experience and then imagine if a drastic change had occurred (such as adoption, a different culture, a different teaching style, a different economic situation, and so on). How might the change have changed you?

3. With a group of peers, discuss whether or not reading is comforting. When is it? When isn't it? Why?

The Grapes of Mrs. Rath

Steve Mockensturm

We are often invited to think about the past as something that is behind us—something to forget about, something that can no longer influence who we are, how we think, what we value. But Steve Mockensturm, an artist, musician, and graphic designer, reminds us that the past looms all around us. The places we drive by, swing into, and rarely notice have absorbed the past and offer it back to us constantly. The buildings where we learned and lived have been defined by our own lives and the social events that swirl around them. And, more importantly for Mockensturm, these places have worked their way into our lives, into our understanding of ourselves and the world we inhabit.

I wonder if Mrs. Hulda Rath ever realized how much she affected my life. Probably not. It's funny how a teacher gets stuck in your head and you find yourself referencing that for the rest of your life.

Mrs. Rath taught English at DeVilbiss High School in 1975—my junior year. I say taught, but she didn't really teach. Didn't even talk that much, just gave us a lot of stories to read. She said they were classic, important books, but I'd never heard of any of them: *Animal Farm, Lord of the Flies, 1984, The Crucible, Cry the Beloved Country.*

DeVilbiss was a rough-and-rowdy school (inner city, a thousand kids, half black, half white) with a lot of distractions. During the '40s and '50s it was THE high school to attend, very academic, but by the mid-'70s it was starting to run down, perhaps stigmatized by a few race riots in '68.

Mrs. Rath had an ability to recognize the kids that actually wanted to read and learn and, often times, would send a few of us down to the library where it was quiet and we could have some sanctuary from the usual classroom shenanigans. Looking back, I realize how amazing and grand that school library was. It was bigger than the local public branch and very church-like with its vaulted ceiling and tall windows. Everything was made of wood—the chairs, the tables, the shelves, the big librarian's station in the middle—and it was always full of light, the windows exposed to the south and west. Three sets of large mahogany doors would clang and creak, echoing down the hall, up around the stairwell, and into our classroom.

It was in this environment that I was introduced to the work of John Steinbeck. Two of the books assigned were *The Grapes of Wrath* and *Of Mice and Men.* I was smitten with these masterpieces and savored Steinbeck's work like a rich meal. Reading these stories in the great, holy library of my young life is one of the happiest memories I have. These were stories about my country and my people. Flawed yet beautiful people in tough situations in an imperfect land. I was discovering America. I suddenly wanted to read everything Steinbeck had ever written.

I checked out *Tortilla Flat* and *The Wayward Bus* from the library and asked Mrs. Rath what else he wrote and where I could get it. She loaned me her copy of "In Dubious Battle." Soon, I wanted to own all of Steinbeck's books. I scoured the bookstores to complete the collection, a collection that has traveled with me for 25 years.

The city sadly closed down DeVilbiss High School a few years after I graduated. It was too big and too expensive to maintain. Thankfully, they never tore it down and trimmed only a few trees from the large oak grove lining the front walkway. For years it sat empty, the massive entrance looking out on Upton Avenue with no expression.

Then, a few years ago, some parts of it reopened for special programs, and the industrial skills center was transformed into a technology academy. My children were enrolled in the Horizons program at the old school. From time to time, during open house, I'll wander the halls and conjure up old voices. Many areas of the building are unsafe; the library is almost unrecognizable. It's a massive storage room now, crap piled to the ceiling, desks and shelves torn out and not a book in sight.

The girls have Russian language lessons in Mrs. Rath's old room at the top of the stairwell. Sometimes I'll stand in the doorway and picture the room as it was back in '75, gazing around, putting old friends in their seats. Whenever I'm reading Steinbeck, my memory goes back to this classroom, the library, and Mrs. Hulda Rath's quiet ways, and I get the urge to plop down and read *Cannery Row.*

Writing Strategies

1. Describe Mockensturm's voice as a writer. That is, how does he come across to readers? Refer to three specific passages to support your description.

2. Choose two sentences in the essay and explain how particular nouns and verbs make them lively and clear.

3. What would you say is Mockensturm's main idea? How does he convey it to readers?

4. Identify the most effective uses of narration (storytelling) and description in Mockensturm's essay, and explain why they work.

Exploring Ideas

1. In groups, discuss how Mockensturm sees high school English differently from the way you see it. (Some may see it the same as he does.) What values, beliefs, or assumptions underlie the different ways people view high school English?

2. Visit your old school, an old playground, a park, or some other place from your past and write down any memories that come to mind. What experience there influenced your identity—or still influence you today?

3. Consider the people from your past. Explain how their behaviors (even the very subtle ones) influenced your outlook on life.

Explaining Relationships

What the Honey Meant

Cindy Bosley

It is easy to see ourselves moving steadily ahead in time. But Cindy Bosley, poet, novelist, and writing teacher, invites us to see how the past circles up into our lives—and how the people from our past linger in the present. In this essay, Bosley's present relationship with her husband involves her past relationship with her father. Although the essay is highly narrative, it is also highly analytical, making intense connections between single moments throughout Bosley's life. And these connections help to reveal significant meaning in a simple honeycomb. (Bosley's writing also appears in Chapter 2.)

My husband disappeared out the back door with an empty bowl in his hand. I did not see him leave, but a few moments later, he came back in and asked me to shut my eyes. I did as he asked. When I opened them, he stood in front of me holding out a bowl of fresh honey and a piece of the comb which had been pulled away from the hive and was still running with the buttery sweet liquid of all my best memories. My husband might as well have gone out just then and shoved his hand, in brown bear fashion, through the stinging, angry bees to release this small brick of honeycomb for all the love and gratitude I felt toward him at that moment. He stood there holding out to me a bowl filled with my life as it should have been, and I wept.

When I think of honeycomb, I think of my father. I first tried a small bite, and then more and more by the spoonful, the day before my father left. He had brought the honey home from a guy at work, he said, and so he set the brick in its jar onto the counter, and found a spoon for himself, plunged the spoon into the hexagon cells and pulled it away with a *suck.* And then he went back for more. I stood over the jar of honeycomb marveling at it—the many sections of honey, the yellowish layer of beeswax sealing the liquid in, the small brown and black flecks of flower remnant, or bee poop, I guessed. My father said nothing to me, and he did not offer me his spoon, but when I got off my chair to get one from the drawer, I stood over the honey jar again waiting for permission, and he said, "Wanna try it?" with surprise and, I think, a little joy, as if it hadn't occurred to him before to offer some to others. That was the way he was. And I ate and ate and ate. I loved the wax like gum, how it stayed behind in my mouth long after the honey part was gone, swallowed, tasted, and replaced with another spoonful.

When my father left that night, I was sleeping and he did not say good-bye. In the years to come as he came and went, moving in and out like a college boy from a dormitory, I would learn that this was how he did things. That first morning, though, I did not know anything had happened, but like a too bulky winter coat a kid inherits from an older sibling, that morning when I woke, the house just *felt* different—a little bigger, a little old. The rooms were quieter. It's hard to believe that was possible, the new quiet, since my father was a too quiet man to begin with, but it was *quiet.* And the browns and golds of our '70s decor were browner, and deeper gold. And my mother was in her bedroom on the phone trying to muffle hard crying. And my younger sister was watching *Land of the Lost,* while my brother played with his Tinker Toys. Something had happened, and I didn't have to ask anyone what that was. The sun was a sawblade in the sky.

I didn't quite know what to feel about this. Part of what I felt was certainly excitement. *Wow. Our dad's gone. Wow.* I also felt a puncture, very small like a needle, that I couldn't locate inside me. And I was, I think now, terrified at the new development that no one had yet explained to me though it was nearing lunch time, though it was time for someone to talk.

I finally had to ask the obvious question, but I didn't know how these things were supposed to go—I had imagined other families, more loving families, sitting down together to talk over the coming changes with the children well before they happened, or maybe even a day before they happened. I had imagined other families dealing with it in other ways—the father kissing the children a special goodnight when he knew he would not be there the next day when they woke up, or maybe he would not save the trauma for the night or morning, but ease out in the smooth part of the afternoon, lots of hugs and tears, but at least the witnessing of leave-taking. And then I remembered the honeycomb.

And if I say: I went to the kitchen to look for something. Like a small and pitiful gesture of his helplessness and regret, there on the counter was a spoon he'd left beside the jar of honey, and I knew he meant it for me.

It feels one way.

But if I say: I went to the kitchen to look for the jar of honey. When I saw the counter, I saw there was nothing there, and I suppose I expected that. He must have taken it with him.

That feels another way.

But what really happened is that I did not have to ask my obvious question, "What happened with Dad?" And I did not have to bother looking for the honey because, yes, he left it—it simply wasn't that important to him. And no, there was no symbolic spoon or other invitation, *Eldest Daughter, please eat,* nearby. What happened was that I took a bite of honey and then I joined my sister and brother, two and ten years younger, watching Saturday morning cartoons together on the black, brown, white carpet, patterned in such a wild way that it was quickly making my head ache.

I heard my mother tell the story five or six times that morning, with different details and emphasis, to the people she talked to most easily. She had moved from the heavy weight of the red and black paisley bedroom to the dimness of the kitchen, a room the sun rarely ventured into, like all the dark rooms of our house. She told Aunt Edith that he better damn well get his stereo cabinet out of this house today. She moaned her money fears to Patty, and there was a hitch in my heart when I heard her mention my violin lessons. While she talked to Marlene, I heard several female names come flying, and with Darla, I understood more clearly that there was somehow another woman involved. What had happened I never did learn exactly, but my father had moved out overnight. Everything felt brand new. And there was a jar half-full of honey in the kitchen that no one but me wanted to eat.

When my husband brought his bowl of honeycomb to me that bright, grown-up day in the kitchen, I did not think *Father.* I did not think *Childhood.* I did not think *Old Pain.* But my husband knows my stories well enough to understand what it might mean to me, and when he heard our neighbor at the door that morning telling him to come get some of this amazing honey someone had given him, my husband knew enough to grab a bowl and bring me some.

Everyone I know has aches so deep that small triggers bring tears to their eyes. The honey gift was clearly that trigger for me. I like to think I cried because seeing that bowl of honey made me miss my father. Or maybe I cried because I don't yet understand all that happened in my life back then, or why people can do the things they do to each other. Maybe I cried because my husband loves me that much, enough to know what the honey would mean. But I do know one thing: I sure do like honey. I wept to see that honey just for me.

Writing Strategies

1. In ¶3, Bosley offers readers details about physical goings-on:

> And the browns and golds of our '70s decor were browner, and deeper gold. And my mother was in her bedroom on the phone trying to muffle hard crying. And my younger sister was watching *Land of the Lost*, while my brother played with his Tinker Toys. Something had happened, and I didn't have to ask anyone what that was. The sun was a sawblade in the sky.

What purpose do these details serve? What point, if any, might they communicate to readers?

2. Notice how Bosley uses her introduction and conclusion (about honey) to frame her essay. Is her framing technique effective? What are such a technique's effects on readers? Can you think of any situations in which this framing technique would be ineffective?

3. Paragraphs 7 and 9 are very short—one sentence each. What effect does their brevity have on the reading of the essay? Why does Bosley offer these particular ideas in one-sentence paragraphs?

4. How does Bosley develop her main idea—with narration (storytelling), description, or both? In what other ways does she develop it?

5. Identify at least one use of figurative language such as hyperbole, metaphor, understatement, or allusion, and explain why it is effective.

Exploring Ideas

1. In a paragraph, explain what the honey means to Bosley. Include in your explanation how the honey comes to have the meaning for her that it does.

2. Revise the paragraph you wrote for item 1 and share it with several classmates. Discuss the differences between your paragraphs.

3. How does Bosley's essay encourage readers to think about everyday things, such as honey?

4. In what ways might you respond to Bosley's essay? What kinds of responses does it invite? List several possibilities and discuss them with your peers.

5. Talk to old friends and relatives, and visit places from your past (a playground, old school, church, and so on). Through writing, explore the memories or emotions you experience.

Dog-Tied

David Hawes

We are surrounded by interesting, complex, and puzzling relationships—which we rarely examine closely. In "Dog-Tied," David Hawes explores the relationship he has with his dog, Logan. His essay prompts the rest of us to consider similar relationships. Hawes's essay demonstrates the curious mind at work, looking not just from the owner's point of view but from the pet's as well.

I realize this is an odd paraphrase of the Beatles, but it certainly seems fitting: I have a dog, or should I say, my dog has me? Often it seems unclear which of us is in charge in this arrangement. As I once explained to a non-dog owner, "Logan and I have a symbiotic relationship: I feed him, walk him, bathe him, take him to the vet, give him his heartworm and flea-and-tick medicines, buy him treats, pet him, and play with him. And what does he do? He lets me." This past summer I even bought him a kiddie pool to lie in when he got too hot. He is, after all, a retriever, so he likes water. Not to mention that he has this hairy coat on all the time that he can't take off when he's too warm. Do I spoil him? Of course I do. Isn't that the whole point of having a dog?

On the other hand, I realize some people don't see things the way I do. Just this morning I saw a man walking his dog past the front of my house. In a loud and commanding voice he kept saying, "Heel! Heel!" Obviously he wanted his dog to make no mistake about who was in charge. However, I did notice that the man kept up his commands all the way down the street. Maybe the dog's name is "Heel." I think most people, though, have a tendency to spoil their dogs. Just go to any pet store and look at the vast array of foods, toys, beds, and treats, not to mention the shampoos and skin treatments.

It wasn't always this way, of course. Dogs were originally domesticated so they could help with the work. And some dogs are still workers, helping herd the sheep or bring in the cattle. But I have to believe these true "working dogs" are a small minority. I think most dogs these days, at least in this country, lead a fairly pampered life, so it certainly gives a different meaning to the old sayings about "a dog's life" and "working like a dog." Personally, I'd love to work as much as my dog does.

Sometimes, though, I have to wonder about him liking his pampered life. Sometimes when he's in a really deep sleep, his legs jerk violently, like he's running. Is he dreaming about retrieving ducks and quail? When fall comes, do those longing looks he gives me mean he's wondering when I'm going to get the shotgun out so he can do what he was bred to do? When he lies down with his head between his paws and heaves one of the heavy dog sighs, is he wishing he could be running through a field somewhere, sniffing out the game? Does he feel like something is missing from his life, but he's not sure what it is? And worst of all, does he blame me for what's missing?

I worry about these things sometimes, but not too much, I guess, because when I leave for work in the morning and he looks very sad, or when I get home from work and he wiggles all over the place in his happiness to see me, or when he comes into the bedroom and lies beside me first thing in the morning waiting for his wake-me-up belly rub, it seems like maybe this relationship is working out OK.

Writing Strategies

1. How does Hawes convey his main idea? Does he state it explicitly or imply it? Does he develop it through narration, description, explanation, or a combination of the three?

2. Hawes describes his relationship with Logan as "symbiotic." What details from the essay support this description?

3. What makes Hawes's essay engaging? Consider particular supporting details, arrangement, writer's voice, sentence vitality, or any other characteristics.

4. Write a new introduction and conclusion for Hawes's essay and then compare it with one a classmate wrote. Discuss the different strategies you chose and the advantages and disadvantages of both.

Exploring Ideas

1. Describe the relationship between Hawes and his dog.

2. Describe the relationship you have with a dog, another pet, a stray or wild animal, or some other life form, such as your prize orchids or herb garden.

3. To further explore people's relationships with other life, interview at least five people about their relationship with any nonhuman life form:

  a. Begin by considering what you want to know. For example, you might ask them to describe the relationship in general, explain what they find rewarding about it, explain what they find frustrating about it, and so on. In groups or alone, compose several clear and purposeful questions that will encourage informative responses.

  b. Conduct the interviews, being certain to accurately record the responses. Then look for interesting ideas that help you to learn something new about people's relationships with other life. Write down the two or three most interesting ideas you discovered and explain what you think is interesting about them.

4. How might you respond to Hawes's essay without writing about dogs or pets? What relationships can you use to illustrate your main idea?

The Holy Land

Kierstin Reszka

Whether or not we want to admit it, we are connected to a range of people—some of whom we see only occasionally, many of whom we keep at a polite distance. In this essay, written for her first-year writing course, Kierstin Reszka examines a web of relationships. She discovers division and unity, artificiality and genuine belonging. As you read, notice how Reszka calls forward layers of communication that otherwise might not be identified, especially in formal situations or polite company.

In our mother's arms we come to be baptized, and from there we learn how to live, come to get married, stumble in to mourn, and are carried in one last time to be mourned over. Inside these walls we are safe. For some, those are the only reasons they come at all. On this relatively mild September morning though, everyone is here because it is Sunday. And that's what Sunday is all about. Church.

It's 11:58 a.m. and the congregation is gathering in the foyer after service in what I like to think of as their usual "Clumps." One of the most prominent Clumps is off to the right, huddled tightly outside the door to the stairs. Ranging in age from eighteen to twenty-six, they are swinging their hips and tossing their hair as they mingle with one another as if there's a song inside begging to be let out. Over the soft scent of cologne and deodorant from the day before rise stories of Saturday, the guy they met at the coffee shop, the friends they saw at the mall, who is going where tonight. These are the Church's Desperately Single College Students. The awkwardness of a junior-higher mixes with the overconfidence left over from high school. Most aren't even in college anymore; instead they've taken a "break" from classes. In this break it is not uncommon for one to become engaged and move on to the Obnoxiously Engaged Pretend-College Students who are located in the center of the foyer, in front of the sanctuary. Here they stand, with their left hand out to reveal a big fat diamond placed just above a purity ring and a smile pasted on their already pasty faces. The majority of this year's batch of engagees graduated last year and spent the following year floundering as college freshmen until their one and only finally dropped down on one knee. I'm standing off from them in my own Clump when—oh, shit—it's Danielle. I swallow, lowering my head, believing in my dark, shallow, sinful heart that the idea of being invisible will somehow make it a fact. She lifts her hand as beaded bracelets slip toward her elbow, and in a high-pitched voice pulls me back toward those chubby cheeks: "Hiiiiiiiiiiiiiiiiiiiiiiiiiiiiiiiii Kierstin!"

"Hiiiiiiiiiiii, Danielle!" I wave. When she waves, the car keys looped around her fingers jingle in the air, breaking apart the thickening hum of conversation circulating around the foyer. Danielle opens her mouth again and asks me how I am. A green shirt is stretched over her stomach and leads into a billowy skirt that stops just above her thickening ankles. Though she's been gaining weight since everyone here found out about her father's affairs last winter, her clothing choices have been more defined and hip, like outfits from the American Eagle catalog with a little bit of chocolate down the sleeve. Danielle doesn't linger long, surprisingly,

---

and when she eyes another person to squeal at, I slip off into a Clump standing in the way of people still stumbling out the doors of the dim-lit sanctuary and out into the gentle sunlight filling the foyer.

This Clump, the one I stand inside, is a dull circle of kids with their hands stuffed in the pockets of their jeans. We wear jeans to church. Parker is one such Jeans Kid. "Say goodbye to Parker," everyone says solemnly, as if Parker is dying in the imminent future. I arch my naturally thin eyebrows and shift my weight to the other leg, looking down at him. He is pretty short. We dull-in-the-way-kids-take-turns interrogate Parker with questions about the army. "Are you scared?" "Why are you going?" In a place where George W. Bush's name is praised to the highest, it's a dangerous question.

We're not The Pretty People; that's almost certain. That would be Sophie and Sara, two sisters who look like twins but are really a couple years apart who happen to have the voices of angels and the bodies of vixens. Even in their church skirts inched just above the knee and chunky headbands, Sophie and Sara look sort of seductive. They know it, and in the way they throw their heads back, tossing rivers of blond hair behind their backs when the boys stop to talk with them, it is obvious.

Oh, the talent you must possess to turn a boy on in the foyer of a church—especially after one of the co-pastor's sermons. Our head pastor was out of town this morning, visiting his son in another state so our children's pastor preached. He spoke about death and the importance of being ready. When I looked around the church, I spotted several men in tan suit coats and scuffed dress shoes with their heads bent low, hands folded in their laps. When the children's pastor walked up to the stage carrying his Bible, there was a collective shift in positions and the congregation's eyes began to close. I was sitting next to my two best friends who, incidentally, began dating over the summer. When she got up to get a tissue, he kept his eyes focused on his own hands and stared, quite foggy, into their dry lines. Sometime later she returned and he raised his face toward her, tracing her body with his eyes as she explained that she had been gone so long because she was choking on her own spit when she went to blow her nose. He still looked at her like she was the most stunning, complex, intriguing creature he'd ever laid eyes on. The pink fuzz of her sweater sleeve caught on his own sleeve as she settled in next to him and they weaved their fingers in and out from the other's. Electric. His older, single sister looked on from the row behind us, her mouth turned down at the corners, but it was much better than having to sit in front of the man who scream-whispers at his squirmy sons throughout the whole service.

The foyer is beginning to thin out, mainly of the older churchgoers and with them the aroma of stale coffee. After a morning of drifting in and out of sleep against the hum of God's word, it's time for their afternoon nap. The Nursery Moms spread out toward the rooms filled with toys and *Winnie the Pooh* books. The new mothers stand in vague circles holding a child with one arm and their stomachs with the other. They are perpetually pregnant or talking of trying to get pregnant. If you get too close to the mommies, you may hear the words "amniotic fluid" or "diarrhea" float up in conversation.

Once in a while one of the Desperate College Students gets pregnant before they migrate to the Blissful Newlyweds or even the Obnoxiously Engaged Pretend-College Students. This is sheer disaster, and offenders must then move on, ashamed, to the realm of Nursery Moms, holding growing tummies and covering their swelling breasts with like six layers of clothing. This once happened to one of the ladies who is now a Nursery Mom. She married the dad and then they had this beautiful baby and named her Emmalee. To some she may have seemed like the result of some horrible mistake. But God doesn't make mistakes and, if He did, they wouldn't be like Emmalee, whose mere presence seems to lift the mood in the foyer by about ten thousand notches.

Sophie and Sara's band of girls, who are beautiful but not as beautiful as them, gather round, orbiting the two girls like they're the sun and the moon until they have the opportunity to break through their atmosphere. The girls stand around, Bibles tucked under their arms, and scan one another. Their eyes move from each other's Spring Pink toenails up their hopefully-not-stubby legs and stop to meet the other's crisp stare.

The only thing anyone here seems to have in common is that their happiness is held by delicate, invisible lines connected from one person to the next. When one tilts forward, the others lean back in an attempt to keep things level. Perhaps it's not the sermon that pulls us from our soft sheets and into this foyer every single Sunday morning. It is this part, the after part, the mingling and talking and reassurance that there are others in the world who think they may have found the point to this seemingly pointless life that keeps us from collectively tilting forward and landing on our faces.

It is nearing 12:30 now and you can actually hear stomachs growling. Someone begins to shut the lights off and lock up the doors to the sanctuary until next Sunday. Emmalee bursts out of nowhere and weaves through a forest of legs as she reaches to catch her cousin and wrap him up in a suffocating embrace. Her closely set eyes are so, so alive underneath neatly trimmed bangs. She's a perfect balance of her mother and father, flouncing around in a simple cotton dress and giving questioning looks to the strange adults who ruffle her precious head of hair. And suddenly Emmalee seems out of place to me—not because she doesn't belong here but perhaps because she is the only one who really belongs here, the only one who has the kind of heart still capable of faith.

I press myself against Parker gently, giving him the Church Hug (when one leans into the hug receiver, pats them on the back, and says "I'll pray for you").

"Thanks," Parker says, nodding. "See you at Christmas." I nod too. My mother wants to leave, it's lunchtime, and there are thunderstorms inside of our tummies.

Another light is shut off, shadows dance against the walls. Emmalee's mother scoops her up. I open the glass door for myself, hold it open for the stragglers behind me, and with my Bible tucked underneath the other arm like a sword, I step out into the fickle September warmth.

So we come. To be baptized, to learn how to live, to get married, to mourn, and to die. And in between all of these things, sometimes we get saved.

Writing Strategies

1. What is Reszka's thesis?
2. How do the labels (such as Desperate College Student, Blissful Newlywed, and Obnoxiously Engaged Pretend-College Students) work in Reszka's essay? What do they reveal about relationships?
3. What is Reszka willing to say that others might want to avoid? What does she say about church and church members that others might politely leave unsaid?
4. Although this essay focuses on a specific church community, it still resonates beyond the particular experience. How does Reszka develop public resonance? Point out and explain specific passages or sentences.
5. Reszka openly admits her biases and complicity in certain ways of thinking. How does her participation in the church activities help or hinder her understanding of others' relationships?

Exploring Ideas

1. According to Reszka, why might people go to church? Why do they leave their beds on a Sunday morning?
2. How is the little girl, Emmalee, both out of place and the only one who belongs?
3. In some ways, Reszka sees through the pretense—the artifice that others use to dramatize their best public selves. What passage do you think best illustrates this? Where does Reszka best get beyond pretense?
4. Why do cliques form? Why do they form at places like a church?

Observing

Onward, Gamers, Onward!

Royce Flores

We have built-up stereotypes, prejudices, and presuppositions about the types of people we encounter on a daily basis. We think we know the people we encounter. But close observation reveals more. In this essay, Royce Flores presents a group of young gamers. In the beginning of the essay, he shows us the most obvious dimension of their public identities. But then he shows us the subtle interactions and nuances of the gamers' culture. His up-close examination of the gamers illustrates a key move in observation: The writer should, at some point, take readers beyond their prejudices and presuppositions.

Within the white, poster-covered walls of "The Fun Factory" is the bantering, bartering, and competing of young minds. Here, young men (and the occasional girl, but this occurrence is as rare as a funny April fool's joke) gather, sit around, chat, and play the occasional card game. The gamers that hang out in the shop are distinct from other kids their age. They are the outcasts of their age group; the kids who do not fit the average profile set by their peers. In every town, in every state, and worldwide, collectable card games have created a sub-culture for these kids to call home and weekly tournaments give them an opportunity to compete. Often, they can be seen dressed in shirts with sayings only they and other gamers can understand, such as "ALL YOUR BASE ARE BELONG TO US." Their pockets are stuffed with moderate sums of saved lunch money eagerly waiting to be spent for three or four packs of the newest Magic the Gathering set. To accompany the players (and their shirts) are black "Ultra Pro" cases that carry the personalized arsenal of decks for ensuing card games. These decks are gamers' most valued possessions—often the product of years' worth of patient building, trading, and purchasing.

"The Fun Factory" is a long, white, rectangle-shaped room with overhead florescent lighting that the owner, Dave, has stated (on numerous occasions) will be removed for track lighting. White plastic tables lay suffocated in bags, drinks, cards, and most importantly, "Ultra Pro" cases. Despite the clutter on top of them, the tables manage to remain in neat rows and columns. The shop reeks, a cocktail mix of young male perspiration and nacho cheese Doritos. The entire shop is glued together by the classic tunes of Double Rock KLT. On the rare occasion, a true classic like Ozzy Osbourne's "Crazy Train" catches the ear of the gamers, prompting outbursts of group singing and occasional air guitar performances.

Yet it is not just for camaraderie that the gamers come here. It is the tournaments, the contests of mental champions, that attract them to this place.

Before a tournament the gamers are lively, eagerly greeting all other participants that enter the store. When players who have not been in a tournament for a while arrive, he (or occasionally she) is met with group hugs, and, "Hey, Ryan, where in the hell have you

---

From Royce Flores, "Onward, Gamers, Onward!" Reprinted with permission of the author.

been?!" Ryan, or whoever the returnee may be, tells a tale of parental strife and how he JUST made it.

Next the group of gamers slips into the second pre-tournament phase, which closely resembles that of the New York stock exchange. Gamers call out for all to hear, "Does anyone have three *Diabolic Edicts*?" If the gamer is lucky, someone will look up and reply, "Yes, but, I need four *Chain Lightnings,* so what else would you be willing to toss in?" This chaotic event is driven by loud requests, denials, and even some begging. As tournament time nears, gamers run from table to table, frantically trying to get that last element added to their decks. The chaos can often last over an hour.

Once it is time for the names to be taken, the store grows silent. Players' faces grow worrisome. Then, one at a time, names get called off, and tournament pairings are made—when officials select opponents. (An occasional sigh or "Fu^%!" pops out when a poor player gets matched up with a superior gamer.)

Contrary to the demeanor at the start of the day, the players now act as if they do not know each other. Their once smiling faces are stern, overthrown by the gamers' will to succeed. The entire atmosphere is thick with the mildew of concentration and brainpower. The friendly conversations have transformed into staccato formalities, announcing the players' turns.

As players are eliminated, via best of three duels, they begin to gather around the better players to watch their games. This process resembles a sort of teacher/student relationship, in which gamers learn from better players on how to improve their games. No one says anything. They just stand intently and watch.

As the tournament winds down, and the final match approaches, the less astute players filter away and the truly intense gamers stay, assured by the fact that if they walk away from watching the final, they'll miss a great play, the huge turn-around victory, or just an absent-minded folly on one of the finalists' part. And this is where the gaming is great. It is the evolution of the mind, a leap from "dorkdom," air guitar, silly tee-shirts, and big public hugs to deep thinking, highly intuitive, focused individuals.

In a society where all information is thrown at the mind in sixty-second intervals, these kids can manage to sit down for two to three hours and play a game that draws so much on concentration and intuition. It is this display of intellect that sets these kids apart from their peers. This respect for the fortitude of thought makes these kids deeper thinkers, able to appreciate when the mind does amazing things through cunning, ingenuity, and knowledge. We see this in their eyes, how one good move lights up the group. There are no fireworks, no dazzling effects, just a mere playing of a card to make onlooking faces smile and nod. By each flop of a card, a gamer's mind is opened up to new possibilities, a chance for victory or to hold out on a loss for one more turn. The watchers of the finals see and respect this; it is why they play, why they watch, why they spend the money to acquire the cards. It is not just a bunch of dorks with nothing to do; this IS what they do.

Writing Strategies

1. How does Flores encourage readers to think differently about gaming?
2. What details help to engage readers? Are any details unnecessary?
3. How do details from the essay support the assertions put forth in the concluding paragraph? What additional details, if any, would be helpful?
4. How does Flores take readers from the common view of gamers to a more accurate view?

Exploring Ideas

1. Based on this essay, what does Flores value? How does Flores appeal to readers' values?
2. Flores writes, "It is this display of intellect that sets these kids apart from their peers." What other activities besides gaming include a "display of intellect" that can go unnoticed by people outside the activity?
3. Interview several gamers or research Magic: the Gathering online. How does your research support or refute Flores's position on gaming?

The Farm on the Hill

Evan Proudfoot

Sometimes we can see more than the present. If we look closely, we can see beyond the values and assumptions of the moment and understand something about the past or future. In this essay, Evan Proudfoot discovers the past in the details of an old barn. Proudfoot wrote this essay for his first-year writing course.

The fields are plowed with tractors now and the red paint has long since faded away, but Albert Slater's barn still stands atop the hill at the end of Montgomery Road. Rusty barbed wire fences stand like sentinels along routes once traversed daily by grazing cows. The old farmhouse has been reduced to a leaning pile of gray boards, and the chicken coop is nowhere to be seen. Cars pass by with hardly a second glance. The seasons change, and the old ways of life embodied by the farm slip further from remembrance.

The farmhouse, too old to stand upright, leans into a grove of young poplar trees, appreciating fully that, after many years of dutiful service, it has earned its repose. Built in the 1930s as the bachelor home of a carpenter, it provided shelter and fond memories for several successive families before falling into disrepair. Leafy branches now poke through the windows, and small shrubs parade through the door like neighbors to a housewarming party.

The barn's endurance is testament to the skill of its maker. It is a study in the complex simplicity that the entropy of time produces. Old and new blend seamlessly into the patchwork quilt of the present. The farmer down the road still works the fields and stores his equipment inside. Rusty sheets of tin and new aluminum plates form the roof; weathered hemlock boards and new white pine planks clothe the old skeleton. These lie upon a base of cracked lime mortar and granite fieldstone. It is the same stone that farmers must laboriously haul from the fields each spring to avoid damaging their teams and equipment. What is troublesome in one place becomes useful in another.

There are two diamond-shaped windows near the apex of the roof. The builders could just as easily have made them square. After all, it was only a storage building for hay and livestock. Instead, they decided to add the elegant diamond windows. And by the northwest basement window, the builder etched his name in the mortar: "A. Slater 3/16—34." Two other names accompany his, neighbors no doubt. The inscription says it all: The men poured the mortar in the spring as the snow was fading and the planting season arrived. They poured it in the cold and were so proud of that barn that each triumphantly marked his participation. For Mr. Slater and countless others like him, the barn was not just a place for storing cattle. It symbolized a way of life. The farm stood for hard work, for doing a job right and putting in the details. It was a life in which neighbors shared each other's burdens and triumphs. It was a time when skill and beauty were born out of necessity.

Family farms have been a sight all over northern Michigan for the past one hundred and fifty years, so the Slater farm isn't unique—except that it is. Every year, another barn falls over or gets torn down. Every year, the land is put to more lucrative uses.

Across the road stands a house of cement block and vinyl siding. It is dreadfully unoriginal. The square angles and perfectly ordered lawns mimic those of every house around it. It also has barns, hastily constructed edifices of Plexiglas and red metal, standing where the little Montgomery schoolhouse once stood.

The Farm Gold Club is two miles to the south. A red barn-shaped sign out front invites in golfers, bar patrons, and homebuyers. It is an empty symbol; the actual barn nowhere to be seen. The owners tore it down when it began to fall apart. The farmhouse remains, as do the fields: subdivided into housing lots, a restaurant, and eighteen exciting holes of golf.

Albert Slater's barn still stands atop its hill, for how much longer, I do not know. It is a nexus point that allows us to reconnect with a different era, with another way of life. For those who take the time to observe and remember old ways, it is a subtle reminder that as society moves into the future, we cannot forget the virtues of the past.

Writing Strategies

1. What single sentence best captures Proudfoot's main insight about the barn?

2. In ¶2, Proudfoot uses a simile to describe the present state of the farmhouse: "Leafy branches now poke through the windows and small shrubs parade through the door like neighbors to a housewarming party." What does this simile do for the essay? How does it influence you?

3. At the end of ¶4, Proudfoot says of the past, "It was a time when skill and beauty were born out of necessity." Explain how the details in the paragraph lead up to this point.

4. In ¶5, Proudfoot offers a contradiction: "Family farms have been a sight all over northern Michigan for the past one hundred and fifty years, so the Slater farm isn't unique—except that it is." What purpose might this serve? How does it work rhetorically?

Exploring Ideas

1. Proudfoot describes some properties surrounding his main focus: "The Farm Gold Club is two miles to the south. A red barn-shaped sign out front invites in golfers, bar patrons, and homebuyers. It is an empty symbol." Why is the red barn-shaped sign an empty symbol?

2. According to Proudfoot, the Slater barn is a nexus point. What other places or buildings can be seen as a nexus point?

3. How else does the past lurk in the present? When you look around your neighborhood or school, what places speak of a different era?

4. Consider the layout of your community. What are the newest buildings? What do they say about the values of your community—what it wants, what it celebrates, what it dislikes, or seeks to ignore?

Analyzing Concepts

Why We No Longer Use the "H" Word

Dan Wilkins

Words such as "handicapped" are automatic. We don't give them much thought until someone like Dan Wilkins shows us something we didn't know about the concept. As with the other readings in this section, this essay not only helps readers to understand a particular concept differently, but it shows us that our concepts are fluid. Concepts can—and do—change.

What is it about the word "handicap" that so offends many of us living with disabilities? Within our disability culture, progressive thinking has steered us away from using the word "handicapped" as a label or descriptor for someone living with a disability for a couple of reasons. To begin with, contrary to longtime societal thinking, it is not synonymous with the word "disabled." More on this in a moment.

Most importantly, it is the very origin of the word that leaves such a bad taste in our mouths. It conjures up imagery that perpetuates archaic misperceptions of the value of people living with disabilities and their potential for contribution to their community and to humanity as a whole.

The word comes from old-world England when the only way many with disabilities could survive was to sit on a corner or on the side of the road with a "handy cap" held out for passersby to fill out of pity. A pretty negative connotation. Not at all an empowering legacy, is it? And, sadly, it is not just a part of our distant past. . . .

I do not wish to break from the "handicap vs. disability" issue, but it is important to point out that this basic premise of projecting pity as a mechanism for exacting funds from the masses is still being used today. If I may rant for a paragraph, children and adults with disabilities continue to be exploited every day, most visibly every Labor Day when Jerry Lewis does his annual Smellathon, er, telethon. Twenty-four hours of patting and hugging "poor, helpless cripples" until FINALLY, in the last five minutes, through red blurry eyes, hair mussed, sleeves uncuffed, bow tie loosened and akimbo, sweat dripping and sleep deprived, he tells us, with all the apparent (or is that transparent) sincerity of a really bad lounge singer, that we "will never walk alone." (Hey, Jerry, I'll never walk AGAIN! and truth be told, that's OK.) He demands that we, the heart-wrenched public, give, GIVE, until it hurts. GIVE, so that, for another year, we can walk the street unashamed to look someone in the eye; unashamed that we might have fearful, discriminatory thoughts toward "those people," unashamed that our society continues to fight equity and access to all it has to offer. Buy the premise, pay the dues, and it's another year of "no fault insurance."

Jerry isn't the only one, just the most notorious. There are others. Be wary. Khalil Gibran said "the gifts which derive from Justice are greater than those which spring from Charity." There is power in this statement. If you want to make a difference and, at the same time, help put an end to the pattern of pity and paternalization, find an organization that is promoting

---

self-control and independent living; one whose mission is that of building confidence and ability, awareness and community. Try your local Center for Independent Living. It'll be money or time well spent.

Back to disability vs. handicap. Now that we know the origin of the word, we realize that there is little dignity to be found there, except when we look into the souls of those who, over history, wrapped themselves in the label like a banner when there was no other word; who lived, fought, and died defending their right to belong in a world trying so hard to eliminate them or hide them away.

All this is not to say that there is no appropriate context in which to use the word "handicap" or "handicapped." There is. Let me explain.

I have a disability. I broke my neck in an auto accident in 1980. It is an integral part of who I am and, to some degree, it impacts the way I do things in the world. I only become "handicapped" when I cannot reach a goal.

It may be a narrow door, or a set of steps, an inaccessible parking structure, or a restaurant with no accessible bathroom. For some it may be no signage or Braille menus, no interpreter or service dogs allowed. It may be someone's attitude out there: "Hey! You can't come in here! We didn't vote for the law and we're not making changes" or my own attitude: "I'm just a quad . . . I'll never amount to anything."

Though I'm not big on continuums, let me illustrate it this way. Two lines. One horizontal. One vertical. They form a big plus sign. (See diagram.) The horizontal line represents disability and the (relative, and I stress relative) significance of its involvement and impact on the person, with minimal impact on the left side and significant impact on the right. The vertical line represents the degree to which the external or internal (self-concept, confidence, etc.) handicap limits one from reaching a goal. We'll put minimal impact at the bottom and significant impact at the top.

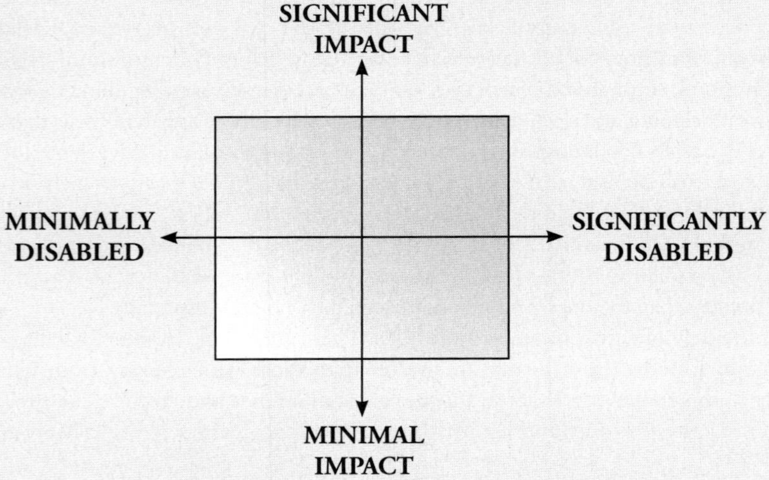

Now let me tell you the story of two friends. "Friend A" (not his real name) has cerebral palsy as his disability. He uses a word board and head stick to communicate with those who do not understand or speak CP. He uses an electric wheelchair and a chin stick to get around. I stressed parenthetically above the issue of relevance with regard to how we perceive the significance of disability. We, not really knowing Friend A but seeing him on the street, might be quick to place him far along the horizontal continuum of disability, considering him to be pretty significantly disabled. And I would tell you that Friend A's self-perception would put him much farther back toward the minimal end. I would also tell you that Friend A is just finishing up his degree in social work at the local university. Here's a guy who most would consider has a significant disability, yet he's out there making a difference in his life and in the lives of others. He's not allowing his disability or society's low expectations to handicap him. He's going to contribute to his community. I would say he sits pretty low on the handicapped scale. Does this make sense?

Adam Clark/StockXchng

On the other hand, I have a friend, "Friend B" (not his real name either). He lost a couple of toes in a farm accident. He walks fine. No pain. No limp. Nothing. Pretty minimally disabled, wouldn't you think? But can I get him to go to the beach with me, or swimming? Absolutely not. He'd like to, but he goes nowhere without shoes on. He won't even wear sandals. Pretty minimally disabled but, again, it's relative. He considers himself pretty significantly disabled. So much so that his own attitude, his own self-concept, has him significantly handicapped.

A final difference: if we were to consider these two continuums over a period of time, we would most likely see that the disability continuum, in most people's lives, would remain relatively static when compared to the handicapped continuum, which would fluctuate with every situation and barrier(s) presented.

It is important to understand the context in which to use the words we use. The best way not to offend someone living with a disability, and I often insert the word "living" because we tend to forget that we are all living, breathing, interacting, supporting, pushing, pulling, etc., basically trying to get from Point A to Point B with as little hassle as possible, the best way not to offend someone living with a disability is to refer to them first as just that: as Someone, as a person, as a teacher, a student, an athlete, whatever they happen to be at that moment. That they have a disability is secondary or even tertiary. People are people. People are not diagnoses, or prognoses. They most certainly are not their disabilities. Their disabilities are a part of who they are, perhaps a tenth or twentieth of who they are completely; affording most of all a unique perspective on the world and one's place in it. It is not something of which to be ashamed but something of which to be proud.

Writing Strategies

1. Describe Wilkins's voice, his persona as a writer. Refer to at least three sentences that illustrate your description.

2. How important is Wilkins's brief etymology (word history) of "handicap"? Does the etymology strengthen his essay? Would the essay do just as well without it? Explain.

3. What tools or strategies does Wilkins use to illustrate his point? What others might he have used?

4. Although Wilkins's essay is focused on the term "handicapped," how does his essay speak to a larger issue?

Exploring Ideas

1. What words, or terms, have been replaced by others, and why? What terms do you think are still in use but shouldn't be?

2. What new term has been most helpful or most harmful? How has the change in terminology affected the concept? How has the change in the term influenced the way people think or act?

Cookies or Heroin?

Marie Winn

The term *addiction* is tossed around in many situations. It gets applied to hard-core drug dependence, the Internet, and to favorite snacks. In this essay from her book *The Plug-In Drug* (2002), Marie Winn invites us to consider addiction—how it works and when we might apply the term to our everyday lives.

The word *addiction* is often used loosely and wryly in conversation. People will refer to themselves as "mystery-book addicts" or "cookie addicts." E. B. White wrote of his annual surge of interest in gardening: "We are hooked and are making an attempt to kick the habit." Yet nobody really believes that reading mysteries or ordering seeds by catalogue is serious enough to be compared with addictions to heroin or alcohol. In these cases the word *addiction* is used jokingly to denote a tendency to overindulge in some pleasurable activity.

People often refer to being "hooked on TV." Does this, too, fall into the lighthearted category of cookie eating and other pleasures that people pursue with unusual intensity? Or is there a kind of television viewing that falls into the more serious category of destructive addiction?

Not unlike drugs or alcohol, the television experience allows the participant to blot out the real world and enter into a pleasurable and passive mental state. To be sure, other experiences, notably reading, also provide a temporary respite from reality. But it's much easier to stop reading and return to reality than to stop watching television. The entry into another world offered by reading includes an easily accessible return ticket. The entry via television does not. In this way television viewing, for those vulnerable to addiction, is more like drinking or taking drugs—once you start it's hard to stop.

Just as alcoholics are only vaguely aware of their addiction, feeling that they control their drinking more than they really do ("I can cut it out any time I want—I just like to have three or four drinks before dinner"), many people overestimate their control over television watching. Even as they put off other activities to spend hour after hour watching television, they feel they could easily resume living in a different, less passive style. But somehow or other while the television set is present in their homes, it just stays on. With television's easy gratifications available, those other activities seem to take too much effort.

A heavy viewer (a college English instructor) observes:

> I find television almost irresistible. When the set is on, I cannot ignore it. I can't turn it off. I feel sapped, will-less, enervated. As I reach out to turn off the set, the strength goes out of my arms. So I sit there for hours and hours.

Self-confessed television addicts often feel they "ought" to do other things—but the fact that they don't read and don't plant their garden or sew or crochet or play games or have conversations means that those activities are no longer as desirable as television viewing. In a way, the lives of heavy viewers are as unbalanced by their television "habit" as drug addicts' or alcoholics' lives. They are living in a holding pattern, as it were, passing up the activities that lead to growth or development or a sense of accomplishment. This is one reason people talk about their television viewing so ruefully, so apologetically. They are aware that it is an unproductive experience, that by any human measure almost any other endeavor is more worthwhile.

It is the adverse effect of television viewing on the lives of so many people that makes it feel like a serious addiction. The television habit distorts the sense of time. It renders other experiences vague and curiously unreal while taking on a greater reality for itself. It weakens relationships by reducing and sometimes eliminating normal opportunities for talking, for communicating.

And yet television does not satisfy, else why would the viewer continue to watch hour after hour, day after day? "The measure of health," wrote the psychiatrist Lawrence Kubit, "is flexibility . . . and especially the freedom to cease when sated." But heavy television viewers can never be sated with their television experiences. These do not provide the true nourishment that satiation requires, and thus they find that they cannot stop watching.

Writing Strategies

1. In ¶3, Winn begins detailing the criteria for addiction—the qualifying factors that would allow someone to accurately apply the term. What are the criteria, or qualifying factors, for determining addiction?
2. Which passage most supports the idea that television viewing can be an addiction?
3. Where might Winn have used an allusion, a scenario, or testimony to illustrate a broader point about television viewing?
4. Winn uses three quotations in the essay, from E. B. White, from a "heavy viewer," and from Lawrence Kubit. Describe how the effect of these quotations differ in the essay. How would you characterize their use?

Exploring Ideas

1. Since Winn's book was published, do you think that television addiction has worsened, stayed the same, or diminished? Is something else taking its place?
2. What kinds of television programs do you think are most addictive? What particular qualities or features of those programs make viewers long to tune in—and consistently feel unsatisfied even as they watch?
3. How do commercials function in the television addiction? (If commercials take up an increasing amount of the viewing experience, how do they keep people glued to the screen?)
4. How might someone argue that television viewing is not an addiction at all?

What Is Education?

Petra Pepellashi

Sometimes the most commonly held assumptions about the most common topics need to be rethought. The prevailing understanding of education, for example, is that its essence is linked to getting a good job. But as Petra Pepellashi explains, such a view, although widely accepted, is limiting and even a little tragic. In this essay, written for her first-year English writing course, Pepellashi tackles the prevailing notion of education by first revealing its historical roots. From there, she invites readers to imagine another, more humane, view of the concept.

During most of my life, I shared the common view of education as providing what I needed to learn in order to "make a good living." In this view, education defines the "correct" and "proper" way to do something: to read, to write, to add/subtract, to draw, to design, to sell, to do whatever necessary to maintain or excel in my work . . . my livelihood. The design and structure of elementary, secondary, higher education revolve primarily around building skill sets related to work/career. If in doubt about the commonly held purpose of education, try talking to a college counselor about a course path outside of a career path. A blank stare meets the inquiry. The stare represents confusion about how to construct the selection of courses without the defining purpose of a career.

Things might have been different if our system of education were more like Thomas Jefferson's vision. Jefferson felt strongly that the average unprivileged man needed to be part of the leadership bodies of the country. As historian James Conant notes, Jefferson's curriculum centered upon developing a critical mind in order to balance the interests of the common man and those of the privileged (whether the privilege came from class, status, or wealth). He was deeply troubled by the control of monarchies in Europe and worried that one of the other privileged groups could easily reign a controlling influence in our nation unless "we are not afraid to follow truth wherever it may lead, nor to tolerate any error so long as reason is free to combat it" (Conant 29). He defined the ideal curriculum of higher education as reading, writing, arithmetic, literature, rhetoric, all the sciences, philosophy, natural philosophy, and ethics. Jefferson included self examination and sincere consideration for all as crucial aspects of critical thinking. As an ardent believer in religious freedom, Thomas Jefferson felt strongly about the importance of secular education as a balance to the indoctrinating aspect of schools operated by religious organizations. Although Jefferson's concept of general public education never came to fruition, he played a major role in establishing the secular University of Virginia, with its curriculum aimed at developing a critical mind.

In fact public school as we know it today did not exist until the industrial revolution needed more highly trained workers. The founders of our school system used the Prussian system as a model, rather than what Jefferson had proposed. The Prussians initially instituted their schools in order to indoctrinate the Prussian worldview and elevate skill sets for improved soldiers and workers. Businessmen and politicians traveling in Europe were so impressed by the success of the Prussian system that they lobbied for its establishment in America (Conant 37).

Maybe we would respect authority more while blindly following authority less if education followed the Jeffersonian definition. Instead, that authority tells us the purpose of education is to succeed as a worker, and we accept the idea. Anyone who has taken Introduction to Social Psychology may remember the experiment conducted by a Midwestern teacher who assigned half her grade-school class as the blue "smart" team and the other half as the brown "dumb" team with the result that the students adhered to the assigned definitions. Amazingly, when the assignment between "smart" and "dumb" switched, it took less than a day for the students to act out their new opposite definitions. Although some may focus upon the aspect of fulfillment of expectations, the most critical factor remains that the adherence was to the expectations of the authority as definer of what "is."

Formal education and therefore educators function as one of the primary authorities in defining and establishing what is "correct," "fact," "truth," "commonly understood" about a wide variety of topics. The lower levels of education, elementary, secondary, and most college and university courses educate/indoctrinate the definitions established by higher education. Typically only the highest levels of education function to define, question, test, refine, and redefine the purpose, content, and context of education in the lower levels.

In addition to formal education, consider all the informal educators such as parents, family, friends, bosses, business leaders, government leaders, special interest groups, athletes, entertainers, musicians, newscasters, talk show hosts, therapists, doctors, religious leaders, etc. whose messages infiltrate our minds through stories, magazine articles, advertising, books, TV programs, films, documentaries, radio talk shows, music, newspaper articles, websites, and more. With so many "authorities," how we evaluate and incorporate their views into our own becomes critical. All too often, the view of an "authority" eludes careful evaluation and becomes unconsciously integrated into our thinking. The danger lies not in authority. Clearly authority provides positive and necessary aspects to society such as order and structure. However, unexamined reliance on authority portends harm. Think of any atrocity throughout history and at the root are many blindly, and therefore ignorantly, following authority.

The harm in unexamined adherence appears in more subtle ways when multiple "authorities" focus our attention on work—on finding that singular career path. No doubt work represents an essential aspect of life, but I can't help but wonder if the tail is wagging the dog. Where do we investigate and define what it means to be human . . . how one relates to one's inner self, the mysteries of life, other people, animals, the planet, the cosmos, and the impact of each on the other? Shouldn't we learn about our own internal operating system before we learn applications such as work? Aren't these topics each one of us should consciously investigate in order to provide the bedrock for building a meaningful life that includes things like work?

I look around to see where one learns a process to define oneself and the criteria by which one chooses to live. I can see glimpses in poetry, in literature, in art, in music, in some sciences, and in nature, but I don't see it in middle or high school when young people are breaking away to define themselves. What tools do they have on the journey of self-discovery or in developing their worldviews? In terms of higher education, one might think ethics or philosophy, but somehow they seem overly cerebral, complicated, and authority bound, focusing upon predefined *whats* instead of explorative *hows*.

Rhetoric most definitely contains the force to shake one to the bones to wake up and redefine and reconsider various aspects of one's world. I'm reminded of Jefferson's inclusion of rhetoric as an important aspect of education. However, it is an elective class taught in college, and it doesn't necessarily point one toward defining oneself and the criteria by which one chooses to live. I thought possibly religion, but it seems the most authority bound, even though the essential principles common to all religions point one down an avenue leading to self-discovery and integration of a worldview large enough to encompass all life. What would our human world look like if the fundamental purpose of education included educating people to define and live their highest human values for the benefit of self, people, animals, and the planet?

Work Cited

Conant, James B. *Thomas Jefferson and the Development of American Public Education.* U of California P, 1962.

Writing Strategies

1. How does Pepellashi's personal statement in the first paragraph function in the essay? What impact does it have on readers—and on the call to rethink education?
2. What is the relationship between Prussian history and present conceptualizations of education? Why is that relationship important to Pepellashi's point?
3. Why the focus on authority? (¶4–7) How does Pepellashi's description of authority figure into her claim about education?
4. Pepellashi points to ethics, philosophy, rhetoric, and religion as possible pathways for education, but she explains that each falls short in some way. What is the effect of her final paragraph—of leaving readers to imagine specifics?
5. What is Pepellashi's most analytical paragraph? Where does she best break down the specific elements or qualities of an idea? How does it serve her essay?

Exploring Ideas

1. Pepellashi is taking on the entire structure of formal schooling in this society. She's calling for a radical reconceptualization. Is such a move warranted? Why or why not?
2. How has your education been limited to the ultimate goal of getting a job?
3. What is the most quiet, least obvious, or invisible way that you obey authority? How does that obedience influence your life? How does that obedience support or oppose Pepellashi's point?
4. Pepellashi concludes ¶4 by writing, "Although some may focus upon the aspect of fulfillment of expectations, the most critical factor remains that the adherence was to the expectations of the authority as definer of what 'is.'" In your life, who defines *what is*?

Analyzing Texts
Impossible Fear
Kathleen Schenck

Kathleen Schenck is a poet, writer, and teacher. She wrote "Impossible Fear," a textual analysis of an article by Mark Synnott about a climbing expedition in Oman. Throughout her analysis, Schenck describes particular textual elements as she finds the broader appeal and value of Synnott's article.

Mark Synnott's article "Impossible Rock" chronicles a climbing expedition in the country of Oman. The article appears in the January 2014 issue of the popular and long-standing magazine *National Geographic*. An international team including two twenty-somethings and Synnott, who is a 44-year-old writer and avid rock climber from New England, visits the remote Musandam Peninsula in the Persian Gulf to explore climbing routes. Synnott provides the first-person narrative as participant observer and leader of the expedition. The team engages in *deepwater soloing* where climbers at the crux of a climb simply (though not necessarily easily) fall or jump off cliffs, towers, and sheer rock faces into the water below. Synnott includes descriptions of the landscape, the people, and the climbs themselves.

The magazine does not provide a bio for Synnott except to declare that this is his "first story for the magazine" (Synnott 138). A quick Internet search yields background information on Synnott, such as his New Hampshire roots, his Middlebury College education, his first chosen profession of carpentry, and the fact that he is an accomplished climber who now writes for several magazines, the latest of which is *National Geographic* ("Mark Synnott"). In this piece he includes no in-text citations, no bibliography or works cited list, and no references to studies. As the story is about climbing, he does quote two experts in the field who accompany him on this expedition: Welsh climber Hazel Findlay, 24, and Californian climber Alex Honnold, 28. As the story takes place in Oman, Synnott also quotes their guide and local police officer, Abdullah Said al Busaidi.

Synnott works facts into the narrative by offering details related to the team's experience as it happens. One example occurs when al Busaidi points out the Iranian smugglers in speedboats. Synnott takes this opportunity to explain how the United Nations' sanctions against Iran have played a part in increasing the demand for household items. This increase in demand fuels a busy black market. But the explanation is void of judgment here; the author condemns neither the UN nor Iran for their actions, and expresses no emotion over the matter.

National Geographic is the magazine of the National Geographic Society, which dates back to 1883. The Society acts "as a nonprofit scientific and educational organization 'for the increase and diffusion of geographic knowledge'" ("National Geographic Society"). In addition to the magazine's association with a well-established nonprofit, its longevity alone gives it a certain status among reliable sources. As a popular magazine, however, it warrants a healthy amount of scrutiny by its readership in regards to possible biases by the editorial team, who are in financial cahoots with the magazine's advertisers. (In the issue with Synnott's article, three car advertisements co-exist with a feature story on the not-so-glamorous temporary, international worker situation in the gulf (and therefore oil-producing) countries of U.A.E., Kuwait, and Qatar. The reader can't know if pejorative information was intentionally left out due to the three car companies and their advertising dollars.)

"Impossible Rock" also takes place in the gulf region. The climbers' guide, al Busaidi, warns the team that a proposed climbing spot is too close to Iran (140). The reader can infer danger here as Synnott uses the adjective "hulking" to describe the silhouettes of oil tankers and as al Busaidi points out the Iranian smugglers in front of them. Without explanation, the author writes that the team does indeed visit the site that very afternoon. They've apparently ignored their guide's implicit advice to steer clear of any area so close to Iran. Again, Synnott remains neutral on matters political and expresses no personal, emotional reaction to the danger of Iran's proximity. He stays true to his primary reason for being here, and that is to climb.

Synnott's story gets told through what is said and what is left unsaid. Synnott is short on dialogue with his teammates. In fact, the only words he speaks to either one of them come in the form of an imperative to arguably the best and most ambitious climber on the team: Alex Honnold. Synnott notes that Honnold has failed to take the usual safety precaution of providing them with the rope he carries in his pack before scurrying up 1,500 feet. "Hold on a second!" Synnott cries (145). But what the author fails to say is *I'm afraid.* He's "slightly annoyed" that his climbing partners have not considered his comfort level and the possibility they are all journeying outside of it; they haven't accommodated his slower climbing speed; they have forgotten his very existence benefits more than just himself as a father responsible for the well-being of small children. He "feel(s) old." But he doesn't express his fear of something most human beings would fear if in his shoes.

As a writer who publishes in magazines marketed primarily toward men, like *Men's Journal*, *Outside*, *Climbing*, and *Rock & Ice,* Synnott's squarely set inside a masculine culture where men are hard-pressed to freely admit fear ("Mark Synnott"). This culture all but forbids it. The culture also fails to recognize it. For example, in a study by Condry and Condry from the 1970s, adult subjects perceive the reaction of a baby to a jack-in-the-box toy (when the "jack" pops up) differently depending on whether they were told the infant was male or female (Romaine 43). The adults describe the assumed male infant as "angry," and the female as "afraid." Men aren't fearful; they're ticked off . . . or "slightly annoyed."

It is rare in the United States today to read an article on the Middle East that does not have as its focus the unrest found there. Oman, while itself not in the nightly news, lies just 24 miles from Iran and is home to "one of the most strategic military locations in the world" (138). But the article does not discuss military affairs; it discusses rock climbing. The fact that the subject matter of the article revolves around an extreme sport as told by the expedition leader instantly makes for novel and surprising reading. The unrest the author relays is his own.

But political commentary and anything resembling an ethnography or cross-cultural understanding remain absent. "Impossible Rock" serves as a vivid entertainment piece for climbers and non-climbers, travelers and homebodies, opponents and supporters of American foreign policy. It was written to appeal to as many readers as it can. In terms of the National Geographic Society's aim to increase knowledge on geographic areas, the article remains neutral as it reveals little more than the fact that these things exist: the craggy landscape and waterways, the villagers, the smuggling operations, and the massive oil industry.

As the narrative progresses, it does find ways to briefly detour into the historical linguistics[1] of the people the team encounters, the navigation of enough intercultural competence to exist temporarily in this locale, and detailed descriptions of climbs (including the villagers' amazement of Alex's *witchy* skills) (139). Ultimately, the article speaks to the author's comparison of himself and his climbing abilities to the two other climbers half his age. It's this comparison and Synnott's reactions that overshadow any political, geographical, or cultural commentary. The author replaces the tension between Iran, Oman, and the United States with the tension he feels within himself, the three-party climbing group, and the climbs. On a surface level, the reader can live vicariously through a tourist's tale of extreme adventure in a remote location. (Synnott refers to the people on his team and in Oman by their first names, a stylistic choice that includes the reader and raises the informality of the piece.) The reader may also relate to situations where gaps in age and/or ability play important roles that help shape the theme of the piece. But the underlying and universal struggle faced by Synnott is his struggle with honesty—first with himself and, as a result, with others. He can't climb as well as his younger counterparts. Perhaps at one time he could; the article doesn't say. He also can't bring himself to ask for help (*No, really, could you please slow down/wait for me/toss me that rope*) or to admit he's afraid (*I'm not as good as you, and I'm scared.*) It's easier for him to say to himself and the reader, *Look, I have kids to consider. They need me.* Never mind *I need me.*

In this way the story has wide appeal. It contains metaphorical value as the outer struggles of climbing mirror the inner struggles of being honest and forthright. It exposes the human desire to simultaneously control fear and save face. It takes place in a region few Americans outside the military will visit, and offers a glimpse of life there. Lastly, it allows for a taste of extreme rock climbing with experts in the sport.

The story ends with Synnott exhaustedly taking a seat atop a highly exposed route just mastered by him and the two antagonists. In the space of three sentences, the younger climbers pop up and exclaim they're already on the prowl for another climb before they lose daylight. The reader is not privy to Synnott's response here, but can imagine the tone (and four-lettered words) of what is left unsaid.

Works Cited

Fromkin, Victoria, et al. *An Introduction to Language*. 7th ed., Wadsworth, 2003.

"Mark Synnott." *The North Face*, www.thenorthface.com/en_US/exploration/athletes/29-mark-synnott/. Accessed 21 Jan. 2014.

[1] The branch of linguistics that deals with how languages change, what kinds of changes occur, and why they occur (Fromkin et al. 584).

"National Geographic Society." *National Geographic*, 2014, nationalgeographic.org/about-us/.
Romaine, Suzanne. *Communicating Gender*. Lawrence Erlbaum, 1999.
Synnott, Mark. "Impossible Rock." *National Geographic,* Jan. 2014, pp. 138-45.

Writing Strategies

1. According to Schenck, what is the purpose of Synnott's article?
2. Textual analysis requires looking at specific textual elements to better understand the larger work. What specific textual elements (of Synnott's article) does Schenck focus on?
3. According to Schenck, why does Synnott's article have wide appeal?
4. What evidence does Schenck provide to help readers accept her assumption that men are hard-pressed to admit being afraid?
5. How would you describe Schenck's voice?

Exploring Ideas

1. Read Synnott's article. Do you share the impression Schenck expresses in her final sentence? Why or why not?
2. Read Synnott's article and then unpack (explain) Schenck's claim that "It contains metaphorical value as the outer struggles of climbing mirror the inner struggles of being honest and forthright."
3. Why might an important magazine like *National Geographic* publish an article about rock climbing in Oman?
4. Most Americans cannot locate Oman on a map of the world. Why is such knowledge important? How might it be related to reading and writing?

Analyzing Images

Cartoons 'n Comics: Communication to the Quick

Joy Clough

Like any art form or highly publicized text, a comic strip is far more than meets the (untrained) eye. It is a complex form of communication, with a set of conventions and a shared history. The comic strip artists practice a particular set of rhetorical tools—different tools than we might see or use for academic writing. In the following essay, Joy Clough, president of the Chicago Community of the Sisters of Mercy of the Americas, explains how comics appeal to readers by connecting with human psychology and the particular culture of the times.

The comics. They may be worth a glance as you check your horoscope. They may provide a chuckle as you sip your morning coffee. But seriously? You can't take the comics seriously!

Au contraire. The comics are taken quite seriously—by fans whose complaints deluge any newspaper that dares cancel a strip, by semi-literate adults who can find in them a sort of pictographic "Ann Landers," and certainly by historians and analysts of popular culture who regard the "funnies" as a revelatory aspect of cultural history.

The comics, say these experts, offer a cross-section of human psychology and capture significant snatches of American life and mores.

The Comics as History

A look at the evolution of the comic strip shows how the "funnies," in their own way, record history. The "Yellow Kid," born in 1895 in the *New York World,* is generally accepted as the first comic character. A violent, gangster-talking figure, the Kid would probably be banned from today's papers. His comments and struggles, however, echoed reality for the city's slum dwellers. Though the Kid died, comics, with their solid psychological appeal, were here to stay.

By the Roaring Twenties, such still-familiar strips as "Mutt and Jeff" and "Gasoline Alley" were populating newspaper pages. "Gasoline Alley" made comic strip history by introducing realism and allowing its characters to age. In keeping with the decade, some strips incorporated the emancipated woman. "Nancy," "Winnie Winkle," and "Blondie" (a high-fashion model) were all born in this era.

The Crash and the troubled '30s saw the rise of action comic strips. "Dick Tracy," "Terry and the Pirates," and "Buck Rogers" could take charge and set things right.

With the war in Europe spreading to the U.S., the 1940s became the decade of the comic strip superhero. Welcome "Superman" and "Wonder Woman," both vigorous fighters in the

---

Allied cause. The comics stepped out of newspapers into books of their own with the creation of additional heroes: Batman, Captain Marvel, the Green Lantern.

The 1950s, by and large, grew reflective. Comment could be humorous or biting. "'Li'l Abner" grew in popularity. "Pogo" and "Peanuts" offered observations on politics and life. The humorous side of the daily lives of ordinary mortals became the subject of such strips as "Dennis the Menace" and "Beetle Bailey."

If the '60s were an era of protest and questioning, the comics felt the mood. As "Doonesbury" was born, superheroes went into a sharp decline. The self-doubting and reluctant Peter Parker (alias Spiderman) is one of the few superheroes of recent vintage.

The Comic Appeal

Old-timer or newcomer, the comic strips apparently owe their ongoing appeal to solid psychology. They mirror human life and respond to the human spirit. When life is bleak, a laugh can help. When life is dull, adventure spells relief. When life seems stupid, humor-become-satire makes its point. When life is lonely, romance provides connections.

These are, in fact, the four major responses the comics offer. Humor strips like "Momma," "Marmaduke," "Hi and Lois," "Hagar," and "For Better or For Worse" allow us to laugh at life's petty but persistent frustrations.

Adventure series like "Steve Canyon," "The Amazing Spiderman," and the perennial "Dick Tracy" and "Superman" spin stories that keep us wondering (but not worrying) about what will happen next.

Comment comics, including "Doonesbury" and "Peanuts," strike with satire at political, social, or human pretensions.

Everett Collection

Romance or soap opera strips like "Mary Worth," "Brenda Starr," and "Dondi" provide a cast of caring characters with which to people our private worlds.

This unique media form has marched out of the "funny papers" to an expanded social role: to educate and irritate, tickle and tease, inform and reform.

The comics' universal appeal to the human psyche is strengthened by their universal distribution. Long before television or radio provided cross-country communication links, comic strip characters were known nationally.

They were fantasy figures inciting the imagination. They were mythic heroes proving in varied situations that right overcomes might. They were storybook characters authorized for adults, reflections of daily life, witty crusaders in a variety of causes, 20th-century successors to the likes of King Arthur and Robin Hood.

An American Art Form

Such literary connections come naturally to the comics, which, as an art form indigenous to America, have verbal as well as visual components. No serious discussion of the "funnies" can proceed far without including words like satire, allegory, fable, personification, comedy (in the classical sense), myth, pun, allusion. All these aspects of literary art exist in the comic strip.

However, it is primarily as a visual art form that the comics have made their contribution. They borrowed and refined the tools of the political cartoonist. Before movies were commonplace or television was conceived, comic strips were the storyboards from which later script writers would learn.

Panel by panel, they set the scene, introduced the characters, unfolded the action. Comic artists taught movie serial makers how to build to a climax and bring the audience back next week.

The strips developed their own "language" or signals: word balloons indicated dialog; sentences strung across a frame suggested narration; and the very way words were printed "produced" sound effects! Any wonder, then, that comic strips have spawned television series and vice versa?

In the enriching mix of today's media, comic strip characters continue to command considerable attention. They entertain us, exercise our fantasy, and reflect wryly on the way life is. They are multiplying. They are leaping off the pages of our papers to live on our movie screens.

In doing so, they continue, like living beings, to adapt to the times. Popeye has proved capable of touching tenderness, Superman and Tarzan have found romance, Zorro has been transformed by satire. The comic strips, in turn, are welcoming into their ranks new figures from other formats—Luke Skywalker, for example, and J. R. Ewing. The comics, quite clearly, remain popular and prosperous. Some are funny. Others, serious. Taken together, however, the comics have much to reveal—about their characters, yes; but more so, about us, their readers!

Writing Strategies

1. According to Clough, why are the comics important? Why should they be taken seriously?
2. What is Clough's purpose in writing? How does she invite readers to see comic strips differently?
3. How does Clough develop her main idea? What support is most effective?
4. Describe Clough's voice as a writer and provide several sentences to support your description.

Exploring Ideas

1. In a group, choose a comic or an animated cartoon and explain how it owes its appeal to "solid psychology" and how it mirrors human life.
2. After completing item 1, consider how your ideas changed because of the group exploration.
3. In a group, create a comic strip that reflects an important aspect of current American culture.
4. Find a comic strip online, study its images and text, and explain what it reveals about its readers.

Condoleezza Rice's Cleveland Browns

Holly A. Putnat

Holly A. Putnat wrote "Condoleezza Rice's Cleveland Browns" for a college writing assignment at Kent State University at Geauga. Students were required to analyze an image that markets the Cleveland Browns, the Cleveland Clinic, or Kent State University. By working through the Analyzing Images chapter to analyze the image, text, subtext, and context of the ad, Putnat discovered a focused and insightful main idea and support.

"Are you ready for some FOOTBALL?" When you hear the recognizable slogan, what do you imagine? You probably envision a group of guys grilling burgers, huddled around a television, and guzzling beer. Since the creation of American football, it has been regarded as a manly, rugged sport. The Cleveland Browns joined a recent NFL Team Shop campaign designed to diversify its fans. Condoleezza Rice wearing Cleveland Browns logo apparel attempts to attract a wider Browns audience including conservatives, intellectuals, and women.

Courtesy NFL

From Holly A. Putnat, "Condaleezza Rice's Cleveland Browns." Reprinted by permisson of the author.

Condoleezza Rice, former Secretary of State, prominently displays a classic Cleveland Browns jersey-style shirt as the focus of the advertisement. Conspicuously shown is the phrase "It's my team," along with the NFL insignia. Less pronounced are the phrases "NFL Women's apparel fit for you" and "Condoleezza Rice, Cleveland Browns fan, former Secretary of State and professor, I never miss a game or a chance to show off my team colors!" (Nudd). The smaller print reinforces the obvious ad message. The background is plain to highlight the heather-grey and orange sweatshirt casually slung over Condoleezza's shoulder, presumably more Browns fan attire. Even her rich, creamy chocolate complexion complements the Browns' team colors and the warm, inviting effect of the ad. Using her as the spokesmodel for Browns gear shows a progressive diversity within the fan base.

Even the details in the image enforce a positive fan association. While Condoleezza abandons her standard conservative blazer in this ad, she keeps her elegant accessories. The simplicity of her stud earrings, chain necklace, and sleek watch suggests a classic conservative look. Though understated, the dainty baubles demonstrate a certain femininity that women rooting for the Browns may wish to emulate. These elements market the Browns toward distinguished women who previously dismissed the sport as undignified. Additionally, as an independent, unmarried woman who rarely dates, she shows women can enjoy the game without a male companion ("Condoleezza Rice").

Highlighting Condoleezza Rice's carefree attitude, the lighting strikes her smiling face in a way that seems to enhance a glow from inside her, suggesting Browns fans feel radiant as well. She normally maintains a serious and reserved persona as a politician. Here, she smiles and relaxes as she steps away from her working role into the playful mode of a Browns fan. She lets other high-ranking and hard-working individuals know that it's acceptable to possess a duality between work and recreation.

Of all the powerful women who could have modeled the clothing in this advertisement, why Condoleezza? She has no major affiliation with the Cleveland area, or Ohio for that matter. However, Condoleezza Rice did not accept the modeling gig haphazardly. Growing up as an only child in Birmingham, Alabama, she learned to love football while watching games on television with her dad. The NFL did not recognize any teams in the segregated South at that time, and the only televised team in her area was the Cleveland Browns. She even admits her dad wanted a boy, but luckily his daughter appreciated the strategy and fun of the contact sport (Florjancic). Women could find reasons to enjoy football if they learn how it is played!

Unquestionably, Condoleezza Rice worked hard for her achievements and positions; and Cleveland remains a laboring, industrial Rust Belt city. Since the Browns returned in 1999, they struggle in creating a winning team, continuously claiming it is a rebuilding year. The economy started declining following 9/11, officially declared as a recession in 2007. Condoleezza served as Secretary of State from 2005 until 2009, the same year the Recession officially ended according to economists (Rampell). Ohio is notoriously known as a major political "swing state" that can make or break a presidential election. Running this advertisement during the final months of the presidential campaign undoubtedly promoted the Republican efforts. Using her for the ad symbolizes a parallel between the persistence and recovery efforts of the Cleveland team.

The Cleveland Browns took a huge risk by placing Condoleezza in fan apparel. Socially we learn how to steer conversations away from hot-button issues such as politics. It is not uncommon to hear a stranger break the ice by asking "How about those Browns?" The advertisement elicits potentially negative emotions from fans with differing political affiliations. Displaying her approachability in this advertisement helps solidify a diverse community coming together for a common interest. The shown jersey number belongs to wide receiver Josh Cribbs, possibly the Browns' best and most likeable player, serving to further her own likeability in the perception of this ad (MJD). The incongruence of Condoleezza's claiming the Browns as her team reaches across party lines by shedding her conservative image in favor of becoming relatable. In this way, the Browns market a sense of unity between upper and lower classes among their fans.

The juxtaposition displayed in the Cleveland Browns apparel advertisement is undeniably thought-provoking. Choosing Condoleezza Rice presents a sports fan diversity trifecta: accomplished African American woman. She empowers the female fan base by demonstrating they can root for the team without resorting to risqué cheerleader attire. The manner in which the NFL Team Shop advertises the women's wear carries the same marketing strategy of the Cleveland Browns by breaking down invisible social barriers.

Works Cited

"Condoleezza Rice Biography." *Biography.com,* A&E Television Networks, www.biography.com/people/condoleezza-rice-9456857. Accessed 9 Apr. 2013.

Florjancic, Matt. "Condoleezza Rice Visits Browns." *Cleveland Browns*, 21 Oct. 2010, www.clevelandbrowns.com/news/article-1/Condoleezza-Rice-visits-Browns/25e2bae9-2ddf-489e-aad9-08958ded13f2.

MJD. "Condoleezza Rice Claims the Browns as Her Team." *Yahoo Sports*, 15 Aug. 2012, sports.yahoo.com/blogs/shutdown-corner/condoleeza-rice-claims-browns-her-team-155047277-nfl.html.

Nudd, Tim. "Cleveland Browns Jersey in NFL Ad: Grey Campaign Pushes League's Women's Apparel." *Adweek*, 15 Aug. 2012, www.adweek.com/adfreak/condoleezza-rice-models-cleveland-browns-jersey-nfl-ad-142766.

Rampell, Catherine. "The Recession Has (Officially) Ended." *The New York Times*, 20 Sept. 2010, nyti.ms/1gsKnq2.

Writing Strategies

1. What is the essay's thesis?
2. What details from the image support the essay's thesis?
3. What other evidence (such as cultural trends, events, or history) support the essay's thesis?

4. What is the relationship between the essay's opening sentence and its thesis?

5. How does the essay use outside sources to analyze the image?

Exploring Ideas

1. Did the Browns take a huge risk in placing Rice in Browns apparel?

2. Why is the juxtaposition displayed in the Cleveland Browns apparel advertisement undeniably thought-provoking?

3. What does Putnat mean when she writes, "The manner in which the NFL Team Shop advertises the women's wear carries the same marketing strategy of the Cleveland Browns by breaking down invisible social barriers"? In what specific way is the manner in which the NFL Team Shop advertises the same marketing strategy as that of the Browns?

The Power of Images: Creating the Myths of Our Time

J. Francis Davis

In the following article, J. Francis Davis, an adult educator and media education specialist, shows how myths—the ideas and stories that motivate daily behavior—are now emerging from the mass of images that surround us. This article appeared in *Media & Values,* a journal published by the Center for Media Literacy.

We see them everywhere: on billboards, in magazines, on bus placards. They come in the mail and in our Sunday newspapers: glossy pictures of women and men in silk robes, pictures of electric twin-foil shavers and Dirt Devil hand-held vacuums. And we see them on TV: living rooms with two sofas, white-lighted football stadiums, even Wild West gunfights and bloodstained murder scenes.

Images. They are so compelling that we cannot not watch them. They are so seductive that they have revolutionized human social communication. Oral and written communication are in decline because a new form of communication, communication by image, has emerged.

The History of Communication

The history of human social interchange has evolved through three distinct phases: oral, text-based, and now image-centered communication. In oral cultures, learning and tradition were passed on by word of mouth, primarily through storytelling. The invention of writing made it possible to preserve information and literary traditions beyond the capacity of memory, but the circulation of handwritten books was still limited to an elite few.

With the invention of the printing press, written texts were in effect transferred from the exclusive property of those wealthy enough to afford hand-copied manuscripts to a broad reading public. Elizabeth Eisenstein, in *The Printing Press as an Agent of Change,* dramatizes this emergence by considering the case of inhabitants of Constantinople born in 1453, the year that the Byzantine capital fell to the Turks.

People born in that pivotal year who lived to be 50 saw more books produced in their lifetimes—some eight million—than had been written in the previous thousand years of Constantinople's existence. The Renaissance, the Protestant Reformation, and the rise of Western science are just a few of the revolutions spurred by the ability to mass-produce books and newspapers and the growing ability of common folk to read them. A similar revolution began about 150 years ago with the invention of photography. For the first time, visual representation of objects in space could be reproduced on a mass scale. Image communication was born.

It only took about 50 years for this new method of representation to become a major player in the communication of social values in American society. The rise of the advertising industry spurred this change, for advertisers quickly learned that the most effective way to sell products was not through stories or plain-text facts, but through the creation of images that appealed to basic human needs and emotions.

Television cemented the era of image communication. In one sense television has turned back the clock to the era of oral storytelling, for television tells stories and we watch and listen just like our ancestors who sat mesmerized around campfires.

But television's most important stories are those not verbalized—the stories and myths hidden in its constant flow of images. These images suggest myths—and thus help construct our world and values—in much the same way that stories did in oral culture.

What Are Images?

Simply put, images are pictures. However, in our culture pictures have become tools used to elicit specific and planned emotional reactions in the people who see them. These pictures—these images—are created to give us pleasure—as when we watch *The Cosby Show*—or to make us anxious when we forget our deodorant or lipstick. Images work best at this task when they are vivid and emotionally saturated. The American flag elicits more powerful emotions than an Idaho potato on a couch, for example. The potato might make us laugh, but the flag is full of multiple and often contradictory meanings and associations—everything from the story of how Francis Scott Key wrote "The Star-Spangled Banner" to flag burning as a protest against the Vietnam War.

The flag works as an image because it suggests a long list of stories and myths that are buried inside us. Image makers hope that in the moment it takes to "consume" an ad or commercial frame, their carefully selected graphics—like the image of the flag—will evoke emotions and memories bubbling deep within us. Pictures that evoke these deep memories can be very powerful—and also very spiritual.

In calling up these deep emotions and memories, however, today's images have taken on new meanings and have created new myths that are shrouded—often deliberately—by these deeper memories. These new myths lie at the heart of modern American culture, and illustrate the double-edged power of today's images.

The New Myths

Traditionally, a myth has been defined as a story or idea that explains the culture or customs of a people. Often myths describe heroes or explain why a people revere the sun, or why elders should be respected. Myths are the motivating stories or ideas of common cultural practices.

This understanding of myth leaves little room for the common misperception that myths are simply false or superstitious ideas. Instead, myths are the ideas and stories that motivate daily behavior.

The key to recognizing the new myths of the image culture is to think of them as ideas that emerge from long exposure to patterns of images—not as myths that can be seen readily in one or two images. In fact, these myths are unconvincing unless one thinks of them as emerging from a huge glut of images which come from many sources, including advertising, entertainment, and news.

Another way to put this is to say that today's images must be read on two levels. First there is the immediate, emotional level on which we recognize the flag or the sexy body and react in a way that taps our inner stories or emotions.

But second, there is a much broader stage on which we can step back and look at one image in context with hundreds of others. This second level is where we can see the new myths of the image clearly—otherwise these basic ideas are obscured by the powerful stories and emotional connections that are used to sell them. Once identified, however, they are easy to recognize, even among all the media messages that daily bombard us.

MYTH#1. The world is a dangerous place and we need guns, police, and military to protect us.

Media critics often focus on violent entertainment dramas such as cop shows and movies like *Terminator 2.* But graphic reports of crime and terror on the news probably have a greater influence in creating our feeling that the world is unsafe. Newsmakers feature shocking, violent stories because they sell newspapers and raise ratings. And our belief that news stories are "real" and thus could happen to us heightens their impact.

MYTH#2. Leave it to the experts (who are usually white men).

Again, "real life" images—or those we assume to be real—are most important here because they set the pattern for our assumptions about who has power. The authority figures we see presenting the national news are white, middle-aged men. And when an "expert" is interviewed about a crisis or program, as in a study of *Nightline* guests by the progressive media criticism organization Fairness and Accuracy in Reporting (F.A.I.R.) the pattern is predictable; nine out of 10 were white males. On *Nightline* and elsewhere, the views of women, persons of color, and representatives of alternate voices of all kinds are customarily absent.

Images found in advertisements and commercials, as well as the national news, reinforce this power structure. Contrast the traditional sex roles of advertisements for Chivas Regal, showing successful professional men in business suits with the stereotypic portraits of women and men in food ads that cast women as kitchen "experts." Many other media images depend on predefined roles based on gender or race.

MYTH#3. The good life consists of buying possessions that cost lots of money.

Living well is synonymous with wealth, according to the pictures and advertisements we see of homes and yards and cars. Big houses, yachts, fancy wine, dinner parties with silver and crystal, romantic evenings overlooking the ocean, vacations to Bermuda, sailing, BMWs, fancy two-oven sunlit kitchens: The list goes on and on. All are part of a luxurious lifestyle that is available for our enjoyment—if only we can afford it.

We can even purchase a little of it vicariously, if we can't have it all, by drinking fancy liquors or by driving a car that's out of our price range and financing it over 10 years. Some people call it status—but the myth behind the status myth is that we are getting the "good life."

MYTH#4. Happiness, satisfaction, and sex appeal, just to name a few, are imminent—and available with the next consumer purchase.

Alas, even when we are wealthy, there's always something missing. We don't have the right woman or man, our car stalls at an intersection, we spend too much time doing housework. But a whole group of images imply that we are on the verge of being happy.

These images are largely advertisements. For example, Hope perfume, Joy dishwashing detergent, or "Oh what a feeling—Toyota!" People in these advertisements are gleefully happy, surrounded by lovers, leaping into the air in rapturous joy. Often, the instrument that brings this instant happiness is technology. We can buy the technology to make us happy.

MYTH#5. Your body is not good enough.

Many—if not most—of the women and men we see in the media are slim, muscular, and good-looking. We, on the other hand, are always too fat, out-of-shape, and smelly—though our friends don't always tell us so forthrightly. We are trained to worry, for example, that people will not even tell us if we smell bad because that kind of criticism is embarrassing.

Most disturbing, however, is the constant stream of perfect people advertising everything from auto parts to Hanes stockings. We are never told that almost all photoadvertisers make their subjects look better, so that legs are slimmer, eyes are bluer, and faces have no freckles.

MYTH#6. Businesses and corporations are concerned for the public welfare.

Short of an environmental disaster like the Alaskan oil spill we see almost no advertisements and few news stories that shed negative light on corporations or businesses. This is not to suggest that all of these organizations are bad. It is worth noting, however, that most corporate images appear in ads purchased or stories placed by the businesses themselves, so it's hardly surprising that the messages we hear are relentlessly positive.

We see full-page color ads for Chevron talking about its concern for the environment. Or news items reporting that gasoline emissions are down because of a new formula developed by ARCO. Ads from tobacco companies like R.J. Reynolds discourage kids under 18 from smoking. And business-oriented magazines and talk shows like *Wall Street Week* cater to the interests of PBS's upscale audience, reporting business and financial trends, while we see none from a labor perspective.

So Why Does This Matter?

To ask the question another way, how are these myths hurting us? The rest of this issue suggests a variety of answers, but in the *Rise of the Image Culture,* Elizabeth Thoman perhaps put it best when she points out that these myths have become a substitute for the search for meaning which other generations sought in more expansive and significant ways. We no longer face uncharted oceans and unexplored continents, but with a universe of space and time to explore and uncounted problems to solve we need not end all our quests at the shopping mall.

Many of us feel a sense of dissatisfaction, a void that the myths of the image culture and the material goods they sell do little to fill. Besides the money, creativity, and resources that the making and selling of these images waste, they also represent a gigantic "red herring," a signpost to an empty journey, a joust with the windmills of our culture, leaving us like confused Don Quixotes looking for a real opponent.

In this sense, the myths of the image culture are "false or superstitious ideas" as well as "motivating stories or ideas behind common cultural practices."

We do have signposts pointing other ways, however, and learning to read images is the first step in the right direction. This issue [of *Media & Values*] and its accompanying Media Literacy Workshop Kit are designed to be a primer on the basic principles of media literacy, using analysis that helps us read images as a beginning point.

Only when we learn to read these myths on a daily basis will we have the power to substitute other motivating ideas and goals of our choosing. Only then can we consciously transcend the Age of Image Communication and stop blindly accepting the myths of the image culture.

Writing Strategies

1. Why is the history of communication important in developing Davis's main idea?
2. How does Davis's definition of "images" go beyond the readers' common understanding of the term?
3. How does Davis define "myths," and how is that definition important to the main idea of the article?
4. What important relationship does Davis draw between myths and images?
5. How would Davis like people to think? What support strategies help readers to think differently?

Exploring Ideas

1. With others, make a list of images that are "so compelling that we cannot not watch them." Why are the images so compelling?
2. Explain how a particular advertising image appeals to basic human needs and emotions.
3. Have any myths Davis talks about changed since the original publication of the article? What myths haven't changed? Are any likely to never change?
4. Why is it difficult for people to question common cultural practices?

Making Arguments
Crimes against Humanity

Ward Churchill

In any culture, people learn to accept some language practices and to avoid others. They learn that some words are hurtful and should be avoided while others are perfectly acceptable. Sometimes, minority voices challenge these linguistic habits and the common assumptions they conceal. In "Crimes against Humanity," Ward Churchill, Keetoowah Band Cherokee, challenges a seemingly harmless trend in popular entertainment, one that mainstream American culture considers "good clean fun." Because he knows that mainstream thinking is not apt to budge easily, he pushes especially hard in his argument. This argument is challenging—even discomforting. Does he go too far? Does he push us to confront something that we would like to dismiss? What will history say about mainstream American culture? What is the value of all this intellectual discomfort? Such questions lurk beneath Churchill's argument.

During the past couple of seasons, there has been an increasing wave of controversy regarding the names of professional sports teams like the Atlanta "Braves," Cleveland "Indians," Washington "Redskins," and Kansas City "Chiefs." The issue extends to the names of college teams like Florida State University "Seminoles," University of Illinois "Fighting Illini," and so on, right on down to high school outfits like the Lamar (Colorado) "Savages." Also involved have been team adoption of "mascots," replete with feathers, buckskins, beads, spears, and "warpaint" (some fans have opted to adorn themselves in the same fashion), and nifty little "pep" gestures like the "Indian Chant" and "Tomahawk Chop."

A substantial number of American Indians have protested that use of native names, images, and symbols as sports team mascots and the like is, by definition, a virulently racist practice. Given the historical relationship between Indians and non-Indians during what has been called the "Conquest of America," American Indian Movement leader (and American Indian Anti-Defamation Council founder) Russell Means has compared the practice to contemporary Germans naming their soccer teams the "Jews," "Hebrews," and "Yids," while adorning their uniforms with grotesque caricatures of Jewish faces taken from the Nazis' anti-Semitic propaganda of the 1930s. Numerous demonstrations have occurred in conjunction with games—most notably during the November 15, 1992 match-up between the Chiefs and Redskins in Kansas City—by angry Indians and their supporters.

In response, a number of players—especially African Americans and other minority athletes—have been trotted out by professional team owners like Ted Turner, as well as university and public school officials, to announce that they mean not to insult but to honor native people. They have been joined by the television networks and most major newspapers, all of which have editorialized that Indian discomfort with the situation is "no big deal," insisting that the whole thing is just "good, clean fun." The country needs more such fun, they've argued, and a "few disgruntled Native Americans" have no right to

"Crimes against Humanity," by Ward Churchill as appeared in *Z Magazine*, March 1993. Reprinted by permission of the author.

undermine the nation's enjoyment of its leisure time by complaining. This is especially the case, some have argued, "in hard times like these." It has even been contended that Indian outrage at being systematically degraded—rather than the degradation itself—creates "a serious barrier to the sort of intergroup communication so necessary in a multicultural society such as ours."

Okay. Let's communicate. We are frankly dubious that those advancing such positions really believe their own rhetoric but, just for the sake of argument, let's accept the premise that they are sincere. If what they say is true, then isn't it time we spread such "inoffensiveness" and "good cheer" around among all the groups so that everybody can participate equally in fostering the national round of laughs they call for? Sure it is—the country can't have too much fun or "intergroup" involvement—so the more, the merrier. Simple consistency demands that anyone who thinks the Tomahawk Chop is a swell pastime must be just as hearty in their endorsement of the following ideas—by the logic used to defend the defamation of American Indians—[to] help us all really start yukking it up.

First, as a counterpart to the Redskins, we need an NFL team called "Niggers" to honor Afro-Americans. Half-time festivities for fans might include a simulated stewing of the opposing coach in a large pot while players and cheerleaders dance around it, garbed in leopard skins and wearing fake bones in their noses. This concept obviously goes along with the kind of gaiety attending the Chop, but also with the actions of the Kansas City Chiefs, whose team members—prominently including black members—lately appeared on a poster, looking "fierce" and "savage" by way of wearing Indian regalia. Just a bit of harmless "morale boosting," says the Chiefs' front office. You bet.

So that the newly-formed Niggers sports club won't end up too out of sync while expressing the "spirit" and "identity" of Afro-Americans in the above fashion, a baseball franchise—let's call this one the "Sambos"—should be formed. How about a basketball team called the "Spearchuckers"? A hockey team called the "Jungle Bunnies"? Maybe the "essence" of these teams could be depicted by images of tiny black faces adorned with huge pairs of lips. The players could appear on TV every week or so gnawing on chicken legs and spitting watermelon seeds at one another. Catchy, eh? Well, there's "nothing to be upset about," according to those who love wearing "war bonnets" to the Super Bowl or having "Chief Illiniwik" dance around the sports arenas of Urbana, Illinois.

And why stop there? There are plenty of other groups to include. Hispanics? They can be "represented" by the Galveston "Greasers" and the San Diego "Spics," at least until the Wisconsin "Wetbacks" and Baltimore "Beaners" get off the ground. Asian Americans? How about the "Slopes," "Dinks," "Gooks," and "Zipperheads"? Owners of the latter teams might get their logo ideas from editorial page cartoons printed in the nation's newspapers during World War II: slanteyes, buck teeth, big glasses, but nothing racially insulting or derogatory, according to the editors and artists involved at the time. Indeed, this Second World War vintage stuff can be seen as just another barrel of laughs, at least by what current editors say are their "local standards" concerning American Indians.

Let's see. Who's been left out? Teams like the Kansas City "Kikes," Hanover "Honkies," San Leandro "Shylocks," Daytona "Dagos," and Pittsburgh "Po-lacks" will fill a certain social void among white folk. Have a religious belief? Let's all go for the gusto and gear up the Milwaukee "Mackerel Snappers" and Hollywood "Holy Rollers." The Fighting Irish of Notre Dame can be rechristened the "Drunken Irish" or "Papist Pigs." Issues of gender and sexual preference can be addressed through creation of teams like the St. Louis "Sluts," Boston "Bimbos," Detroit "Dykes," and the Fresno "Fags." How about the Gainsville "Gimps" and the Richmond "Retards," so the physically and mentally impaired won't be excluded from our fun and games?

Now, don't go getting "overly sensitive" out there. None of this is demeaning or insulting, at least not when it's being done to Indians. Just ask the folks who are doing it, or their apologists like Andy Rooney in the national media. They'll tell you—as in fact they have been telling you—that there's been no harm done, regardless of what their victims think, feel, or say. The situation is exactly the same as when those with precisely the same mentality used to insist that Step 'n Fetchit was okay, or Rochester on the Jack Benny show, or Amos and Andy, Charlie Chan, the Frito Bandito, or any other cutesy symbols making up the lexicon of American racism. Have we communicated yet?

Let's get just a little bit real here. The notion of "fun" embodied in rituals like the Tomahawk Chop must be understood for what it is. There's not a single non-Indian example used above which can be considered socially acceptable in even the most marginal sense. The reasons are obvious enough. So why is it different where American Indians are concerned? One can only conclude that, in contrast to the other groups at issue, Indians are (falsely) perceived as being too few, and therefore too weak, to defend themselves effectively against racist and otherwise offensive behavior.

Fortunately, there are some glimmers of hope. A few teams and their fans have gotten the message and have responded appropriately. Stanford University, which opted to drop the name "Indians" from Stanford, has experienced no resulting drop in attendance. Meanwhile, the local newspaper in Portland, Oregon recently decided its long-standing editorial policy prohibiting use of racial epithets should include derogatory team names. The Redskins, for instance, are now referred to as "the Washington team," and will continue to be described in this way until the franchise adopts an inoffensive moniker (newspaper sales in Portland have suffered no decline as a result). Such examples are to be applauded and encouraged. They stand as figurative beacons in the night, proving beyond all doubt that it is quite possible to indulge in the pleasure of athletics without accepting blatant racism into the bargain.

Nuremberg Precedents

On October 16, 1946, a man named Julius Streicher mounted the steps of a gallows. Moments later he was dead, the sentence of an international tribunal composed of representatives of the United States, France, Great Britain, and the Soviet Union having been imposed. Streicher's body was then cremated, and—so horrendous were his crimes thought to have been—his ashes dumped into an unspecified German river so that "no one should ever know a particular place to go for reasons of mourning his memory."

Julius Streicher had been convicted at Nuremberg, Germany of what were termed "Crimes against Humanity." The lead prosecutor in his case—Justice Robert Jackson of the United States Supreme Court—had not argued that the defendant had killed anyone, nor that he had personally committed any especially violent act. Nor was it contended that Streicher had held any particularly important position in the German government during the period in which the so-called Third Reich had exterminated some 6,000,000 Jews, as well as several million Gypsies, Poles, Slavs, homosexuals, and other *untermenschen* (subhumans).

The sole offense for which the accused was ordered put to death was in having served as publisher/editor of a Bavarian tabloid entitled *Der Sturmer* during the early to mid-1930s, years before the Nazi genocide actually began. In this capacity, he had penned a long series of virulently anti-Semitic editorials and "news."

Stories, usually accompanied by cartoons and other images, graphically depicted Jews in extraordinarily derogatory fashion. This, the prosecution asserted, had done much to "dehumanize" the targets of his distortion in the mind of the German public. In turn, such dehumanization had made it possible—or at least easier—for average Germans to later indulge in the outright liquidation of Jewish "vermin." The tribunal agreed, holding that Streicher was therefore complicit in genocide and deserving of death by hanging.

During his remarks to the Nuremberg tribunal, Justice Jackson observed that, in implementing its sentences, the participating powers were morally and legally binding themselves to adhere forever after to the same standards of conduct that were being applied to Streicher and the other Nazi leaders. In the alternative, he said, the victorious allies would have committed "pure murder" at Nuremberg—no different in substance from that carried out by those they presumed to judge—rather than establishing the "permanent benchmark for justice" which was intended.

Yet in the United States of Robert Jackson, the indigenous American Indian population had already been reduced, in a process which is ongoing to this day, from perhaps 12.5 million in the year 1500 to fewer than 250,000 by the beginning of the 20th century. This was accomplished, according to official sources, "largely through the cruelty of Euro American settlers," and an informal but clear governmental policy which had made it an articulated goal to "exterminate these red vermin" or at least whole segments of them.

Bounties had been placed on the scalps of Indians—any Indians—in places as diverse as Georgia, Kentucky, Texas, the Dakotas, Oregon, and California and had been maintained until resident Indian populations were decimated or disappeared altogether. Entire peoples such as the Cherokee had been reduced to half their size through a policy of forced removal from their homelands east of the Mississippi River to what were then considered less preferable areas in the West.

Others, such as the Navajo, suffered the same fate while under military guard for years on end. The United States Army had also perpetrated a long series of wholesale massacres of Indians at places like Horseshoe Bend, Bear River, Sand Creek, the Washita River, the Marias River, Camp Robinson, and Wounded Knee.

Through it all, hundreds of popular novels—each competing with the next to make Indians appear more grotesque, menacing, and inhuman—were sold in the tens of millions of copies in the U.S. Plainly, the Euro American public was being conditioned to see Indians in such a way so as to allow their eradication to continue. And continue it did until the Manifest Destiny of the U.S.—a direct precursor to what Hitler would subsequently call *Lebensraumpolitik* (the politics of living space)—was consummated.

By 1900, the national project of "clearing" Native Americans from their land and replacing them with "superior" Anglo American settlers was complete; the indigenous population had been reduced by as much as 98 percent while approximately 97.5 percent of their original territory had "passed" to the invaders. The survivors had been concentrated, out of sight and mind of the public, on scattered "reservations," all of them under the self-assigned "plenary" (full) power of the federal government. There was, of course, no Nuremberg-style tribunal passing judgment on those who had fostered such circumstances in North America. No U.S. official or private citizen was ever imprisoned—never mind hanged—for implementing or propagandizing what had been done. Nor had the process of genocide afflicting Indians been completed. Instead, it merely changed form.

Between the 1880s and the 1980s, nearly half of all Native American children were coercively transferred from their own families, communities, and cultures to those of the conquering society. This was done through compulsory attendance at remote boarding schools, often hundreds of miles from their homes, where native children were kept for years on end while being systematically "deculturated" (indoctrinated to think and act in the manner of Euro Americans rather than as Indians). It was also accomplished through a pervasive foster home and adoption program—including blind adoptions, where children would be permanently denied information as to who they were/are and where they'd come from—placing native youths in non-Indian homes.

The express purpose of all this was to facilitate a U.S. governmental policy to bring about the "assimilation" (dissolution) of indigenous societies. In other words, Indian cultures as such were to be caused to disappear. Such policy objectives are directly contrary to the United Nations 1948 Convention on Punishment and Prevention of the Crime of Genocide, an element of international law arising from the Nuremberg proceedings. The forced "transfer of the children" of a targeted "racial, ethnical, or religious group" is explicitly prohibited as a genocidal activity under the Convention's second article.

Article II of the Genocide Convention also expressly prohibits involuntary sterilization as a means of "preventing births among" a targeted population. Yet, in 1975, it was conceded by the U.S. government that its Indian Health Service (IHS), then a subpart of the Bureau of Indian Affairs (BIA), was even then conducting a secret program of involuntary sterilization that had affected approximately 40 percent of all Indian women. The program was allegedly discontinued, and the IHS was transferred to the Public Health Service, but no one was punished. In 1990, it came out that the IHS was inoculating Inuit children in Alaska with Hepatitis-B vaccine. The vaccine had already been banned by the World Health Organization as having demonstrated a correlation with the HIV syndrome, which is itself correlated to AIDS. As this is written [March 1993], a "field test" of Hepatitis-A vaccine, also HIV-correlated, is being conducted on Indian reservations in the northern plains region.

The Genocide Convention makes it a crime against "humanity" to create conditions leading to the destruction of an identifiable human group, as such. Yet the BIA has utilized the government's plenary prerogatives to negotiate mineral leases "on behalf of" Indian peoples paying a fraction of standard royalty rates. The result has been "super profits" for a number of preferred U.S. corporations. Meanwhile, Indians, whose reservations ironically turned out to be in some of the most mineral-rich areas of North America, which makes us the nominally wealthiest segment of the continent's population, live in dire poverty.

By the government's own data in the mid-1980s, Indians received the lowest annual and lifetime per capita incomes of any aggregate population group in the United States. Concomitantly, we suffer the highest rate of infant mortality, death by exposure and malnutrition, disease, and the like. Under such circumstances, alcoholism and other escapist forms of substance abuse are endemic in the Indian community, a situation which leads both to a general physical debilitation of the population and a catastrophic accident rate. Teen suicide among Indians is several times the national average.

The average life expectancy of a reservation-based Native American man is barely 45 years; women can expect to live less than three years longer.

Such itemizations could be continued at great length, including matters like the radioactive contamination of large portions of contemporary Indian country, the forced relocation of traditional Navajos, and so on. But the point should be made: Genocide, as defined in international law, is a continuing fact of day-to-day life (and death) for North America's native peoples. Yet there has been—and is—only the barest flicker of public concern about or even consciousness of, this reality. Absent any serious expression of public outrage, no one is punished and the process continues.

A salient reason for public acquiescence before the ongoing holocaust in Native North America has been a continuation of the popular legacy, often through more effective media. Since 1925, Hollywood has released more than 2,000 films, many of them rerun frequently on television, portraying Indians as strange, perverted, ridiculous, and often dangerous things of the past. Moreover, we are habitually presented to mass audiences one-dimensionally, devoid of recognizable human motivations and emotions: Indians thus serve as props, little more. We have thus been thoroughly and systematically dehumanized.

Nor is this the extent of it. Everywhere we are used as logos, as mascots, as jokes: "Big Chief" writing tablets, "Red Man" chewing tobacco, "Winnebago" campers, "Navajo" and "Cherokee" and "Pontiac" and "Cadillac" pickups and automobiles. There are the Cleveland "Indians," the Kansas City "Chiefs," the Atlanta "Braves," and the Washington "Redskins" professional sports teams—not to mention those in thousands of colleges, high schools, and elementary schools across the country, each with their own degrading caricatures and parodies of Indians and/or things Indian. Pop fiction continues in the same vein, including an unending stream of New Age manuals purporting to expose the inner works of indigenous spirituality

Library of Congress

in everything from pseudo-philosophical to do-it-yourself styles. Blond yuppies from Beverly Hills amble about the country claiming to be reincarnated 17th-century Cheyenne Ushamans ready to perform previously secret ceremonies.

In effect, a concerted, sustained, and in some ways accelerating effort has gone into making Indians unreal. It is thus of obvious importance that the American public begin to think about the implications of such things the next time they witness a gaggle of face-painted and war-bonneted buffoons doing the "Tomahawk Chop" at a baseball or football game. It is necessary that they think about the implications of the grade-school teacher adorning their child in turkey feathers to commemorate Thanksgiving. Think about the significance of John Wayne or Charlton Heston killing a dozen "savages" with a single bullet the next time a western comes on TV. Think about why Land-o-Lakes finds it appropriate to market its butter with the stereotyped image of an "Indian princess" on the wrapper. Think about what it means when non-Indian academics profess—as they often do—to "know more about Indians than Indians do themselves." Think about the significance of charlatans like Carlos Castaneda and Jamake Highwater and Mary Summer Rain and Lynn Andrews churning out "Indian" bestsellers one after the other, while Indians typically can't get into print.

Think about the real situation of American Indians. Think about Julius Streicher. Remember Justice Jackson's admonition. Understand that the treatment of Indians in American popular culture is not "cute" or "amusing," or just "good, clean fun."

Know that it causes real pain and real suffering to real people. Know that it threatens our very survival. And know that this is just as much a crime against humanity as anything the Nazis ever did. It is likely the indigenous people of the United States will never demand that those guilty of such criminal activity be punished for their deeds. But the least we have to expect—indeed to demand—is that such practices finally be brought to a halt.

Writing Strategies

1. Describe Churchill's voice as a writer. Refer specifically to several sentences that support your description. Then explain how Churchill's particular writer's voice might affect his readers. What seems to be Churchill's strategy regarding his writer's voice?
2. Identify a particular support strategy (such as personal anecdote, literary or historical allusion, a scenario, logical reasoning) and explain how it helps readers understand and accept the essay's thesis.
3. Identify places in Churchill's essay where he anticipates his readers' thoughts. How is he able to anticipate them, and how successful is he at responding to them?
4. Consider Churchill's opening and closing strategies. Why are they successful? How else might he have gotten into and out of his essay?

Exploring Ideas

1. Although some people argue that the use of Native American names, images, and symbols is harmless, others argue that it is actually a tribute to Native Americans. Why does Churchill think it isn't a tribute? What values, beliefs, or assumptions create the difference of opinion?
2. Take Churchill's side and respond to the following statement: "I am Irish, and I'm not offended that Notre Dame's mascot is a leprechaun."
3. Why shouldn't a school or team change its name from Redskins to Bears?
4. Search the Internet for websites against the use of Native American names for sports teams. How are the arguments put forth on such sites more effective or less effective than Churchill's argument?

Beware of Drug Sales

Therese Cherry

Extensive use of outside sources can be difficult in a short essay. The writer's voice can easily be drowned out by reliance on statistics and authorities, and the writer's own line of reasoning can be sidetracked by secondary sources. But Therese Cherry manages to use sources in her essay while maintaining a consistent voice and a coherent line of reasoning. Cherry wrote this essay for a first-semester English course at the University of Toledo. The topic emerged from her field of study. At the request of her instructor, she expressed the ideas of the essay in a letter that appears at the end of this essay.

Prescription drug ads are everywhere. You can't turn on the TV or open a magazine these days without finding out if Claritin is "right for you" or being told to ask your doctor about Viagra. Obviously, the makers of prescription drugs want the public to know that there are pills to cure what ails us, and that they don't mind making a little money off our relief. This is how business is run, spending money to make money, marketing the product so that as many consumers as possible are aware of it and will buy it. However, it seems that pharmaceutical companies have taken their role a bit far, marketing their drugs so aggressively that they are actually creating the demand for them. In an industry that sells cars, an ad campaign that sold cars to people who hadn't even realized they wanted to buy one would definitely be a triumph. But to advertise prescription drugs to the extent that people who don't even need them want to buy them is irresponsible and dangerous.

According to the United Nations International Narcotics Control Board (INCB), advanced countries are overdosing on quick-fix pills to ease "non-medical" problems like fat and stress ("Rich States"). INCB also stated that mood-altering drugs are often prescribed for social problems, such as unemployment or relationship problems ("Prescription"). Consumers around the globe are taking medication for this disease called life. The fact that people are spending their hard-earned money on medicine they do not need is bad enough, but the harm these unnecessary drugs can do is a much bigger issue. Yet the drug companies keep on telling us, "It's okay, just ask your doctor." The problem is, the doctors don't have all the answers, either.

Some statistics cited by the FDA reported that toxic reactions to marketed drugs are estimated to cost more than 30 billion dollars per year and to be among the ten leading causes of death in the United States (Pomper 6). So if these drugs are having these kinds of negative effects on people, why are doctors prescribing them? For one, pharmaceutical companies are advertising more aggressively than they have in the past, in part because of loosened restrictions. In 1997 the FDA caved to heavy pressures from the industry, which made it possible for drug companies to advertise on TV without spending huge chunks of time describing side effects (Pomper 6). Now that drug companies can market directly to consumers, suddenly patients are telling their doctors what drugs they want to use. A recent study published by *Health Affairs* reported that three-quarters of the respondents who saw a drug on TV and asked their doctors for it were successful (Pomper 6).

Another reason these drugs are being prescribed is because some doctors are influenced to prescribe drugs that are marketed more aggressively, according to the January 2000 *Journal of the American Medical Association.* And since the most heavily advertised drugs tend to be the newest drugs, the long list of possible side effects cannot be known. In fact, six new drugs approved since mid-1996 have been pulled off the market, and 150 deaths were linked to the drugs before they were pulled (Pomper 8).

Perhaps the most unjust and appalling fact about this considerably new trend of pharmaceutical peddling is the industry's knowledge of the damage this marketing technique is causing to the health of the public: "Even people in the industry will concede off the record that groups acting as advertising agents for manufacturers should be subject to FDA regulations" (Pomper 10). The INCB stated in its 2000 report that there was a "continuing existence of aggressive sales methods and even some cases of financial support to various advocacy groups to foster sales" and appealed to the pharmaceutical industry to demonstrate social responsibility and voluntary cooperation ("Rich States"). We all need to make this same appeal to the drug companies. A business has every right to turn a profit, but should it really be at the risk of good health? Without your health, money means nothing. So, until the pharmaceutical industry can agree with that, buyer beware.

Works Cited

Pomper, Stephen. "Drug Rush." *Washington Monthly*, May 2000, www.washingtonmonthly.com/features/2000/0005.pomper.html.

"Prescription Drugs 'Over-Used.'" *BBC News*, 21 Feb. 2001, news.bbc.co.uk/2/hi/health/1182115.stm.

"Rich States Overdosing on Feel-Good Pills." *Dawn*, 21 Feb. 2001, pp. 5+.

Writing Strategies

1. What strategy, or strategies, does Cherry use to draw the readers' attention to the point of her essay?
2. What type of evidence does Cherry provide to support her claim? How successful is her evidence? What other evidence might she have provided?
3. Identify any concessions Cherry makes in this essay. That is, where does she acknowledge the validity of a differing viewpoint?
4. Choose two sentences and explain how their nouns and verbs make them especially clear and lively.

Exploring Ideas

1. In groups, explore Cherry's question: "A business has every right to turn a profit, but should it really be at the risk of good health?" (¶5). Consider each part of her implied stance:
   - Does a business have every right to turn a profit? What businesses don't?
   - What businesses, besides major pharmaceutical companies, threaten their customers' health?

- How do pharmaceutical companies actually threaten their customers' health?
- What businesses should be prohibited from advertising on television and why?
- What legal businesses should be illegal? What illegal ones should be legal?

After exploring through discussion, explain in what ways the issue has become more complex.

2. Is it okay for Americans to take prescription drugs to ease nonmedical problems like fat and stress (¶2)? What problems should prescription drugs be used for? Consider the following problems: fat, stress, attention, anger, worry, doubt, blood pressure, fear, vision, hearing, sleep, energy, income. Add several more items to the list and explore their relationship to the prescription drug solution.

3. Why do Americans take so many prescription drugs?

This professional letter is based on the invention strategies Therese Cherry used to write the previous essay.

205 West 5th Street
Kenmore, OH 46904
(213) 555-9086
April 22, 2005

Ruth Weisheit, Public Affairs Specialist
Brunswick Resident Post
Food and Drug Administration
3820 Center Road
Brunswick, OH 44212

Dear Ms. Weisheit:

As a concerned citizen and patient, I have become very alarmed at the growing addiction to prescription drugs in the United States. Though the medical advancements of our time are to be applauded, it seems that stricter regulations on the marketing and prescribing of these drugs may be in order to help ensure public health.

According to the United Nations International Narcotics Control Board, advanced countries are overdosing on quick fix pills to ease non-medical problems like fat and stress. The INCB also reported that mood-altering drugs are often prescribed for social problems, such as unemployment or relationship problems. Not only are many of these drugs being prescribed unnecessarily, they are increasingly dangerous. According to Stephen Pomper's May 2000 article "Drug Rush" in the *Washington Monthly,* toxic reactions to marketed drugs are estimated to cost more than 30 billion dollars per year and to be among the ten leading causes of death in the U.S. Six new drugs approved since mid-1996 have been pulled off the market, and 150 deaths were linked to these drugs before they were pulled.

Although part of the problem involves unnecessary prescriptions being written, the aggressive marketing of these drugs appears to play a key role in this addiction issue. "Drug Rush" also reported that in 1997, the FDA loosened restrictions on the marketing of pharmaceutical companies, due in large part to heavy pressure from the pharmaceutical industry. This made it possible for drug companies to advertise on T.V. without spending huge chunks of time describing risks and side effects. And the 2000 *Journal of the AMA* has researched and shown findings that doctors are influenced to prescribe drugs that are marketed more heavily. Recent studies in *Health Magazine* stated that three-quarters of the respondents who saw one of these ads on T.V. and asked their doctors to prescribe it were successful.

Apparently, many factors have contributed to this growing epidemic, but none so fully or irresponsibly as the marketing companies that are pushing these drugs. The INCB stated in its 2000 report that there was a "continuing existence of aggressive sales methods and even some cases of financial support to various advocacy groups to foster sales" and appealed to the pharmaceutical industry to demonstrate social responsibility and voluntary cooperation. Even people in the industry will concede off the record that groups acting as advertising agents for manufacturers should be subject to FDA regulations. Since this voluntary cooperation does not seem likely, I would like to know what actions the FDA, as well as other organizations, are taking to curb the aggressive sales tactics of these pharmaceutical drugs.

The growing use of new and heavily marketed drugs for the ease of social conditions is not going to just go away. I am concerned about this issue and would like to learn how I can get involved with organizations that understand the importance of placing stronger restrictions on advertisers. Thank you for taking the time to address my concerns and I would appreciate any information you can send me.

Sincerely,

Therese Cherry

Writing Strategies

1. How does Cherry support her main claim?

2. Describe Cherry's writer's voice, using several sentences from her letter to support your description.

3. Give some examples of good sentence vitality in Cherry's letter.

Internet Addiction

Greg Beato

"Internet Addiction," published in the August–September 2010 issue of *Reason* magazine, says students who "went on a 24-hour media fast . . . described how 'jittery,' 'anxious,' 'miserable,' and 'crazy' they felt without Twitter, Facebook, iPods, and laptops." The article explores the extent and consequences of Internet addiction that most college students and others experience.

In 1995, in an effort to parody the way the American Psychiatric Association's hugely influential *Diagnostic and Statistical Manual of Mental Disorders* medicalizes every excessive behavior, psychiatrist Ivan Goldberg introduced on his website the concept of "Internet Addiction Disorder." Last summer Ben Alexander, a 19-year-old college student obsessed with the online multiplayer game *World of Warcraft,* was profiled by CBS News, NPR, the Associated Press, and countless other media outlets because of his status as client No. 1 at reSTART, the first residential treatment center in America for individuals trying to get themselves clean from Azeroth, iPhones, and all the other digital narcotics of our age.

At reSTART's five-acre haven in the woods near Seattle, clients pay big bucks to detox from pathological computer use by building chicken coops, cooking hamburgers, and engaging in daily therapy sessions with the program's two founders, psychologist Hilarie Cash and clinical social worker and life coach Cosette Rae. With room for just six addicts at a time and a $14,500 program fee, reSTART isn't designed for the masses, and so far it seems to have attracted more reporters than paying clients. When I spoke with Rae in May, she said "10 to 15" people had participated in the 45-day program to date.

Still, the fact that reSTART exists at all shows how far we've progressed in taking Dr. Goldberg's spoof seriously. You may have been too busy monitoring Kim Kardashian's every passing thought-like thing on Twitter to notice, but Digital Detox Week took place in April, and Video Game Addiction Awareness Week followed on its heels in June. Internet addiction disorder has yet to claim a Tiger Woods of its own, but the sad, silly evidence of our worldwide cyber-bingeing mounts on a daily basis. A councilman in the Bulgarian city of Plovdiv is ousted from his position for playing *Farmville* during budget meetings. There are now at least three apps that use the iPhone's camera to show the world right in front of you so you can keep texting while walking down the street, confident in your ability to avoid sinkholes, telephone poles, and traffic. Earlier this year, 200 students taking a class in media literacy at the University of Maryland went on a 24-hour media fast for a group study, then described how "jittery," "anxious," "miserable," and "crazy" they felt without Twitter, Facebook, iPods, and laptops. "I clearly am addicted," one student concluded, "and the dependency is sickening."

In the early days of the Web, dirty talk was exchanged at the excruciatingly slow rate of 14.4 bits per second, connectivity charges accrued by the hour instead of the month, and the only stuff for sale online was some overpriced hot sauce from a tiny store in Pasadena. It took the patience of a Buddhist monk, thousands of dollars, and really bad TV reception to overuse

---

Greg Beato, "Internet Addiction." From Reason.com Sept. 2010 http://reason.com/archives/2010/07/26/internet-addiction. Reprinted with permission.

the Web in a self-destructive manner. Yet even then, many people felt Ivan Goldberg's notes on Internet addiction worked better as psychiatry than comedy. A year before Goldberg posted his spoof, Kimberly Young, a psychologist at the University of Pittsburgh, had already begun conducting formal research into online addiction. By 1996 the Harvard-affiliated McLean Hospital had established a computer addiction clinic, a professor at the University of Maryland had created an Internet addiction support group, and *The New York Times* was running op-eds about the divorce epidemic that Internet addiction was about to unleash.

Fifteen years down the line, you'd think we'd all be introverted philanderers by now, isolating ourselves in the virtual Snuggie of *World of Warcraft* by day and stepping out at night to destroy our marriages with our latest hook-ups from AshleyMadison.com. But the introduction of flat monthly fees, online gaming, widespread pornography, MySpace, YouTube, Facebook, WiFi, iPhones, netbooks, and free return shipping on designer shoes with substantial markdowns does not seem to have made the Internet any more addictive than it was a decade ago.

In 1998 Young told the Riverside *Press-Enterprise* that "5 to 10 percent of the 52 million Internet users [were] addicted or 'potentially addicted.'" Doctors today use similar numbers when estimating the number of online junkies. In 2009 David Greenfield, a psychiatrist at the University of Connecticut, told the *San Francisco Chronicle* that studies have shown 3 percent to 6 percent of Internet users "have a problem." Is it possible that the ability to keep extremely close tabs on Ashton Kutcher actually has reduced the Internet's addictive power?

Granted, 3 percent is an awful lot of people. Argue all you like that a real addiction should require needles, or spending time in seedy bars with people who drink vodka through their eyeballs, or at least the overwhelming and nihilistic urge to invest thousands of dollars in a broken public school system through the purchase of lottery tickets. Those working on the front lines of technology overuse have plenty of casualties to point to. In our brief conversation, Cosette Rae tells me about a Harvard student who lost a scholarship because he spent too much time playing games, a guy who spent so many sedentary hours at his computer that he developed blood clots in his leg and had to have it amputated, and an 18-year-old who chose homelessness over gamelessness when his parents told him he either had to quit playing computer games or move out.

A few minutes on Google yields even more lurid anecdotes. In 2007 an Ohio teenager shot his parents, killing his mother and wounding his father, after they took away his Xbox. This year a South Korean couple let their real baby starve to death because they were spending so much time caring for their virtual baby in a role-playing game called *Prius Online*.

On a pound-for-pound basis, the average *World of Warcraft* junkie undoubtedly represents a much less destructive social force than the average meth head. But it's not extreme anecdotes that make the specter of Internet addiction so threatening; it's the fact that Internet overuse has the potential to scale in a way that few other addictions do. Even if Steve Jobs designed a really cool-looking syringe and started distributing free heroin on street corners, not everyone would try it. But who among us doesn't already check his email more often than necessary? As the Internet weaves itself more and more tightly into our lives, only the Amish are completely safe.

As early as 1996, Kimberly Young was promoting the idea that the American Psychiatric Association (APA) should add Internet addiction disorder to the *Diagnostic and Statistical Manual of Mental Disorders* (*DSM*). In February, the APA announced that its coming edition of the *DSM,* the first major revision since 1994, will for the first time classify a behavior-related condition—pathological gambling—as an "addiction" rather than an "impulse control disorder." Internet addiction disorder is not being included in this new category of "behavioral addictions," but the APA said it will consider it as a "potential addition . . . as research data accumulate."

If the APA does add excessive Internet use to the *DSM,* the consequences will be wide-ranging. Health insurance companies will start offering at least partial coverage for treatment programs such as reSTART. People who suffer from Internet addiction disorder will receive protection under the Americans with Disabilities Act if their impairment "substantially limits one or more major life activities." Criminal lawyers will use their clients' online habits to fashion diminished capacity defenses. Which means that what started as a parody in 1995 could eventually turn more darkly comic than ever imagined. Picture a world where the health care system goes bankrupt because insurers have to pay for millions of people determined to kick their Twitter addictions once and for all. Where employees who view porn at work are legally protected from termination. Where killing elves in cyberspace could help absolve you for killing people in real life. Is it too late to revert to our older, healthier, more balanced ways of living and just spend all our leisure hours watching *Love Boat* reruns?

Writing Strategies

1. What evidence does Beato provide of Internet addiction?
2. What reasoning does Beato use to compare/contrast Internet and meth addictions?
3. According to Beato, what might be the wide-ranging consequences of the APA adding excessive Internet use to the *Diagnostic and Statistical Manual of Mental Disorders*?
4. Beato uses sentence fragments in his concluding paragraph. How do those fragments influence his voice? How do they impact your reading?

Exploring Ideas

1. Are you addicted to the Internet or some other technology? Provide evidence that you are or are not.
2. Make an argument for why Internet addiction is or is not a serious problem.
3. Which forms of technology are most addicting and why?

Trees Please

Michael Rust

Michael Rust wrote "Trees Please" for his first-semester college writing course at Kent State University at Geauga. Rust's previous assignment was to do intensive invention writing about a choice of topics: Rust chose *trees*. After doing a couple thousand words of invention writing and then examining that writing for possible insights, Rust created this focused and insightful essay.

I live on a road called Forest Drive. The name certainly matches the street; every day I can look in all four directions and observe the quiet peace of trees encompassing my house. When a driver turns onto the street, he or she passes under this canopy of maple trees and enters into a forest filled with calmness. This calmness, accompanied by a soothing security and serenity, stimulates a positive and focused attitude. The difference between being, living, and working in a place with trees and then doing the same in an environment without trees can change relationships and lives.

Locally, trees in neighborhoods subtly impact an individual's everyday emotional disposition because a person subconsciously associates feelings, emotions, and concepts with trees. As a human's natural backdrop, trees help people to feel at ease. More than that, trees profoundly shape one's attitudes and impressions. Trees affect people in this way because trees reflect ideas, some of which are these: the beauty of nature, the security of home (trees mark the horizon, the end of the community, and the start of the outside), life and growth, freedom yet control, and endurance or perseverance.

Trees create a sense of security—an important factor in moods—by enveloping people in a comforting area. In an article by Tina Prow from *The Illinois Steward*, it states that people "identified settings with trees as places where they would feel safe." A place environed by trees seems natural and controllable, one that does not promote instability, fear, or lack of composure. People may also psychologically acknowledge trees as their natural surroundings and consequently feel less afraid and act more relaxed and confident. When not erased by a sense of security, stress can make a person anxious, irritable, depressed, and worn out. The presence of trees makes a person feel calmer and ready to take on challenges one at a time. If one feels secure, then he/she will also be more focused. According to the researcher Frances Kuo, people, who have ADHD (attention deficient/hyperactivity disorder), if exposed to nature, will have significantly reduced symptoms. Similar to this, "hospital patients have been shown to recover from surgery more quickly when their hospital room offered a view of trees" ("Benefits"). The patients had a renewed positive attitude from drinking in the fresh sight of trees outside.

Obtaining an added sense of security from trees will also build relationships in the community. The article "Power of Trees" asserts: "[b]y drawing people out of their homes, . . . trees created an opportunity for neighbors to interact and develop community relationships" (Prow). Trees draw people to them; people like to feel relaxed, secure, and safe so they move closer to the source. When community members reach out of their houses more, relationships can form and when people have friends and neighbors they can rely on, then people do not resort as much to violence. As Prow puts it, "Having neighbors you can call on for support means you have an alternative way of dealing with your frustrations other than striking out against someone." Citing a study, Prow provides evidence: "14% of residents living in barren conditions have threatened to use a knife or gun against their children versus 3% for the residents living in green conditions." Those statistics show the significant effect trees produce. The effects of trees come, in part, from the concepts affiliated with trees.

Trees cause people to feel secure because of their underlying representations coming from experiences. Consider this analogy: When one touches a hot stove for the first time, he or she realizes that touching the stove causes pain. This experience immediately changes the perception in which a person views the stove. It now has an added characteristic because of the experience. Likewise, most everyone has experiences having trees as a protective border and having trees provide shade or shelter from the rain. People also witness the staunch endurance of the trees, firmly rooted and stable. Trees give impressions of a reliable environment to people. For one, trees emulate life. They grow up and out with secure roots tethering them to the ground. They invite people to look up, to imagine new possibilities, and to think differently.

In the *Odyssey*, Odysseus builds his wedding bed using an olive tree, still firmly rooted into the ground, as one of his bedposts. Because trees are both stable and can grow, this symbolizes the immovable foundation of his marriage, yet the ability to have his marriage continue to grow and flourish. Humans correlate positive emotions with trees because of two things: the good things caused by trees and the good things represented and reflected by trees. Sometimes the latter is caused by the former.

People associate positive emotions with trees because trees emulate other positive concepts. Not only do people feel better around trees because they subconsciously recognize the good physical benefits of them, such as shelter, shade, oxygen, and beauty, but also because of the abstract concepts trees' characteristics exhibit. To the Greeks, olive trees mean peace, wisdom, and triumph. When a victor becomes crowned with laurels, the honor is extraordinary. The olive tree reflects the ideals of society; it represents all of Athens at its height. So, why is this tree held in such high regard? Why did the Greeks attribute the olive tree with Athena, the goddess of wisdom? The Greeks recognized that, first these trees played an important part in the economy (olives and olive oil were precious), and secondly these trees populated their lands, and third, these trees represented their homes. When they thought of home, they might have thought of a villa on a hillside dotted with olive trees. When the Greeks placed laurels on the victor's head, they weren't putting some leaves and twigs on the champion, instead they bestowed a crown declaring what the winner deserves: the wealth of the olive industry, the wisdom of Athena, the love and peace of their homes, and their ascension to king-like status. The powerful symbols of the olive tree in Greece influenced that culture and their way of living.

Admittedly, some contrary opinions to the concept of trees influencing people in such a manner arise. Some people say that one can choose happiness no matter the circumstance, and happiness is a matter of the right attitude. This is mostly true. Trees do not automatically make someone happy; they do not come as an elixir of pure joy. Instead trees create a conducive environment in which happiness and positivity come more easily. Trees provide less resistance to a positive attitude and stimulate a calmer and more relaxed emotional state of mind.

Others may argue that people in barren, rocky lands are not bad, violent people. People who live in sparse or barren areas, as a whole, are not much different than any other population. However, for a specific person trees could alter his temperament for the better in a way that might change his intimate relationships and his perspective and attitude. People who do not live in forested places are not bad people; they simply do not live in an ideal human habitat.

Another opposing concept comes from the ideology that one must put something in (usually work or time) to get something out (a benefit). Then, it follows that most people do not put much time, effort, or money directly into trees, so why do trees affect them, if trees do? At first glance, it might appear that a person puts very little into trees, but that is false. An individual invests his/her time into observing trees grow. The time spent around trees is enormous—driving by them, walking around them, looking at them through a window.

Because people correlate trees with particular concepts, feelings, and emotions, trees in the neighborhood affect everyone's attitude. So, what should people do with this knowledge? Taking the initiative to plant trees in communities of low-tree density can help improve communities and lower crime. People do not need to immediately plant a tree into their front yard or petition the mayor for a tree to be planted on every block in the city (though that would be nice), but maybe one could just take a five-minute walk in the trees every day or take more time to appreciate what is in front of his/her eyes. People recognize the profound effect of trees; they need to value their environment.

Works Cited

"Benefits of Trees." *TreesAreGood*, International Society of Arboriculture, 2011, www.treesaregood.com/treecare/resources/benefits_trees.pdf.

Prow, Tina. "The Power of Trees." *The Illinois Steward*, vol. 7, no. 4, Winter 1999. *Landscape and Human Health Laboratory*, U of Illinois at Urbana-Champaign, lhhl.illinois.edu/media/thepoweroftrees.htm.

Writing Strategies

1. According to Rust, how do trees change lives and relationships?

2. Throughout his essay, Rust uses words, phrases, and sentences to connect ideas for readers—to lead readers by the hand, so to speak, through his line of reasoning. In ¶3 ("Trees create a sense of security. . . ."), what words, phrases, or sentences function as connectors (or transitions) to help lead readers from one idea to the next? Select one other paragraph and list words, phrases, or sentences that effectively connect ideas for readers.

3. Where in his essay does Rust qualify an important point?

4. Describe Rust's conclusion. How does it do more than just summarize his main points?

5. What is the essay's thesis?

Exploring Ideas

1. What do you think is Rust's most insightful (most interesting and least obvious) idea about trees?

2. Rust says, "To the Greeks, olive trees mean peace, wisdom, and triumph." What does some other type of tree mean to a particular group of people?

3. How did Rust's argument help you think differently about trees?

Responding to Arguments

A New Map of How We Think: Top Brain/ Bottom Brain

Stephen M. Kosslyn and G. Wayne Miller

In the following article, cognitive neuroscientist Stephen M. Kosslyn and author G. Wayne Miller challenge a commonly accepted way of thinking about thinking, and they offer what they say is a better way of understanding the brain. "A New Map of How We Think: Top Brain/Bottom Brain" was published in *The Wall Street Journal* (2013).

Who hasn't heard that people are either left-brained or right-brained—either analytical and logical or artistic and intuitive, based on the relative "strengths" of the brain's two hemispheres? How often do we hear someone remark about thinking with one side or the other?

A flourishing industry of books, videos and self-help programs has been built on this dichotomy. You can purportedly "diagnose" your brain, "motivate" one or both sides, indulge in "essence therapy" to "restore balance" and much more. Everyone from babies to elders supposedly can benefit. The left brain/right brain difference seems to be a natural law.

Except that it isn't. The popular left/right story has no solid basis in science. The brain doesn't work one part at a time, but rather as a single interactive system, with all parts contributing in concert, as neuroscientists have long known. The left brain/right brain story may be the mother of all urban legends: It sounds good and seems to make sense—but just isn't true.

The origins of this myth lie in experimental surgery on some very sick epileptics a half-century ago, conducted under the direction of Roger Sperry, a renowned neuroscientist at the California Institute of Technology. Seeking relief for their intractable epilepsy, and encouraged by Sperry's experimental work with animals, 16 patients allowed the Caltech team to cut the corpus callosum, the massive bundle of nerve fibers that connects the two sides of the brain. The patients' suffering was alleviated, and Sperry's postoperative studies of these volunteers confirmed that the two halves do, indeed, have distinct cognitive capabilities.

But these capabilities are not the stuff of popular narrative: They reflect very specific differences in function—such as attending to overall shape versus details during perception—not sweeping distinctions such as being "logical" versus "intuitive." This important fine print got buried in the vast mainstream publicity that Sperry's research generated.

There is a better way to understand the functioning of the brain, based on another, ordinarily overlooked anatomical division—between its top and bottom parts. We call this approach "the theory of cognitive modes." Built on decades of unimpeachable research that has largely remained inside scientific circles, it offers a new way of viewing thought and behavior that may help us understand the actions of people as diverse as Oprah Winfrey, the Dalai Lama, Tiger Woods and Elizabeth Taylor.

Our theory has emerged from the field of neuropsychology, the study of higher cognitive functioning—thoughts, wishes, hopes, desires and all other aspects of mental life. Higher cognitive functioning is seated in the cerebral cortex, the rind-like outer layer of the brain that consists of four lobes. Illustrations of this wrinkled outer brain regularly show a top-down view of the two hemispheres, which are connected by thick bundles of neuronal tissue, notably the corpus callosum, an impressive structure consisting of some 250 million nerve fibers.

If you move the view to the side, however, you can see the top and bottom parts of the brain, demarcated largely by the Sylvian fissure, the crease-like structure named for the 17th-century Dutch physician who first described it. The top brain comprises the entire parietal lobe and the top (and larger) portion of the frontal lobe. The bottom comprises the smaller remainder of the frontal lobe and all of the occipital and temporal lobes.

Our theory's roots lie in a landmark report published in 1982 by Mortimer Mishkin and Leslie G. Ungerleider of the National Institute of Mental Health. Their trailblazing research examined rhesus monkeys, which have brains that process visual information in much the same way as the human brain. Hundreds of subsequent studies in several fields have helped to shape our theory, by researchers such as Gregoire Borst of Paris Descartes University, Martha Farah of the University of Pennsylvania, Patricia Goldman-Rakic of Yale University, Melvyn Goodale of the University of Western Ontario and Maria Kozhevnikov of the National University of Singapore.

This research reveals that the top-brain system uses information about the surrounding environment (in combination with other sorts of information, such as emotional reactions and the need for food or drink) to figure out which goals to try to achieve. It actively formulates plans, generates expectations about what should happen when a plan is executed and then, as the plan is being carried out, compares what is happening with what was expected, adjusting the plan accordingly.

The bottom-brain system organizes signals from the senses, simultaneously comparing what is being perceived with all the information previously stored in memory. It then uses the results of such comparisons to classify and interpret the object or event, allowing us to confer meaning on the world.

The top- and bottom-brain systems always work together, just as the hemispheres always do. Our brains are not engaged in some sort of constant cerebral tug of war, with one part seeking dominance over another. (What a poor evolutionary strategy that would have been!) Rather, they can be likened roughly to the parts of a bicycle: the frame, seat, wheels, handlebars, pedals, gears, brakes and chain that work together to provide transportation.

But here's the key to our theory: Although the top and bottom parts of the brain are always used during all of our waking lives, people do not rely on them to an equal degree. To extend the bicycle analogy, not everyone rides a bike the same way. Some may meander, others may race.

Beyond what is required by a particular situation (your reaction, say, to a car speeding toward you), all of us can use each system in optional ways. You can use the top-brain system to develop simple and straightforward plans, as required by a situation—or you have the option to use it to develop detailed and complex plans (which are not imposed by a situation).

For example, instead of just catching dinner in an unfamiliar city by finding the nearest restaurant, you might formulate a more detailed and complex plan that involves coordinating schedules with a friend, finding the best way to reach different parts of town, discovering which restaurants have tables at specific times and so on. And you can use the bottom-brain system to get a quick sense of what you perceive—or you can use it in optional ways to go "deeper," interpreting even the subtleties of a situation. For example, instead of just noticing the type and size of a restaurant, you might check out how many other people are dining there, the types of cars in the parking lot and so on.

Our theory predicts that people fit into one of four groups, based on their typical use of the two brain systems. Depending on the degree to which a person uses the top and bottom systems in optional ways, he or she will operate in one of four cognitive modes: Mover, Perceiver, Stimulator and Adaptor.

Mover mode results when the top- and bottom-brain systems are both highly utilized in optional ways. Oprah Winfrey, who overcame a difficult childhood to create a formidable TV and publishing empire, illustrates such behavior. According to the theory, people who habitually rely on Mover mode are most comfortable in positions that allow them to plan, act and see the consequences of their actions. They are well suited to being leaders.

Others who seem to typify the Mover mode include: the Wright Brothers, who incorporated lessons from their many failures into designing the successive models that finally led to the first airplane; Franklin Delano Roosevelt, who brought the U.S. out of the Great Depression and led the country during World War II; and the late Nascar chairman Bill France Jr., who began by parking cars and working the concession stands at his father's speedway and eventually grew the sport into a multibillion-dollar business.

Perceiver mode results when the bottom-brain system is highly utilized in optional ways but the top is not. Think of the Dalai Lama or Emily Dickinson. People who habitually rely on Perceiver mode try to make sense in depth of what they perceive; they interpret their experiences, place them in context and try to understand the implications.

But they don't make and execute grand plans. By definition, such people—including naturalists, pastors, novelists—typically lead lives away from the limelight. Those who rely on this mode often play a crucial role in a group; they can make sense of events and provide a bigger picture. In business, they are key members of teams, providing perspective and wisdom but not always getting credit.

Then there is Stimulator mode, which results when the top-brain system is highly utilized but the bottom is not. According to our theory, people who interact with the world in Stimulator mode often create and execute complex and detailed plans (using the top-brain system) but fail to register consistently and accurately the consequences of acting on those plans (using the bottom-brain system). They don't update or correct their plans when events unfold in unexpected ways.

Such people may be creative and original, able to think outside the box even when everybody around them has a fixed way of approaching an issue. At the same time, they may not always note when enough is enough. Their actions can be disruptive, and they may not adjust their behavior appropriately.

Examples of people who illustrate Stimulator mode would include Tiger Woods, who clearly makes ample use of his top-brain system but does not always respond well to the consequences of carrying out his plans, and the late social activist Abbie Hoffman, who effectively organized major protests in the 1960s but reacted poorly when some of his plans went off track.

Finally, there is Adaptor mode, which results when neither the top- nor the bottom-brain system is highly utilized in optional ways. People who think in this mode are not caught up in initiating plans, nor are they fully focused on classifying and interpreting what they experience. Instead, they become absorbed by local events and the immediate requirements of the situation. They are responsive and action-oriented and tend to "go with the flow." Others see them as free-spirited and fun to be with.

Because they can easily embrace the plans of others, those who typically operate in Adaptor mode can be valuable team members. In business, they often form the backbone of an organization, carrying out essential operations.

The New York Yankee slugger Alex Rodriguez and the late Elizabeth Taylor show evidence of often functioning in this mode. Coming to the Yankees in 2004 from the Texas Rangers, where he played Gold Glove-winning shortstop, Mr. Rodriguez agreed to switch to third base to accommodate his new teammate Derek Jeter—"the ultimate team move," as Mr. Rodriguez himself called it. But his ongoing troubles over his alleged use of steroids suggest that Mr. Rodriguez has not learned from his experiences. As for Taylor, she was a great actress—and fun to be around, by all accounts—but her eight marriages suggest that she had difficulty understanding her experiences and making detailed plans.

In applying this new way of looking at the brain at work, it is important to avoid the pitfalls of the left-brain/right-brain story. The top-brain and bottom-brain systems should not be seen in isolation. The key is how they interact—both within individuals and in groups where individuals tend to favor one mode over another.

Individuals who operate in different modes can complement each other to form a successful team. Consider, say, a mayor who has an efficient staff. Her policy experts may be people who habitually operate in Perceiver mode; the person answering phone calls from constituents perhaps habitually uses Adaptor mode; the chief of staff might be someone who often operates in Mover or Stimulator mode (but, if the latter, someone will need to exert quality control on the ideas). All the while, the mayor could be operating in Mover mode. She is at the center, drawing on help as needed.

No one mode is "better" than the others. Each is more or less useful in different circumstances, and each contributes something useful to a team. Our theory leads us to expect that you can work with others most productively when you are aware not just of the strengths and weakness of their preferred modes but also of the strengths and weakness of your own preferred mode.

The injunction to "know thyself" is not exactly news, but science is regularly advancing toward this ancient goal—and we hope that our new theory proves to be a step forward.

Writing Strategies

1. What argument are Kosslyn and Miller responding to?
2. Specifically where does the article shift from explaining the original argument (the one to which it is a response) to the response itself? Try to pinpoint the particular sentences where it moves from original argument to response.
3. Kosslyn and Miller allude to popular and historical figures such as Oprah Winfrey and Elizabeth Taylor. How do these allusions function in the article? What ideas do they support or develop?
4. Kosslyn and Miller say, "The key is how they [the top-brain and bottom-brain systems] interact." What does this statement mean? And why is it important to the response?

Exploring Ideas

1. A complex article like Kosslyn and Miller's requires careful reading, rereading, highlighting or note taking, and other strategies. What about the particular content of this article requires readers to slow down? What strategies did you use to slow down and comprehend the ideas? What other strategies might you have used?
2. It is difficult to read an article like this one without wondering what cognitive mode you fit into: Mover, Perceiver, Stimulator, or Adaptor. Which mode best fits you and why? What, if anything, makes it difficult or uncomfortable for you to describe your thinking this way?
3. Kosslyn and Miller say, "Our theory leads us to expect that you can work with others most productively when you are aware not just of the strengths and weakness of their preferred modes but also of the strengths and weakness of your own preferred mode." Identify several key people in your life (close co-workers, family, friends). What do you think is their preferred cognitive mode, and how might knowing this make you a more productive (or better) team?

A More Perfect Union

Barack Obama

Barack Obama delivered the following speech in Philadelphia, Pennsylvania, on March 18, 2008, during the primary campaign for U.S. president. The speech was a response to controversy about comments made by Obama's former pastor, Reverend Jeremiah Wright. When news programs played Wright's most controversial comments and critics connected them to Obama and his campaign, Obama responded by encouraging the nation to explore and grapple with the complexity of race in America.

"We the people, in order to form a more perfect union."

Two hundred and twenty one years ago, in a hall that still stands across the street, a group of men gathered and, with these simple words, launched America's improbable experiment in democracy. Farmers and scholars, statesmen and patriots who had traveled across an ocean to escape tyranny and persecution finally made real their declaration of independence at a Philadelphia convention that lasted through the spring of 1787.

The document they produced was eventually signed but ultimately unfinished. It was stained by this nation's original sin of slavery, a question that divided the colonies and brought the convention to a stalemate until the founders chose to allow the slave trade to continue for at least twenty more years, and to leave any final resolution to future generations.

Of course, the answer to the slavery question was already embedded within our Constitution—a Constitution that had at is very core the ideal of equal citizenship under the law; a Constitution that promised its people liberty, and justice, and a union that could be and should be perfected over time.

And yet words on a parchment would not be enough to deliver slaves from bondage, or provide men and women of every color and creed their full rights and obligations as citizens of the United States. What would be needed were Americans in successive generations who were willing to do their part—through protests and struggle, on the streets and in the courts, through a civil war and civil disobedience and always at great risk—to narrow that gap between the promise of our ideals and the reality of their time.

This was one of the tasks we set forth at the beginning of this campaign—to continue the long march of those who came before us, a march for a more just, more equal, more free, more caring, and more prosperous America. I chose to run for the presidency at this moment in history because I believe deeply that we cannot solve the challenges of our time unless we solve them together—unless we perfect our union by understanding that we may have different stories, but we hold common hopes; that we may not look the same and we may not have come from the same place, but we all want to move in the same direction—towards a better future for our children and our grandchildren.

This belief comes from my unyielding faith in the decency and generosity of the American people. But it also comes from my own American story.

From Barack Obamba, March 18, 2008, Phil. Penn.

I am the son of a black man from Kenya and a white woman from Kansas. I was raised with the help of a white grandfather who survived a Depression to serve in Patton's army during World War II and a white grandmother who worked on a bomber assembly line at Fort Leavenworth while he was overseas. I've gone to some of the best schools in America and lived in one of the world's poorest nations. I am married to a black American who carries within her the blood of slaves and slave owners—an inheritance we pass on to our two precious daughters. I have brothers, sisters, nieces, nephews, uncles, and cousins, of every race and every hue, scattered across three continents, and for as long as I live, I will never forget that in no other country on Earth is my story even possible.

It's a story that hasn't made me the most conventional candidate. But it is a story that has seared into my genetic makeup the idea that this nation is more than the sum of its parts—that out of many, we are truly one.

Throughout the first year of this campaign, against all predictions to the contrary, we saw how hungry the American people were for this message of unity. Despite the temptation to view my candidacy through a purely racial lens, we won commanding victories in states with some of the whitest populations in the country. In South Carolina, where the Confederate flag still flies, we built a powerful coalition of African Americans and white Americans.

This is not to say that race has not been an issue in the campaign. At various stages in the campaign, some commentators have deemed me either "too black" or "not black enough." We saw racial tensions bubble to the surface during the week before the South Carolina primary. The press has scoured every exit poll for the latest evidence of racial polarization, not just in terms of white and black, but black and brown as well.

And yet, it has only been in the last couple of weeks that the discussion of race in this campaign has taken a particularly divisive turn.

On one end of the spectrum, we've heard the implication that my candidacy is somehow an exercise in affirmative action; that it's based solely on the desire of wide-eyed liberals to purchase racial reconciliation on the cheap. On the other end, we've heard my former pastor, Reverend Jeremiah Wright, use incendiary language to express views that have the potential not only to widen the racial divide, but views that denigrate both the greatness and the goodness of our nation; that rightly offend white and black alike.

I have already condemned, in unequivocal terms, the statements of Reverend Wright that have caused such controversy. For some, nagging questions remain. Did I know him to be an occasionally fierce critic of American domestic and foreign policy? Of course. Did I ever hear him make remarks that could be considered controversial while I sat in church? Yes. Did I strongly disagree with many of his political views? Absolutely—just as I'm sure many of you have heard remarks from your pastors, priests, or rabbis with which you strongly disagreed.

But the remarks that have caused this recent firestorm weren't simply controversial. They weren't simply a religious leader's effort to speak out against perceived injustice. Instead, they expressed a profoundly distorted view of this country—a view that sees white racism as endemic, and that elevates what is wrong with America above all that we know is right with America; a view that sees the conflicts in the Middle East as rooted primarily in the actions of stalwart allies like Israel, instead of emanating from the perverse and hateful ideologies of radical Islam.

As such, Reverend Wright's comments were not only wrong but divisive, divisive at a time when we need unity; racially charged at a time when we need to come together to solve a set of monumental problems—two wars, a terrorist threat, a falling economy, a chronic health care crisis, and potentially devastating climate change; problems that are neither black or white or Latino or Asian, but rather problems that confront us all.

Given my background, my politics, and my professed values and ideals, there will no doubt be those for whom my statements of condemnation are not enough. Why associate myself with Reverend Wright in the first place, they may ask? Why not join another church? And I confess that if all that I knew of Reverend Wright were the snippets of those sermons that have run in an endless loop on the television and YouTube, or if Trinity United Church of Christ conformed to the caricatures being peddled by some commentators, there is no doubt that I would react in much the same way.

But the truth is, that isn't all that I know of the man. The man I met more than twenty years ago is a man who helped introduce me to my Christian faith, a man who spoke to me about our obligations to love one another; to care for the sick and lift up the poor. He is a man who served his country as a U.S. Marine; who has studied and lectured at some of the finest universities and seminaries in the country; and who for over thirty years led a church that serves the community by doing God's work here on Earth—by housing the homeless, ministering to the needy, providing day care services and scholarships and prison ministries, and reaching out to those suffering from HIV/AIDS.

In my first book, *Dreams from My Father,* I described the experience of my first service at Trinity:

> People began to shout, to rise from their seats and clap and cry out, a forceful wind carrying the reverend's voice up into the rafters. . . . And in that single note—hope!—I heard something else; at the foot of that cross, inside the thousands of churches across the city, I imagined the stories of ordinary black people merging with the stories of David and Goliath, Moses and Pharaoh, the Christians in the lion's den, Ezekiel's field of dry bones. Those stories—of survival, and freedom, and hope—became our story, my story; the blood that had spilled was our blood, the tears our tears; until this black church, on this bright day, seemed once more a vessel carrying the story of a people into future generations and into a larger world. Our trials and triumphs became at once unique and universal, black and more than black; in chronicling our journey, the stories and songs gave us a means to reclaim memories that we didn't need to feel shame about . . . memories that all people might study and cherish—and with which we could start to rebuild.

That has been my experience at Trinity. Like other predominantly black churches across the country, Trinity embodies the black community in its entirety—the doctor and the welfare mom, the model student and the former gang-banger. Like other black churches, Trinity's services are full of raucous laughter and sometimes bawdy humor. They are full of dancing, clapping, screaming, and shouting that may seem jarring to the untrained ear. The church contains in full the kindness and cruelty, the fierce intelligence and the shocking ignorance, the struggles and successes, the love, and yes, the bitterness and bias that make up the black experience in America.

And this helps explain, perhaps, my relationship with Reverend Wright. As imperfect as he may be, he has been like family to me. He strengthened my faith, officiated my wedding, and baptized my children. Not once in my conversations with him have I heard him talk about any ethnic group in derogatory terms, or treat whites with whom he interacted with anything but courtesy and respect. He contains within him the contradictions—the good and the bad—of the community that he has served diligently for so many years.

I can no more disown him than I can disown the black community. I can no more disown him than I can my white grandmother—a woman who helped raise me, a woman who sacrificed again and again for me, a woman who loves me as much as she loves anything in this world, but a woman who once confessed her fear of black men who passed by her on the street, and who on more than one occasion has uttered racial or ethnic stereotypes that made me cringe.

These people are a part of me. And they are a part of America, this country that I love.

Some will see this as an attempt to justify or excuse comments that are simply inexcusable. I can assure you it is not. I suppose the politically safe thing would be to move on from this episode and just hope that it fades into the woodwork. We can dismiss Reverend Wright as a crank or a demagogue, just as some have dismissed Geraldine Ferraro, in the aftermath of her recent statements, as harboring some deep-seated racial bias.

But race is an issue that I believe this nation cannot afford to ignore right now. We would be making the same mistake that Reverend Wright made in his offending sermons about America—to simplify and stereotype and amplify the negative to the point that it distorts reality.

The fact is that the comments that have been made and the issues that have surfaced over the last few weeks reflect the complexities of race in this country that we've never really worked through—a part of our union that we have yet to perfect. And if we walk away now, if we simply retreat into our respective corners, we will never be able to come together and solve challenges like health care, or education, or the need to find good jobs for every American.

Understanding this reality requires a reminder of how we arrived at this point. As William Faulkner once wrote, "The past isn't dead and buried. In fact, it isn't even past." We do not need to recite here the history of racial injustice in this country. But we do need to remind ourselves that so many of the disparities that exist in the African-American community today can be directly traced to inequalities passed on from an earlier generation that suffered under the brutal legacy of slavery and Jim Crow.

Segregated schools were, and are, inferior schools; we still haven't fixed them, fifty years after *Brown v. Board of Education,* and the inferior education they provided, then and now, helps explain the pervasive achievement gap between today's black and white students.

Legalized discrimination—where blacks were prevented, often through violence, from owning property, or loans were not granted to African-American business owners, or black homeowners could not access FHA mortgages, or blacks were excluded from unions, or the police force, or fire departments—meant that black families could not amass any meaningful wealth to bequeath to future generations. That history helps explain the wealth and income gap between black and white, and the concentrated pockets of poverty that persists in so many of today's urban and rural communities.

A lack of economic opportunity among black men, and the shame and frustration that came from not being able to provide for one's family, contributed to the erosion of black families—a problem that welfare policies for many years may have worsened. And the lack of basic services in so many urban black neighborhoods—parks for kids to play in, police walking the beat, regular garbage pick-up, and building code enforcement—all helped create a cycle of violence, blight, and neglect that continue to haunt us.

This is the reality in which Reverend Wright and other African Americans of his generation grew up. They came of age in the late fifties and early sixties, a time when segregation was still the law of the land and opportunity was systematically constricted. What's remarkable is not how many failed in the face of discrimination, but rather how many men and women overcame the odds; how many were able to make a way out of no way for those like me who would come after them.

But for all those who scratched and clawed their way to get a piece of the American Dream, there were many who didn't make it—those who were ultimately defeated, in one way or another, by discrimination. That legacy of defeat was passed on to future generations—those young men and increasingly young women who we see standing on street corners or languishing in our prisons, without hope or prospects for the future. Even for those blacks who did make it, questions of race, and racism, continue to define their worldview in fundamental ways. For the men and women of Reverend Wright's generation, the memories of humiliation and doubt and fear have not gone away; nor has the anger and the bitterness of those years. That anger may not get expressed in public, in front of white coworkers or white friends. But it does find voice in the barbershop or around the kitchen table. At times, that anger is exploited by politicians, to gin up votes along racial lines, or to make up for a politician's own failings.

And occasionally it finds voice in the church on Sunday morning, in the pulpit and in the pews. The fact that so many people are surprised to hear that anger in some of Reverend Wright's sermons simply reminds us of the old truism that the most segregated hour in American life occurs on Sunday morning. That anger is not always productive; indeed, all too often it distracts attention from solving real problems; it keeps us from squarely facing our own complicity in our condition, and prevents the African American community from forging the alliances it needs to bring about real change. But the anger is real; it is powerful; and to simply wish it away, to condemn it without understanding its roots, only serves to widen the chasm of misunderstanding that exists between the races.

In fact, a similar anger exists within segments of the white community. Most working- and middle-class white Americans don't feel that they have been particularly privileged by their race. Their experience is the immigrant experience—as far as they're concerned, no one's handed them anything, they've built it from scratch. They've worked hard all their lives, many times only to see their jobs shipped overseas or their pension dumped after a lifetime of labor. They are anxious about their futures, and feel their dreams slipping away; in an era of stagnant wages and global competition, opportunity comes to be seen as a zero sum game, in which your dreams come at my expense. So when they are told to bus their children to a school across town; when they hear that an African American is getting an advantage in landing a good job or a spot in a good college because of an injustice that they themselves never committed; when they're told that their fears about crime in urban neighborhoods are somehow prejudiced, resentment builds over time.

Like the anger within the black community, these resentments aren't always expressed in polite company. But they have helped shape the political landscape for at least a generation. Anger over welfare and affirmative action helped forge the Reagan coalition. Politicians routinely exploited fears of crime for their own electoral ends. Talk show hosts and conservative commentators built entire careers unmasking bogus claims of racism while dismissing legitimate discussions of racial injustice and inequality as mere political correctness or reverse racism.

Just as black anger often proved counterproductive, so have these white resentments distracted attention from the real culprits of the middle-class squeeze—a corporate culture rife with inside dealing, questionable accounting practices, and short-term greed; a Washington dominated by lobbyists and special interests; economic policies that favor the few over the many. And yet, to wish away the resentments of white Americans, to label them as misguided or even racist, without recognizing they are grounded in legitimate concerns—this too widens the racial divide, and blocks the path to understanding.

This is where we are right now. It's a racial stalemate we've been stuck in for years. Contrary to the claims of some of my critics, black and white, I have never been so naïve as to believe that we can get beyond our racial divisions in a single election cycle, or with a single candidacy—particularly a candidacy as imperfect as my own.

But I have asserted a firm conviction—a conviction rooted in my faith in God and my faith in the American people—that working together we can move beyond some of our old racial wounds, and that in fact we have no choice if we are to continue on the path of a more perfect union.

For the African American community, that path means embracing the burdens of our past without becoming victims of our past. It means continuing to insist on a full measure of justice in every aspect of American life. But it also means binding our particular grievances—for better health care, and better schools, and better jobs—to the larger aspirations of all Americans—the white woman struggling to break the glass ceiling, the white man whose been laid off, the immigrant trying to feed his family. And it means taking full responsibility for our own lives—by demanding more from our fathers, and spending more time with our children, and reading to them, and teaching them that while they may face challenges and discrimination in their own lives, they must never succumb to despair or cynicism; they must always believe that they can write their own destiny.

Ironically, this quintessentially American—and yes, conservative—notion of self-help found frequent expression in Reverend Wright's sermons. But what my former pastor too often failed to understand is that embarking on a program of self-help also requires a belief that society can change.

The profound mistake of Reverend Wright's sermons is not that he spoke about racism in our society. It's that he spoke as if our society was static; as if no progress has been made; as if this country—a country that has made it possible for one of his own members to run for the highest office in the land and build a coalition of white and black, Latino and Asian, rich and poor, young and old—is still irrevocably bound to a tragic past. But what we know—what we have seen—is that America can change. That is the true genius of this nation. What we have already achieved gives us hope—the audacity to hope—for what we can and must achieve tomorrow.

In the white community, the path to a more perfect union means acknowledging that what ails the African American community does not just exist in the minds of black people; that the legacy of discrimination—and current incidents of discrimination, while less overt than in the past—are real and must be addressed. Not just with words, but with deeds—by investing in our schools and our communities; by enforcing our civil rights laws and ensuring fairness in our criminal justice system; by providing this generation with ladders of opportunity that were unavailable for previous generations. It requires all Americans to realize that your dreams do not have to come at the expense of my dreams; that investing in the health, welfare, and education of black and brown and white children will ultimately help all of America prosper.

In the end, then, what is called for is nothing more, and nothing less, than what all the world's great religions demand—that we do unto others as we would have them do unto us. Let us be our brother's keeper, Scripture tells us. Let us be our sister's keeper. Let us find that common stake we all have in one another, and let our politics reflect that spirit as well.

For we have a choice in this country. We can accept a politics that breeds division, and conflict, and cynicism. We can tackle race only as spectacle—as we did in the OJ trial—or in the wake of tragedy, as we did in the aftermath of Katrina—or as fodder for the nightly news. We can play Reverend Wright's sermons on every channel, every day, and talk about them from now until the election, and make the only question in this campaign whether or not the American people think that I somehow believe or sympathize with his most offensive words. We can pounce on some gaffe by a Hillary supporter as evidence that she's playing the race card, or we can speculate on whether white men will all flock to John McCain in the general election regardless of his policies.

We can do that.

But if we do, I can tell you that in the next election, we'll be talking about some other distraction. And then another one. And then another one. And nothing will change.

That is one option. Or, at this moment, in this election, we can come together and say, "Not this time." This time we want to talk about the crumbling schools that are stealing the future of black children and white children and Asian children and Hispanic children and Native American children. This time we want to reject the cynicism that tells us that these kids can't learn; that those kids who don't look like us are somebody else's problem. The children of America are not those kids, they are our kids, and we will not let them fall behind in a 21st century economy. Not this time.

This time we want to talk about how the lines in the emergency room are filled with whites and blacks and Hispanics who do not have health care; who don't have the power on their own to overcome the special interests in Washington, but who can take them on if we do it together.

This time we want to talk about the shuttered mills that once provided a decent life for men and women of every race, and the homes for sale that once belonged to Americans from every religion, every region, every walk of life. This time we want to talk about the fact that the real problem is not that someone who doesn't look like you might take your job; it's that the corporation you work for will ship it overseas for nothing more than a profit.

This time we want to talk about the men and women of every color and creed who serve together, and fight together, and bleed together under the same proud flag. We want to talk about how to bring them home from a war that never should've been authorized and never should've been waged, and we want to talk about how we'll show our patriotism by caring for them, and their families, and giving them the benefits they have earned.

I would not be running for President if I didn't believe with all my heart that this is what the vast majority of Americans want for this country. This union may never be perfect, but generation after generation has shown that it can always be perfected. And today, whenever I find myself feeling doubtful or cynical about this possibility, what gives me the most hope is the next generation—the young people whose attitudes and beliefs and openness to change have already made history in this election.

There is one story in particularly that I'd like to leave you with today—a story I told when I had the great honor of speaking on Dr. King's birthday at his home church, Ebenezer Baptist, in Atlanta.

There is a young, twenty-three-year-old white woman named Ashley Baia who organized for our campaign in Florence, South Carolina. She had been working to organize a mostly African American community since the beginning of this campaign, and one day she was at a roundtable discussion where everyone went around telling their story and why they were there.

And Ashley said that when she was nine years old, her mother got cancer. And because she had to miss days of work, she was let go and lost her health care. They had to file for bankruptcy, and that's when Ashley decided that she had to do something to help her mom.

She knew that food was one of their most expensive costs, and so Ashley convinced her mother that what she really liked and really wanted to eat more than anything else was mustard and relish sandwiches. Because that was the cheapest way to eat.

She did this for a year until her mom got better, and she told everyone at the roundtable that the reason she joined our campaign was so that she could help the millions of other children in the country who want and need to help their parents too.

Now, Ashley might have made a different choice. Perhaps somebody told her along the way that the source of her mother's problems were blacks who were on welfare and too lazy to work, or Hispanics who were coming into the country illegally. But she didn't. She sought out allies in her fight against injustice.

Anyway, Ashley finishes her story and then goes around the room and asks everyone else why they're supporting the campaign. They all have different stories and reasons. Many bring up a specific issue. And finally they come to this elderly black man who's been sitting there quietly the entire time. And Ashley asks him why he's there. And he does not bring up a specific issue. He does not say health care or the economy. He does not say education or the war. He does not say that he was there because of Barack Obama. He simply says to everyone in the room, "I am here because of Ashley."

"I'm here because of Ashley." By itself, that single moment of recognition between that young white girl and that old black man is not enough. It is not enough to give health care to the sick, or jobs to the jobless, or education to our children.

But it is where we start. It is where our union grows stronger. And as so many generations have come to realize over the course of the two hundred and twenty one years since a band of patriots signed that document in Philadelphia, that is where the perfection begins.

Writing Strategies

1. What is Obama's main claim? What support strategies does he use to help readers understand and accept it?
2. How does Obama use the concept of "a more perfect union" as a unifying device throughout his speech?
3. Explain how two passages from Obama's speech illustrate a Rogerian approach to argument.
4. How does Obama's concluding anecdote about Ashley help readers understand and accept his argument?
5. Describe the "racial stalemate" to which Obama refers. How does Obama suggest we approach the stalemate?

Exploring Ideas

1. Why does Obama think the U.S. Constitution was "signed but ultimately unfinished"? Summarize his argument about this point, and then imagine how others might respond. Write down one argument that supports Obama's position and one that refutes it.
2. With a group of peers, discuss your responses to item 1. Which group members think the constitution was, and is, ultimately unfinished, and why? Which group members disagree, and why?
3. According to Obama, Reverend Wright "contains within him the contradictions—the good and the bad—of the community that he served diligently for so many years." (¶21) What contradictions—good and bad—of your community do you contain?
4. Obama writes, "The fact is that the comments that have been made and the issues that have surfaced over the last few weeks reflect the complexities of race in this country that we've never really worked through—a part of our union we have yet to perfect" (¶26). Why haven't we worked through these issues?

Military Fraud: The Myth of Automatic Virtue

Steve Gillman

In the following article, which was published at RadicalNewThoughts.com, Steve Gillman responds to an argument that we should praise soldiers. Gillman introduces his response in the opening paragraph, explaining that the article is "about the cultural mythology that has been created in the United States, which makes all soldiers into 'heroes.'"

This is about a military fraud. It isn't the usual story of soldiers tempted into enlisting by unkept promises, nor of cover-ups of failed or immoral operations during war. It is about the cultural mythology that has been created in the United States, which makes all soldiers into "heroes."

True Story:

"I want to go to Iraq," he told me. He was thirty-nine years old, and he added "I always liked guns and the idea of going around fighting and blowing things up with a group of other guys." He also likes the idea of the $30,000 bonus the army was promising him. I suggested that he might get killed, but he mentioned that it's better than the job opportunities he had around town.

I certainly won't claim that this is a typical recruit. People join the army for all sorts of reasons. Some join for adventure, some to travel, some for the money and educational opportunities, and some for reasons they'll never know. Some even join because of a desire to serve their country.

Let's be honest about that last one, though. Notice that very few young men and women who are making a great living doing something they enjoy choose to quit that in order to "serve the country." This and close attention to what those who enlist say suggests that this supposedly "noble" intention is rare at best, at least as a primary motivation. Maybe as much as 10% of the total join primarily to "serve their country."

Looking at it this far, already the idea that there is some special virtue in those that join the military is suspect. But what about that small subsection of soldiers who do want only to serve? Do they deserve automatic praise, or some special respect or admiration? Many people think so.

What if they are engaged in wars I disagree with? More to the point, what if what they're doing is actually against our interests? Whether they actually serve some real value should have some relevance, right? Those who killed Native American children in the 1800s or the few misguided soldiers who slaughtered innocent Vietnamese in that war are not honored just because they wore an American uniform—even if they were just following orders.

So what makes soldiers worthy of some special respect and appreciation? Perhaps nothing. Perhaps they are normal human beings like the rest of us, who are sometimes

---

Radical New Thoughts.com, "Military Fraud: The Myth of Automatic Virtue," from http://www.radicalnewthoughts.com/military-fraud.html. Reprinted with permission.

courageous, and sometimes cowardly, sometimes well intentioned and often confused. To the extent that we assess their character, shouldn't we do this on an individual basis like we do with everyone else? Isn't this a more realistic and objective view if we are honest enough to look plainly at the facts?

Sometimes, in some places, soldiers may actually protect those who live in the U.S.—although it's getting harder to find actual examples of this as time goes by. And there are incredible acts of courage in individual situations—just as there are among all people in all places. But in the end, these are men and women hired to do a dangerous job, and they do it largely without regard to whether it needs to be done or in any way protects human rights, because once they sign up they have no choice.

They are used and abused by elements of society which convince them that it's their "duty" to die for various purposes. They are deceived about the nature of the "work" in order to get them to risk their lives. The entire "let's honor our soldiers" custom is just another way to keep the game going, to convince young people to throw away their lives for the political and economic purposes of others.

What is it about killing people who have not attacked us (the majority of war causalities) that makes it more worthy of praise than a millionaire creating a thousand life-sustaining jobs, or a teacher opening and enriching the minds of thousands of children? Nothing.

This is not a rant against soldiers, nor against defense. Those in the armed services are our brothers, mothers, fathers and friends. They do a dangerous job that sometimes protects us, and they do the best they can according to the understanding they have. But they chose that job, and for their own reasons. If they think that part of their payment is my praise, I am announcing here that I offer none. When we are attacked we fight to defend ourselves and our families—no outside praise or other reward is needed.

If we perpetuate this pretense that it is heroic to fight regardless of the cause, and that stated intent deserves praise regardless of the outcome, we encourage the support of bad causes done in the name of good, and of killing in the name of peace. And if we perpetuate the myth that a scared kid who wanted to get college paid for is a hero because a stray bullet kills him in a foreign land while he happens to wear the right uniform, we will have more innocent and scared young men dying for no good reason.

To potential soldiers: Go to war if you feel you must, and I will not condemn you, but you'll also get no automatic praise from me. Your choice will have its consequences for yourself and many others. Make that choice without looking back to see the cheering faces of those who tell you your duty is to do what they are not doing for purposes you may not know nor share. Think for yourself and let your own satisfaction be your reward if there is one. There is no automatic virtue in joining a cause just because others happen to call it noble. This myth is a cultural and military fraud perpetrated on young men and women to encourage them to risk their lives and souls for purposes which may or may not be of any value.

Writing Strategies

1. What is the article's thesis?
2. How does the article appeal to logic?
3. What important point or points does the writer concede, and how might the concession(s) help readers accept the thesis?
4. What point or points work to complicate the reader's thinking, and how?
5. Describe the writer's voice, and explain how it invites or alienates readers.

Exploring Ideas

1. Does this article offend you or make you uncomfortable? If so why? Does the writer do anything to try not to offend readers or make readers uncomfortable? Explain.
2. With a group of peers, discuss the statement: "The entire 'let's honor our soldiers' custom is just another way to keep the game going, to convince young people to throw away their lives for the political and economic purposes of others." How is or isn't "let's honor our soldiers" a custom? To what extent does it "keep the game going"?
3. With a group of peers, explore the following statement: "And if we perpetuate the myth that a scared kid who wanted to get college paid for is a hero because a stray bullet kills him in a foreign land while he happens to wear the right uniform, we will have more innocent and scared young men dying for no good reason." First, explain the logic of the statement. Then discuss why someone might dispute the logic.

Evaluating

The Day the Music Died: A Tribute to Rock Band

Chay Close

The following article, first published April 4, 2014, at *VentureBeat*, a website about technology, eulogizes—and argues the value of—a video game: Harmonix's Rock Band series. Author Chay Close explains that he can better understand Rock Band as a video game now that it is gone. His article explains that new understanding and helps readers see the game's value.

Like it or not, the age of the plastic instrument was never going to last. After burning perhaps a bit too brightly over the course of the last decade, Guitar Hero and its ilk fizzled out in 2011, passing their collective torch to a lone survivor: Harmonix's Rock Band series. For a long while, we watched in awe as Harmonix continued to float a sinking ship, playing catch-up with the spectre of an industry that just didn't exist anymore.

So it's no surprise that this week, with the addition of Don McLean's "American Pie" to the library, Harmonix is taking its leave from the franchise. After more than five years of weekly downloadable content support, Rock Band is no more, along with the genre it helped make popular.

Melodramatic? Maybe, but I suppose my desire to eulogize plastic instruments speaks to the effect they had on me. Ever since that first horrific failure playing "Free Bird" on Hard, I've been a loyal devotee of anything vaguely molded in the shape of an instrument—whether it be a drum kit, a microphone (come to think of it, those things are real), or even a set of turntables.

Hundreds if not thousands of hours and banknotes later, I suppose a healthy question to ask myself is, why?

Aptly enough, when the first Guitar Hero released, I was actively concerned with that very question—albeit from a different perspective. "This isn't a game," I would have said at the time. "Why would anyone want to play a fake guitar?" I had once touched a real guitar, and by that virtue, anything less was a gimmick. It was only with the release of Guitar Hero II that I began to warm to the obvious appeal of the rhythm genre and its cabin-fever approach to the discovery of music—not to mention that it let me outfit my avatar in dungarees and rock the virtual globe to my heart's content.

If anything, my sudden change in attitude only stood testament to the genre's prevailing problems with identity. Ridiculous as their premise may be, plastic-instrument games are so conceptually obtuse that it's easy to get caught on the surface—so involved with watching YouTube videos of "Jordan" on Expert difficulty that the real substance gets lost.

Which perhaps explains why, when Rock Band entered the plastic-arms race back in 2007, it was held in a vacuous space known only as the rhythm genre, which was seemingly absent from design talks and the medium at large. The disparity between note highways and traditional 3D spaces had become so vast that the genre no longer aligned with common interests. It became a self-contained entity, sitting on the sidelines and quietly amassing a small fortune. Consciously or otherwise, the "this isn't a game" thinking had inherited some truth.

It's only now, after the genre's removal from the limelight, that I feel like I can understand Rock Band as a video game and not as a gross amalgamation of its expectations. It seems so obvious now, but at heart, it was a class-based multiplayer game—one that set the stage for concepts as familiar as microtransactions and community integration long before they hit the zeitgeist. In retrospect, Rock Band should have been vital to discourse on multiplayer game design (if not game design as a whole), yet very rarely did it transcend conversations about gimmickry and longevity. Although it predicted and mastered market trends en masse, Rock Band's design went unsung even as it rode through a perfect storm—setting, following, and bucking trends as it became the sole survivor in a notoriously saturated marketplace.

I can imagine some eyes rolling as I write this, but from within the constraints of the rhythm genre, I feel like we failed to notice the real nuts-and-bolts appeal of Harmonix's work. It's easy to assume that the physical qualities (your specific interactions with the controller or the friends you play with) are what makes Rock Band so enjoyable, but this ignores the fact that the game's mechanics are never far from sight.

Rock Band's emphasis on the interaction between band members distilled the plastic instrument down to its fundamental principles: social interaction and showboating. Like any good multiplayer game, Rock Band specialised in social engineering. It led players into a mindset conducive to the game's interests and used this to orchestrate a shared experience, one with a competitive undercurrent.

In Rock Band, songs as docile as The Foo Fighters' "Doll" become running gags against the drummer while the painfully difficult swings of Malmsteen's "Caprici di Diablo" become a means of putting the guitarist in his place. Series favorites like "Green Grass and High Tides," on the other hand, are all-hands-on-deck co-operative ventures—sprawling tests of endurance defined by the players' collective ability to avoid severe cramps. It's a dynamic that creates an inclusive social space and only furthers the desire to play on and engage with those around you, if just because you have something to prove.

Then, of course, there's the meta-game—the desire to get better not just to climb the leaderboards but because the vocalist wants a new toga. The bassist wants to try to buy some self-respect. The drummer wants enough money to see the band's logo, a flying set of male genitalia, printed on the front of a solid gold drum kit. Once you're hooked, the focus is no longer on the controller. The systems are deep, layered, and above all, balanced enough that you're never just playing another rhythm game; you're on a campaign as valuable as that of any traditional blockbuster.

Ultimately, from a design and marketing standpoint, Rock Band rarely compromised when it came to letting the player have fun. It became an entertainment platform unto itself, and as such, created a DLC and purchasing model that worked to the tune of one billion dollars years before the likes of Dead Space 3 and Sim City struggled to get their own ideas off the ground.

Elsewhere in the industry, iteration has grown to carry a bitter taste, yet here, it served as the vehicle that kept a sprawling franchise relevant for over five years. Whether Harmonix was conscious in its decisions or not, in Rock Band, we were given a taste of where the game industry was going—executed with a success and confidence that few developers manage even to this day.

If I go back to my question of why, the answer is obvious. It may be tempting to define Rock Band by its surface interaction—by the promise of embodying a world-famous rock star or discovering new music. But peel back the facade, and Rock Band held on for so long because it valued good design above the cheap promise of the plastic instrument. Whether people realized it or not, that translated into a loyal fan base for years to come.

"Be a rock star" was always going to be a hollow venture. Harmonix saw depth in an otherwise ridiculous marketplace and led the charge not just for the genre but for the medium as a whole. From a consumer perspective, Rock Band will be remembered as a great piece of software, independent of the hardware that shaped it. And if the continued growth and prosperity of Harmonix is anything to go by, it didn't do too badly for the developer, either. In the end, it's only fitting that the company should be able to pull the plug on its own terms.

We shouldn't lament the demise of the plastic instrument but instead the fall of a franchise that, despite racking up more than 5,000 playable tracks, made a firm statement for quality over quantity.

Here's to you, Rock Band.

Writing Strategies

1. What is Close's main evaluative claim (thesis) about Harmonix's Rock Band series?

2. Close generally avoids the use of "I," but he uses it sparingly in places. Why? When he shifts to "I," is it to provide personal testimony, to distinguish his claim from someone else's, or for some other reason? (If for some other reason, explain.)

3. What criteria does Close use to determine the value—the worth—of Harmonix's Rock Band series?

4. Who is the intended audience for the original publication of this article (at the *VentureBeat* website)? What specific language from the article can you provide to support your response? Can other readers, besides the intended (or primary) audience, still understand and find valuable meaning in the article? Why or why not?

5. According to Close, why did Rock Band hold on for so long?

Exploring Ideas

1. You can think seriously about any topic: reality shows, cartoons, cotton candy, and so on. In this article, Close thinks seriously about a video game. What passages most reflect his seriousness of thought, and why?

2. According to Close, what are the fundamental principles of Rock Band? Explain why he might describe these principles as *fundamental*.

3. What are the fundamental principles of some other game you have played or of some other activity you have participated in? Try getting beneath the surface and identifying the less obvious fundamental principle(s).

Revealing the Ugly Cartoonish Truth: *The Simpsons*

Simon Benlow

Evaluating entertainment can be dangerous because writers might be tempted to give a list of likes and dislikes. Based on this essay, we can assume that Simon Benlow "likes" *The Simpsons,* but the essay does more than share Benlow's approval of the show. It argues about the purpose of mainstream entertainment—what it should or could do for American audiences. While celebrating *The Simpsons* and analyzing its specific qualities, Benlow reveals the shortcomings of mainstream American entertainment and even pokes fun at the institutions of everyday life.

It's not often that a television sitcom does more than tickle our most simplistic pleasures. The vast majority of sitcoms, past and present, fill twenty-two minutes (or is it nineteen?) with cliché moralism, empty characters, and adolescent dialog. Every fall we can look forward to a new parade of bad jokes and simpleton plots—created primarily to allow American viewers to gawk at the latest celebrity hairstyles and tight shirts.

However, amidst an exhausting list of here-and-then-gone "real-life" sitcoms, *The Simpsons* has managed to create a new class of television. It has stretched what can (and should) be expected in prime-time entertainment. It goes where most sitcoms, most American entertainment, will not. It satirizes everything (and nearly anything) mainstream America cherishes. From SUVs to friendly fast-food chains, the familiar elements of everyday life are revealed as ridiculous creations of a culture blind to its own vices. Certainly, it takes shots at big targets: nuclear power, organized labor, corporate fraud, slick politicians, organized religion, hyper-consumerism, hyper-consumption, and even television programming (often slamming its own network, FOX). But these are more than easy targets; these are the entities that seem to run amuck consistently, the institutions that maintain their status despite repeated failings, the bullies of our culture that always seem in need of a punch to their maniacal eye sockets.

In "Homer's Odyssey," an episode from the first season, the show does its usual deconstruction of everyday life. The episode reveals some ugly truth: Beneath the daily façade, there lurks an entire set of systems barely working, hardly accomplishing anything beyond their own survival. In the first scene, in front of Springfield Elementary, the children wait for the tardy, pot-smoking bus driver, Otto (who loves to "get blotto"). Once they get settled, they drive in circles through town. They pass by the toxic waste dump where happy workers casually pour mysterious fluid into the river; they pass the prison where they are greeted by hosts of prisoners (who were set free during the children's last field trip). They pass the Springfield tire yard (which becomes the Springfield tire fire in later episodes), and finally arrive at the nuclear power plant. At the gate, several signs announce "employees only," but the guard is sucking on a beverage and watching Krusty the Clown on television, so the children pass on through unnoticed.

In the power plant, we see the gross fumblings and even grosser cover-ups of an unchecked system. While Joe Fission, a cartoon icon, feeds the children pro-nuclear propaganda, Homer flummoxes his job and wreaks havoc in the plant. Homer is the poster boy of incompetence—yet he's granted a typical place in the ill-defined bureaucracy of power: Is he the "supervising technician" or the "technical supervisor"? No one knows. Through the episode, Homer is fired and then, for no good reason, hired back. The status quo prevails; three-eyed fish swim happily in the lake and the town continues to live on the brink of nuclear disaster.

In the animated town of Springfield, nothing is worthy of the praise it wants. Schools are not great institutions of learning; they are poorly funded bureaucracies run by flawed and desperate individuals. Government is not "of the people"; it is a mob of self-perpetuating boozers and womanizers. Business is not ethical or productive; it is a race to monopolize and swindle everyone in sight. These are the hard truths that *The Simpsons* offers us. Of course, we get these truths thrown at us in sanctimonious movies and bad morning talk shows, but *The Simpsons* manages to reveal these ideas without romanticizing its own characters or actors.

The Simpsons throws at us what we all might be thinking had we not been programmed to dismiss it. We all might briefly consider the lies the nuclear power industry feeds us, the laziness and self-righteousness of city governments, or the emptiness and humiliation of most jobs, but we've been trained out of being appalled. We've become distracted by our own lives, and the constant barrage of material goodness, so we allow our own institutions to bully us, to humiliate us, to dismiss our general welfare entirely. But *The Simpsons* reminds us of the slip-shod work and flagrant thievery going on just outside our own television sets.

Some may argue that *The Simpsons* is just a show; it can't possibly have that much meaning. However, one thing we've learned in America is that our entertainment has more significance than history, literature, philosophy, and politics. Mainstream society gets its values, its slogans, its hairstyles, even its dialects from entertainment. We are, as the world knows, an over-entertained nation. The average American citizen reads very little (maybe a few books per year), but fills thousands of hours being massaged by the television. As the last thirty years proves undoubtedly, Americans can change their minds at the drop of a hat (about almost anything) if the television set prompts us to do so. When television maintains such influence, it is significant and meaningful when the television itself plays with, pokes at, and parodies that influence.

In a swirling array of giddy and capricious entertainment, *The Simpsons* is far more real than any "real-life" sitcom hopes to be (or wants to be). In its relentless pursuit to overturn our romantic notions of ourselves and our lovely creations, it is probably more real than the audience it attracts (and certainly more real than those whom it doesn't). In fact, if we take the show as seriously as it deserves, we might even see the broad strokes of its irony: that *we* are the cartoons, drawn and colored by the ridiculous institutions that constitute our society. However, as soon as we go that far, Homer belches, Bart moons a head of state, and Grandpa soils himself; *The Simpsons* won't allow anything, including itself, to be taken seriously.

Writing Strategies

1. According to Benlow, what is the purpose of The Simpsons?

2. In your own words, what is Benlow's main idea?

3. What details from Benlow's essay are most helpful in developing his main idea?

4. Identify one counterargument Benlow makes and explain how it is important to his essay.

Exploring Ideas

1. Why does Benlow think *The Simpsons* is important?

2. Watch several episodes of *The Simpsons,* finding support for Benlow's argument.

3. After exploring the following statement with others, explain what Benlow means when he says we are "drawn and colored by the ridiculous institutions that constitute our society":

> In fact, if we take the show as seriously as it deserves, we might even see the broad strokes of its irony: that we are the cartoons, drawn and colored by the ridiculous institutions that constitute our society. (¶8)

Hip-Hop: A Roadblock or Pathway to Black Empowerment?

Geoffrey Bennett

Throughout American history, popular art forms and entertainment have pushed against mainstream tastes and mores: slam poetry, jazz, vaudeville, swing, rock and roll, punk, heavy metal, rap, hip-hop. Each of these shocked the sensibilities of the mainstream culture. And when they gained popularity, writers, politicians, church groups, sociologists, and thinkers of all stripes asked questions about the state of the civilization. In the past twenty years, hip-hop music has been the source (and target) of such commentary. In this article, Geoffrey Bennett (former editor-in-chief of the *Maroon Tiger* college newspaper at Morehouse College) explores the relationship between hip-hop and the black community. The article originally appeared in the *Black Collegian Online* (2001).

In the early 1980s, a highly percussive, cadenced, and repetitious musical form seeped from the inner city streets of the South Bronx to a virtually exclusive African-American audience. Harbingered by originators such as Run DMC, the Sugar Hill Gang, Public Enemy, Afrika Bambaataa, and others, the medium was a simple reflection of the daily lives of its creators with topics ranging from the trivial, such as the style of one's new Adidas sneakers, to the significant, like the infuriation spurred by police harassment.

Rap music, as it came to be known, lacked major commercial support in its early stages, and, as a result, it was authentic and unaffected; it was truly "CNN for the streets," as Chuck D once commented. Twenty years later, however, hip-hop culture has since flooded mainstream culture, and rap music is as prevalent in suburban homes as it once was in its native environment, moving from American subculture to the forefront of American attention. "Hip-hop is more powerful than any American cultural movement we've ever had," said rap music impresario Russell Simmons.

Hip-hop is one of the fastest-growing music genres in the United States, accounting for $1.84 billion in sales last year out of a $14.3 billion total for the U.S. recording industry, according to industry statistics. Interestingly, nearly 70 percent of those sales are to white suburban youth, a striking transformation considering rap music's beginnings. Most importantly, perhaps, rap music and its associated hip-hop culture have become a new component of the Black cultural aesthetic. With its rhythmical roots firmly planted in African tradition, hip-hop music is more than just musical expression. For some, it is a way of life, affecting their speech, style of dress, hairstyle, and overall disposition.

Like any other expressive art form, rappers have tested the boundaries of social responsibility, legality, free speech, and old-fashioned "good taste." Labeled as misogynistic, reckless, and even criminal, rappers endured years of public scrutiny with African Americans among some of their most relentless critics. After years of incessant scrutiny, hip-hop mogul Russell Simmons organized a three-day hip-hop music summit for 200 rappers, industry executives, and African-American politicians, the first event of its kind. Sean Combs, LL Cool J, Queen

Latifah, Wyclef Jean, Wu-Tang Clan, Chuck D, Jermaine Dupri, KRS-1, Luther Campbell, Ja Rule, and Talib Kweli were just a few of the influential hip-hop artists in attendance at the conference held last June in New York City.

Stars joined forces with some of Black America's intellectual and political elite, including NAACP president Kweisi Mfume; Urban League president Hugh Price; Nation of Islam minister Louis Farrakhan; Martin Luther King, III, leader of the Southern Christian Leadership Council; Georgia Democratic congressional representative Cynthia McKinney; and authors Cornel West and Michael Eric Dyson. The summit ended with musicians and industry executives agreeing to follow voluntary guidelines to advise parents of music's lyrical content while vowing to protect rap artists' freedom of speech by fighting Congressional efforts to censor the music. Minister Louis Farrakhan of the Nation of Islam, one of the political activists who attended the summit, told rappers, "You've now got to accept the responsibility you've never accepted. You are the leaders of the youth of the world."

Today's African-American college students, many of whom as youth were the original fans during rap music's formative years, still remain avid rap music connoisseurs. Rap music, however, has taken a decidedly different direction in recent years. Since rap music is clearly a profitable commercial commodity, rappers consequently perpetuate images and stereotypes that will sell their products, ranging from the excessively violent to the extravagantly wealthy. "Many rappers do not live the type of lives they claim. Those that claim to be affluent often are not, and those that claim to be poor gang-bangers are often millionaires. Fortunately, most college students have the ability to decipher between rap's glamorous image and the realities of life. A problem arises for the younger, impressionable audience, many of whom buy into rap's surface image," said Morehouse College Student Government Association president Christopher J. Graves.

As role models, accepting of the designation or not, rappers have a unique responsibility to be cognizant of their message and their intended audience. Since American pop culture reveres stardom, rappers often garner more attention and respect than they deserve. Consequently, rap music and hip-hop culture have the power to either adversely or positively affect African Americans in specific, and the larger culture in general. While a summit on rap music cannot adequately address all of its dilemmas, a dialogue between interested parties must continue in order to preserve the distinctive art form, while protecting the rich heritage of the African-American cultural aesthetic.

Writing Strategies

1. Describe how Bennett's introduction functions. What is he attempting to do? How does it assist readers in understanding the rest of the article?
2. Describe Bennett's voice and evaluate its appropriateness for this subject matter. Provide several passages to support your evaluation.

3. How does Bennett support his main claim? What type of background information and evidence does he provide?

4. Evaluate the effectiveness of Bennett's sources. How do they help readers to understand his argument or to accept his claims?

Exploring Ideas

1. How does Bennett encourage readers to look at hip-hop?

2. How does Bennett's idea fit into a larger discussion? That is, how can what he says be applied not just to hip-hop but also to other art forms?

3. Observe the relationship between different art forms (hip-hop, country music, film, painting, etc.) and people in your community. How does art seem to influence their thoughts and behavior? How do they seem to influence the art form?

4. In addition to art, what influences people? Go out and observe how people in your community choose to live—how they move around, shop, eat, work, and play. What are the major influences on what they wear, what they eat, how they get around, what they do for a living and what they do in their spare time?

The Parting Breath of the Now-Perfect Woman

Chester McCovey

Literature often comments on human foibles and social ills. Authors allow fictional characters to live out the worst and best human traits and reveal their psychological and social effects. But the commentary, the meaning behind characters' actions, often lurks quietly in the events of a story; the points are not blatant. Writers like Chester McCovey bring that meaning to the surface. In this essay, McCovey sheds light on the meaning lurking in Nathaniel Hawthorne's short story "The Birthmark." Notice that McCovey works to make this nineteenth-century story relevant to the lives of his readers.

A masterpiece of literature offers its readers unlimited opportunities for thought, analysis, discovery, insight, interpretation. Though an old story's language may be difficult for some, if that old story is a masterpiece, its characters and plot develop a timeless theme as relevant today as it was yesterday. Nathaniel Hawthorne's "The Birthmark" is such a story.

Hawthorne's theme is clear. In the story's opening paragraph we read:

> The higher intellect, the imagination, the spirit, and even the heart might all find their congenial ailment in pursuits which, as some of their ardent votaries believed, would ascend from one step of powerful intelligence to another, until the philosopher should lay his hand on the secret of creative force and perhaps make new worlds for himself. We know not whether Aylmer possessed this degree of faith in man's ultimate control over Nature.

See what I mean about the language? But the point here is that even though we now speak—and write—differently, Aylmer *did* apparently possess this degree of faith in man's ultimate control over nature. And in attempting to remove his young wife's only blemish—a small, hand-shaped birthmark on her left cheek—he "removes" her very life. The story's climax comes when after much science, Aylmer is successful—the birthmark is gone:

"By Heaven! It is well-nigh gone!" said Aylmer to himself, in almost irrepressible ecstasy. "I can scarcely trace it now. Success! success! And now it is like the faintest rose color. The lightest flush of the blood across her cheek would overcome it. But she is so pale!"

And while Georgiana is now "perfect" and Aylmer's science has been "successful," Georgiana is, of course, not just "pale." She is dying . . . then dead. And the young beauty—who because she had been told so often that her birthmark was a charm was, in her own words, "simple enough to imagine that it might be so"—now speaks her dying words:

> "My poor Aylmer," she repeated, with a more than human tenderness, "you have aimed loftily; you have done nobly. Do not repent that with so high and pure a feeling, you have rejected the best the earth could offer. Aylmer, dearest Aylmer, I am dying."

Reading "The Birthmark" for a second time, one plainly sees that the author laid everything out in the first paragraph. It could, of course, turn out no other way. And today's reader, raised on "Frankenstein" and stories like it, is probably not surprised by the ending. After the bombing of Hiroshima and Nagasaki, Americans spent their 1950s watching ("Birthmark"-like) movies in which havoc-wreaking mutants warned us about the dangers of man's faith in his ultimate control over Nature. Yet Hawthorne's masterpiece is so perfectly crafted, one eagerly reads on to find out what is about to happen.

As a masterpiece of literature, "The Birthmark" deserves much attention: attention to Hawthorne's plot, which contains perfect foreshadowing throughout; attention to his characters—poor Aylmer, and simple Georgiana who one cannot help but fall in love with; attention to word choice and sentence structure, though these are not so easy to be attracted to because of our modern tastes in writing. And also deserving attention, the theme of the story—a story written in the early nineteenth century—is not only *worth* pondering today—at the dawn of a twenty-first century—but it would be, in fact, difficult to imagine how someone could *not* ponder it.

The attentive reader is already a step ahead of me: cloning, stem cell research, genetic engineering. The incidents of humans "perfecting" nature—or fiddling with nature in attempts to perfect it—are forever in today's headlines. But cloned sheep and the possibility of cloned people is not the only science "The Birthmark" asks today's reader to think about.

While Georgiana's birthmark represents abstract imperfection, and Aylmer's faith in man represents humankind's efforts to perfect nature in general, the birthmark obviously reminds us of today's little "imperfections": (too small) breasts, a (too large) nose, (no) chin, (fat) thighs, and so on. The reader should not miss the point. No one is saying that cleft palates or clubbed feet should not be corrected—at least no one is saying that in this essay. But Georgiana's birthmark was "of the smallest pygmy size" and her lovers were "wont to say that some fairy at her birth hour had laid her tiny hand upon the infant's cheek, and left this impress there in token of the magic endowments that were to give her such sway over all hearts. Many a desperate swain would have risked life for the privilege of pressing his lips to the mysterious hand." The "mad scientist" is us—eager to erase these "imperfections" of Nature.

Perhaps the story's most important warning—indeed! It *is* the story's most important warning—comes so subtly that one might overlook it. When Georgiana, for the first time, goes into her husband's off-limits laboratory where he is working on one last concoction, she is scolded for her lack of faith in him. But she *has* faith and tells him so, and then she fails to tell him her reason for coming. She has felt a "sensation in the fatal birthmark, not painful, but which induced a restlessness throughout her system." One can hardly imagine the sensation was nothing at all, that it was just an excuse for a master storyteller to prolong his story. It is also unlikely that this sensation was a *negative* reaction to Aylmer's first treatment—after all, it was a "sensation" and it was not "painful." We thus imagine that Aylmer's first treatment was on its way to working, then he went too far.

Earlier in the story Aylmer shows Georgiana a powerful drug, and says, "With a few drops of [it] in a vase of water, freckles may be washed away as easily as the hands are cleansed." When asked, "Is it with this lotion that you intend to bathe my cheek?" Aylmer replies, "Oh, no . . . this is merely superficial. Your case demands a remedy that shall go deeper." And so, Aylmer's remedy ends up going too far. To him, the birthmark is not "superficial," but something that "has clutched its grasp into [her] being." His cure *does* work. The birthmark is removed. And his young wife is perfect, just as he planned . . . but only for a moment.

Great literature survives—it survives time, and multiple readings, and critical analysis, and skeptical hearts and minds. And it not only survives, but it thrives. Read "The Birthmark" twice and you will know what I mean. Hawthorne's theme is just as relevant today. And Georgiana's dying words express the real complexity of the issue.

As for physical imperfection in the twenty-first century, it seems odd that on one level we promote respect for all sorts of human "imperfections," yet on another level, we strive as we do to eliminate them whenever we can. It seems odd because so many times they are not imperfections at all.

> Alas! It was too true! The fatal hand had grappled with the mystery of life, and was the bond by which an angelic spirit kept itself in union with a mortal frame. As the last crimson tint of the birthmark—that sole token of human imperfection—faded from her cheek, the parting breath of the now-perfect woman passed into the atmosphere, and her soul, lingering a moment near her husband, took its heavenward flight.

Writing Strategies

1. Describe McCovey's voice and identify several specific passages to support your description.
2. Identify at least one counterargument McCovey makes. What other counterargument might he have made to strengthen his argument?
3. Study the ways in which McCovey refers to the story "The Birthmark" in his essay. Look for quotes and paraphrases. When he quotes, look for (a) long passages set off by themselves, (b) shorter passages quoted within McCovey's sentences, and (c) individual words from the story worked into McCovey's sentences. Based on McCovey's essay (and at least two others in this text) write a one- or two-page essay explaining various ways in which writers can refer to sources (in this case a story) in their text.
4. What is McCovey's thesis? Is it implied or stated explicitly?

Exploring Ideas

1. In a paragraph, explain how McCovey connects Hawthorne's story to twenty-first-century America.
2. State McCovey's main idea in no more than a few sentences and then compare your statement with those of several classmates. Discuss the similarities and differences in the way you and your classmates understand McCovey's essay. Then revise your statement of his main idea and explain how your understanding changed, if it did, through discussion.
3. Explain McCovey's main idea to several friends, coworkers, and family members, and then ask for their input. Do others agree or disagree with McCovey's ideas? Why?

Searching for Causes

Sex, Lies, and Conversation: Why Is It So Hard for Men and Women to Talk to Each Other?

Deborah Tannen

The essays in this section are argumentative in nature; that is, they argue that a particular cause is responsible for a behavior. As with any argument, the writers must rely on ample and reasonable evidence, which can take many forms: examples, testimony, anecdotes, statistics, allusions, all the appeals, and so on. In her argument, Deborah Tannen, a linguist and author of many books, relies on testimony and anecdotes to build a case for gender-specific behaviors—a slippery and complex phenomenon. She also points to her own research to support the claims.

I was addressing a small gathering in a suburban Virginia living room—a women's group that had invited men to join them. Throughout the evening, one man had been particularly talkative, frequently offering ideas and anecdotes, while his wife sat silently beside him on the couch. Toward the end of the evening, I commented that women frequently complain that their husbands don't talk to them. This man quickly concurred. He gestured toward his wife and said, "She's the talker in our family." The room burst into laughter; the man looked puzzled and hurt. "It's true," he explained. "When I come home from work I have nothing to say. If she didn't keep the conversation going, we'd spend the whole evening in silence."

The episode crystallizes the irony that although American men tend to talk more than women in public situations, they often talk less at home. And this pattern is wreaking havoc with marriage.

The pattern was observed by political scientist Andrew Hacker in the late '70s. Sociologist Catherine Kohler Riessman reports in her new book *Divorce Talk* that most of the women she interviewed—but only a few of the men—gave lack of communication as the reason for their divorces. Given the current divorce rate of nearly 50 percent, that amounts to millions of cases in the United States every year—a virtual epidemic of failed conversation.

In my own research, complaints from women about their husbands most often focused not on tangible inequities such as having given up the chance for a career to accompany a husband to his, or doing far more than their share of daily life-support work like cleaning, cooking, social arrangements, and errands. Instead, they focused on communication: "He doesn't listen to me," "He doesn't talk to me." I found, as Hacker observed years before, that most wives want their husbands to be, first and foremost, conversational partners, but few husbands share this expectation of their wives.

In short, the image that best represents the current crisis is the stereotypical cartoon scene of a man sitting at the breakfast table with a newspaper held up in front of his face, while a woman glares at the back of it, wanting to talk.

Linguistic Battle of the Sexes

How can women and men have such different impressions of communication in marriage? Why the widespread imbalance in their interests and expectations?

In the April [1990] issue of *American Psychologist,* Stanford University's Eleanor Maccoby reports the results of her own and others' research showing that children's development is most influenced by the social structure of peer interactions. Boys and girls tend to play with children of their own gender, and their sex-separate groups have different organizational structures and interactive norms.

I believe these systematic differences in childhood socialization make talk between women and men like cross-cultural communication, heir to all the attraction and pitfalls of that enticing but difficult enterprise. My research on men's and women's conversations uncovered patterns similar to those described for children's groups.

For women, as for girls, intimacy is the fabric of relationships, and talk is the thread from which it is woven. Little girls create and maintain friendships by exchanging secrets; similarly, women regard conversation as the cornerstone of friendship. So a woman expects her husband to be a new and improved version of a best friend. What is important is not the individual subjects that are discussed but the sense of closeness, of a life shared, that emerges when people tell their thoughts, feelings, and impressions.

Bonds between boys can be as intense as girls', but they are based less on talking, more on doing things together. Since they don't assume talk is the cement that binds a relationship, men don't know what kind of talk women want, and they don't miss it when it isn't there.

Boys' groups are larger, more inclusive, and more hierarchical, so boys must struggle to avoid the subordinate position in the group. This may play a role in women's complaints that men don't listen to them. Some men really don't like to listen, because being a listener makes them feel one-down, like a child listening to adults or an employee to a boss.

But often when women tell men, "You aren't listening," and the men protest, "I am," the men are right. The impression of not listening results from misalignments in the mechanics of conversation. The misalignment begins as soon as a man and a woman take physical positions. This became clear when I studied videotapes made by psychologist Bruce Dorval of children and adults talking to their same-sex best friends. I found that at every age, the girls and women faced each other directly, their eyes anchored on each other's faces. At every age, the boys and men sat at angles to each other and looked elsewhere in the room, periodically glancing at each other. They were obviously attuned to each other, often mirroring each other's movements. But the tendency of men to face away can give women the impression they aren't listening even when they are. A young woman in college was frustrated: Whenever she told her boyfriend she wanted to talk to him, he would lie down on the floor, close his eyes, and put his arm over his face. This signaled to her, "He's taking a nap." But he insisted he was listening extra hard. Normally, he looks around the room, so he is easily distracted. Lying down and covering his eyes helped him concentrate on what she was saying.

Analogous to the physical alignment that women and men take in conversation is their topical alignment. The girls in my study tended to talk at length about one topic, but the boys tended to jump from topic to topic. The second-grade girls exchanged stories about people they knew. The second-grade boys teased, told jokes, noticed things in the room, and talked about finding games to play. The sixth-grade girls talked about problems with a mutual friend. The sixth-grade boys talked about 55 different topics, none of which extended over more than a few turns.

Listening to Body Language

Switching topics is another habit that gives women the impression men aren't listening, especially if they switch to a topic about themselves. But the evidence of the 10th-grade boys in my study indicates otherwise. The 10th-grade boys sprawled across their chairs with bodies parallel and eyes straight ahead, rarely looking at each other. They looked as if they were riding in a car, staring out the windshield. But they were talking about their feelings. One boy was upset because a girl had told him he had a drinking problem, and the other was feeling alienated from all his friends.

Now, when a girl told a friend about a problem, the friend responded by asking probing questions and expressing agreement and understanding. But the boys dismissed each other's problems. Todd assured Richard that his drinking was "no big problem" because "sometimes you're funny when you're off your butt." And when Todd said he felt left out, Richard responded, "Why should you? You know more people than me."

Women perceived such responses as belittling and unsupportive. But the boys seemed satisfied with them. Whereas women reassure each other by implying, "You shouldn't feel bad because I've had similar experiences," men do so by implying, "You shouldn't feel bad because your problems aren't so bad."

There are even simpler reasons for women's impression that men don't listen. Linguist Lynette Hirschman found that women make more listener-noise, such as "mhm," "uhuh," and "yeah," to show "I'm with you." Men, she found, more often give silent attention. Women who expect a stream of listener-noise interpret silent attention as no attention at all.

Women's conversational habits are as frustrating to men as men's are to women. Men who expect silent attention interpret a stream of listener-noise as over-reaction or impatience. Also, when women talk to each other in a close, comfortable setting, they often overlap, finish each other's sentences and anticipate what the other is about to say. This practice, which I call "participatory listenership," is often perceived by men as interruption, intrusion, and lack of attention.

A parallel difference caused a man to complain about his wife, "She just wants to talk about her own point of view. If I show her another view, she gets mad at me." When most women talk to each other, they assume a conversationalist's job is to express agreement and support. But many men see their conversational duty as pointing out the other side of the argument. This is heard as disloyalty by women, and refusal to offer the requisite support. It is not that women don't want to see other points of view, but that they prefer them phrased as suggestions and inquiries rather than as direct challenges.

In his book *Fighting for Life,* Walter Ong points out that men use "agonistic" or warlike, oppositional formats to do almost anything; thus discussion becomes debate, and conversation a competitive sport. In contrast, women see conversation as a ritual means of establishing rapport. If Jane tells a problem and June says she has a similar one, they walk away feeling closer to each other. But this attempt at establishing rapport can backfire when used with men. Men take too literally women's ritual "troubles talk," just as women mistake men's ritual challenges for real attack.

The Sounds of Silence

These differences begin to clarify why women and men have such different expectations about communication in marriage. For women, talk creates intimacy. Marriage is an orgy of closeness: You can tell your feelings and thoughts, and still be loved. Their greatest fear is being pushed away. But men live in a hierarchical world, where talk maintains independence and status. They are on guard to protect themselves from being put down and pushed around.

This explains the paradox of the talkative man who said of his silent wife, "She's the talker." In the public setting of a guest lecture, he felt challenged to show his intelligence and display his understanding of the lecture. But at home, where he has nothing to prove and no one to defend against, he is free to remain silent. For his wife, being home means she is free from the worry that something she says might offend someone, or spark disagreement, or appear to be showing off; at home she is free to talk.

The communication problems that endanger marriage can't be fixed by mechanical engineering. They require a new conceptual framework about the role of talk in human relationships. Many of the psychological explanations that have become second nature may not be helpful, because they tend to blame either women (for not being assertive enough) or men (for not being in touch with their feelings). A sociolinguistic approach by which male–female conversation is seen as cross-cultural communication allows us to understand the problem and forge solutions without blaming either party.

Once the problem is understood, improvement comes naturally, as it did to the young woman and her boyfriend who seemed to go to sleep when she wanted to talk. Previously, she had accused him of not listening, and he had refused to change his behavior, since that would be admitting fault. But then she learned about and explained to him the differences in women's and men's habitual ways of aligning themselves in conversation. The next time she told him she wanted to talk, he began, as usual, by lying down and covering his eyes. When the familiar negative reaction bubbled up, she reassured herself that he really was listening. But then he sat up and looked at her. Thrilled, she asked why. He said, "You like me to look at you when we talk, so I'll try to do it." Once he saw their differences as cross-cultural rather than right and wrong, he independently altered his behavior.

Women who feel abandoned and deprived when their husbands won't listen to or report daily news may be happy to discover their husbands trying to adapt once they understand the place of small talk in women's relationships. But if their husbands don't adapt, the women may still be comforted that for men, this is not a failure of intimacy. Accepting the difference, the wives may look to their friends or family for that kind of talk. And husbands who can't provide it shouldn't feel their wives have made unreasonable demands. Some couples will still decide to divorce, but at least their decisions will be based on realistic expectations.

In these times of resurgent ethnic conflicts, the world desperately needs cross-cultural understanding. Like charity, successful cross-cultural communication should begin at home.

Writing Strategies

1. Describe Tannen's voice as a writer, and refer to several passages to support your description.
2. In your own words, write down Tannen's main idea.
3. Discuss with several peers what you wrote down for item 2. How is your understanding of Tannen's idea similar to or different from your peers' understanding? After discussing, write one statement of Tannen's main idea that you and your group members agree on.
4. What support, or evidence, does Tannen provide to explain a cause? That is, does she tell stories, provide statistics, or something else?
5. How does Tannen's article invite others to think about communication?

Exploring Ideas

1. Reflect on your communication habits. You might first jot down any initial ideas you have, and then recall comments others have made about the way you communicate. In several paragraphs, describe your own conversational behavior.
2. Over the course of several days, make your own observations about the way men and women communicate. How are your observations similar to or different from Tannen's?
3. Is it acceptable to generalize, as Tannen does, about men and women? What makes her generalizations valid? Or, why aren't they valid?

Why We Binge-Watch TV

Kevin Fallon

"Why We Binge-Watch TV" was published on *The Daily Beast* website in 2014. The article explores an interesting phenomenon: that in a fast-paced and distracted society, people are slowing down and watching multiple episodes of the same TV show, perhaps all day or even all weekend.

We correspond with each other in 140-character bursts. We consume news in sound bites and blog posts. We're, by all accounts, an increasingly distracted society, with the attention span of a house fly sipping on Red Bull in a room lit by a strobe light while dubstep plays. Knowing that, it makes absolutely no sense that we are also a society that enjoys binge-watching TV.

But we do. Oh, for the love of Walter White, we do.

According to a new study by Harris Interactive on behalf of Netflix, 61 percent of us binge-watch TV regularly, which is to say that we watch at least 2 to 3 episodes of a single series in one sitting. Or, some of us (many of us), devour 14 in a row with breaks just for bathroom and answering the door for the deliveryman. Almost three-quarters of us view binge-watching as a positive experience, and nearly 80 percent say that feasting on a show actually makes it better.

Given how many times we've heard people use the word "binge-watch" this past year and how many times we've alarmed our friends by disappearing from society for a week to marathon a show, it shouldn't be surprising that the practice is quickly becoming the new normal when it comes to consuming television. But it is remarkable that such a highly fragmented world is actively seeking out—and even preferring—longer form, more complex storytelling at the same time we want everything else in life easy and breezy.

It shouldn't compute. So why does it?

All of the elements of a perfect storm brewed at the same time, explains Grant McCracken, a cultural anthropologist who worked on the study. More accurately, it's a storm cycle: TV has gotten better, making viewers smarter, making TV even more complex, making binge-watching more fun. And because we're living in a world where too many things are constantly competing for our attention, developing a habit of binge-watching is like seeking shelter in the calm eye of that storm.

"I was illuminated to hear people say, 'Look, it's precisely because there's so much distraction that this is a special pleasure,'" McCracken says of the 1,500 streamers he interviewed as part of the study. While TV marathons have always been events, the rise of binge-watching is a byproduct of necessary and sufficient conditions that have only surfaced in recent years, with the easy availability of streaming, season DVDs, and TiVos compounded with the rise in quality of the shows available.

Plus, there's the undeniably fun appropriation of the word "binge."

"You hear that people are slightly embarrassed to spend four or five hours watching TV, that there's something reckless or indulgent or ill-advised about it," McCracken says. "That was the origin of the research project: to find out if 'binge' is the right metaphor, and if not then what is."

As it turns out, the entire connotation of "binge"—a word tinged with the shame of eating an entire roll of cookie dough—has changed into something prideful and brag-worthy. "Finally some people get that there's something ironic about the term," McCracken says. "People aren't watching Dukes of Hazard. They're watching great TV, not bad TV."

Indeed, the successive-episode viewing couldn't be as popular as it is—especially, again, in the age where people discuss everything and anything on social media and attempting to avoid a major plot spoiler online is a fool's errand—if the series being binged weren't as creatively evolved and dramatically complex as *Breaking Bad, The Wire, Game of Thrones, Orange Is the New Black,* and other popular bingeing series are.

The entire connotation of "binge"—a word tinged with the shame of eating an entire roll of cookie dough—has changed into something prideful and brag-worthy.

"Remember on Dallas when somebody shot J.R.?" says McCracken. "If you found out who did it after the fact, what would be the point of going back and watching that season? But with something like *The Wire,* even if a friend accidentally let a key character's death slip it doesn't really destroy the point of watching the show." There's so much more to pick apart, dissect, and become emotionally and intellectually engaged with that watching it, despite the unintended spoiler, is still enjoyable.

The late-in-its-run success of *Breaking Bad* is the perfect example of that. The show's final season premiered to double the series' previous ratings high and almost four times the ratings for the show's debut in 2008. The five years in between saw hordes of people finally caving to the "you have to watch *Breaking Bad!"* pressure of their colleagues, thanks to the availability of the entire series for streaming on Netflix.

"I think Netflix kept us on the air," Vince Gillian, *Breaking Bad*'s creator, said after his show won the Emmy for Best Drama Series in September. "Not only are we standing up here [with the Emmy], I don't think our show would have lasted beyond Season Two. It's a new era in television and we've been very fortunate to reap the benefits."

Netflix is notorious for keeping its data locked away in that same bunker where the UFOs and the still-alive Elvis Presley are kept, but the company does confirm that bingeing is more popular than ever with its subscribers. "Our viewing data shows that the majority of streamers would actually prefer to have a whole season of a show available to watch at their own pace," said Ted Sarandos, Chief Content Officer of Netflix.

The habits even shape its original programming choices, including *House of Cards* and *Orange Is the New Black.* "Netflix has pioneered audience choice in programming and has helped free consumers from the limitations of linear television. Our own original series are created for multi-episodic viewing, lining up the content with new norms of viewer control for the first time."

The result, not just because of strides in original programming from Netflix but because of the "bingeing" now becoming a legitimate alternative to most first-run broadcast airings, is that we are rejecting, in at least one crucial aspect of our lives—entertainment—the idea of instant gratification. It's what McCracken calls the "in case of emergency, break glass" phenomenon. And we all can identify with it.

There's a new series that you're excited about. You can't wait to try it out. "Then there's a small tension," McCracken says. "Do you watch it right away or do you set it aside for some eventuality like a terrible flu or a terrible snow storm?" Anyone who just snuggled under a blanket with Olivia Pope during Snowstorm Hercules to watch an entire season of *Scandal* and gasped because OMG HE'S HER FATHER!? knows exactly what he means. "You have a great show on hand. You're protected in event of emergency. And then there's something delicious about having a great show on standby, in reserve."

Bingeing, as we used to do it, was a hindsight act of embarrassment, an action realized only after its completion when staring at an empty Doritos bag. Now we're planning to do it. In a world moving faster than ever and our focus more split than ever, who would have thought that it would be the medium of television, once called "a vast wasteland" by former FCC Chairman Newton Minow, that would finally slow us down.

Writing Strategies

1. Why does Fallon think the cause of binge-watching is worth explaining?
2. According to Fallon, what causes binge-watching?
3. Fallon spends time exploring the meaning of *binge.* How is the word's meaning key to his article?
4. Describe Fallon's voice. Explain how specific writing strategies (word choice, sentence structure, paragraphs, punctuation, types of support, and so on) help to create his voice.

Exploring Ideas

1. Why does Fallon think "it is remarkable that such a highly fragmented world is actively seeking out—and even preferring—longer form, more complex storytelling at the same time we want everything else in life easy and breezy"? Do you agree that it is remarkable?
2. If you have binge-watched TV, how would you describe the experience? Why did you do it? What was its value? Was it more like an event, a vacation, an obligation, or would you describe it some other way?
3. What else is like binge-watching TV?

Are Female Long-Distance Runners More Prone To Suicidal Depression?

Emily de la Bruyere

The following article, published in 2014 in *The Daily Beast*, explores why some female long-distance runners may be prone to suicidal depression. Emily de la Bruyere is a writer and long-distance runner at Princeton University. Her article can be viewed as both explaining a relationship and arguing cause.

At 7 PM on the evening of Friday, January 17th, University of Pennsylvania freshman Madison Holleran jumped off a Philadelphia parking garage to her death.

Less than seven months earlier, Madison—then a New Jersey high-school runner—had beat out the state's top varsity runners in the 800 meters, running 2:08.87, the fastest New Jersey time that season. She earned all-State accolades in both soccer and track that year, and matriculated to Penn, where she became a scoring member of the cross-country squad. Her first-semester GPA was a 3.5. Madison was motivated, accomplished, beautiful, and talented. But, it seems, for the driven, ambitious girl, that wasn't enough. "There was a lot more pressure in the classroom," her father said of Madison's transition to college.

Madison's story is tragic and shocking. But what is most shocking about it is that in many ways it is not unprecedented. Madison is not the first high-achieving individual to become depressed. She is not the first woman to feel she has to succeed in every realm. Nor is she the first female distance runner to turn to suicide.

In June of 1986, Kathy Ormsby—a 21-year-old junior from North Carolina State and an American collegiate record holder—ran off the track with less than two laps to go in the NCAA championship race. She didn't break stride. She just raced off the field, under a railing, up the stadium, across a softball diamond, over a seven-foot fence, down a main thoroughfare—and over the side of a bridge. She fell 35 feet. She survived, but was paralyzed from the waist down. Off the track, she had been a perfectionist pre-med student with a perfect GPA. She had planned to pursue a career as a medical missionary.

Four years earlier, high-school distance running phenomenon Mary Wazeter jumped off a railway bridge over the Susquehanna River. She, too, survived, but was paralyzed from the chest down. The former straight-A student was on a leave of absence from Georgetown, where severe anorexia had left her emaciated, disoriented, and depressed.

Fortunately, suicides among high-performing distance runners are rare. What are not rare are feelings of inadequacy and even suicidal despair. After Ormsby's attempted suicide, the former director of Athletics West in Eugene, Oregon told the *Los Angeles Times* that he knew a number of female distance runners who had contemplated killing themselves, had prepared to do so, or had attempted to do so. The 1981–85 North Carolina cross-country coach reported a runner who overdosed on cold-remedy pills, and another who told her teammates about suicidal fantasies. The women who succumb to those impulses are consumed by the need to win a battle that simply cannot be won; a battle to be the best at everything, all at once.

Like the gymnast and the ballerina, the distance runner is often defined by drive and compulsion. She is an endurance athlete. As such, her days revolve around the demands of her sport: 50, 60, 70, 80-mile weeks, weights, cross-training—and, above all, a complete focus on her body, its abilities, and its inabilities. Hers is a sport without mercy. Every race has one, and only one, winner—often determined by a fraction of a second. In running, results are clearly defined and indelible. Unsurprisingly, the distance runner has a tendency towards obsessive-compulsive behavior. She is willing to spend every day fretting over the extra mile or half-mile, the quarter of a second, the extra hour of sleep, and the infinitesimal margin of victory. She is competitive, driven, and, sometimes, crazy. She is Captain Ahab, and victory is her white whale.

Perhaps even more than their male counterparts, female distance runners are perfectionists and control freaks. This is hardly unusual in a society where the woman is expected to do it all. But it is particularly apparent—and, often, destructive—among the already-driven and already high-achieving population of distance runners. Stories of eating disorders abound. In many cases, those are only the tip of the iceberg. For women like Holleran, Ormsby, and Wazeter, the obsession is not just about training. Nor is the compulsion solely about food. The drive for success—or, rather, victory—extends to the classroom, society, and every other aspect of life. In the same way that the woman on Wall Street is expected to be a perfect mother, the woman on the track is often expected to be a straight-A student, team leader, social role model, and everything in between. Kathy Ormsby was known for taking her class notes to workouts. Madison Holleran's depression was apparently triggered by what she considered a sub-par 3.5 GPA.

Of course, there are expectations for men, too. But somehow, the male athlete can be just a varsity athlete. The woman has to make varsity in every realm. Little has changed since, in a 2007 *New York Times* article, Sara Rimer called girls' drive for perfection "anorexia of the soul." In the high-achieving Yale ecosystem, some label it the "Rory Gilmore syndrome." A Brooklyn-based life coach said it best in an interview with *Today:* "Girls get the message . . . that they need to excel at everything, academically, professionally, physically, emotionally, spiritually, and be in perfect balance . . . be a 'perfect 10' in every area." Running appeals to exactly that sort of girl: The world is intense, the work taxing, and the success (when it comes) tangible.

Success in running is about toeing the edge. If the athlete is too fit, or trains too hard, injury becomes inevitable. One step too far, and ambition turns into unrealistic expectations, compulsion into craziness. Perfectionism becomes a sort of impossible perfectionism-plus.

The same line exists in all realms of high accomplishment, from John Nash in mathematics to Van Gogh and art to Nina and dance in *Black Swan*. There's a thin line between total dedication and self-immolation. For Madison Holleran, Kathy Ormsby, and Mary Wazeter, it was an easy commute from ambition to unattainable expectation.

The precise backstory of Madison Holleran's tragic death is still unknown. But what facts do exist fit seamlessly, if heart-wrenchingly, into the larger narrative. The distance runner is a good actor; the first lesson she learns is how to fool herself out of pain. Generally thin, rule-abiding, and responsible, she fits the mold of the golden girl. But that veneer hides an inner drive so powerful that it risks turning on itself. Her very strength is rooted in an Ahab-like quest that risks overwhelming her. In these three tragic cases, the definition of success—a particularly female definition of success, perhaps—leads her over the brink.

Writing Strategies

1. What is the article's thesis?

2. What main support strategies help readers understand and accept the thesis?

3. At the end of ¶7, de la Bruyere makes a literary allusion: "She is Captain Ahab, and victory is her white whale." Explain the allusion and how it supports the author's thesis.

4. Consider the qualifier "may have" in de la Bruyere's statement, "the perfectionist pressure of [Madison Holleran's] sport may have pushed her to suicide." Qualifiers help determine the force of the argument being made. How might de la Bruyere have argued differently—and provided different support—if she had qualified her claim differently? For instance, what if instead of "may have," she said "definitely," "most likely," or "probably didn't"?

Exploring Ideas

1. The article says the female distance runner "fits the mold of the golden girl. But that veneer hides an inner drive so powerful that it risks turning on itself." Explain what this means. What is the inner drive and how or why does it risk turning on itself?

2. De la Bruyere claims, "But somehow, the male athlete can be just a varsity athlete." Unpack "somehow." That is, provide a persuasive explanation and actual evidence, if you can, that male athletes are different in this respect than female athletes.

3. The article provides three examples of female long-distance runners, but it does not follow a formulaic five-paragraph essay format. Identify the three examples (Madison Holleran, Kathy Ormsby, and Mary Wazeter). Then imagine if de la Bruyere had written a five-paragraph essay (intro, example 1, example, 2, example 3, conclusion). How would the article be different? What ideas (what complexity) might be missing?

4. De la Bruyere focuses on the stories of particular women to make a larger point about a sport (female long-distance running) and an even larger point beyond that sport (about types of sports or activities and the characteristics of people who participate in them). What sport or activity requires (and reinforces) a particular type of inner drive, and therefore attracts a particular type of person? How does that inner drive, then, risk turning on itself (as the article states in its last paragraph)?

5. What causes someone to think he/she is a perfectionist?

Proposing Solutions

Technology, Movement, and Sound

Ed Bell

Good solutions can be involved and complex. Or they can be simple. In this essay, Ed Bell takes a "back-to-the-basics" approach. Such approaches are dangerous—they often rely on oversimplistic thinking or the assumption that *things were a whole lot better back in the good old days.* A successful "back-to-basics" argument, however, gets at the root of a problem. This essay questions our unquestioning faith in technological "advancements." As you read Bell's essay, consider the value, and dangers, of such "back-to-basics" thinking.

Although technology has improved society in many ways, we use it indiscriminately, not distinguishing the good uses from the bad. We could talk about cell phones, oversized SUVs, fast food, or a variety of other advancements. But the cool air and falling leaves of autumn bring to mind the leaf blower—a monster whose decibel level far exceeds her practical value.

While I'm willing to admit that under certain circumstances the leaf blower can be useful, I think most people are missing out on the natural benefits of using a rake:

1. Raking does just as good a job as blowing.
2. If it actually does take longer to rake (a fact of which I'm not certain), the time "saved" and used otherwise would in many ways have been better spent raking.
3. Raking provides more exercise—the necessary physical movement our twenty-first-century bodies are lacking.
4. Raking makes *only* the most wonderful sound as it scratches across the leafy ground.

As for point one, beautifully raked yards existed long before noisy leaf blowers—there's no denying that it is, at the very least, possible to rake leaves and not have to blow them. As for point two, how many Americans who argue they don't have time to rake all those leaves will stand there blowing them, then rush off to the health club to use a rowing machine or a stair-climber? How long will it be until the most popular workout machine is the one that simulates leaf raking? But if you don't rush off to a health club (no doubt because you don't have the time), you're probably too busy working. After all, you have bills to pay: the new leaf blower, the new cell phone, the new computer, the new car, and that badly needed vacation to get away from it all.

But even if it does take longer to rake than to blow, the extra time spent raking provides the exercise that we need. One look at the human body will tell you it is built for raking—it *wants* to rake! According to Pete Egoscue, renowned anatomical functionalist and author of *The Egoscue Method of Health Through Motion,* "movement is as much a biological imperative as food and water." Many people today, he says, don't "move enough to beat the overwhelming

---

odds that one day this motionless lifestyle will catch up with them." Do we sit at computers and cash registers doing repetitive movements, then relax with a little TV? Should we add standing and holding a noisy leaf blower to our routine? Just think about all the various body movements required by leaf raking.

The human body is built to move, yet we treat our physical human movement as an inconvenience. Egoscue says that "what all of us must do is deliberately and systematically get our bodies back in motion despite a modern lifestyle that discourages movement, and even encourages us to believe that we can survive and prosper as sedentary beings who treat motion as an inconvenience that can be minimized with the help of technology." A few sore muscles (and blisters) from a little leaf raking is, I would say, just what we need.

The man who blows the leaves on my campus wears special equipment—big spaceman goggles for his eyes and headphone-like muffs to protect his ears. His get-up alone indicates a problem to me: If you can't gather up leaves without protecting your own eyes and ears, perhaps there's a better way of doing it. Stop and compare the man with the rake to the one with the leaf blower. Which one is better off? The rake is simple; it stores easily; it doesn't cost much; it is quiet and doesn't bother the neighbors; it encourages necessary body movement; it's not very dangerous; and so on. But the leaf blower is bound to break down; it takes up more space and, combined with its cousins (the weed-whacker, the electric hedge trimmers, and so on), it will eventually convince you to build a bigger garage; it (and machines like it) costs more money, which is why you are working too much to rake leaves; it is loud, which is unpleasant, if not for you, for the neighbors; it is apparently dangerous—I'm assuming this because of the equipment the man on campus wears.

Technology is likely to come along and solve all of these problems. It's not hard to imagine a quieter leaf blower someday. Of course, the old-fashioned leaf-blowing folk will long for the good old days when a leaf blower could be heard for blocks away. But soon enough they'll all have the newer, lighter, more ergonomically correct models too. And then, of course, we'll have another problem to deal with—a problem that we can't even imagine until it occurs. Through all of that, however, two things will remain true: (1) We should not make too much noise around other people and (2) we should get our bodies moving. We should, I suggest, use our technology more discriminately—instead of using it just because we can.

Work Cited

Egoscue, Pete. *The Egoscue Method of Health through Motion: Revolutionary Program That Lets You Rediscover the Body's Power to Rejuvenate It*. HarperCollins Publishers, 1992.

Writing Strategies

1. What types of evidence (statistics, facts, allusions, anecdotes, scenarios, analogies) does Bell use to support his claims?

2. Write down any concessions (acknowledging possible weaknesses in his argument or value in opposing positions) or counterarguments (anticipating and responding to his readers' possible questions and

concerns) Bell makes. Write down at least one concession and one counterargument that he might have made, but didn't.

3. Bell uses one secondary source, Pete Egoscue. How does he let readers know when he is referring to Egoscue and when he is not?

4. Bell uses nearly every form of punctuation. Did you notice his punctuation throughout the essay? Or was it invisible to you? Where might he have punctuated differently in order to help you more readily understand his points?

5. Explain how Bell's essay moves from an individual concern to a community concern.

Exploring Ideas

1. Explain the relationship Bell sees among technology, movement, and sound.

2. In your own words, describe the problem Bell writes about and the solution he proposes.

3. Share your description (from item 2) with several classmates, and discuss the similarities and differences in the way you and they understood Bell's essay.

4. Share Bell's ideas with several people outside of class and get their responses. (You may have them read the essay, or you may summarize it for them.) How is the way others think about technology and movement different from the way Bell thinks about it? What difference might be worth further exploration?

Television: Destroying Childhood

Rose Bachtel

Even though people commonly say television is bad (especially for children), mainstream America remains enamored with, and locked into, television life. In this essay, Rose Bachtel argues that television destroys something in children. As you read, imagine how you might expand on what Bachtel says or how you might offer an alternate way of seeing the problem.

When my grandparents were little, they spent their free time riding bicycles outside, playing dolls or dress-up, or curling up with a good book. Nowadays, my younger siblings consume every free moment they have in front of a television. "Times have changed. It is just another form of entertainment," some say. Should this obsession be handled so lightly? Is there nothing wrong with sitting in front of a television set all day? Of course this poses a problem, especially where children are concerned! They are at a vital growing period in their lives, and how they are raised will play a strong role in who they will become. Watching television will not work any muscle groups, so a child will not get the proper amount of exercise he or she needs. This will lead to future health problems, whether it be in the near future or years down the road. Also, because TV does not demand effort or interaction of the person watching it, children who watch television often become lazy and expect that everything should come to them instantaneously and without work. This lowers a child's patience because he or she wants instant gratification and will not engage in activities or events that require time or complicated components. These same children will also experience a decline in creativity because the television is creative for them. This is not healthy because childhood is the most vital time for stimulating a young person's mind and forcing him or her to develop it.

How can parents stop their children's bodies and minds from eroding? My solution is quite simple. Parents should not keep a television in the home. It may sound a bit drastic at first, but when analyzed, it makes sense. Without the convenience of a television, children are forced to think of other forms of keeping themselves entertained. This would lead them to exercise more, since most activities involve using more muscle groups than are involved in stagnantly watching television. Also, since children would be forced to seek out other forms of entertainment, they would be, in turn, forced to use their brains more and think creatively in order to come up with something to do. They would have to use their minds to search for information about their world instead of having it handed to them by TV. Also, since a child is no longer confined to inside the house, he or she can venture outside and explore nature while getting fresh air and vitamin D from the sun's rays. Another problem with TV is that many television show producers feel that sex and violence sell, so consequently many of today's programs contain these elements. Since people at a young age are very impressionable, they pick up on these messages and are influenced by them. Without a television set in the home, children will be less exposed to sex and violence. Another benefit of my proposal is the fact that parents do not have to worry about monitoring the content of the television shows their children watch if there is no TV set in the home to begin with. Their kids will not be able to watch unapproved shows when the parents are not home to supervise.

Still, many people may feel apprehensive towards this proposal because they have lived with televisions for so long that they cannot imagine functioning without them. "How will we know what's going on in the world or what the weather is going to be like?" they might ask. Sure, television stations provide very useful information, but so do other forms of communication, such as newspapers and magazines. These sources of information can be just as convenient as television. Of course, a news program can give more up-to-date information, but written periodicals are not far behind. There is also the Internet, which is perhaps more current than television. "What about all of the shows on TV that the adults want to watch?" Television does offer a great deal of American entertainment, but it is not the only way to be entertained. People could try reading a good book, going out on the town, or enjoying the outdoors. Adults will find that if there is not TV in the house to distract them, they will have a lot more free time on their hands to really enjoy life. A good argument brought up by television supporters is the point that there are a lot of educational programs that teach children. These programs keep the attention of children and help them grow mentally. Yes, these stations are helpful, but what would be better and more effective to children is if someone taught them about the world in a "hands on" fashion instead of through a television set. Another protest against my proposal is that TV acts as a sort of babysitter for children. It keeps them quiet and entertained so that the parents can get all of their tasks accomplished. My response to that argument is that raising the children should be a parent's number one priority. The best way to raise a child is to constantly interact with him or her, spending many hours of quality time, because it shows the child that he or she is important and loved. This aspect of raising a young one will be lost if he or she is constantly sat in front of the TV.

Granted, many television shows are not moral and should be kept away from children. That is not the problem. The real problem with TV is the fact that it consumes so much of an American's time that could be invested into a more productive activity. Sure, television use could just be minimized, but I think that it would be better to get rid of televisions in the home altogether. The problem with owning one but not watching it as often is that it is easier said than done. When the temptation is there, it is hard to resist. Paul Klein, who worked for NBC in the 1950s, believed that people would watch TV just to watch TV, meaning that even if nothing interesting is on, people will still sit in front of a television set. For example, when I first moved into my apartment, I did not have a TV for a few days. During those few days, I was very efficient, using every minute of my time to study, clean, or perform any other needed task. I accomplished a lot of things in those first few days. However, when my television finally arrived, I found myself turning on the set and watching shows that I did not necessarily have any interest in. I was also not keeping up on my studies as well as I had before or cleaning as much. This scenario is true for many Americans. The television does not have one single essential use. People functioned perfectly fine before this invention. Sure, it is entertaining, informative, and convenient, but it also has many hidden side effects that are hurting the younger generations. By getting rid of televisions in the home, children will spend their childhood as they should, not watching television, but playing, creating, and learning about their world through their own eyes.

Writing Strategies

1. What evidence does Bachtel provide to explain the problem? What evidence does she provide to support her solution?
2. Describe Bachtel's voice as a writer, referring to several passages as evidence.
3. Write a new introduction and conclusion for Bachtel's essay, taking a very different approach for each.
4. Provide several examples of how Bachtel helps readers go from one idea to another.

Exploring Ideas

1. Based on this essay, describe how Bachtel is concerned about community and others.
2. How is the way that you see television similar to or different from the way Bachtel sees it?
3. Briefly summarize Bachtel's main idea, and then ask others to respond. Write down the three responses that interest you the most and explore what you find to be interesting about them. How is each response similar to or different from what Bachtel says?

Medicine after Oil

Daniel Bednarz

Insightful essays and articles don't just say what a writer thinks or report researched facts and opinions. They help readers understand a new way of thinking. As you read "Medicine after Oil" by health care consultant Daniel Bednarz, do you come to think differently about the topic? Do you respond like the public health official in the closing paragraph who says, "Oh my, I never thought of it that way. This is serious"?

The scale and subtlety of our country's dependency on oil and natural gas cannot be overstated. Nowhere is this truer than in our medical system.

Petrochemicals are used to manufacture analgesics, antihistamines, antibiotics, antibacterials, rectal suppositories, cough syrups, lubricants, creams, ointments, salves, and many gels. Processed plastics made with oil are used in heart valves and other esoteric medical equipment. Petrochemicals are used in radiological dyes and films, intravenous tubing, syringes, and oxygen masks. In all but rare instances, fossil fuels heat and cool buildings and supply electricity. Ambulances and helicopter "life flights" depend on petroleum, as do personnel who travel to and from medical workplaces in motor vehicles. Supplies and equipment are shipped—often from overseas—in petroleum-powered carriers. In addition there are the subtle consequences of fossil fuel reliance. A recently retired doctor informs me, "In orthopedics we used to set fractures mostly by feel and knowing the mechanics of how the fractures were created. I doubt that many of the present orthopedists could do a good job if you took away their [energy-powered] fluoroscope or X-ray."

Despite this enormous vulnerability, public discussions of health care routinely ignore the prospect of peak oil. The proposed reforms, which seek to cover more people while holding down escalating costs, amount to little more than fiscal maneuvers. They take no notice of ecological resource constraints that will set limits on our ability to give people access to medical care.

The coming scarcity of fossil fuels, on top of inflationary costs in medicine (the prices of oil and natural gas are approximately four times what they were in 1999 and rising) and the expenses of treating Baby Boomers (a cohort twice the size of its predecessor), could overwhelm a medical system already in crisis. We can avoid collapse, however, by reducing medicine's present consumption of energy and creating a health-care system that reflects our actual relationship to resources. Ironically, peak oil can be a catalyst for creating a health-care system that is cost-effective, ecologically sustainable, and congruent with a democratic social ethos.

At present we have a tiered health-care system. At the top is a Ferrari model of care that reflects our affluence, fascination with technology, and extravagance. Ferrari care has made possible the treatment of rare life-threatening diseases and expensive procedures like organ transplants, but it has also been used for esoteric and often redundant testing and vanity procedures such as Botox injections. At the bottom is a jalopy model serving over 50 million un-and underinsured Americans who very often receive no treatment, defer treatment until

---

From Daniel Bednarz, "Medicine After Oil," from *Orion Magazine* July/August 2007, http://www.orionmagazine.org/index.php/articles/article/314/. Reprinted with permission of the author.

their condition cannot be ignored, or face economic ruin when they seek adequate care. If the two tiers persist after peak oil, they will eventually be preserved by force—armed guards at gated medical facilities—for the few able to pay, while the rest of Americans are relegated to the jalopy and faced with overt rationing, triage, and curtailment of medical care. Such an outcome would be an overt contravention of democratic values—most Americans tell pollsters they believe that health care is a human right, not a privilege awarded those with higher income.

What then should we do? The best democratic option is to replace both the Ferrari and the jalopy with a Honda. The post-peak Honda health-care model will of necessity operate with fewer overall resources and less energy than today's health-care system, and at lower cost. But it need not result in poorer quality of care. Although the United States spends more on health than any other nation—per capita health-care costs in this country are three times those in Great Britain and more than twice those in Canada—we do not have the best health outcomes. A study in the *Journal of the American Medical Association* in 2006, for example, reported that "white, middle-aged Americans—even those who are rich—are far less healthy than their peers in England."

The commonsensical Honda model will emphasize public health—the prevention of disease and the promotion of health within the population as a whole—over treatment medicine, which focuses on restoring health to chronically or acutely ill individuals. Typically accomplished through the diffusion of information, low-cost therapies, and the promotion of healthful nutrition and lifestyle, preventive medicine allows people to avoid or postpone disease, and to stay clear of the costliest and most energy-intensive sectors of the medical system—doctors' offices, pharmacies, and the hospital. In the Honda model, treatment medicine would continue, but its role would be brought into better balance with the vastly more cost-effective and energy-efficient mode of preventive health care.

The public health system arose in the early decades of the last century as a response to fears of infectious diseases in our country's crowded cities. Its outlook is inherently egalitarian—if the entire community is not protected, then no one's health is assured. Public health is no longer the force it was when it sent "ladies in white uniforms" into communities to preach the Gospel of Germs, explaining the relationship between hygiene and disease prevention. Today, public health is overburdened and underfunded, receiving about 5 percent of health-care dollars, with the balance going to treatment medicine and to biomedical research.

Despite funding inadequacies, public health is in place and functioning. Public health workers, for example, educate about and test for HIV/AIDS and other sexually transmitted diseases; they interdict infectious diseases like avian flu; they create emergency plans to deal with a variety of disaster scenarios; they monitor waste management and air and water quality. No new system needs to be invented or institutionalized to meet the health-care challenges of the coming energy transition, or, for that matter, those of climate change.

Already, some public health officials are beginning to address peak oil's effect on health care. On the national level, the Center for Environmental Health at the Centers for Disease Control is investigating impacts of petroleum scarcity on pharmaceuticals. In Congress, a

Peak Oil Caucus led by Roscoe Bartlett (R-MD) and Tom Udall (D-NM), is looking into the health risks posed by economic decline and mass unemployment, which peak oil is likely to trigger. At the local level, Indianapolis's Marion County Health Department is the first in the country to begin *planning for maintaining public health services* under differing scenarios of energy scarcity.

Late though the hour is, we can still avert the worst health consequences of an energy downturn, but doing so will require transforming our entire health-care system. The elitist impulse to perpetuate Ferrari care for the explicit benefit of the few at the expense of the many will persist after peak oil, and substantial citizen action will be needed to put into effect the affordable, egalitarian Honda model. Medicine itself could play a central role in this effort, by educating those who are unaware of the sweeping changes peak oil will initiate. Reprising its inaugural campaign against germs, public health could become a platform for disseminating a Gospel of Energy Conservation. For the most part, the medical community is as naive about peak oil as the rest of the citizenry. As one public health official told me after hearing about medicine's reliance on oil, "Oh my, I never thought of it that way. This is serious."

Writing Strategies

1. What is the article's thesis?
2. Explain why the opening paragraph is or isn't effective.
3. What is the purpose of the article's second paragraph? How does it support or relate to Bednarz's thesis?
4. Describe Bednarz's strategy for helping readers understand the current "tiered health-care system."
5. What solution does Bednarz propose?

Exploring Ideas

1. What is the relationship between medicine and oil?
2. Using this article as a model, imagine another topic (besides medicine) and its relationship to (or dependence on) oil. Describe the relationship.
3. With several peers, list reasons why "transforming our entire health-care system" would be difficult. What would the major obstacle be? How could that obstacle be overcome?

Thinking Radically

Not Homeschooling? What's Your Excuse?

Tricia Smith Vaughan

Is school boring? Is school harmful? In the following article, published on NewsWithViews.com, Tricia Smith Vaughan puts forth a radical argument about why public, or government, schooling should be avoided.

My favorite excuse is "but the schools here are so wonderful!" The parent will go on and on about how little Johnny or JoEllen is learning the clarinet or Chinese or times tables in their local public kindergarten, something that Johnny or JoEllen's mommy and daddy claim not to be smart enough to teach. If you think that I'm being demeaning to the mommy or daddy, I am merely repeating what he or she has told me.

I've had moms of four-year-olds tell me how much their child is learning, things that the mom says that she couldn't possibly teach. When I pry with a question or two, I find that what I'm teaching my child at home is at least as good as what Johnny or JoEllen is learning at preschool or kindergarten. And if we need to find a clarinet teacher, we will.

My just-turned-five-year-old has not spent a day in a government institution of learning and yet, he talks with ease to adults, knows his alphabet, writes words correctly with an adult's spelling help, and works hard at learning to read. From all accounts, he's just as smart as the heavily schooled.

What's placed the idea in our heads that the government can educate our children better than we can is none other than our public school system, the government darling of our unconstitutional Department of Education. Most of us grew up with the government's feeding us lunch, teaching us knowledge and values, and suggesting what careers we should have, all under the guise of educating us. Is it any wonder that we allow this seemingly benevolent entity to provide an education to our children?

As parents, we have grown to believe something that our ancestors of one hundred years ago would be shocked to see happening. The millennia-old concept of self-sufficient parents who educated their children at home has given way to a system in which parents believe that we are not smart enough to teach our children the alphabet and basic math.

We over-educated post-feminist moms allow the joyful opportunity to educate our children at home pass; we send our child to a government school that teaches not only the alphabet and numbers, but a little socialist school-to-work agenda along with it. Things have changed in the government schools, even in the past five years. Some call it progress; others call it a few steps closer to socialism.

One thing that hasn't changed, however, is that little Johnny and JoEllen will learn their place in a government school. Maybe they'll do well in group activities and the teacher will deem them fine to work in the new planned world order. But maybe not. A little deviation from the supposed norm and the little tykes can be diagnosed and sent to special education

---

classes, something that John Taylor Gatto claims places them at a much lower level of the "reproductive sweepstakes."

According to Gatto, government schools encourage these sweepstakes by ranking children in groups and assigning those deemed not worthy to reproduce to special education classes. Let us not forget that these days, children deemed special by government change agents will be drugged, at least if President Bush and Congress continue to have their way via the Orwellian-named New Freedom Commission on Mental Health. Ah, the land of the free!

How else can I describe a country that requires its children to sit in a classroom all day? I must admit that I had never thought much about this strange paradox of freedom and confinement until I read John Taylor Gatto's *The Underground History of American Education.* It's available free online at his website, www.johntaylorgatto.com; no one I've ever told this to, to my knowledge, has ever read the book. And yet moms continue to tell me how wonderfully their children are thriving in the government schools, never knowing the true history behind those schools.

According to Gatto, our public schools were set up to dumb us down so that we can be happy to be a cog in the planned economy. We have to understand that government schools in the U.S. were created to dull children's potential. Yes, read that part again—government schools were never about truly educating your child; they were and are about creating happy workers and taxpayers, people afraid to challenge the status quo and unable to read and think for themselves.

I used to teach students who'd been educated in government schools; I've seen the products of this lovely system. And as a product myself, I can tell you that the students I taught at a major research university in the 1990s were less able to read, write, and think for themselves, as a whole, than were the people whom I graduated with at my public high school in the 1980s.

Most of us can give examples of crappy experiences we had in public schools—my husband remembers a teacher's berating a girl who'd wet her pants in first grade; the teacher forced the class to laugh at the little girl. And this wonderful government school moment occurred in the 1970s.

If you think that kind of thing would never happen in your child's wonderful government school today, don't talk with the parents in Elizabeth, Pennsylvania. A principal there recently resigned because parents were outraged when they found out that she paraded a third-grader from class to class, calling the young child a "liar and thief." The principal didn't bother to investigate the accuser's story; the young accuser later "recanted the story."

Have you ever thought about the crappy overall experience you had in a government school? Even if you graduated at the top of your class? Even if you loved it at the time? Have you ever wondered what things you might have accomplished had you not been forced to attend high school? If schooling is such a wonderful thing, why don't we have the freedom to choose it for ourselves, instead of having it chosen for us? Personally, I can remember wanting to attend college when I was 13. No such luck—I was stuck in high school prison.

Take some time to understand why Our Government Masters developed the system that they did for dumbing us down. Learn how even the best of teachers must work in an atmosphere every day that does not allow the freedom to worship God as one wishes. If you don't believe me, try saying a softly spoken prayer before a meal or studying the Bible as God's sacred word at a government school, things we are able to do rather easily in a private restaurant or even in a public library.

Learn how your children are being tested for their values instead of their knowledge. And please, stop complaining about sex education classes that preach homosexuality or about recitation of the Pledge of Allegiance in the classroom that doesn't say "under God." Parents in San Francisco who complained recently that a sex survey was given to their children, some of whom were in first grade—yes, first grade!—were told by the court system that they had no rights. If you're surprised at this decision, do some reading on the true history of education.

Expecting the government schools to acquiesce to your demands is useless. Occasionally, the parents will win, as they did when they insisted that the Pennsylvania principal resign, but most of the time, parents lose. Do yourself a favor and stop trying to win. Take your children out of those schools.

The government schools are not going to teach your child Judeo-Christian values; they are going to teach him or her how to survive in a group, good practice for a future as a soldier of the United Nations. Your child, in a subtle or blatant way, will learn how to outbully and outsmart his or her classmates and vie for the teacher's attention in a classroom of twenty or so other children the same age. The experts will tell you that this socialization is wonderful for a child, but even in college, I have never encountered such a blatantly homogeneous group of people as I did in public school classrooms. My children are learning manners, which will allow them to be kind and polite to people of all ages, ethnicities, and religions; I am thankful that they are not having to fight for a teacher's attention in order to be properly socialized, whatever that vague term means.

It's tempting to blame the public school's state on politicians. It becomes easy to cite Bush, or Clinton, or any other politician, for doing or not doing something to help education. And then there's the other little blame darling: funding; public schools seem always to blame things on lack of funding. As long as you do this blaming thing and don't understand the full picture, you will consider the public schools a good thing. You will try to obtain your money's worth as a taxpayer and you may try to change the system: You will fail.

Only when you understand what the government's biggest propaganda campaign and cash cow is doing to your children, and has done to you, will you take your child away from the governmental change agents that our public schools contain. And only then will you refuse government money, even for a public charter school that allows you to teach your child at home.

On the other hand, if you've read John Taylor Gatto, Charlotte Iserbyt, and Beverly Eakman, and you're still okay with the U.S. government schools, keep your children in them. If you're okay with the links to the two largest U.S. teacher's unions, the NEA and the AFT, on the Communist Party USA's website, don't bother either to homeschool or to send your child to a private school with no financial ties to the federal government. If having the government interfere in your life and the life of your family, often without your consent, is okay with you, then leave your children exactly where they are.

But if you are interested in teaching your child about the true freedom of the individual that this country was founded upon, take your child as far from the government schools as possible. I know that in a few cases, it's difficult to homeschool. But for the most part, if you're literate, you can teach your child! Some single parents even homeschool. Don't let the government have control of your children's most precious asset: their mind. Take control yourself and thrive in the responsibility that God has given you. Take true responsibility for your child and for his or her education. And do it today!

Writing Strategies

1. What is Vaughan's main claim?
2. What support strategies does Vaughan use to help readers understand and accept her position?
3. According to Vaughan, what is the relationship between drugs and government schools?
4. Vaughan writes, "As long as you do this blaming thing and don't understand the full picture, you will consider the public schools a good thing" (¶19). What is the full picture, according to Vaughan?
5. How does Vaughan's argument go beyond the basic argument for homeschooling? Alternatively, how does it fit in with more common arguments for homeschooling?

Exploring Ideas

1. Vaughan states, "What's placed the idea in our heads that the government can educate our children better than we can is none other than the public school system. . . ." (¶4) What evidence does Vaughan provide to support this assertion? What additional evidence can you provide to support it? What evidence might refute it?
2. How is government education like a school-to-work agenda? What, if anything, about government education challenges a school-to-work agenda?
3. Vaughan questions an educational system "that requires its children to sit in a classroom all day" (¶9). Why is or isn't a system like this effective? Is Vaughan's description accurate? (Do children sit in a classroom pretty much all day? Did you?)
4. Interview a variety of Americans of different ages and backgrounds to find out if they think "our public schools were set up to dumb us down so that we can be happy to be a cog in the planned economy" (¶10). How many people you interviewed seem open to the possibility? How many reject it immediately?

Why Tough Teachers Get Good Results

Joanne Lipman

In "Why Tough Teachers Get Good Results," published in *The Wall Street Journal* (2013), Joanne Lipman questions some of the most common and agreed-upon ideas in current education. Her article offers support (from current research) for new alternatives based on old approaches.

I had a teacher once who called his students "idiots" when they screwed up. He was our orchestra conductor, a fierce Ukrainian immigrant named Jerry Kupchynsky, and when someone played out of tune, he would stop the entire group to yell, "Who eez deaf in first violins!?" He made us rehearse until our fingers almost bled. He corrected our wayward hands and arms by poking at us with a pencil.

Today, he'd be fired. But when he died a few years ago, he was celebrated: Forty years' worth of former students and colleagues flew back to my New Jersey hometown from every corner of the country, old instruments in tow, to play a concert in his memory. I was among them, toting my long-neglected viola. When the curtain rose on our concert that day, we had formed a symphony orchestra the size of the New York Philharmonic.

I was stunned by the outpouring for the gruff old teacher we knew as Mr. K. But I was equally struck by the success of his former students. Some were musicians, but most had distinguished themselves in other fields, like law, academia and medicine. Research tells us that there is a positive correlation between music education and academic achievement. But that alone didn't explain the belated surge of gratitude for a teacher who basically tortured us through adolescence.

We're in the midst of a national wave of self-recrimination over the U.S. education system. Every day there is hand-wringing over our students falling behind the rest of the world. Fifteen-year-olds in the U.S. trail students in 12 other nations in science and 17 in math, bested by their counterparts not just in Asia but in Finland, Estonia and the Netherlands, too. An entire industry of books and consultants has grown up that capitalizes on our collective fear that American education is inadequate and asks what American educators are doing wrong.

I would ask a different question. What did Mr. K do right? What can we learn from a teacher whose methods fly in the face of everything we think we know about education today, but who was undeniably effective?

As it turns out, quite a lot. Comparing Mr. K's methods with the latest findings in fields from music to math to medicine leads to a single, startling conclusion: It's time to revive old-fashioned education. Not just traditional but old-fashioned in the sense that so many of us knew as kids, with strict discipline and unyielding demands. Because here's the thing: It works.

Now I'm not calling for abuse; I'd be the first to complain if a teacher called my kids names. But the latest evidence backs up my modest proposal. Studies have now shown, among other things, the benefits of moderate childhood stress; how praise kills kids' self-esteem; and why grit is a better predictor of success than SAT scores.

All of which flies in the face of the kinder, gentler philosophy that has dominated American education over the past few decades. The conventional wisdom holds that teachers are supposed to tease knowledge out of students, rather than pound it into their heads. Projects and collaborative learning are applauded; traditional methods like lecturing and memorization—derided as "drill and kill"—are frowned upon, dismissed as a surefire way to suck young minds dry of creativity and motivation.

But the conventional wisdom is wrong. And the following eight principles—a manifesto if you will, a battle cry inspired by my old teacher and buttressed by new research—explain why.

1. A little pain is good for you.

Psychologist K. Anders Ericsson gained fame for his research showing that true expertise requires about 10,000 hours of practice, a notion popularized by Malcolm Gladwell in his book "Outliers." But an often-overlooked finding from the same study is equally important: True expertise requires teachers who give "constructive, even painful, feedback," as Dr. Ericsson put it in a 2007 *Harvard Business Review* article. He assessed research on top performers in fields ranging from violin performance to surgery to computer programming to chess. And he found that all of them "deliberately picked unsentimental coaches who would challenge them and drive them to higher levels of performance."

2. Drill, baby, drill.

Rote learning, long discredited, is now recognized as one reason that children whose families come from India (where memorization is still prized) are creaming their peers in the National Spelling Bee Championship. This cultural difference also helps to explain why students in China (and Chinese families in the U.S.) are better at math. Meanwhile, American students struggle with complex math problems because, as research makes abundantly clear, they lack fluency in basic addition and subtraction—and few of them were made to memorize their times tables.

William Klemm of Texas A&M University argues that the U.S. needs to reverse the bias against memorization. Even the U.S. Department of Education raised alarm bells, chastising American schools in a 2008 report that bemoaned the lack of math fluency (a notion it mentioned no fewer than 17 times). It concluded that schools need to embrace the dreaded "drill and practice."

3. Failure is an option.

Kids who understand that failure is a necessary aspect of learning actually perform better. In a 2012 study, 111 French sixth-graders were given anagram problems that were too difficult for them to solve. One group was then told that failure and trying again are part of the learning process. On subsequent tests, those children consistently outperformed their peers.

The fear, of course is that failure will traumatize our kids, sapping them of self-esteem. Wrong again. In a 2006 study, a Bowling Green State University graduate student followed 31 Ohio band students who were required to audition for placement and found that even students who placed lowest "did not decrease in their motivation and self-esteem in the long term." The study concluded that educators need "not be as concerned about the negative effects" of picking winners and losers.

4. Strict is better than nice.

What makes a teacher successful? To find out, starting in 2005 a team of researchers led by Claremont Graduate University education professor Mary Poplin spent five years observing 31 of the most highly effective teachers (measured by student test scores) in the worst schools of Los Angeles, in neighborhoods like South Central and Watts. Their No. 1 finding: "They were strict," she says. "None of us expected that."

The researchers had assumed that the most effective teachers would lead students to knowledge through collaborative learning and discussion. Instead, they found disciplinarians who relied on traditional methods of explicit instruction, like lectures. "The core belief of these teachers was, 'Every student in my room is underperforming based on their potential, and it's my job to do something about it—and I can do something about it,'" says Prof. Poplin.

She reported her findings in a lengthy academic paper. But she says that a fourth-grader summarized her conclusions much more succinctly this way: "When I was in first grade and second grade and third grade, when I cried my teachers coddled me. When I got to Mrs. T's room, she told me to suck it up and get to work. I think she's right.I need to work harder."

5. Creativity can be learned.

The rap on traditional education is that it kills children's creativity. But Temple University psychology professor Robert W. Weisberg's research suggests just the opposite. Prof. Weisberg has studied creative geniuses including Thomas Edison, Frank Lloyd Wright and Picasso—and has concluded that there is no such thing as a born genius. Most creative giants work ferociously hard and, through a series of incremental steps, achieve things that appear (to the outside world) like epiphanies and breakthroughs.

Prof. Weisberg analyzed Picasso's 1937 masterpiece *Guernica,* for instance, which was painted after the Spanish city was bombed by the Germans. The painting is considered a fresh and original concept, but Prof. Weisberg found instead that it was closely related to several of Picasso's earlier works and drew upon his study of paintings by Goya and then-prevalent Communist Party imagery. The bottom line, Prof. Weisberg told me, is that creativity goes back in many ways to the basics. "You have to immerse yourself in a discipline before you create in that discipline. It is built on a foundation of learning the discipline, which is what your music teacher was requiring of you."

6. Grit trumps talent.

In recent years, University of Pennsylvania psychology professor Angela Duckworth has studied spelling bee champs, Ivy League undergrads and cadets at the U.S. Military Academy in West Point, N.Y.—all together, over 2,800 subjects. In all of them, she found that grit—defined as passion and perseverance for long-term goals—is the best predictor of success. In fact, grit is usually unrelated or even negatively correlated with talent.

Prof. Duckworth, who started her career as a public school math teacher and just won a 2013 MacArthur "genius grant," developed a "Grit Scale" that asks people to rate themselves on a dozen statements, like "I finish whatever I begin" and "I become interested in new pursuits every few months." When she applied the scale to incoming West Point cadets, she found that those who scored higher were less likely to drop out of the school's notoriously brutal summer boot camp known as "Beast Barracks." West Point's own measure—an index that includes SAT scores, class rank, leadership and physical aptitude—wasn't able to predict retention.

Prof. Duckworth believes that grit can be taught. One surprisingly simple factor, she says, is optimism—the belief among both teachers and students that they have the ability to change and thus to improve. In a 2009 study of newly minted teachers, she rated each for optimism (as measured by a questionnaire) before the school year began. At the end of the year, the students whose teachers were optimists had made greater academic gains.

7. Praise makes you weak . . .

My old teacher Mr. K seldom praised us. His highest compliment was "not bad." It turns out he was onto something. Stanford psychology professor Carol Dweck has found that 10-year-olds praised for being "smart" became less confident. But kids told that they were "hard workers" became more confident and better performers.

"The whole point of intelligence praise is to boost confidence and motivation, but both were gone in a flash," wrote Prof. Dweck in a 2007 article in the journal *Educational Leadership*. "If success meant they were smart, then struggling meant they were not."

8. . . . while stress makes you strong.

A 2011 University at Buffalo study found that a moderate amount of stress in childhood promotes resilience. Psychology professor Mark D. Seery gave healthy undergraduates a stress assessment based on their exposure to 37 different kinds of significant negative events, such as death or illness of a family member. Then he plunged their hands into ice water. The students who had experienced a moderate number of stressful events actually felt less pain than those who had experienced no stress at all.

"Having this history of dealing with these negative things leads people to be more likely to have a propensity for general resilience," Prof. Seery told me. "They are better equipped to deal with even mundane, everyday stressors."

Prof. Seery's findings build on research by University of Nebraska psychologist Richard Dienstbier, who pioneered the concept of "toughness"—the idea that dealing with even routine stresses makes you stronger. How would you define routine stresses? "Mundane things, like having a hardass kind of teacher," Prof. Seery says.

My tough old teacher Mr. K could have written the book on any one of these principles. Admittedly, individually, these are forbidding precepts: cold, unyielding, and kind of scary.

But collectively, they convey something very different: confidence. At their core is the belief, the faith really, in students' ability to do better. There is something to be said about a teacher who is demanding and tough not because he thinks students will never learn but because he is so absolutely certain that they will.

Decades later, Mr. K's former students finally figured it out, too. "He taught us discipline," explained a violinist who went on to become an Ivy League-trained doctor. "Self-motivation," added a tech executive who once played the cello. "Resilience," said a professional cellist. "He taught us how to fail—and how to pick ourselves up again."

Clearly, Mr. K's methods aren't for everyone. But you can't argue with his results. And that's a lesson we can all learn from.

Writing Strategies

1. What is the article's thesis? How does it unify Lipman's eight principles?
2. What does Lipman say is at the core of Mr. K's approach to teaching (and the eight principles)?
3. Why does Lipman say, "Decades later, Mr. K's former students finally figured it out, too"? How is this statement key to her argument?
4. Describe Lipman's main support strategies: What type of support does she provide to help readers understand and accept her main claim?
5. Why does Lipman rely on the first-person "I" in her first seven paragraphs and then avoid it later in the article?

Exploring Ideas

1. Why would Jerry Kupchynsky be fired today? What has changed? Do you think a teacher like him should be fired?
2. Lipman says Jerry Kupchynsky was "undeniably effective." Why might some of his students disagree with her claim?
3. Have you ever received painful feedback from a teacher? If so, how did it affect you? How did you respond to it in the short term and then later?

21 Rhetorical Handbook

John Metz

Where to Find It

How Sentences Work: An Overview

Every sentence is made up of words that cluster into related groups. If a group has a subject and a verb, it is called a *clause*. If it doesn't, it is called a *phrase*. When a noun (such as *dog*) and a verb (such as *sleeps* or *eats* or *barks* or *bites*) group together, a sort of reaction occurs. Other words group together around *dog* and *sleeps* to fill in the story.

Some words describe the dog (*big, black, furry, stray*), while others describe the sleeping (*soundly, restlessly, peacefully*). Other words connect, explaining the relationship between one word or word group and another. And, as you know, words change their forms to express number and time so that instead of "one dog sleeps" we can say "two dogs slept" or "two big dogs slept soundly" and so on.

Words—Parts of Speech

1. **Noun**—A noun names a person, place, or thing.
2. **Pronoun**—A pronoun takes the place of a noun.
3. **Verb**—A verb expresses an action or a state of being.
4. **Adjective**—An adjective modifies a noun or pronoun.
5. **Adverb**—An adverb modifies a verb, adjective, or adverb.
6. **Interjection**—An interjection expresses surprise or strong emotion.
7. **Conjunction**—A conjunction connects words, phrases, and clauses and shows a relationship.
8. **Preposition**—A preposition, placed before a noun and its modifiers, creates a modifying phrase.

Words (parts of speech) are combined into phrases and clauses to create sentences (see next page).

Phrases

1. **Prepositional**—Consisting of a preposition, modifiers, and a noun, the prepositional phrase functions most often as an adjective or adverb.
2. **Participial**—Consisting of a participle, modifiers, and a noun, the participial phrase functions as an adjective.
3. **Gerund**—Consisting of a gerund, modifiers, and a noun, the gerund phrase functions as a noun.
4. **Infinitive**—Consisting of an infinitive, modifiers, and a noun, the infinitive phrase functions as a noun, adjective, or adverb.

5. **Appositive**—An appositive (which may also be a single noun) describes or restates a noun.
6. **Absolute**—Consisting of a noun, modifiers, and often a participle, the absolute phrase modifies an entire clause.

Clauses

1. **Independent**—An independent clause (main clause) contains a subject and a verb and is not preceded by a subordinating conjunction.
2. **Dependent**—A dependent clause (subordinate clause) contains a subject and a verb and is preceded by a subordinating conjunction or a relative pronoun.
   - **Noun clause**—Noun clauses function as subjects, objects, or complements.
   - **Adjective clause**—Adjective clauses modify nouns or pronouns.
   - **Adverb clause**—Adverb clauses modify verbs, adjectives, or adverbs.

Sentences

Classified by Structure

1. **Simple**—A simple sentence contains one independent clause.
2. **Compound**—A compound sentence contains two independent clauses.
3. **Complex**—A complex sentence contains one independent and one dependent clause.
4. **Compound-complex**—A compound-complex sentence contains at least two independent clauses and at least one dependent clause.

Classified by Purpose

1. **Declarative**—A sentence that makes a statement and ends with a period.
2. **Imperative**—A sentence that expresses a command.
3. **Interrogative**—A sentence that asks a question.
4. **Exclamatory**—A sentence that expresses an emphatic statement and ends with an exclamation mark.

How Parts of Speech Function in a Sentence

Words can function in different ways within a sentence. For example, *fish* can be a noun or a verb. (*Fish are fun to watch. I fish with Cousin Dan at Carpenter Lake.*) Parts of speech may also function in different ways. For example, a noun—such as *fish*—may be the subject of a sentence or the object. (*Fish are fun to watch. I saw a fish.*)

1. **Subject**—The subject of a sentence is a noun (or noun phrase, noun clause, or pronoun). It normally precedes the verb (predicate), and it names who or what the sentence is about.

   The dog barked at Mary.

   Finishing the race was Mark's only goal.

   She drove Gary crazy.

2. **Verb (Predicate)**—The predicate of a sentence (a verb and the words that complete its meaning) usually follows the subject and expresses what the subject does, what it is, or what has been done to it.

   The dog barked at Mary.

   Finishing the race was Mark's only goal.

   She drove Gary crazy.

3. **Objects**—Objects are nouns (or noun phrases, noun clauses, or pronouns). They usually follow the verb and can be direct objects or indirect objects.

   A **direct object** receives the action of the verb. It is what the verb is being done to.

   Joe fed the dog.

   The dog (the direct object) is what is being fed.

   An **indirect object** precedes the direct object and tells to whom or for whom the action of the verb is done and who is receiving the direct object.

   Mary gave Joe the dog food.

   Indirect objects are usually found with verbs of giving or communicating (give, tell, show, take, etc.).

4. **Complements**—Complements are nouns (noun phrases, noun clauses, or pronouns) and adjectives (or adjective phrases) that complete a thought. That is, they complete the sense of a subject, object, or verb.

   A **subject complement** (either noun or adjective) follows a linking verb and renames or defines the subject.

   Mary is the president. (subject complement or predicate noun)

   Larry is tall. (subject complement or predicate adjective)

   Noun complements are also called **predicate nouns**; adjective complements are also called **predicate adjectives**.

An **object complement** (either noun or adjective) follows and modifies or refers to a direct object.

The manager saw the security guard sleeping.

We painted the house red.

Sleeping and *red* complete the idea of the object, *security guard* and *house.*

5. **Adverbials**—Adverbials are adverbs (or adverb phrases or adverb clauses) that refer to or modify the verb. For example,

   We went to the doctor's office. (The phrase *to the doctor's office* modifies where we *went.*)

   The dog barked from midnight until 3:00 a.m. (The phrase *from midnight until 3:00 a.m.* modifies when the dog *barked.*)

   The team cheered maniacally. (*Maniacally* is a word that modifies how the team *cheered.*)

Activity

Identify the parts of speech, particularly subjects and verbs, in the following sentences.

1. As health care professionals, we must regard this crisis with the utmost importance.
2. I like the story because it is put together so well.
3. As a concerned citizen and patient, I have become very alarmed at the growing addiction to prescription drugs in the United States.
4. At the same time, each fearless and self-sacrificing helper shows each victim a human face, stands for respect for that person's dignity, and is a source of hope for peace and reconciliation.
5. The president will address the nation tonight, upon his return to the White House.

How Sentences Work (Expanded)

Words—Parts of Speech

Noun A noun names a person, place, thing, idea, quantity, or condition. Nouns can be proper, common, collective, abstract, or concrete.

Proper nouns name specific people, places, and things. They are always capitalized.

Jane	Zaire
Eatonton, Georgia	the Red Cross
John Kenneth Galbraith	Mexican American
Gutenberg College	English
Star Wars	the Middle East

Common nouns name people, places, and things by general type. They are not capitalized.

woman	nation
town	organization
economist	nationality
college	language
movie	region

Collective nouns name groups of people or things and are treated as singular, not plural.

jury	band
congress	public
committee	

Abstract nouns name ideas, qualities, and conditions.

patriotism	despair
hatred	freedom
love	perfection
integrity	respect
joy	

Concrete nouns name things or qualities that are perceptible by the senses.

reporter	book
ball	hot dog
cricket	flower
letter	bed
check	

Activity

What type of noun (proper, common, collective, abstract, concrete) is each of the following?

hope	London
rainbow	paint
dog	loyalty
choir	Main Street
secret	main street
fence	

(Depending upon the context, some nouns may fit into different categories.)

Pronoun A pronoun takes the place of a noun. Pronouns can be personal, possessive, reflexive, interrogative, demonstrative, indefinite, or relative.

Personal pronouns refer to specific people or things.

	Subject Form		**Object Form**	
	Singular	*Plural*	*Singular*	*Plural*
first person	I	we	me	us
second person	you	you	you	you
third person	he		him	
	she	they	her	them
	it		it	

Possessive pronouns indicate ownership.

	Singular	*Plural*
first person	my, mine	our, ours
second person	your, yours	your, yours
third person	his, his	
	her, hers	their, theirs
	its, its	

Reflexive pronouns show that someone or something is acting for or on itself.

	Singular	*Plural*
first person	myself	ourselves
second person	yourself	yourselves

third person	himself	
	herself	themselves
	itself	

Interrogative pronouns are used to ask questions.

Subject	*Object*	*Other*
who / whoever	whom / whomever	what / which / whose

Demonstrative pronouns point out particular people or things.

Singular	*Plural*
this / that	these / those

Indefinite pronouns serve as general subjects or objects in a sentence.

Singular	*Plural*
another / any* / anybody /	all* / both / few
anyone / anything	
each / either / everybody /	many / several
everyone / everything	
neither / nobody / no one /	some*
nothing / one	
somebody / someone / something	

*Some indefinite pronouns can be either singular or plural: singular if they refer to a unit or quantity and plural if they refer to individuals. For example, "Some of the money **is** gone" (singular); "Some of my friends **are** leaving" (plural).

Relative pronouns connect adjective clauses to nouns or pronouns.

Refer to People	*Refer to Things*	*Refer to People or Things*
who / whom	that / what / whatever	that / whose
whoever / whomever	which / whichever	

Activity

Read through one of your essays and then one of the essays in *The Composition of Everyday Life* and identify as many types of pronouns as you can: personal, possessive, reflexive, interrogative, demonstrative, indefinite, relative.

Verb A verb expresses an action or a state of being. The three types of verbs are *action, linking,* and *auxiliary.* Verbs can take other forms and become *verbals*—words formed from verbs that do not function as verbs. (See Verbals at the end of this section.)

Action verbs express action, either physical or mental. Action verbs are either transitive or intransitive.

Transitive verbs require direct objects to complete their meaning.

Joe sold . . .

subject verb

Joe sold the boat.

The direct object names whom or what is directly acted upon.

Joe finally sold Tom the old sailboat in the backyard.

An indirect object names who or what was indirectly affected by the action of the verb. *Finally* modifies *sold. Old* modifies *sailboat,* as does the prepositional phrase *in the backyard.*

I love . . .

subject verb

I love baseball.

The direct object names whom or what is directly acted upon.

I still love baseball after all these years.

Other words fill out the sentence. *Still* modifies *love,* as does the prepositional phrase *after all these years.*

Intransitive verbs do not require direct objects to complete their meaning.

The ship sank.

Chelsea skipped.

Scott flipped.

Other words—such as modifiers—can be added to the sentences, but as long as no object is required, the verb is considered to be intransitive.

The ship sank off the coast of South America.

Off the coast of South America is two prepositional phrases.

Chelsea, the little girl next door, skipped down the sidewalk.

The little girl next door is an appositive that describes *Chelsea; down the sidewalk* is a prepositional phrase.

Scott flipped. (intransitive)

Scott flipped a pancake. (transitive)

If Scott did a flip, then *flipped* requires no object and is intransitive. But if Scott flipped a pancake, then *flipped* has a direct object, *a pancake,* and the verb is therefore transitive. Thus, the same verb can be intransitive or transitive, depending upon whether an object is required to complete its meaning.

Linking verbs express a state of being or a condition, not an action.

The dialog is quiet, engaging, funny, real. (Ed Bell)

We were a young culture with no parents. (Simon Benlow)

The biggest problem as I see it is that although students are able to graduate from high school (and even some colleges) with minimal effort, those students may find themselves cheated in the long run. (Daniel Bruno)

Common Linking Verbs—Forms of *to be*

is	am	are	was
were	be	being	been

Common Linking Verbs—Other Forms

appear	feel	grow	look	become
make	seem	smell	taste	sound

Auxiliary verbs (also called helping verbs) work with other verbs to create verb tenses or form questions.

My mug is insulated so it delivers hot, delicious, organically shade-grown, fair trade coffee for a couple of hours at a time, and in so doing, helps me directly support the small coffee growers and their cooperatives around the world. (Jim Crockett)

The verb of the main clause consists of two words: *is* (a helping verb) and *insulated* (a past participle).

Modern society has adopted the historically recent perspective that the purpose of education is training for the workplace.

The verb of the main clause consists of two words: *has* (a helping verb) and *adopted* (a past participle).

Activity

Which of the underlined words function as linking verbs and which function as auxiliary verbs?

1. Pittsburgh <u>is</u> the second largest city in Pennsylvania.
2. Rusty <u>is</u> going to call me later this evening.
3. I <u>was</u> reading an interesting article when the phone rang.
4. The Cowlicks <u>are</u> playing at the Dance Hall tonight.
5. They are the best band ever.

Verb Forms Verbs take different forms that can be categorized as infinitive, third-person singular present, past, present participle, and past participle.

Infinitive: The base form of a verb, often used with the word *to,* the infinitive (the form one would look up in the dictionary) indicates action that occurs in the present, occurs habitually, or is generally true.

infinitive	(I, you, we) walk	say, sing, care

Third-person singular present: Frequently ending in *-s* or *-es,* the third-person singular indicates action that occurs in the present, occurs habitually, or is generally true.

third-person singular present	(he, she, it) walks	says, sings, cares

Past: Ending in *-d* or *-ed* (except in irregular verbs), the past tense indicates that something happened before now.

past	(I, she, they) walked	said, sang, cared

Present participle: Ending in *-ing,* the present participle with an auxiliary forms a verb; without an auxiliary verb, it functions as an adjective or a noun.

present participle	(am, was) walking	saying, singing, caring

Past participle: Usually ending in *-d* or *-ed* (except in irregular verbs), the past participle with an auxiliary forms a verb; without an auxiliary, it functions as an adjective.

past participle	(have, has, was) walked	said, sung, cared

Many common English verbs are irregular and form their past tense and participle forms in unpredictable ways. Following is a partial list.

	Infinitive	*Past Tense*	*Past Participle*
Regular Verbs (most verbs in English are regular verbs)	walk	walked	walked
	jump	jumped	jumped
	follow	followed	followed
Irregular Verbs (many verbs in English are irregular verbs)	be	was/were	been
	begin	began	begun
	bite	bit	bitten
	blow	blew	blown
	break	broke	broken
	come	came	come
	cost	cost	cost
	do	did	done
	draw	drew	drawn
	drink	drank	drunk
	drive	drove	driven
	eat	ate	eaten
	fly	flew	flown
	freeze	froze	frozen
	give	gave	given
	go	went	gone
	read	read	read
	ring	rang	rung
	see	saw	seen
	shoot	shot	shot
	spring	sprang	sprung
	swear	swore	sworn
	swim	swam	swum
	take	took	taken

tear	tore	torn
throw	threw	thrown
wear	wore	worn
write	wrote	written

Verb Talk

Action verbs express action, either physical or mental.

Transitive verbs transfer the action from an actor to a direct object.

Intransitive verbs show action that is limited to the subject.

Linking verbs allow the word or words following them to complete the meaning of the subject.

Auxiliary verbs, or **helping verbs,** combine with the base or a participle form of another verb to create tense, mood, and voice (active or passive).

Verbals are formed from verbs and act as adjectives, adverbs, and nouns.

Verb tense indicates when an action or state of being occurs.

Verb mood expresses whether the speaker considers a thing to be a fact, a command, or an unreal or hypothetical condition contrary to fact.

Voice can be active or passive, depending upon whether the grammatical subject is doing the action or is being acted upon.

Verbals Verbals are formed from verbs but do not function as verbs. There are three types: *participles* (verbals that function as modifiers or as part of the verb), *gerunds* (verbals that function as nouns), and *infinitives* (verbals that function as nouns or modifiers). For example, a verb such as *fish* can be used as a participle, gerund, or infinitive.

I fish with Cousin Dan.

Fish is a verb in this sentence. We might have used any other action verb: *swim, work, play, argue, eat,* etc.

Participles look like verbs and are formed from verbs but cannot function as verbs in a sentence. Participles can be present or past (present participles end in *-ing,* and past participles end in *-ed* or an irregular past tense form). Participles are used (1) in participial phrases that modify other sentence parts, (2) as modifying words, or (3) with a helping word or words to create a verb.

Participial phrase

Fishing with Cousin Dan, I lost my wallet.

While fishing with Cousin Dan, I lost my wallet.

I lost my wallet fishing with Cousin Dan.

Participle as modifier

Cousin Dan is my fishing guru.

I am Cousin Dan's favorite fishing partner.

Cousin Dan and I both enjoy the fishing life.

Participle as part of a verb

I go fishing with Cousin Dan.

I am fishing with Cousin Dan.

I have never been fishing with Cousin Dan.

Gerunds are verbals that act as nouns.

Fishing is fun.

No one likes fishing like I do.

You can watch TV shows about cooking, painting, hunting, and fishing.

Infinitives, like gerunds, can act as nouns.

To fish is fun.

No one likes to fish like I do.

Activity

In the following sentences, how does each of the underlined verbals function: participial phrase, participle as modifier, participle as part of a verb, gerund, or infinitive?

1. Everyone had a <u>jumping</u> good time at the shindig last night.
2. <u>Jumping</u> on a trampoline isn't much fun for me now.
3. <u>To jump</u> out of second-story window is frightening.
4. Everybody was <u>jumping</u> around and singing.
5. While <u>jumping</u> over the moon, the cow saw a laughing dog.

Verb Tense

Tense indicates time. Verbs have three simple tenses (present, past, and future) along with three perfect tenses (present perfect, past perfect, and future perfect) and six progressive tenses, one corresponding to each simple and perfect tense.

present	I dance. She sings.
past	I danced. She sang.
future	I will dance. She will sing.
present perfect	I have danced. She has sung.
past perfect	I had danced. She had sung.
future perfect	I will have danced. She will have sung.
present progressive	I am dancing. She is singing.
past progressive	I was dancing. She was singing.
future progressive	I will be dancing. She will be singing.
present perfect progressive	I have been dancing. She has been singing.
past perfect progressive	I had been dancing. She had been singing.
future perfect progressive	I will have been dancing. She will have been singing.

Tenses are indicated by the form of the main verb (*dance* and *sing* in the preceding examples) and the auxiliary verbs. Notice that *dance* is a regular verb: *dance, danced, danced.* And *sing* is an irregular verb: *sing, sang, sung.*

Verb Mood *Mood* reflects a writer's attitude toward a statement.

Indicative mood expresses a declarative statement or question.

Daffodils are a sign of spring.

Students make clear distinctions between different writing situations.

Imperative mood expresses a command or a direct request.

Vote.

Help yourself to another burger.

Invent your way to an insightful thesis.

Subjunctive mood expresses a conditional situation, a hypothetical, a wish, or some statement contrary to fact.

If I were the president, I would make some changes around here.

I wish I were the president.

Name the verb mood in the following sentences:

1. Workers of the world, unite!
2. My parents built a house in the country.
3. Everyone should sit down.
4. If I were you, I'd take the train instead.
5. Remember to set your clocks one hour ahead tonight.

Adjective An adjective modifies a noun or pronoun. The three articles—*a, an,* and *the*—mark, or precede, certain nouns and therefore function as a special type of adjective. An adjective answers one of the following questions:

What kind?	How many?
Which one?	Whose?

Adjectives modifying nouns

red balloon	Orwellian partyspeak
big river	skulking rhetoric
little women	bright, doomed city
recent layoffs	endless, obsessive preoccupation
practical goal	pure elation
blatant manipulation	everyday lives
amusing instance	simple euphemism

Adverb An adverb modifies a verb, adjective, or adverb. Adverbs frequently end in *-ly* and answer the following questions:

How?	How often?
When?	To what extent?
Where?	

Adverbs modifying verbs

clearly said	reluctantly explained
jump quickly	suddenly stopped
constantly sang	replied sheepishly
will happily move	land smoothly
willingly applauded	dropped instantly

Interjection

An interjection expresses surprise or strong emotion.

Hey!	Eek!
Oh!	Yikes!
Okay!	Ugh.
Wow!	Duh.

Good and Well

In casual, everyday speech, people often use the adjective good instead of the adverb well. For example:

> "I did good at bowling last night." OR "I bowled good."

Or, if asked, "How did you bowl?" someone might respond,

> "I did good."

Or someone might just say,

> "Good."

Yet *good* is an adjective, and *well* is an adverb; adjectives modify nouns and pronouns while adverbs modify verbs, adjectives, and adverbs.

1. Do you consider *good* to be incorrect in the preceding sentences? Why or why not?
2. Why should, or shouldn't, you avoid using *good* as an adverb?
3. Interview several classmates and others outside of class to get their views on using *good* and *well* correctly.
4. Consider the following sentences. Would you say *good* or *well,* and why?
   Lisa does ______ at whatever she does.
   She hasn't felt ______ about New England since she left.
   Lorenzo is ______ at playing the spoons.
   Diamonds don't look ______ in that ring.
   I don't feel ______.
5. *Bad* and *badly* pose a similar problem. Which word would you use in the sentences below, and why?
   Martha golfed ______.
   I have never done so ______ on a math test.
   The ______ thing about it is the grinding sound.
   Dan is ______ at being on time.
   I feel ______ when it rains.

Conjunction A conjunction connects words, phrases, and clauses and shows a relationship. Conjunctions may be coordinating, subordinating, or correlative.

Coordinating conjunctions link sentence parts of equal grammatical rank. There are only seven coordinating conjunctions:

I went, and she stayed.

She and I went to dinner and a movie.

We went to a movie but not to dinner.

and, or, nor, for, yet, but, so

Subordinating conjunctions link clauses, making one clause dependent on, or subordinate to, the other. Many words act as subordinating conjunctions.

Because I went, she stayed.

I went although she stayed.

Even though I went and she stayed, we still had fun.

after	however	that
although	if	though
as	in case	till
as if	in order that	unless
as far as	in that	until
as soon as	no matter how	when
as though	now that	whenever
because	once	where
before	since	wherever
even if	so that	whether
even though	supposing that	while
how	than	why

Correlative conjunctions work in pairs to link sentence parts.

Whether it rains or not, I am washing my pickup truck tomorrow.

I could go for either a bath or a shower right now.

both . . . and	either . . . or	whether . . . or
neither . . . nor	not only . . . but also	

Preposition A preposition placed before a noun and its modifiers creates a prepositional phrase. Prepositional phrases function as either adverbs or adjectives.

> Paul left his umbrella by the door.
>
> The woman at the counter said the bus leaves at noon.
>
> Who said the majority of customers in the carryout were buying emergency supplies?

Common one-word prepositions

about
above
across
after
against
along
among
around
at
before
behind
below
beneath
beside
besides
between
beyond
but
by
concerning
despite
down
during
except
for
from
in
inside
into
like
near
of
off
on
onto
out
outside
over
past
since
through
throughout
till
to
toward
under
underneath
until
up
upon
with
within
without

Common multiple-word prepositions

according to
ahead of
along with
apart from
as for
as to
as well as
because of
by way of
due to
except for
in addition to
in case of
in front of
in spite of
inside of
instead of
on account of
out of
up to
with regard to
with respect to
with the exception of

Activity

Some words can function as conjunctions or prepositions. Identify the underlined word as either a subordinating conjunction or a preposition:

1. Nobody can leave <u>until</u> you tell us a story.
2. Larry drove Raquel home <u>after</u> the Raspberry Festival.
3. Ace has to be home <u>before</u> midnight or he can't go out tomorrow.
4. I haven't seen Mike <u>since</u> he moved to Alabama.

Phrases

A phrase is a group of related words without a subject and a verb. Phrases can be categorized as prepositional, participial, gerund, infinitive, appositive, or absolute.

Prepositional: Consisting of a preposition, modifiers, and a noun, the prepositional phrase functions most often as an adjective or adverb.

> Barney chased a rabbit <u>under the porch</u>.
>
> The top executives met <u>in the conference room for about two hours</u>.

Participial: Consisting of a participle, modifiers, and a noun, the participial phrase functions as an adjective.

> <u>Running after the rabbit,</u> Barney disappeared under the porch.
>
> <u>While meeting in the conference room,</u> the executives voted to study the issue further.

Gerund: Consisting of a gerund, modifiers, and a noun, the gerund phrase functions as a noun.

> <u>Running after a rabbit</u> is hard work for a small dog.
>
> <u>Meeting in the conference room</u> is convenient for everyone except Mary.

Infinitive: Consisting of an infinitive, modifiers, and a noun, the infinitive phrase functions as a noun, adjective, or adverb.

> <u>To run after a rabbit all day</u> is good exercise.
>
> The most convenient place <u>to meet the new employee</u> is the conference room.

Appositive: An appositive (which may also be a single noun) describes or restates a noun.

> Barney, <u>a short-haired terrier,</u> chased a wild rabbit under the porch.
>
> Mary, <u>the only executive with an office across the street,</u> didn't mind meeting in the conference room.

Absolute: Consisting of a noun, modifiers, and often a participle, the absolute phrase modifies an entire clause.

> The rabbit hiding under the porch, Barney barked frantically at the stairs.
>
> Mary arrived at the meeting late, her office being across town.

Activity

Identify each of the underlined phrases: prepositional, participial, gerund, infinitive, appositive, or absolute:

1. Coming around the bend, Jackie saw a moose.
2. The city council voted to close the school at the end of the year.
3. The fiddle contest, a big event in these parts, has been cancelled.
4. His bike with a flat tire, Bill decided to walk instead.
5. For some people, going with the flow isn't all that easy.
6. To call Doug fantastic is an understatement.

Clauses

A clause is a group of words with a subject and a verb (or predicate). The two types of clauses are *independent* (or main) and *dependent* (or subordinate).

Independent: An independent (main) clause contains a subject and a verb not preceded by a subordinating conjunction.

> Joe passed his math test.
>
> Independent clause: subject (*Joe*) + verb (*passed*)
>
> Gutenberg College is a great books college. (David Crabtree)
>
> Independent clause: subject (*Gutenberg College*) + verb (*is*)

Dependent: A dependent (subordinate) clause contains a subject and a verb and is preceded by a subordinating conjunction or a relative pronoun. Some dependent clauses function as nouns, adjectives, or adverbs.

> Because Joe passed his math test, he ordered a pizza with all the toppings.
>
> Dependent clause: subordinating conjunction (*because*) + subject (*Joe*) + verb (passed)
> Independent clause: subject (*he*) + verb (*ordered*)
>
> As soon as he had the paper, he thumbed through it, looking for jobs he could feasibly apply to.

Dependent clause: subordinating conjunction (*As soon as*) + subject (*he*) + verb (*had*) Independent clause: subject (*he*) + verb (*thumbed*)

Anyone who sends a text message while driving is not responsible enough to operate a motor vehicle.

The relative clause *who sends a text message while driving* modifies the noun *anyone.* A relative clause modifies the noun that comes before it. Other relative pronouns include *that* and *which.* Relative pronouns are followed either by a subject and a verb or just a verb. In this example, the relative pronoun *who* is followed by the verb *sends.*

Examples of relative clauses

the lion that roared at Dorothy . . .

the band that the club owner hired . . .

the woman who won the marathon . . .

the team that wins the championship . . .

the boy who finds the egg . . .

Activity

Identify the underlined clauses as either dependent or independent. Which, if any, is a relative clause?

1. Jane was going to the acupuncturist <u>when she heard the news</u>.
2. After his first semester, <u>Tim decided to get organized</u>.
3. We missed our turn <u>even though the road sign was large and in plain view.</u>
4. When he got back from the seminar, <u>Gary was, somehow, full of misinformation.</u>
5. The house <u>that has been empty for two years</u> is now for sale.

Sentences—Classified by Structure

Simple: A simple sentence contains one independent clause.

Bobby played the banjo on the back step.

Independent clause: subject (*Bobby*) + verb (*played*)

My daughter doesn't ask for $72 pants from the Gap or $58 shirts from Abercrombie & Fitch.

Independent clause: subject (*daughter*) + verb (*doesn't ask*)

Compound: A compound sentence contains two independent clauses.

Bobby played the banjo on the back step; he made a musical dent in the night.

Independent clause: subject (*Bobby*) + verb (*played*)
Independent clause: subject (*he*) + verb (*made*)
The independent clauses are connected with a semicolon.

The road was slippery, but the car had good tires.

Independent clause: subject (*road*) + verb (*was*)
Independent clause: subject (*car*) + verb (*had*)
The coordinating conjunction that connects the two clauses is *but*.

Complex: A complex sentence contains one independent and one dependent clause.

When Bobby played the banjo on the back step, he made a musical dent in the night.

Dependent clause: subordinating conjunction (*when*) + subject (*Bobby*) + verb (*played*)
Independent clause: subject (*he*) + verb (*made*)

If you feed the ducks, they will follow you home.

Dependent clause: subordinating conjunction (*If*) + subject (*you*) + verb (*feed*)
Independent clause: subject (*they*) + verb (*will follow*)

Compound-complex: A compound-complex sentence contains at least two independent clauses and at least one dependent clause.

When Bobby played the banjo on the back step, he made a musical dent in the night, and the neighbors complained.

Dependent clause: subordinating conjunction (*when*) + subject (*Bobby*) + verb (*played*)
Independent clause: subject (*he*) + verb (*made*)
Independent clause: subject (*neighbors*) + verb (*complained*)

Swimming is good exercise, and if you need to think about an essay, you can do it in the pool.

Independent clause: subject (*swimming*) + verb (*is*)
Dependent clause: subordinating conjunction (*if*) + subject (*you*) + verb (*need*)
Independent clause: subject (*you*) + verb (*can*)

Sentences—Classified by Purpose

Declarative: A sentence that makes a statement and ends with a period.

We cooked hamburgers on the grill last night.

After they painted the trim on the old house green, it looked a million times better.

Birds are chirping.

Imperative: A sentence that expresses a command.

Lift up your feet so that I can vacuum under the chair.

Turn left at the intersection and look for the donut shop.

Stop talking.

Interrogative: A sentence that asks a question.

Who is the first person to have made a snow angel?

How many times do you have to invite Janice to dinner before she accepts your invitation?

Where are my shoes?

Exclamatory: A sentence that expresses an emphatic statement and ends with an exclamation mark.

If we are going to win the election, we must unite!

How about that soup!

Look out!

Activity

Identify each of the following sentences as declarative, imperative, interrogative, or exclamatory:

1. Imagine all the possibilities.
2. The best solutions are often dismissed without serious consideration.
3. Why do we accept these bad ideas?
4. It's time for a change!

Nine Ways of Combining Simple Sentences (Independent Clauses)

Combining sentences helps readers see the relationship between ideas. For example, "I went. She stayed." can mean "I went because she stayed" or "I went although she stayed." Combining the sentences with a subordinating conjunction clarifies the relationship. The strategies in this section can be helpful for combining sentences and for eliminating fused sentences and comma splices. For example, the comma splice "I went, she stayed." can be rewritten using strategies 1, 2, 3, 4, 5, or 6.

1. Subject + verb. Subject + verb. (two simple sentences)

Mary was relaxing in the meadow. Mary saw a dragonfly.

Larry had never flown a plane before. He landed the 747 safely.

A nickel isn't worth much anymore. George gave Susie a dime.

2. Subject + verb; subject + verb. (one compound sentence)

Mary was relaxing in the meadow; Mary saw a dragonfly.

Larry had never flown a plane before; he landed the 747 safely.

A nickel isn't worth much anymore; George gave Susie a dime.

3. Subject + verb, coordinating conjunction + subject + verb. (one compound sentence)

Mary was relaxing in the meadow, and she saw a dragonfly.

Larry had never flown a plane before, yet he landed the 747 safely.

A nickel isn't worth much anymore, so George gave Susie a dime.

4. Subject + verb; conjunctive adverb, subject + verb. (one compound sentence)

Mary was relaxing in the meadow; therefore, she saw a dragonfly.

Larry had never flown a plane before; nevertheless, he landed the 747 safely.

A nickel isn't worth much anymore; hence, George gave Susie a dime.

5. Subject + verb + subordinating conjunction + subject + verb. (one complex sentence)

Mary was relaxing in the meadow when she saw a dragonfly.

Larry had never flown a plane before until he landed the 747 safely.

A nickel isn't worth much anymore though George gave Susie a dime.

6. Subordinating conjunction subject + verb, subject + verb. (one complex sentence)

Because Mary was relaxing in the meadow, she saw a dragonfly.

Although Larry had never flown a plane before, he landed the 747 safely.

Now that a nickel isn't worth much anymore, George gave Susie a dime.

7. Subject + relative clause (relative pronoun + verb) + verb. (one complex sentence)

Mary, who was relaxing in the meadow, saw a dragonfly.

Larry, who had never flown a plane before, landed the 747 safely.

A nickel isn't worth much anymore. George gave Susie a dime. [A relative clause will not work.]

8. Subject + verb + verb. (one simple sentence)

Mary was relaxing in the meadow and saw a dragonfly.

Larry had never flown a plane before but landed the 747 safely.

A nickel isn't worth much anymore. George gave Susie a dime. [A compound verb will not work.]

9. Phrase, subject + verb. (one simple sentence)

Relaxing in the meadow, Mary saw a dragonfly.

Never having flown a plane before, Larry landed the 747 safely.

A nickel not being worth much anymore, George gave Susie a dime.

Activity

Combine the following simple sentences in each of the nine ways:

Samantha and Steve went to the Kentucky Derby. They'd never been to a horse race before.

Word Choice

Mark Twain wrote, "The difference between the almost right word & the right word is really a large matter—it's the difference between the lightning bug and the lightning." Choosing the right word begins with understanding language as something that is shared. For example, people generally agree on what a cat is, and on what to call it. Thus, the word *cat* accurately expresses the idea *cat,* which corresponds to the material reality of a cat. This simple example illustrates how we share language. What I call a cat, you, too, call a cat. And we not only share the word *cat*—we also share the concept *cat.* Other, more abstract concepts—such as *patriotism, honesty, love, service,* and so on—can vary more in meaning from one person to another. As humans, we share not only words but categories of thoughts. When we refer to a category of thought (*cat, family, responsibility, success, intimacy*), we choose a word that will accurately express our thought to others and allow us to be heard.

When choosing words, writers consider the following:

- Am I using this word in the way that it is usually understood?
- If I am using this word in an unusual sense, will my reader understand it? Should I define the word and/or illustrate it with an example?
- Could I replace this word with one that more accurately expresses my meaning?
- Have I used unusual words in an attempt to impress my readers with my vocabulary? If so, should I replace these words with plain, straightforward language?
- Am I comfortable with my word choice? How does it make me sound?

A writer's word choice might be accurate but still not appropriate. For example, words might be too casual or too formal for a particular writing situation; they might be gender-biased, overly technical, insensitive, or archaic. Writers determine whether or not words are appropriate by sizing up each writing situation and considering how their word choice might influence readers.

Level of Formality Formality in word choice varies depending upon the writing situation. An e-mail to a friend might be casual, a scientific report formal. And the level of formality can vary from essay to essay. Slang (informal words common in speech and restricted to particular audiences and situations) can be used effectively in an essay, but used indiscriminately slang can suggest a lack of serious thought or sensitivity for readers. Archaic (old and outdated) language, which some writers use to sound more formal or learned, often strikes modern readers as odd or insincere and should be used cautiously if at all. Flowery writing (characterized by elaborate word choice and phrases) can sometimes be effective, but it often draws attention to itself instead of to the ideas being expressed. This type of writing can make for slow and difficult reading.

Gender Bias Writers must be aware of the consequences of gender-biased language. A job ad that states, "The candidate must own his own tools" appears to be excluding female candidates. Thus, third-person singular pronouns such as *he, she, he/she, s/he,* and so on should be chosen carefully. Words once common, such as *congressman, policeman,* and *chairman,* have been replaced with gender-neutral terms, such as *representative, police officer,* and *chair.* Nurses are not assumed to be women, and CEOs are not assumed to be men. Showing awareness and sensitivity through one's choice of words invites readers to listen. Showing insensitivity gives readers a reason for tuning out.

Jargon The technical language of a field (jargon) must be used carefully with an audience that is not expert in that field. Experts use jargon to talk shop, but because nonexperts do not share the same language, jargon must be defined or replaced with more common terms. Good writers explain complex ideas in plain language so that readers don't become frustrated or suspicious of all the technical vocabulary. Using technical jargon is a matter of audience awareness. Will your audience understand the jargon or not?

General and Specific Language When choosing the exact right word, writers must decide upon the appropriate level of abstraction. Some words are specific, or concrete, whereas other words are general, or abstract. Abstract words express general qualities but do not provide specific detail about those qualities. More specific words eliminate possibilities of meaning. For example, *farm animals* (a general term) includes cows, pigs, mules, goats, sheep, ducks, chickens, and geese. But *fowl* (which is more specific) eliminates cows, pigs, mules, goats, and sheep. *Fowl* can mean ducks, chickens, or geese. *Rooster* (which is even more specific) eliminates ducks and geese. And *Jim,* our rooster, is even more specific. He is one particular rooster. And we can refer to *Jim* either generally over the course of his life or even more specifically, such as "Jim when he was a chick," "Jim the day we got him," or "Jim the day he died."

Levels of Abstraction

life	*general* ↑	transportation	*general* ↑
animal life		public transportation	
farm animals		bus	
fowl		school bus	
rooster		bus #8	
Jim, our rooster	↓ *specific*	bus #8, yesterday	↓ *specific*

When we refer to examples, statistics, or colors, we are being specific. But specifics are not always desirable; readers can get bogged down in too much detail or sidetracked by irrelevant detail. Although a more specific word choice can be more accurate, at times it is better to speak more generally. Writers keep in mind two tips about levels of abstraction:

- Move back and forth between general and specific information.
- Consider replacing general language with more specific language.

Notice how the following excerpt from Rebecca Hollingsworth's "An Imperfect Reality" provides readers with an appropriate balance of general and specific information.

> The 2006 autism awareness campaign sponsored by Autism Speaks challenges common notions of the "perfect kid" by revealing how the reality of autism crushes unrealistic ideals of young American girls and boys. The campaign features a series

> of television, radio, online, magazine, and billboard advertisements that emphasize the prevalence of the disorder. The campaign's magazine ads show kids doing "kid things"—that is, playing dress-up for girls and playing sports for boys. In one ad (see below), a young girl adorns herself with brightly colored clothes and jewelry as proud mom looks on.

This paragraph begins with a general statement and then provides more specific information about the campaign. The next paragraph gets even more specific:

> The girl wears a cropped, short-sleeved, light pink jacket unzipped to reveal a billowing fuchsia-and-black striped tie and matching fuchsia beaded necklace. She commands the attention of the mother and of us; she stands in a fashionable pose with one leg slightly bent as she looks down to tie a light pink belt around her waist. [. . .]

For more on specific nouns and verbs, refer to the discussion on pages 592–593. [reference is to "Getting Specific" section in Chapter 19]

Activities

1. Read through some of your own writing and identify words that may be inaccurate. How might a different word choice allow readers a better chance of understanding what you meant?
2. Read through some of your own writing and identify words that may be accurate yet inappropriate. Explain why the word choice might be inappropriate and how a different word choice might be better.
3. Take one paragraph from your own writing and rewrite it two ways: (1) using more formal language, and (2) using less formal language. Do not make your changes too drastic—instead, experiment with fine adjustments in your writer's voice.
4. Find three paragraphs in this book that include both general and specific information. How many levels of abstraction can you identify? How does the writer move from one level to another?
5. Study one essay in this book to see how it presents general and abstract information. Describe how the writer moves back and forth throughout the essay from general to specific.

Complete Sentences

In written English, sentences generally contain at least one **independent clause** (a group of related words with a subject and verb). Consider the following sentences and their independent clauses:

> The pH of the tomato juice was 4.1. (subject: pH; verb: was)
>
> The hecklers interrupted the president's speech. (subject: hecklers; verb: interrupted)
>
> Even though we arrived late, we sat in the front row. (subject: we; verb: sat)

Each sentence has one independent clause, and the third sentence also has a dependent clause, *even though we arrived late* (subject: we; verb: arrived). A complete sentence can have several independent and dependent clauses. Now consider the following sentence basics:

- A group of words without an independent clause is a **sentence fragment.**
- A group of words made up of two independent clauses not connected by either a coordinating conjunction (*and, or, nor, for, yet, but, so*) or a semicolon is a **run-on sentence.**
- There are two kinds of run-on sentences: a **fused sentence** and a **comma splice.**

Sentence Fragments and Run-On Sentences

Sentence Fragments

A sentence fragment, because it contains no independent clause, can be a single word, a phrase, a dependent clause, or any combination of the three *without an independent clause.* Writers sometimes use fragments purposely for effect. Such as here. This strategy is acceptable and can be effective if used sparingly, although fragments should not creep into one's writing by accident.

Phrases are not complete sentences.

Falling off his horse and getting right back on it.

The neighbor's new Siamese kitten, Lorenzo.

Dependent clauses are not complete sentences.

When Joe passed his algebra test.

As long as you and Susie are going to the game.

Combinations of phrases and dependent clauses are not complete sentences.

Running to catch the bus so I won't be late for class.

George Washington who was the first president of the United States and general of the Continental Army.

Run-On Sentences

In a run-on sentence, two independent clauses are "run together" either with a comma (a comma splice) or with no punctuation at all (a fused sentence).

Comma splice

I went home, she stayed at the party.

I am tired of reading, I am going to bed now.

Joe flew the 767, he had never landed a plane before.

There is a mouse in the closet, we need a better mousetrap.

Fused sentence

I went home she stayed at the party.

I am tired of reading I am going to bed now.

Joe flew the 767 he had never landed a plane before.

There is a mouse in the closet we need a better mousetrap.

How to Identify Sentence Fragments and Run-On Sentences

To identify sentence fragments and run-on sentences, you must take a grammatical approach. Nongrammatical approaches can be unhelpful. For example, fragments are not just incomplete thoughts. All sentences are somewhat incomplete when it comes to meaning. *He was there* doesn't say who he is or where he is. Thus, its meaning is not complete, even though it is a grammatically complete sentence because it contains an independent clause. Run-on sentences are not just long sentences or sentences with a lot of ideas in them. *I went she stayed* is a run-on sentence even though it is short and contains only a couple of ideas. And a much longer sentence—even 100 words—can be a complete sentence, not a run-on. And comma splices are not just the misuse of a comma. *I, went, and, she, stayed* is not a comma splice even though commas are misused in the sentence. Feeling like a sentence might be a fragment or run-on is a starting place, but to be certain, you must take the following grammatical approach to the problem:

1. Identify the independent clauses in your sentence.

- If there are no independent clauses, the sentence is a fragment.
- If there is only one independent clause, the sentence is a complete sentence.
- If there are two or more independent clauses, go to step 2.

2. If you found two or more independent clauses, how are they connected?
   - If with a coordinating conjunction *(and, or, nor, for, yet, but, so),* you have a complete sentence.
   - If with a semicolon, you have a complete sentence.
   - If with a comma, you have a comma splice.
   - If with no punctuation, you have a fused sentence.
3. If you have a fragment, comma splice, or a fused sentence, you may revise your sentence in several ways.

Activity

Which of the following are sentence fragments? Which are run-on sentences?

1. Even when the radio is turned up loud.
2. Fall is in the air, it feels like marching bands and football.
3. Miles Davis was a trumpeter, his magnum opus is *Kind of Blue.*
4. As darkness fell and the temperature dropped, making us wonder whether or not we should have worn heavier jackets.
5. The day after the game when everybody was still talking about the upset.

How to Revise Fragments

Writers sometimes use fragments to achieve a desired effect. But fragments should not occur by accident. Most sentence fragments should be identified and revised to read as complete sentences. This can be done in various ways. The writer can either (1) attach the fragment to an independent clause, (2) add an independent clause to the fragment, or (3) restructure the sentence to create an independent clause.

Revising fragments that are phrases

(A **phrase** is a group of related words without a subject and a verb.)

Falling off his horse and getting right back on it.

a fragment because it is a phrase and has no independent clause

Joe fell off his horse and got right back on it.

a complete sentence because an independent clause—*Joe* (subject) *fell* and *got* (verb)—has been added

Falling off his horse and getting right back on it, Joe joined the posse and captured the bandits.

a complete sentence because the phrase has been connected to an independent clause—*Joe* (subject) *joined* and *captured* (verb)

Revising fragments that are dependent clauses

(A **dependent clause** is a clause preceded by a subordinating conjunction.)

> When Joe passed his algebra test.
>
> a fragment because it is a dependent clause and has no independent clause
>
> Joe passed his algebra test.
>
> a complete sentence because the subordinating conjunction—*when*—has been eliminated, thus creating an independent clause
>
> When Joe passed his algebra test, he let out a sigh of relief.
>
> a complete sentence because the dependent clause has been attached to an independent clause

How to Revise Run-On Sentences

Run-on sentences, either fused sentences or comma splices, are frowned upon in academic and professional writing. Although fragments are sometimes used intentionally for effect, run-on sentences are rarely (almost never) used this way. Writers fix run-on sentences by making certain that two independent clauses in the same sentence are connected in one of two ways, with either a semicolon (;) or a coordinating conjunction *(and, or, nor, for, yet, but, so)*.

> Comma splice: I went home, she stayed at the party.
>
> Fused sentence: I went home she stayed at the party.
>
> Complete sentence: I went home; she stayed at the party.
>
> Complete sentence: I went home, and she stayed at the party.

A run-on sentence can be corrected in other ways. For example, one of the clauses can be made dependent by adding a subordinating conjunction. Or, the two independent clauses can be made separate sentences:

> Complete sentence: Because I went home, she stayed at the party.
>
> Two sentences: I went home. She stayed at the party.

For more information about how to combine independent clauses, see pages 749–751.

Agreement

Agreement refers to the grammatical relationship between words, such as a subject and a verb or a pronoun and its antecedent. For example, a writer will decide to write in a particular tense—such as past or present—and then stick to that tense until there is a good reason to change. Unnecessary shifts in tense, or other faulty agreement, can be confusing and distracting.

Verb Tense Agreement

A piece of writing has one controlling tense, such as past, present, future. However, verb tense may shift to indicate a change in time:

> Liz **left** the football game early and **went** to a movie. She **is** not a big fan of the game. I **doubt** that she **will** ever **enjoy** football.

The first sentence uses past-tense verbs (*left* and *went*). But the follow-up sentence is written in present tense because Liz still *is* not a fan of the game. The third sentence uses a present tense verb (*doubt*) and a future tense verb (*will enjoy*). These shifts in tense accurately express the time relationship among several ideas; thus, there is a good reason to change tense. Some shifts, however, are less purposeful, distracting, and confusing. Unnecessary tense shifts sometimes occur during narration when the writer shifts unexpectedly from past to present tense:

> When I first **got** off the plane in Belgrade, I **noticed** how cool and crisp the air felt. I **see** the mountains in the distance and **want** to drive out to them and begin climbing.

The verb *see* in the second sentence marks an unnecessary shift from past tense to present. Because the verb tense is not consistent and because the change does not express an actual change in time, the shift is likely to distract readers.

Pronoun/Antecedent Agreement

Pronouns take the place of nouns; the nouns they replace (or refer back to) are called their antecedents. For example, in the following sentence, *her* takes the place of *the little girl*—that is, it allows the writer to not repeat *the little girl.* Because *girl* is (1) singular, (2) feminine, and (3) in the third person, so is the pronoun that replaces it.

> The little **girl** enjoyed **her** ride on the giant Ferris wheel.

↑ antecedent ↑ pronoun

Pronoun/antecedent agreement can be tricky in sentences more complex than the previous one. When several sentences work together to form a paragraph or several paragraphs, more vigilance is required to make sure pronouns and antecedents agree. In the following example, Daniel Bruno consistently uses the third-person plural pronouns *them/they* because the passage begins with the plural noun *students:*

> Students would do well to look around **them,** at the room full of fellow classmates. **They** should imagine that many of those students will be graduating one day. And **they** should imagine the students in the classroom next door and across the hall and in all the other buildings on campus. **They** will be graduating, too.

Third-person singular Pronouns and antecedents require special attention when it comes to the third-person singular (*he, she, it*). In the following example, the writer uses the feminine pronoun *she* to refer to both men and women.

> The injustice, then, has been done to the students (as Sacks says, the students are the victims). **While the student** has happily skipped (or unhappily slogged) along through sixteen years of formal education, **she** is allowed, if **she** wants, to come away with very little in terms of education. **She** is allowed, unfortunately, to escape practically unscathed by learning.

The use of a feminine pronoun to refer to both men and women might be considered unusual here. In the past, the masculine pronoun (*he, him, his*) was commonly used to refer to both men and women:

> While the student has happily skipped (or unhappily slogged) along through sixteen years of formal education, **he** is allowed, if **he** wants, to come away with very little in terms of education.

Writers sometimes use some form of *he/she, she/he,* or *he and she* to agree with a singular third-person antecedent:

> While the student has happily skipped (or unhappily slogged) along through sixteen years of formal education, **he or she** is allowed, if **he or she** wants, to come away with very little in terms of education.
>
> This approach can be effective as long as the text does not get bogged down in *he/she, she/he,* or *he and she.* Third-person singular situations provide writers with a difficult decision: to use just *he,* just *she,* a form of *he/she,* or to change the antecedent to plural, which is often the best option.

Writers can also avoid the pronoun/antecedent agreement problem by changing singular antecedents (such as *student*) to the plural (*students*) and using *they* as the pronoun:

> While students have happily skipped (or unhappily slogged) along through sixteen years of formal education, **they** are allowed, if **they** want, to come away with very little in terms of education.

Pronoun Consistency

Pronouns that refer to the same idea should be consistent in person. For example, the following passage shifts not only from past to present tense, but also from a first to a second-person pronoun—from *I* to *you.* An unnecessary shift in person may distract or confuse the reader.

> When **I** first got off the plane in Belgrade, **I** noticed how cool and crisp the air felt. **You** see the mountains in the distance and want to drive out to them and begin climbing.

Pronouns can be first, second, or third person. First-person pronouns refer to the person speaking (*I, me, mine; we, our, ours*); second-person pronouns refer to the person being spoken to (*you, your, yours*); and third-person pronouns refer to the person or thing being spoken about (*he, him, his; she, her, hers; it, its; they, them, theirs*). In the preceding example, the writer refers to himself in the first person (*I*), then shifts unnecessarily to the second person (*you*). The following passage is consistent in tense (past) and person (first).

> When **I** first **got** off the plane in Belgrade, **I noticed** how cool and crisp the air felt. **I saw** the mountains in the distance and **wanted** to drive out to them and begin climbing.

Subject/Verb Agreement

In addition to indicating tense (past, present, future), verbs indicate number—they can be singular or plural. Nouns, too, indicate number (*dog* is singular; *dogs* is plural). Singular nouns take singular verbs and plural nouns take plural verbs.

> My **sister takes** the train to work.
>
> My **sisters take** the train to work.

A singular noun (*sister*) with a plural verb (*take*) conveys the same meaning as when the subject and verb agree. But in academic and professional written English, subjects and verbs agree in number.

Other Subject/Verb Agreement Issues

Phrases or clauses that act as subjects take singular verbs.

> Having a kennel full of hungry puppies and no dog food is Marcia's biggest fear.

In academic and professional written English, collective nouns take singular verbs.

> The government is taxing the citizens more now than in previous years.

(Other collective nouns to look for include *team, class, congress, orchestra,* and *administration.*)

Compound subjects joined by *and* take a plural verb; some other compound subjects take plural or singular verbs, depending upon the meaning.

> Bob and Sue share a common interest in painting. (*Share* is plural—two people share.)
>
> Bob shares a common interest with Sue. (*Shares* is singular—one person shares.)

Either Bob or Sue shares a common interest with Sally. (*Shares* is singular—one or the other shares.)

Neither Bob nor Sue shares a common interest with Sally. (*Shares* is singular—not one or the other shares.)

Indefinite pronouns, such as everyone, everybody, all, and anybody, usually take a singular verb and singular pronoun.

Everyone in our family goes to the annual ice cream social at the volunteer fire department. (The verb *goes* is singular and agrees with the singular subject *everyone.*)

Activities

1. Write a paragraph that changes verb tense to indicate different times. What is the controlling tense of your paragraph? Did you use any tenses besides simple past, present, and future? That is, did you use a perfect or progressive tense?
2. Write a paragraph with a controlling tense. Then try to distract and confuse readers by shifting verb tenses unnecessarily.
3. Before turning in your next essay, check your pronoun/antecedent agreement. First, circle every *they, their,* and *them.* Then identify the word to which the pronoun refers (draw a line from the circled word to the word it replaces). Because *they, their,* and *them* are plural, the antecedent must also be plural. If it is not, revise the sentence accordingly.

Parallelism

Parallelism means using the same grammatical form (noun, verb, participial phrase, etc.) to help indicate that ideas are related. Like agreement, parallelism contributes to a piece of writing's coherence, or how it flows. In the following, the first sentence is parallel; the second is not:

Herbert **ate** a big dinner, **sat down** in his favorite chair, and **put on** his slippers.

We see that Herbert did three things. Each is expressed by the same grammatical form—a verb phrase.

Herbert **ate** a big dinner, **sat down** in his favorite chair, and **putting on** his slippers.

Here, the third thing, *putting on his slippers,* is expressed in a different grammatical form—a participial phrase instead of a verb.

Coordinating Conjunctions

One way to ensure better parallelism is to identify all coordinating conjunctions (*and, or, nor, for, yet, but, so*) and then to make sure the sentence parts they connect are grammatically equal. For example, because *and* connects parallel (or coordinate) sentence parts, the words, phrases, or clauses connected by *and* should take the same grammatical form. This helps readers more easily pick up on the relationship between the ideas.

> Bob went fishing **and** fell into the lake.
>
> *And* connects two verbs—*went* and *fell.*
>
> The man in the green hat **and** the woman with the umbrella are old friends.
>
> *And* connects two *nouns*—*man* and *woman.*
>
> I went to the market **and** to the bookstore before it rained.
>
> *And* connects two prepositional phrases—*to the market* and *to the bookstore.*
>
> The doctor was two hours behind schedule, **and** all the patients had to wait.
>
> *And* connects two independent clauses—*The doctor was* **. . .** and *all the patients had.* **. . .**
>
> It was raining, **yet** everyone had fun.
>
> *Yet* connects two independent clauses—*It was raining* and *everyone had fun.*
>
> We finished cleaning the garage, **but** not the basement.
>
> *But* connects two nouns—*the garage* and *the basement.*

Semicolons

Like coordinating conjunctions, semicolons express a coordinate relationship. The sentence parts connected by a semicolon should be grammatically equal. In the following sentence, the semicolons connect independent clauses: (1) *Engineers will build defective bridges;* (2) *doctors will botch their operations;* (3) *marketers will have no clue how to market.*

> For example, one might argue that students find themselves cheated because upon graduation they will not be prepared to do their jobs: Engineers will build defective bridges; doctors will botch their operations; and marketers will have no clue how to market.

Comparisons/Contrasts

The parallel structure of comparison/contrast helps readers more easily notice the relationship between ideas. In the following sentence, comparison/contrast relationship is indicated through parallelism: *the one on the higher level* and *the one on the lower level.*

> The problem, of course, is that the two students have entered college on different academic levels and **the one on the higher level** has graduated on an even higher level while **the one on the lower level** has remained pretty much the same.

Lists

A grocery list provides a good example of how meaning and grammatical form work together. When meaning is parallel or equal (all things we can pick up at a grocery store), form tends also to be parallel or equal (all nouns).

> eggs, cheese, butter, bagels, cookies, sauce, milk, bread, beans, soap, light bulbs

Notice that the following listed items are all nouns and are expressed in parallel terms:

> We bought eggs, cheese, butter, and milk.

The items in the following list are verb phrases:

> They have at least three options: (1) take advantage of the easy system and learn a little along the way; (2) motivate themselves, working harder (and learning more) than the system requires them to; and (3) attend a more academically rigorous school (of course, such schools still exist, though they are likely to cost more to attend).

Activities

1. Before turning in an essay, check for parallel structure.
   - **a.** Identify all coordinating conjunctions *(and, or, nor, for, yet, but, so),* and make sure that the words or group of words they connect are the same grammatical form. This includes items in a series, such as *bread, cheese, butter,* and *milk.* (Note: The word *for* most often functions as a prepositional phrase and not a coordinating conjunction.)
   - **b.** Find semicolons, and make sure that the words or group of words they connect have the same grammatical form.
2. Exchange essays with a peer and check for parallel structure.

Punctuation

Understanding punctuation allows writers to more clearly and concisely communicate their ideas. For example, notice how the basic end punctuation marks affect the following three sentences:

> Have a seat, George.
>
> Have a seat, George!
>
> Have a seat, George?

Because of punctuation, each sentence speaks differently. The same point could be illustrated by looking at how commas, dashes, and parentheses are used to set off a sentence part.

The situation itself, small-town people in a small town, is comforting.

The situation itself—small-town people in a small town—is comforting.

The situation itself (small-town people in a small town) is comforting.

Because of punctuation, each sentence speaks differently. Different forms of punctuation, like different words, allow writers to communicate more effectively. For example, many readers know that when a writer places ideas within dashes, he or she means to emphasize those ideas while ideas placed within parentheses are thought to be less important. Understanding these subtleties, which can be learned through reading about punctuation as well as noticing how others punctuate, can help you as both a writer and a reader.

Commas

Commas help to indicate the relationship between parts of a sentence.

While I was talking on the phone, I was watering my plants.

The preceding comma separates the two main parts of the sentence: *While I was talking on the phone* (a dependent clause) and *I was watering my plants* (an independent clause).

Mike Easler, left-handed power hitter for the Pirates, slugged one out of the park.

The two commas in this example, like bookends, stand at the beginning and ending of a sentence part (*left-handed power hitter for the Pirates*). That sentence part interrupts the main part of the sentence (*Mike Easler slugged one out of the park*). The interrupting part, an appositive, restates the noun that it follows (Mike Easler = left-handed power hitter for the Pirates). Commas separate ideas for readers who quickly make sense of the relationship.

Commas are Often Used in the Following Ways:

Before independent (or main) clauses Whenever an introductory phrase, word, or clause begins a sentence, a comma comes directly after it. The comma helps separate the introductory material from the main part of the sentence. Put another way, the comma comes before the independent clause and can be viewed as a sort of road sign indicating an independent clause is beginning:

Going down the road, the truck stopped to pick up the hitchhiker.
introductory phrase

While I was talking on the phone, I was watering my plants.
introductory clause

Sadly, the Comets came out flat for the second half.
introductory word

Before coordinating conjunctions when they join two independent clauses Commas usually appear before coordinating conjunctions connecting two independent clauses. But when coordinating conjunctions connect two dependent clauses, phrases, or words, commas are not used.

> The fire was burning brightly, and the rain was still falling gently.
> *and* connects two independent clauses

> The Rangers were sitting around and talking.
> *and* connects two participles—*sitting around* and *talking*

> Herbert felt awful after the firefighters' cookout and called his sister for advice.
> *and* connects two verbs—*felt* and *called*

The seven coordinating conjunctions

and	yet
or	but
nor	so
for	

Not before dependent (or subordinate) clauses Commas don't usually precede subordinating conjunctions (*because, since, although,* etc.) the way they do coordinating conjunctions (*and, or, nor, for, yet, but, so*). The sentence parts (an independent clause and a dependent clause) are distinct because of the subordinating conjunction and thus don't require a comma. At times, however, a comma may be used to build an even stronger distinction between the two clauses. For example, S. I. Hayakawa writes, "All new ideas sound foolish at first, because they are new." Writers size up the situation and decide whether or not inserting a comma before a dependent clause will help readers to better see the intended relationship between ideas.

A Partial List of Subordinating Conjunctions

after	how
although	if
as	inasmuch
as if	in order that
as much	lest
as soon as	now that
as though	provided that
because	since
before	so that
even if	than

that	when
though	whenever
till	where
unless	wherever
until	while

To set off interrupting elements Some sentence parts interrupt. For example, *The dog, as you know, barked at the biker* can be viewed as having two parts: the main clause (*The dog barked at the biker*) and an interrupting element (*as you know*). Interrupting elements can be one word, a phrase, or a clause.

French fries, although I haven't had any for a while, sure do taste good.

French fries, an American classic, are sold all around the world.

French fries, yum, are my favorite kind of potatoes.

Notice how the interrupting elements are punctuated in the following sentences:

A sadder truth, I am afraid, is that because of skills and attitudes developed in high school, for some students the reality of genuine learning (as opposed to just getting by) might already be too late. (Daniel Bruno)

Soon, I predict, they and other companies will not be able to sell us out. (Michael Moore)

I crouched low to avoid destroying a jewelled spider's web that stretched, exquisite and fragile, across the trail. (Jane Goodall)

Interrupting elements can also be set off with parentheses or dashes. In general, parentheses suggest that the inserted information is somehow less important compared to the main point being made, and dashes—unlike parentheses—draw attention to the interrupting bit of information.

To separate items in a series Placing a comma between each item in a series helps readers know where one item stops and another begins. Thus, we punctuate the following sentence this way: *As individuals in a society, we conform to laws, clothing styles, hairstyles, and even culinary tastes (most Americans like French fries but not raw oysters)*. Not punctuating the list *laws clothing styles hairstyles and even culinary tastes* would have been, at the least, distracting to readers.

Just go to any pet store and look at the vast array of foods, toys, beds, and treats, not to mention the shampoos and skin treatments. (David Hawes)

If a person is unaware of common references—the Battle of the Bulge, Normandy, Existentialism, T. S. Eliot, World War I, Rasputin, John the Baptist, Gandhi, apartheid,

> Jonas Salk, Johnny Appleseed, Lewis and Clark, the Trail of Tears, slavery, the Donner Party, and so on—he misses out on conversations, on meaning, on connecting with his fellow inmates. (Daniel Bruno)

To separate coordinate modifiers When side-by-side modifiers describe the same word independently of each other, the modifiers are usually separated with a comma.

> the big, black dog

Each modifier (*big* and *black*) modifies the dog independently of the other. The dog is big. And the dog is black. Notice the use of coordinate modifiers (*black, brown, white carpet*) in the following passage:

> What happened was that I took a bite of honey and then I joined my sister and brother, two and ten years younger, watching Saturday morning cartoons together on the black, brown, white carpet, patterned in such a wild way that it was quickly making my head ache.

Another type of modifier, the compound modifier, is punctuated with a hyphen. See Hyphens on page 770.

Quick Guide to Commas

1. Commas come after introductory clauses or phrases:

   After the party at Jake's house, we sang Calypso songs for days.

   Although they were tired from hunting, the hounds chased the children around the backyard.

2. Commas separate items in a series:

   Alice gave Ralph a necktie, a bottle of cologne, and some chocolates.

   We ate good food, drank some tasty apple cider, and sang songs around the campfire.

   The Big Reds were moving the ball down the field, scoring touchdowns, and taking all the fun out of the game for the Spartans.

3. Commas are used between coordinate modifiers:

   Suzette is a lovely, intelligent girl.

   Some large, purple birds swooped down from above.

4. Commas set off an interrupting element:

   The rest of our group, for example, is going home tomorrow.

   The parking on campus, though it doesn't bother me, has become a hot topic.

   Ella Fitzgerald, the famous jazz singer, was born in Newport News, Virginia.

5. Commas are used in dates, addresses, place names, and long numbers:

We drove through Whitley City, Kentucky, on August 16, 1972.

John's truck has 124,618 miles on it.

Please mail my refund to 35 Flarton Place, Burton, Maine 00178.

6. Commas are used when a quotation follows a speaking verb:

She said, "Are you coming?"

After it rained for three days straight, Mrs. Merriweather asked, "Who wants to mop up all this water?"

Activities

1. Scan the essays in this book, noticing how commas are used. Find two examples of each of the following: (1) a comma before a main clause (or setting off an introductory element), (2) two commas setting off an interrupting element, (3) a comma between items in a series, and (4) a comma between coordinate modifiers.

2. Scan your own writing—an essay, letter, e-mail—and notice how commas are used. Find two examples of each of the following: (1) a comma before a main clause (or setting off an introductory element), (2) two commas setting off an interrupting element, (3) a comma between items in a series, and (4) a comma between coordinate modifiers.

Semicolons

Semicolons are stronger than commas and weaker than periods. They are used to connect sentence parts that are equal grammatically, such as two independent clauses, two dependent clauses, two phrases, or two words. They are not used to connect sentence parts that aren't grammatically equal, such as a clause and a phrase or an independent clause and a dependent clause.

> Every morning Chuck made his bed, took a shower, and fed the cat; every evening he walked the dog and did his homework.
>
> The sky is clear and blue; however, the game has been postponed.
>
> Last summer I drove through Bangor, Maine; Hanover, New Hampshire; and Halifax, Nova Scotia.

In the first two examples, the semicolon is used to connect two independent clauses. Notice that in the second example, the conjunctive adverb *however* is also used. Semicolons precede conjunctive adverbs when they connect two independent clauses. In the third example, the semicolons are used to connect (or separate) locations: Bangor, Maine; Hanover,

New Hampshire; and Halifax, Nova Scotia. Semicolons are used because the sentence already contains commas between the cities and states.

Colons

Colons are useful for connecting a list, explanation, or quotation to the statement introducing it. Properly used colons can save time while connecting ideas clearly. The statement preceding the list, explanation, or quotation should be able to stand on its own as a complete sentence. For example in the following, the sentence part preceding the list could be a complete sentence without the list:

> We bought a lot of supplies before the game: hand warmers, wool socks, thermal underwear, boots, and knit hats.

A colon would not be used if the words to the left of the colon could not stand alone:

> We bought hand warmers, wool socks, thermal underwear, boots, and knit hats.

Activities

1. Create a comma quiz for your peers by removing the commas from one page of your recent writing. Allow your peers ten minutes to punctuate the text, and then discuss how their punctuation compares to the original.
2. Find or create at least one example of the following: (1) a sentence that is clearer to readers because it is punctuated one way instead of another, and (2) a sentence that is clear but distracting to readers because it is punctuated one way instead of another.

Hyphens

Hyphens are used to connect compound modifiers—two or more words combined to function as one modifier.

> We had thirty-five minutes to write an in-class essay.

The words *in* and *class* combine to modify *essay.* Each word alone is unable to modify *essay.* It is not an *in* essay or a *class* essay. It is an *in-class* essay. Thus, *in-class* is hyphenated. Notice also that numbers from twenty-one through ninety-nine are hyphenated. Consider these additional examples of compound modifiers: —*give-it-to-me-now race for more, water-covered land:*

> Although we probably would not have relented in our give-it-to-me-now race for more, we would have taken a solemn moment to raise a toast and drink to your hardship. (Simon Benlow)
>
> I'd lost the contest with the engagement ring on my seventeen-year-old finger. (Cindy Bosley)

Coordinate modifiers (page 768) are punctuated with a comma—not a hyphen.

Dashes

Dashes—like this—are used to set off interrupting elements. As discussed on page 767, interrupting elements can be set off with commas, parentheses, or dashes. In general, dashes draw attention to the interrupting information, while parentheses suggest that the information is somehow less important compared to the main point being made.

> So, a need or desire—to stay cool, to be entertained, to keep up with what's going on—is replaced not by a different need or desire but instead by a new way of meeting it. (Chester McCovey)

> While *Three's Company* or *Dharma and Greg* or *MASH* may also wind things up happily after 30 minutes, there is—even though the complication of that particular week's crisis has been worked out—always a sense on those shows that things are not quite right. (Ed Bell)

Parentheses

Parentheses (like this) are used to set off interrupting elements. As discussed on page 767, interrupting elements can be set off with commas, parentheses, or dashes. Parentheses suggest that the information is somehow less important compared to the main point being made. Yet, because this information is still included, it is somehow important and interesting.

> After my mother's never-subtle hints that if I'd just lose 20 pounds boys would like me and I might even win a beauty contest, it was my friend Bridget who wanted us to enter the Ottumwa (pronounced Uh-TUM-wuh) Junior Miss Pageant together. (Cindy Bosley)

> Doubtless, my sense of education at that time (as well as my sense of what constituted good writing) was more than mildly seasoned by huge doses of the Beats—Allen Ginsburg, Gregory Corso, William Burroughs, Kenneth Patchen, LeRoi Jones, and, of course, Jack Kerouac. (Leonard Kress)

> Wrought in stainless steel and plastic, this bit of industrial-designer paraphernalia (it holds my drug of choice) is every cup holder's dream. (Jim Crockett)

Activities

1. Write a paragraph in which you set off interrupting elements, one with commas, one with parentheses, and one with dashes. Use the forms of punctuation rhetorically, making sure the idea you set off with parentheses is less important and that you mean to emphasize the idea within dashes.
2. Make your draft more lively and concise by using colons to connect a list, explanation, or quotation to the words introducing it.

Paragraphs

Paragraphs serve different purposes. Some introduce the main idea of an essay; others support that idea; some transition from one idea to another; and others bring the essay to a satisfying conclusion.

Opening and Closing Paragraphs

Shorter essays often have an opening paragraph, several supporting paragraphs, and a closing paragraph. In longer essays, an introduction or conclusion may take several paragraphs, and one supporting point may require more than just one paragraph. Opening paragraphs bring readers into the essay, introducing the subject and setting the tone. Closing paragraphs take readers out of the essay, back to the outside world. Although a conclusion could just summarize the main points, a summary is often unnecessary. Instead, a strong conclusion might suggest or emphasize the public resonance of the essay, create a lasting image, call readers to action, and so on. The particular ways of beginning and ending essays are unlimited. But readers respond well to introductions that open a door to a new way of thinking and conclusions that emphasize the most important idea in the essay.

Strategies for Introductions

1. Begin with a statistic, quotation, or anecdote.
2. Ask a question.
3. Create a strong visual image.
4. Provide necessary background.
5. Make a comparison.
6. Briefly explain what the essay is responding to.
7. Allude to the public resonance of the essay.
8. Create a tone for the essay.

Test the approach: Will the introduction invite readers into a new way of thinking?

Strategies for Conclusions

1. Suggest or emphasize the public resonance.
2. State and explain the main idea.
3. Create a strong image.
4. Ask an important question.
5. Relate back to a point from the introduction.
6. Call readers to thought or action.
7. Make a recommendation.
8. Suggest a consequence.

Test the approach: Will the conclusion reinforce a new way of thinking, or will it just repeat what readers might have already considered?

For more, see "Beginning" (pages 549–552) and "Concluding" (pages 557–559) in Chapter 17.

Supporting Paragraphs

The supporting paragraphs in an essay, everything except the introduction and conclusion, help readers understand and accept the essay's thesis. Three important qualities of supporting paragraphs (and essays overall) are unity, development, and coherence.

> **Unity** means that each paragraph is about one thing; that is, it has a purpose and it goes about achieving that purpose without significant digression.
>
> **Development** means that each paragraph is sufficiently thorough. This can only be determined by considering each paragraph's purpose and what must be done to achieve that purpose.
>
> **Coherence** means that the relationship between ideas is clear to readers—that the writing flows. The writer assists readers by arranging ideas in an appropriate order and by providing transitions, repeating key terms, and following conventions of grammar.

Organization Paragraphs are often organized deductively, stating the main idea first and then support. They also can be organized inductively, giving support first and then the main idea. Some paragraphs (called "turnabout paragraphs" in this text) begin with a point and then pivot, or move, readers to a related point. Other paragraphs serve as transitions between paragraphs.

Deductive If information is organized deductively, the main idea is presented first and the support for that idea follows. Stating the main idea first often helps readers understand the point of the paragraph more easily.

> **Sadly, the gap between these two groups grows even wider.** The motivated student with good study skills (the one who has had at least an adequate high school education) attends class, takes notes, understands reading assignments, follows instructions, develops even better habits of mind, gains even more knowledge, and learns ways of making that knowledge work for her and his fellow humans. But in a system where B's are average and C's might indicate that although a student "tried" she did not demonstrate understanding or skill, the poorer students continue to advance through the system while remaining trapped at the bottom. Their level of thinking does not change much, while that of their better-prepared peers does.

Here the opening sentence expresses a main idea: The gap between two groups of students grows wider. The rest of the paragraph explains *why.*

Inductive If information is organized inductively, the main idea comes after the support. The preceding deductive paragraph can be reorganized by placing the main idea last.

> The motivated student with good study skills (the one who has had at least an adequate high school education) attends class, takes notes, understands reading assignments, follows instructions, develops even better habits of mind, gains even more knowledge, and learns ways of making that knowledge work for her and his fellow humans. But in a system where B's are average and C's might indicate that although a student "tried" she did not demonstrate understanding or skill, the poorer students continue to advance through the system while remaining trapped at the bottom. Their level of thinking does not change much, while that of their better-prepared peers does. **Sadly, the gap between these two groups grows even wider.**

Turnabout Writers often pivot from one idea to another within the same paragraph—the second idea playing off the first. The pivot, or turnabout, is usually signaled by a transition word or expression such as *but, however, on the other hand, still, yet,* and so on.

> In his book *Generation X Goes to College,* Peter Sacks describes, among other things, the sense of entitlement that some students in today's consumerist culture have toward a college education. One entire chapter explores this issue alone, providing examples of this "sense" and looking into its "humble beginnings." Sacks shows how consumerism has invaded education, leading some students to expect good grades for little effort. **But** he fails, it seems, to emphasize enough a most harmful effect of this sense of entitlement. The biggest problem, as I see it, is that although students are able to graduate from high school (and even some colleges) with minimal effort, those students may find themselves cheated in the long run.

Notice how the preceding paragraph turns on the word *But,* building on the previous point and moving in a different, yet appropriate, direction. The first part of the paragraph tells what Peter Sacks writes about; the second part tells what he fails to emphasize.

Transition Some paragraphs, especially in longer pieces, function as transitions that take readers from one idea to another.

> True enough, these are all ways that students who are allowed to just slide by end up getting cheated. But another way (and one less talked about) strikes me as being far more offensive. This reason hinges on the fact that many students are not just sliding by.

This paragraph moves readers from the previously mentioned ways that students are cheated to a far more offensive way that students are cheated. Then the rest of the essay develops this point.

Activities

1. Read the introductions of three essays in this book. Describe each strategy. (Is it a strategy from this chapter or a different strategy?)
2. Read the conclusions of three essays in this book. Describe each strategy. How does each conclusion work? Does it leave readers with something to ponder? (Keep in mind that some conclusions may be more than one paragraph long.)
3. Rewrite your introduction with an eye toward getting into the essay more quickly. Cut anything that unnecessarily delays getting to the main point or that takes away from the essay's forward momentum.
4. Read one essay in this book and study its paragraphs. Note each paragraph's organization (deductive, inductive, turnabout) and function (transition, support). Do you think each paragraph is unified, developed, and coherent? Explain why or why not.
5. Revise one of your essays by writing out a main idea for each paragraph. Place the main idea at the beginning of the paragraph, and then try moving the main idea to different places.

Beyond the Five-Paragraph Essay

One typical organization, often helpful but ultimately limiting, is the five-paragraph essay. It includes a brief introduction, three supporting paragraphs, and a conclusion. Notice in the following example how each supporting paragraph will develop or support a clearly stated main idea. Notice also how key terms from the controlling idea are repeated, word for word or with synonyms, in the topic sentences (the main ideas for the supporting paragraphs):

Controlling Idea: Myrtle Beach is a great place to go on vacation.

Supporting Paragraph #1: Myrtle Beach has many nice golf courses.

Supporting Paragraph #2: Myrtle Beach has a beautiful, long beach.

Supporting Paragraph #3: Myrtle Beach has plenty of good nightlife.

Concluding Paragraph

This example provides plenty of potential for going beyond the five-paragraph essay. By narrowing the essay's focus, making counterarguments and concessions, and establishing a purpose beyond merely describing some positive aspects of Myrtle Beach, the writer would create a more complex and less limiting essay. Instead of explaining three nice things about Myrtle Beach, a writer might show why Myrtle Beach is preferable to Daytona Beach, Panama City, Acapulco, or the New Jersey shore. This approach would likely include making counterarguments and concessions. Or the writer might narrow his or her focus to *just the beach*. Such an approach might deal briefly with the region's golf courses, nightlife, and other matters, then focus more specifically on the virtues of the beach. Going beyond the five-paragraph approach requires more analysis and will produce a more engaging essay.

The five-paragraph essay can have more than five paragraphs and still be limiting. The problem is not with the number of points or paragraphs but with the lack of exploration and discovery. Often, the writer using the five-paragraph strategy avoids asking hard questions, dissecting points, analyzing assumptions—all strategies that create an engaging essay.

Coherence

Coherence means connecting ideas so that writing flows smoothly from one idea to another. You might think of it as taking readers by the hand and leading them carefully through your essay. Notice how the following strategies work to create coherence in "Entitlement Education":

- A title that expresses the focus of the essay
- A purposeful introduction that moves steadily toward a main point
- Accurate word choice
- Sentence vitality (eliminating expletives, wordiness, etc.)
- Explicit statements (including statements of main ideas and statements of support)
- Summary of appropriate information
- Consistent verb tense
- Conventional punctuation (commas, colons, quotation marks, etc.)
- Transitional words, expressions, sentences, and paragraphs
- Pronoun/antecedent agreement
- Subject/verb agreement
- Parallelism
- Parenthetical information
- Subordination/coordination
- Relevant use of sources
- Integration of borrowed material
- In-text documentation and a corresponding Works Cited page

Daniel Bruno

Composition I

Dr. Fritz Strisky

5 November 2013

Entitlement Education

In his book *Generation X Goes to College,* Peter Sacks describes, among other things, the sense of entitlement that some students in today's consumerist culture have toward a college education. One entire chapter explores this issue alone, providing examples of this "sense" and looking into its "humble beginnings." Sacks shows how consumerism has invaded education, leading some students to expect good grades for little effort. But he fails, it seems, to emphasize enough a most harmful effect of this sense of entitlement. The biggest problem, as I see it, is that although students are able to graduate from high school (and even some colleges) with minimal effort, those students may find themselves cheated in the long run.

Title provides coherence by providing readers with an overall focus.

Clear reference to Sacks's book provides coherence—the rest of the essay is about this.

Consistent verb tense—present—provides coherence.

How might they be cheated? One might argue that students get cheated because entitlement doesn't go on forever. At some point it stops. For example, a college graduate with a marketing degree, but especially weak thinking or writing skills, may find himself disadvantaged on the job. It is not that his boss puts her foot down; instead, the job does. Our student finds himself not well prepared for it. He gets cheated because he is disadvantaged at his job—a job that he paid money to learn how to do. Of course the point isn't about marketing majors. The same is true of students in any field. (Marketing is just what came to mind.)

Transitional expressions such as "for example" provide coherence by clarifying the relationship between ideas.

One might also claim that students will be cheated because their lives will somehow *be less.* This argument claims that a person's intelligence contributes to his quality of life. Here we must remember that "intelligence" is not just "knowledge." Instead, it is

"Also" indicates a relationship between this claim and the previous one.

Pronouns such as "this" provide coherence by connecting ideas.

Parallelism provides coherence (to use; to make; to see OR may have much knowledge; but not have much intelligence).

being able to use knowledge, to make connections and figure things out, to see causes and solve problems. A person may have much knowledge—that is, he may have accumulated a lot of facts—but not have much intelligence . . . or so the argument goes. As one goes from first grade to twelfth, from twelfth grade to college, and from freshman to senior, education shifts focus from mere accumulation of information (knowledge) to application of information (intelligence). And while we may accumulate more knowledge as a senior in college than we did as a senior in high school, the focus in college has (or should have) shifted from mere knowledge to intelligence—that is, to the ability to make good use of one's knowledge.

"Other," "for example," "but," "of course," and "and" show the relationship between ideas.

Other standard arguments claim other ways students might be cheated. For example, we might feel sorry for someone who doesn't get a joke—or a reference. Allusions to literature, history, philosophy and so on allow us to say much in few words. But does the listener understand? If a person is unaware of common references—the Battle of the Bulge, Normandy, Existentialism, T. S. Eliot, World War I, Rasputin, John the Baptist, Gandhi, apartheid, Jonas Salk, Johnny Appleseed, Lewis and Clark, the Trail of Tears, slavery, the Donner Party, and so on—he misses out on conversations, on meaning, on *connecting with his fellow inmates.* Of course, here one might counter that you don't need to know all of these things. And, I agree, you don't. People tend to hang out with people who have similar interests and tastes.

Items in a series (on conversations, on meaning, on connecting) expressed in parallel grammatical form contribute to coherence.

Explicit statements of main ideas, followed with support for that idea, contribute to coherence.

One more argument claims that because we live in a democracy, we must be well-educated. Since all the citizens are responsible for the government, our forefathers promoted public education so that all citizens—not just the wealthy and elite—would know how to read and write. Thomas Jefferson wrote,

> I know no safe depository of the ultimate powers of society but the people themselves; and if we think them not enlightened enough to exercise their control with a wholesome discretion, the remedy is not to take it from them, but to inform their discretion by education. This is the true corrective of abuses of constitutional power. (278)

In what ways can educated citizens correct abuses in a democracy? A person's way of life, his purchases and activities—not just a person's vote or protest march—is part of the responsibility. Thus, consumers and neighbors and co-workers and so on should behave responsibly and think intelligently. It is our responsibility as citizens of a democracy.

True enough, these are all ways that students who are allowed to just slide by end up getting cheated. But another way (and one less talked about) strikes me as being far more offensive. This reason hinges on the fact that many students are not just sliding by.

In Generation X Goes to College, Peter Sacks illustrates that all of today's college students cannot just be thrown in the same big barrel. In describing the modern/post-modern clash in education, he spends the majority of his time talking about those students who are underprepared, who lack the basic study skills required in academic work, and who demonstrate little real commitment to their own education. Yet, he does not discuss this problem in isolation. He also mentions another type of student. For example, he introduces the reader to Marissa and Carol: "As very good students, [their views] were virtually excluded by The College in order to accommodate the whiners and complainers" (61). And he says they "suffered not only educationally" (63). In addition to discussing specific good students, an entire chapter presents survey results about students' attitudes toward education. While he makes claims such as "nearly a quarter of the students . . . harbored

Smoothly integrating appropriate outside information and documenting correctly contribute to coherence.

The quoted material is discussed.

This entire paragraph provides coherence between two sections by taking readers from the previous ideas to "another way."

Main ideas at the beginning of paragraphs provide coherence by letting readers know the reason for the information that follows.

A properly used colon—to introduce a quote with words that could be punctuated as a sentence—provides coherence. Readers know immediately the relationship of the words on the left and right of the colon. Quotation marks provide coherence by making clear that the words inside them are from a source.

In-text documentation that corresponds to a Works Cited page provides coherence by being unobtrusive while at the same time providing important information.

a disproportionate sense of entitlement," this very statement tells the reader that a full three-quarters (that is, three out of four) students *do not* "harbor a disproportionate sense of entitlement" (54–59). He wraps up the book by focusing on another student, Andie, who he describes as "a good student, constantly picking [his] brain for information and feedback on her work" (186–87). His final paragraph, before the Epilogue, says, "Let's create a system that encourages people like Andie at least as much as the ones who don't give a damn" (187). Thus, Sacks shows that today's students are a more diverse group—in skill level, background, and attitude toward education—than has ever before been gathered together in the college classroom.

Works Cited

Jefferson, Thomas. *The Writings of Thomas Jefferson.* Edited by Andrew Adgate Lipscomb and Albert Ellery Bergh, vol. 15, Thomas Jefferson Memorial Association of the United States, 1904. *Google Books*, books.google.com/books/about/The_Writings_of_Thomas_Jefferson.html?id=SRoxygL334cC.

Sacks, Peter. *Generation X Goes to College.* Open Court Publishing, 1996.

Activities

1. Check your own essay for coherence by referring to the strategies in Bruno's essay. For example, how does the title help focus readers on the main idea, or how does your purpose in writing help to make the essay coherent and concise?
2. Examine the table of contents of this book. What strategies do authors seem to use when titling their essays? What makes some titles more intriguing than others? Which essays do you want to read based on just the title? Describe how the most successful titles help focus readers on the writer's purpose.

Index

A

B

C

E

F

J

K

L

M

P

S

U

V

W

Y

Z

20 mg olanzapine
— $9 for 30 days —

Anal – 100 4 month

Fluvoxamine – 33.08
2 wks
CVS

goodrx.com